The **20th Century**

1901-1940

Great Events from History

The 20th Century

1901-1940

Volume 6
1937-1940

Editor
Robert F. Gorman
Southwest Texas State University

Salem Press
Pasadena, California   Hackensack, New Jersey

Editor in Chief: Dawn P. Dawson

Editorial Director: Christina J. Moose

Acquisitions Editor: Mark Rehn

Research Supervisor: Jeffry Jensen

Manuscript Editors: Judy Selhorst, Andy Perry, Anna A. Moore

Research Assistant Editor: Tim Tiernan

Production Editor: Andrea E. Miller

Design, Layout, and Graphics: James Hutson

Additional Layout and Graphics: William Zimmerman

Photo Editor: Cynthia Breslin Beres

Editorial Assistant: Dana Garey

Cover photos (pictured clockwise, from top left): Marlene Dietrich in *The Blue Angel*, 1930. (The Granger Collection, New York); Orville Wright in flight, 1909. (The Granger Collection, New York); Hammer and Sickle. (The Granger Collection, New York); Gold coffin of King Tut, photographed in 1922. (The Granger Collection, New York); Picasso's *Guernica*. (The Granger Collection, New York); American troops landing in France, 1918. (The Granger Collection, New York)

Some of the essays in this work originally appeared in the following Salem Press sets: *Chronology of European History: 15,000 b.c. to 1997* (1997, edited by John Powell; associate editors, E. G. Weltin, José M. Sánchez, Thomas P. Neill, and Edward P. Keleher); *Great Events from History: North American Series, Revised Edition* (1997, edited by Frank N. Magill); *Great Events from History II: Science and Technology* (1991, edited by Frank N. Magill); *Great Events from History II: Human Rights* (1992, edited by Frank N. Magill); *Great Events from History II: Arts and Culture* (1993, edited by Frank N. Magill); *Great Events from History II: Business and Commerce* (1994, edited by Frank N. Magill), and *Great Events from History II: Ecology and the Environment* (1995, edited by Frank N. Magill). New material has been added.

Library of Congress Cataloging-in-Publication Data

Great events from history. The 20th century, 1901-1940 / editor, Robert F. Gorman.

    p. cm.

Some of the essays in this work originally appeared in various Salem Press publications.

Includes bibliographical references and index.

ISBN 978-1-58765-324-7 (set : alk. paper) -- ISBN 978-1-58765-325-4 (v. 1: alk. paper) -- ISBN 978-1-58765-326-1 (v. 2 : alk. paper) -- ISBN 978-1-58765-327-8 (v. 3 : alk. paper) -- ISBN 978-1-58765-328-5 (v. 4 : alk. paper) -- ISBN 978-1-58765-329-2 (v. 5 : alk. paper) -- ISBN 978-1-58765-330-8 (v. 6 : alk. paper) 1. Twentieth century. I. Gorman, Robert F. II. Title: 20th century, 1901-1940. III. Title: Twentieth century, 1901-1940.

D421.G629 2007
909.82'1—dc22

2007001930

First Printing

Contents

1937 (continued)

1938

1939

CONTENTS

KEYWORD LIST OF CONTENTS

LIST OF MAPS, TABLES, AND SIDEBARS

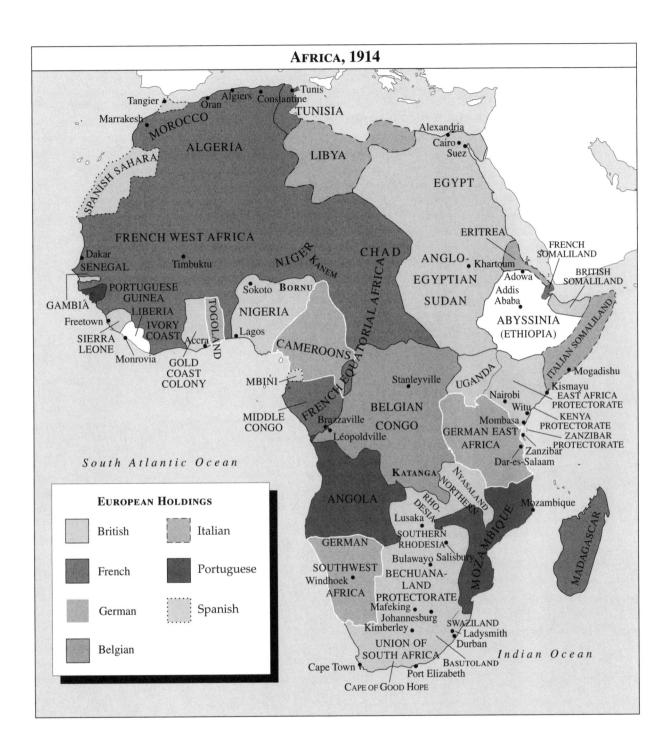

AFRICA, 1914

Tangier
Marrakesh
MOROCCO
Oran • Algiers • Constantine
TUNISIA
• Tunis
Alexandria
Cairo •
Suez •
SPANISH SAHARA
ALGERIA
LIBYA
EGYPT

FRENCH WEST AFRICA
ERITREA
ANGLO-
EGYPTIAN
SUDAN
FRENCH
SOMALILAND
BRITISH
SOMALILAND

Dakar •
SENEGAL
Timbuktu •
NIGER
KANEM
CHAD
Khartoum •
Adowa •
Addis
Ababa •
PORTUGUESE
GUINEA
GAMBIA
LIBERIA
Freetown •
IVORY
COAST
SIERRA
LEONE
Monrovia •
GOLD
COAST
COLONY
Accra •
TOGOLAND
Sokoto •
BORNU
NIGERIA
Lagos •
CAMEROONS
ABYSSINIA
(ETHIOPIA)
ITALIAN SOMALILAND

MBINI
FRENCH EQUATORIAL AFRICA
Stanleyville •
UGANDA
Mogadishu •
Kismayu
EAST AFRICA
PROTECTORATE
MIDDLE
CONGO
Brazzaville •
Léopoldville •
BELGIAN
CONGO
Nairobi •
Witu •
Mombasa •
GERMAN EAST
AFRICA
Dar-es-Salaam •
KENYA
PROTECTORATE
ZANZIBAR
PROTECTORATE
Zanzibar •

South Atlantic Ocean

KATANGA
NYASALAND
NORTHERN

ANGOLA
RHO-
DESIA
Mozambique •
Lusaka •
SOUTHERN
RHODESIA
Bulawayo • Salisbury •
MOZAMBIQUE
MADAGASCAR

GERMAN
SOUTHWEST
AFRICA
Windhoek •
BECHUANA-
LAND
PROTECTORATE
Mafeking •
Johannesburg •
Kimberley •
UNION OF
SOUTH AFRICA
SWAZILAND
Ladysmith •
Durban •
BASUTOLAND
Indian Ocean
Cape Town •
Port Elizabeth •
CAPE OF GOOD HOPE

EUROPEAN HOLDINGS

British   Italian
French   Portuguese
German   Spanish
Belgian

EUROPE, 1914

Arctic Ocean

Iceland

*Atlantic
Ocean*

NORWAY

SWEDEN

Baltic Sea

RUSSIA

Northern
Ireland

North Sea

DENMARK

NETHERLANDS

IRELAND

GREAT BRITAIN

BELGIUM

GERMAN
EMPIRE

FRANCE

SWITZER-
LAND

AUSTRO-HUNGARIAN
EMPIRE

ROMANIA

Black Sea

PORTUGAL

SPAIN

Corsica

ITALY

Adriatic Sea

MONTE-
NEGRO

SERBIA

ALBANIA

BULGARIA

GREECE

Thrace

OTTOMAN
EMPIRE

Sardinia

Sicily

Cyprus

ALGERIA

TUNISIA

*Mediterranean
Sea*

Crete

MOROCCO

AFRICA

LIBYA

EGYPT

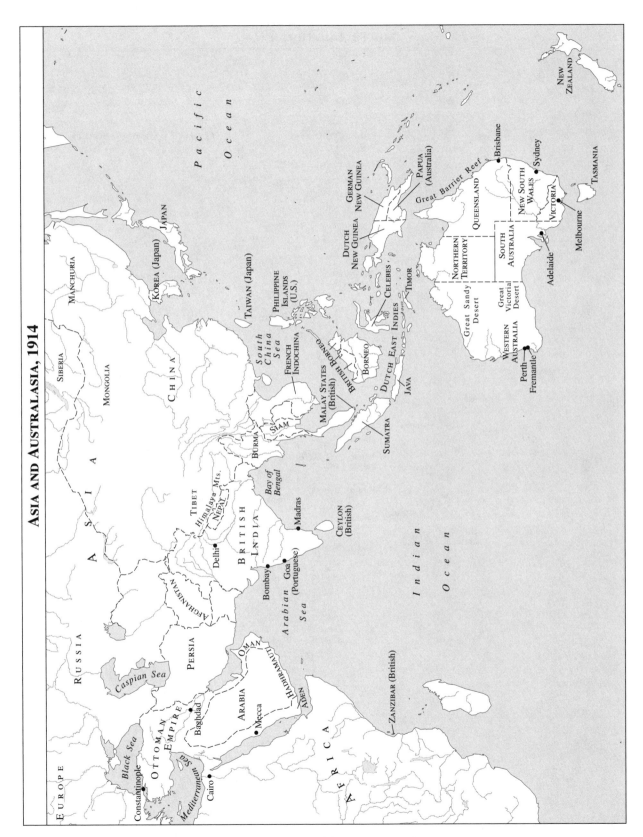

ASIA AND AUSTRALASIA, 1914

EUROPE

RUSSIA

SIBERIA

MONGOLIA

MANCHURIA

JAPAN

KOREA (Japan)

CHINA

TAIWAN (Japan)

Pacific Ocean

PHILIPPINE ISLANDS (U.S.)

South China Sea

FRENCH INDOCHINA

SIAM

BURMA

TIBET

Himalaya Mts.

NEPAL

BRITISH INDIA

Bay of Bengal

Delhi

Bombay

Madras

Goa (Portuguese)

CEYLON (British)

AFGHANISTAN

PERSIA

Caspian Sea

Black Sea

Constantinople

OTTOMAN EMPIRE

Mediterranean Sea

Cairo

Baghdad

ARABIA

Mecca

OMAN

HADHRAMAUT

ADEN

Arabian Sea

AFRICA

ZANZIBAR (British)

Indian Ocean

MALAY STATES (British)

BRITISH BORNEO

SUMATRA

JAVA

BORNEO

Dutch East Indies

CELEBES

TIMOR

DUTCH NEW GUINEA

GERMAN NEW GUINEA

PAPUA (Australia)

Great Barrier Reef

QUEENSLAND

Great Sandy Desert

WESTERN AUSTRALIA

Great Victoria Desert

NORTHERN TERRITORY

SOUTH AUSTRALIA

NEW SOUTH WALES

VICTORIA

Perth

Fremantle

Adelaide

Melbourne

Sydney

Brisbane

TASMANIA

NEW ZEALAND

NORTH AMERICA, 1914

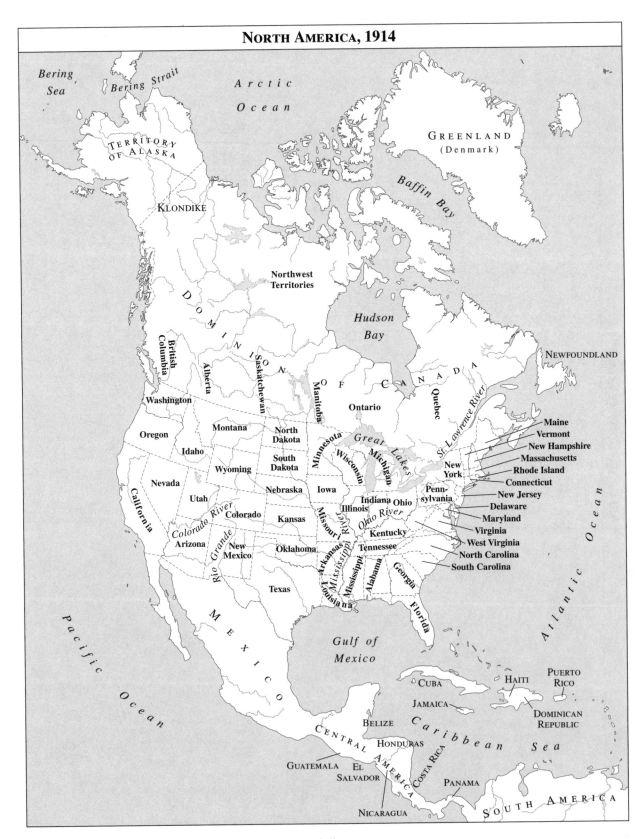

Bering Sea

Bering Strait

Arctic Ocean

TERRITORY OF ALASKA

KLONDIKE

GREENLAND (Denmark)

Baffin Bay

Northwest Territories

Hudson Bay

D O M I N I O N

British Columbia

Alberta

Saskatchewan

Manitoba

Ontario

O F   *C A N A D A*

Quebec

St. Lawrence River

NEWFOUNDLAND

Washington

Oregon

Idaho

Montana

North Dakota

South Dakota

Wyoming

Nevada

Utah

Colorado River

Colorado

Nebraska

Iowa

Minnesota

Wisconsin

Great Lakes

Michigan

New York

Maine

Vermont

New Hampshire

Massachusetts

Rhode Island

Connecticut

New Jersey

Pennsylvania

Delaware

Maryland

Virginia

West Virginia

North Carolina

South Carolina

California

Arizona

Rio Grande

New Mexico

Kansas

Oklahoma

Missouri River

Indiana

Illinois

Ohio

Ohio River

Kentucky

Tennessee

Arkansas River

Mississippi River

Mississippi

Alabama

Georgia

Texas

Louisiana

Florida

M E X I C O

Gulf of Mexico

Pacific Ocean

Atlantic Ocean

CUBA

HAITI

PUERTO RICO

JAMAICA

DOMINICAN REPUBLIC

BELIZE

Caribbean Sea

HONDURAS

CENTRAL AMERICA

GUATEMALA

EL SALVADOR

COSTA RICA

PANAMA

NICARAGUA

SOUTH AMERICA

SOUTH AMERICA, 1914

North
Atlantic
Ocean

Caracas

BRITISH
GUIANA

DUTCH
GUIANA

FRENCH
GUIANA

VENEZUELA

Bogotá
COLOMBIA

Galápagos
Islands

ECUADOR   Quito

Amazon River

Amazon Basin

BRAZIL

São Francisco River

PERU

Lima

Andes

La Paz
BOLIVIA

Sucre

South
Pacific
Ocean

Mountains

Paraná River

PARAGUAY

Rio de Janeiro

Negro River

CHILE   Santiago

ARGENTINA

Buenos Aires

URUGUAY
Montevideo

South
Atlantic
Ocean

Falkland
Islands
(British)
Stanley

South
Georgia

Cape
Horn

Great Events from History

The 20th Century

1901-1940

February 5-July 22, 1937
SUPREME COURT-PACKING FIGHT

When the executive and judicial branches of the U.S. government confronted each other over social legislation, a battle to pack the Supreme Court ensued. President Franklin D. Roosevelt was ultimately able to name eight justices and one chief justice to the Court, but in the process he catalyzed the creation of an anti-New Deal coalition that stymied many of his later efforts at social reform.

LOCALE: Washington, D.C.

CATEGORIES: Government and politics; laws, acts, and legal history

KEY FIGURES

Franklin D. Roosevelt (1882-1945), president of the United States, 1933-1945

Homer S. Cummings (1870-1956), U.S. attorney general

Charles Evans Hughes (1862-1948), chief justice of the United States

Owen J. Roberts (1875-1955), associate justice of the United States

Joseph Taylor Robinson (1872-1937), U.S. senator from Arkansas

Burton Kendall Wheeler (1882-1975), U.S. senator from Montana

SUMMARY OF EVENT

In November, 1936, President Franklin D. Roosevelt was returned to office by one of the widest election margins in history. Even conservative journalists spoke of a mandate for further New Deal reform. Indeed, the president's second inaugural address spoke of the problems with "one-third of a nation ill-housed, ill-clad, ill-nourished." In what was a surprise to many, including some members of his own party, however, the president's first message to Congress on February 5, 1937, called not for social programs but for adjustments to the U.S. Supreme Court. By July, 1937, the president had been defeated in his attempts to reorganize the Court, and he was faced with the growing disintegration of congressional support for his other legislative initiatives.

The Court that sat in judgment on Roosevelt's reform measures consisted of pre-New Deal appointees. Roosevelt had not had an opportunity to appoint a single justice during his first term. James C. McReynolds, George Sutherland, Willis Van Devanter, and Pierce Butler (known as the Four Horsemen) were all staunch conservatives who considered private property sacred and laissez-faire the best policy. The liberal wing of the Court consisted of Louis D. Brandeis, Benjamin N. Cardozo, and Harlan Fiske Stone. Chief Justice Charles Evans Hughes and Associate Justice Owen J. Roberts were both Republicans, and although they did not share the uncompromising laissez-faire attitude of the conservative bloc, they were reluctant to see an expansion of government involvement in the economy.

However, in 1935, the Court delivered a series of decisions that virtually overturned the early New Deal's recovery programs. In January, the Court, by a vote of eight to one, invalidated parts of the National Industrial Recovery Act (NIRA). At that point, the president was ready to attack the Court's power of judicial review publicly as "unconscionable" if the justices ruled against the government's power to regulate the currency in the Gold Clause cases. Confrontation was temporarily averted when the Court sustained the administration's monetary policy by a vote of five to four. Three months later, the Court, in a five-to-four division, declared the Railway Retirement Act of 1934 unconstitutional. New Dealers feared that their programs would be destroyed by a narrowly divided Court, especially if Justice Owen Roberts, an unpredictable jurist, had permanently joined the conservatives.

Their worst fears were confirmed when, on May 27, a day that became known as Black Monday, the Court handed down three unanimous antiadministration decisions. In *Louisville Bank v. Radford*, the justices declared the Frazier-Lemke Act (Farm Bankruptcy Act), which provided mortgage assistance to farmers, unconstitutional. The Court limited the president's power to remove members of regulatory bodies in *Humphrey's Executor v. United States*, and in *Schechter Poultry Corporation v. United States*, it found that the NIRA was unconstitutional because of an illegal delegation of legislative authority to the executive branch of the government in the form of code-making procedures. In the last of these cases, the Court also narrowly defined Congress's power to regulate interstate commerce. In a press conference, Roosevelt criticized the ruling, calling it a "horse-and-buggy definition of interstate commerce." Also, to some advisers he expressed a brief interest in a constitutional amendment that would limit the Court's power of judicial review.

In early 1936, in *United States v. Butler*, the Court ruled that the Agricultural Adjustment Act (AAA) was also unconstitutional. In a six-to-three decision, the Court held that the AAA involved an illegal use of federal taxing power. Finally, during the summer of 1936, in the *Tipaldo* decision, the Court struck down a New York State minimum wage law by a five-to-four vote in terms that seemed to indicate that the National Labor Relations Act (Wagner Act) and the recently passed Social Security Act were both in danger. The president accused the Court of creating a regulatory "no man's land," where neither states nor the federal government was allowed to function.

During 1936, more than one hundred bills that would curb the Court's power were introduced in Congress without Roosevelt's endorsement. Even before the election of 1936, Roosevelt had undoubtedly decided to take some action to protect his program from judicial nullification. His advisers believed that it was an opportune time to act, but there was disagreement about the best

method to employ. A constitutional amendment was rejected because it would be too difficult to draft and ratification would take too long. Change needed to occur before the Court had an opportunity to decimate more New Deal programs.

Roosevelt was convinced that the real problem with the Court was one of personnel. The method finally selected was designed to foil the conservative bloc by an outflanking strategy. Ironically, it incorporated an approach once advocated by Justice McReynolds, the most intractable of the Four Horsemen on the Court. The administration bill, which was drawn up by Attorney General Homer S. Cummings, provided that whenever a federal judge failed to retire after reaching the age of seventy, the president could appoint a new judge to that bench. The number of new appointments, however, was limited to six on the Supreme Court and forty-four in the lower federal courts. The chief attraction of this plan, according to Roosevelt, was that it emphasized efficiency in the entire federal judicial system rather than singling out the high court or dwelling on politics and personalities. The president made reference to the overcrowded dockets of the federal courts and the resulting expense and delay to litigants. He claimed that younger judges could handle the courts' business with more vigor and new vision. Although many people shared Roosevelt's frustration with the Court, opposition to the bill developed immediately from Republicans, anti-New Deal Democrats, members of the bar, and newspaper editors. More serious was the resistance from party regulars and liberals such as Senator Burton K. Wheeler.

Chief Justice Hughes soon made it clear to Senator Wheeler that the Court was not behind in its business. Wheeler had been a supporter of many New Deal measures in the past but was now heading the opposition to the bill from his post on the Senate Judiciary Committee. In addition, many elder statesmen resented the president's oblique slap at people over the age of seventy. One of these was the most liberal member of the

Editorial cartoon published in March, 1937, ridicules President Franklin D. Roosevelt's efforts to reorganize the Supreme Court to protect his New Deal programs. (FDR Library)

bench, Justice Brandeis, who was eighty years old. Helping to strengthen this opposition were the incredibly clumsy political tactics employed by the administration. Keeping even the floor leaders in ignorance until the last minute, Roosevelt did little to prepare Congress for the measure. Finally, the administration was surprised at the level of reverence many Americans expressed for the judiciary as a guardian of personal liberties and the separation of powers.

In the midst of the debate, the Supreme Court itself spoke out in a manner that did much to undermine the president's already faltering support in Congress. In March, 1937, in *West Coast Hotel Company v. Parrish*, the Court, in a move that appeared to reverse its *Tipaldo* ruling, upheld a Washington state minimum wage law by a five-to-four vote. In April, *National Labor Relations Board v. Jones & Laughlin Steel Corp.* upheld the Wagner Act by the same margin. On May 24, 1937, the Court upheld the Social Security Act in all particulars. It was clear that at least one member of the court, Justice Roberts, had shifted from opposition to support of the New Deal legislation. Roberts's move, which appeared to seal the doom of the Court-packing bill, is often referred to as "the switch in time that saved nine."

In addition, Justice Van Devanter announced his plans to retire. Roosevelt would at last be presented with the opportunity to nominate a member of the Court with a philosophy compatible with the New Deal, and presumably to assure approval of his legislation by a six-to-three margin.

While the president publicly announced his great satisfaction with the Court's apparent change of ideology, the news actually helped to kill his floundering Court reform bill. He was also acutely aware of the dissension the bill was creating within the Democratic Party. The Court reform bill gave conservative Democrats (who had been temporarily intimidated by the Depression) an opportunity to take a popular stand and at the same time to free themselves from the irritating confines of the presidential directions. When Senate majority leader Joseph Taylor Robinson of Arkansas, who was guiding the bill through Congress, died suddenly, the future of the legislation became hopeless. On July 22, 1937, the Senate sent the bill back to committee. It was never seen again.

SIGNIFICANCE

If the public was initially surprised at Roosevelt's "Court-packing" proposal, the idea of judicial reform had long appealed to some members of the administration. A number of considerations led to Roosevelt's decision to place judicial reorganization ahead of social legislation. The Supreme Court, as then composed, favored a conservative interpretation of the U.S. Constitution, but the president and others had hoped that the Court would make allowances for the emergency atmosphere when considering New Deal legislation.

Many historians have commented that Roosevelt lost the battle over the Court-packing law but won the war to achieve a more compatible Supreme Court. Before he left office, Roosevelt would name eight justices and one chief justice. In the process of winning the war, however, he may have lost his army, for after the court fight, an anti-New Deal coalition formed. After 1937, Roosevelt was never again able to count on widespread congressional support for his social reform programs.

—George Q. Flynn and Mary Welek Atwell

FURTHER READING

Abraham, Henry J. *Justices and Presidents: A Political History of Appointments to the Supreme Court*. 3d ed. New York: Oxford University Press, 1992. This volume provides a basic discussion on the Court's nomination process. Bibliography.

Baker, Leonard. *Back to Back: The Duel Between FDR and the Supreme Court*. New York: Macmillan, 1967. Details the politics of the Court-packing fight.

Burns, James Macgregor. *Roosevelt: The Lion and the Fox*. New York: Harcourt, Brace & World, 1956. Classic political biography of Franklin D. Roosevelt.

Hall, Kermit L. *The Magic Mirror: Law in American History*. New York: Oxford University Press, 1989. A chapter on the New Deal-era Court puts it into the context of legal thought and culture.

_____. *The Oxford Guide to United States Supreme Court Decisions*. New York: Oxford University Press, 1999. Multiauthored collection of essays on more than four hundred significant Court decisions, with supporting glossary and other aids.

_____, ed. *The Oxford Companion to the Supreme Court of the United States*. New York: Oxford University Press, 1992. Provides a detailed and useful outline of the history of the Court, major decisions and doctrines that have guided and influenced Court rulings dating back to 1789, and brief biographies of every justice who has served on the Court as well as other historically significant characters. Concise but detailed entries help to make landmark cases and legal terms accessible to a variety of users.

Irons, Peter. *A People's History of the Supreme Court*. New York: Penguin Books, 2000. Chronicles the development of the Court and argues that its history is largely characterized by its tendencies toward discrimination on the basis of race, sex, and socioeconomic status, at least before the entrance of Chief Justice Earl Warren. The author's passion injects new life into old arguments. Recommended.

Leuchtenburg, William E. *The Supreme Court Reborn: The Constitutional Revolution in the Age of Roosevelt.* New York: Oxford University Press, 1995. The definitive study of the Court-packing battle.

SEE ALSO: Oct. 29, 1929-1939: Great Depression; Jan. 22, 1932: Reconstruction Finance Corporation Is Created; Mar. 23, 1932: Norris-La Guardia Act Strengthens Labor Organizations; Nov. 8, 1932: Franklin D. Roosevelt Is Elected U.S. President; Mar. 9-June 16, 1933: The Hundred Days; Apr. 5, 1933: U.S. Civilian Conservation Corps Is Established; June 16, 1933: Roosevelt Signs the National Industrial Recovery Act; Apr. 8, 1935: Works Progress Administration Is Established; May 27, 1935: Black Monday.

March, 1937
DELAWARE RIVER PROJECT BEGINS

New York City, facing water-supply demands of more than one billion gallons per day, expanded its supply system by constructing the water system known as the Delaware River Project.

LOCALE: New York, New York; southeastern New York State

CATEGORIES: Environmental issues; natural resources; government and politics; engineering

KEY FIGURES

John B. Jervis (1795-1885), chief engineer who directed and completed the Croton Aqueduct project

Fiorello Henry La Guardia (1882-1947), mayor of New York City, 1934-1944, who supported the Delaware River Project

Herbert Lehman (1878-1963), governor of New York and supporter of the Delaware River Project

Walter E. Spear (fl. twentieth century), chief engineer of the Delaware River Project and department engineer on the Catskill Aqueduct project

SUMMARY OF EVENT

The Delaware River Project, including the Delaware Aqueduct, quickly became an important component of the water-supply system for New York City, one of the largest cities in the world. This system continues to help the city meet its massive demand for water by using its supply capacity of more than one billion gallons per day. From its inception, the Delaware River Project promised to be an engineering marvel, and it remains the longest continuous tunnel in the world. Since the Delaware River Project is part of a larger water system that developed over the past two hundred years, a study of its evolution is valuable.

Prior to 1800, inhabitants of New York City had no public water-supply system. Water was drawn from public or private wells. (One famous well, the Tea Water Pump, provided water that was especially pure and fit for making tea. Some merchants, known as tea-water men, sold the water from carts they wheeled through the city's streets.) In 1799, a private company began work on the first public water system, which consisted of twenty-five miles of wooden water mains made from logs that had been bored hollow. This system delivered 700,000 gallons of water daily to about two thousand homes. In 1829, a new system was built. It used an elevated cast-iron tank to hold 230,000 gallons of water. This system pumped 21,000 gallons of water per day through twelve-inch-diameter cast-iron water mains.

In 1834, the New York state legislature authorized construction of the Croton Aqueduct project, which began in 1837. The initial cost was estimated at $5.4 million, but by 1842, when the project was completed, its cost had risen to $13 million. The Croton Aqueduct supplied 90 million gallons of water per day to a city population of 360,000. The Murray Hill Reservoir was constructed at Forty-second Street and Fifth Avenue, the modern-day site of the main branch of the New York Public Library. By 1885, New York City's population was approaching two million, and new demands were being placed on the city's water system. The New Croton Aqueduct project began in 1885 and was completed in 1893. It was capable of supplying 340 million gallons of water per day to the city. This aqueduct included a thirty-mile tunnel, which was the longest tunnel in the world at that time.

In 1905, the New Croton (Cornell) Dam was completed, which expanded Croton Lake to a length of nineteen miles. This dam was 300 feet high and contained 35 billion gallons of water.

The Catskill water-supply system was initiated in 1907 and was completed in 1927. This system transported water from Esopus Creek and the Ashokan Reservoir, eighty miles northwest of New York City, to the Kensico Reservoir near White Plains, New York. The Catskill Aqueduct is fourteen feet in diameter and is constructed of seventeen-inch-thick concrete walls. It passes eleven hundred feet below the Hudson River between Newburgh and West Point.

From the Kensico Reservoir, the aqueduct continues fifteen miles south to the Hill View Reservoir near Yonkers. Two distribution tunnels emanate from Hill View Reservoir. Tunnel number 1, completed in 1907, distributes water to Manhattan, while tunnel number 2, completed in 1937, carries water through the Bronx, Queens, and Brooklyn. The two distribution tunnels eventually meet in Western Brooklyn and continue on to supply Staten Island. These tunnels, lined with concrete, were bored through solid rock, at some locations as far as 750 feet below the ground.

By 1933, New York City realized that even more water was needed for the future. Since watersheds northwest of New York City had already been included in the Catskill Aqueduct, the Delaware River basin, farther west, was identified as the next water source. The new system became known as the Delaware River Project and would consist of four reservoirs and miles of new tunnels to be constructed in three stages. A lawsuit by the state of New Jersey, in which the U.S. Supreme Court limited New York to 440 million gallons per day from the Delaware River basin, held up the project for more than two years. Construction of stage 1 began in March, 1937, with an estimated cost of $272 million over twelve years. Stage 1 included construction of the Neversink and Rondout Reservoirs. The Delaware Aqueduct, which extends forty-five miles, connects these reservoirs with the Croton Watershed. Additional tunnels extend twenty-seven miles to connect with the Kensico Reservoir, then thirteen miles to the Hill View Reservoir. Water then enters one of the two city distribution tunnels and is carried into New York City. The total tunnel length of this aqueduct system is 105 miles.

The aqueduct has a circularly shaped cross section that ranges from 13.5 feet to 19.5 feet in diameter. It is situated between 300 and 2,500 feet below the ground surface. Machinery used to bore the tunnels was lowered down vertical shafts that were up to 19 feet in diameter and up to 1,500 feet deep. Tunnel excavation progressed

at the rate of 135 to 270 feet per week, and workers toiled around the clock. Although the project was not interrupted during World War II, available material and human resources were limited and the project was guarded against possible enemy attack or sabotage. The first water from the Delaware Aqueduct reached New York in 1944; stage 1 was completed in 1954 and provided 889 million gallons per day. Stage 2 of the Delaware River Project included a 25.5-mile extension, the East Delaware tunnel, which connected the Rondout Reservoir with the Pepacton Reservoir on the east branch of the Delaware River. Stage 2 was completed in 1955 and carried 375 million gallons per day. The East Delaware tunnel has a diameter of 11.25 feet. Finally, Stage 3 of the Delaware River Project was completed in 1966. Stage 3 included the 39-mile-long West Delaware tunnel, which connected Cannonsville Reservoir on the west branch of the Delaware River with the Rondout Reservoir. The West Delaware tunnel varies in diameter from 11.3 feet to 13.3 feet and has a capacity of 310 million gallons per day.

The Delaware River Project water system was expected to satisfy water requirements for New York City through the year 2000, but given declining overall water usage and per-capita usage, it seems that the water system might well serve the city's needs indefinitely. In 1970, in order to satisfy New York's water demand of 1.5 billion gallons per day, digging began on water tunnel number 3 to add 55 miles of tunnel to the existing system; this project was planned to be completed in 2020. Usage generally and steadily declined from the highs of the 1970's, however, to less than 1.1 million gallons per day in 2003. Per-capita consumption also dropped from a high of 208 gallons in 1988 to a low of 136.6 gallons in 2003.

The demand for water by the people of New York City has grown with the city's increasing population and burgeoning manufacturing and commercial activities. Development of New York City's water-supply system has been characterized by its success not only in meeting the demand for quantity but also in delivering high-quality soft water. This availability of ample high-quality water has had a positive economic impact and has contributed to desirable living and working conditions, which attract residents and businesses. The Delaware River Project was completed over a period of time during which water demand increased from 870 million gallons per day in 1927 at the completion of the Catskill Aqueduct to 1 billion gallons per day in 1930, to 1.2 billion gallons per day in 1948. The Delaware River portion of the entire system provides 920 million gallons per day, or one-half of the entire water-system capacity of 1.82 billion gallons per day. This total capacity, given the decline in demand since the 1980's, seems largely adequate to the area's needs for the foreseeable future.

SIGNIFICANCE

Construction of the Delaware River Project had an immediate impact on the environment and on the people of New York in several areas. The most important immediate impact was the provision of sufficient quantity and quality of water to one of the world's largest metropolitan populations. Other effects included the displacement of people and their homes from land needed for reservoirs, the economic stimulation of the area through job creation and material purchases, and side effects from construction, including noise, dust, and earth displacement.

Each construction phase of the New York City water-supply system included the building of dams to create reservoirs. For the Delaware River Project, damming of rivers created the Rondout, Neversink, Pepacton, and Cannonsville reservoirs. When a reservoir is created, water covers previously dry land. In some cases, entire valleys are filled with water. Land purchased for the Delaware River Project included woods, tillable farmland, and small villages, from which residents were displaced to accommodate the reservoirs. The Rondout Reservoir occupies 3,513 acres and displaced three small villages and 329 people. The Neversink Reservoir covers an area of 93 square miles.

Another immediate impact of aqueduct construction was the creation of jobs. Construction of the Rondout Reservoir, for example, employed 329 people, and the number of employees at the New York Board of Water Supply increased substantially, from 219 to 720, when the Delaware River Project began. The estimated project cost of $272 million was an enormous amount of money, especially in the 1930's, to add to the economy. Interstate and intrastate competition for water use from the Delaware River Project in the New York City metropolitan area led to the establishment of the State Commission on the Water Supply Needs of Southeastern New York in 1969. This commission was charged with laying the foundation for meeting Southeastern New York's water needs through the twentieth century, including determining long-range needs, evaluating water resources, analyzing alternative methods for financing, and constructing necessary facilities. The commission also reported on a range of issues affecting future water supply.

Environmental impact on fish and wildlife was cited as a problem resulting from water released from New York City reservoirs. Extreme variations in the quantity, temperature, and time of water release inhibited fish populations and adversely affected recreational opportunities. There was also discussion of a water withdrawal plant on the Hudson River near Hyde Park, New York, to utilize river water, and expansion of the Hinckley Reservoir by ten thousand acres to provide an additional five hundred million gallons of water per day.

The commission contemplated several water-supply technology options. Its considerations included large-scale desalting operations to utilize salt water from the ocean, weather modification using chemicals spread by airplane to seed clouds, and direct and indirect wastewater recycling and reuse, in which wastewater would be treated and injected back into the water-supply system either directly (direct reuse) or at a point in the initial stage of the supply cycle (indirect use) in a process similar to the feeding of a reservoir by a tributary. The commission examined methods of reducing water consumption, such as leakage control of water-main breaks; incentives to use water-saving appliances such as special toilets, showerheads, and washing machines; and innovative water pricing that could penalize any user's excessive consumption demands.

The Delaware River Project helped to provide water to people in the suburbs of New York City on a long-term basis. Many other municipal water systems were able to obtain water from the New York City system. The New York City water system also allowed conservation of important groundwater resources beneath Long Island, providing water for millions of people, in addition to the people served by the New York City system. Access to and development of watershed areas surrounding the reservoirs was strictly limited to protect water purity; hence natural habitats for wildlife were simultaneously created and protected. Finally, the system yielded exceptionally good water, especially compared with systems of other large metropolitan areas.

—*Garrett L. Van Wicklen*

FURTHER READING

Chiles, James R. "The Fearless Forty of New York's Water Tunnel." *Smithsonian* 25 (July, 1994): 60-69. A description of tunnel excavators working on the expansion of New York City's water system, which is due for completion in 2020. Provides a brief history and good maps of New York City's system. Describes the equipment, working conditions, danger, and excitement of excavating tunnel number 3. A very readable article.

Conway, E. Virgil. *Water for Tomorrow: Recommenda-*

tions of the Temporary State Commission on the *Water Supply Needs of Southeastern New York*. Albany: New York State Government Printing, 1973. A report on water use circa 1973, thirty years after the completion of the Delaware Aqueduct. Presents the strategies for water use and production methods dictated by technology during 1973. Good maps of the New York City water system are provided.

Galusha, Diane. *Liquid Assets: A History of New York City's Water System*. Harrison, N.Y.: Harbor Hill Books, 2002. An excellent work of regional history and a thorough, detailed examination of water in New York City.

Garrison, E. G. "Sanitary and Hydraulic Engineering." In *A History of Engineering and Technology: Artful Methods*. Boca Raton, Fla.: CRC Press, 1991. A short but interesting discussion of New York City's water supply. A good review of other hydraulic-engineering projects.

Kirby, R. S., S. Withington, A. B. Darling, and F. G. Kilgour. "Sanitary and Hydraulic Engineering." In *Engineering in History*. New York: McGraw-Hill, 1956. Excellent chapter dealing with the history of New York City's water supply, beginning with the late eighteenth century. Excellent illustrations. Map of the reservoir and aqueduct system.

Koeppel, Gerard T. "A Struggle for Water." *Invention and Technology* 9 (Winter, 1994): 18-31. Excellent historical account of the New York City water system from its inception through development of the Croton Aqueduct in 1842. Includes several enlightening paintings, photographs, and diagrams of the water system.

_____. *Water for Gotham: A History*. Princeton, N.J.: Princeton University Press, 2001. Sometimes slow-paced but well-researched and extremely detailed account.

Weidner, C. H. *Water for a City: A History of New York City's Problem from the Beginning to the Delaware River System*. Piscataway, N.J.: Rutgers University Press, 1974. This text provides one of the most complete histories of New York City's water system and includes many details of the system's development.

SEE ALSO: 1908: Chlorination of the U.S. Water Supply Begins; Nov. 5, 1913: Completion of the Los Angeles Aqueduct; Dec. 19, 1913: U.S. Congress Approves a Dam in Hetch Hetchy Valley; May 21, 1924: Farmers Dynamite the Los Angeles Aqueduct; 1930's: Wolman Begins Investigating Water and Sewage Systems; Sept. 8, 1933: Work Begins on the Grand Coulee Dam; Mar. 11, 1936: Boulder Dam Is Completed.

March, 1937
KREBS DESCRIBES THE CITRIC ACID CYCLE

Hans Adolf Krebs postulated the operation of a series of chemical oxidation and reduction reactions that convert the food humans eat to energy in a form useful to the cells of the body.

ALSO KNOWN AS: Krebs cycle; tricarboxylic acid cycle
LOCALE: University of Sheffield, England
CATEGORIES: Science and technology; biology; chemistry

KEY FIGURES
Hans Adolf Krebs (1900-1981), British biochemist
William Arthur Johnson (1913-1993), British student of Krebs
Hans Leo Kornberg (b. 1928), British biochemist

SUMMARY OF EVENT
The foods humans eat consist largely of carbohydrates, fats, and proteins; each of these classes represents a

source of energy and molecules required for growth and repair of tissue. A detailed understanding of the conversion of foods into energy and chemical building blocks is necessary to any attempt to use particular foods to maintain or restore health. The central problem in the early 1930's was that of describing exactly how this conversion is conducted in the cell.

When Sir Hans Adolf Krebs first became interested in these questions, it had already been established that carbohydrates, or sugars and starches, are converted to carbon dioxide, a gas. As these names imply, the chemical structures involve the carbon atom. It had been known for many years that this single element is the main constituent of all living matter. It is not obvious from the names that many complex molecules, or unique collections of six to thousands of carbon atoms, are converted to a specific substance of a single carbon atom. This idea is important because it suggests that such a process might

THE KREBS (CITRIC ACID) CYCLE

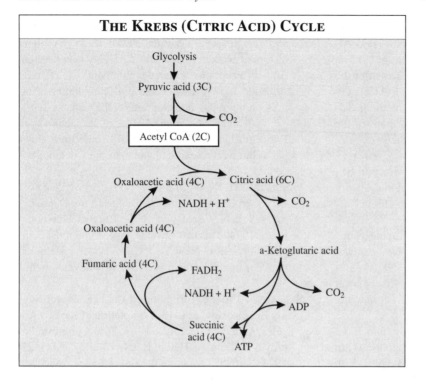

food substance citric acid, which had long been known to be connected directly with the healthy operation of the body. Not only does citrate—the form of an acid in cells—undergo oxidation rapidly, but it also speeds up, or catalyzes, respiratory chemistry. This effect of a compound causing a greater increase in the rate of a reaction had been demonstrated in 1935 for several acids by Hungarian biochemist Albert Szent-Györgyi. Unlike those acids, citrate possesses three acidic carbon atoms. Furthermore, in 1937, organic chemists Carl Martius and Franz Knoop showed exactly how citrate is converted into succinate. Now, Krebs had all the information he needed to propose a pathway describing the conversion of a carbohydrate into carbon dioxide.

The key feature of Krebs's hypothesis is that the process is cyclic in design. It is apparent that each step, or individual change of one molecule into another, must be connected to the next. Biochemists refer to such an arrangement as a pathway. In asserting that the pathway is cyclic, Krebs linked the last chemical reaction to the first as well. The scheme involves some material being constantly fed into the pathway and reacting, or undergoing a chemical change, with one of the products of the last reaction of the sequence.

To be specific, acetate, already proposed by other scientists, enters from the food supply. Reaction takes place with a four-carbon acid, oxaloacetate, which Krebs suggests is a product of the final chemical conversion in his cycle. The product, by a well-known chemical reaction, is citrate.

There is an unexpected characteristic of many pathways that leads to the breakdown of substances: They may require first the synthesis of a more complicated structure, in this case, citrate. Such apparently wasteful indirect steps can be explained by considerations such as efficiency and control of the complex process.

Krebs's proposal for what he called the tricarboxylic, or citric, acid cycle has come to be known as the Krebs cycle. Citrate contains as part of its structure a carbon atom linked sequentially to an oxygen atom and a hydrogen atom. Such an arrangement is characteristic of the common substance alcohol and may be easily lost, or

take place in a series of steps rather than all at once. In fact, it was well known that energy is transformed more efficiently in such a series.

Little was known at that time about the nature of these steps as applied to the carbohydrates, although some progress had been made with the fats and proteins. Krebs had heard of a proposal that combined two acetate fragments, each containing two carbon atoms, to form a four-carbon structure called succinate. Both of these structures are acids that had been shown to involve carbon atoms that had reacted with the element oxygen. These facts and ideas were entirely consistent with respiration, which involves breathing in oxygen and breathing out carbon dioxide. More important, they suggested a research lead that turned out to be vital: the study of acid oxidation.

Krebs appreciated that the most promising approach to the problem of describing the chemistry that takes place in the cell was the study of the rates, or velocity, at which possible intermediate molecules are oxidized. He made an important contribution in the development of a sensitive method of following the changes of pressure in oxygen as the acid was being transformed. In this way, he found that a number of acids are oxidized rapidly enough to play a role in the overall conversion sequence.

His most important discovery concerned the common

eliminated, along with another hydrogen atom as a molecule of water; this process is known as dehydration. The product formed, aconitate, can undergo the reverse process of hydration and produce another alcohol, called isocitrate. This sequence is a clear example of apparently unproductive chemistry. Although the chief concern is oxidation, none has taken place in three chemical reactions. These mysteries can be explained by the fact that citrate is very difficult to oxidize, whereas isocitrate undergoes such chemical change easily.

The next step in the Krebs cycle involves oxidation, but in a surprising way. The element oxygen is not directly involved. Such chemistry had been known long before Krebs's work, and required chemists to look at oxidation in more general terms. The most satisfactory view is that oxidation demands that a substance lose electrons from its structure. Such a definition includes, but is much broader than, reaction with oxygen.

The very nature of this extended view brings about a fundamental chemical concern of direct interest in terms of the Krebs cycle. When chemists say a substance must lose electrons, they must not be taken too literally. The electrons are transferred actually to some other chemical; that is, they are gained also in a process called reduction. First, it is necessary to look at another basic understanding of the biochemist. In essentially every chemical reaction that makes up the myriad chemical processes called metabolism, a highly specific and efficient catalyst, called an enzyme, is found. For many of these enzymatic reactions to occur, a second component, or coenzyme, is also required. In the Krebs cycle, specific coenzymes are reduced by accepting the electrons lost, as, for example, when isocitrate is oxidized. As isocitrate is oxidized, it becomes a very unstable substance known as a beta-ketoacid. In spontaneously losing a molecule of carbon dioxide, it provides a route to one of the known final products of respiration. This event does not prove that Krebs is right, but it demonstrates that his proposal is in accord with experimental observations.

The subsequent steps in the Krebs cycle are similar in that they involve oxidations and loss of carbon dioxide, coupled with the reduction of coenzymes. The final production of oxaloacetate is the result of an oxidation of malate whose structure involves an alcohol similar to isocitrate. Thus the cycle is prepared to begin again with the arrival of another acetate group.

Many men and women worked untold years to provide evidence that Krebs's brilliant hypothesis is a valid approximation of the truth.

SIGNIFICANCE

At the beginning of the nineteenth century, chemists were fascinated by the extraordinary changes that matter undergoes in living organisms. It is from this interest that the designation "organic" was used for the ubiquitous carbon compounds of nature. It was generally believed, however, that these reactions could not be studied outside of living beings.

In the century between the 1830's and the 1930's, this "vital force theory" was so completely abandoned that a new science, biochemistry, was born. Krebs, as one of the principal founders of such studies, provided a vital link between biology and chemistry. In the early years of the twentieth century, a great interest was developing in the exact and quantitative study of chemical reactions. Krebs contributed to both of these modern movements by his leadership in using and developing precise instruments and techniques for the examination of metabolic reactions.

The proposal of the citric acid cycle was met with characteristic scientific skepticism, because it was a breath-

Hans Adolf Krebs. (The Nobel Foundation)

taking leap into uncharted territory. It was about a decade before the conversion of pyruvate to citrate was demonstrated experimentally. There were severe criticisms directed toward the hypothesis, especially because so much of its experimental justification remained to be found.

In time, most working biochemists came to accept the cycle as a hypothesis, and a huge amount of extremely important experimental work was conducted. Much of the refinement was done by Krebs and his students, but in a review characteristic of his generosity, he gives full credit to many other workers who contributed significantly to the development of his basic scheme, such as William Arthur Johnson and Hans Leo Kornberg.

Of central importance is the fact that Krebs's original proposal, although greatly enhanced and extended, has stood the test of many studies. For example, although the proposal was originally conceived to explain the oxidation of carbohydrates, it was shown later that all major foodstuffs are readily accommodated by its chemistry. Furthermore, the functioning of the cycle in plant, as well as animal, tissue soon became apparent. About two-thirds of all the oxidation that takes place in plants and animals using carbohydrate, fat, or protein takes place through the Krebs cycle.

The discovery of the Krebs cycle has been called the greatest imaginative and experimental accomplishment of the science of biochemistry. The breadth of application of the cycle is so great that it lies at the very heart of life, a concept that is not understood completely. Its greatest feature is demonstrated in its delicate control of chemical rates of conversion and balanced supply of vital molecular building blocks for the growth and repair of tissue.

In 1970, a volume of essays was dedicated to Krebs on the occasion of his seventieth birthday. In a dedication, his research director asked, "What had he [Krebs] achieved since 1925?" The answer: "He had discovered the essential chemical reactions of energy-transformations in life."

—*K. Thomas Finley and Patricia J. Siegel*

FURTHER READING

Bartley, W., H. L. Kornberg, and J. R. Quayle, eds. *Essays in Cell Metabolism: Hans Krebs Dedicatory Volume*. New York: Wiley-Interscience, 1970. Collection of highly technical essays also includes vivid and unique personal recollections by Krebs's former students and colleagues. Essential for a full appreciation of Krebs as a scientist and as a person.

Igelsrud, Donald E. "How Living Things Obtain Energy: A Simpler Explanation." *American Biology Teacher* 51 (February, 1989): 89-93. Well-written presentation for the biology teacher and the nonspecialist, with classroom suggestions that aid understanding.

Kornberg, H. L. "H. A. Krebs: A Pathway in Metabolism." In *The Metabolic Roles of Citrate*, edited by T. W. Goodwin. New York: Academic Press, 1968. Fascinating biographical sketch by one of Krebs's students and close collaborators. Full of highly personal observations and rare insights.

Krebs, H. A. "The History of the Tricarboxylic Acid Cycle." *Perspectives in Biology and Medicine* 14 (Autumn, 1979): 154-170. Not only describes the origin of Krebs's ideas and their development but also offers details concerning their success. A revealing analysis of how one scientist finds a solution when others, just as brilliant, overlook it.

Krebs, H. A., and H. L. Kornberg. *Energy Transformations in Living Matter: A Survey*. Berlin: Springer-Verlag, 1947. Careful review of the citric acid cycle as a means of changing energy from foods to forms directly useful for the organisms.

Krebs, H. A., and M. B. V. Roberts. *The Citric Acid Cycle: An Historical Analysis*. New Rochelle, N.Y.: Audio Learning, 1973. Package consisting of manual, audiocassette, and eleven slides presents discussion between Krebs and an English scientist and illustrates chemical reactions. Invaluable description of the history and goals of biochemistry.

McMurray, W. C. *Essentials of Human Metabolism*. 2d ed. New York: Harper & Row, 1983. Places the Krebs cycle within the context of the overall metabolic picture. Treats the regulation of the cycle and the role of the mitochondria in some detail. Includes excellent glossary.

Piel, Gerard. *The Age of Science: What Scientists Learned in the Twentieth Century*. New York: Basic Books, 2001. An overview of the scientific achievements of the twentieth century. Chapter 5 includes brief discussion of Krebs's work. Includes many illustrations and index.

Quayle, J. R. "Obituary: Sir Hans Krebs, 1900-1981." *Journal of General Microbiology* 128 (1982): 2215-2220. Far more than the usual obituary, written by a colleague and admirer. Full of inside detail on Krebs as a person, scientist, and coworker. Provides important information about the development of the entire field of biochemistry.

Rensberger, Boyce. *Life Itself: Exploring the Realm of*

the Living Cell. New York: Oxford University Press, 1996. Comprehensive examination of scientific knowledge about human cells and the frontiers of cell research. Includes glossary and index.

Steiner, Robert F., and Seymour Pomerantz. *The Chemistry of Living Systems.* New York: D. Van Nostrand, 1981. Well-written, detailed review of the chemistry of the Krebs cycle and its relationship to oxidative phosphorylation. Includes an array of thought-

provoking questions and a list of suggested readings at various levels.

SEE ALSO: 1901: Grijns Suggests the Cause of Beriberi; 1901: Hopkins Announces the Discovery of Tryptophan; 1906: Hopkins Postulates the Presence of Vitamins; 1925: Whipple Discovers Importance of Iron for Red Blood Cells; 1928-1932: Szent-Györgyi Discovers Vitamin C.

March 14, 1937
PIUS XI URGES RESISTANCE AGAINST NAZISM

In the midst of Adolf Hitler's assault on organized Christianity and the early stages of the Holocaust, Pope Pius XI issued an encyclical to the German bishops urging them to resist Nazi attempts to destroy Catholicism in Germany.

ALSO KNOWN AS: *Mit brennender Sorge*
LOCALE: Vatican City; Germany
CATEGORIES: Civil rights and liberties; human rights; religion, theology, and ethics; World War II; wars, uprisings, and civil unrest

KEY FIGURES

Pius XI (Ambrogio Damiano Achille Ratti; 1857-1939), Roman Catholic pope, 1922-1939

Eugenio Maria Giuseppe Giovanni Pacelli (1876-1958), cardinal and Vatican secretary of state, 1930-1939, and later Pope Pius XII, 1939-1958

Adolf Hitler (1889-1945), chancellor of Germany, 1933-1945

Michael von Faulhaber (1869-1952), German cardinal and archbishop of Munich who opposed the Nazis

SUMMARY OF EVENT

On July 20, 1933, after six months of negotiation, Cardinal Eugenio Maria Giuseppe Giovanni Pacelli, the Vatican's secretary of state and future Pope Pius XII, signed a concordat with the vice chancellor of the new German regime, Franz von Papen. Pope Pius XI ratified the agreement on the Vatican's behalf on September 10. The concordat guaranteed the Catholic Church and its personnel freedom of action in organizing, preaching, teaching, and conducting religious rites in the secular state. In exchange, the Vatican agreed to keep the Church out of German politics.

The Weimar government had refused to make the for-

mal reassurances that the pope saw as vital in the highly secularized nation, which had a high percentage of Protestants and a history of anti-Catholic government actions. The Vatican felt that the agreement to such guarantees by the new National Socialist (Nazi) government, which was doctrinally anti-Christian, was a major diplomatic achievement and vital to the safety and security of the Church in Germany and its adherents. The concordat also appeared to give formal Church recognition of the Nazi state, which was a boost to the new government's legitimacy and an opportunity for the Nazis to calm German Christians' fears of repression.

German leader Adolf Hitler broke the terms of the agreement again and again. Catholic clergy were ridiculed and physically assaulted, worshipers were harassed, and Catholic schools were oppressed or closed by state organs such as the SA (Sturm Abteilung, also called the Brownshirts) and the Gestapo. The rise of the blatantly pagan Hitler Youth movement, led by Baldur von Schirach, undermined moral and religious teaching in every Catholic school and actively sought to supplant every Catholic youth organization.

Nazi attempts to undermine Catholicism were fed by Hitler's plans for a German national church that would absorb all forms of Christianity. At the same time, Nazi anti-Semitism ran rampant, expressed in both state-sanctioned and private murders of Jews and in the destruction of Jewish property. The unbridled power of Hitler's Germany confronted every institution or organization that seemed to pose a threat to Nazi hegemony. Official state religiosity teetered somewhere between atheism and mythical Germanic neopaganism, with the cult of a semideified Hitler as its focus.

Between the signing of the concordat and the middle of 1937, Pius XI and Pacelli issued nearly sixty formal, private diplomatic letters to the German government in which they protested the unwarranted and illicit treatment of Catholics and the Church in Germany. Pacelli had earlier served in Germany as papal nuncio to the state of Bavaria and then to the Weimar government, so his knowledge of German affairs and his rapport with the German Church were quite strong. Typically, however, the Nazis paid no attention to the Vatican's pleas. The protests were ultimately recorded in three volumes that were secretly provided to German bishops as a way of informing them of papal activities.

Papal concerns, however, were not limited to the status of Catholics. Leaders in the Vatican worried about

---

MIT BRENNENDER SORGE

Pope Pius XI's famous encyclical Mit brennender Sorge *surprised the world by blatantly condemning the Nazi regime.*

Take care, Venerable Brethren, that above all, faith in God, the first and irreplaceable foundation of all religion, be preserved in Germany pure and unstained. The believer in God is not he who utters the name in his speech, but he for whom this sacred word stands for a true and worthy concept of the Divinity. Whoever identifies, by pantheistic confusion, God and the universe, by either lowering God to the dimensions of the world, or raising the world to the dimensions of God, is not a believer in God. Whoever follows that so-called pre-Christian Germanic conception of substituting a dark and impersonal destiny for the personal God, denies thereby the Wisdom and Providence of God who "Reacheth from end to end mightily, and ordereth all things sweetly" (Wisdom viii. 1). Neither is he a believer in God.

Whoever exalts race, or the people, or the State, or a particular form of State, or the depositories of power, or any other fundamental value of the human community— however necessary and honorable be their function in worldly things—whoever raises these notions above their standard value and divinizes them to an idolatrous level, distorts and perverts an order of the world planned and created by God; he is far from the true faith in God and from the concept of life which that faith upholds.

Source: Pope Pius XI, *Mit brennender Sorge*, Encyclical of Pope Pius XI on the Church and the German Reich to the Venerable Brethren the Archbishops and Bishops of Germany and Other Ordinaries in Peace and Communion with the Apostolic See. Given at the Vatican on March 14, 1937.

Christians in general and about the German Jews, who were the special targets of Nazi hatred and oppression, especially after the 1935 passage of the Nuremberg Laws, which stripped Jews of their citizenship. Hitler, however, saw the concordat as a guarantee against papal meddling in German politics, including the "urgent struggle against international Jewry," as he put it to his cabinet in 1933. For his part, Pacelli spoke out forcefully against Nazi atheism, racism, and use of terror in a speech in Lourdes and in an open letter to the archbishop of Cologne in 1935. By 1936, the position of the Catholic Church in Germany had deteriorated even further, and the Church was also under assault in such places as Mexico, war-torn Spain, and the Soviet Union.

The situation in Germany worsened, and in August of 1936, German bishops urged Pius XI to issue a formal protest against the Nazis' doctrines and actions. The following winter, the ailing pope decided to issue two encyclicals, or formal letters, that would be read to Catholic congregations and published in the Catholic press.

Pius issued his anti-Nazi encyclical, *Mit brennender Sorge*, on March 14, 1937. Pacelli was charged with drawing up the statement against the Nazi regime, a task in which he was aided by three German cardinals and two German bishops. Cardinal Michael von Faulhaber, archbishop of Munich, drafted the initial document for the group, and Pacelli lengthened and intensified it. Breaking with tradition, Pacelli made sure that the encyclical was composed in German rather than in Latin, and he took the work's title from its opening words: "with burning anxiety." It is addressed to the bishops of Germany and expresses Pius's pain at learning of the persecution of Catholicism in Germany and of the many Catholics who abandoned the Church for Nazi secularism.

Mit brennender Sorge reviewed the history of the 1933 concordat and lamented the Nazi violations of it. It attacked Nazi neopaganism and the cult that had formed around Hitler while simultaneously reaffirming Christ and the Church as the only sources of religious truth. Furthermore, the encyclical addressed Nazi assaults on the use of Hebrew Scriptures in Christian education and emphasized the importance of the Old Testament and its people in a statement many viewed as a protest against anti-Semitism. *Mit brennender Sorge* defined freedom of conscience and worship as human rights that the German state was wrong to abridge or even attack, and although its references to faith were clearly intended as statements about the Catholic faith, the principles expressed extend to Protestants and Jews alike.

After the encyclical's secret publication on March 14,

the text was smuggled into Germany and read from every Catholic pulpit on Palm Sunday, March 21, 1937. Bold printers produced tens of thousands of copies, and the German government quickly reacted. So did the Vatican, however, and a second encyclical, *Divini Redemptoris*, appeared on March 19, 1937. It targeted totalitarian, atheistic, and violently anti-Christian forms of communism in the Soviet Union and Western Europe.

SIGNIFICANCE

The Nazis had no prior knowledge of the *Mit brennender Sorge* encyclical, and they were caught off guard by its publication. They condemned what they claimed was an open breach of the concordat and did all they could to stop the document's spread. Printers who published it were punished, and possession of a copy was declared illegal. Even mention of the encyclical's title was outlawed. Nazi propaganda as well as Nazi thugs went after the Catholic clergy with increased intensity, and Joseph Goebbels, Hitler's minister of propaganda, started a clumsy campaign claiming that Pius had Jewish ancestry. Internationally, *Mit brennender Sorge* was viewed as a bold and greatly needed condemnation of a vile regime and a powerful statement of universal rights—especially of conscience and worship—in an age of ever-increasing official repression. Shortly after its publication, Pius ordered a new encyclical aimed directly at Nazi racial and anti-Semitic doctrines and practices, although this document, *Humani Generis Unitas*, was never promulgated.

Given the horrors of the Holocaust, historians have either defended *Mit brennender Sorge* as an outspoken, if oblique, defense of Jews and an attack on anti-Semitism or decried it as a lost opportunity for the pope to confront Nazi Germany's anti-Jewish atrocities directly. In fact, Pius's intent was clearly to defend Roman Catholic principles of human dignity and to assert the Church's right to the freedom it needed to minister. Pius was deeply concerned about the integrity and liberty of the Catholic Church in Germany, but the Nazis had essentially declared war on the Vatican even before the encyclical's publication, and Pius was loath to meddle in what the

Nazi regime insisted were internal political matters. Even though no specific reference to the Nazis is ever made in the encyclical, it remains a powerful condemnation of the movement and one of the most forthright papal attacks ever made on a sitting political regime.

—*Joseph P. Byrne*

FURTHER READING

Cornwall, John. *Hitler's Pope: The Secret History of Pius XII.* New York: Penguin Books, 2000. Highly controversial study that criticizes Pacelli, later Pius XII, for his failure to confront or condemn the Nazi state; downplays the importance of *Mit brennender Sorge*.

Godman, Peter. *Hitler and the Vatican: Inside the Secret Archives That Reveal the New Story of the Nazis and the Church.* New York: Free Press, 2004. Another controversial work based upon a rather narrow reading of relevant sources and underestimation of the brutality of the Nazi regime.

Lewy, Guenther. *The Catholic Church and Nazi Germany.* New York: Da Capo Press, 2000. Fairly even-handed treatment of the relationship of the Nazi regime with the Catholic hierarchy in Germany and the Vatican.

Passelcq, Georges, and Bernard Suchecky. *The Secret Encyclical of Pius XI.* New York: Harcourt, 1997. Emphasizes the importance of *Humani Generis Unitas* and *Mit brennender Sorge*.

Pius XI. *"Mit Brennender Sorge": Encyclical on the Church and the German Reich.* The Vatican. http://www.vatican.va/holy_father/pius_xi/encyclicals/documents/hf_p-xi_enc_14031937_mit-brennender-sorge_en.html. The encyclical is available online in English at this Web site.

SEE ALSO: Aug. 9, 1903: Pius X Becomes Pope; June 7, 1912: Pope Pius X Condemns Slavery; Feb. 11, 1929: Lateran Treaty; Jan. 30, 1933: Hitler Comes to Power in Germany; Mar. 2, 1939: Pius XII Becomes Pope.

1937

April 1, 1937
BRITAIN SEPARATES BURMA FROM INDIA

After the three Anglo-Burmese wars of the nineteenth century, Great Britain finally absorbed Burma into its empire on February 26, 1886. Burma was then ruled by the viceroy of India from Calcutta and Delhi as a province of India. With the Government of India Act of 1935, Burma was separated from India; it became a separate colony when the act took effect in 1937.

LOCALE: Burma (now Myanmar)
CATEGORIES: Colonialism and occupation; laws, acts, and legal history

KEY FIGURES
Sir Archibald Douglas Cochrane (1885-1958), governor of Burma, 1936-1941
Aung San (1915-1947), Burmese nationalist leader
Ba Maw (1893-1977), Burmese nationalist leader and prime minister, 1937
Ne Win (Shu Maung; 1911-2002), Burmese nationalist leader
U Nu (1907-1995), Burmese nationalist leader
Saya San (Ya Gyaw; 1874-1931), self-proclaimed leader of Burma, 1930-1932
Lawrence Dundas (second marquis of Zetland; 1876-1971), British secretary of state for India, 1935-1937, and secretary of state for Burma, 1937-1940

SUMMARY OF EVENT

Since 1886, Burma had been ruled by the British as a province from India, which brought to Burma a modern administrative and police system and absorbed it into the global system of finance and trade. The British also created a new, nonhereditary, urban, elite landlord class that was educated at the University of Rangoon, which had been founded in 1920. British citizens acquired increasingly larger amounts of land, and Indian moneylenders and Chinese businessmen moved to Burma to provide the credit for a growing market-driven economy.

Meanwhile, a resistance movement led by monks and former monks developed. In 1906, the Young Men's Buddhist Association was established. Although it was initially a modernist organization concerned with cultural and religious revival, it became increasingly nationalistic and political. In 1909, the British introduced the Government of India Act, which created a Legislative Council with a nonofficial Burmese majority. The

Burmese, however, were not mollified. In response, the British declared that the Burmese were not ready for responsible government and excluded them from the Government of India Act of 1919, which extended the provisions of the 1909 act. This statement aroused considerable resentment among the Burmese and led to such an increase nationalist agitation that the British gave Burma five seats in the Indian Legislative Assembly in Delhi. By the end of the 1920's the idea of separating Burma from India had become popular—it was welcomed by the British business classes—but the Burmese were concerned that the British wanted Burma to be a Crown Colony whose constitutional freedoms could be denied. In the House of Commons in London on January 20, 1931, the secretary of India insisted this charge was inaccurate, and he stated that the British were committed to the introduction of responsible government in both Burma and India.

A former monk named Saya San crowned himself king of Burma in 1930 and led his Galon Army against the government. His rebellion was snuffed out after two years, and he was captured and hanged, but his death became a rallying point for nationalists. In 1930 the Dobama Asiayone (which translates as the "We Burmese Association") was founded by a number of graduates of the University of Rangoon. They called themselves Thakin (master), and they became the recognized leaders of the Burmese nationalist movement. Aung San, one of the Thakin, had became one of the most important leaders of the nationalist movement by the mid-1930's.

The growth and organization of the nationalist movement in Burma prompted the British to reduce the movement's support by co-opting increasing numbers of conservative and opportunistic members of the educated classes into the Burmese civil service and the imperial government. The result was that the Government of India Act of 1935 separated Burma from India, and the country received a fully elected assembly. The Burmese gained considerable authority—more than the Indians—over their own affairs.

In the only general election held in Burma by the British, which took place in December of 1936, 24 percent of the population was allowed to vote for a 132-member House of Representatives. Burmese became ministers responsible for all aspects of their government, except for foreign relations, defense, and the financial system, which remained under the direct control of the governor, who administered these offices through official counsellors and a financial adviser. In addition, the British kept control of the "excluded areas," the tribal areas of the Shan States and the Karen Hills in the east, Kachin in the north, and the Chin Hills in the west. Burma was separated on April 1, 1937, and Sir Archibald Douglas Cochrane was appointed governor in February of 1936. His appointment was also a concession to Burmese nationalism: In the past, the governors of Burma had been senior members of the Indian Civil Service, but Cochrane was a former submarine commander and member of Parliament.

The secretary of state for India, Lawrence Dundas, continued to be the British cabinet minister responsible for Burmese affairs, but he did so through the new Burma office. Ba Maw, the leader of the Sinyetha (translated as the "poor men" or "proletarian") Party became the prime minister after he received the support of the thirty-four seats held by non-Burmese groups—Europeans, Indians, and non-Burmese minorities—but he quickly lost power in Burma's faction-ridden politics. He was followed by three other prime ministers, none of whom could command the support of the majority of the Burmese politicians.

During World War II, Aung San fled to China, where the Japanese took him and his group, called the Thirty Comrades, to Japan for military training. By May of 1942, the Japanese had captured all of Burma, and the British retreated to Imphal, India, where they established a government in exile. On August 1, 1943, Aung San was appointed Burma's war minister, and U Nu became the country's foreign affairs minister. Ne Win formed the Burma National Army in 1943, and Aung San formed the Anti-Fascist People's Freedom League, which became the most popular nationalist organization in Burma.

The Japanese retreated in May of 1945, and in October of 1946, Aung San and his allies were appointed to Britain's Governor's Council. In September of 1946, Aung became head of the provisional government, but on July 19, 1947, he and six colleagues were murdered at a cabinet meeting. U Nu succeeded Aung after October 17, 1947, and he signed the treaty with the British that gave Burma its independence as of January 4, 1948.

SIGNIFICANCE

The separation of Burma from India through the Government of India Act of 1935 accelerated the pace of reforms in Burma. The British colony was given a large dose of self-rule, even though the British remained firmly in control of the police and the army, which were backed by the British navy. However, these reforms merely encouraged the Burmese, especially the younger generation of Thakins (many of whom had become Communists), to demand complete independence. They became frustrated with Britain's hold on power and with what they saw as the collaborationist and compromising attitude of the older generation of Burmese leaders.

As this younger generation became increasingly radicalized, they turned first to the Kuomintang in China and then to the Japanese—who ultimately became Burma's ally—for assistance in expelling the British. In the short term, the separation of Burma from India led to the introduction of a modern political system roughly modeled on the British system of representative government. This began the short-lived practice of democracy and responsible government. In the long term, however, the separation of Burma from India made little difference to Burma. By the end of World War II, Great Britain was a bankrupt nation with little financial or political choice but to grant independence to its colonies, including Burma.

—*Roger D. Long*

FURTHER READING

Kitchen, Martin. *The British Empire and Commonwealth: A Short History*. London: Palgrave Macmillan, 1996. The book concentrates on the nineteenth and twentieth centuries. It explains how Britain came to have the only true empire in the Victorian era and how it emerged victorious in two world wars.

Rose, J. Holland, A. P. Newton, and E. A. Benians, eds. *The Cambridge History of the British Empire*. 8 vols. Cambridge, England: Cambridge University Press, 1929-1963. This is the definitive history of the Commonwealth, although it has become somewhat dated.

Tarling, Nicholas, ed. *From c.1800 to the 1930's*. Vol. 3, part 1 in *The Cambridge History of Southeast Asia*. 4 vols. Cambridge, England: Cambridge University Press, 1999. Different sections of the five parts of this volume offer authoritative details of the history of Burma leading up to the separation of Burma from India and its aftermath. Includes segments written by Tarling, one of the foremost authorities on modern Southeast Asian history.

Tinker, Hugh. *The Foundations of Local Self-Government in India, Pakistan, and Burma*. New York: Praeger, 1968. The importance of the history of the

British parliament to British political development made Parliament see constitutional development as a key to national development and as the means toward freedom for colonies. Accordingly, the British colonial model was to establish local government and then follow it with a responsible provincial government before granting full independence. Tinker's book is considered a classic in the field.

SEE ALSO: Dec. 30, 1906: Muslim League Protests Government Abuses of Minority Rights in India; Mar., 1915: Defense of India Act Impedes the Freedom Struggle; Apr. 13, 1919: British Soldiers Massacre Indians at Amritsar; Aug., 1921: Moplah Rebellion; Mar. 5, 1931: India Signs the Delhi Pact; Dec. 11, 1931: Formation of the British Commonwealth of Nations.

April 26, 1937
RAIDS ON GUERNICA

Raids on Guernica made civilians the targets of military assaults in the Spanish Civil War, indicating Francisco Franco's ties to other fascist governments.

LOCALE: Guernica, Spain
CATEGORIES: Wars, uprisings, and civil unrest; atrocities and war crimes

KEY FIGURES
Francisco Franco (1892-1975), leader of the Nationalist forces rebelling against the Spanish Republic
Adolf Hitler (1889-1945), chancellor of Germany, 1933-1945
Benito Mussolini (1883-1945), premier of Italy, 1922-1943

SUMMARY OF EVENT

Probably the most notorious event linked with war to precede Hitler's "final solution," the bombing of a completely civilian target in the Basque area of Spain—the town of Guernica—revealed to the world the tactics of Spain's General Francisco Franco and his ability to enlist the aid of fascist dictators Benito Mussolini and Adolf Hitler.

By April, 1937, the civil war in Spain between Republicans and Nationalist troops fighting under Franco had been raging for some months. Many Republicans fled to France to live and carry out raids across the border. Ill equipped, they depended on the hospitality of and news carried by peasants in the Basque region of Spain, including Guernica.

The Republican forces had also received much-needed assistance from the American volunteer fighters of the Abraham Lincoln Brigade, although that brigade failed in its objectives and was ultimately disbanded without having contributed to the war in a palpable way.

Nevertheless, writers and authors began to take notice of this war, most notably Ernest Hemingway in *For Whom the Bell Tolls* (1940) and several short stories. These works were precursors to reactions to the bombing of Guernica, which created the largest artistic protest since the introduction of the use of mustard gas in World War I.

A number of studies have shed light on the genesis of the bombing raid on Guernica. One actor in this drama who has often been ignored is Italian dictator Benito Mussolini. Apparently, Mussolini had been in constant contact with Franco about the "Basque problem." With intelligence assistance from Franco's troops, Mussolini had singled out the town of Guernica as a target whose destruction would send a message to the provinces. Having chosen Guernica as a likely target, Mussolini met on several occasions with Hitler. Hitler's role in the bombing went far beyond his action in dispatching the German bombers that attacked Guernica. All three dictators knew that Guernica constituted a civilian target. Only with Mussolini's discussion with Hitler was the bombing of Guernica finalized as part of Hitler's plans to "impress" the world with the extent of Germany's military might. Hitler's easy agreement to bomb civilians in another country served to prefigure future German actions during World War II.

The attack on Guernica surprised many contemporary observers because Germany had largely left Spain to its own struggles in its civil war. Although Franco and Hitler shared similar right-wing philosophies, they were not on particularly friendly terms with each other. Mussolini and Hitler had developed far more amicable relations, however, and that is why Mussolini's actions as a go-between were so important to carrying out the bombing raid on Guernica.

Early on the morning of April 26, 1937, while it was still dark, the people of Guernica were awakened by the

A devastated section of the Basque village of Guernica following the German air attacks of April 26, 1937. (AP/Wide World Photos)

unfamiliar sound of waves of high-flying German bombers. No fighter planes accompanied these bombers because no resistance was expected. The bombers soon released their payloads of solid and shrapnel bombs over the town. When they landed, the solid bombs obliterated entire buildings and started fires throughout the town. The shrapnel bombs split apart on impact, spraying fragmented pieces across a wide area.

As more people were roused from sleep or interrupted in their chores by German planes and the sound of falling bombs, they rushed into the streets, where most were cut down by pieces of shrapnel bombs. Unsure of what was happening, many people who lived on nearby farms made the mistake of running to Guernica in a vain attempt to rescue relatives and friends. Some survivors later spoke of climbing into their root cellars until they could hear nothing overhead; a few managed to escape into the countryside and found shelter in areas less devastated by the bombing. Reports about how long the bombing lasted differ, but some scholars have estimated that the attack it-self may have lasted little more than an hour. A tremendous number of bombs were dropped in that time, destroying people, houses, churches, and a hospital.

Other Basque villages tried to assist the survivors of Guernica, sharing the few medical supplies they had, and additional assistance came from France. The destruction was so complete that at the conclusion of World War II, some eight years later, the town of Guernica had not been rebuilt.

SIGNIFICANCE

Despite this attempt to halt their efforts, the Republicans continued to conduct even more raids from across the French border against Nationalist targets. Although most Basque residents stopped taking up arms against Franco, they provided secret assistance to the rebels. Franco had proved that he could call on Germany's powerful military resources with the intercession of the Italian government, but the destruction of Guernica was not truly a triumph for the leadership of Spain, Italy, or Germany.

THE BASQUE RESPONSE TO THE ATTACK ON GUERNICA

On the day after the attack on Guernica, the Basque Country's president, José Antonio de Aguirre, issued the following statement to the press:

The German airmen, in the service of the Spanish rebels, have bombarded Guernica, burning the historic town which is held in such veneration by all Basques. They have sought to wound us in the most sensitive of our patriotic sentiments, once more making it entirely clear what Euzkadis may expect of those who do not hesitate to destroy us down to the very sanctuary which records the centuries of our liberty and our democracy.

Before this outrage all we Basques must react with violence, swearing from the bottom of our hearts to defend the principles of our people with unheard-of stubbornness and heroism if the case requires it. We cannot hide the gravity of the moment; but victory can never be won by the invader if, raising our spirits to heights of strength and determination, we steel ourselves to his defeat.

The enemy has advanced in many parts elsewhere to be driven out of them afterwards. I do not hesitate to affirm that here the same thing will happen. May to-day's outrage be one spur more to do it with all speed.

The bombing of civilians spoke volumes about Franco's character and encouraged a growing distrust of Hitler and his motives—a conviction that was reinforced during the years leading up to the outbreak of World War II. Artists throughout the world responded to the horror of the bombing. Pablo Picasso created his powerful and enduring antiwar painting titled *Guernica*, and Paul Éluard was inspired to write his famous poem "La Liberté," copies of which were later dropped in bundles across war-torn France by the RAF in 1940. It has been estimated that some twenty thousand poems were written by five thousand poets in response to the Spanish Civil War, and many of these poems were written about Guernica.

—*John Jacob*

FURTHER READING

Alpert, Michael. *A New International History of the Spanish Civil War*. 2d ed. New York: Palgrave Macmillan, 2004. Well-researched analysis of all the international elements involved in the Spanish Civil War. Chapter 10 discusses the events at Guernica. Includes map, bibliography, and index.

MacDonald, Nancy. *Homage to the Spanish Exiles: Voices from the Spanish Civil War*. New York: Human Sciences Press, 1987. Discusses the value of the work of the Basque rebels and those exiled to France during the war.

Martin, Russell. *Picasso's War: The Destruction of Guernica and the Masterpiece That Changed the World*. New York: E. P. Dutton, 2002. Follows the literal and figurative journey of the painting since its creation to present an examination of art's importance to human lives.

North American Committee to Aid Spanish Democracy. *The Crime of Guernica*. New York: Author, 1937. One of the first published reactions of North Americans (particularly U.S. citizens) to the bombings.

Oppler, Ellen C., ed. *Picasso's Guernica: Illustrations, Introductory Essay, Documents, Poetry, Criticism, Analysis*. New York: W. W. Norton, 1988. Collection of materials presents scholarly discussion of the political motives behind the raids on Guernica and the artistic impulse these actions unleashed.

Pérez, Janet, and Wendell Aycock, eds. *The Spanish Civil War in Literature*. Lubbock: Texas Tech University Press, 1990. Collection of essays discussing literary reactions to the Spanish Civil War, including the bombing of Guernica.

Thomas, Gordon. *The Day Guernica Died*. London: Hodder & Stoughton, 1975. Presents a blow-by-blow account of the atrocities at Guernica.

Thomas, Gordon, and Max Morgan Witts. *Guernica, the Crucible of World War II*. 1975. Reprint. Chelsea, Mich.: Scarborough House, 1991. Discusses how Guernica prefigured further atrocities and military campaigns during World War II and the relationships among Franco, Mussolini, and Hitler.

SEE ALSO: July 17, 1936: Spanish Civil War Begins; Aug. 2-18, 1936: Claretian Martyrs Are Executed in Spain; Jan. 6, 1937: Embargo on Arms to Spain; July, 1937: Picasso Exhibits *Guernica*.

May 6, 1937
HINDENBURG DIRIGIBLE BURSTS INTO FLAMES

The disastrous explosion of the zeppelin dirigible
Hindenburg, *the largest rigid aircraft ever constructed,*
caused the deaths of thirty-five on board. The crash
marked the end of the age of lighter-than-air
commercial passenger aircraft.

LOCALE: Lakehurst, New Jersey

CATEGORIES: Disasters; transportation; space and
aviation

KEY FIGURES

Max Pruss (1891-1960), German captain of the
Hindenburg

Ernst Lehmann (1886-1937), German naval officer
who was Eckener's right-hand man at the Zeppelin
Company

Herbert Morrison (1905-1989), journalist who
witnessed the *Hindenburg*'s destruction

Charles E. Rosendahl (1892-1977), American
commander of the naval air station at Lakehurst,
New Jersey

Hugo Eckener (1868-1954), zeppelin pioneer and
successor to Count Ferdinand von Zeppelin and
head of the Zeppelin Airship Construction
Company

SUMMARY OF EVENT

On May 6, 1937, on its first scheduled transatlantic
crossing, the LZ-129 zeppelin *Hindenburg* was preparing to land at Lakehurst, New Jersey, when its hydrogen
ignited and it suddenly burst into flames. As stunned
spectators watched, the burning mass crashed to the
ground within seconds. Thirteen of the thirty-six passengers and twenty-two of the sixty-one crew members died
in the disaster, and one ground crew member was also
killed. Miraculously, almost two-thirds of the ninety-
seven people on board survived the crash.

The flight from Frankfurt, Germany, had been
smooth, and a routine landing was expected. The *Hindenburg* could carry seventy-two passengers, but it did
not have a full passenger load on this flight; May was not
peak flying season. No celebrities were onboard, and
most of the crowd on the ground were family members
and friends, ground crew, journalists, and customs, immigration, and public health officials.

The arrival of the airship had been scheduled for 8:00
A.M., but it was running behind schedule. As the ship
neared the air station at about 4:00 P.M., Captain Max

Pruss, the flight's commander, signaled his intention to
cruise and delay landing until 6:00 P.M. because of threatening storm clouds. Sudden showers drenched the crowd
and landing crew, but at 6:12 P.M., Commander Charles
E. Rosendahl, who was in charge of landing operations
on the ground, signaled to Pruss that the landing could
proceed. The ceiling was 200 feet, visibility was 5 miles,
and the wind was from the west-northwest at 8 knots.
Pruss headed the ship back toward the landing field,
passed over it, and made a tight turn to return to the landing area. Passengers were waving from the windows as
landing ropes were let down to the waiting ground crew
and officials prepared to receive the passengers.

The Chicago-based radio station WLS had sent re-
porter Herbert Morrison and sound engineer Charles
Nehlsen to make a disc recording of the *Hindenburg*'s arrival. As the airship approached, 200 feet above the field,
Morrison described its awesome beauty and grace. At
7:25 P.M., a strange quiet fell on the ship as it neared the
mooring mast. Some spectators reported they saw a blue
flame along its back, and these flames suddenly mush-
roomed from the top of the *Hindenburg*. Landing personnel began scrambling away from under the ship as fire
spread from one gas cell to another and the burning stern
fell to the ground. Commander Rosendahl, who had survived the *Shenandoah* airship wreck, cried out in disbelief as tiny figures fell like ants from the dirigible. Some
passengers walked from the burning wreckage in flames,
some jumped to their death, others jumped to safety, and
a few dazed, but relatively unharmed, passengers escaped with the help of the heroic crew and rescuers.

As the tragedy unfolded, Morrison sobbed and was
unable to speak, but Nehlsen kept him talking and he resumed his historic account of the horrific scene. Photographers and newsreel cameramen also recorded the disaster live. Shocking photos of the catastrophe appeared
on the front pages of morning editions of American
newspapers and were carried by wire services to papers
overseas. Later in the day, newsreels carried the images
to horrified theatergoers, and Herbert Morrison's emotional account was heard on radio across the country.
Captain Pruss survived the wreck, but he underwent
months of plastic surgery and was scarred for life. Captain Ernst Lehmann, a senior captain and German naval
officer who had flown zeppelins on reconnaissance and
bombing raids in World War I, was on board as an adviser.
He was badly burned in the crash and died on May 7.

The Hindenburg *flies over New York City on its way to Lakehurst, New Jersey, on May 6, 1937.* (Courtesy, Navy Lakehurst Historical Society, Inc.)

The world was stunned. The loss of the *Hindenburg* was a serious blow to the German people. Named for their revered late president, Paul von Hindenburg, it was the symbol of German technology and progress. The largest airship ever built, it was 804 feet long (comparable to a thirteen-story building and only 79 feet shorter than the *Titanic*), with a maximum diameter of 135 feet. The ship contained sixteen cells, filled with more than seven million cubic feet of hydrogen gas, and traveled on the lower currents of the air. Living space was only 1 percent of the ship's volume. Powered by four 1,200-horsepower Daimler-Benz diesel engines, the *Hindenburg* had a cruising speed of 78 miles per hour (126 kilometers per hour), and a maximum speed of 84 miles per hour (135 kilometers per hour). Airplanes of the day could carry only the pilot and crew, but zeppelin dirigibles offered intercontinental passengers luxurious service and faster travel than ocean liners at less expensive fares.

After construction was completed in 1935, the *Hindenburg* inaugurated the first scheduled transatlantic air service between Frankfurt, Germany, and Lakehurst, New Jersey, in March, 1936, logging 60 hours for the first trip and 50 hours for the return. In ten round-trips

that year, it carried more than 1,300 passengers and thousands of pounds of cargo and mail (the *Graf Zeppelin*, the *Hindenburg*'s predecessor, had flown 590 flights, including 144 ocean crossings, for ten years, carrying a total of 13,110 passengers.) Since 1910, zeppelins had flown 2,300 flights and carried more than 50,000 passengers. Until the *Hindenburg* catastrophe, zeppelins had never lost a passenger. Only Germany enjoyed such an enviable safety record, and most countries, plagued by catastrophes, had given up building airships.

Adolf Hitler recognized the zeppelins' potential as a propaganda tool and a symbol of the "new Germany" that could reinforce the image of German superiority and invincibility. The Nazi government took over the Zeppelin Company in 1935 (renaming it Deutschezeppelin Reederei) and financed the *Hindenburg*'s completion. Huge swastikas were painted on its fins, and Dr. Hugo Eckener, Count Zeppelin's successor and an international celebrity unsympathetic to the Nazis, was installed as a figurehead chairman of the board. After the crash, ten thousand people witnessed the Nazi rites for the twenty-eight European victims, whose coffins were then transported by ship to Germany.

Controversies raged about the disaster's cause. Given the zeppelins' safety record, many believed that the ship had been sabotaged. An American commission and German investigators, led by Eckener, however, found no evidence of sabotage. The most commonly held belief was that the thunderstorm's conditions had ignited a static electrical charge (known as St. Elmo's Fire) that resulted in the loss of hydrogen gas. (A U.S. embargo on the exportation of helium had forced Germany to use highly flammable hydrogen to lift the aircraft.) A few modern revisionist theorists claimed that the cover of the ship was ignited by static electricity rather than hydrogen. These theorists contended that reflective, flammable aluminum paint reacted with the fabric, hydrogen in the gas cells, and oxygen in the air to cause the crash.

SIGNIFICANCE

The *Hindenburg* crash was not the worst aircraft disaster in history, but it was the greatest disaster captured live by the media up to that time. Herbert Morrison's account became a landmark in the history of broadcasting and was later synchronized to newsreel footage. It foreshadowed the importance of the media in portraying world events. The demise of the *Hindenburg* ended the golden age of lighter-than-air ships: The public was no longer willing to trust airships. The United States was the world's only source of helium, the safer, nonflammable gas, and its refusal to release it to any foreign concern also contributed to the end of commercial-airship construction.

However, advances in airplane design and technology

The Hindenburg *seconds after bursting into flames.* (Courtesy, Navy Lakehurst Historical Society, Inc.)

were the most important factors behind the end of airship construction. After the *Hindenburg* disaster, Hitler was convinced that zeppelins had no military potential and that military superiority in the air would depend on heavier-than-air vessels. Zeppelins were never again used for commercial service, and by the start of World War II, Nazi authorities declared the dirigibles obsolete. On the third anniversary of the *Hindenburg* disaster, the German air ministry destroyed all of its airships. Still, long after the end of the age of airships, the debate over the cause of the *Hindenburg* disaster continued, as did fascination with lighter-than-air vessels.

—Edna B. Quinn

FURTHER READING

Archbold, Rick. *Hindenburg: An Illustrated History.* New York: Warner Books, 1994. Discusses events leading up to the disaster and its possible causes, but the book's strength is its wealth of photographs and illustrations.

Botting, Douglas. *Dr. Eckener's Dream Machine: The Great Zeppelin and the Dawn of Air Travel.* New York: Henry Holt, 2001. Discusses Eckener's invention, its successful flight history, and examines the possible cause of the *Hindenburg* disaster, concluding that the zeppelins' inherently flammable nature was responsible.

Dick, Harold G., and Douglas Robinson. *Golden Age of the Great Passenger Airships: Graf Zeppelin and Hindenburg.* Reprint. Washington, D.C.: Smithsonian Books, 1992. Illustrated volume concerning the evolving designs of the German airships.

Stephenson, Charles. *Zeppelins: German Airships, 1900-1940.* New York: Osprey, 2004. Provides a detailed history of zeppelins.

Syon, Guillaime de. *Zeppelins: Germany and the Airship, 1900-1939.* Baltimore: The Johns Hopkins University Press, 2002. Excellent resource on the political importance of the German airships to Nazi Germany.

Toland, John. *The Great Dirigibles: Their Triumphs and Disasters.* Rev. ed. New York: Dover, 1972. Chapter titled "Twilight of the Gods" discusses the *Hindenburg* disaster and points out the possibility of sabotage by an anti-Nazi crew member.

SEE ALSO: Dec. 17, 1903: Wright Brothers' First Flight; July 25, 1909: First Airplane Flight Across the English Channel; Jan. 19, 1915: Germany Launches the First Zeppelin Bombing Raids; May, 1915: Fokker Aircraft Are Equipped with Machine Guns; May 20, 1927: Lindbergh Makes the First Nonstop Transatlantic Flight; May 27, 1931: Piccard Travels to the Stratosphere by Balloon; May 20-21, 1932: First Transatlantic Solo Flight by a Woman.

May 26, 1937
EGYPT JOINS THE LEAGUE OF NATIONS

Although still limited in its sovereignty by Britain's four "reserved points" in the Anglo-Egyptian Treaty of 1936, Egypt decided to join the League of Nations as a nationalist assertion of its independence.

LOCALE: Cairo, Egypt; Geneva, Switzerland
CATEGORIES: Diplomacy and international relations; organizations and institutions

KEY FIGURES
Muṣṭafā an-Naḥḥās Pasha (1875-1965), head of Egypt's nationalist Wafd Party, 1927-1952, and prime minister of Egypt, 1928, 1930, 1936-1937, 1942-1944, 1950-1952
William Makram Ebeid (1889-1961), prominent Coptic, Wafd Party secretary-general, and frequent minister of finance
Wasef Boutros Ghali (Wasif Butrus Ghali; 1878-1958), Coptic foreign minister, 1924-1937
Alī al-Shamsī (1885-1962), prominent businessman and Wafd Party member, first Egyptian representative at the League of Nations, 1937-1939

SUMMARY OF EVENT
After receiving invitations from twenty-two members of the League of Nations, Egypt formally applied for admission to the League on March 6, 1937. The first invitation to join had come on February 14, 1937 from Iraq, which at the time was the only Arab member of the League. The original vote on Egypt's application had been scheduled for the regular League Assembly meeting in September of 1937, but since both Egypt and Britain were anxious to settle the issue, a special session was held on May 26, 1937. The proceedings began and ended on the same day, and Egypt's application was unanimously approved in a secret ballot by all fifty members present.

Egypt thus became the fifty-ninth member (although some counts list it as the fifty-sixth member, given the intervening defections by Germany, Italy, Japan, and others). According to the statement by Antonio Quevedo of Ecuador, the outgoing League Council president, Egypt's admission was a sign of the League's vitality and of its readiness to be available to those who put their trust in it. The members of the Egyptian delegation were invited to take their seats by the League Assembly's president, Tevfik Rüştü Aras of Turkey. They included Muṣṭafā an-Naḥḥās Pasha at their head, Makram Ebeid, Wasef Boutros Ghali, and Alī al-Shamsī.

Even though Egypt's formal independence had been declared on February 28, 1922, the fifteen-year delay in its admission to the League was a result of Britain's opposition; the British feared that the matter of its various "reserved points" would not hold up to international forum international scrutiny. The reserved points involved defense matters that Egypt had brought up at every round of negotiations with British prime minister Austen Chamberlain in 1928 and Prime Minister Arthur Henderson in 1930. Britain kept reasserting Egypt's right to join the League, but the British did not fully support Egyptian membership until the signing of the Anglo-Egyptian Treaty of August 26, 1936, which established the stationing of British troops in Egypt. As *Al-Ahram*, Egypt's semiofficial newspaper, editorialized, "Egypt, which has regained its independence, is keen to register this achievement through its membership in the League of Nations, thereby rendering its independence an incontrovertible international reality." Elaborate celebrations were planned for the delegates on their return from League headquarters in Geneva, Switzerland.

It was perhaps surprising, then, that the headline announcing Egypt's admission into the League in *The New York Times* of May 28, 1937, read, "Egypt Not Excited by League's Action: Admission by Unanimous Vote Seen Merely as Final Step in Rise to Independence." There are two reasons for this perception. First, while the Anglo-Egyptian Treaty of 1936 had advanced Egypt's aim of limiting the British military presence in the country to certain bases, especially in the Suez Canal Zone, and of promising an end to the Capitulations System under which foreign nationals enjoyed certain extraterritorial rights in the court system, Egypt continued to be riled by Britain's hold on various aspects of Egyptian politics and especially by its privileges in the Anglo-Egyptian region of the Sudan and the Nile Valley.

The second major reason for Egypt's muted rejoicing at joining the League's other independent states was the League's increasing fragility. By 1937, Japan, Germany, and Italy had been pursuing their own aggressive policies in violation of the League's Covenant, defections from world membership were increasing, and the world body was losing both effectiveness and credibility. In fact, at the very session when Egypt was admitted, Italy's invasion of Ethiopia was the issue that most concerned the League's members.

Egypt's admission into the League was also complicated by the problems of unemployment and poverty created by the Great Depression. Even the success of Alī al-Shamsī's efforts to include Arabic as an official League language (side by side with English and French) on September 16, 1937, did not convince Egypt that it had achieved the complete and unmitigated sovereignty for which it had aimed since achieving nominal independence in 1922.

SIGNIFICANCE

By the time Egypt was admitted to the League of Nations, U.S. president Woodrow Wilson's dream (described in his Fourteen Points) of an alternate forum that would peacefully settle political differences was deteriorating. The United States had never joined the world body, and Japan, Germany, Italy, and others had decided to withdraw from the League altogether. For all intents and purposes, the League had stopped being an effective body. In fact, Egypt was the last country to be admitted before the debacle that ended with the Soviet Union's ouster for its invasion of Finland in 1939. In this context, then, Egypt's induction into the League turned out to be something of a Pyrrhic victory.

—Peter B. Heller

FURTHER READING

"Egypt Not Excited by League's Action: Admission by Unanimous Vote Seen Merely as Final Step in Rise to Independence." *The New York Times*, May 28, 1937, p. 9. Reports that Egypt's admission was viewed by Egyptian leaders as only one of several steps in the country's progress to complete independence.

Goldschmidt, Arthur, Jr. *Biographical Dictionary of Egypt*. Cairo, Egypt: American University of Cairo Press, 2000. Profiles the major actors involved in Egypt's entry into the world organization.

Gorman, Anthony. *Historians, State, and Politics in Twentieth-Century Egypt: Contesting the Nation*. London: Routledge Curzon, 2003. Discusses the ways in which Egypt tried to offset Britain's "veiled protectorate" by asserting its independence through League membership.

"League Admits Egypt as Fifty-Ninth Member; Ethiopia Casts Shadow on Geneva Session." *The New York Times*, May 27, 1937, p. 14. Describes the League's special assembly to consider, among other things, Egypt's application for membership.

League of Nations. "Legal and Constitutional Questions." *The Monthly Summary of the League of Nations* 17 (1937): 89-92. Section headed "Admission of Egypt to the League" provides the verbatim statements of Egyptian Prime Minister Muṣṭafā an-Naḥḥās Pasha and British Foreign Secretary Anthony Eden on the occasion.

Rizk, Yunan Labib, "Ministry of Education Centennial," *Al-Ahram Weekly Online* 757 (August, 2005). http://weekly.ahram.org.eg/2005/757/chrncls.htm. The Egyptian government's semiofficial newspaper comments on the country's joining the world organization on May 26, 1937, and identifies the architects of that initiative.

Walters, F. P. *A History of the League of Nations*. Westport, Conn.: Greenwood Press, 1986. Still considered a classic on the world body, the work includes a synopsis of Egypt's admission to membership.

SEE ALSO: Dec. 21, 1908: Cairo University Is Inaugurated; Apr. 28, 1919: League of Nations Is Established; Dec. 13, 1920: Permanent Court of International Justice Is Established; July 24, 1922: League of Nations Establishes Mandate for Palestine; Sept. 25, 1926: League of Nations Adopts International Slavery Convention; Mar., 1928: Muslim Brotherhood Is Founded in Egypt; Oct. 11, 1935-July 15, 1936: League of Nations Applies Economic Sanctions Against Italy; Sept. 13, 1940: Italy Invades Egypt.

May 27, 1937
GOLDEN GATE BRIDGE OPENS

In the years immediately following World War I, the number of commuters crossing into San Francisco became so great that the existing ferry system could no longer accommodate the traffic without long delays. The Golden Gate Bridge, built to relieve the problem, was the longest suspension bridge constructed up to that time.

LOCALE: San Francisco, California
CATEGORIES: Engineering; transportation

KEY FIGURES
Joseph B. Strauss (1870-1938), civil engineer and builder of the Golden Gate Bridge
Charles A. Ellis (1876-1949), civil engineer, professor of engineering, and codesigner of the Golden Gate Bridge
Leon Moisseiff (1872-1943), civil engineer and codesigner of the Golden Gate Bridge

SUMMARY OF EVENT
In the post-World War I era, San Francisco was beginning to feel the need to expand northward. Unfortunately, the Golden Gate, the scenic entrance to San Francisco Bay, prevented easy travel to and from the city. Regular ferry service was available, but it was operating at near capacity and passengers had to wait for several hours on heavy travel days. Dreams of a bridge across the

Golden Gate had been periodically discussed since the latter half of the nineteenth century, but no one considered it feasible or affordable. In 1917, San Francisco's chief engineer, Michael O'Shaughnessy, began contacting engineers around the country about the possibility of building a bridge, but many of the engineers estimated the cost of such a bridge at more than $100 million. Joseph B. Strauss, a Chicago engineer who had made his name designing drawbridges, stood out from the other engineers: He estimated that the bridge could be built for less than $30 million.

In 1921, Strauss submitted preliminary plans for a hybrid bridge with a 2,640-foot suspension span flanked on each end by 685-foot cantilevered-truss spans. Most people disliked the aesthetics of his original design, which probably would have been structurally sound but would have ruined the view of the San Francisco Bay. A greater source of initial concern, however, was that many feared that the cost would be too great and would likely be significantly above Strauss's estimate. The city felt it would be unable to cover the cost, and the counties to the north were even less able to help. The ferry operators were also opposed; they saw the bridge as direct competition that would endanger their business. In spite of clear opposition, Strauss became a crusader for the project, traveling throughout the counties north of San Francisco to convince them that they stood to gain if the bridge was built.

In spite of his best efforts, however, Strauss made little progress on finding approval for the bridge until 1929, when he decided to get help in redesigning his proposed structure.

With the assistance of the engineers Charles A. Ellis and Leon Moisseiff, the bridge's design was extended to a suspension span of 4,000 feet. Instead of the clunky hybrid design originally proposed, the new design was more sweeping, and it promised to be the world's largest suspension bridge. Once the new design was unveiled, preliminary approval was given, and Strauss was appointed chief engineer. For final approval, however, the engineers needed a completed design, including all the engineering calculations. Strauss relentlessly pushed Ellis to get him to finish the calculations, and finally, on August 30, 1930, the completed report and plans were presented to the city. Even though Ellis had done the majority of the design work, he was simply listed as "chief assistant" and received only secondary credit. Rivalry between Ellis and Strauss soon led to Ellis's dismissal.

By 1930, the U.S. War Department determined that the bridge would not cause navigational problems and gave its approval. While the design was being finished, the search for funding also continued, although it was made more difficult by the onset of the Great Depression. After finding no interest in the project at the state or federal levels, full attention was turned to local sources. Convinced of the bridge's economic benefits and after heavy lobbying efforts by Strauss and his supporters, the northern counties decided to join a bridge district that would issue bonds to raise the estimated $35 million needed for construction. In November of 1930, the voters overwhelmingly approved the bonds, but no bond house or bank would agree to take them. The bonds remained in limbo until 1932, when A. P. Gianini, whose bank later became the Bank of America, agreed to lend the needed money.

Construction on the Golden Gate Bridge began in 1933. The first major project was to build the two towers

Military biplanes fly between the towers of the Golden Gate Bridge as pedestrians walk across the span during the bridge's opening ceremonies. (AP/Wide World Photos)

that would support the suspension span. Because the length of the span was so great—4,200 feet in the final design—they had to bear tremendous forces. Each tower was to extend 746 feet above the water. The north tower was relatively easy to construct as it was in shallow water, but the south tower was to be built in deep water 1,100 feet from shore, where wave action from the open ocean would leave it very exposed. To provide adequate anchorage, 1.6 million cubic yards of rock had to be blasted and dredged from the south tower's site. Much of the blasting work required that divers enter the water to place the charges, but strong currents meant that there were only small windows of time in which diving was possible.

After excavation was complete, a protective bumper was built around the spot where the caisson for the base of the tower was to be placed. Wave action was so intense that the first attempt failed, and the caisson shifted. After further engineering calculations, a sturdier method was designed, and the tower began to take shape. The Art Deco design of the towers was the work of architect Irving F. Morrow.

Once the towers were complete, in the fall of 1935, the Roebling company was hired to spin the cables that would support the road bed. The contract with the Roebling company specified that Roebling would complete the cables in one year; after the year had passed, the company would lose money for each additional day needed. The bridge required 80,000 miles of wire, enough to span the equator more than three times. Thousands of strands were laboriously spun together to produce the largest suspension cable of that time, which was 36.5 inches in diameter. The towers and cables were designed to withstand a broadside wind of 100 miles per hour; at this speed, the bridge would be able to sway as much as 27 feet at midspan. The cables were completed on May 20, 1936, well ahead of schedule and four times faster than predicted.

The final part of the project was to complete the road bed, the most dangerous part of the job. At the time, the rule of thumb was one fatality for each $1 million in cost. Strauss, who was obsessed with safety, spent $130,000 for a safety net to be placed beneath the developing road bed. In spite of this precaution, one major accident left ten fatalities, but the overall fatality figures were well below the typical rate. By 1937, the bridge was completed, sixteen years after Strauss first submitted plans. The official opening day was May 27, 1937. More than two hundred thousand people turned out for the celebration and were given the chance to be the first pedestrians to cross the bridge. Joseph B. Strauss gave one of the speeches that day, but he died within a year after the bridge's opening.

SIGNIFICANCE

When the Golden Gate Bridge was opened to traffic, drivers had to pay a toll that was intended to pay off the bonds used to build the bridge. Drivers of passenger cars were charged fifty cents, with an additional five cents for each passenger. The bridge remained in operation and tolls continued to be charged, not to pay off the bonds, which were retired, but to pay for the continuing maintenance required to keep the bridge safe. After 1997, the bridge began a three-phase seismic retrofit, a significant portion of which was funded by bridge tolls.

—*Bryan Ness*

FURTHER READING

Dillon, Richard H., Don Denevi, and Thomas Moulin. *High Steel: Building the Bridges Across San Francisco Bay*. Berkeley, Calif.: Celestial Arts, 1980. Recounts the history of the two largest bridges in the San Francisco Bay: the Golden Gate and Bay Bridges.

Schock, James W. *The Bridge: A Celebration*. Sherman Oaks, Calif.: Shock Ink, 1997. Considered by many to be a definitive account of the history of the Golden Gate Bridge.

Van Der Zee, John. *The Gate: The True Story of the Design and Construction of the Golden Gate Bridge*. New York: Simon & Schuster, 1987. Delves into the personalities involved in the building of the Golden Gate Bridge.

Wells, Matthew. *Thirty Bridges*. New York: Watson-Guptill, 2002. As the title suggests, this book looks at thirty different bridges worldwide, including the Golden Gate Bridge. Gives a nice perspective on how the Golden Gate fits into history.

SEE ALSO: Apr. 18, 1906: San Francisco Earthquake; Mar. 19, 1932: Dedication of the Sydney Harbour Bridge; Nov. 7, 1940: Tacoma Narrows Bridge Collapses.

June, 1937
THEILER DEVELOPS A TREATMENT FOR YELLOW FEVER

Max Theiler conducted research that led to the 17D vaccine for yellow fever, one of the deadliest diseases of the nineteenth and twentieth centuries.

LOCALE: New York, New York
CATEGORY: Health and medicine

KEY FIGURES
Max Theiler (1899-1972), South African
microbiologist and specialist in tropical medicine
Wilbur Augustus Sawyer (1879-1951), American
physician
Hugh Smith (b. 1902), American physician

SUMMARY OF EVENT
Yellow fever, caused by a virus and transmitted by mosquitoes, infects humans and monkeys. After the bite of the infecting mosquito, it takes several days before symptoms appear. The onset of symptoms is abrupt, with headache, nausea, and vomiting. Because the virus destroys liver cells, yellowing of the skin and eyes is common. Approximately 10 to 15 percent of patients die after exhibiting the terrifying signs and symptoms. Death occurs usually from liver necrosis (decay) and liver shutdown. Victims who survive, however, recover completely and are immunized.

At the beginning of the twentieth century, there was no cure for yellow fever. The best that medical authorities could do was to quarantine the afflicted. Those quarantines usually waved the warning yellow flag, which gave the disease its colloquial name, "yellow jack."

After the *Aëdes aegypti* mosquito was clearly identified as the carrier of the disease in 1900, efforts were made to combat the disease by wiping out the mosquito. Most famous in these efforts were the American army surgeon Walter Reed and the Cuban physician Carlos Juan Finlay. This strategy was successful in Panama and Cuba and made possible the construction of the Panama Canal. Still, the yellow fever virus persisted in the tropics, and the opening of the Panama Canal increased the danger of its spreading aboard the ships using this new route.

Moreover, the disease, which was thought to be limited to the jungles of South and Central America, had begun to spread around the world to wherever the mosquito *Aëdes aegypti* could carry the virus. Mosquito larvae traveled well in casks of water aboard trading vessels and spread the disease to North America and Europe.

Max Theiler received his medical education in London. Following that, he completed a four-month course at the London School of Hygiene and Tropical Medicine, after which he was invited to come to the United States to work in the department of tropical medicine at Harvard University.

While there, Theiler started working to identify the yellow fever organism. The first problem he faced was finding a suitable laboratory animal that could be infected with yellow fever. Until that time, the only animal successfully infected with yellow fever was the rhesus monkey, which was expensive and difficult to care for under laboratory conditions. Theiler succeeded in infecting laboratory mice with the disease by injecting the virus directly into their brains.

Laboratory work for investigators and assistants coming in contact with the yellow fever virus was extremely dangerous. At least six of the scientists at the Yellow Fever Laboratory at the Rockefeller Institute died of the disease, and many other workers were infected. In 1929, Theiler was infected with yellow fever; fortunately, the attack was so mild that he recovered quickly and resumed his work.

During one set of experiments, Theiler produced successive generations of the virus. First, he took virus from a monkey that had died of yellow fever and used it to infect a mouse. Next, he extracted the virus from that mouse and injected it into a second mouse, repeating the same procedure using a third mouse. All of them died of encephalitis (inflammation of the brain). The virus from the third mouse was then used to infect a monkey. Although the monkey showed signs of yellow fever, it recovered completely. When Theiler passed the virus through more mice and then into the abdomen of another monkey, the monkey showed no symptoms of the disease. The results of these experiments were published by Theiler in the journal *Science*.

This article caught the attention of Wilbur Augustus Sawyer, director of the Yellow Fever Laboratory at the Rockefeller Foundation's International Health Division in New York. Sawyer, who was working on a yellow fever vaccine, offered Theiler a job at the Rockefeller Foundation, which Theiler accepted. Theiler's mouse-adapted, "attenuated" virus was given to the laboratory workers, along with human immune serum, to protect them against the yellow fever virus. This type of vaccination, however, carried the risk of transferring other diseases, such as hepatitis, in the human serum.

THEILER'S CONTRIBUTION

In 1951, Max Theiler received the Nobel Prize in Physiology or Medicine for his work on the yellow fever vaccine. In a presentation speech at the awards ceremony, Professor H. Bergstrand, chairman of the Nobel Committee for Physiology or Medicine of the Royal Caroline Institute, noted why Theiler's discovery was worthy of recognition:

The significance of Max Theiler's discovery must be considered to be very great from the practical point of view, as effective protection against yellow fever is one condition for the development of the tropical regions—an important problem in an overpopulated world. Dr. Theiler's discovery does not imply anything fundamentally new, for the idea of inoculation against a disease by the use of a variant of the etiologic agent which, though harmless, produces immunity, is more than 150 years old. Jenner used a natural virus variant, cowpox virus, against smallpox, and Pasteur produced a similar variant of the rabies virus by repeated passage through animals. So far there have been only a few successful attempts to master a disease by such measures, but Dr. Theiler's discovery gives new hope that in this manner we shall succeed in mastering other virus diseases, many of which have a devastating effect, and against which we are still entirely powerless. Max Theiler, therefore, has rendered mankind such a service as Nobel made a condition for the awarding of this prize.

Source: H. Bergstrand, "Presentation Speech," in *Nobel Lectures, Physiology or Medicine 1942-1962* (Amsterdam: Elsevier, 1964).

ler's assistant, called to his attention an odd development as noted in the laboratory records of strain 17D. In its 176th culture, 17D had failed to kill the test mice. Some had been paralyzed, but even these eventually recovered. Two monkeys who had received a dose of 17D in their brains survived a mild attack of encephalitis, but those who had taken the infection in the abdomen showed no ill effects whatever. Oddly, subsequent subcultures of the strain killed monkeys and mice at the usual rate. The only explanation possible was that a mutation had occurred unnoticed.

The batch of strain 17D was tried over and over again on monkeys with no harmful effects. Instead, the animals were immunized effectively. Then it was tried on the laboratory staff, including Theiler and his wife, Lillian. The batch injected into humans had the same immunizing effect. Neither Theiler nor anyone else could explain how the mutation of the virus had occurred. Attempts to duplicate the experiment, using the same Asibi virus, failed. Still, this was the first safe vaccine for yellow fever. In June, 1937, Theiler reported this crucial finding in the *Journal of Experimental Medicine*.

In 1930, Theiler worked with Eugen Haagen, a German bacteriologist, at the Rockefeller Foundation. The strategy of the Rockefeller laboratory was a cautious, slow, and steady effort to culture a strain of the virus so mild as to be harmless to a human but strong enough to confer a long-lasting immunity. (To "culture" something—tissue cells, microorganisms, or other living matter—is to grow it in a specially prepared medium under laboratory conditions.) They started with a new strain of yellow fever harvested from a twenty-eight-year-old West African named Asibi; it was later known as the "Asibi strain." It was a highly virulent strain that in four to seven days killed almost all the monkeys that were infected with it. From time to time, Theiler or his assistant would test the culture on a monkey and note the speed with which it died.

It was not until April, 1936, that Hugh Smith, Thei-

Max Theiler. (The Nobel Foundation)

SIGNIFICANCE

Following the discovery of the vaccine, Theiler's laboratory became a production plant for the 17D virus. Before World War II (1939-1945), more than one million vaccination doses were sent to Brazil and other South American countries. After the United States entered the war, eight million soldiers were given the vaccine before being shipped to tropical war zones. In all, approximately fifty million people were vaccinated during the war years.

Although the vaccine, combined with effective mosquito control, eradicated the disease from urban centers, yellow fever is still present in large regions of South and Central America and of Africa. The most severe outbreak of yellow fever ever known occurred from 1960 to 1962 in Ethiopia; out of one hundred thousand people infected, thirty thousand died. Severe outbreaks of yellow fever occurred in the 1980's in Ghana, Burkina Faso, and Nigeria. In 2001 the World Health Organization reported that the incidence of yellow fever rose during the 1980's and 1990's, infecting up to two hundred thousand people and causing thirty thousand deaths per year. This resurgence of the disease was attributed to deforestation, the proliferation of environments in which mosquitoes breed, and large unvaccinated populations in developing countries of Africa and Latin America.

More than fifty years after its development, the 17D yellow fever vaccine prepared by Theiler in 1937 continues to be the only vaccine against the disease used by the World Health Organization, which is involved in a continuous effort to prevent infection by immunizing the people living in tropical zones.

—*Gershon B. Grunfeld*

FURTHER READING

Bendinger, Elmer. "Max Theiler: Yellow Jack and the Jackpot." *Hospital Practice*, June 15, 1988, 211-244. An excellent article on the life story of Max Theiler. Opens with Theiler's childhood in South Africa, where he began his fascination with biology, and continues through his brilliant scientific career.

Bres, P. L. J. "A Century of Progress in Combating Yellow Fever." *Bulletin of the World Health Organization* 64 (December, 1986): 775-786. Surveys the epidemiological situation of yellow fever in the fifty years that followed the discovery of the vaccine. Discusses major scientific advancements in the study of the virus and the disease. Includes a short description of the history of yellow fever epidemics and research on yellow fever.

Hill, Ralph Nading. *The Doctors Who Conquered Yellow Fever*. New York: Random House, 1957. Depicts the story of the fight against yellow fever through the life story of Walter Reed. Includes a brief description of the developments in the fight against the disease following Reed's death up to Theiler's development of the 17D vaccine.

Oldstone, Michael B. A. *Viruses, Plagues, and History*. New York: Oxford University Press, 1998. Examines the effects of deadly viruses on human history and discusses scientists' efforts to eradicate such viruses. Chapter 5 is devoted to the successful fight against yellow fever.

Pierce, John R., and Jim Writer. *Yellow Jack: How Yellow Fever Ravaged America and Walter Reed Discovered Its Deadly Secrets*. New York: John Wiley & Sons, 2005. Focuses on the impact of yellow fever epidemics in the United States and on Walter Reed's work to determine the disease's mode of transmission.

Strode, George K., ed. *Yellow Fever*. New York: McGraw-Hill, 1951. The most authoritative book on yellow fever at the time of its publication. Chapters were written by the foremost experts in the field, including one by Max Theiler on the virus. Covers topics such as the history of the fight against yellow fever, the search for a vaccine against the disease, and the cost of this effort.

Williams, Greer. *Virus Hunters*. New York: Alfred A. Knopf, 1959. Describes the development of a vaccine against yellow fever in chapter 15, titled "Theiler: Yellow Fever's Second Exit." Includes annotated bibliography.

SEE ALSO: Feb. 4, 1901: Reed Reports That Mosquitoes Transmit Yellow Fever; Dec. 2-5, 1902: Founding of the International Sanitary Bureau; 1904-1905: Gorgas Develops Effective Methods of Mosquito Control.

June-September, 1937
REBER BUILDS THE FIRST INTENTIONAL RADIO TELESCOPE

Grote Reber's construction of the first reflecting radio telescope for the systematic study of radio emission from space marked the beginning of intentional radio astronomy.

LOCALE: Wheaton, Illinois
CATEGORIES: Science and technology; astronomy

KEY FIGURES
Grote Reber (1911-2002), American radio engineer and amateur astronomer
Karl G. Jansky (1905-1950), American radio engineer
Bernard Lovell (b. 1913), English radio astronomer
Heinrich Hertz (1857-1894), German physicist
Guglielmo Marconi (1874-1937), Italian electrical engineer

SUMMARY OF EVENT
Intentional radio astronomy began in 1937 when Grote Reber built the first reflecting radio telescope at his home in Wheaton, Illinois, only fifty years after the discovery of radio waves by Heinrich Hertz in 1887 and five years after the first report of radio waves from space. Hertz had produced radio waves with a spark generator at about 50 million oscillations per second (50 megahertz) and measured a wavelength of about 6 meters (almost 20 feet), indicating a wave velocity equal to the speed of light (approximately 300 million meters, or 186,000 miles, per second). His work demonstrated that radio waves and light waves are both electromagnetic waves differing only in frequency and wavelength. Radio waves are the longest waves in the electromagnetic spectrum, which also includes infrared, visible light, ultraviolet, and X rays at increasingly higher frequencies and shorter wavelengths.

The early study of radio was directed toward the development of wireless communications, leading to transatlantic transmission and reception of radio signals in 1901 by Guglielmo Marconi. In 1932, Karl G. Jansky reported his accidental discovery of radio waves from space. At the Bell Telephone Laboratories in New Jersey, he built a rotating dipole-array wire antenna sensitive to 15-meter (49.2-foot) radio waves to study the static noise that interferes with radio communications. In addition to the usual atmospheric static, he detected a weak, steady hiss that appeared four minutes earlier each day. As this corresponds to the twenty-three-hour, fifty-six-minute apparent daily motion of the stars, he concluded that he was receiving cosmic radio noise from outside the solar system.

Jansky's work was published in a series of scientific papers starting in 1932. His results made the front page of *The New York Times*, and a national radio network broadcast ten seconds of radio hiss from space. Despite this publicity, no scientist followed up on Janksy's discovery until Grote Reber, a twenty-five-year-old radio engineer and amateur astronomer, decided to build a large parabolic dish for radio reception in the side yard at his home in Wheaton, Illinois, 40 kilometers (about 25 miles) west of Chicago. It was the first intentional radio telescope and the only one in operation until after World War II.

Reber was an avid radio amateur who built his first transceiver at age fifteen and began to communicate with other amateurs around the world. He received an electrical engineering degree in 1933 from what is now the Illinois Institute of Technology and began working for the Stewart-Warner Company in Chicago. After reading Jansky's papers, he recognized the importance of his discovery. He also realized that greater progress could be made with equipment specially designed to measure cosmic static at radio frequencies. He began to plan the construction of a large reflecting dish with associated receiving equipment that could measure the detailed distribution of radiation intensities throughout the sky at different wavelengths.

Although he had no outside support, Reber decided to build as large a reflector as he could in order to obtain maximum resolution (separation of sources) at radio frequencies. His reflector design also had the capability of tuning to different wavelengths by changing the antenna feed at the focus of the parabolic dish. He decided on a 6.1-meter (20-foot) focal length and a dish diameter of 9.4 meters (31 feet), based on the length of the longest two-by-fours available locally. Working with only a minimum of help from June to September, 1937, he completed his radio telescope at a cost of thirteen hundred dollars of his own money. This instrument remained in his yard for ten years; it was a source of amazement and wild rumors among local residents and visitors.

To minimize expense, Reber used a meridian-transit mounting that could be pointed up and down in a north-south plane (declination), while scanning east and west (right ascension) was provided by Earth's rotation. The differential gear from a Ford Model T truck was used to change the elevation angle of the dish. The reflecting

The reflecting radio telescope built by Grote Reber in Wheaton, Illinois, in 1937.

to find any radiation of celestial origin. A still longer wavelength could be conveniently detected with a cylindrical cavity made from a sheet of aluminum measuring 2 meters by 4 meters (approximately 6.6 feet by 13.1 feet), setting the operating wavelength at 1.87 meters (6.14 feet). A dipole antenna in the cavity resonator at the dish's focus gave positive results by the spring of 1939, after two years of persevering work.

Reber did most of his observing from midnight to dawn to avoid interference from automobile ignitions. By April, the plane of the Milky Way crossed the meridian late at night, and it became apparent that our galaxy emitted 1.87-meter radio waves. The intensity of the cosmic radiation was determined by reading a microammeter at one-minute intervals while monitoring the audio signal to detect and remove periods of local interference. His initial results were published in February, 1940, in the *Proceedings of the Institute of Radio Engineers*, where he noted that his estimated intensity was far below that reported by Jansky at the 15-meter (49.2-foot) wavelength. This led Reber to the conclusion that the source of the cosmic radiation could be explained by interactions between electrons and positive ions (charged atoms) in an ionized gas rather than from thermal emission. Over the next five years, he obtained the first radio maps of the galaxy at two different wavelengths and identified a number of important radio sources in different parts of the galaxy.

dish consisted of seventy-two radial wooden rafters cut to parabolic shape with a tolerance of about 0.5 centimeter (about 0.02 inch), with forty-five pieces of galvanized sheet metal screwed over the rafters to form the reflecting surface. The entire structure weighed nearly two tons.

Using custom-made vacuum tubes from the University of Chicago and other radio components from his employer, Reber began with a receiver designed for the shortest possible operating wavelength of 9 centimeters (3.5 inches). This would give the best angular resolution and would be more sensitive to thermal radiation than at the longer wavelength detected by Jansky. Unfortunately, scanning at 9 centimeters gave no response, so he began to doubt that thermal radiation was the source of Jansky's observations. By the summer of 1938, Reber had upgraded his receiver to detect 33-centimeter (13-inch) waves at a greater sensitivity, but still failed

As virtually the only active radio astronomer in the world, Reber operated his telescope in Wheaton for ten years before it was finally moved to a U.S. Bureau of Standards field station in 1947. The telescope was again relocated in 1960 to the National Radio Astronomy Observatory at Green Bank, West Virginia, where it remains on public view and is occasionally used for demonstration purposes. In 1954, Reber moved to Tasmania, Australia, where he constructed a huge wire-antenna array telescope to measure radiation at a wavelength of 150 meters (approximately 492 feet) in the Southern Hemisphere.

SIGNIFICANCE

The success of Reber's pioneering radio telescope led to the rapid development of radio astronomy after World War II and the construction of increasingly larger and more sophisticated radio telescopes. Early work in radio astronomy was done by adapting radar scanning dishes retired from wartime service. Their electronic receivers were much more sensitive than the relatively simple devices used by Jansky and Reber. In fact, radio emission from the Sun was first observed accidentally by James S. Hey, when antiaircraft radars, operating between 4- and 8-meter (about 13- and 26-foot) wavelengths in England, experienced severe noise jamming on February 27 and 28 of 1942. Analysis of this phenomenon showed that the signals came from the Sun during unusual sunspot activity, but publication was withheld until after the war. Reber also detected solar radio emissions in 1943.

One of the first applications of radar to radio astronomy began in 1946 at Jodrell Bank, an experimental botanical site of Manchester University. Here, a group led by Sir Bernard Lovell used radar astronomy to study daytime meteor activity in great detail, even though it was invisible to ordinary sight. In 1947, they constructed a fixed, upward-looking parabolic reflector, 66 meters (216.5 feet) in diameter, with a reflecting surface consisting of wire mesh spread over a frame on the ground. This instrument was limited to vertical reception, with scanning mainly from Earth's rotation. Lovell soon began to plan a giant fully steerable reflector that could explore radio phenomena throughout the universe. Construction of the 76-meter (249.3-foot) radio telescope at Jodrell Bank Experimental Station took six years, with the turret rack of a battleship to move the huge dish. It was designed to operate at 21 centimeters (about 8.3 inches) after it was discovered that interstellar atomic hydrogen radiates at that wavelength. The telescope was completed in 1957, in time to track the first human-made satellite, *Sputnik 1*. This instrument gave productive results in many investigations, including emissions from the Sun, the galaxy, and several discrete radio sources.

In the United States, the National Radio Astronomy Observatory began operation at Green Bank, West Virginia, with a 26-meter (85.3-foot) dish in 1959, followed by a 91-meter (298.6-foot) transit telescope in 1962 and a 43-meter (141.1-foot) steerable telescope in 1965. For more than twenty-five years, the 91-meter telescope, with its wire-mesh reflecting dish, was the largest movable telescope in the United States until it collapsed from metal fatigue in 1989. In 1970, a 100-meter (328.1-foot) fully steerable radio telescope was completed at Effels-burg near Bonn, West Germany, and in 1963, a 305-meter (1,000-foot) fixed bowl built of wire mesh was constructed in a natural valley near Arecibo, Puerto Rico.

Larger telescopes provide sharper images, but the best resolution can be achieved through the electrical connection of two or more radio telescopes in an array; this configuration gives a resolving power equivalent to a single dish with a diameter equal to the size of the array. The Very Large Array (VLA) in the high desert near Socorro, New Mexico, began operation in 1980 with twenty-seven dishes, each 25 meters (about 82 feet) in diameter, forming a Y-shaped array 27 kilometers (about 16.8 miles) long, with a resolution comparable to that of the best optical telescopes.

—*Joseph L. Spradley*

FURTHER READING

Abell, George O., David Morrison, and Sidney C. Wolff. *Exploration of the Universe*. 6th ed. Philadelphia: Saunders College Publishing, 1991. Standard college astronomy textbook includes a good chapter on radio telescopes that presents some discussion of Reber's work. Describes many of the most important radio telescopes and features a good variety of photographs.

Burke, Bernard F., and Francis Graham-Smith. *An Introduction to Radio Astronomy*. 2d ed. New York: Cambridge University Press, 2002. Authoritative graduate-level text provides an introduction to radio telescopes as well as an overview of radio astronomy. Includes references, index, and an appendix on the origins of radio astronomy.

Hey, J. S. *The Evolution of Radio Astronomy*. New York: Science History Publications, 1973. Useful history of radio astronomy by one of the pioneers in its development. Describes the work of Jansky and Reber as well as the rise of radio astronomy after World War II. Includes illustrations and references.

Malphrus, Benjamin K. *The History of Radio Astronomy and the National Radio Astronomy Observatory: Evolution Toward Big Science*. Melbourne, Fla.: R. E. Krieger, 1996. Presents the history of the field of radio astronomy along with that of one of the world's most important radio astronomy observatories. Accessible to both lay readers and readers with science backgrounds.

Spradley, Joseph L. "The First True Radio Telescope." *Sky and Telescope* 76 (July, 1988): 28-30. Introductory article on Reber's background and work describes the design, construction, and operation of the first intentional radio telescope. Includes photographs of the telescope and the original model used in its design.

Sullivan, Woodruff T., III, ed. *The Early Years of Radio Astronomy: Reflections Fifty Years After Jansky's Discovery*. 1984. Reprint. New York: Cambridge University Press, 2005. Collection of articles by the pioneers of radio astronomy on the field's early development. Includes a 1958 article by Reber, originally published in *Proceedings of the Institute of Radio Engineers*, titled "Early Radio Astronomy at Wheaton, Illinois" and an article by Lovell titled "The Origins and Early History of Jodrell Bank." Features many historical photographs.

Verschuur, Gerrit L. *The Invisible Universe Revealed: The Story of Radio Astronomy*. 2d ed. New York:

Springer-Verlag, 1987. Provides good description of the results of radio astronomy with more than one hundred photographs and radio contour maps. Concluding chapters give a history of the field since Jansky and Reber and present an overview of the most important radio telescopes.

SEE ALSO: Mar. and June, 1902: Kennelly and Heaviside Theorize Existence of the Ionosphere; 1919: Principles of Shortwave Radio Communication Are Discovered; 1927: Oort Proves the Spiral Structure of the Milky Way; 1930-1932: Jansky's Experiments Lead to Radio Astronomy; 1934-1945: Radar Is Developed; 1935: Chapman Determines the Lunar Atmospheric Tide at Moderate Latitudes.

June 2, 1937
BERG'S *LULU* OPENS IN ZURICH

Alban Berg's opera Lulu, *written in a personalized version of the twelve-tone compositional style, premiered in Zurich in truncated form; the completed version would not premiere until 1979.*

LOCALE: Zurich, Switzerland
CATEGORIES: Music; theater

KEY FIGURES
Alban Berg (1885-1935), Austrian composer
Helene Berg (1887-1976), wife of Alban Berg
Frank Wedekind (1864-1918), German playwright

SUMMARY OF EVENT
The performance history of the opera *Lulu* is one of the most complicated in musical history. It took three quarters of a century between the opera's conception and its world premiere in the definitive form intended by its composer, Alban Berg, before an audience could comfortably say it had seen the "real" *Lulu*. The tortuous stage history of *Lulu* involves the composer's premature death, a world war, a succession of provocative but inadequate productions, a good deal of scholarly bickering, and even a ghost.

As a young man, Alban Berg was deeply impressed by a May, 1905, performance of Frank Wedekind's play Die Büchse der Pandora (pr., pb. 1904; *Pandora's Box*, 1918). Wedekind himself had been inspired by reports of the gruesome murders of Jack the Ripper in London and wrote a play on the topic. To avoid almost cer-

tain difficulties with the German censor, in 1895 he published only the first three acts of the play as *Der Erdgeist* (*Earth Spirit*, 1914), and eventually the remaining portions of the play were published as *Pandora's Box*. Like Freud before him, Wedekind discovered that German and Austrian audiences at the turn of the century were not willing to tolerate his radical views. What made the work so shocking was its implicit call for complete female sexual freedom and its depiction of human sexuality as an endlessly disruptive force. One prominent scholar has called Wedekind's plays "sex tragedies *par excellence*, a ferocious battle in the Nietzschean sense between the sexes and ultimately a conflict between spirit (man) and flesh (woman)."

When Berg died on Christmas Eve, 1935, he had completed the short score for the entire opera, but not the full orchestral score. Erwin Stein had prepared the complete piano-vocal score (the reduction of the full score for voice parts and piano), but the engraving by Berg's publisher, Universal Editions, was halted by the onset of World War II and never completed. Although he was not Jewish, Berg was denounced by the German press for sharing the "decadence" of the Arnold Schoenberg circle of composers.

For the opera's world premiere in Zurich, Switzerland, on June 2, 1937, at which Nuri Hadzic sang the role of Lulu and Robert Denzler conducted, the musicians had full access only to the first two acts of the piece. In place of the crucial third act, the musicians made use of fragments from Berg's previously published *Lulu Symphony*, which was a sort of advertisement for the opera in progress. (The *Lulu Symphony* had premiered in Berlin in November, 1934.) The woefully truncated third act, used until 1979, consisted of twelve minutes of music, ending with the murder of Lulu and her companion, the Countess Geschwitz, by Jack the Ripper. The use of fragments of the *Lulu Symphony* was a stage director's attempt to round out the action and had not been sanctioned by Berg.

The first concert performance of *Lulu* after the interruption of World War II occurred in Berg's native Vienna on March 16, 1949, and the first postwar stage production took place at Essen, Germany, on March 7, 1953, still with the truncated, improvised third act. This was the version that served for the production of the Hamburg State Opera, a version that was widely influential during the 1960's, for the American premiere, in Santa Fe, New Mexico, on August 7, 1963 (sung in English), and the Metropolitan Opera's premiere, on March 18, 1977 (in German).

What had become of Berg's third act? Why did forty-three years elapse between the composer's death and its premiere? The answer lies with a misguidedly loyal widow. Helene Berg was determined to prevent the completion of her late husband's final opera. A spiritualist, she claimed to be in constant contact with the ghost of her husband, who, she said, urged her to prevent any attempts to complete the score, and she preserved the Bergs' residence in the way that it stood on the day of Alban's death. She also claimed to have been told by Berg's friends, the composers Schoenberg, Anton von Webern, and Alexander von Zemlinsky, that the opera was "unfinishable." Although her word was accepted as fact for many years, the few critics who gained access to the manuscript materials reported that the score was basically complete and could easily be performed; it remains puzzling why Universal Editions collaborated with the widow's obstinacy.

Not until Helene Berg's death in 1976 did the publisher relent and allow wider access to the manuscript. The Austrian scholar Friedrich Cerha was chosen to examine and complete the orchestral score, and the Paris Opera was chosen to offer the world premiere on February 24, 1979, with the soprano Teresa Stratas in the title role and Pierre Boulez conducting; the production was staged by Patrice Chereau. Despite some complaints about Chereau's direction, the production was widely celebrated as a success, and it confirmed the integrity and vision of Berg's total conception.

SIGNIFICANCE

For his first opera, *Wozzeck*, which premiered in 1925, Alban Berg reordered the scenes of Georg Büchner's tragedy *Woyzeck* (wr. 1836; English translation, 1927); when he began to compose *Lulu* in 1929, Berg had to cut an enormous amount of material, shorten the dialogue, and combine Wedekind's two Lulu plays into one. The surprise is that Berg was able to compress Wedekind's vast and philosophically meaningful materials into seven long operatic scenes that critics generally regard as more coherent and dramatically effective than the Lulu plays. Although *Wozzeck* remains one of the monuments of twentieth century music, Berg's goals for *Lulu* were even greater. Critic George Perle has argued that "between *Wozzeck* and *Lulu* Berg's musical language was transformed."

As a student and disciple of the German composer Arnold Schoenberg, Berg was a proponent of Schoenberg's twelve-tone compositional theory, known as serialism. Schoenberg's theory challenged the traditional use of tonality in Western music by advocating the complete equality of twelve tones in the musical scale. The basic melodic strategy of the opera would be dictated by Berg's choice of tone row (a nonrepeating series of the twelve tones of the scale) to depict the character of Lulu. Berg's devotion to Schoenberg's ideal, however, was tempered by his own lyrical and melodic gifts. Although expressionism as an artistic style, whether in music or painting, is often accused of exaggerating the horrific and grotesque, Berg's musical expressionism shows a preference for the lyrical and romantic, resulting in the often-repeated critical putdown that Berg is the "twelve-tone Puccini."

Having made the basic decision that character would determine the musical structure, Berg then made the even more provocative decision that the tone row associated with Lulu (the twelve notes of the scale, used in equal measure) would determine the entire musical action of the opera. All the other characters in the opera are lovers, victims, or attempted manipulators of Lulu. In her key aria in the second act, usually called "Lied der Lulu," Lulu asserts her innocence, depicting herself as a natural woman who cannot help being universally desired.

Among the victims of Lulu are Doctor Goll, who succumbs to a heart attack; a painter, who slits his throat in a fit of jealousy; and Doctor Schon, the most important male figure in the opera, who is shot by Lulu with the very pistol with which he demands that Lulu kill herself. In the descending half of the opera, Lulu finds that even as a prostitute she is less and less in demand. By selling her sexual favors, she has repudiated her claim to be free and has set the pattern for her ultimate victimization when both she and her lesbian admirer, the Countess Geschwitz, are stabbed by Jack the Ripper. Lulu's death scream ("Todesschrei") and Geschwitz's subsequent tender death song ("Lulu, my angel") bring the opera to its conclusion.

That scream, like its famous visual counterpart, Edvard Munch's painting *The Cry* (1893; also known as *The Scream*), is practically the signature of the expressionist style, and the cry of Lulu, like the opera to which she lends her name, provides vivid articulation of the desire and suffering of mankind in the twentieth century. As Douglas Jarman notes in his study of Berg's music, the third act of *Lulu* is largely recapitulatory, bringing Lulu from her amoral innocence of the first act to her final degradation and death at the hands of Jack the Ripper. Jarman's thesis, that Berg's obsession with symmetry in his composition reflects his pessimistic assessment of life (with characters who are trapped in a cycle of ascent invariably followed by descent and death), perhaps offers a hint at the true motivation of Helene Berg: By preventing the release of the third act, she could keep hidden the bleak pessimism of Berg's vision of life. The complete version of the opera perhaps reveals Berg's indebtedness to one of his philosophical heroes, Friedrich Nietzsche. According to Nietzsche's theory of "eternal return," mankind is doomed to enact endless repetitions of the events of life; in this light, the actions of Lulu, her lovers, and her victims are irrelevant. All one can do, argued Nietzsche, is affirm life, for all its pain and problems; and the affirmation of life, finally, is what *Lulu* glowingly provides. The opera has increasingly been recognized as one of the towering artistic masterpieces of the century, and even as serialism has declined in prestige, popular appreciation of *Lulu* has continued to grow.

—*Byron Nelson*

FURTHER READING

Carner, Mosco. *Alban Berg: The Man and the Work*. 2d rev. ed. New York: Holmes & Meier, 1983. Solid musical and dramatic study, with Freudian hints, by the most prominent student of Giacomo Puccini. The dissimilar composers, near contemporaries, shared only the determination to depict sexual neuroses on the operatic stage.

Grout, Donald J., and Claude V. Palisca. "Atonality, Serialism, and Recent Developments in Twentieth-Century Europe." In *A History of Western Music*. 6th ed. New York: W. W. Norton, 2000. Covers the full range of Schoenberg's innovations and provides a balanced overview with examples, illustrations, and bibliography. Accessible to the general reader.

Jarman, Douglas. *The Music of Alban Berg*. London: Faber, 1979. Argues that Berg's music reflects his deeply pessimistic view of life.

Perle, George. *Lulu*. Vol. 2 in *The Operas of Alban Berg*. Berkeley: University of California Press, 1985. Exhaustive study by the American composer and musicologist who argued tirelessly for the release of the third act of *Lulu*.

_____. *Serial Composition and Atonality: An Introduction to the Music of Schoenberg, Berg, and Webern*. 6th ed., rev. Berkeley: University of California Press, 1991. Excellent treatment of twelve-tone technique intended for readers with background in music.

Reich, Willi. *Alban Berg*. Reprint. New York: Vienna House, 1974. Useful introductory study of the life and works of Berg by a Viennese friend.

Rosen, Charles. *Arnold Schoenberg*. 1975. Reprint. Chicago: University of Chicago Press, 1996. Lucid and sympathetic introduction to the seminal figure in musical expressionism and serialism. Includes illustrations, bibliography, and index.

Schmidgall, Gary. *Literature as Opera*. New York: Oxford University Press, 1977. A provocative study of the literary sources of great operas. Claims that the difficult playwrights Büchner and Wedekind find their ideal musical interpreter in Berg, as Berg's style is marked by "rootlessness and flexibility, extreme distortion and nervous tension."

Simms, Bryan R., ed. *Schoenberg, Berg, and Webern: A Companion to the Second Viennese School*. Westport, Conn.: Greenwood Press, 1999. Examines the works of these composers in the context of earlier Viennese musical developments and compares the modernism in their music with that in the nonmusical arts in Vienna during the same period. Includes bibliography and index.

SEE ALSO: 1908-1909: Schoenberg Breaks with Tonality; Mar. 31, 1913: Webern's Six Pieces for Large Orchestra Premieres; 1921-1923: Schoenberg Develops His Twelve-Tone System; Dec. 14, 1925: Berg's *Wozzeck* Premieres in Berlin.

July, 1937
PICASSO EXHIBITS *GUERNICA*

Created for the Paris International Exposition, Pablo Picasso's Guernica *expressed the great artist's horror at the bombing of the Basque capital Guernica during the Spanish Civil War.*

LOCALE: Paris, France
CATEGORY: Arts

KEY FIGURES
Pablo Picasso (1881-1973), Spanish artist
Francisco Franco (1892-1975), Spanish dictator

SUMMARY OF EVENT
Spanish by birth, Pablo Picasso spent most of his working life in France, in or near Paris. His political sympathies were always on the left (he joined the Communist Party in 1944), although his art did not begin to contain explicit political themes until the beginning of the Spanish Civil War, when a group of right-wing military officers, headed by Francisco Franco, attacked the democratically elected government of Spain. Outgunned by Franco and his allies (the fascist regimes of Germany and Italy), the Spanish Republic waged a losing battle over a three-year period, gradually relinquishing territory to the rebels, who mercilessly bombed the civilian population.

In early 1937, Picasso had written a poem ridiculing Franco, rejecting his rebellion, treating him as a subhuman type, and evoking the violence of war: the screaming of women, children, and animals, of inanimate objects such as beds, chairs, and curtains, and of nature itself—a holocaust of screaming that could be seen and smelled because it permeated everything. Picasso's strongest statement against the assault on the republic, however, came after the bombing on April 26, 1937, of the Basque capital Guernica, where sixteen hundred of seven thousand inhabitants were killed and 70 percent of the town was destroyed during an attack by forty-three German bombers and low-flying planes armed with machine guns. Working at a furious rate over the course of a month, the artist produced a monumental canvas (twenty-five feet by eleven feet), fulfilling a commission given to him by the Spanish Republic for the Paris International Exhibition. The painting was received not merely as a protest against a horrible act of war but as a symbol of the irrational forces of terror that had been loosed not only on Spain but also on humanity as a whole in the twentieth century.

The stark brutality of this enormous painting is emphasized by Picasso's use of shades of black and white against a rectangular background, creating a field of violence, a killing ground. This mythic scene, expressive of the world's cruelty and not solely the product of a particular evil act, seems timeless, universal. The scene is dominated by the fragmented figures of human beings and animals arranged both horizontally and vertically—all with mouths open, screaming: a man tumbling from a burning building, a woman lamenting the dead baby in her arms, a dead soldier, fallen from his horse, his body in pieces. Another woman, dazed by the desolation and chaos, is on one knee, her head thrust upward on a diagonal toward a light held over the soldier by another screaming woman. As in so much of Picasso's painting, human faces and bodies are distorted (heads elongated, eyes, hands, and limbs enlarged), shown frontally and in profile at the same time, and flattened against the picture plane in order to increase the emotional impact of the setting and the conception of a people, a whole nation, suffering.

Several commentators have remarked that images of a horse and a bull are at the heart of the painting, linking it to Picasso's earlier bullfight paintings, which employed symbolic evocations of these animals to suggest the power and mobility the artist found compelling. In *Guernica*, the horse is clearly under attack; the bull, however, stands apparently unharmed and impassive, perhaps as an evocation of the impersonal brutality that attracts certain human beings to the bullfight but also of the terrible force the ritual of the bullfight seeks to master. At least one critic has interpreted the bull as hovering protectively above the woman wailing over her dead child, although the bull may have more to do with presenting death as part of the ritualistic recurrence of events such as the bullfight and war. In this respect, human beings and animals suffer the same fate. By juxtaposing horse and bull, Picasso seems to acknowledge his identification with the victims while frankly confessing that violence is inherent in the makeup of the universe. It is an austere vision and highly abstract, as befits a painting purporting to encompass the core conflict in the nature of the world and the inevitability of death—so often seen in the human and animal skulls Picasso painted and sculpted before *Guernica*.

The lightbulb shining at the top center and the tile floor visible at the bottom of the painting suggest Picasso's effort to render the horror of war within the confines of art. This is not a naturalistic painting, in which the artist tries to re-create the look and the feel of the actual setting and event or the perspective of an eyewitness; instead, the painting offers a highly personal and aesthetic reaction to death and destruction, a deliberate distancing of the artist from the historical facts in order to portray the human condition.

The heavy symbolic load of *Guernica* is balanced by the fluidity of Picasso's line, the deftly drawn, flaring nostrils, teeth, and tongue of the horse, the almost equally wide open, concave mouths of the human victims who shout out the vitality of the life that is extinguished. This grim lyricism heightens emotional identification with the lives lost. The expressiveness of the art is at one with the expressiveness of its doomed figures. *Guernica* has been considered one of Picasso's finest paintings since his cubist period because it manages to suffuse the personal symbols and figures of his work with the struggles of a whole people and the fate of twentieth century civilization.

SIGNIFICANCE

Until *Guernica*, exactly where Picasso stood on the great issues of his time was not understood. It was supposed that he sympathized with leftist and democratic causes, but his art was not interpreted as having a particularly political orientation, even though many 1930's artists, writers, and musicians had created works that were socially and politically oriented—even directly supportive of political ideologies such as communism and anarchism.

In *Guernica*, Picasso fused his great reputation with the aspirations not only of the Spanish Republic but also of all those politically progressive artists and activists who regarded Spain as the testing ground for the defense against fascism. The prestige he lent to the cause of saving Spain can hardly be exaggerated. He had been previously attacked by certain Communist Party ideologues for finding refuge in what they regarded as a solely personal, idiosyncratic, and decadent art that did not reflect the aspirations of the masses or dignify their struggle. Although *Guernica* is hardly

an example of Socialist Realism, the kind of art the Communist Party saw as faithfully rendering the everyday as well as the heroic actions of the people, there is a sense of collective humanity in the painting that made it possible for Picasso to earn his place on the left (having been dismissed as a "degenerate" modern artist by the Nazis) while maintaining his standing as the foremost artist of his time. In 1939, the Museum of Modern Art in New York City gave Picasso his largest retrospective to date, calling it "Picasso: Forty Years of His Art." The exhibition included more than three hundred works, including *Guernica*, which had already been shown to great acclaim in London, Chicago, Los Angeles, and San Francisco.

Picasso ensured his standing among radicals by issuing in pamphlet form a series of etchings called *The Dream and Lie of Franco* (1937), later produced as post-

Pablo Picasso. (AP/Wide World Photos)

cards and sold to raise money for the Republican cause. The image of Picasso as an aloof artist alienated from his society gave way to the image of the artist expressing solidarity with the people, thus ratifying the social and political involvements of many of his contemporaries in art throughout the 1930's. On December 18, 1937, Picasso sent a statement of his political commitment to the American Artists' Congress in New York, affirming that the most important values of humanity were at stake in the attack on Spain. From that point on, he would periodically issue political statements, often drafted by his close Communist friends. Picasso would continue his involvement with the Communist Party in the postwar years, attending and designing posters for party congresses.

Guernica was only one of a series of works that Picasso and other artists created in the years immediately preceding World War II that expressed a sense of foreboding, even of apocalypse. The somber and savage quality of many of his paintings produced during the war period express a personal despair, best evoked in a series of still lifes depicting the skulls of bulls' heads, their flesh flayed and lit by a naked candle flame, that Picasso produced during the Occupation.

Picasso's adamant refusal to leave Paris during the Occupation and his spurning of German offers of fuel to warm his studio made the artist a symbol of resistance. In one often-told story, Picasso is said to have been visited in his studio by a German officer who spotted a photograph of *Guernica* and wanted to know if Picasso had done it. "No," Picasso reportedly replied, "you did." In fact, there is some doubt about exactly how uncompromising Picasso's position toward the Germans actually was, but his loyalty to Paris became the stuff of legend, making him into a symbol of freedom and the unvanquished spirit and elevating him to a category all his own.

Throughout the war, the artist continued to create chilling examples of the impact of war on his consciousness. In *Death's Head* (1943), he strips away most of the human features from the face, leaving only rounded, hollow eyes and jagged slits for the nose and mouth, suggesting the darkness and hollowness of war at a point when the wrenching emotions of *Guernica* have been spent. Similarly, *The Charnel House* (1945) goes beyond *Guernica* in presenting war's aftermath; in the later painting, the earth has become a mortuary, the resting place of the dead, where there is no screaming, where everything has been reduced to a ghastly silence in a world that is just discovering the atrocities of the concentration camps. Instead of the moving figures of *Guernica*, the bodies in *The Charnel House* are tumbled together as in a

mass grave, with parts of bodies twisted together or gouging into one another; a frozen gasp of agony is expressed on the face of a woman upended and pressing down on the bodies below her. Humanity itself is rent and mangled in the painting.

Perhaps what is most gruesome about *The Charnel House* is that it is not, like *Guernica*, associated directly with war or with a catastrophic event, for the heap of broken corpses is shown beneath a mundane domestic scene: a white table with an empty jug and an empty saucepan. It is as if the war—not shown on the canvas—has resulted in the bankruptcy of everyday life, which rests on (or covers up) a mountain of death.

In the long term, Picasso's *Guernica* contributed to a postwar questioning of the foundations of civilization. The Spanish Civil War and World War II were not seen merely as aberrations, savage interludes between periods of peace, but as the outcomes of malevolent strains within civilization itself, a much more frightening vision of the end of things than the insight that first prompted Picasso to paint *Guernica*.

—*Carl Rollyson*

FURTHER READING

Beardsley, John. *First Impressions: Picasso*. New York: Harry N. Abrams, 1991. A lucid introductory study with a chapter on *Guernica* and a large foldout illustration of the painting. Describes several other works Picasso created during the Spanish Civil War and World War II and situates both paintings and sculptures in their historical context. Includes color plates and index.

Blunt, Anthony. *Picasso's "Guernica."* 1969. Reprint. New York: Oxford University Press, 1985. Heavily illustrated study (many of the plates are of the forty-five preliminary drawings) with photographs of the painting at various stages of realization. Discusses *Guernica* in the context of Picasso's other work and in terms of European traditions that go back to antiquity. Includes large foldout of the painting and notes.

Gilot, Françoise. *Matisse and Picasso*. London: Bloomsbury, 1990. Presents incisive comments on *Guernica* and other works created during the Spanish Civil War and World War II in the light of Picasso's friendship and rivalry with his great contemporary. Having lived with Picasso for several years, and as an artist herself, the author provides a unique and sensitive reading of his art and its development. Includes notes and index.

Hilton, Timothy. *Picasso*. 1975. Reprint. London: Thames and Hudson, 2002. Includes discussion of

Guernica, with several illustrations and examination of preliminary drawings and the artist's related works. Notes the impact of Surrealism on Picasso's poetry and painting and some of the negative American responses to the style. Concludes that *Guernica* is a competent but not a breakthrough work.

Huffington, Arianna Stassinopoulos. *Picasso: Creator and Destroyer*. New York: Simon & Schuster, 1988. Biography provides very little discussion of Picasso's art, but summarizes reactions to it and analyzes biographical background relevant to his paintings, including *Guernica*. Sensationalizes some aspects of Picasso's life but contains important information drawn from extensive interviews with his friends and associates. Includes photographs, extensive bibliography, and index.

Martin, Russell. *Picasso's War: The Destruction of Guernica and the Masterpiece That Changed the World*. New York: E. P. Dutton, 2002. Follows the literal and figurative journey of the painting since its creation to present an examination of art's importance to human lives.

Sommer, Robin Langley. *Picasso*. New York: Smith-

mark, 1988. Sumptuous reproductions of Picasso's paintings and drawings, including a huge foldout of *Guernica*, enlargements of the bull and the horse, and pencil-on-paper and pencil-and-crayon-on-paper sketches for the painting. Includes a full-page illustration of *The Charnel House* and many other color plates, with accompanying text.

Walther, Ingo E. *Pablo Picasso, 1881-1973*. 2d ed. Translated by Hugh Beyer. Cologne, Germany: Benedikt Taschen, 2000. Introductory study includes a chapter on Picasso's wartime experience, a two-page layout of *Guernica*, and several black-and-white and color plates of work done during the war, including *The Charnel House*. Informative text accompanied by sidebars quoting the artist on various aspects of his work and his attitudes toward art. Includes illustrated chronology of Picasso's life and work and extensive bibliography.

SEE ALSO: 1906-1907: Artists Find Inspiration in African Tribal Art; Summer, 1908: Salon d'Automne Rejects Braque's Cubist Works; 1913: Apollinaire Defines Cubism; Apr. 26, 1937: Raids on Guernica.

July 7, 1937
CHINA DECLARES WAR ON JAPAN

After the Battle of the Marco Polo Bridge, the Chinese Kuomintang government declared war on the nation of Japan. This military action was the result of Japan's aggressive expansionist policies.

ALSO KNOWN AS: Marco Polo Bridge incident
LOCALE: China; Manchuria
CATEGORIES: Military history; wars, uprisings, and civil unrest

KEY FIGURES
Chiang Kai-shek (1887-1975), leader of the Kuomintang, president of China, 1948-1949, and president of the Republic of China (Taiwan), 1950-1975
Mao Zedong (Mao Tse-tung; 1893-1976), chairman of the Chinese Communist Party, 1935-1976
Henry L. Stimson (1867-1950), U.S. secretary of state, 1929-1933, secretary of war, 1940-1945
Hirota Kōki (1878-1948), prime minister of Japan, 1936-1937

SUMMARY OF EVENT
The Second Sino-Japanese War (1937-1945) was the result of the political, economic, and geopolitical factors that directed the struggle for control of China in the years following the end of World War I. When the founder of the Chinese Republic, Sun Yixian (also known as Sun Yat-sen), died in 1925, the leadership of the Chinese Kuomintang Party passed into the hands of a young military officer named Chiang Kai-shek. During this period, China was a decentralized state with large regions, especially in the north, which was controlled by independent warlords. Chiang Kai-shek's Kuomintang Party joined forces with the Chinese Communists led by Mao Zedong and launched a military campaign called the Northern Expedition to reclaim the northeast part of China from the warlords.

By 1927, the majority of the warlords in the region had been pacified, and Chiang took advantage of his success to launch a campaign against Mao and his Communist forces. The Kuomintang army inflicted heavy casualties, and the Communists retreated into the safety of the Chinese countryside. By 1928, Chiang felt secure enough to declare that the Kuomintang government was in control of China, and he established his capital in Nanjing. In reality, however, Chiang's power was tenuous at best, and he had to deal with challenges to his government's sovereignty from a number of internal and foreign threats. The Kuomintang Party had failed to implement the needed economic reforms, especially in the agricultural sector, that would have helped alleviate the widespread poverty among peasants, and Chiang's government also faced serious challenges from the warlords, who still pledged their allegiance to the Kuomintang regime but maintained large, independent standing armies and controlled a significant percentage of China's natural resources.

Chiang also faced a political challenge from Mao and the Communists, who had taken advantage of Chiang's failed economic reforms to establish strong ties with the peasantry. On an international level, the Chinese Communist Party had called for a military campaign against Japanese incursions into northern China, and Mao also argued for an alliance with the Soviet Union; he believed such an alliance would give China the military strength needed to stop Japan's aggressive policies.

Japanese expansion into mainland Asia was the most pressing national security threat facing Chiang's government. Japan's first target was Manchuria, which occupied territory directly northeast of China. There were three major reasons that the Japanese military sought to control this vital region. Economically, Manchuria possessed great quantities of industrial raw materials, the most important of which were iron ore and coal, which were needed to maintain growth in Japan's manufacturing and defense sectors. Manchuria also had thousands of square miles of rich, productive farmland, which would help feed Japan's growing population. Location also played an important role in Japan's geopolitical worldview, and Manchuria's strategic position would allow the Japanese to use it as a base of operations against three possible military targets: the Soviet Union, China, and the United States.

In 1894 and 1895, Japan had fought a successful war

Chinese soldiers defend Beijing from behind a sandbag barricade on the Marco Polo Bridge. (AP/Wide World Photos)

against China for the control of the Korean Peninsula. The object of this conflict was to drive China from the region because its weak and inefficient military was unable to maintain order in this pivotal strategic area. In addition, the Japanese wanted to block Russian expansion into what Japan believed was its own sphere of influence. Ten years later, in 1904 and 1905, Russia was soundly defeated in the Russo-Japanese War, which established Japan as the premier military power in Asia. If Japan could gain control of Manchuria, it could block any attempts by the new Soviet government to link up with the Chinese Communist army and destabilize the region. Japan could also use Manchuria as a staging area for a future invasion of China. Using the detonation of a small bomb on the Southern Manchurian Railway near the outskirts of Mukden as a sign of Chinese aggression, the Japanese quickly overran Manchuria and established the puppet state of Manchukuo.

In the meantime, relations between Japan and the United States were already tense: The two nations were on a geopolitical collision course over the Nine-Power Treaty, which assured China's territorial integrity and served as a bulwark against Japanese domination. As a result of this Japanese aggression, the Western democracies issued a series of condemnations, the most forceful of which came from the U.S. secretary of state, Henry L. Stimson. He convinced the United States to issue the Stimson Doctrine, which refused to recognize Manchukuo's political legitimacy. Stimson wanted to take more aggressive action, but President Herbert Hoover, like his counterparts in the other capitalist democracies, was too bogged down in the economic chaos of the Great Depression to become involved in an international incident thousands of miles from the borders of the United States. The League of Nations openly condemned the aggressive act, and Japan responded by giving up its membership in the international body.

The lack of international response to this blatant aggression unleashed powerful political forces in both China and Japan. In China there was a rapprochement between the Kuomintang government and the Chinese Communist Party; this reconciliation was coordinated by the Soviet Comintern. Communist leaders were concerned about the Japanese drive to control Manchuria, which they believed would isolate the Chinese Communists from their Soviet counterparts. This geopolitical reality convinced Mao to enter into an alliance with Chiang Kai-shek, at least until the threat of Japanese aggression had been overcome.

Japan was also experiencing a period of domestic un-

rest caused by the struggle between the military and the civilian government. A group of chauvinistic army officers had attacked the civilian government for what they perceived was its weak and incompetent handling of the nation's diplomacy; they believed the government had disgraced itself in accepting the provisions of the two major treaties of the Washington Disarmament Conference of 1922. They viewed the Five-Power Treaty, which assigned Japan the smallest ratio of battleships among the world's major naval powers, and the Nine-Power Treaty, which assured China's territorial integrity, as betrayals of Japan's national security. These army officers called for a military takeover of the government, and army death squads assassinated a number of important Japanese officials.

With the approval of the young militarists, a former foreign minister named Hirota Kōki became leader of the new Japanese government. This marked a turning point in the history of Japan and placed the nation's foreign policy directly in the hands of the military. Once in control, the army began to finalize plans to invade China; their rationale was based on the belief that it was Japan's responsibility to control events in East and Southeast Asia. This control would be assumed through swift military action followed by the occupation of strategically important areas and, eventually the complete colonization of the region. The Japanese military elite believed that China was decadent, corrupt, and antimodern and that it had abrogated its traditional position of dominance in East Asia.

Japan initiated a series of preliminary military actions to both probe China's weaknesses and establish staging areas for a massive invasion of the mainland. By the summer of 1937, Chinese and Japanese forces had clashed in battles in both northern and eastern China. The tension between the two nations finally exploded in the Marco Polo Bridge incident just outside Beijing. The nationalist government responded to this incident by declaring war on Japan.

SIGNIFICANCE

The Japanese army inflicted heavy casualties on the Chinese military and on the segments of the civilian population unfortunate enough to be caught between the two opposing forces. The worst example of Japanese brutality was the Rape of Nanjing. Using a deadly combination of armor, as well as tactical air and ground forces, the Japanese launched a blitzkrieg-like attack against the defenses around Nanjing. The Chinese military was unable to repulse the assault, and the city was quickly overrun.

Once inside Nanjing, the Japanese violated and slaughtered thousands of innocent citizens. The military's failures in Nanjing and other areas caused a significant number of Chinese, especially the peasants, to lose faith in the Kuomintang government. Mao and the Communists would eventually use this lack of confidence to gain power after World War II.

—*Richard D. Fitzgerald*

FURTHER READING

Graff, David A., and Robin Higham. *A Military History of China.* Boulder, Colo.: Westview Press, 2002. One of the best surveys of Chinese military history available. Includes maps, bibliography, and index.

Hoyt, Edwin P. *Japan's War: The Great Pacific Conflict.* New York: Da Capo Press, 1986. Provides a detailed study of Japanese military operations during the period 1931-1945. Includes maps, bibliography, and index.

Hsü, Immanuel Chung-yueh. *The Rise of Modern China.* New York: Oxford University Press, 2000. Among the best single-volume treatments of modern Chinese history. Includes maps, bibliography, and index.

SEE ALSO: Feb. 9, 1904-Sept. 5, 1905: Russo-Japanese War; 1926-1949: Chinese Civil War; Feb. 24, 1933: Japan Withdraws from the League of Nations; Oct. 16, 1934-Oct. 18, 1935: Mao's Long March; Dec. 29, 1934: Japan Renounces Disarmament Treaties; Dec., 1937-Feb., 1938: Rape of Nanjing; June 7, 1938: Chinese Forces Break Yellow River Levees; Aug., 1940: Japan Announces the Greater East Asia Coprosperity Sphere; Sept., 1940: Japan Occupies Indochinese Ports.

July 19-November 30, 1937
NAZI GERMANY HOSTS THE *DEGENERATE ART EXHIBITION*

A display of modern art confiscated by the Nazis from German museums and labeled "degenerate" foreshadowed the later purging of artists by Adolf Hitler's regime.

ALSO KNOWN AS: *Entarte Kunst*
LOCALE: Hofgarten Arcades, Munich, Germany
CATEGORY: Arts

KEY FIGURES

Adolf Hitler (1889-1945), Nazi dictator who believed that Germany needed to be cleansed of modern art
Joseph Goebbels (1897-1945), Nazi minister of propaganda who was responsible for overseeing German cultural life
Adolf Ziegler (1892-1959), president of the Reich Chamber of Visual Arts and organizer of the *Degenerate Art Exhibition* and the *Great German Art Exhibition*
Otto Dix (1891-1969), artist and World War I veteran whose work was attacked by the Nazis
George Grosz (1893-1959), artist who satirized German economic and political life during the Weimar Republic
Wassily Kandinsky (1866-1944), expressionist painter derided by the Nazis
Emil Nolde (1867-1956), expressionist painter whose Nazi Party membership did not protect his work from confiscation

SUMMARY OF EVENT

The *Degenerate Art Exhibition* was opened in Munich on July 19, 1937, by Adolf Ziegler, the president of the Reich Chamber of Visual Arts, one day after Adolf Hitler had dedicated the city's House of German Art and the first of eight official "Great German Art Exhibitions." Speaking in the city where the Nazi movement was born and shortly before the height of his prewar success, Hitler described the House of German Art as a temple for an eternal German art that would not welcome modern art. Ziegler's speech, which summarized thoughts previously articulated by Hitler and his minions, condemned modern art as "the monstrous offspring of insanity, impudence, ineptitude, and sheer degeneracy." These complementary speeches and exhibits clarified the role of art in the Third Reich; they established the parameters for what would be officially promoted and made clear what would be condemned, removed from public view, and concealed or destroyed.

Visitors to the *Degenerate Art Exhibition* viewed a display of more than 650 modern paintings, prints, books, and sculptures that had been hastily removed from thirty-two public museums in Germany by Ziegler, with the authorization of Nazi propaganda chief Joseph Goebbels. The works were carefully displayed in the most defamatory manner possible: Some paintings were stripped of their frames, and the labels that provided information about the works, including their original purchase prices, were often erroneous and simply tacked or pasted in place. Scattered haphazardly throughout the exhibit were phrases and slogans denigrating modern art, quotations by avant-garde artists taken out of context and selected to seem threatening or ridiculous, and passages about the nature of art and its place in Nazi Germany by Hitler and other party functionaries. The exhibition appeared crowded, jumbled, and claustrophobic—an effect the organizers wished to impress on the viewer, because the event reflected a concept of modern art as both degenerate and the product of artistic incompetence. In the opinion of Hitler, the modern art that had flourished in Germany before World War I and then during the 1920's was a symptom not only of political and cultural decline but also of racial, physical, and mental pathology.

Art confiscated for the *Degenerate Art Exhibition* was arranged in nine loosely themed groups. Visitors saw first Ludwig Gies's *Crucified Christ*, a war memorial that had once hung in Lübeck Cathedral and that the Nazis branded a horror, and then Emil Nolde's multipaneled altarpiece *The Life of Christ*, both of which purportedly mocked Christianity. Next came paintings by Jewish artists such as Marc Chagall and Ludwig Meidner. The third room housed more than seventy pieces,

---

PRODUCTS OF MADNESS

In 1937, president of the Reich Chamber of Visual Arts Adolf Ziegler expressed his frustration with "degenerate" artists as he contemplated the forthcoming Entartete Kunst (Degenerate Art) exhibition:

Our patience with all those who have not been able to fall in line is at an end. . . . What you are seeing here are the crippled products of madness, impertinence, and lack of talent. . . . I would need several freight trains to clear our galleries of this rubbish. . . . This will happen soon.

German expressionist painter Karl Schmidt-Rottluff, whose works showed the influence of cubism and African art, received the following letter from Ziegler in 1938:

In connection with the task, entrusted to me by the Führer, of eradicating the works of degenerate art from our museums, no fewer than 608 paintings of yours had to be seized. A number of these paintings were displayed at the exhibits of Degenerate Art in Munich, Dortmund, and Berlin. This fact could leave no doubt in your mind that your paintings did not contribute to the advancement of German culture in its responsibility toward people and nation. Although you must also have been aware of the policy-setting speech of the Führer at the opening of the Great German Art Exhibit in Munich, the recent paintings of yours which you have now submitted to us indicate that even at this date, you are still far removed from the cultural foundations of the National Socialist state. On the basis of these facts, I am unable to grant that you possess the necessary reliability for belonging to my Chamber. On the basis of Paragraph 10 of the first executive Order implementing the Law Concerning the National Chambers of Culture of November 1, 1933 (*Official Gazette*, I, 797) I hereby expel you from the National Chamber of Fine Arts and forbid you, effective immediately, any activity—professional or amateur—in the field of graphic arts. Membership book no. M 756 issued in your name is no longer valid, and you are requested to send it back to me by return mail.

Source: The Nazi Years: A Documentary History, edited by J. Remak (New York: Prentice-Hall, 1969).

---

among them nudes by Karl Hofer, Ernst Ludwig Kirchner, and Otto Mueller headed "An Insult to German Womanhood," images of World War I labeled "Deliberate Sabotage of National Defense," and portrayals of peasants by Kirchner and Karl Schmidt-Rottluff that were identified as "German Farmers: A Yiddish View." Singled out for ridicule was Dadaist art; on the so-called Dada wall, works by Kurt Schwitters and Paul Klee appeared beneath a quotation from George Grosz and against a backdrop copied from an abstract but hardly Dadaist painting by Wassily Kandinsky. Similar displays filled the remaining rooms. Prominently featured works included townscapes by Lyonel Feininger, compositions by professors and teachers of art who allegedly were corrupting German youth, etchings by Otto Dix,

and miscellaneous works by Klee, Schmidt-Rottluff, George Grosz, and Max Beckmann, among others. In the lobby stood Otto Freundlich's sculpture *The New Man*, which appeared on the cover of the exhibition guide.

The names of the 112 artists exhibited testify to the dynamism of modern German art during the first third of the twentieth century; the artists listed represented movements as diverse as the Bauhaus style, cubism, Dadaism, expressionism, the New Objectivity, and abstractionism. Artists represented with ten or more works, excluding those named above, included Erich Heckel, Oskar Kokoschka, Max Pechstein, and Christian Rohlfs. The selection criteria, however, remain obscure. Despite the Nazi insistence that modern art was foreign, Jewish, or left-wing in inspiration, only six artists were Jewish, and non-German artists were rare. Troublesome was the inclusion of works by the expressionist Franz Marc, who had been killed in World War I; the German Officers' Federation protested the use of his work, and his *Tower of Blue Horses* was removed from the exhibit. The presence of works by Nolde, a Nazi Party member whose art had once found favor with such high officials as Goebbels, was controversial for similar reasons. The case of the sculptor Rudolf Belling was particularly ironic; Belling had two works shown in the *Degenerate Art Exhibition* at the same time his bronze of the boxer Max Schmeling stood in the nearby *Great German Art Exhibition*.

More than two million people visited the *Degenerate Art Exhibition*, making it the most popular exhibit of modern art ever; less than one-fifth as many viewers attended the *Great German Art Exhibition*. From February, 1938, to April, 1941, the *Degenerate Art Exhibition* traveled to twelve cities in Germany and Austria, usually under the patronage of local branches of the Nazi Party. Although the traveling exhibition was changed and reduced in size from the Munich showing, it also attracted large audiences, with attendance in excess of one hundred thousand in Berlin, Düsseldorf, Hamburg, and Vienna, and a total of more than one million additional viewers. Added in Düsseldorf was an exhibit of "degenerate music" that excoriated jazz, so-called Jewish music, and the compositions of Arnold Schoenberg, Igor Stravinsky, and Kurt Weill, to name a few. A catalog accompanied the touring exhibition, although none was available for the original in Munich. The catalog juxtaposed a programmatic statement and excerpts from Hitler's speeches with quotations from the exhibit's walls and photographs of exhibited works. Readers were invited, in one notorious instance, to view three drawings and guess which was by an inmate of an insane asylum and which were by a modern artist.

The brand of art favored by the Nazis was made evident at the *Great German Art Exhibition*. Displayed were almost nine hundred paintings and sculptures by Arno Breker, Josef Thorak, Ziegler, and other politically acceptable artists. Landscapes, portraits of Nazi officials, and images of idealized men and women, farmers and artisans, and public buildings or works predominated. The large number of male and female nudes achieved what George L. Mosse has called "beauty without sensuality." Also shown was *In the Beginning Was the Word*, an image by Hermann Otto Hoyer of Hitler speaking before his earliest followers. Notable by their absence were urban scenes and any art that raised questions or stimulated

thought. In brief, the *Great German Art Exhibition* presented idealized images of Nazi ideology, just as the *Degenerate Art Exhibition* summarized, again with images, not only what the Nazi regime rejected as diseased but also what it intended to purge from German cultural life.

SIGNIFICANCE

The *Degenerate Art Exhibition* and the *Great German Art Exhibition* cannot be understood apart from Hitler's ideas concerning art. According to his worldview, the Nazi movement stood at the forefront of a cultural revolution destined to usher in a creative new age, that of the thousand-year Reich, and the arts were to play a formative role in the revolution's genesis. Nazi doctrine held that artistic creativity and inspiration originated in the *Volkgemeinschaft*, the racial community, and that the duty of the artist was to express what Hitler called the essential character of that people or community; the artist's task was therefore not to create images for other artists to admire but rather to present an ideal for the people to emulate. Further, said Hitler, art should embody eternal values and be easily understood and appreciated by the average person. However specific their formulation by the Nazis, these ideas derived from racist concepts long in circulation and from an ongoing debate that had set in opposition so-called pure German art and modern art.

The Munich *Degenerate Art Exhibition* completed a series of attacks launched by Hitler and his government after 1933 on artists, teachers, collectors, museum administrators, and critics connected with avant-garde movements. Such actions had been anticipated by a 1933 report by Goebbels that had proposed a five-point program for the purge of modern art and were in keeping with the Nazi policy of *Gleichschaltung*, the goal of which was ideological and administrative control of all German associations, institutions, and aspects of individual life. Artists whose work was categorized as degenerate—including, for the most part, those even remotely associated with expressionism, the German defeat in World War I, the Weimar Republic, Jewishness, Marxism, or abstract art—were excluded from membership in the Reich Chamber of Culture and therefore forbidden to practice their profession. Likewise, the modern wing of the National Gallery in Berlin was closed in 1936, the same year that Goebbels banned art criticism.

Not content merely to silence modern artists and their advocates, the Nazis organized nearly a dozen exhibitions slandering modern art in the period 1933-1937, giving the shows such titles as *The Chamber of Horrors* and *Images of Cultural Bolshevism*. Indeed, the prototype for the 1937 *Degenerate Art Exhibition* may have been a Dresden exhibition of the same title organized in 1933 and shown at eight other locations, including the 1935 Nazi Party rally at Nuremberg. Before long, however, ridicule gave way to a systematic purge. While the *Degenerate Art Exhibition* still hung in Munich, a committee appointed by Goebbels and headed by Ziegler undertook additional confiscations, and some sixteen thousand pieces of modern art by more than a thousand artists were seized and removed to Berlin for storage. A few hundred, including a self-portrait by Vincent van Gogh, were sold abroad at auctions or exchanged from 1939 to 1941. Approximately five thousand other works of art were reportedly burned at the central fire department in Berlin in March, 1939, while thousands more simply vanished.

The fate of the artists classified as degenerate by the Third Reich was similarly grim. Those who were able, including Max Bechmann, Jacob Feininger, and George Grosz, left Germany. Some committed suicide; Otto Freundlich and others died in concentration camps. Many, including Nolde, retreated into silence after having lost their teaching or other public positions. Following the end of World War II, those who survived often resumed their work, taking on teaching and administrative positions both in the East and the West.

In the long term, of course, the Nazis failed. The Thousand Year Reich lasted but twelve years, and its creators succeeded neither in imposing their ideology and their concept of art on Germany and Europe nor in purging Germany of modern art. Museum visitors today are thus able to view paintings and sculptures by the expressionists, the New Objectivists, the Surrealists, and the members of other schools attacked by the Nazis. In contrast, the officially sanctioned art of the Third Reich is all but unknown. Nevertheless, the *Degenerate Art Exhibition* should be not forgotten, for it is an example of what is possible when a government manipulates for its own purposes the bewilderment or the discomfort felt by many in the presence of modern art.

—*Robert W. Brown*

FURTHER READING

Adam, Peter. *Art of the Third Reich*. New York: Harry N. Abrams, 1992. Understanding the *Degenerate Art Exhibition* is impossible without an understanding of the exhibit's context, the official Nazi art discussed and reproduced in this book.

Barron, Stephanie, ed. *Degenerate Art: The Fate of the Avant-Garde in Nazi Germany*. New York: Harry N. Abrams, 1991. Essential source; its ten essays by mostly German authors include a complete re-creation of the exhibit, photographs of works exhibited, a facsimile and translation of the 1937 catalog, and an outstanding bibliography of literature, mostly in German.

_____. *Exiles and Emigres: The Flight of European Artists from Hitler*. Los Angeles: Los Angeles County Museum of Art, 1997. Barron selected twenty-three famous artists exiled from Austria and Germany in the period 1933-1945. More than three hundred images and essays from nineteen contributors are compiled in this stunning catalog.

Crockett, Dennis. "The Most Famous Painting of the 'Golden Twenties'? Otto Dix and the *Trench* Affair." *Art Journal* 51 (Spring, 1992): 72-80. Solid discussion of the controversy raised during the Weimar period by a painting shown at the *Degenerate Art Exhibition*.

Dunlop, Ian. *The Shock of the New: Seven Historic Exhibitions of Modern Art*. New York: American Heritage, 1972. Final chapter deals with the *Degenerate Art Exhibition*. Extensive quotes from German documents and reviews in the German press make this a valuable source.

Evans, Richard J. *The Third Reich in Power, 1933-1939*. New York: Penguin Books, 2005. Carefully crafted and thorough analysis of Hitler's rise to power and the development of his social and economic policies. Argues that Hitler's vision of a new, "pure" Europe could only have been created by war.

Grosshans, Henry. *Hitler and the Artists*. New York: Holmes & Meier, 1983. A general account of the development of Hitler's ideas on art and culture, with a chapter on the *Degenerate Art Exhibition*.

Hinz, Berthold. *Art in the Third Reich*. Translated by Robert Kimber and Rita Kimber. New York: Pantheon Books, 1979. Well-illustrated study, with chapters that treat the *Great German Art Exhibition*, the *Degenerate Art Exhibition*, and Nazi concepts of art.

Sax, Benjamin, and Dieter Kuntz, eds. *Inside Hitler's Germany: A Documentary History of the Third Reich*. Lexington, Mass.: D. C. Heath, 1992. Contains a translation of Hitler's speech opening the House of German Art.

SEE ALSO: 1919: German Artists Found the Bauhaus; Mar. 31, 1924: Formation of the Blue Four Advances Abstract Painting; Jan. 30, 1933: Hitler Comes to Power in Germany; June 30-July 2, 1934: Great Blood Purge; Nov. 9-10, 1938: Kristallnacht.

August 17, 1937
MILLER-TYDINGS ACT LEGALIZES RETAIL PRICE MAINTENANCE

By allowing manufacturers to maintain minimum prices, the Miller-Tydings Act promised small retailers protection from chain-store competition, but adverse court decisions and changing economic circumstances diminished the impact of the law.

LOCALE: Washington, D.C.
CATEGORIES: Trade and commerce; laws, acts, and legal history

KEY FIGURES

Herbert Levy (fl. twentieth century), lawyer for the National Association of Retail Druggists
John E. Miller (1888-1981), U.S. congressman from Arkansas
Millard Tydings (1890-1961), U.S. senator from Maryland
Emanuel Celler (1888-1981), U.S. congressman from New York

SUMMARY OF EVENT

The Miller-Tydings Act of 1937 amended the Sherman Antitrust Act of 1890. It legalized retail price maintenance, and in doing so it allowed manufacturers to maintain minimum prices for the sale of their goods. Manufacturers used retail price maintenance to protect their goodwill, hoping that high prices would keep retailers from cutting services to customers. Independent retailers hoped that retail price maintenance would eliminate price competition from chain stores. Prior to the act, the courts had held retail price maintenance to be in violation of the 1914 Federal Trade Commission Act.

The Miller-Tydings Act embodied the anti-chain-store sentiment prevalent in the 1920's and 1930's. During the early twentieth century, independent retailers had confronted new types of competition as department stores appeared in large cities and mail-order houses began to sell goods throughout the nation. The rapid rise of chain stores in the 1920's further eroded the market share of small businesses. Chain stores attracted customers by offering prices lower than those of their single-store competitors. This form of mass marketing spread rapidly as the automobile connected small towns to larger urban markets. Chain-store sales continued to increase during the cost-conscious Depression years, and by 1935 the chains handled nearly one-fourth of all retail sales.

Independent retailers responded by sponsoring advertising campaigns encouraging Americans to "trade at home" and by boycotting those manufacturers that sold to chain stores. Ambitious politicians also seized on anti-chain-store sentiment to attract the votes of independent merchants and others critical of big business. The anti-chain-store movement gained additional momentum in the South and West, where politicians played on the populist fear of "outside" corporations that could control local economies. This movement found expression in state laws that discriminated against chain stores. During the 1920's and 1930's, almost every state imposed punitive taxes on chain stores.

During the early twentieth century, organized merchants had tried to overcome the competitive advantage of mass marketers by urging manufacturers to fix minimum retail prices, a practice known as retail price maintenance or "fair trade." The Supreme Court, however, ruled against retail price fixing. Manufacturers and retailers interested in retail price maintenance then sought to secure the passage of laws legalizing fair trade. The American Fair Trade League (AFTL) and the National Association of Retail Druggists (NARD) led this drive for fair trade. The AFTL represented manufacturers of trademarked goods that wished to use fair trade as a means to protect their goodwill. By maintaining minimum prices, manufacturers hoped to attract those retailers interested in emphasizing quality and service rather than price. As chain stores increased their market share, however, many manufacturers sought higher sales volume and abandoned retail price maintenance.

The druggists hoped to increase their profit margins and reduce chain-store competition. The NARD, widely considered to be one of the most powerful trade associations in the country, conducted intense, well-organized campaigns in support of fair trade legislation. In 1931, California enacted a fair trade law drafted by the NARD, and several other states quickly followed suit. In 1936, the Supreme Court upheld the constitutionality of these laws. Thereafter, fair trade advocates met with virtually no opposition on the state level. In 1937 alone, twenty-eight states passed fair trade laws, and by 1940, a total of forty-four had enacted some form of this legislation.

At the federal level, however, proponents of fair trade met resistance from within the executive and legislative branches of the government. The Federal Trade Commission had always opposed fair trade legislation on the grounds that it lessened competition and violated the spirit of antitrust legislation. Since 1914, Congress had also rejected bills aimed at legalizing retail price maintenance. As a result, the impact of state fair trade laws remained limited because products sold in interstate commerce, under federal law, could not be subject to fair trade agreements.

Having failed to secure a national fair trade law, the proponents of retail price maintenance sought the passage of permissive legislation allowing states to settle the issue. In 1935, the NARD enhanced its influence by hiring Herbert Levy, a law partner of Senator Millard Tydings (Democrat of Maryland). Levy persuaded Tydings to sponsor a bill drafted by the NARD. Representative John E. Miller (Democrat of Arkansas) introduced a companion bill in the House of Representatives.

Tydings's bill met with opposition from Representative Emanuel Celler (Democrat of New York), who feared it would reduce price competition. President Franklin D. Roosevelt also expressed his belief that the bill would increase the cost of living and slow recovery by removing purchasing power from the economy. Congressional supporters, however, played on sentiments in favor of states' rights by emphasizing that the law merely gave the states the right to determine their position on fair trade. In July, 1937, Tydings hoped to avoid a presidential veto by attaching his bill as a rider to a bill granting appropriations to the District of Columbia. Despite the opposition of consumer groups and nearly all economists, Congress passed this legislation by an overwhelming margin. President Roosevelt criticized the use of this evasive tactic but signed the bill into law on August 17, 1937.

By amending the Sherman Act, the Miller-Tydings Act granted an antitrust exemption for retail price maintenance agreements. Manufacturers of trademarked or brand-name goods could now prohibit retailers from selling their product below a minimum price. Tydings neglected to incorporate a nonsigner clause that would make retail price-maintenance agreements binding on all merchants within a state. This defect would later allow the U.S. Supreme Court effectively to nullify the law. Although technically an antitrust law, the Miller-Tydings Act did not authorize the Federal Trade Commission to police resale price agreements; instead, Congress left it to manufacturers to enforce their own fair trade contracts.

The Miller-Tydings Act failed to satisfy the demands of independent retailers hungry for higher margins. Ironically, the high margins on fair trade products attracted mass marketers, and thereby intensified competition. Although the price of fair trade products increased after passage of this act, the NARD and other trade associations still criticized manufacturers for setting their minimum prices too low. These associations also found it difficult to persuade many manufacturers to abandon volume sales and adopt fair trade. As a result, several of these organizations decided to engage in coercive practices prohibited by the Miller-Tydings Act. The act allowed manufacturers to set minimum prices voluntarily, but retailers could not legally conspire to force manufacturers into fair trade. Nevertheless, the NARD proceeded to boycott and blacklist manufacturers that did not maintain minimum prices.

The rise of new types of competition also limited the impact of fair trade. During the 1950's, discount chains spread rapidly, and department stores responded by carrying a greater number of private brands. R. H. Macy & Company, for example, carried more than fourteen hundred products under its own name. By 1954, fewer than nine hundred manufacturers sold fair trade products, and the number continued to dwindle through the end of the decade. In 1956, a Senate Small Business Committee survey of retailers revealed widespread pessimism about the future of retail price maintenance.

During the late 1930's and the 1940's, the courts upheld the constitutionality of the Miller-Tydings Act, but this favorable treatment did not last into the 1950's. In 1951, the Supreme Court ruled that fair trade agreements could not be enforced against nonsigners in interstate commerce. Congress overrode the Court by passing the McGuire Act (1952), but the Court's strongly worded indictment of fair trade continued to influence the thinking of lower courts. Critical studies by economists and the Federal Trade Commission also fostered a judicial climate of opinion hostile to fair trade. During the 1950's and 1960's, state courts throughout the United States invalidated all or part of their fair trade laws, and by 1975 only eleven states had fair trade laws on the books.

The Miller-Tydings Act finally fell victim to the inflationary climate of the 1970's. In 1937, the sponsors of the act had hoped to raise prices in a deflationary period, but policy makers in the inflationary postwar years became more concerned with reducing prices. Economists estimated that fair trade raised the nation's cost of living by several billion dollars per year. In 1975, President Gerald Ford urged repeal of fair trade legislation as part of his WIN (Whip Inflation Now) program. Senator Edward W. Brooke (Republican of Massachusetts) introduced legislation to repeal the Miller-Tydings Act. His bill gathered overwhelming support from both liberals and conservatives. The resulting Consumer Goods Pricing Act repealed the Miller-Tydings Act and ended the experiment with retail price maintenance.

SIGNIFICANCE

The Miller-Tydings Act of 1937 expanded the marketing options of manufacturers by allowing them to emphasize quality and service rather than price. The act also reflected congressional concern with the fate of small business. Along with other legislation, such as the Robinson-Patman Act of 1936 (which limited the quantity discounts available to chain stores), the Miller-Tydings Act aimed to reduce the competitive advantage of discounters. Independent retailers hoped that the elimination of price competition would enable them to compete more successfully with mass marketers.

The impact of the Miller-Tydings Act varied from trade to trade. Retail price maintenance flourished in oligopolistic industries with trade associations strong enough to enforce compliance with fair trade agreements. Manufacturers found that they could maintain minimum prices on luxury goods that already sold at a high profit margin. Thus retail price maintenance spread most rapidly in drugs, cosmetics, jewelry, alcoholic beverages, tobacco, books, electrical appliances, cameras, and hardware. In 1950, the number of manufacturers engaged in retail price maintenance peaked at approximately sixteen hundred.

Despite the success of retail price maintenance in these fields, less than 10 percent of all goods were sold under fair trade contracts. Several factors limited the appeal of retail price maintenance. First, manufacturers using this tactic still faced price competition, so the minimum prices set could not be too high. In addition, mass marketers responded to retail price maintenance by adopting an increasing number of private brands, especially in the grocery trade. Discounters also found ways to evade retail price agreements, such as by offering rebates and accepting trade-ins. Many price cutters simply flouted the law, confident that manufacturers could not afford to enforce their fair trade contracts. Indeed, several leading consumer goods manufacturers, including General Electric and the Sheaffer Pen company, initially pursued a policy of price maintenance but abandoned this marketing strategy because the costs of enforcement were too high. Other manufacturers paid lip service to fair trade while at the same time seeking high sales volume through chain stores.

—Jonathan Bean

FURTHER READING

Blackford, Mansel G. *A History of Small Business in America.* New York: Twayne, 1991. Provides an overview of the changing role played by small business in the American economy as well as its impact on society at large. Chapter 3, "Government Policies for Small Business, 1921-1971," examines the political influence of small business. A good general history of American small business.

Bork, Robert H. *The Antitrust Paradox: A Policy at War with Itself.* New York: Basic Books, 1978. A critical study of the American antitrust tradition. The author shows how government enforcement of antitrust laws has deviated from original legislative intent. Bork combines economic theory with legal analysis in arguing for a consumer welfare test of antitrust policy. In chapter 14, "Resale Price Maintenance and Vertical Market Division," Bork develops arguments in favor of legalizing retail price maintenance. Assumes some knowledge of antitrust law.

Crews, Wayne. "Reexamining Antitrust: Can 'Anticompetitive' Business Practices Benefit Consumers?" *USA Today* (Society for the Advancement of Education) 130, no. 2862 (March, 2002): 1-28. Advocates a skeptical approach to study of antitrust policy, particularly with regard to modern corporations such as Microsoft.

Gellhorn, Ernest, William E. Kovacic, and Stephen Calkins. *Antitrust Law and Economics in a Nutshell.* St. Paul, Minn.: Thomson/West, 2004. This volume is a consistently accurate guide to the confusing world of antitrust law. It gives special attention to the roles of evidence, the granting of immunity, and government intervention.

Hawley, Ellis W. *The New Deal and the Problem of Monopoly: A Study in Economic Ambivalence.* Princeton, N.J.: Princeton University Press, 1966. A well-researched study of business-government relations in the New Deal period. Hawley presents a picture of an administration hopelessly divided among antitrusters, central planners, and those favoring close cooperation between government and business. The attention to detail is sometimes overwhelming, but the author provides an excellent summary of his findings in the concluding chapter.

Palamountain, Joseph Cornwall, Jr. *The Politics of Distribution.* Cambridge, Mass.: Harvard University Press, 1955. The standard work on the politics surrounding the anti-chain-store movement of the 1920's and the 1930's. The author analyzes the legislative history of the Miller-Tydings Act from the perspectives of manufacturers, retailers, and wholesalers. Heavy on theory in some parts but generally easy to read.

Strasser, Susan. *Satisfaction Guaranteed: The Making of*

the American Mass Market. New York: Pantheon Books, 1989. A lively account of the rise of mass marketing and its impact on the business practices of large and small firms. Chapter 8, "The Politics of Packaged Products," discusses the debate over retail price maintenance. Written for a general audience.

U.S. Federal Trade Commission. *Report of the Federal Trade Commission on Resale Price Maintenance.* Washington, D.C.: Government Printing Office, 1945. Summarizes the findings of a six-year study of the effects of retail price maintenance. This work provides a wealth of data, including results of public opinion surveys and the changing price levels of fair trade products.

Yamey, B. S., ed. *Resale Price Maintenance.* Chicago: Aldine, 1966. A collection of essays examining the impact of fair trade legislation in the United States and abroad. In "United States of America," Stanley Hollander discusses the efforts of congressional small-business advocates to strengthen fair trade legislation in the aftermath of adverse court decisions.

SEE ALSO: Sept. 26, 1914: Federal Trade Commission Is Organized; Oct. 15, 1914: Clayton Antitrust Act; June 16, 1933: Roosevelt Signs the National Industrial Recovery Act; Oct. 18, 1933: Roosevelt Creates the Commodity Credit Corporation; June 19, 1936: Robinson-Patman Act Restricts Price Discrimination; June 21, 1938: Natural Gas Act.

September, 1937
TOLKIEN REDEFINES FANTASY LITERATURE

With the publication of The Hobbit, *the first of his successful and imaginative books that would later include the trilogy* The Lord of the Rings, *J. R. R. Tolkien established a new benchmark for the fantasy genre of literature: fully realized imaginary worlds, epic in nature, including relevant moral themes, and appealing to adults as well as children.*

ALSO KNOWN AS: *The Hobbit*
LOCALE: Oxford, England
CATEGORY: Literature

KEY FIGURES
J. R. R. Tolkien (1892-1973), English writer and professor of early English language and literature
C. S. Lewis (1898-1963), English author and close friend of Tolkien
Stanley Unwin (1884-1968), English publisher responsible for publication of *The Hobbit* and *The Lord of the Rings*

SUMMARY OF EVENT
J. R. R. Tolkien was educated at Oxford, where he earned a degree in English language and literature in 1915. He served in France during World War I, married, and had four children from 1917 to 1929. He was a respected scholar and professor of Anglo-Saxon language and literature at Leeds University and, beginning in 1925, at Oxford.

Tolkien had a deep love for language and mythology, and he learned Old English, Old Norse, and Finnish so that he could read the myths he loved in their original languages. In addition, he invented languages from childhood through adulthood and then invented worlds and civilizations to go with those languages. After World War I, he began to write about a complex fantasy world in a series of stories that later became *The Silmarillion* (published in 1977); these stories lay the groundwork for *The Hobbit* (1937) and *The Lord of the Rings* (1955). At the same time, Tolkien lived the life of an English academic, teaching, writing poetry, and publishing scholarly works.

The Hobbit grew out of a family mythology that Tolkien created while telling stories to his children. He began to invent a complex English mythology, using English landscapes, elves, dwarves, wizards, and dragons. Among the characters he created were those known as hobbits, small furry creatures who love order and the comforts of home. Tolkien based the hobbits on English peasant and middle-class types.

C. S. Lewis, who later published his own works of fantasy fiction, including *The Chronicles of Narnia* (1950-1956), played an extremely important role in the development of Tolkien's fantasy world. Tolkien and Lewis were close friends and colleagues at Oxford for many years, and both men were members of the Inklings, a group of writers at Oxford who critiqued each other's unpublished works. Tolkien began writing *The Hobbit* in 1930, and by 1933 he had much of the book completed. Tolkien and Lewis were both interested in fantasy worlds, which at the time were considered only suitable

J. R. R. Tolkien. (Courtesy, Houghton Mifflin Company)

In the final third of the book, the threads of the tale come together: Once Bilbo has helped the dwarves reach their treasure, Bilbo takes a moral stand against materialism, greed, and war and tries to reach a compromise between the dwarves on one side and the elves and men on the other. The climax of the story comes when the dragon is finally killed and the dwarves, elves, and men unite against a common enemy, the goblins. The treasure is divided fairly, and Bilbo returns to the Shire with a comfortable amount of gold, a reputation for adventure, and a treasure in memories. Bilbo's growth and development is a major theme of the story: Within himself he finds the wit, strength, and courage to help his friends and himself and proves himself to be a resourceful and down-to-earth hero.

By the time Tolkien showed the manuscript to C. S. Lewis in 1933, *The Hobbit* was mostly complete. It remained rough and incomplete until 1936, when Tolkien showed it to a former student and friend of the family who had a job at the London publishing firm Allen & Unwin. The publisher asked Tolkien to complete the book and submit it for publication. With this incentive, he finalized the manuscript and publisher Stanley Unwin gave it to his ten-year-old son to read. *The Hobbit* was published in September of 1937, and it was an immediate success: Critics pronounced it genial, attractive, and fresh. The initial printing sold out before Christmas, and a second printing was rushed through the presses. Unwin immediately asked for a sequel and for more stories about hobbits. Tolkien soon began work on *The Lord of the Rings*, although that trilogy was not published until 1955. *The Hobbit* stands as an independent work and as an introduction to the more mature work of the trilogy.

Although *The Hobbit* originated as a story for his children, Tolkien did not conceive of the written work as a children's book. The clarity and simplicity of the style, which appealed to young readers, was necessary to make the complex, imaginary world understandable and clear, and it helped the book to be enjoyed at several different levels by children and adults. *The Hobbit*'s fully realized

for children's books, and they encouraged each other's work. As a result, Lewis was the first person to read *The Hobbit*, which at the time was still in manuscript form.

The hero of the novel is Bilbo Baggins, a hobbit who lives in a fairy-tale country called the Shire (based on the landscape of the English countryside). Content with the simple pleasures of home, Baggins is a reluctant hero who is recruited by the wizard Gandolf to help a company of dwarves recover their treasure from the dragon Smaug. Together they undergo a journey to the territory laid waste by Smaug: They travel through mountains and forest, brave the dangers of trolls and goblins, enjoy the hospitality of elves, and share in the company of giants and heroes. Through a series of episodic adventures, Bilbo acquires a ring that can make him invisible, and he grows in confidence and competence as he moves through a world of epic danger, heroism, war, and complex cultures in which new civilizations and languages are introduced. His cleverness in wordplay and language wins battles of wits that help Baggins overcome obstacles, especially as he attempts to obtain the precious ring from a subterranean creature named Gollum.

imaginary worlds, its exploration of nature of heroism, it moral themes and their relation to contemporary politics and events, its epic scope, and its detailed descriptions (including maps) of imaginary people and places became the characteristics of a new genre of fantasy for adults.

SIGNIFICANCE

The Hobbit is considered a transitional work in Tolkien's career and in literary history. In the context of Tolkien's writing, the development of *The Hobbit* formed a crucial link between the stories Tolkien told to his children and the rich, mature narrative of the *Lord of the Rings* trilogy. *The Hobbit* also connected the genre of British children's literature and a new fantasy genre meant to appeal to adults' imaginations. Together, Tolkien and C. S. Lewis were largely responsible for the creation of an adult readership for fantasy literature. Their careful construction of alternative universes that combined quest tales and exploration of the nature of heroism with the appeal of mythology, wordplay, and a variety of linguistic styles gave the genre a life beyond the confines of children's literature.

—*Susan Butterworth*

FURTHER READING

Carpenter, Humphrey. *J. R. R. Tolkien: A Biography.* Boston: Houghton Mifflin, 2000. The authorized biography of Tolkien, originally published in the 1980's. Carpenter also edited a published a collection of Tolkien's letters and a book on the Inklings.

De Koster, Katie, ed. *Readings on J. R. R. Tolkien.* San Diego, Calif.: Greenhaven, 2000. Collection of critical articles including a comprehensive section on aspects of *The Hobbit*, such as its roots in British children's novels, adult themes, and the nature of heroism.

Heims, Neil. *J. R. R. Tolkien.* Philadelphia: Chelsea House, 2004. Engaging literary biography drawing on the work of previous Tolkien scholars. Accessible portrait of the man and his ideas that strives to illuminate his works.

Manlove, Colin. *The Fantasy Literature of England.* New York: Palgrave, 1999. Places Tolkien's work in the context of the history and conventions of the fantasy genre in England.

O'Neill, Timothy R. *The Individuated Hobbit: Jung, Tolkien, and the Archetypes of Middle-Earth.* Boston: Houghton Mifflin, 1979. Demonstrates the connection between Carl Jung's theories of the struggle for self-realization and Tolkien's mythology and characters.

Rosebury, Brian. *Tolkien: A Cultural Phenomenon.* New York: Palgrave, 2003. Clear, lucid criticism and analysis of Tolkien's work and his place in twentieth century literature and culture.

Shippey, Tom. *The Road to Middle-Earth: How J. R. R. Tolkien Created a New Mythology.* Boston: Houghton Mifflin, 2003. A respected Tolkien scholar discusses the sources and creation of Tolkien's complex world.

SEE ALSO: 1918: Cather's *My Ántonia* Promotes Regional Literature; Feb. 21, 1925: Ross Founds *The New Yorker*; Sept., 1929-Jan., 1930: *The Maltese Falcon* Introduces the Hard-Boiled Detective Novel; Fall, 1933-Oct. 20, 1949: Lewis Convenes the Inklings; 1938-1950: Golden Age of American Science Fiction.

September 2, 1937
PITTMAN-ROBERTSON ACT PROVIDES STATE WILDLIFE FUNDING

The Pittman-Robertson Act authorized funding of state wildlife agencies through federal excise taxes on sporting guns and ammunition used in hunting.

ALSO KNOWN AS: Federal Aid in Wildlife Act
LOCALE: Washington, D.C.
CATEGORIES: Environmental issues; laws, acts, and legal history

KEY FIGURES

Carl D. Shoemaker (1882-1969), special investigator for the U.S. Senate Special Committee on Conservation of Wildlife Resources and secretary of the National Wildlife Federation
Key Pittman (1872-1940), U.S. senator from Nevada who introduced Shoemaker's draft in the Senate and speeded the act's passage
A. Willis Robertson (1887-1971), U.S. congressman from Virginia who introduced the bill in the House and served as its sponsor
Jay Darling (1876-1962), American political cartoonist and advocate of wildlife conservation
Scott Lucas (1892-1968), U.S. congressman from Illinois who, as chairman of the Agriculture Committee, supported the bill through the House

SUMMARY OF EVENT

On September 2, 1937, President Franklin D. Roosevelt signed the Pittman-Robertson Act, which authorized the federal government to collect manufacturers' excise taxes on sporting guns and ammunition and to transfer the money to state wildlife agencies. This law originated through the cooperation of conservationists, primarily hunters, and manufacturers of sporting arms and ammunition. The revenues collected have been used to support wildlife management, including purchase of critical habitat, management of existing refuges, hunter training, and wildlife restoration. Many species whose survival had once been threatened have thereby been able to thrive. The law, also known as the Federal Aid in Wildlife Act, was initiated by Carl D. Shoemaker, a conservationist, and was sponsored through Congress in less than three months by Senator Key Pittman and Representative A. Willis Robertson.

In the early years of the twentieth century, as sport hunting became increasingly popular and wildlife habitat and wildlife itself became increasingly scarce, lead-

ing conservationists tried to develop and fund a refuge system that would benefit both wildlife and sportsmen. Several laws were passed as a result. The Migratory Bird Conservation Act of 1929 set up a refuge system to be financed by congressional appropriations. In 1934, largely through the efforts of Jay Darling as chief of the Bureau of Biological Survey, the Duck Stamp and Fish Wildlife Coordination Acts, which provided funding for wetland conservation, were passed.

Darling and Shoemaker, as special investigator of the Senate Special Committee on Conservation and Wildlife Resources, helped to organize the first North American Wildlife Conference in 1936, out of which the National Wildlife Federation was created. At the second North American Wildlife Conference in 1937, Shoemaker and others started to develop what would become the Pittman-Robertson law by modifying suggestions made by John B. Burnham and T. Gilbert Pearson in 1925. Burnham and Pearson had suggested that the 10 percent excise tax on sporting arms and ammunition be used to finance refuges instead of being considered part of general funds, but the proposed financing did not go through because Congress repealed all excise taxes, although they were reinstated in 1932.

In 1937, Shoemaker suggested that the current 11 percent manufacturers' excise tax on sporting guns and ammunition be allocated to the states equitably. In order to apportion funding equitably and to balance the small populations of the western states with the high populations of the East, his formula included the number of paid license holders as well as the area of the states. This approach would balance the western states with their relatively small populations but large land area with the larger number of licensed hunters in the more populous but smaller eastern states. The draft bill was supported by the Bureau of Biological Survey, state wildlife agencies, and conservation organizations. The firearms industry supported it as well after Shoemaker agreed to the suggestion of Charles L. Horn of the Federal Cartridge Company to lower the percentage of tax collections used for administrative costs by the Biological Survey from his proposed 10 percent to 8 percent.

Shoemaker enlisted the support of Senator Key Pittman of Nevada, chairman of the Special Committee on Wildlife, and Representative A. Willis Robertson of Virginia, chairman of the House Select Committee on Conservation of Wildlife Resources. Robertson had been a member of the Virginia Game and Inland Fisheries Commission and knew that state legislatures sometimes used funds from license receipts for state programs other than those of the wildlife agencies. He therefore added to Shoemaker's bill the prohibition of the diversion of funds for purposes other than the administration of the state fish and game department. The modified bill moved through the Senate very quickly. In the House, however, the Agriculture Committee, not the Wildlife Committee, had jurisdiction over the bill. In order to entice Representative Scott Lucas from Illinois, chairman of the Agriculture Committee, to move the bill through the House more quickly, Shoemaker encouraged Illinois women's groups and garden clubs to contact Lucas. The bill passed the House on August 17 and was signed by Franklin D. Roosevelt on September 2, 1937.

Ira N. Gabrielson, chief of the Bureau of Biological Survey, and his assistant, Albert M. Day, implemented the Pittman-Robertson Act. Day determined that the funds were to be used for three types of state projects: to purchase land to rehabilitate wildlife, to develop and improve land's suitability for birds and mammals, and to research ways to solve problems of wildlife restoration. In order to ensure that management of state wildlife programs was performed by professionals and not political appointees, Gabrielson and Day also required that management personnel hired through Pittman-Robertson funds be trained and competent.

Despite excise tax revenues of around three million dollars in 1938, Congress allocated only one million dollars that first year and continued to refuse to allocate the funds to the state wildlife agencies until the 1950's. In 1939, the Bureau of Biological Survey was removed from the Department of Agriculture and placed in the Department of the Interior, where it was combined with the Bureau of Fisheries of the Department of Commerce. This new agency was called the Fish and Wildlife Service. In 1951, as part of the Appropriations Act, Congress agreed to transfer all the tax collections to the state wildlife agencies. In 1956, Congress agreed to release thirteen million dollars in back tax revenues. As a result, excise tax revenues collected from hunters have been used to replenish wildlife and their habitat throughout the United States.

Over the years, as the act's influence has grown, it has financed scientific research of particular species and their habitats, habitat restoration, hunter education, and wildlife research in general. As a result, the decline of many species has been reversed, habitat has been re-

stored, and hunting accidents and fatalities in many states have declined. The Pittman-Robertson Act has increased the professionalism of wildlife research and management by setting professional standards for management personnel as well as requiring that projects meet national standards. It also has served as a dependable source of money so that states may engage in long-term programs, and it has provided professionals with a means of exchanging information to ensure that managers are aware of projects in different states. Funds have also been used to support cooperative programs with nongovernment organizations.

Funds are distributed based on the number of paid license holders and the area of each state. No state may receive more than 5 percent or less than 1 percent of the total funds. Puerto Rico receives one-half of 1 percent and Guam, Northern Mariana Islands, and the U.S. Virgin Islands each receives one-sixth of 1 percent. For every dollar a state receives it must contribute twenty-five cents. In 1970, Pittman-Robertson's funding base was expanded to include a 10 percent excise tax on handguns, and in 1971, an 11 percent tax on archery equipment. Half of these revenues are used for hunter education and half for traditional wildlife restoration. The use of the funds has changed over the years. In 1970, Congress allowed states to finance not only specific projects but also wider-ranging comprehensive plans. All in all, eligibility has become more complicated as environmental attitudes and regulations have changed and as new federal requirements, including laws pertaining to civil rights and age discrimination, have been instituted.

More than $800 million (or around 60 percent of the money) has been used to obtain land for feeding, resting, and breeding places for wildlife. States have provided around $270 million of their own money, largely from license fees from hunters. Wetlands were of particular concern. In the first fifty years of the law's existence, the states acquired more than two million acres of waterfowl habitat. This and other acquisition and control of land through leasing and cooperation with farmers and other landowners has been very important in preventing further deterioration and loss of natural habitat. The law also has facilitated modification of the land, through stream diversion and improvement of drainage and nesting cover, all beneficial to wildlife.

SIGNIFICANCE

The Pittman-Robertson Act was enacted to reverse the decline of wildlife in the United States. It has led to very

1937

successful restorations of specific species, including the wild turkey and white-tailed deer. Through the application of knowledge gained about such factors as habitat, food habits, and predators, and by regulating human hunting, the number of white-tailed deer has drastically increased so that in some areas of the country there are too many deer. Heightened awareness of the wild turkey's needs, combined with the development of traps and transfer techniques, has led to successful turkey restoration in many states. Turkey populations have increased so much that the number of states with legal hunting seasons has grown from sixteen in 1952 to forty-six in 1987.

Improved trapping and transfer techniques for big-horn sheep have also been developed with funds from Pittman-Robertson and from such groups as the Foundation for North American Wild Sheep and the Society for the Conservation of Bighorn Sheep. Bighorn sheep have been transferred back to parts of their historic ranges in the intermountain plateau region between the Rockies and the Cascades and Sierra Nevada in the western United States. Development and construction of artificial water-collecting devices have also improved conditions for the bighorn and other animals such as the elk, mule deer, and pronghorn antelope. Although the bighorn sheep are not flourishing to the degree of the wild turkey and the white-tailed deer, their number are much larger than they would have been without the money and cooperation fostered by Pittman-Robertson.

Pittman-Robertson matching funds have also contributed to the comeback of black bear populations. States have been able to buy and manage lands and to support long-term studies. By trapping and tranquilizing bears so that they can be tagged and collared with radio transmitters, wildlife researchers have greatly expanded their knowledge of the black bear. New hunting regulations, changes in the public's attitudes about bears, and the recovery of its forest habitat have all combined with scientific research to contribute to the increase in bear population.

Other animals whose numbers have increased include the prairie chicken, the mountain lion, the Canadian goose, the pronghorn antelope, the elk, the caribou, the beaver, the sea otter, the gray and fox squirrels, the mule deer, the wood duck, the chukar partridge, the bobcat, and the ring-necked pheasant. The benefits of the Pittman-Robertson Act extend beyond the hunters who pay the excise taxes funding the program. Because of the act, wildlife has become more plentiful, some spe-

cies have been saved from extinction, and natural habitats have been improved and expanded throughout the United States.

—Margaret F. Boorstein

FURTHER READING

National Research Council of the National Academy of Sciences. *Land Use and Wildlife Resources.* Washington, D.C.: National Academy of Sciences, 1970. Focuses on the interactions between wildlife management and agriculture. In examining the relationship of the Pittman-Robertson Act with other legislation, the book provides some context for its role in wildlife restoration.

Owen, A. L. Riesch. *Conservation Under F. D. R.* New York: Praeger, 1983. Examines conservation during Franklin D. Roosevelt's administration. Discusses the historical context in which Pittman-Robertson Act was enacted and the law's relation to other legislation and policies.

_____. "Wildlife Aid from Gun Taxes." *Nature Magazine* 30 (December, 1937): 361-362. This magazine states that its purpose is to assist Americans in playing a militant part in attaining constructive conservation aims. The editorial, written a few months after the Pittman-Robertson Act became law, predicted that both migratory and resident game would be harmed because more hunting would be encouraged to raise more tax money.

Sheldon, H. P. "Game Restoration." *Country Life and the Sportsman* 74 (June, 1938): 28, 90. A brief summary of the act. Discusses how the act expanded federal authority to nonmigratory wildlife, previously considered property of the states but now seen as a national resource. It warns that although Congress has authorized funds, wildlife interests must ensure that the moneys are actually appropriated.

Sinclair, Anthony R. E., John M. Fryxell, and Graeme Caughley. *Wildlife Ecology, Conservation, and Management.* Malden, Mass.: Blackwell, 2006. An excellent introduction to ecology and conservation studies. Includes a CD that helps students create computer-based models of different ecological scenarios.

Taber, Richard D., and Neil F. Payne. *Wildlife, Conservation, and Human Welfare: A United States and Canadian Perspective.* Malabar, Fla.: Krieger, 2003. Attempts to chronicle the history of human impact on wildlife and analyzes the response to its destruction.

United States Department of the Interior, Fish and Wildlife Service. *Restoring America's Wildlife: 1937-1987: The First 50 Years of the Federal Aid in Wildlife Restoration (Pittman-Robertson) Act.* Washington, D.C.: Author, 1987. Provides an overall summary of the evolution and implementation of the act and many detailed examples of its impact on specific species, habitats, and hunters. Includes maps and pho-tographs, statistical tables, and a state-by-state summary of actions taken by wildlife agencies.

SEE ALSO: Mar. 14, 1903: First U.S. National Wildlife Refuge Is Established; July 3, 1918: Migratory Bird Treaty Act; Feb. 4, 1936: Darling Founds the National Wildlife Federation; July 1, 1940: U.S. Fish and Wildlife Service Is Formed.

Fall, 1937-Winter, 1938
WEIDENREICH RECONSTRUCTS THE FACE OF PEKING MAN

When Franz Weidenreich reconstructed the face of the oldest known hominid and provided the first glimpse of Peking man, he clarified the path of human evolution.

ALSO KNOWN AS: Beijing man
LOCALE: Beijing, China; Zhoukoudian, China
CATEGORIES: Anthropology; prehistory and ancient cultures

KEY FIGURES

Franz Weidenreich (1873-1948), German anatomist, physical anthropologist, and paleoanthropologist
Davidson Black (1884-1934), Canadian physician, anatomist, and paleoanthropologist
Pierre Teilhard de Chardin (1881-1955), French Jesuit, philosopher, archaeologist, and paleontologist
Pei Wenzhong (W. C. Pei; 1904-1982), Chinese archaeologist
Johan Gunnar Andersson (1874-1960), Swedish geologist and paleoanthropologist

SUMMARY OF EVENT

As early as 1900, Western scientists knew that China was an ideal place to look for fossil humans. Western visitors had discovered isolated humanlike teeth in Chinese drugstores, where they were called "dragon's teeth" and sold as medicine. In 1918, the Swedish geologist Johan Gunnar Andersson discovered a major deposit of Pleistocene fossils in a cave outside the village of Zhoukoudian, located near Beijing (then known in the West as Peking). These fossils appeared to be about 500,000 years old. Looking for fossil mammals and hoping for fossil humans, Andersson began excavating the site in 1921. Shortly thereafter, Davidson Black, a professor of anatomy at the Peking Medical Union, persuaded the Rockefeller Foundation to establish the Cenozoic Research Laboratory in Beijing. It became the center for excavations at Zhoukoudian and for the analysis of material found at that site.

Based on isolated teeth, Black formally identified Peking man in 1927, calling him *Sinanthropus pekinensis*. In 1929, the Chinese archaeologist Pei Wenzhong discovered the first nearly complete skullcap of a *Sinanthropus pekinensis*, providing the first real evidence that early man existed in China. This discovery seemed to confirm Black's belief that humanity's ancestor was to be found in the Far East. Furthermore, stone tools, burned animal bones, and animal bones with clear-cut marks were found in association with the skullcap, giving definite evidence of culture. When Black died of a heart attack in 1934, he was succeeded by Franz Weidenreich, who had been firmly established in Germany as an anatomist and physical anthropologist. Already renowned for his work in hematology and osteology, in 1928 he had written the definitive account of a Neanderthal-like skull found at Weimar-Ehringsdorf, Germany. In Beijing, he cooperated with the archaeologists who were actively involved in excavations such as Pei and Pierre Teilhard de Chardin. Weidenreich supervised the extraction of the bones from their rocky matrices, directed the scientific drawing of the fossils, and wrote reports of findings.

Although many human fossils had been found at Zhoukoudian by 1937, nearly all were damaged skullcaps. The skull below the level of the ears was frequently destroyed, as were most facial bones. Bones from the lower skeleton were rare, but those that had been found were broken in a way that implied extraction of marrow. It has generally been assumed that Peking man had been the agent of this destruction and that he had been removing and eating brains and bone marrow. With the advent of the study of taphonomy—the natural conditions affecting preservation of human activities—it has been recognized that fossils as old as Peking man are frequently crushed and that the thinnest part of the bone in Peking man's skull was below the ears. Consequently, it is possible that the damage to these bones may have been caused by natural agencies. Nevertheless, it was impossible for modern scholars to reconstruct his face. They knew that he had a massive ridge of bone above his eyes, little or no forehead, his skull was long and low, and his brain was somewhat more than twice the size of a modern chimpanzee, but the scarcity of facial bones meant that they did not know what he looked like.

This knowledge was pieced together after the end of fall, 1937. This was to be the last season at Zhoukoudian before the Japanese invasion put an end to fieldwork. Three fairly well-preserved skulls, all adults, were found in the same location. None of these individuals had complete faces. Nevertheless, enough of the three faces had survived that it was possible to reconstruct the appearance of Peking man.

Actually, it was a Peking woman who was recon-

structed. One of the skulls, a female's, included a large fragment of the upper jaw. This was the important piece needed to fill in the picture of the *Sinanthropus* face. Only the nasal bones, a portion of the front of the upper jaw, the cheekbones, and part of the area around the eyes needed to be adapted from other individuals. The lower jaw was adapted from the lower jaw of a female found in 1936. Weidenreich was satisfied that his reconstruction was correct, given that it was based on real bones and had no imaginary details. According to Weidenreich's reconstruction, the face of Peking woman was heavy and large. Her eye sockets were larger than those of modern humans, and her eyes were set wide apart. Her nose was low and wide, but within the range of variation in modern humans. Her face was wide and jutted forward slightly. She had the usual *Sinanthropus* chin and forehead and the usual heavy brow ridge over her eyes and nose. Her head was small in comparison to modern humans but is larger than any ape's. Her skull was widest above the ears and then sloped upward and inward, and she had a slight ridge running from front to rear along the top of her head.

She had a bony ridge at the back of her head, set slightly above a very thick neck. Despite these characteristics, she undeniably represents an ancestor of modern human beings.

Weidenreich left China in 1941, barely escaping incarceration in a Japanese prison camp. He had attempted to send the Peking man fossils out of China with the help of the United States Army. The bones of forty individuals—men, women, and children—from an important stage of human evolution were packed in footlockers and sent to the coast with American soldiers to be delivered to the S. S. *President Harrison* at the port of Zhingwangdao. Unfortunately, they disappeared after they left Beijing. It is not known whether they were stolen, lost, or destroyed by Japanese soldiers. Weidenreich and others attempted to locate the fossils after World War II, but to no avail. Although a number of mysterious stories were told about their whereabouts, the Peking fossils were never found. The disaster of this loss has been partly compensated for by the excellent casts, photographs, and drawings made by laboratory technicians in China. That is all that is left of the major finds from Zhoukoudian.

In recent years, archaeologists in China have continued the search for Peking man. No further fossils of Peking man have been found at

Franz Weidenreich. (American Museum of Natural History)

Zhoukoudian, but they have been found elsewhere in China. It is regrettable that the bones so carefully studied by Weidenreich and others are no longer available for further research. New and sophisticated methods of analysis could have been used to extract further secrets from them, and it is unlikely that such a large population of early man will ever be found again.

SIGNIFICANCE

At the time that Weidenreich made his reconstruction, Peking man, together with his cousin, Java man, was the earliest accepted ancestor of modern people. Neanderthals and related types from Europe and the Middle East were far too recent and far too similar to modern humans to qualify as early ancestors. Although the Australopithecines had been discovered in South Africa as early as 1924, they were not accepted as being on the human line of evolution until the 1950's. At the time of the great discoveries of Peking man, an acrimonious debate was percolating over whether the Australopithecines were large apes or early hominids. The discoveries in Zhoukoudian excited the world, because Peking man and his Javanese cousins stood alone as humankind's undisputed ancestors. In a certain sense, they still stand alone. In later years, Peking man, Java man, and other related types later found in Africa and Europe were reclassified as *Homo erectus*, thought to have lived between one million years ago and about 150,000 years ago. They are the first members of the genus *Homo* and the immediate forerunners of the modern human species, *Homo sapiens*. They were the first to use fire, first to have habitations, first to use stone tools with a definite style, and first to inhabit the temperate regions of Europe and Asia; they are indisputably human.

Furthermore, the fossils found at Zhoukoudian remain unique in the annals of human prehistory. Although *Homo erectus* has been found elsewhere, the remains have most often consisted of fragmentary and isolated finds that natural processes have often removed from where the individuals died. Nowhere else have so many individuals been found who are more or less contemporaneous and who died on the spot, surrounded by their tools, their hearths, and their garbage. As a result, the fossils from Zhoukoudian reveal what the range of variation was for this species, and their relatively in situ position tells much about how they lived and what they ate. They are fundamental in defining the species *Homo erectus*, and they are unique pieces in the puzzle of human evolution.

—*Lucy Jayne Botscharow*

FURTHER READING

Brace, C. Loring. *The Stages of Human Evolution: Human and Cultural Origins*. 4th ed. Englewood Cliffs, N.J.: Prentice Hall, 1991. Well-written general account of human evolution also presents a short history of evolutionary thought, together with descriptions of the discovery of important human fossils and the controversies that often ensued. Includes illustrations, bibliography, and index.

Howells, W. W. "*Homo Erectus* in Human Descent: Ideas and Problems." In *Homo Erectus: Papers in Honor of Davidson Black*, edited by Becky A. Sigmon and Jerome S. Cybulski. Toronto: University of Toronto Press, 1981. Provides a clear and succinct summary of current scientific thought regarding Peking man's position in human evolution. Somewhat technical, but indispensable for an understanding of the current status of *Homo erectus*. Includes illustrations, a map of fossil hominid sites, and excellent bibliography.

Koenigswald, Gustav Heinrich Ralph von. *Meeting Prehistoric Man*. Translated by Michael Bullock. New York: Harper & Brothers, 1956. Although outdated scientifically, provides enjoyable discussion of "dragon's bones" and of the exhilaration of the early finds in Java and China. Koenigswald worked in Java and later at the American Museum of Natural History and was a close associate of Weidenreich. Includes illustrations.

Oosterzee, Penny van. *Dragon Bones: The Story of Peking Man*. New York: Perseus Books, 2000. Historical account for lay readers describes the activities that led to the discovery of Peking man and the events that followed. The author is an Australian ecologist and science writer.

Shapiro, Harry L. *Peking Man: The Discovery, Disappearance, and Mystery of a Priceless Scientific Treasure*. New York: Simon & Schuster, 1974. Combines good scholarship with exciting narrative. Shapiro was associated with the American Museum of Natural History for more than fifty years and knew Weidenreich well. Includes illustrations and charts of geological time and of Peking man's place on the evolutionary tree.

Tattersall, Ian. *The Last Neanderthal: The Rise, Success, and Mysterious Extinction of Our Closest Human Relatives*. Rev. ed. Boulder, Colo.: Westview Press, 1999. Examination for a lay audience of the evidence concerning humans' relation to the Neanderthals. Provides background on paleoanthropology in general and current knowledge about the hominid line. Includes illustrations and index.

Weidenreich, Franz. "The Face of Peking Woman: Latest Developments Regarding Our Celebrated Apelike Relative." *Natural History* 41 (May, 1938): 358-360. A description of the reconstructed face of Peking woman written for the general public. Clearly conveys the satisfaction that Weidenreich felt regarding

his reconstruction. Includes excellent illustrations and bibliography.

SEE ALSO: Dec., 1908: Boule Reconstructs the First Neanderthal Skeleton; Summer, 1923: Zdansky Discovers Peking Man; Summer, 1924: Dart Discovers the First Australopithecine Fossil; Sept. 12, 1940: Lascaux Cave Paintings Are Discovered.

October, 1937
THE DIARY OF A COUNTRY PRIEST INSPIRES AMERICAN READERS

During the Great Depression, while many Americans were turning in despair to mass political movements and charismatic leaders, Georges Bernanos's story of an unprepossessing man who becomes a vehicle for God's grace suggested that the answer lay elsewhere.

LOCALE: Europe; United States
CATEGORY: Literature

KEY FIGURE
Georges Bernanos (1888-1948), French novelist

SUMMARY OF EVENT
George Bernanos's 1936 novel *Journal d'un curé de campagne*, the winner of France's Femina Prize and the Grand Prix of the Académie Française, became available in English translation as *The Diary of a Country Priest* in October, 1937. The book had been a great success in France, the author's native country (although he wrote the work while living in Spain), but its focus on a Catholic priest's struggles was more problematic in the United States. Could a literary work that sought to address the great problems of society through a Roman Catholic cleric's eyes speak to a nation that had, within the past decade, rejected a Democratic candidate for president largely because of his membership in the Catholic Church?

The Catholic press in the United States celebrated the work as emphatically as the French had. Bernanos's most valuable praise came from John Kenneth Merton, who wrote for the lay Catholic weekly *Commonweal*. Merton characterized the book as "unusually touching and beautiful," a work that, "despite its exquisite restraint, makes the reader breathless with intensity." He called some of the characters "beautiful" and extolled the protagonist's "spirit of heroism that is so perfect as not to be conscious of itself." He further praised *The Diary of a Country*

Priest as "a remarkable book, one written with beautiful art, full of a searching and delicate psychology, and revealing a simplicity so crystalline and a courage so humble as to lift what might have been a sordid tragedy to heroic heights."

What of the American literary world outside the Catholic orbit? Would others also see the beauty of the work? *The New York Times* trumpeted the publication with a glowing review on the front page of its book review section in which Katherine Woods pronounced the novel to be a work of "deep, subtle and singularly encompassing art" likely to "fill a quite definite place in the interest of readers here." Woods celebrated the work's "greatness as creative art" and called it a "strange and sad, yet beautiful and triumphant, story." Reviewers and critics for other publications also welcomed the work with high praise and suggested its import for the American audience.

However, the simplicity so often cited as the principal source of *The Diary of a Country Priest*'s value, when coupled with the Catholic focus, militated against the book's success in the literary market. The book has little action and no excitement. Even Merton admitted that the work had "very little" plot "in the ordinary sense." The novel consequently never made it onto any best seller lists, and it subsequently fell into relative obscurity. Even so, it remained available in English translation for more than fifty years and continued to draw praise from those who read it even decades after its initial publication.

What little action the novel contains takes place in an obscure French village. The protagonist is a young, frail, and dying Roman Catholic priest who is largely incapable of inspiring those around him and whose greatest attribute is the ability to absorb lectures from those seemingly more confident, secure, and wise than himself. The book consists of a series of these lectures (and the reflections they inspire) presented as discussions, bracketed between bouts of personal anxiety and small defeats. The plot develops from the reflections these experiences inspire. The work takes place within the individual priest's consciousness as he grapples to comprehend his place and role in the largely unpleasant developments around him.

The priest comes new to his assignment in a small village and worries that the residents neither like nor respect him. His physical and social impairments sap his confidence and impede his efforts to relate to his parishioners; the parish children make fun of his efforts to teach them the faith he sometimes wonders if he still holds. The local merchant seems to take advantage of his impoverished state, and his peculiar diet of bread dipped in wine (necessitated by a growing stomach cancer) causes parishioners to suspect him of alcoholism.

Despite the unrelenting frustration the curate experiences in the town—perhaps because of it—he rises to heroic heights. His earnest ineffectualness and his genuine and seemingly losing battle with despair render him a transcendent hero to whom all who suffer can relate. Although he accomplishes no final feat that might render him "heroic" in the sense that many understand the term, his continued charity throughout his suffering suggests a spiritual triumph.

SIGNIFICANCE

Contemporary American reviewers located the value of *The Diary of a Country Priest* in its transcendence of the French village setting and in the lessons the book provided for all who struggled in those turbulent times. Bernanos wrote as much about the world as he did about the tiny French village, and the young priest is not so much a denominational manifestation as a representative of every person searching for the good in a society steeped in despair and ugliness. The priest grapples with the very issues that consumed Americans in the late 1930's, questions of social justice and human dignity. Bernanos located much of the cause of these concerns in the very institutions that were supposed to eliminate (or at least ameliorate) them: the Church and the community. The Church sought institutional survival rather than social salvation, and the community blunted and dwarfed its members rather than nurtured them.

If Bernanos seemed cynical about the ability of the Church and the community to solve serious social problems, he also suggested that individuals could successfully find solutions through inner, individual, efforts. Although the Church did not always foster virtue and

dignity (and often seemed to impede the achievement of those aims), people could find such values in the world around them. The dying priest's last words, spoken in answer to his friend's concern that a priest will not arrive soon enough to provide final absolution, suggest an extrainstitutional route to salvation and dignity. The priest asks if it matters that he will not receive the Church's final rite; he then answers his own question by

THE COUNTRY PRIEST'S DESPAIR

In the opening paragraphs of The Diary of a Country Priest, *the narrator's gloomy state of mind is evident:*

Mine is a parish like all the rest. They're all alike. Those of to-day I mean. I was saying so only yesterday to M. le Curé de Norenfontes—that good and evil are probably evenly distributed, but on such a low plain, very low indeed! Or if you like they lie one over the other; like oil and water they never mix. M. Le Curé only laughed at me. He is a good priest, deeply kind and human, who at diocesan headquarters is even considered a bit of a free-thinker, on the dangerous side. His outbursts fill his colleagues with glee, and he stresses them with a look meant to be fiery, but which gives me such a deep sensation of stale discouragement that it almost brings tears into my eyes.

My parish is bored stiff; no other word for it. Like so many others! We can see them being eaten up by boredom, and we can't do anything about it. Some day perhaps we shall catch it ourselves—become aware of the cancerous growth within us. You can keep going a long time with that in you.

This thought struck me yesterday on my rounds. It was drizzling. The kind of thin, steady rain which gets sucked in with every breath, which seeps down through the lungs into your belly. Suddenly I looked out over the village, from the road to Saint Vaast along the hillside—miserable little houses huddled together under the desolate, ugly November sky. On all sides damp came steaming up and it seemed to sprawl there in the soaking grass like a wretched worn-out horse or cow. What an insignificant thing a village is. And this particular village was my parish! My parish, yes, but what could I do? I stood there glumly watching it sink into the dusk, disappear. . . . In a few minutes I should lose sight of it. I had never been so horribly aware both of my people's loneliness and mine.

Source: Georges Bernanos, *The Diary of a Country Priest*, translated by Pamela Morris (New York: Macmillan, 1937).

noting that "grace is everywhere," which is itself a teaching of the Church.

Bernanos, however, came to this conclusion slowly. He was born in the late nineteenth century, when many Frenchmen were divided over the issue of whether they owed their loyalty to the republic or to the monarchy and Church. Bernanos grew up strongly in the royal camp and was highly supportive of the Catholic Church in its struggle to regain preeminence. He developed this position from his early life experiences, such as his Jesuit education, and bolstered his monarchical bent with political commitments. He joined the reactionary Action Française movement and edited the royalist weekly *L'Avant-garde de Normandie*. He fought in the French army during World War I. His views began to change shortly after the war, when he began to question the Catholic Church's strong alignment with the wealthy rather than with the poor. He became even more critical of the Church during the Spanish Civil War.

Bernanos became disillusioned with his fellow conservative Catholics as he witnessed firsthand the gross violations of human rights perpetrated by Francisco Franco's supporters in the Spanish Civil War. The more he spoke out about the violations, the more isolated he became from the community in which he had long situated himself. He wrote *The Diary of a Country Priest* in the midst of this profound personal transformation, this disillusionment with the institutions he had so long supported. Evidence of his disillusionment permeates the novel and culminates in the young priest's conclusion that grace abounds outside the Church.

Many of these concerns, particularly regarding the French Catholic Church, might reasonably be considered more European matters than American. What might explain the favorable reception of *The Diary of a Country Priest* in the American literary world of 1937? Much can be explained by the state of the American social, economic, and cultural scene at the time. Drained by nearly a decade of terrible economic depression, Americans sought solace from their misery. The earlier optimism about the New Deal's ability to move society completely out of the Depression waned by 1937—despite the relative success various programs had achieved. For a short while, such demagogues as Huey Long and Father Charles Coughlin promised to lift the country from its economic malaise, but they too foundered. An assassin felled Long, and with him the promise of his share-the-wealth solutions to the sufferings many Americans endured. Coughlin turned vitriolic in his social criticism, and his increasingly strident and hateful message came to alienate many who had placed with him their own hopes for a solution to their suffering. Cultural historians suggest that Americans had begun to turn inward for relief by 1937, and away from social interpretations of their persistent suffering.

By the late 1930's, Americans had come to seek personal rather than societal solutions for their problems. *The Diary of a Country Priest* provided a portrait of a young man in much the same state as many Americans during the Depression. He was anxious and near despair. If Americans worried about the seeming inability of collective social reform to regenerate society, the French country priest shared their troubling concerns. He too located much of his anxiety in larger social developments that impeded the formation and survival of a just society, but he located his solace, his resolution to the problems he identified for himself and his world, in an individual, deeply personal commitment to the struggle for human dignity and grace.

Another key theme perhaps often missed in this work is the central Christian teaching about the need for humility in a world governed by pride. The young priest's relationship as confessor to the haughty Mme la Comtesse, and to others, is rooted in humility and charity facing down pride and hard hearts. The majesty of the interior life of the soul, Bernanos holds, in keeping with the Sermon on the Mount and Church teachings, is built paradoxically on the foundation of humility, from which well-ordered love, justice, mercy, and peace then grow.

Many American critics could appreciate this struggle and resolution because they too saw the causes of their concerns, and the answers to their uncertainties, to be individual and personal. They too had become cynical about the possibility of societal transformation, about the potential for social justice in the world, and they saw in the young priest's simplicity and honesty, in his earnest struggle to do right, the dignity Americans sought in their own lives. The young curate's final peace provided hope for Americans frustrated with persistent social and economic dislocation, and in creating such a character, Bernanos provided reason for optimism in a troubled world.

—*Timothy Kelly*

FURTHER READING

Bernanos, Georges. *The Diary of a Country Priest*. Translated by Pamela Morris. 1965. Reprint. New York: Carroll & Graf, 2002. Reprinting of the novel includes an introduction by novelist and cloistered monk Rémy Rougeau.

_____. *The Last Essays of Georges Bernanos*. Translated by Joan Ulanov and Barry Ulanov. Westport, Conn.: Greenwood Press, 1968. Collection of six essays Bernanos wrote roughly a decade after he published *The Diary of a Country Priest* and shortly before his death. Centers on the evils of the times and covers some of the same issues as the earlier novel.

Bush, William. *Georges Bernanos*. New York: Twayne, 1969. Surveys Bernanos's artistic vision, summarizes his novels, and provides a brief analysis of each. One of the most approachable works on Bernanos available in English. Chapters are organized around Bernanos's works, and each provides a brief conclusion. Chapter on *The Diary of a Country Priest* argues that the original English-language edition mistranslates the priest's final words, and so misses the centrality of Saint Thérèse of Lisieux to Bernanos's work.

Cooke, John E. *Georges Bernanos: A Study of Christian Commitment*. Amersham, England: Avebury, 1981. Brief examination of Bernanos's religious life centers on the author's focus on the human struggle for redemption. Suggests that all of Bernanos's work can rightly be understood as his attempt to point the modern, corrupted world back toward a spiritual orientation, to the search for grace and societal salvation.

Greeley, Andrew. *The Catholic Imagination*. Berkeley: University of California Press, 2000. Examination of the Catholic worldview through discussion of central themes such as the Sacrament, salvation, and community, particularly as these themes have been addressed by Catholic artists, including novelist Bernanos.

Pells, Richard. *Radical Visions and American Dreams: Culture and Social Thought in the Depression Years*. 1973. Reprint. Champaign: University of Illinois Press, 1998. Solid one-volume survey of the American cultural scene during the Great Depression helps to set the context for the positive reception *The Diary of a Country Priest* received in the United States. Includes bibliography and index.

Speaight, Robert. *Georges Bernanos: A Study of the Man and the Writer*. London: Collins & Harvill Press, 1973. Comprehensive biography examines in depth both Bernanos's literary work and his life, explaining his writing in the context of his experiences.

SEE ALSO: 1925: Gide's *The Counterfeiters* Questions Moral Absolutes; May 17, 1925: Thérèse of Lisieux Is Canonized; Oct. 29, 1929-1939: Great Depression; 1932: Céline's *Journey to the End of the Night* Expresses Interwar Cynicism.

December, 1937-February, 1938
RAPE OF NANJING

After having captured the Nationalist Chinese capital city of Nanjing, three divisions of Japanese troops were allowed to kill, rape, loot, and burn.

LOCALE: Nanjing, China

CATEGORIES: Atrocities and war crimes; diplomacy and international relations; military history; wars, uprisings, and civil unrest; terrorism

KEY FIGURES

Chiang Kai-shek (1887-1975), president of China, 1948-1949, and military commander in chief who rejected negotiations

Iwane Matsui (1878-1948), overall commander of the expeditionary force that captured Nanjing, later executed for war crimes

Yasuhiko Asaka (1887-1981), commander who succeeded Matsui at Nanjing and presided over the atrocities but was not prosecuted

Akira Muto (1892-1948), officer who ordered troops into Nanjing and was in closest contact with the atrocities

Kingoro Hashimoto (1890-1957), officer who ordered the sinking of the USS *Panay* and other vessels

SUMMARY OF EVENT

Japan had begun absorbing parts of China in 1895 with the annexation of Taiwan, followed by Manchuria in 1932, Jehol Province in 1933, and Inner Mongolia in 1935. In the latter three, a pattern was established: Local Japanese field commanders initiated military action, after which the Tokyo higher command would debate but finally back up their actions, and then the Chinese Nationalist government under Chiang Kai-shek would submit to a local settlement to avoid major confrontation. The Japanese attitude toward the Nationalist government and the Chinese people came to be contemptuous. In July, 1937, a clash occurred outside Beijing and, when the Chinese did not back down, the Japanese army was

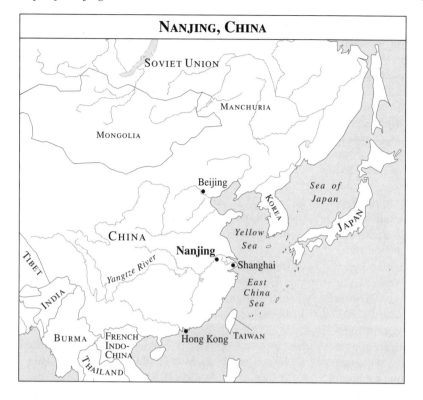

NANJING, CHINA

The flanking forces he drove toward Nanjing, however, were hard to control. Indications of their mood were shown in the bombing, strafing, and looting of cities and villages along the way.

Many in the Japanese high command, including Matsui, believed that negotiations for a cease-fire should have been initiated before attacking Nanjing. Chiang had indicated willingness to negotiate, although at the same time he issued orders that Nanjing was to be defended to the last, despite its indefensible position and its lack of military value. In any case, Japanese moderates were overridden and no terms were offered. The assault began on December 9, with a creeping artillery and air barrage that shattered all resistance by December 13. On December 17, with the Nanjing atrocities already beginning, Chiang, who had moved his government inland, issued his historic address rejecting all negotiations and calling for a people's war to the bitter end.

As the attack on Nanjing began, General Matsui was removed from personal supervision of field operations and confined to theater command. Emperor Hirohito's uncle, General Prince Yasuhiko Asaka, was appointed to the Nanjing operation. His headquarters issued secret orders to kill all captives, referring presumably to the Chinese troops trapped in the besieged city. Under him were the field commanders whose troops perpetrated the Nanjing outrages: Lieutenant General Kesago Nakajima of the Sixteenth Division, General Heisuke Yanagawa of the Nineteenth Corps, Lieutenant General Hisao Tani of the Sixth Division, and Colonel Akira Muto. Muto was in charge of billeting troops, and he moved soldiers from encampments safely outside Nanjing into the city, where the holocaust took place.

forced to choose between withdrawal and full military assault. Dismissive of Chinese military capability, they chose the latter course, hoping that a quick defeat would topple Chiang, neutralize China, and free Japanese troops for expected confrontations with the Soviet Union.

The key to rapid conquest was Shanghai, the gateway to the Yangtze Valley and central China. Once Shanghai was taken, the passage to Nanjing, the Nationalist capital 170 miles inland, would be easy. Chiang committed the cream of his officer corps and best-trained troops to the battle for Shanghai, but he lost the majority of them in a suicidal stand against naval and air bombardment that began in August and lasted into November. With the Japanese forces bogged down in street fighting, the higher command formulated a strategy that would outflank the Shanghai fortifications and expedite the drive on Nanjing, which many in the Japanese army and government expected to be the final campaign. The overall commander of the expeditionary force was General Iwane Matsui, a slight, tubercular man pulled out of retirement by the emperor himself. He had been a pan-Asian idealist earlier and, although he advocated the drive on Nanjing, there is nothing to indicate that he held any enmity toward the Chinese, whose language he spoke fluently.

The Chinese never formally surrendered the city. Their retreat was unplanned and disjointed, and about seventy thousand troops were trapped inside. About three-fourths of the city's population of one million fled, with Japanese firing on boats in the Yangtze, killing thousands as overloaded junks capsized. Many people were trampled in the confusion. As the Chinese authorities departed, they turned over supplies and effective authority to a self-appointed committee of twenty-seven foreign residents—American, British, German, and Danish missionaries, academics, and businesspeople—who established a safety zone of about two square miles in the northwest part of the city. Working tirelessly to protect a refugee population that reached a total of one-quarter million, they protested to Japanese authorities without result and restrained countless acts of individual brutality by their sheer presence, although they were never formally recognized by the Japanese. It was their diaries, letters, reports, film, and reminiscences that provided the four-thousand-page record of the atrocities in Nanjing for history and for the Allied war crimes trials.

Systematic looting began as soon as Japanese troops reached the city. Evidence of command complicity lay in the organized nature of the looting and the fact that army trucks were used. Later, even refugees were stripped of their pitiful possessions. Arson was also systematic; efficient thermite strips were used to burn whole sections of what had been one of the loveliest cities in China. Tricked by notices promising good treatment, disarmed Chinese soldiers, and later virtually all males of military age, were bound and murdered by machine gun or bayonet. Many were staked and used for bayonet or sword

practice. Prisoners were roasted over fires, doused with kerosene and set on fire, burned with chemicals, disemboweled, or buried up to the neck before torture.

Rapes occurred more and more frequently and increasingly flagrantly, often on the street in broad daylight. Pregnant women, girls as young as nine, and women as old as seventy-six fell victim. Some women were gang-raped, were raped and then murdered, or saw their children murdered. Others were rounded up and kept for months in sexual bondage at camps.

The grisly statistical totals for the seven weeks from December, 1937, to February, 1938, when the carnage finally subsided, are difficult to determine; official sources are often biased and the eyewitnesses were unaware of the bigger picture. Many deaths went unrecorded because of the difficulty of keeping wartime records in China. A high estimate of the death toll is 300,000; the true number is almost certainly more than 150,000. There were more than twenty thousand rapes. The overall economic loss was impossible to determine. Japanese army warehouses were filled with looted valuables. Some officers, including Nakajima, retained small fortunes in plunder, but most items were sold to defray army expenses. A study on a limited sample of individuals estimated that the average farmer lost the equivalent of 278 days of labor and the average city dweller lost 681 days. Nanjing would take more than a year to begin its economic revival.

On December 12, as Nanjing was falling, Japanese forces under Colonel Kingoro Hashimoto bombed and sank an American gunboat, the USS *Panay*, twenty-five miles upriver from Nanjing. Lifeboats were strafed and the craft was machine-gunned from a nearby Japanese gunboat. Two American tankers, two British gunboats, and two British-flag steamers were also bombed. Four American crew members were killed and sixty were wounded; two British crew members and countless refugees were also killed. Hashimoto, an ultranationalist zealot, had done this on his own initiative in defiance of standing policy to avoid provoking the West. In contrast to the Nanjing outrages, the Japanese government apologized officially and privately

The remains of South Station in Shanghai, which the Japanese ravaged before attacking Nanjing. (NARA)

and offered indemnities, which were accepted by the United States and Great Britain with little protest.

SIGNIFICANCE

The attitude of the Japanese army and government at first was to ignore the events at Nanjing, treating them as a matter for the army and accepting the army's bland fictions minimizing the horror. Later, however, Nanjing veterans on leave boasted openly of their depredations. In December, newspapers had even reported a grotesque sort of contest between two lieutenants racing to see who could cut down the most Chinese with their swords, referring to the race as "fun." The authorities were forced to suppress virtually all mention of atrocities. Even decades later, Japanese school texts avoided the subject, and prominent officials have asserted that it never happened.

The Imperial Japanese Army almost never punished a soldier for excesses (punishment was reserved for lack of aggressiveness), so punishment had to wait for the war's end. Matsui, who had scolded his subordinates for their complicity (they laughed at him), retired after Nanjing, built a temple, and held services for the dead of Nanjing. Even though he was less guilty than most, he offered no defense and so was the only prominent officer executed specifically for the Nanjing atrocities at the Tokyo war crimes tribunal. Muto was executed for war crimes in the Philippines, Hashimoto was given a life sentence, and Prince Asaka, protected by his royal connections, escaped prosecution.

Nanjing had a crucial effect on the course of the war. Japan might have won the war either with an acceptable offer of terms or with an immediate drive past Nanjing into the interior. Instead, the brutal tactics at Nanjing clearly failed to shock the Nationalists into negotiating and allowed them time to reorganize to carry on the war. This left the Japanese with the sole alternative of creating collaborationist governments, which were divided and subject to the same independent field commands that had produced the Nanjing incident. Japan's actions in China cost it any credibility in negotiations with the United States. The breakdown of these negotiations produced the impasse that made Japan's attack on Pearl Harbor possible.

The atrocities in Nanjing had a consciousness-raising effect on Japan's reputation in the court of world opinion, particularly on American public opinion. Newspapers in the United States began reporting on the sinking of the USS *Panay* almost immediately. Reports on the larger disaster at Nanjing came more gradually but were regular after December 30. Photographs were taken by foreigners, and even by the ingenuous Japanese, of horrible scenes. Chinese shops that processed the film smuggled out duplicate prints. There was even motion-picture footage taken by the Reverend John Magee of the carnage, footage that was later used by the isolationist organization America First to frighten Americans into staying out of war. So many, however, were moved to anger and sympathy that the film was withdrawn. Nanjing was one of the great atrocities of World War II. Never quite overshadowed by the more massive but impersonal Holocaust, it remained the benchmark for personal savagery and exemplified the dilemma posed by the rights of noncombatants in any profound nationalistic or ideological conflict.

—*David G. Egler*

FURTHER READING

Brook, Timothy, ed. *Documents on the Rape of Nanking*. Ann Arbor: University of Michigan Press, 1999. Collection of primary sources that document the rape of Nanjing. Divided into two parts addressing both letters and documents during the time of the invasion and records of the judicial proceedings that followed.

Butow, Robert J. C. *Tojo and the Coming of the War*. Princeton, N.J.: Princeton University Press, 1961. More than a biography of Prime Minister Tojo, this book delineates the military-bureaucratic environment that produced the decision to go to war with the United States. A classic and a foundation for subsequent scholarly works on the political history of Japan's part in World War II. Excellent bibliography and index.

Chang, Iris. *The Rape of Nanking: The Forgotten Holocaust of World War II*. New York: Basic Books, 1997. Vivid, horrifying account of the Nanjing attack from viewpoints of Japanese soldiers, Chinese civilians, and Westerners.

Coox, Alvin D., and Hilary Conroy, eds. *China and Japan: Search for Balance Since World War I*. Santa Barbara, Calif.: ABC-Clio, 1978. Predominantly analytic account that discusses the emperor's role in the war. The Nanjing atrocities are seen as a watershed in the "pure military" line toward China. Some of the articles later became major works.

Crowley, James B. *Japan's Quest for Autonomy: National Security and Foreign Policy, 1930-1938*. Princeton, N.J.: Princeton University Press, 1966. The major monograph on diplomacy, bureaucracy, and military decision-making. Particularly good resource for information on Sino-Japanese relations behind the scenes, in which Nanjing becomes only a part of a larger picture composed of hard decisions, misperceptions, lost opportunities, and situational imperatives. A thorough and scholarly work covering territory not dealt with elsewhere.

Eastman, Lloyd. "Facets of an Ambivalent Relationship: Smuggling, Puppets, and Atrocities During the War, 1937-1945." In *The Chinese and the Japanese: Essays in Political and Cultural Interactions*, edited by Akira Iriye. Princeton, N.J.: Princeton University Press, 1980. A thoughtful and intriguing glimpse behind the obvious national hatreds at the fraternization, trade, and other cooperative ventures between the two sides. Offsets the brutality of Nanjing with instances of mutual accommodation. Eastman makes no apology for the widely observed Japanese arrogance.

Fogel, Joshua A., ed. *The Nanjing Massacre in History and Historiography*. Berkeley: University of California Press, 2000. This collection of essays analyzes the Nanjing massacre and the ways in which the issue has become a political controversy.

Hsue, Shu-hsi. *The War Conduct of the Japanese*. Shanghai, China: Kelly & Walsh, 1938. Includes hastily compiled essays on Japanese atrocities in China. Exceedingly detailed, this volume is designed as an archive for war crimes charges and to inform public opinion. Based on International Safety Zone Committee sources and international publications.

Morley, James W., ed. *The China Quagmire: Japan's Expansion on the Asian Continent, 1933-1941*. New York: Columbia University Press, 1983. Part of the seven-volume Japanese *Taiheiyo senso-e no michi*, translated with additional chapters and commentary. Reflecting a Japanese academic (liberal) view, it accepts all of the occurrences at Nanjing but tends to dwell on the decision-making context of the war as a whole.

Wilson, Dick. *When Tigers Fight: The Story of the Sino-Japanese War, 1937-1945*. New York: Viking Press, 1982. One of the most balanced condensed military histories of the war available. Presents astute judgments of all the major military leaders on both sides. Heavily anecdotal, with a preference for extensive quotes. Accessible style makes this an excellent work to start with on this subject.

SEE ALSO: Aug. 22, 1910: Japanese Annexation of Korea; Jan. 7, 1932: Stimson Doctrine; Feb. 24, 1933: Japan Withdraws from the League of Nations; Dec. 29, 1934: Japan Renounces Disarmament Treaties; July 7, 1937: China Declares War on Japan; June 7, 1938: Chinese Forces Break Yellow River Levees; Aug., 1940: Japan Announces the Greater East Asia Co-prosperity Sphere.

December 21, 1937
DISNEY RELEASES *SNOW WHITE AND THE SEVEN DWARFS*

Snow White and the Seven Dwarfs *became a milestone in cinema history as the first full-length animated feature film.*

LOCALE: United States
CATEGORIES: Motion pictures; entertainment

KEY FIGURES
Walt Disney (1901-1966), producer and creator of the cartoon legend Mickey Mouse and the genius behind the idea of full-length animated films
Frank Thomas (1912-2004), Disney studio animation artist
Eric Larson (1933-1988), Disney studio animation artist
Ward Kimball (1914-2004), Disney studio animation artist
Wolfgang Reitherman (1909-1985), Disney studio animation artist
Milt Kahl (1909-1987), Disney studio animation artist
Les Clark (1907-1979), Disney studio animation artist

SUMMARY OF EVENT
By 1937, Walt Disney was well known by filmmakers and audiences across the country. His animated hero, Mickey Mouse, was a nationally recognized figure and had been enormously popular since *Steamboat Willie* was released with sound in 1928. Disney's 1933 cartoon version of *The Three Little Pigs* often received larger marquee billing than the feature films at the theaters where it played. Disney's Silly Symphony series had successfully wedded classical music to the use of color animation, and one entry in the series, *Flowers and Trees*, had won several film awards.

Yet Walt Disney was far from being content with his position as a leading producer of short animation; he had a grander design in mind. One warm evening in 1934, Disney called his animators together on a soundstage at the studio. He told them the story that would become *Snow White and the Seven Dwarfs*, acting out principal parts complete with voice intonations and facial gestures. He created suspense, filled in details, and even provided jokes and sight gags. At the end of the story, when Snow White was awakened from her deadly sleep by Prince Charming and carried away to his castle, many of the hard-boiled animators were in tears. Disney then told them that he planned to make a feature film of the story—not an eight-minute short—as complete and detailed as the story they had just heard.

Financing was a problem from the outset. Despite Disney's success with short cartoon features, few lenders were willing to risk the $500,000 that Disney originally projected as the cost of a feature film. The Depression was still stifling the American economy, and no one was

Walt Disney poses with characters from his animated works after receiving an honorary master of arts degree at Harvard University in 1938. (AP/Wide World Photos)

sure that Disney could find audiences of adults as well as children who would pay to watch a feature-length cartoon. As production costs skyrocketed toward the $1,488,000 that the finished *Snow White* cost, Hollywood insiders dubbed the project "Disney's Folly." Desperate for financing to complete the film, Disney was forced to show the incomplete film to his banker. He watched, horrified, as the banker remained grim and unmoved throughout the film. At the film's end, however, the banker turned to Disney and said, "Walt, that film is going to make you a hatful of money." It did.

Technically, the film was incredibly complex. Although actual animation did not begin until 1936, story work had been proceeding on an almost daily basis since 1934. It is estimated that more than one million drawings were made during the production of the film. Hollywood knew that a big project was afoot when Disney sent out a call for 300 artists—a staggering number for a single film, but short of the real total needed. In fact, more than 750 artists worked on the film, including 32 animators, 102 assistants, 107 "in-betweeners" (who filled in bits of action between the animator's drawings), 20 layout artists, 25 background artists, 65 special-effects animators, and 158 inkers and painters.

Technicolor was still a new process in 1937; most films, live action and animated, were still produced in black and white. Studio chemists and artists mixed more than fifteen hundred shades of paint to determine the best hues for painting characters and backgrounds. This care provided a far more subtle and realistic effect than did the bright primary colors of other animation. To create the most realistic possible drawings, live models were used for several principal characters. The best known was Marge Belcher, who modeled for Snow White (she later achieved fame as Marge Champion of the Marge and Gower Champion dance team). As was always true in animation, finding the right voices for characters was vital. After auditioning more than 150 women, including the popular singing actor Deanna Durbin, Disney chose Adriana Caselotti, daughter of a Los Angeles vocal coach, to be Snow White. Harry Stockwell voiced the Prince, and Pinto Colvig, better known as the voice of the Disney character Goofy, did the voices of Sleepy and Grumpy.

Disney, sparked by childhood memories of a 1917 silent-film version of *Snow White* starring Marguerite Clark, nevertheless returned to the classic Brothers Grimm fairy tale as the basis for his film. Parts of the tale were deleted; the film witch, for example, presents Snow White with only a poison apple rather than with the poison lace and combs of the original. Parts of the tale were expanded, especially the roles of the dwarfs, which are only vaguely sketched in the original. Disney experimented with as many as twenty-four dwarf names and personalities (including such alternatives as Deafy, Awful, and Burpy) before settling on the seven that achieved cinematic immortality. The ending was rendered more traditionally romantic; in the Grimm tale, Snow White awakens when the bearers drop her glass coffin and the apple flies from her throat, but Disney had the Prince awaken Snow White with love's first kiss.

Snow White had its premiere at the Carthay Circle Theater in Hollywood on December 21, 1937, and it was an enormous success with audiences, both immediately and over time. The film made $8.5 million during its first release, an astonishing figure given the fact that in 1937 a child paid a dime for theater admission. Although surpassed in 1939 by *Gone with the Wind*, *Snow White* for a time held the record as the highest-grossing motion picture ever. Furthermore, the film had several financially successful rereleases, including a special fiftieth anniversary release in 1987. *Snow White* was also a critical success. The *New York Daily News* reported in January, 1938, that "Disney has maintained faith with the Brothers Grimm in transferring the broad outline of the plot of the fairy tale to the screen, but he has drawn on his own delicious sense of humor, and that of his staff, for the delightful details that have been worked into the story." The *New York Herald Tribune* also reported in January, 1938, that Disney had "taken a Grimm fairy tale and brought it to such hauntingly beautiful pictorial realization that fantasy and reality are inextricably mingled in a world of fresh wonder and enchantment."

As a further indication of the acceptance of animation as a serious art form, *Snow White* received an Academy Award nomination for best score (for Frank Churchill, Paul Smith, and Leigh Harline) and won a special award for Walt Disney for having produced "a significant screen innovation which has charmed millions and pioneered a great new entertainment field for the motion picture cartoon." The award, presented by child star Shirley Temple, consisted of one full-size Oscar and seven dwarf Oscars. The *Snow White* record album was the first "original soundtrack" recording ever released; prior to that time, film music was rerecorded for release on records. Disney's use of music as a significant feature of his films, not just as background, began with *Snow White* and continues in the Disney studio's productions in the twenty-first century.

Significance

The impact of *Snow White* on both Walt Disney's career and on worldwide filmgoing audiences is hard to overstate. For Disney, the success of *Snow White* meant a financial and critical base from which he could launch new experiments. *Snow White*'s pioneering animation was succeeded by more complex animated features such as *Pinocchio* (1940), *Fantasia* (1940), *Alice in Wonderland* (1951), and *Sleeping Beauty* (1959); by ambitious films that combined live action and animation, such as *Song of the South* (1946) and *Mary Poppins* (1964); by highly successful pioneer work in television, both fantasy and documentary; and finally by the entertainment triumphs of the Disneyland and Walt Disney World theme parks. As the concrete figures that appear to hold up the roof of the Disney headquarters building in Burbank, California, attest, Disney was indeed an empire built not only by Mickey Mouse but by seven dwarfs as well.

With *Snow White*, animation came into its own. It was no longer only a backup for feature films or a clever device for commercials; it was a medium for capturing fantasy for an international audience of all ages. Walt Disney steadfastly maintained that he did not make films for children but for the child in himself and in all viewers. The strong personal will and tenacity that propelled him to make *Snow White* are reflected in his comment: "Sheer animated fantasy is still my first and deepest production impulse. The fable is the best storytelling device ever conceived, and the screen is its best medium."

—*Evelyn Romig*

Further Reading

Canemaker, John. *Walt Disney's Nine Old Men and the Art of Animation*. New York: Disney Editions, 2001. Aimed at young adults, this book focuses on the nine men who created many of the most recognizable Disney films. Fully illustrated.

The Complete Story of Walt Disney's "Snow White and the Seven Dwarfs." New York: Harry N. Abrams, 1987. Illustrated anniversary edition of the Grimm tale that formed the basis of the Disney film. Good beginning point for reference work.

Finch, Christopher. *The Art of Walt Disney*. Rev. ed. New York: Harry N. Abrams, 1975. A concise edition of Finch's much larger earlier work by the same name. Provides a chapter of information on the making of *Snow White* and places the movie in the larger context of Disney's developing art form. Contains 251 illustrations, including 170 full-color plates.

Hollis, Richard, and Brian Sibley. *"Snow White and the Seven Dwarfs": The Making of the Classic Film.* New York: Simon & Schuster, 1987. The best single book on the making of the film. Contains backgrounds, sources, anecdotes, and a wealth of early sketches and film plans.

Johnston, Ollie, and Frank Thomas. *The Illusion of Life: Disney Animation.* New York: Disney Editions, 1995. Johnston and Thomas were two of Disney's original animators, and in this book they manage to both clearly explain the animation process and to give a readable history of the Disney brand.

Schickel, Richard. *The Disney Version: The Life, Times, Art, and Commerce of Walt Disney.* Rev. ed. Chicago: Ivan R. Dee, 1997. A powerful, provocative analysis.

Probably the best biographical study of Disney. This edition adds a new introduction to the 1985 version.

Thomas, Bob. *Disney's Art of Animation: From Mickey Mouse to "Beauty and the Beast."* New York: Hyperion, 1991. A panoramic look at the films of Disney, including those made after Walt's death. Excellent chapter on the making of *Snow White*, with technical information made available in simple language. Illustrated.

SEE ALSO: May 11, 1928: Sound Technology Revolutionizes the Motion-Picture Industry; May 16, 1929: First Academy Awards Honor Film Achievement; 1930's: Hollywood Enters Its Golden Age; 1930's-1940's: Studio System Dominates Hollywood Filmmaking; Aug. 17, 1939: *The Wizard of Oz* Premieres; Nov. 13, 1940: Disney's *Fantasia* Premieres.

1938
BARNARD PUBLISHES *THE FUNCTIONS OF THE EXECUTIVE*

In The Functions of the Executive, *Chester Irving Barnard established an intellectual foundation for America's leadership by a professionalized managerial elite.*

LOCALE: Cambridge, Massachusetts
CATEGORIES: Business and labor; publishing and journalism

KEY FIGURES

Chester Irving Barnard (1886-1961), American management theorist
Vilfredo Pareto (1848-1923), Italian economist sociologist
Frederick Winslow Taylor (1856-1915), American efficiency expert
Mary Parker Follett (1868-1933), American management theorist
Walter S. Gifford (1885-1966), president of American Telephone and Telegraph
John R. Commons (1862-1945), American labor historian and institutional economist

SUMMARY OF EVENT

Published in 1938, Chester Irving Barnard's *The Functions of the Executive* filled an immense theoretical and practical void in knowledge of executive goals and of executives' institutional and public responsibilities. De-

spite the fact that a managerial class had been the principal force in modernizing the United States, wielding immense power as a consequence, executives carried out their functions and met responsibilities chiefly through reliance on habit and intuition. Formal analyses of what they did or how and why they did it, except in reference to profits and losses, were almost as unknown to them as their names were to the general public. Guides to rationalizing and improving their performance and to coping with their expanding responsibilities were notably lacking. Fewer still were studies produced by the kinds of people whose works executives were likely to read or whose advice they might follow—namely, other successful and experienced executives. The seminal studies of organization theorist Henri Fayol, for example, went untranslated for years.

A "science" of management—of the executive's roles in regard to the organization, the public, and the government—was still being explored in the United States by a handful of positivist and progressive social scientists in 1938, but their inquiries were far from complete. Moreover, most studies originated with academics. Their approaches to what occurs—or ought to occur—inside the organizational world of executives was marked by an understandable caution characteristic of outsiders.

To be sure, a new breed of executives had appeared during the 1920's and 1930's. They brought fresh precepts and practices to running their corporations, thus developing their own contributions to a systematized knowledge of management that was commensurate with a mature industrial economy. Pierre S. du Pont undertook the decentralization of the Du Pont Corporation, for example, and Julius Rosenwald and Robert E. Wood restructured Sears, Roebuck. Such novel successes were swiftly studied by consultants and by academic specialists. These operations, as perceived by other executives, however, seemed idiosyncratic and thus unworthy of conscious imitation. Only much later did literature flow from them. Alfred P. Sloan, for example, did not publish what he had learned from restructuring General Motors until 1964. Thus, despite the changes and successes in management during the 1920's and 1930's, analyses of managerial tasks and responsibilities were still far removed from the public domain. They had little effect on the formal training of prospective executives until after World War II.

This was the gap that was filled by Barnard's pathbreaking work, combining as it did the fruits of his eclectic readings, particularly in philosophy and the social sciences, with the dividends of his high-level executive experience. Barnard received preparatory education and Christian moral instruction at Mount Hermon School and then attended Harvard University. Under the mentorship of Walter S. Gifford, Barnard joined the statistics department of American Telephone and Telegraph (AT&T) in 1909. Gifford's promotion to chief executive officer of AT&T in 1925 resulted in Barnard's promotion to the presidency of AT&T's subsidiary, New Jersey Bell Telephone Company, in 1927. He held that position until 1948. Over time, he accompanied his presidency with the direction of several foundations as well as with government service and continuing close rapport with his Harvard faculty friends. This was the career that generated *The Functions of the Executive*, originally a series of eight lectures delivered at Boston's Lowell Institute in 1937.

The book carefully defines in scholarly language the nature of cooperative systems and the role of individuals within them. It examines both formal and informal organizational theory and structure as well as the bases of specialization, economic incentives, the decision-making environment, and specific executive roles and responsibilities. Recognizing the abundant technical literature available to executives on accounting, personnel, technology, and the like, Barnard stressed instead the need for a science of management that synthesizes materials from the physical, biological, and social sciences. His

cooperative system of management was based on this catholic amalgam of knowledge.

Barnard's explicit assumptions were that highly complex private and public organizations are the permanent and central characteristics of modern societies. The key role in these organizations is that of the executive. By Barnard's estimate, five million executives were working in the United States at the time he was writing, of whom approximately one hundred thousand occupied major, mostly corporate, positions. Their authority was immense, and, in his mind, they ran American society. One issue was the legitimacy of their position in a democratic setting. According to Barnard, that legitimacy depended on their ability to satisfy the needs of individuals in their workforces and in society by efficiently delivering material goods in socially responsible ways and by enhancing the quality of individual lives. To the extent that executives meet these criteria of performance, they ensure a stable social system as well as their own longevity in authority.

SIGNIFICANCE

Barnard's *The Functions of the Executive* was a functionalist manifesto. Barnard regarded systems of cooperation as being alive. His concept of businesses, particularly of corporations and their executives, was therefore an organic one.

The book was also a guide to scientific management that drew speculation and evidence from some of the finer minds of Barnard's era. Barnard generously acknowledged his debts to them. His organic theories, for example, derived from works by the brilliant Italian economist and sociologist Vilfredo Pareto, from the distinguished English philosopher and mathematician Alfred North Whitehead, and from Barnard's Harvard colleagues Lawrence Henderson (a specialist on Pareto) and Mary Parker Follett (an authority on the dynamics of administrative control). His concepts of cooperation came from one of the great American administrators, Herbert Hoover, as well as from Gestalt psychologist Kurt Koffka. Barnard borrowed from sociologist Eugene Ehrlich and from the famed labor historian and institutional economist John R. Commons the idea that law itself does not confer legitimacy on authority, but, rather, legitimacy comes from the people. These are only a few of the impressive figures whose works contributed to blending Barnard's own executive experiences with scholarly theory and abstractions.

This range of creatively synthesized learning, abstrusely explained by Barnard, was heavy reading for

1938

working executives and heady fare for prospective managers. Nevertheless, it possessed the authentic smack of science and represented the first work of its type in the United States. Business management schools, foremost Dean Wallace B. Donham's Harvard Graduate School of Business Administration, burgeoned during the decades of the management boom and a spreading awareness of the critical importance of managers. *The Functions of the Executive* was a perfect fit as a text for these schools and met the needs of the times.

Barnard's book was more than a timely set of nostrums that happened to appear during the years prior to World War II, a time that Peter F. Drucker, a prolific and influential American authority on management and an ideological descendant of Barnard, has described as years of management innocence, obscurity, and ignorance. By 1968, the thirtieth anniversary of the book's first publication, it had been reprinted eighteen times. Its usefulness and relevance, and consequently its impact, had grown during the astounding organizational, managerial, and technological changes that had occurred through the decades.

Barnard's work is cited as pioneering in nearly every book Drucker wrote on managers and management. Drucker's first influential book, *The Practice of Management* (1954), was designed to carry forward, clarify, and amend Barnard's central themes. This was particularly true of Barnard's view that managers constitute— and should constitute—the force behind the formal organizations that serve as the "concrete social process by which social action is largely accomplished."

Barnard believed that order and freedom in the United States could be combined best under the leadership of a managerial elite that knows its business, can deliver material goods, and can maintain a quality of life that ensures social stability. Because most Americans are employees, he noted, some loss of liberty is required for order to prevail, a point he stressed by quoting Aristotle. In Barnard's view, application of the kind of knowledge dealt with in his book, in combination with refined rational and moral sensibilities among managers, legitimates managerial authority.

American Progressivism furnished the context into which Barnard fit. Predominantly represented by well-educated, urban, middle-class professionals and businessmen, the Progressives sought between the 1890's and the 1930's to recast American life and to reorder it by applying scientific principles to nearly everything that fell under their scrutiny. Like Frederick Winslow Taylor, who premised his study of work on scientific principles so as to bring efficiency into the workplace, or Barnard's

colleague, Mary Parker Follett, who among many others sought scientific principles that might be applied to dynamic administration, the Progressives sanguinely believed that applications of knowledge—whether to government, to politics, or to enterprise—would ensure both a healthier democracy and social stability. Both goals could be achieved at small expense. Seen as part of this tradition, Barnard was the first American to attempt to ground executive functions on the most advanced, relevant knowledge and thereby convert management into a discipline rather than an art.

The American managerial revolution was well under way when Barnard published his seminal work. Executives, among them Barnard's friend and mentor Gifford, by 1938 were already running the United States. John Kenneth Galbraith, the liberal economist and public servant, recognized in his international best sellers *The Affluent Society* (1958) and *The New Industrial State* (1967) the triumph of managerialism. Despite worries about the conformity demanded of the "Organization Man," Galbraith predicted that managerialism and the technostructure surrounding it would prove to be permanent. Barnard's cooperative collectivism, which champions effectiveness over hierarchy, became the boardroom norm.

Beginning in the 1970's and continuing into the early 2000's, evidence flowed in from social commentators, the press, polls, scholars, and even novelists that confidence in managerial leadership was undergoing a precipitous decline. This erosion, observers noted, was specific to executive leadership and did not extend to basic American institutions. Successions of business failures and scandals certainly quickened the loss of respect, as did the general perception that American technology and the quality of major American products lagged behind those of foreign competition. The erosion of confidence came from within as well. A number of major executives expressed the opinion that the vast majority of their colleagues working in *Fortune*'s top five hundred corporations held their jobs only for what they could get out of them and were failing in their performance if measured against legal, moral, and ethical criteria. More philosophical observers simply wondered whether any elite, no matter how golden its moments, can enjoy great longevity in a democratic society.

—*Clifton K. Yearley*

FURTHER READING

Barnard, Chester Irving. *The Functions of the Executive.* 30th anniversary ed. Cambridge, Mass.: Harvard University Press, 2005. Reprint edition of Barnard's original work includes an introduction by Harvard Business School professor Kenneth Richmond Andrews.

Drucker, Peter F. *Management: Tasks, Responsibilities, Practices.* 1974. Reprint. New York: HarperCollins, 1993. Readable work by an acknowledged authority on all aspects of management. Includes discussion of the legitimacy of management.

Gabor, Andrea. *The Capitalist Philosophers: The Geniuses of Modern Business—Their Lives, Times, and Ideas.* New York: Crown Business, 2000. Examines the history of American business by focusing on important individuals. Chapter 3 is devoted to discussion of Barnard. Includes selected bibliography and index.

Lipset, Seymour Martin, and William Schneider. *The Confidence Gap: Business, Labor, and Government in the Public Mind.* Rev. ed. Baltimore: The Johns Hopkins University Press, 1987. Presents information from polls, the press, and many other sources confirming a steady decline in public confidence in managerial leadership. Includes figures, tables, index of poll results, and general index.

Scott, William G. *Chester I. Barnard and the Guardians of the Managerial State.* Lawrence: University of Kansas Press, 1992. Well-written and well-researched work discusses Barnard and his influences. Places Barnard within the context of his times.

Williamson, Oliver E., ed. *Organization Theory: From Chester Barnard to the Present and Beyond.* Expanded ed. New York: Oxford University Press, 1995. Excellent collection of essays provides information on the theoretical context into which Barnard fits. Includes index.

SEE ALSO: Apr. 8, 1908: Harvard University Founds a Business School; Mar., 1914: Gilbreth Publishes *The Psychology of Management*; July, 1916: Fayol Publishes *General and Industrial Management*; 1920's: Donham Promotes the Case Study Teaching Method at Harvard; Mar. 14, 1923: American Management Association Is Established; 1925: McKinsey Founds a Management Consulting Firm; 1932: Berle and Means Discuss Corporate Control.

1938

1938
CALLENDAR CONNECTS INDUSTRY WITH INCREASED ATMOSPHERIC CARBON DIOXIDE

Guy Stewart Callendar noted the increasing level of carbon dioxide in the earth's atmosphere and traced it to human activity.

ALSO KNOWN AS: Greenhouse effect; Callendar effect
LOCALE: England
CATEGORIES: Science and technology; earth science; physics; chemistry; environmental issues

KEY FIGURES
Guy Stewart Callendar (1898-1964), English physicist
Svante August Arrhenius (1859-1927), Swedish physicist and chemist
Charles D. Keeling (1928-2005), American marine geochemist
Bert R. Bolin (b. 1925), Swedish meteorologist

SUMMARY OF EVENT
Carbon dioxide is a colorless, tasteless, transparent gas that is present in very small quantities, about 0.03 percent by volume, in the air that humans breathe in and in larger quantities in the air that is breathed out, because it is a waste product of the process by which life is maintained.

It also has the interesting property that, while it allows the electromagnetic energy of sunlight to pass through it unhindered to the surface of the earth, when the warm surface of the ground or ocean radiates heat upward at infrared frequencies, this heat is absorbed by carbon dioxide. This process by which heat is trapped near the surface of the earth is known as the greenhouse effect. It operates for other gases in the air, but, unlike other gases, the proportion of carbon dioxide in the air is increasing steadily as a result of human activity. There is no doubt that the burning of fossil fuels—coal, oil, and natural gas—releases carbon dioxide into the atmosphere.

A few decades after the beginning of the industrial age, scientists began to question the effect of increased burning of carbon-based fossil fuels on the atmosphere. Carbon-based fuels are the chief energy source for the earth's population, and, as a result, the human impact on the global carbon cycle is far-reaching. Fossil fuels are hydrocarbon molecules whose chemical energy is released when they are burned, the principal emission from this combustion being carbon dioxide gas. The effect of carbon dioxide gas is that it heats the lower atmosphere as carbon dioxide concentrations increase. Svante August Arrhenius, a Swedish physicist and chemist, was one of the first to write about increased carbon dioxide levels in the atmosphere. In the mid-1880's, he announced his survey of the first few decades of the Industrial Revolution and concluded that humans were burning coal at an unprecedented rate. Arrhenius knew that carbon dioxide trapped infrared radiation that would otherwise have reflected back out to space. He used measurements of infrared radiation from the full moon in his first calculations of the possible effects of anthropogenic (of human origin) carbon dioxide. His conclusions were that the average global temperature would rise as much as 9 degrees if the amount of carbon dioxide in the air doubled from its preindustrial level.

Arrhenius's work did not gain acceptance until Guy Stewart Callendar, an English physicist, speculated in 1938 that increasing carbon dioxide levels were the probable cause

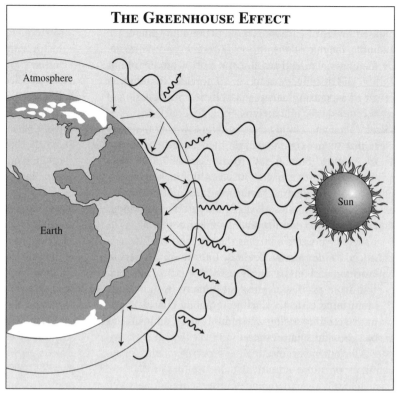

THE GREENHOUSE EFFECT

In the so-called greenhouse effect, some of the heat from the Sun is reflected back into space (wavy arrows), but some becomes trapped by Earth's atmosphere and radiates back toward Earth (straight arrows), heating the planet.

for a warming of North America and Northern Europe that meteorologists had begun to observe in the 1880's. Carbon dioxide is transparent to incoming ultraviolet but opaque to the resulting reradiation in the infrared. Because carbon dioxide also absorbs incoming infrared radiation, it is an integral part of the mechanism of global heat balance. Without compensating charges, increased levels of carbon dioxide will result in higher temperatures. The increase in the effective emissivity of infrared radiation from the earth, with resulting atmospheric heating, is responsible for the so-called greenhouse effect. Callendar was the first to assemble a large body of measurements from several scientific sources and predict significant temperature change from anthropogenic carbon dioxide.

Direct measurements of the temperature effects of carbon dioxide are difficult because the underlying natural fluctuations in temperature do not provide a stable baseline against which to reference anthropogenic disturbances. Callendar, working from this disadvantage, collected data from several scientists. They were odd, rather

unsystematic, and somewhat unreliable data; however, they agreed with later, more precise observations.

Several factors worked against widespread acceptance of Callendar's study, one of which was that a warming seemed to be replaced by a temperature decline around 1940. Another was that most scientists in the 1930's were too busy with the exploitation of petroleum for new products and believed that the problem of excess carbon dioxide would be absorbed in the oceans, not the atmosphere. Callendar remained convinced by his 1938 study and noted in 1958, that since 1942, the carbon dioxide content had continued to rise at a rate of about 0.2 percent per year. Concern about atmospheric pollution as a direct result of humans virtually exploded in the late 1960's, when many of the industrial nations began to promulgate laws and write regulations covering atmospheric pollution by manufacturers. The early work done by investigators such as Callendar was remarkably correct considering the fact that the work was done during a time when there were no computers to allow for the development of models to add innumerable variables and analyze them.

There are uncertainties about what has caused the increased levels of carbon dioxide in the atmosphere; for example, the rate of absorption of excess carbon dioxide by the ecosystem and oceans, the rate of production of carbon dioxide by destruction of forests, the cooling effect of increasing aerosols—both anthropogenic and from revived volcanic activity—and feedback effects of water vapor and clouds. Nevertheless, it is abundantly clear that there is a connection, as Callendar noted in 1938, between human activity and air pollution. The energy crisis in the mid-1970's and the increasing sophistication of numerical atmospheric circulation models have led to greatly increased interest and investigation of the carbon dioxide greenhouse effect. In 1975, V. Ramanathan pointed out that the greenhouse effect is enhanced by the continued release into the atmosphere of chlorofluorocarbons, even though their combined concentration is less than a part per billion by volume.

Many physicists look to the computer models and view the steadily rising concentration of atmospheric carbon dioxide as a prelude to climatological catastrophe; at the other extreme, another group of scientists concentrates on more empirical data. Empirical data are those that rely on experience or observation alone, often without regard for system and theory. The empiricists believe that any change in the climate caused by rising levels of carbon dioxide will be indistinguishable from natural climatic fluctuations. They foresee that higher concentrations of carbon dioxide will tend to stimulate photosynthesis and so increase the productivity of crops and the efficiency with which plant life uses water. The empirical approach depends on finding some natural event that temporarily disturbs the heat balance of the atmosphere, such as the great dust storms of the 1930's in the southern plains of the United States. By monitoring the temperature changes and flow of radiative heat during such natural events, scientists can measure the response of the real world to the perturbation.

SIGNIFICANCE

In the several decades after Callendar first noted that humans were causing increased levels of carbon dioxide in the atmosphere, it has been found that the much more abundant constituent carbon monoxide is also increasing as a result of automobile exhausts and other combustion processes. Although carbon monoxide does not make a direct impact in enhancing the greenhouse effect, it does play an indirect role by serving as a sink for the hydroxyl radical, which acts as a catalyst in modulating the increase of nitrous oxide from combustion processes. Also

contributing to carbon monoxide is the use of chemical fertilizers and the increase of methane from biogenic and industrial production.

From 1957 to 1975, the amount of carbon dioxide in the air increased from 312 to 326 parts per million, almost 5 percent. American scientists have measured this trend since 1957, initially under the leadership of marine geochemist Charles D. Keeling (until his death in 2005), and Swedish meteorologists, led by Bert R. Bolin, have taken measurements since 1963. Both groups of scientists have made their measurements in areas far away from any localized sources of carbon dioxide so that they might observe the background and thus the worldwide trends in carbon dioxide: the Americans on Mauna Loa, Hawaii, and at the South Pole, and the Swedes on the air-intake systems of commercial aircraft flying the polar route.

In addition to research in the atmosphere, considerable research has been carried out in glacial areas of the world. In 1990, two teams of European and American researchers drilled through more than two miles of ice searching for trapped air bubbles and entombed crystals in order to discover what the weather was like during the past 200,000 years. On the summit of Greenland, the highest point on the vast ice mound that almost completely covers the world's largest island, scientists are seeking an answer to the most pressing question in climatology: Will rising levels of carbon dioxide and methane heat the earth and melt the polar ice caps? Evidence from ice cores drilled by Soviet researchers in Antarctica have indicated that rising levels of carbon dioxide in the atmosphere have resulted in warmer temperatures on the earth several times during the past 200,000 years.

—*Earl G. Hoover*

FURTHER READING

Breuer, Georg. *Air in Danger: Ecological Perspectives on the Atmosphere.* New York: Cambridge University Press, 1980. Very good account of the atmosphere covers carbon dioxide increase and features a good discussion of the risks associated with higher levels of carbon dioxide in the atmosphere. Includes a few illustrations.

Callendar, Guy S. "The Artificial Production of Carbon Dioxide and Its Influence on Temperature." *Quarterly Journal of the Royal Meteorological Society* 64 (1938): 223-240. Interprets and analyzes worldwide temperature measurements and the effects of production of carbon dioxide. Includes interesting temperature charts from the great cities and oceans. Valuable primarily for historical reasons.

1938

Gore, Al. *Earth in the Balance: Ecology and the Human Spirit*. New York: Houghton Mifflin, 1992. Argues that only a drastic rethinking of humankind's relationship with nature can preserve the earth for the future. Includes bibliography and index.

Goudie, Andrew. *The Human Impact on the Natural Environment: Past, Present, and Future*. 6th ed. Malden, Mass.: Blackwell, 2006. Excellent general reference accessible to lay readers. Chapter 7 focuses on the human impact on climate and the atmosphere. Includes glossary, bibliography, and index.

Idso, Sherwood B. "Carbon Dioxide Can Revitalize the Planet." In *The Greenhouse Effect*, edited by Matthew Kraljic. New York: H. W. Wilson, 1992. Contends that the rising carbon dioxide content of the atmosphere is beneficial and that the small amount of greenhouse warming it causes may actually enhance the biosphere.

Keller, Edward A. *Environmental Geology*. 8th ed. Upper Saddle River, N.J.: Prentice Hall, 1999. Includes a well-illustrated chapter on urban air with diagrams showing the effects of various factors on potential air pollution: smog, future trends for urban areas, and the control of particulates in air pollution.

Lyman, Francesca. *The Greenhouse Trap*. Boston: Beacon Press, 1990. One of a series of books by the World Resource Institute Guides to the Environment. Discusses the basic concerns about atmosphere and climate and the steps necessary to achieve climate stability.

McKibben, Bill. *The End of Nature*. 10th anniversary ed. New York: Random House, 1999. Addresses the scientific evidence about the greenhouse effect, the depletion of the ozone layer, and an array of other ecological ills. Written in a narrative style accessible to the lay reader.

Revkin, Andrew. *Global Warming: Understanding the Forecast*. New York: Abbeville Press, 1992. Discusses Callendar's and Arrhenius's early studies as well as more recent developments such as the Persian Gulf War of 1990 and the effects of industrial development in emerging nations. Includes tables and color plates.

Schneider, Stephen H. *Global Warming: Are We Entering the Greenhouse Century?* San Francisco: Sierra Club Books, 1989. Examines the causes of world climate change and provides an authoritative, entertaining look at the science, personalities, and politics behind the problem of global warming. Explains in clear, nontechnical language what is scientifically known, what is speculative, and where major uncertainties lie.

SEE ALSO: 1913: First Geothermal Power Plant Begins Operation; 1926: Vernadsky Publishes *The Biosphere*; Dec., 1930: Du Pont Introduces Freon.

1938
HOFMANN SYNTHESIZES THE POTENT PSYCHEDELIC DRUG LSD-25

While pursuing ergot alkaloid medicinal chemistry research, Albert Hofmann synthesized LSD-25 (lysergic acid diethylamide-25), a drug with potent psychogenic properties that were not recognized until 1943.

LOCALE: Basel, Switzerland
CATEGORIES: Science and technology; chemistry

KEY FIGURES
Albert Hofmann (b. 1906), Swiss research chemist
Arthur Stoll (1887-1971), Swiss chemist
Werner Stoll (b. 1915), Swiss psychiatrist

SUMMARY OF EVENT
For thousands of years, human beings have searched for tranquillity, spiritual enlightenment, and guidance in understanding and defining their role in the natural world.

Both primitive and modern religions frequently advocate individuals' use of aids such as meditation, fasting, and ritual ingestion of psychoactive plants to alter perception of the world and to achieve a harmonious state of being. Mescaline, a natural substance occurring in peyote cactus, and psilocybin, found in various species of mushrooms, have been used in religious rituals in Mexico since the Aztec era; these are only two examples of the dozens of psychoactive plants distributed throughout the world. Such plants contain substances that have a profound ability to influence consciousness—the innermost essence of being.

Mystical experiences are difficult to express and are often beyond words, thus a number of words have been fashioned to define and describe the psychic effects of such natural substances. Because these compounds often induce visual hallucinations (colors, patterns, objects, flights of imagination) perceived by the taker as either drug-induced fantasy or less often as reality, the term "hallucinogen" is commonly employed. Such compounds also have been called "psychotomimetic" drugs because people suffering from psychoses are often plagued by hallucinations and altered states of reality.

The term "psychedelic" (mind-expanding), coined by British psychiatrist Humphry Osmond, was widely used in the 1960's. Since then, the hallucinogenic drug lysergic acid diethylamide (LSD) stands alone as having achieved a notoriety matched only by its potency. On the basis of weight, LSD is ten thousand times more active than mescaline.

As told firsthand by the "father" of LSD, Albert Hofmann, in his 1980 book *LSD, My Problem Child*, the discovery of LSD began not as a quest for a drug with fantastic properties but as a disappointment to the chemist working in a research laboratory that was investigating derivatives of natural products for use as medicines. After completing his dissertation research at the University of Zurich, in which he determined the chemical constituents of chitin (the structural material of wings, shells, and claws of insects and crustaceans) in only three months, Hofmann joined the pharmaceutical research group at Sandoz Limited in Basel, Switzerland, in 1929. Hired by Arthur Stoll, director of the laboratory, Hofmann spent several years working with ergot alkaloids. These natural compounds are produced by a parasitic fungus of rye and were an area of interest to Stoll. In 1918, Stoll had isolated the pure active principle of ergot, ergotamine, and this natural product was used widely as a treatment for migraine and as a hemostatic remedy in obstetrics to stop uterine bleeding after childbirth. In the early 1930's, several research groups, including Sandoz, published simultaneous reports that the principal active ingredient of ergotamine was a simple alkaloid, subsequently named ergobasine by Stoll. By chemical degradation, it was determined that ergobasine was composed of two chemical constituents: lysergic acid and the amino alcohol, propanolamine. With this knowledge and further research into the chemistry of these compounds, Hofmann began to synthesize many artificial ergot alkaloids, all derivatives of lysergic acid.

In 1938, Hofmann produced his twenty-fifth substance in a series of lysergic acid derivatives, lysergic acid diethylamide, abbreviated LSD-25 (based on the German name for the compound, *Lysergsaure-diathylamid*). This synthesis had been planned to produce a compound with properties similar to the drug Coramine, a circulatory and respiratory stimulant. Animal tests with

Albert Hofmann. (Hulton Archive/Getty Images)

1938

LSD-25, however, aroused no special interest at Sandoz. Further testing was discontinued and LSD was forgotten.

Over the next five years, Hofmann developed several commercially successful drugs including Hydergine, an effective geriatric remedy that was Sandoz's most successful pharmaceutical product. Despite his obvious successes, Hofmann decided to produce LSD-25 once again to provide samples to the pharmacology department for further testing, an unusual undertaking as the compound had been rejected already for further testing. On April 16, 1943, when Hofmann was performing the final purification step of the synthesis of LSD-25, he was affected by dizziness and a remarkable restlessness. He stopped working and went home, where, as he later reported to Stoll, he "sank into a not unpleasant intoxicatedlike condition, characterized by an . . . uninterrupted stream of fantastic pictures, extraordinary shapes with intense, kaleidoscopic play of colors."

Hofmann attributed this remarkable experience to working with LSD-25, but he was skeptical. He was a chemist who had worked with very toxic compounds for

HOFMANN ON LSD

In the foreword to his 1980 book LSD, My Problem Child, *Hofmann both extolled and warned of the hallucinogenic properties of the drug:*

There is today a widespread striving for mystical experience, for visionary breakthroughs to a deeper, more comprehensive reality than that perceived by our rational, everyday consciousness. Efforts to transcend our materialistic world view are being made in various ways, not only by the adherents to Eastern religious movements, but also by professional psychiatrists, who are adopting such profound spiritual experiences as a basic therapeutic principle.

I share the belief of many of my contemporaries that the spiritual crisis pervading all spheres of Western industrial society can be remedied only by a change in our world view. We shall have to shift from the materialistic, dualistic belief that people and their environment are separate, toward a new consciousness of an all-encompassing reality, which embraces the experiencing ego, a reality in which people feel their oneness with animate nature and all of creation.

Everything that can contribute to such a fundamental alteration in our perception of reality must therefore command earnest attention. Foremost among such approaches are the various methods of meditation, either in a religious or a secular context, which aim to deepen the consciousness of reality by way of a total mystical experience. Another important, but still controversial, path to the same goal is the use of the consciousness-altering properties of hallucinogenic psychopharmaceuticals. LSD finds such an application in medicine, by helping patients in psychoanalysis and psychotherapy to perceive their problems in their true significance.

Deliberate provocation of mystical experience, particularly by LSD and related hallucinogens, in contrast to spontaneous visionary experiences, entails dangers that must not be underestimated. Practitioners must take into account the peculiar effects of these substances, namely their ability to influence our consciousness, the innermost essence of our being. The history of LSD to date amply demonstrates the catastrophic consequences that can ensue when its profound effect is misjudged and the substance is mistaken for a pleasure drug.

Source: Albert Hofmann, foreword to *LSD, My Problem Child,* translated by Jonathan Ott (New York: McGraw-Hill, 1980).

years and had meticulous work habits. He wondered if a drop of the chemical had touched his fingertips. If so, LSD-25 was a very potent psychogenic compound. With the full knowledge of Stoll and his assistants, Hofmann carefully planned a self-experiment with LSD-25. As recorded in his laboratory notebook, Hofmann took merely 0.25 milligram of the drug dissolved in water at 4:20 P.M. on April 19, 1943. At 5:00 P.M., he recorded that he felt dizzy, anxious, and had visual distortions and an urge to laugh. That was his last entry in the notebook. Hofmann became overwhelmed by the hallucinogenic experience and asked his assistant to escort him home by bicycle.

Hofmann later described the next two hours as a nightmare. He was convinced that he had poisoned himself and that he was going to die, but neither his assistant nor the doctor who was summoned to attend him observed anything out of the ordinary about him physically other than extremely dilated pupils. His respiration and heartbeat were normal, and the assistant said they had bicycled to his home at a good speed. With the constant assurances of his companions, by 8:00 P.M. Hofmann was no longer panic-stricken, although this LSD experience was much stronger than his previous experience a few days earlier. One hallucinogenic feature of the drug that astounded Hofmann was synesthesia, the overflow from one sensory modality to another in which colors are "heard" and sounds may be "seen." The effects subsided gradually and he was able to sleep.

The next morning, feeling refreshed and without a hangover, Hofmann went to work and reported on the previous day's experiences to Stoll and Ernst Rothlin, director of the pharmacology laboratory. Both expressed disbelief that the dose of a fraction of a milligram of LSD could have such effects; a psychoactive compound of such potency seemed unbelievable. Several days later, Rothlin and two colleagues repeated Hofmann's LSD experiment but took only one-third the dose that Hofmann had ingested. The effects they experienced were remarkable, and all doubts about Hofmann's statements were eliminated.

It was determined later that for his first self-experiment, Hofmann ingested five to eight times the optimal dose of LSD necessary to achieve the psychedelic state. LSD is such a potent substance that experimental doses in humans are calculated in micrograms (one microgram equals one-millionth of a gram) per kilogram body weight.

Laboratory animal studies proved to be of little value in examining the psychic effects of LSD because lower animals do not respond to the drug except at extremely high doses. Animal studies have demonstrated that LSD has an extremely low toxicity potential in comparison to its effective dose in humans. There are no recorded deaths attributed to the direct action (overdose) of LSD, although deaths have been recorded as accidents or as suicides accomplished under the influence of LSD. The danger of the drug lies not in its toxicity, but rather in the unpredictability of its psychic effects.

SIGNIFICANCE

In 1947, Werner Stoll, a Zurich psychiatrist and the son of Arthur Stoll, was the first to publish reports of self-experiments with LSD and results of experimental studies involving both healthy normal volunteers and psychiatric patients. In 1953, Sandoz applied to the U.S. Food and Drug Administration to study LSD as an investigational new drug and supplied the drug to authorized investigators.

In the 1950's, hundreds of scientific papers were written that examined the use of LSD as a model for psychosis, as a psychotherapeutic aid to help patients see themselves and their problems from a detached perspective, in the treatment of alcoholism, and as therapy for terminal cancer patients to help them deal with their own mortality.

A darker side of investigations with LSD evolved as well. The U.S. Army and the Central Intelligence Agency both conducted experiments with LSD as a chemical warfare agent and as a sort of "truth serum" for interrogating spies and prisoners of war. Many of the subjects were dosed secretly with LSD. It was later revealed that the Army sponsored LSD experimental research on more than fourteen hundred people between 1956 and 1967 that often blatantly violated ethical codes of conduct established for experiments with human subjects.

In the mid-1950's, Aldous Huxley, a philosopher and writer, published two books (*The Doors of Perception*, 1954; *Heaven and Hell*, 1956) describing his experiences with the peyote cactus hallucinogen, mescaline. Huxley's concept of "chemical keys" as an alternative to meditation to alter one's perception attracted the attention of two Harvard University professors, Timothy Leary and Richard Alpert. These researchers began studies with graduate students using the mushroom hallucinogen psilocybin but later used LSD as the drug of choice. Although the original work was conducted under proper scientific controls and with a physician present, by 1963, the studies apparently had become little more than off-campus LSD parties, with no semblance of scientific method applied. Leary and Alpert were dismissed from the university. Alpert moved to the West Coast and

abandoned the drug, but Leary continued to advocate the use of LSD, encouraging people to "turn on, tune in, drop out."

The LSD movement expanded rapidly to students, writers, and artists who were more interested in the possibilities of self-exploration of the psychedelic experience than in scientific experimentation. By 1967, the "psychedelic age" had arrived and evolved into a distinct subculture with its own language, music, and art forms. LSD came to be known as "acid," and users were "acid heads." An LSD experience was a "trip." Words like "bummer" and "bad trip" were used to describe panic or psychotic reactions to LSD. Bright fluorescent colors appeared in the palettes of psychedelic artists. Many popular music groups of the day recorded songs with veiled references to drugs in their lyrics; the music of several San Francisco-based bands—including Jefferson Airplane and the Grateful Dead—became known as "acid rock."

The use of LSD declined sharply at the end of the 1960's because of widely publicized concern over "bad trips," prolonged psychotic reactions, and personality changes in some people who took the drug. Other publicized adverse effects of LSD (chromosome damage and birth defects), although never validated, contributed to this decline. By 1970, U.S. law included LSD in the same regulatory category as the narcotic heroin, as a drug with no proven, effective use in medicine or scientific investigations.

—*Brian L. Roberts*

FURTHER READING

Bowman, William C., and Michael J. Rand. *Textbook of Pharmacology*. 2d ed. Oxford, England: Blackwell Scientific Publications, 1980. Chapter titled "Psychotropic Drugs" offers brief treatment of the history and pharmacology of major hallucinogens. Chapter titled "Social Pharmacology: Drug Use for Nonmedical Purposes" describes the spread of LSD from controlled clinical experiments to street use and discusses adverse psychiatric reactions and social consequences of LSD use; dismisses some of the dangers attributed to LSD.

Hoffer, A., and Humphry Osmond. *The Hallucinogens*. New York: Academic Press, 1967. Indispensable resource for any serious student of hallucinogens. Extensive literature review covers the history, pharmacology, and psychiatric uses of LSD, how the drug works, and the psychedelic state of mind induced by the drug.

Hofmann, Albert. *LSD, My Problem Child*. Translated by Jonathan Ott. New York: McGraw-Hill, 1980. Excellent firsthand account of the history of LSD. Describes Hofmann's career as a chemist at Sandoz and conveys the excitement and joys of a scientist immersed in his work. Details his collaboration with Albert Stoll on ergot alkaloids, his self-experiments with LSD, and his later work with other hallucinogens. The last third of the book is devoted to Hofmann's encounters with people such as Huxley and Leary.

Jaffe, Jerome H. "Drug Addiction and Drug Abuse." In *Goodman and Gilman's the Pharmacological Basis of Therapeutics*, edited by A. S. Gilman, L. S. Goodman, I. W. Rall, and F. Murad. 7th ed. New York: Macmillan, 1985. Presents a good explanation and description of the altered states of consciousness and the hallucinations induced by LSD as well as standard pharmacology text discussions of the pharmacology and toxicity of LSD.

Julien, Robert M. *A Primer of Drug Action: A Concise, Nontechnical Guide to the Actions, Uses, and Side Effects of Psychoactive Drugs*. Rev. ed. New York: Owl Books, 2001. Comprehensive coverage of psychoactive substances for general readers. Chapter 12 discusses psychedelic drugs, including LSD.

Ray, Oakley, and Charles Ksir. *Drugs, Society, and Human Behavior*. 10th ed. New York: McGraw-Hill, 2004. Thorough treatment of hallucinogens includes an interesting discourse on the history, use, and politics of LSD during the 1960's. Suitable for nonscientists.

Stevens, Jay. *Storming Heaven: LSD and the American Dream*. New York: Perennial Library, 1987. Looks back at the 1960's psychedelic movement as part comedy, part tragedy. Presents sketches of many of the advocates of LSD use, including Leary, poet Allen Ginsberg, and novelist Ken Kesey. Describes the CIA's experiments with LSD and discusses the impact of the era on American life.

SEE ALSO: Winter, 1932: Huxley's *Brave New World* Forecasts Technological Totalitarianism; June 25, 1938: Federal Food, Drug, and Cosmetic Act.

1938
JOHN MUIR TRAIL IS COMPLETED

With the completion of Forester Pass, the 212-mile John Muir Trail, which runs along the crest of the Sierra Nevada, made a unique wilderness experience possible for more people.

LOCALE: California
CATEGORIES: Environmental issues; travel and recreation

KEY FIGURES
John Muir (1838-1914), American naturalist and wilderness preservation advocate
Theodore S. Solomons (1870-1947), charter member of the Sierra Club
William E. Colby (1875-1964), secretary of the Sierra Club

SUMMARY OF EVENT
Forester Pass in the Sierra Nevada, 13,150 feet above sea level, was the last portion of the John Muir Trail to be completed. Work began on the pass in 1930; because the pass was located on the boundary of the Sequoia National Forest and the Sequoia National Park, both the Department of Agriculture and the Department of the Interior provided crews for the project. Forester Pass, sometimes called the Golden Staircase, is a narrow notch 187 miles from the north end of the trail, beginning at Happy Isles, 4,035 feet above sea level. The view from the pass includes several lakes, Kern Canyon, the Kings-Kern Divide, and the treacherous Kaweah Peaks.

It was appropriate that this mountain trail should be named for naturalist and mountaineer John Muir. Muir had come to Yosemite in 1868 after emigrating to Wisconsin from Dunbar, Scotland, and the beauty of the region had captivated him. The following year, he worked as a shepherd in the High Sierras, exploring and recording his experiences. Later, he wrote books and articles, published his drawings, and gave lectures on his wilderness experiences.

In 1892, Muir helped to found the Sierra Club. Initially, the club limited its efforts to the conservation of wildlife and the natural formations of the Sierra Nevada. In 1903, Muir and President Theodore Roosevelt camped together in Yosemite, an experience that underlay the significant conservation efforts of the Roosevelt administration.

Sierra Club members, who explored, photographed, and mapped the High Sierra region, were pioneers in generating the public support needed for developing the John Muir Trail. The club published information that enabled many hikers to experience the wonders of the area, and club members led small expeditions. The club made handbooks available that explained the geography, geology, and plant and animal life of the High Sierra region, provided information on side routes along the major sections of the trail, and described techniques for living in the wilderness.

Once the John Muir Trail was completed, hikers could begin at the northern end in Yosemite Valley and follow the natural ridges and valleys of the High Sierra. Some portions were old sheep and Indian trails. South of the Yosemite area, the trail never drops below 7,500 feet, and the altitude increases steadily to Cathedral Pass at 9,700 feet, 17.3 miles from the trail's beginning. At this point, the trail affords a view of Upper Cathedral Lake. Over the next 4.2 miles, the trail descends 1,100 feet to the Tuolumne Meadows and, 0.7 miles further on, to Soda Springs, Muir's favorite campsite. After that, the trail ascends again to Donohue Pass, at the southeastern boundary of Yosemite National Park.

Devils Postpile National Monument lies 56 miles south of the trailhead. The area is marked by a wall of polygonal columns created by basalt that poured from a volcano about 100,000 years ago. Most of the columns are five- or six-sided, and some are sixty feet tall. Another climb of 2,500 feet and 12.4 miles brings the trail to Duck Pass, which lies at one end of Duck Lake, one of the largest lakes in the High Sierra; it can be reached only by trails.

Over the next 54.9 miles, the trail's altitude fluctuates between 10,860 and 7,750 feet. Sapphire Lake lies at 11,000 feet and Wanda Lake at 11,500 feet. The Muir Pass is at 11,955 feet. The next high points on the trail are Mather Pass at 12,000 feet, Pinchot Pass at 12,100 feet, and Forester Pass. After that, the trail does not drop below 10,000 feet as it

climbs to the summit of Mount Whitney, at 14,494 feet the highest point in the contiguous United States. Thirty-eight lateral trails connect the John Muir Trail to automotive routes, and there is an 8-mile extension to the trail on which hikers can wind down the eastern side of Mount Whitney to Whitney Portal.

The idea for the trail began in 1888 in the mind of fourteen-year-old Theodore S. Solomons, who was working on a cattle ranch in the High Sierra. Solomons could see the mountain peaks in the distance, and he envisioned a route that horses and mules could travel while carrying heavy camping items. In 1888, twenty-three years before the trail actually began to be constructed, Solomons explored the possibility of a trail southward from Yosemite Valley, and three years later, he forged a trail from Yosemite Valley one hundred miles south. Many of these paths form portions of the northern half of the John Muir Trail. Beginning in 1898, Joseph N. Le-

1938

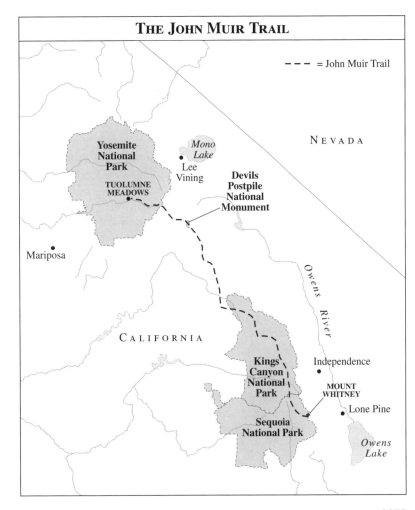

THE JOHN MUIR TRAIL

- - - = John Muir Trail

NEVADA

Yosemite National Park

Mono Lake

Lee Vining

Devils Postpile National Monument

TUOLUMNE MEADOWS

Mariposa

CALIFORNIA

Owens River

Kings Canyon National Park

Independence

MOUNT WHITNEY

Lone Pine

Sequoia National Park

Owens Lake

Conte and other Sierra Club members explored the difficult passes and canyons of the southern section near the Kings-Kern Divide; this area was later found to require much more blasting and construction than the northern half of the trail.

The specific proposal for the trail was formulated in 1914, the year John Muir died. The project was funded by the California legislature and placed under the direction of state engineer Wilbur F. McClure. Construction began in 1917. The U.S. Forest Service contributed to the development of the trail, and the Sierra Club lobbied for state appropriations until the trail was completed in 1938. The total cost was $50,000.

SIGNIFICANCE

Even during the twenty-one years of the construction of the John Muir Trail, many people enjoyed the completed sections of trail. By 1934, the increased use of Tioga Road to Tuolumne Meadows required that it be improved. William E. Colby, a Sierra Club secretary who had worked to develop the John Muir Trail and make the mountains accessible to many people, petitioned the National Park Service not to reroute the road, as had been suggested, because the rerouted road would harm the wilderness that Muir wished people to enjoy. The Park Service followed Colby's and the Sierra Club's recommendations.

The completion of Forester Pass made one of the most scenic spots in the High Sierra accessible to many people, even the occasional hiker. Previously an animal crossing on the Kings-Kern Divide, the pass had been difficult for any but trained mountaineers to reach. A plaque at the pass, erected by fellow workers, honors Donald Davis, who died on September 2, 1930, at the age of nineteen in a rock slide during construction of Forester Pass.

In 1939, the Sierra Club made the protection of the high country around the John Muir Trail one of its main priorities. In 1940, the club supported a bill that established the King's Canyon National Park in 1940. Together with the Sequoia National Park, this area formed an 11,320-square-mile twin-park wilderness region.

The completion of the John Muir Trail through Forester Pass also helped promote the development of the Pacific Crest Trail System, which Clinton Clark initiated in the 1930's and which eventually ran along the entire length of the West Coast. This trail was linked to the 442-mile Oregon Skyline Trail and to 185 miles of the John Muir Trail—the area from Forester Pass through Devils Postpile National Monument and Donahue Pass to Tuol-

umne Meadows. Later, these trails were connected with the 445-mile Cascade Crest Trail in Washington, which was completed in 1941.

Eventually, the John Muir Trail passed through three national parks (Yosemite, Sequoia, and Kings Canyon), one national monument (Devils Postpile), and four national wilderness areas (John Muir, Sequoia, Minarets—now known as Ansel Adams—and Kings Canyon). This caused some problems, because each park and area had its own regulations. For example, the Forest Service, under the Department of Agriculture, promoted an "adopt-a-trail" policy in the wilderness areas and allowed in-season hunting, guns, and dogs on trails adjacent to the John Muir Trail itself. The service considered site restoration and trail maintenance to be priorities; over the years, however, the service's focus gradually shifted from conservation toward preservation. The parks administered by the Department of the Interior employed park rangers who enforced strict regulations, including rules against pack trains, which the early developers of the trail saw as the only way some people could enjoy the trail. Hunting and firearms were not allowed in these park areas, and vehicles, even helicopters, were used to move working crews to their assignments, to remove garbage, and to undertake rescue work.

Because the John Muir Trail proved so popular, permits became necessary to control the number of people using it. This presented many questions, among them whether the land is more important than the people. Use of the trail showed the need for the application of scientific management techniques, not only to care for the land but also to influence government and private action. Since its completion, the John Muir Trail has offered a prime example of the need to maintain a delicate balance between policies that protect wilderness and policies that allow people to enjoy it.

—Rose A. Bast

FURTHER READING

Cohen, Michael P. *The History of the Sierra Club, 1892-1970*. San Francisco: Sierra Club Books, 1988. Provides excellent background information on the organization primarily responsible for the development of the John Muir Trail.

Fishbein, Seymour L. *Wilderness U.S.A.* Washington, D.C.: National Geographic Society, 1973. Excellent collection of photographs taken in wilderness areas, including the four through which the John Muir Trail passes.

Lantis, David W., Rodney Steiner, and Arthur E. Karinen. *California: Land of Contrast.* 3d rev. ed. Dubuque, Iowa: Kendall/Hunt, 1981. Provides a short summary of the history of the John Muir Trail and a detailed account of the various areas through which the trail passes. Also discusses trails that join the John Muir Trail. Includes many black-and-white photographs.

Lowe, Don, and Roberta Lowe. *The John Muir Trail: A Complete Hiking Guide.* 1982. Reprint. Caldwell, Idaho: Caxton, 2001. Presents a historical summary as well as a careful description of the trail. Describes wildlife and rock formations to be found along the trail as well as road exits and side trails. Includes black-and-white photographs and detailed maps.

Muir, John. *The Yosemite.* 1912. Reprint. New York: Modern Library, 2003. Excellent source of insight into Muir's personality and his struggle to protect his beloved Yosemite. The tone is lyrical in places, providing the reader with vivid word pictures of the High Sierra scenery.

Nash, Roderick Frazier. *Wilderness and the American Mind.* 4th ed. New Haven, Conn.: Yale University Press, 2001. Intellectual history of Americans' rela-

tionship with the wilderness. Begins with the earliest days of European contact.

Roth, Hal. *Pathway in the Sky: The Story of the John Muir Trail.* Berkeley, Calif.: Howell North Books, 1965. Provides a history of the trail and information on its geology and wildlife. Also describes the area around Forester Pass.

Starr, Walter A., Jr. *Starr's Guide to the John Muir Trail and the High Sierra Region.* San Francisco: Sierra Club Books, 1974. Trail guide continually revised and updated since it was first published in 1934. Includes detailed map and description of the trail as well as an excellent history.

SEE ALSO: Mar. 14, 1903: First U.S. National Wildlife Refuge Is Established; May, 1903: Roosevelt and Muir Visit Yosemite; Jan. 3, 1905: Pinchot Becomes Head of the U.S. Forest Service; Jan. 11, 1908: Roosevelt Withdraws the Grand Canyon from Mining Claims; May 13-15, 1908: Conference on the Conservation of Natural Resources; Dec. 19, 1913: U.S. Congress Approves a Dam in Hetch Hetchy Valley; Aug. 25, 1916: National Park Service Is Created; 1923: Federal Power Commission Disallows Kings River Dams.

1938-1950
GOLDEN AGE OF AMERICAN SCIENCE FICTION

The entry of scientifically trained writers and editors into the science-fiction magazine market significantly increased the quality of the genre, making the 1940's the Golden Age of American science fiction.

LOCALE: United States
CATEGORY: Literature

KEY FIGURES

John W. Campbell, Jr. (1910-1971), engineer turned science-fiction writer and editor who launched the careers of virtually all the great writers of the period

Isaac Asimov (1920-1992), scientist, science writer, and science-fiction writer first published, by Campbell, at the age of eighteen

Robert A. Heinlein (1907-1988), most popular writer of the Golden Age, controversial for the strong political views in his fiction

Theodore Sturgeon (1918-1985), most consciously prose-oriented stylist of the Golden Age, known for taking science fiction beyond various taboos

A. E. van Vogt (1912-2000), influential science-fiction writer of the 1940's whose ideas about non-Aristotelian logic form the premise for his stories, most of which have superhuman protagonists

SUMMARY OF EVENT

The story of America's Golden Age of science fiction is the story of the "pulp" magazines. Until the end of the 1940's, little science fiction was published in book form. Novels usually were serialized in the pulps, cheap magazines named for the rough, cheap, pulpy newsprint on which they were printed. The pulps were the major forum for adventure stories of the mystery, detective, Wild West, and sea-adventure genres. In the beginning, science fiction simply followed the established pulp-adventure formula.

The roots of the Golden Age can be dated quite specifically. In April of 1926, the first magazine devoted exclusively to science fiction appeared: *Amazing Stories,* edited by Hugo Gernsback. To be sure, science fiction appeared in other periodicals, and Gernsback's science and technology monthlies, such as *Modern Electrics*, had published and encouraged science stories as early as 1911. In *Amazing Stories*, however, science fiction for the first time could find its own identity without competing with other forms of fiction. Gernsback's ideal was a fiction that combined literary skill with scientific plausibility. That ideal was not achieved for another decade, and then by another editor.

In September of 1937, a young engineer who had been publishing science fiction in *Amazing Stories* since 1930 (Gernsback was no longer editor) was invited to take over as editor of a magazine with a similar title: *Astounding Stories*. His name was John W. Campbell, Jr., and he remained at the helm of the magazine—which changed its name twice during his tenure—until his death in 1971. He introduced more talented writers than any other editor of the period.

The writers who dominated the Golden Age of the 1940's were almost all first published by Campbell: Lester del Rey and L. Ron Hubbard in 1938; Isaac

Isaac Asimov. (Library of Congress)

Asimov, Robert A. Heinlein, Fritz Leiber, Theodore Sturgeon, and A. E. van Vogt in 1939; C. M. Cornbluth in 1940; Hal Clement in 1942; Arthur C. Clarke in 1946; Poul Anderson in 1947; and Judith Merril in 1948. The few science-fiction writers of any stature who did not come through Campbell's stable in the 1940's—James Blish, Ray Bradbury, and Damon Knight—were influenced by those who did.

Campbell's high editorial standards were largely responsible for the quality of the work produced during the Golden Age. The pieces he chose told readers and writers what the new measure of science fiction would be. Notably, Campbell avoided the scientifically absurd travesties scornfully dubbed "space operas" by science-fiction fans. In editorials and letters pages, his principles were articulated more directly: He required solid scientific plausibility and the same basic standards of literary quality set by any other genre.

Four writers who delivered both, and who came to dominate the genre, owed their start to Campbell. Their first works in *Astounding Stories* all appeared in 1939. The first was Isaac Asimov, whose short story "Marooned off Vesta" appeared in the March issue. As a chemistry major at Columbia University preparing for graduate school, Asimov was confident of the scientific quality of his writing. Under Campbell's guidance, he soon developed a literary craftsmanship to match. Campbell's influence can be seen in Asimov's two most important contributions to science fiction: the three laws of robotics and the psychohistory that is the basis of his *Foundation* series. The three laws explained how robots would be governed in their relationships with humans. Psychohistory, involving prediction of the future and guidance of its course through human psychology, was born out of a discussion Asimov had with Campbell about Edward Gibbon's *The Decline and Fall of the Roman Empire* (1776-1788).

The second Campbell find of 1939 was Robert A. Heinlein, an older man who also had done graduate study in the sciences. His major contribution to the Golden Age, the "future history" concept, also owed much to Campbell's influence. Campbell had noticed that many of Heinlein's stories referred to the same characters and events, as if Heinlein had a coherent picture of a possible future. He had, and Campbell began referring to Heinlein's "future history" in the February, 1941, issue of *Astounding Stories*, in which an outline of the concept was eventually published.

Campbell's influence on his third discovery of 1939, Theodore Sturgeon, may have been more negative than positive, in that Campbell represented the moral taboos against which Sturgeon would later struggle to break free. Sturgeon's Golden Age work stayed within Campbell's guidelines, but the language and style of his stories of the 1940's pushed the limits of science fiction. Sturgeon was the first true stylist of American science fiction; he had a sophisticated ear for the sound and rhythm of prose. Sturgeon made science fiction sing without endangering its value as story or science.

A. E. van Vogt, the last science-fiction giant to emerge in 1939, is the only one of the four whose influence has not lasted. His novel *Slan*, serialized in *Astounding Stories* in 1940, introduced the first of a series of superhuman heroes persecuted by an inferior majority who feared them. The stories were tremendously popular until it became uncomfortably obvious that they presented an ugly potential for science-fiction writers and readers to see themselves as just such misfits with a supposed superiority. Nevertheless, van Vogt remained one of Campbell's most popular writers through the end of the Golden Age.

Although the beginning of the Golden Age was signaled by Campbell's rise as editor, its end was not dependent on Campbell's retirement, and he remained an influential editor until his last issue of *Analog* (formerly *Astounding Stories*) in December of 1971. However, several developments conspired to lessen Campbell's influence, and most of these had nothing to do with the nature of science fiction. The first major influence was World War II. Campbell lost his best writers to the war effort. The most scientifically gifted were assigned to war-related scientific research; Asimov and Heinlein, in fact, worked in the same laboratory in Philadelphia. Moreover, the government appropriated more than Campbell's writers. The war effort needed paper, and science fiction, like all literary fields, lost many magazine titles during the war. In 1941, there were twenty major science-fiction magazines; by the end of the war, there were seven.

The influence of a watershed event like World War II is not, of course, limited to personnel and paper. As Asimov later pointed out in his essays on the Golden Age, a single moment at the end of the war changed the world's attitude toward science fiction forever. That was the world's abrupt entry into the atomic age, when atomic bombs were dropped on Hiroshima and Nagasaki. Suddenly, everything the science-fiction writers had suggested about atomic power became horribly real. The concurrent fight for Adolf Hitler's rocket scientists and the subsequent race with the Soviets to get into space

quickly made the American public aware that science had caught up with fiction.

Another boom time for science fiction came immediately after the war. The major writers from before the war began writing again, and several new writers appeared. Many influential British science-fiction magazines appeared in 1946, emulating (and sometimes reprinting) the best stories of the American Golden Age. Arthur C. Clarke was published in these British pulps, although his first publication was in Campbell's *Astounding Stories* in 1946.

The American magazines that had survived the war were stronger than ever, but new developments in publishing occurred in the last years of the Golden Age that would end the pulp magazines' exclusive hold on science fiction. The first was the advent of paperback publishing during the war. Many publishing houses at that time produced inexpensive newsprint versions of their bestselling titles, with spaces on the back cover for addressing. The intent was for civilians to buy them and mail them to servicemen overseas. The paperback form, without the address labels, remained after the war, and science fiction found a home in the paperback industry.

SIGNIFICANCE

The end of the 1940's also saw Golden Age science fiction published for the first time in hardcover form, as short-story anthologies and novels previously serialized in the pulps. Four small presses specializing in science fiction sprang up in the 1940's: Advent, Fantasy, Gnome, and the horror-story publisher Arkham House. When these houses proved that it was economically feasible to publish science fiction outside pulp magazines, Doubleday became the first mainstream publisher to try it. Charles Scribner's Sons launched a series of "boys' books" by Robert A. Heinlein, beginning with *Rocket Ship Galileo* in 1947.

For the most part, paperback and hardcover science fiction continued the style and themes of the Golden Age. Hugo Gernsback's emphasis on gadgets had changed to John Campbell's focus on people. The scope of stories broadened, however, following the Golden Age. Instead of reading about individuals encountering new ideas and technologies, readers began to see stories about the effects of those ideas and technologies on society at large. To put it another way, the science of science fiction had been drawn from the physical sciences in the Golden Age. In the second half of the twentieth century, it would be drawn from the social sciences, including anthropology, sociology, and psychology.

1938

To some extent, Heinlein and Asimov, both Campbell-trained Golden Age writers, had anticipated this shift. From the beginning, many of Heinlein's stories dealt with psychological issues. Heinlein complained that editors were rejecting such stories for lack of "scientific" content. Asimov's *Foundation* series, similarly, had sociological and psychological premises in its use of psychohistory. Both Heinlein and Asimov, however, were trained in the physical sciences and always had some of that orientation in their stories.

The rise of two new and different science-fiction magazines, *Fantasy and Science Fiction* (which began in the fall of 1949) and *Galaxy* (beginning in October of 1950), proclaimed the end of the Golden Age by taking science fiction in a new direction. A greater emphasis on prose style, the courting of mainstream writers, and an aim at a more adult audience characterized these two titles. Although it differed in many respects from the science fiction that preceded it, this newer fiction still showed the influence of the Golden Age, in which a successful balance was found between science and fiction.

—*John R. Holmes*

FURTHER READING

Aldiss, Brian W. *Billion Year Spree*. New York: Schocken Books, 1973. A history of science fiction that takes into account concurrent movements in literature outside the field. Written by an important science-fiction writer of the later "New Wave" movement who is not blinded by nostalgia for the Golden Age.

Asimov, Isaac. *Asimov on Science Fiction*. New York: Avon Books, 1981. A collection of periodical essays, mostly editorials from Asimov's science-fiction magazine. Chapters are arranged by topic. Two chapters deal with the Golden Age in general, and two specifically with Campbell.

Disch, Thomas M. *The Dreams Our Stuff Is Made Of: How Science Fiction Conquered the World*. New York: Free Press, 1998. An excellent introduction to the genre. The author treats his material seriously and without bias. Among other discussions, Disch makes an interesting case for Edgar Allan Poe as the father of modern science fiction and analyzes the successful development of L. Ron Hubbard's Scientology.

Fiedler, Leslie A., ed. *In Dreams Awake*. New York: Dell Books, 1975. A critical anthology of short stories, with helpful introductions to each section. Both the general introduction and the introduction to the Golden Age section contain vital insights regarding the period. Fiedler is the most important mainstream critic to write on the Golden Age.

Moskowitz, Sam. *Seekers of Tomorrow*. New York: Ballantine, 1967. A series of critical biographies of the major writers in science fiction up to the mid-1960's. Chapters on Asimov, Campbell, Heinlein, Sturgeon, and van Vogt are included. Moskowitz, the editor of Gernsback's last science-fiction magazine, knew most of the major writers professionally.

Robinson, Frank M. *Science Fiction of the Twentieth Century*. Tigard, Oreg.: Collector's Press, 1999. Although some of the text lacks substance, this book's vast array of beautiful, full-color images is worth noting. The latter sections of the book focus more on the role of science fiction in film than on its literary history.

Wingrove, David. *The Science Fiction Source Book*. New York: Van Nostrand, 1984. The bulk of this book is an encyclopedia of science-fiction writers, rarely with more than one hundred words per entry. A brief history of science fiction by Brian W. Aldiss opens the book, and an essay on science-fiction magazines by Wingrove appears as an appendix. Both essays provide insight into the Golden Age.

SEE ALSO: 1915: *The Metamorphosis* Anticipates Modern Feelings of Alienation; Winter, 1932: Huxley's *Brave New World* Forecasts Technological Totalitarianism; 1935: Penguin Develops a Line of Paperback Books; Sept., 1937: Tolkien Redefines Fantasy Literature.

January, 1938
KAPITSA EXPLAINS SUPERFLUIDITY

Pyotr Leonidovich Kapitsa developed ideas relating to superfluidity in liquid helium and techniques that remain basic to modern low-temperature physics.

LOCALE: Institute for Physical Problems, Moscow, Soviet Union (now Russia)

CATEGORIES: Science and technology; physics

KEY FIGURES

Pyotr Leonidovich Kapitsa (1894-1984), Soviet physicist
Heike Kamerlingh Onnes (1853-1926), Dutch physicist
Ernest Rutherford (1871-1937), English physicist
Lev Davidovich Landau (1908-1968), Soviet physicist

SUMMARY OF EVENT

A thorough and systematic study of the properties of materials whose temperature is close to absolute zero was made possible when, in 1908, Heike Kamerlingh Onnes of the University of Leiden succeeded in liquefaction of helium. Among many unexpected properties, it was found that electrical resistance of many metals approached a constant as the temperature was lowered, and in some cases it vanished entirely at some characteristically low temperature, found to depend on the magnetic field. Kamerlingh Onnes thus had discovered superconductivity in liquefying helium, and for his many achievements in the area of low-temperature physics, he was awarded the Nobel Prize in Physics in 1913.

By 1920, as the properties of various metals near liquid helium temperature (4.20 Kelvins) were being investigated, it became evident that liquid helium exhibits strange and unusual properties around 2.20 Kelvins, thus making it a subject of intense study. In 1924, Kamerlingh Onnes and coworkers found that liquid helium density has a maximum at around 2.30 Kelvins, and a graph of density versus temperature shows a cusp rather than a smooth curve as in the analogous case of water. After several attempts, Willem Hendrik Keesom of Leiden succeeded in solidifying liquid helium under several atmospheric pressures and showed that the melting curve (pressure versus temperature) bends at the lower end so as to appear almost parallel to the temperature axis. This led Kamerlingh Onnes to surmise that under atmospheric pressure, helium may remain a liquid down to absolute zero temperature. By 1927, Keesom and coworkers observed an increase in the dielectric constant of liquid helium, as well as peculiar variations in the specific heat at

around 2.20 Kelvins. It was suggested that a phase change in liquid helium occurs at 2.19 Kelvins such that normal "liquid helium I" prevails at higher temperature and stable "liquid helium II" exists at lower temperature. A curve of specific heat of liquid helium as a function of temperature resembles the Greek letter lambda, and the critical temperature at which phase transition occurs is known as the "lambda point."

In addition to these accumulated perplexing properties of liquid helium, in 1935, Keesom and his daughter A. P. Keesom discovered that helium II exhibits a seemingly infinite thermal conductivity. At the University of Cambridge, John Frank Allen and his collaborators, in addition to confirming Keesom's result, showed that the thermal conductivity of helium II differed from the ordinary because of its dependence on the temperature gradient. In 1938, Allen and his coworkers were to find two of the three important properties of helium II.

Pyotr Leonidovich Kapitsa arrived at Cambridge's Cavendish Laboratory in 1921. After initially working under the supervision of Ernest Rutherford, he received his Ph.D. in 1923 and remained at Cambridge until 1934. By early 1930, he was honored by the Royal Society of Science and installed as a Royal Society Professor and as director of the newly constructed Mond Laboratory. During this time, Kapitsa had achieved "liquefaction of helium by an adiabatic method without precooling with liquid hydrogen," a common procedure since Kamerlingh Onnes's work. Kapitsa returned to the Soviet Union in 1934 for a visit and was not permitted to leave (until 1965); he was named director of the new Institute for Physical Problems in Moscow in 1935.

The apparent lack of "explanation to the abnormal thermal conductivity of helium II" evident from Keesom's experimental results, confirmed by Allen and collaborators, provided the setting for Kapitsa's work. In an article that appeared in *Nature* in January, 1938, he suggested that the thermal conductivity of helium II, below the lambda point, occurs via the convection currents rather than the normal conduction process. He pointed out that such convection current can be maintained only if the viscosity of helium II is exceedingly low. The experimental data pointed to the fact that viscosity of helium II was at least eight times less than that slightly above the lambda point (2.20 Kelvins). Kapitsa showed experimentally that the viscosity of "helium II was at least ten thousand times less than that of gaseous hydro-

1938

Pyotr Leonidovich Kapitsa.

gen at low temperature," supposedly the least viscous of fluids. Based on these supporting arguments, Kapitsa proposed that helium II "below the lambda point assumes a special kind of state," which he called "superfluid." He was able to demonstrate the low viscosity (the internal resistance to flow) by allowing helium to flow through a narrow slit of 5×10^{-7} meters formed by two polished glass disks. He found that helium II passed through the slit rapidly below the lambda point but scarcely flowed above it.

A few months later, Allen and his collaborators at Cambridge discovered that around 1.08 Kelvins, a small heat flow, which was passed electrically, produced a rise in the liquid helium level in a closed bulb at the heated end. It should have fallen because of increased vapor pressure, and this was found to be the case for larger heat flows. When the experiment was repeated with a modi-

fied apparatus such that the top of the bulb at the hot end of the capillary was open, thus sharing the vapor pressure with the helium bath, no difference in the result was noted. They also found "fountain effect," in which a hydrodynamic flow through a capillary resulted when liquid helium was heated by radiation. In 1938, John Gilbert Daunt and Kurt Mendelssohn of the University of Oxford reported yet another property of superfluid, the phenomenon of the "creeping film." They demonstrated that when an empty beaker was lowered into the liquid, it filled to the level of the helium bath even though the rim of the beaker was above the liquid level. It was observed that the level of the liquid in the beaker dropped at the same rate at which the beaker filled when it was partly lifted above the bath.

In a 1941 paper, Kapitsa proved, in addition to his original hypothesis, that helium II flow was composed actually of two currents: one flowing along the wall of the capillary and the other through the center in the opposite direction. He showed further that heat transfer in helium II is produced by these oppositely directed convection currents of different heat content. Kapitsa also assumed that the heat content of the flow of thin films along the wall was different, resulting from the molecular force of the surface, as opposed to the flow along the center. Through a series of experiments, Kapitsa established that below the lambda point, helium II is a mixture of normal fluid and superfluid and that the concentration of the latter increases as the temperature is lowered. He showed that superfluid has zero entropy and as one approaches absolute zero, helium II is transformed entirely into superfluid, which flows without friction, unlike the normal fluid, which experiences drag as it transports heat. He also confirmed Daunt and Mendelssohn's result; namely, if the fluid is forced out through a fine capillary, its temperature falls as much as three- to four-tenths of a degree.

Seeking to demonstrate that heat transport in helium II is the result of movement of fluid, Kapitsa fashioned a movable vane and suspended it at the mouth of a flask filled with fluid so that any flow would be observable by the deflection of the vane. He then filled the electrically heatable flask with liquid helium and immersed it in a helium bath. By placing the movable vane at the mouth of the flask and applying heat to it, he was able to observe the deflection of the vane, proving conclusively that the liquid flows. During World War II, research activities in the area of low-temperature physics were suspended in the West, while in the Soviet Union, Kapitsa and other prominent physicists such as Lev Davidovich Landau progressed at a rapid rate, the latter formulating an elaborate quantum theory of liquid helium during 1940 to 1941.

SIGNIFICANCE

Following Kapitsa's hypothesis of superfluidity, numerous unexpected and puzzling properties of liquid helium were discovered, but none could be explained theoretically. From 1940 to 1941, Landau, of Kapitsa's institute, advanced an elaborate quantum theory of liquid helium. Independently, Laslo Tisza of the College de France advanced some of the qualitative aspects of the theory of helium II, such as zero entropy and "second sound." Landau's theory of superfluidity describes quantum mechanically all observed macroscopic properties of liquid helium below the lambda point at 2.19 Kelvins. The two

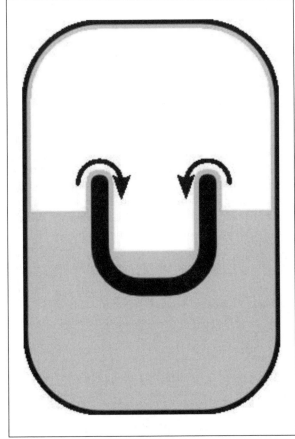

In 1938, John Gilbert Daunt and Kurt Mendelssohn reported a property of superfluidity known as the "creeping film" phenomenon: When an empty beaker is lowered into a bath of liquid helium, it fills to the level of the helium bath even though the rim of the beaker is above the liquid level. Liquid helium, in other words, will "creep" along surfaces to find its own level.

fluids, each in a different state, are assumed to coexist as a mixture of separate quantum states capable of independent simultaneous motion, free of mutual drag, as if through each other. The new state—the superfluid state emerging through a phase change in the normal fluid—is nonviscous and has zero entropy. The transition from normal to superfluid increases with decreasing temperature and tends to complete at 0 Kelvins. The normal viscous fluid transports heat, and in a sense, it is heat itself, flowing against the background of superfluid at ground state or zero energy.

Kapitsa had shown in one of his experiments that although normal fluid escaping from a flask that was being electrically heated deflected the movable vane, the quantity of liquid helium remained unchanged. The explanation of this phenomenon is that superfluid countercurrent flowed back into the flask, keeping the quantity of fluid constant. Landau's theory assumes the superfluid flow to be "irrotational," and, according to the theory of hydrodynamics by the well-known eighteenth century Swiss mathematician Leonhard Euler, the flow of such nonviscous fluid past a solid surface should not exert a force on the body. Thus normal fluid current in one direction and the countercurrent in the opposite direction would keep the quantity of fluid in a container unchanged.

The theory of liquid helium predicts the so-called second sound. Based on the propagation of two different kinds of waves, one associated with the normal fluid and the other with the superfluid, both moving simultaneously in opposite directions with different velocities, Landau's theory should lead to a second sound in addition to the ordinary sound. The initial effort to detect the "second sound" failed in 1940. It soon became evident, however, that whereas the ordinary sound waves are associated with cyclical compression and rarefaction of fluid that propagates through the fluid, the second sound waves oscillating in opposite directions would be too weak to detect. Such counteroscillations of normal and superfluid were realized as giving rise to oscillations of heat relative to cold superfluid background of ground state. Thermal waves can be expected to radiate and are susceptible to excitation (hence detection) by appropriately tuned temperature oscillators. A. P. Peshkov successfully confirmed the occurrence of second sound in helium II. In recognition of his theory of liquid helium, Landau was awarded the 1962 Nobel Prize in Physics.

Eminent Soviet physicists such as Ilya Mikhailovich Lifshitz, Isaak Yakovlevich Pomeranchuk, and Nikolai Nikolaevich Bogoliubov continued to explore superfluidity after Landau's death. The work done on liquid helium in the United States pointed to the fact that critical phase change in helium II is brought on by the formation of microscopic vortices, experimentally verified by William Frank Vinen of Mond Laboratory in Cambridge. It soon became obvious that as helium is composed of two stable isotopes—helium-4 and helium-3—it should exhibit different statistical characteristics. Helium-4 would obey Bose-Einstein statistics, whereas helium-3 atoms conform to Fermi-Dirac statistics, and therefore liquid helium composed of pure helium-3 isotope would show totally different characteristics. In 1949, Edward Roger Grilly, Edward Frederic Hammel, and Stephen George Sydoriak, of Los Alamos showed that helium-3 liquefies at 3.20 Kelvins. Experiments indicate that helium-3 does not become superfluid and that it is a new and even more interesting quantum fluid in comparison with helium-4.

The study of superfluid and low-temperature physics progressed at a rapid rate after Kapitsa formulated his hypothesis and conducted his experiments. Kapitsa is said to have believed firmly that the secrets of nature are revealed only at the limits of physical phenomena. After nearly half a century, he was awarded the 1978 Nobel Prize in Physics for his contribution to low-temperature and plasma physics.

—*V. L. Madhyastha*

FURTHER READING

Kapitza, P. L. *The Collected Papers of P. L. Kapitza.* Edited by D. ter Haar. 4 vols. Oxford, England: Pergamon Press, 1926-1970. Highly technical volumes demonstrate Kapitsa's contributions to physics. Papers appearing in volume 2, pertaining to superfluidity, are relatively simple to follow.

Kedrov, Fedor B. *Kapitza: Life and Discoveries.* Translated by Mark Fradkin. Moscow: Mir, 1984. A journalistic account of Kapitsa's scientific career and his life in the Soviet Union under Joseph Stalin. Includes a complete list of Kapitsa's scientific and nontechnical writings and related works.

Lifshitz, Eugene M. "Superfluidity." *Scientific American* 198 (June, 1958): 20. Well-written account of Kapitsa's discovery of the phenomenon of superfluidity and the historical development of low-temperature physics. Written for the general reader by a well-known Soviet scientist.

Lubkin, Gloria B. "Nobel Prizes: To Kapitza for Low Temperature Studies." *Physics Today* 31 (December, 1978): 17-19. Explains the essence and importance of Kapitsa's work.

Perry, Albert. Introduction to *Peter Kapitza on Life and Science*, by Pyotr L. Kapitza. New York: Macmillan, 1968. Provides a brief sketch of Kapitsa's life and discusses his work at the Cavendish Laboratory.

Spruch, Grace Marmor. "Pyotr Kapitza, Octogenarian Dissident." *Physics Today* 32 (September, 1979): 34-36. Brief account of Kapitsa's career shows the physicist's development from a prisoner in a gilded cage to an effective dissident treading a narrow path.

Trigg, George L. *Landmark Experiments in Twentieth Century Physics.* 1975. Reprint. Mineola, N.Y.: Dover, 1995. Provides highly readable and accurate technical accounts of developments in low-temperature physics from 1908, when Kamerlingh Onnes succeeded in liquefaction of helium. Includes extensive excerpts from Kapitsa's original papers that appeared in *Nature*.

Wilson, David. *Rutherford: Simple Genius.* Cambridge, Mass.: MIT Press, 1983. Interesting biography of a man who played a crucial role in Kapitsa's life. Chapter 16 presents an account of the special bond that existed between Rutherford and his unique student.

SEE ALSO: Mar. 7, 1912: Rutherford Describes the Atomic Nucleus; 1930-1931: Pauling Develops His Theory of the Chemical Bond; 1934: Zwicky and Baade Propose a Theory of Neutron Stars; Feb. 15, 1939: Oppenheimer Calculates the Nature of Black Holes.

February 4, 1938
OUR TOWN OPENS ON BROADWAY

The Broadway opening of Thornton Wilder's Our Town *signaled an American revolt against traditional "box set" staging that kept spectators at a distance from the play.*

LOCALE: New York, New York
CATEGORY: Theater

KEY FIGURES
Thornton Wilder (1897-1975), American novelist and playwright
Jed Harris (1900-1979), American theater producer

SUMMARY OF EVENT

Having achieved worldwide recognition at the early age of thirty with his second published novel, *The Bridge of San Luis Rey* (1927), Thornton Wilder, who had been fond of the theater since childhood, harbored an ambition to write plays. By the age of forty, Wilder had published two additional novels to somewhat mixed reviews and had begun to set his sights and expectations on the stage. As early as 1931, he had published a volume of collected short plays, and since then he had translated and adapted at least two European plays for performance on the Broadway stage for such recognized performers as Katharine Cornell and Ruth Gordon. Many of Wilder's good friends, including Gordon and her then-consort Jed Harris, were Broadway theater people, and Wilder, along with most of his students at the University of Chicago, saw the theater as the most rewarding outlet (personally and professionally, if not financially) then available to creative writers.

Although not born to wealth, Wilder had acquired, with the unexpected success of his second novel, sufficient means and income not only to buy a house for his parents and siblings but also to travel wherever he pleased, with added remuneration along the way for lectures and other public appearances. While traveling in Europe, he had kept his eyes and ears open to various developments in the arts, particularly in the theater.

As a student at Yale University recently mustered out of stateside service during World War I, Wilder had been impressed by the minimalist, "theatricalist" staging of the French director Jacques Copeau, then on worldwide tour with the repertory company he had founded in 1913 at the Théâtre du Vieux-Colombier in Paris. While traveling through Europe in the mid-1930's, Wilder had reexperienced both French theatricalism (recently re-

freshed by the import of plays by Luigi Pirandello of Italy) and German expressionism; he had also discussed the elements of literary art at great length with the American expatriate poet and theorist Gertrude Stein, whom he first met when Stein came to Chicago as a visiting lecturer. Drawing eclectically from such "foreign" influences, as well as from his own earlier experiments in playwriting, Wilder in late 1936 conceived and subsequently developed what would in time be seen as the quintessential American play, which would eventually be seen and heard by a larger worldwide audience than any previous American play.

Its plotting grounded in classical and medieval literature, *Our Town* highlights life and death in a New England town between 1899 and 1913. Time and place, however, soon recede into the background; spectators see a bare stage that remains to be furnished by their imaginations, with only occasional help from the Stage Manager, Wilder's one-man adaptation of the classical Greek chorus. Ladders and shelving are moved around the bare stage by the actors to simulate houses, rooms, and furniture; many props, however, are left to be imagined.

Years earlier, Wilder had accorded to his Yale and Broadway acquaintance Jed Harris the rights of refusal to his first full-length play. In fact, Wilder in 1937 had two such efforts in his briefcase: *Our Town* and *The Merchant of Yonkers* (pr. 1938), which he later reworked as *The Matchmaker* (pr. 1954) and which became the source of the 1964 musical comedy *Hello, Dolly!* Harris, already well known for his devotion to the bottom line, was quick to choose *Our Town*, because it offered him and his actors, yet to be chosen, an easy compromise between creative freedom and practical economy. Harris had long sought to combine art with craft and profit. *Our Town*, perhaps a bit exotic for the prevailing Broadway taste, nevertheless opened at the Morosco Theater on Broadway early in 1938, with future film star Martha Scott in the pivotal role of Emily Webb.

Our Town got off to a slow start, but it gained momentum as the months passed. Failing to acquire the New York Drama Critics Circle Award for which it was nominated, the play nevertheless won the 1938 Pulitzer Prize for drama, with several amateur and student groups quite literally waiting in the wings for performance rights to be released in the spring of 1939. In 1940, *Our Town* was successfully filmed in Hollywood from a screenplay prepared free of charge by Wilder himself, who had rejected an earlier scenario written by playwright Lillian Hellman.

Significance

A quarter century after its less-than-spectacular debut, *Our Town* had become perhaps the most often read and most frequently performed text in American dramatic history, known at least by name to most literate Americans and respected and performed by theater professionals in Europe. More than a few American theatergoers versed also in the European tradition yet jaded by repeated exposure to bad productions of *Our Town* in American high schools, where countless prom queens sought to play Emily, would first rediscover the play's abiding virtues through the medium of European productions, not only in a foreign country but also in a foreign language. After fifty years, the place of *Our Town* in the worldwide dramatic repertory was even more secure, proving the wisdom and foresight implicit in Wilder's

apparently peculiar blend of foreign and domestic elements.

Unlike many of his predecessors and contemporaries writing for the Broadway stage, Wilder in *Our Town* rejected the somber, detailed realism of plot and staging, itself a European legacy most frequently associated with the work of the Norwegian Henrik Ibsen, whose work Wilder had himself translated and adapted for the stage. Breaking with recently hallowed tradition, following even more recent German and French trends that harked back to the ancient Greeks, Wilder presented his archetypal town, Grover's Corners, New Hampshire, as less fictional than mythical; the town is constructed and furnished through the collaboration of the play's spectators, who contribute their imaginations in order to make the play succeed as an act of communication.

"Do any human beings ever realize life while they live it?—every, every minute?" wonders Emily Webb Gibbs, dead in childbirth at age twenty-six. Emily is allowed by the Stage Manager to reexperience one full day in her short life, and she chooses her twelfth birthday, February 11, 1899. The Stage Manager replies to her question in the negative, adding, after a pause, "The saints and poets, maybe—they do some." The deceptive homespun simplicity of Wilder's carefully crafted dialogue earmarks the play as quintessentially American, but it also misleads some observers to find in the play only nostalgia and sentimentality. What Wilder has done, however, is to place each human life against the broadest possible background—described elsewhere in the play as "The Mind of God"—highlighting both the unique and the universal elements implicit in all human experience. The American audience for which he was writing is thus "repatriated" into the world community of theater, at once giving and receiving; thus does *Our Town* remain in the dramatic repertory, often revived in New York and elsewhere, despite the grumblings of those who still regard the play as sentimental.

The 1940 film version of the play, notable mainly for its impact on the Hollywood career of William Holden, who starred as George Gibbs, was recirculated some forty years later on videotape. A somewhat ill-advised television musical version from the mid-1950's, starring Frank Sinatra as the Stage Manager, remains in the collective American memory primarily as a consequence of its theme song, "Love and Marriage," performed and recorded by Sinatra. Televised productions of *Our Town*, without music, have continued well past Wilder's death in 1975, as have live productions both domestic and foreign. In the meantime, the creative freedom exercised by

Thornton Wilder. (AP/Wide World Photos)

WILDER ON *OUR TOWN*

In his preface to a 1957 volume containing three of his plays, Thornton Wilder sheds some light on his decisions regarding the staging of Our Town:

Our Town is not offered as a picture of life in a New Hampshire village; or as a speculation about the conditions of life after death (that element I merely took from Dante's *Purgatory*). It is an attempt to find a value above all price for the smallest events in our daily life. I have made the claim as preposterous as possible, for I have set the village against the largest dimensions of time and place. The recurrent words in this play (few have noticed it) are "hundreds," "thousands," and "millions." Emily's joys and griefs, her algebra lessons and her birthday presents—what are they when we consider all the billions of girls who have lived, who are living, and who will live? Each individual's assertion to an absolute reality can only be inner, very inner. And here the method of staging finds its justification—in the first two acts there are at least a few chairs and tables; but when she revisits the earth and the kitchen to which she descended on her twelfth birthday, the very chairs and table are gone. Our claim, our hope, our despair are in the mind—not in things, not in "scenery." Molière said that for the theatre all he needed was a platform and a passion or two. The climax of this play needs only five square feet of boarding and the passion to know what life means to us.

Source: Thornton Wilder, preface to *Three Plays* (New York: Harper & Brothers, 1957).

Wilder in *Our Town* helped to open up the American stage to greater measures of spectator participation. By the late 1960's, many American productions, on and off Broadway, were performed with few or no props and frequently on three-dimensional "thrust" stages, which were all but unknown to American audiences before their use for *Our Town* productions during the 1950's.

Beneath the surface of Wilder's plays, especially *Our Town*, lies an intelligent acquaintance with developing psychoanalytic theory. Wilder's biographers have documented his meetings during the 1930's with pioneer psychiatrist Sigmund Freud and Wilder's public denunciation of the elderly, terminally ill doctor's mistreatment by the Nazis. In retrospect, however, Wilder's theater seems to bear an even stronger imprint from Freud's erstwhile colleague Carl Jung's explorations of myth and the collective unconscious. In any case, Wilder, through the contemplation of death, managed in *Our Town* to breathe fresh life into the mainstream of American theater, and his contribution still survives him.

—*David B. Parsell*

FURTHER READING

Burbank, Rex. *Thornton Wilder*. 2d ed. New York: Twayne, 1978. Second edition of a volume that was among the first full-length studies of Wilder's work. Remains authoritative, if not definitive.

Cowley, Malcolm. *A Second Flowering: Works and Days of the Lost Generation*. New York: Viking, 1973. Devotes a useful, perceptive chapter to Wilder's "universality" and its sources.

Goldstein, Malcolm. *The Art of Thornton Wilder*. Lincoln: University of Nebraska Press, 1965. A reader's guide to Wilder's novels and plays, notable for its brevity and insights.

Goldstone, Richard. *Thornton Wilder: An Intimate Portrait*. New York: E. P. Dutton, 1975. Prepared over the course of many years, originally planned—or presented—as a work of literary criticism. Draws on previously unavailable letters and documents. Appeared in print shortly before Wilder's death, and much against Wilder's wishes. Wilder questioned Goldstone's critical talents, seriously opposed biographical studies of persons still living, and in effect forced a cancellation of Goldstone's original contract with Harper & Row, Wilder's own longtime publisher.

Haberman, Donald. *The Plays of Thornton Wilder: A Critical Study*. Middletown, Conn.: Wesleyan University Press, 1967. Study of Wilder's plays remains fresh and provocative, reaching back toward sources and forward toward results.

Harrison, Gilbert A. *The Enthusiast: A Life of Thornton Wilder*. New York: Ticknor & Fields, 1983. Full-scale biography of Wilder begun after his death. Somewhat better grounded than Goldstone's (cited above), although short on literary analysis. Authoritative on production history of *Our Town*.

Konkle, Lincoln. *Thornton Wilder and the Puritan Narrative Tradition*. Columbia: University of Missouri Press, 2006. Scholarly study places Wilder's work within the context of American, and specifically New England, culture and literary tradition. Includes a chronology of Wilder's works, bibliography, and index.

Siebold, Thomas, ed. *Readings on "Our Town."* San Diego, Calif.: Greenhaven Press, 2000. Collection of critical essays examines various aspects of the play, including Wilder's experimental approach to theater. Features chronology and index.

1938

SEE ALSO: 1905: Baker Establishes the 47 Workshop at Harvard; May 10, 1921: Pirandello's *Six Characters in Search of an Author* Premieres; 1929-1930: *The Bedbug* and *The Bathhouse* Exemplify Revolutionary Theater; 1931-1941: The Group Theatre Flourishes; Jan. 2, 1933: Coward's *Design for Living* Epitomizes the 1930's; Feb. 19, 1935: Odets's *Awake and Sing!* Becomes a Model for Protest Drama; Aug. 29, 1935-June 30, 1939: Federal Theatre Project Promotes Live Theater.

February 10, 1938
FANNIE MAE PROMOTES HOME OWNERSHIP

Establishment of the Federal National Mortgage Association facilitated the move out of the Great Depression and assisted families in achieving home ownership.

LOCALE: Washington, D.C.
CATEGORIES: Banking and finance; organizations and institutions

KEY FIGURES
Robert J. Bulkley (1880-1965), Democratic member of the Senate Committee on Banking and Currency and influential supporter of the National Housing Act Amendments of 1937
Henry Bascom Steagall (1873-1943), Democratic congressman from Alabama and chair of the House Committee on Banking and Currency
Robert F. Wagner (1877-1953), chair of the Senate Committee on Banking and Currency
T. Alan Goldsborough (1877-1951), Democratic congressman from Maryland and member of the House Committee on Banking and Currency
Franklin D. Roosevelt (1882-1945), president of the United States, 1933-1945

SUMMARY OF EVENT
The Federal National Mortgage Association (FNMA), organized on February 10, 1938, was designed to create and maintain an active market for insured mortgages and a steady flow of mortgage money at relatively favorable interest rates. It provided an avenue of investment for individuals and institutions previously unable to benefit directly from insured mortgage programs.

The U.S. housing industry is made up of hundreds of thousands of small builders, carpenters, and real estate agents, making supervision and control difficult. The construction industry operates in thousands of small, separate sites. The industry is significantly affected by interest rates, which are influenced by fiscal and monetary policies of the U.S. government. The construction industry is an important segment of the economy that can provide a great stimulus to the overall employment level and the economy or can drag it down. Construction activity usually changes in advance of changes in the economy as a whole.

The U.S. housing industry suffered a severe setback as a consequence of the stock market crash of 1929. Investors lost approximately seventy-five billion dollars in the market. Builders stopped work overnight, millions of construction workers lost employment, housing starts plunged, funds for mortgage financing dried up, and more than 1.5 million homes eventually came under foreclosure. Apart from directly affecting the housing industry, the Depression and foreclosures resulted in a large-scale failure of financial institutions, which were left holding foreclosed properties that had declined significantly in value.

By the end of 1930, the housing industry was in disarray as a result of the Depression, poorly planned projects, badly designed homes and apartments, overextended financing, and second and third mortgages on homes at high interest rates. The mortgage finance structure was weak and almost insolvent. Housing starts declined from a high of 937,000 units in 1925 to 93,000 in 1933. A severe decline in deposits at banks and saving institutions, a natural consequence of unemployment, made home financing difficult to find, and many people were unwilling to buy homes and thereby obligate themselves to make mortgage payments. Inability to meet mortgage payments by many home owners resulted in unusually high rates of foreclosure. The foreclosures and a resulting drop in new construction as foreclosed properties came on the market threw more than two million construction workers out of employment.

In 1932, President Herbert Hoover attempted to alleviate the problem by creating the Reconstruction Finance Corporation (RFC), with capital of $500 million and the authority to borrow $1.5 billion to make loans to banks, insurance companies, building and loan associations, and others. Hoover also signed the Federal Home Loan Bank Act of 1932, which created the Federal Home Loan Bank (FHLB). The FHLB was to act as a reserve system for major mortgage financiers such as savings and loan associations. These actions did not succeed in revitalizing the housing industry.

It was left to the next president, Franklin D. Roosevelt, to stimulate the economy and the construction and financing of housing throughout the country. To get the home-construction industry going, he signed the National Housing Act, which created the Federal Housing Administration (FHA), in June of 1934. The FHA established standards for insurance and property and standards for economic soundness in lending. The FHA was also authorized to insure regulated financial institutions that were engaged in mortgage financing and to insure mortgages, to encourage private financial institutions to provide financial resources for real estate purchases. To allow the FHA to borrow funds in the market at a relatively low cost, the interest paid by the FHA on its obligations was freed from all taxes. The FHA revolutionized mortgage financing with its long-term amortized mortgages and acceptance of low down payments. The development of long-term amortized loans eliminated the need to frequently refinance short-term mortgages and significantly reduced borrowers' financing costs.

The RFC Mortgage Company was organized in 1935 as a subsidiary of the RFC to help maintain a market for mortgages. The agency was moved among various departments of the federal government before being abandoned in 1947. By 1937, it had become clear that although the FHA had significantly succeeded in improving the financing of and growth in the real estate industry, it still had not succeeded in attracting private money to the housing market. The construction of housing facilities had not kept pace with the needs and the growth of the population or with recovery in other fields. Industrial production as a whole was more than 90 percent of the average for the period 1925-1930, but residential construction was limping along at only 34 percent of its level during the same period.

The lack of activity had a retarding effect on the recovery of all industries and trade. There was a shortage of affordable housing, especially for lower- and middle-class families. It was estimated that it would be necessary to provide new units at the rate of 760,000 per year for the next ten years to meet the accumulated deficit. The federal government had hoped that private lenders, especially commercial banks, would increase their mortgage holdings in response to federal insurance of mortgages.

A lack of an efficient secondary mortgage market, however, kept private resources away from mortgage investments. A secondary market would allow lenders to sell loans they had made, thus allowing diversification.

On February 10, 1938, under provisions of the National Housing Act of 1934 as amended in 1937, the National Mortgage Association of Washington was organized by the RFC. On April 5, 1938, the name of the National Mortgage Association of Washington was changed to the Federal National Mortgage Association, commonly known as FNMA and later as Fannie Mae. The FNMA began as a wholly owned corporation of the federal government, with initial capital of $10 million, a reserve of $1 million, and borrowing capacity limited to twenty times its equity capital.

The FNMA essentially took over the role of the RFC Mortgage Company. The basic goals of the FNMA included utilization of the best available means of achieving sustained long-term residential construction, with a minimum expenditure of federal funds and a maximum reliance on private business enterprise.

During its first ten years of operation, the FNMA performed a useful secondary market function by buying FHA mortgages when private financial institutions were unable to meet the demand and selling mortgages when housing activity, especially during World War II, fell behind the available supply of funds. By 1942, its investment in mortgages amounted to $211 million. Low interest rates and low levels of real estate activity made mortgage investment an attractive vehicle for private investors from 1942 to 1947, and the FNMA sold much of its portfolio.

During the prewar period, the FNMA remained a minor factor in the mortgage market. Its holdings never exceeded 1 percent of the total outstanding mortgage debt on nonfarm properties. During the period from 1948 to 1954, the size and scope of FNMA operations increased sharply. It became a large primary source of funds for real estate. Mortgage bankers and lenders started playing the role of loan originators for the agency. In 1948, Congress authorized the FNMA to purchase Veterans Administration (VA) authorized loans. In 1948, through an amendment to the National Housing Act of 1934, Congress authorized the FNMA to support mortgages for special federal housing programs in cases in which private money was not available. By the end of 1954, 20 percent of the FNMA's portfolio and 70 percent of its FHA-guaranteed holdings were loans on disaster relief and defense projects.

The FNMA was reorganized in November, 1954. It

1938

was to be a true secondary market facility that would eventually be privately owned and financed. To avoid excessive use of its secondary market facilities, it paid going market prices for loans, and sellers were required to purchase equity interests in the agency. The FNMA was to provide special assistance on certain residential mortgages and housing programs as designated by the government. It was to manage and liquidate its mortgage portfolio in an orderly manner, with a minimum of unfavorable effects on the market and a minimum loss to the government.

At the end of 1954, the FNMA's mortgage portfolio stood at more than $2.4 billion. The FNMA had thus far depended primarily on the Treasury for its financing needs. It experienced substantial growth in its operations after 1954. The most notable change after 1954 was a greater use of private funds to finance FNMA operations. By the end of 1960, $2.5 billion of the FNMA's secondary market obligations were held by the public. Private investment in its common stock amounted to another $73 million. Early in 1960, the FNMA introduced a new method of financing by selling discount notes with maturities ranging from 30 to 270 days. Rates on these discounts changed periodically to reflect market interest rates. The availability of these investment alternatives proved attractive to private investors and reduced the FNMA's dependence on Treasury funds. Although mortgage sellers were required to buy FNMA stock, the stock subscriptions were not large. Attainment of private ownership, it became clear, would require a higher rate of stock subscription.

The FNMA was reorganized as a privately owned corporation under the Housing and Urban Development Act of 1968. At that time, all stock, both common and preferred, owned by the U.S. Treasury was redeemed and replaced by the sale of common stock to the public, and the FNMA came to be known as Fannie Mae. The common stock was listed on the New York Stock Exchange. After the reorganization, the FNMA retained its secondary market mortgage operations. Its special assistance and management and liquidation functions were assigned to a new organization, the Government National Mortgage Association, popularly known as GNMA or Ginnie Mae. Ginnie Mae was to remain under the direction of the Department of Housing and Urban Development.

The 1968 act provided for a transitional period for the FNMA's shareholders to assume control over the FNMA. Although the 1968 act removed all federal ownership interests, significant federal regulation of the

FNMA remained. The secretary of the treasury retained the authority to regulate the issuance of the association's debt instruments. In addition, the secretary of the Department of Housing and Urban Development had the authority to require that a reasonable portion of FNMA mortgage loan purchases be related to the national goal of providing adequate housing to low and moderate-income families, but with a reasonable rate of return to the FNMA. Five of the thirteen members of the FNMA's board of directors were to be appointed by the president of the United States, with the others elected by shareholders.

SIGNIFICANCE

By the time the FNMA was created, the FHA insurance program was four years old but not well established. Immediately upon its creation, the FNMA started its secondary market operations by buying, selling, and holding federally underwritten mortgages. It issued short-term and long-term debentures for sale in the markets to raise additional resources. To stimulate recovery, the FNMA purchased FHA mortgages on new houses from all types of mortgage lenders and mortgage companies. Until its dissolution in 1947, the RFC Mortgage Company continued to finance mortgages on existing properties, which were not authorized to be financed by the FNMA.

Although the FNMA operated under strict federal regulations, it also had certain privileges and immunities. Securities issued by the FNMA were considered to be exempt securities not required to be registered with the Securities and Exchange Commission before their issuance. The FNMA was also exempt from all taxation (except for real estate taxes) by any state, county, city, or municipality. The FNMA issued different types of debt instruments to suit different investor needs. Traditionally, its debt traditionally was treated as government-agency debt in the credit markets. The FNMA, then, enjoyed ready access to funds in the credit markets at rates that are slightly lower than those on comparable U.S. Treasury obligations. Over the years, the FNMA evolved from a taxpayer-supported government agency into a federally chartered private company that by 2005 had provided hundreds of billions of dollars in affordable mortgages and helped sixty-three million American families to own their own homes.

—Rajiv Kalra

FURTHER READING
Brueggeman, William G., Jeffrey D. Fisher, and Leo D. Stone. *Real Estate Finance*. 8th ed. Homewood, Ill.:

Irwin, 1989. This comprehensive text on real estate finance provides a general look at the subject, including legal instruments, institutional sources of funds, and secondary mortgage markets.

Bryant, Willis R. *Mortgage Lending: Fundamentals and Practices*. New York: McGraw-Hill, 1956. A good resource for fundamental aspects of mortgage lending, sources of funds, VA loan programs, and general mortgage loan services.

Dasso, Jerome, and Gerald Kuhn. *Real Estate Finance*. Englewood Cliffs, N.J.: Prentice-Hall, 1983. A detailed book about financial institutions in the real estate industry, primary and other sources of funds, laws relating to real estate finance, and arrangements for financing.

De Souza Briggs, Xavier, and William Julius Wilson, eds. *The Geography of Opportunity: Race and Housing Choice in Metropolitan America*. Washington, D.C.: Brookings Institution, 2005. Contemporary experts in housing and urban policy studies examine the relationship between housing and America's history of racial, social, and economic segregation.

Federal National Mortgage Association. *Introducing Fannie Mae*. Washington, D.C.: Author, 1992. Twelve-page booklet provides a brief history of the FNMA and its activities in the real estate market. Lists sources of income, securities issued to raise funds, and international activities.

Jones, Oliver, and Leo Grebler. *The Secondary Mortgage Market: Its Purpose, Performance, and Potential*. Los Angeles: University of California, Graduate School of Business Administration, 1961. Excellent work, although somewhat dated, provides a detailed look at the growth and development of the secondary mortgage markets. A good source of data on market activity for the period up to 1960.

Mason, Joseph B. *History of Housing in the U.S., 1930-1980*. Houston: Gulf, 1982. Chapter 1 provides a review of the Depression years and the federal government's efforts to restart the housing industry.

Ward, Colin. *Cotters and Squatters: The Hidden History of Housing*. Nottingham, England: Five Leaves, 2002. Draws parallels between the history of informal settlements that have been erected throughout human history and the modern debate over zoning, planning, and the availability and cost of housing.

SEE ALSO: Dec. 23, 1913: Federal Reserve Act; June 16, 1933: Banking Act of 1933 Reorganizes the American Banking System; Aug. 23, 1935: Banking Act of 1935 Centralizes U.S. Monetary Control.

1938

February 12-April 10, 1938
THE ANSCHLUSS

After being thwarted in a 1934 attempt to subvert and overthrow the government of the neighboring Republic of Austria, Adolf Hitler capitalized on the growing friction between Italy and the Allied Powers to bluff, cajole, and intimidate his way into initiating a bloodless invasion that incorporated the formerly independent Austrian state into the greater German Reich.

LOCALE: Germany, Austria
CATEGORIES: Diplomacy and international relations; wars, uprisings, and civil unrest; World War II

KEY FIGURES
Adolf Hitler (1889-1945), chancellor of Germany, 1933-1945
Kurt von Schuschnigg (1897-1977), chancellor of Austria, 1934-1938
Arthur Seyss-Inquart (1892-1946), Austrian Nazi Party leader and chancellor of Austria, 1938
Wilhelm Miklas (1872-1956), president of Austria, 1928-1938
Guido Schmidt (1901-1957), Austrian foreign affairs secretary, 1936-1938
Benito Mussolini (1883-1945), prime minister and dictator of Italy, 1922-1943
Hermann Göring (1893-1946), German field marshal and head of the armed forces
Franz von Papen (1879-1969), German ambassador to Austria
Joachim von Ribbentrop (1893-1946), German foreign minister, 1938-1945
Neville Chamberlain (1869-1940), prime minister of Great Britain, 1937-1940

SUMMARY OF EVENT
An Austrian German by birth, Adolf Hitler had long harbored a desire to implement Anschluss, a concept that might be broadly defined as the union of all Germans in

GERMANY AFTER THE ANSCHLUSS, 1938

Nazis, now led by lawyer Arthur Seyss-Inquart, were waging a terrorist campaign against the Austrian government, and Seyss-Inquart accelerated his efforts in early 1938 so that the German government would have a greater pretext for armed intervention.

Confident of success, Hitler summoned von Schuschnigg and his foreign secretary, Guido Schmidt, to a conference at Berchtesgaden on February 12, 1938. The German chancellor launched a hysterical, abusive verbal attack and threatened the Austrians with dire consequences if they did not meet his demands. This invective so unnerved von Schuschnigg that he signed the document presented to him by the new Nazi foreign minister, Joachim von Ribbentrop, and Franz von Papen, Germany's ambassador to Austria. In doing so, von Schuschnigg also pledged to meet a number of Nazi demands: Before February 18, he would appoint Seyss-Inquart as his interior minister, free all imprisoned Austrian Nazis, and name Nazis to head the ministries of war and finance. Von Schuschnigg's concessions went quite a distance toward surrendering Austrian sovereignty.

Somewhat recovered from his return to Vienna, the shaken von Schuschnigg attempted to undo some of the damage. In a defiant speech in the Austrian parliament on February 24, von Schuschnigg ruled out further concessions and reaffirmed Austria's sovereignty. Seyss-Inquart's response was to unleash mobs of Nazis to riot and terrorize the population; since the Interior Ministry directed the police, nothing was done to prevent the violence. The chaos provided an excellent subterfuge for German military intervention, and so von Schuschnigg resorted to two desperate expedients: He sought assistance from Mussolini and announced, in a speech on March 9, that a plebiscite on the question of whether or not to unite Austria with Germany would be presented to the Austrian electorate on March 13. Had they been allowed to vote, Austrians surely would have rejected the Anschluss, and this would have seriously undercut Hitler's assertions that the vast majority of Austrians wanted to merge with the Third Reich.

one land. When Hitler became Germany's chancellor on January 30, 1933, and established a totalitarian regime, Anschluss and the incorporation of Austria into his Germanic Third Reich became not only a possibility but also a priority. On July 25, 1934, Austrian Nazis assassinated Austrian chancellor Engelbert Dollfuss and attempted a coup, but they were stymied when Dollfuss's successor, Kurt von Schuschnigg, assumed control. Matters were made more complicated when Italian dictator Benito Mussolini threatened to deploy Italian troops to the Brenner Pass to prevent the German military from advancing into Austrian territory. Hitler had hoped to use the Nazi uprising in Vienna as a justification for taking control of the area, but he was compelled to abandon the idea.

Although on that occasion Hitler had been forced to back down, the situation had changed by early 1938. The German military machine had been transformed into a powerful entity through Hitler's repeated violations of the rearmament clauses of the treaties signed at Versailles and Locarno, and German-Italian relations had undergone a complete turnaround: Hitler and Mussolini were now on the most cordial of terms. The Austrian

After an initial burst of rage, Hitler ordered that preparations for a military move into Austria be prepared under the code name Case Otto. On March 10, responding to Hitler's request, Mussolini abandoned Austria and stated his support for Anschluss. On March 11, von Schuschnigg was confronted with the massing of German troops along his borders and a demand from Hitler and Field Marshal Hermann Göring that the plebiscite be canceled. No sooner had von Schuschnigg done so than Göring upped the ante, insisting that von Schuschnigg be replaced by Seyss-Inquart. Although von Schuschnigg resigned, Austrian president Wilhelm Miklas refused to confirm Seyss-Inquart as chancellor. The stalemate lasted into the evening: The sixty-six-year-old Miklas refused to bend, even under intense pressure, until nearly midnight. By this time the invasion was already under way; Seyss-Inquart had long since agreed to authorize the arrival of German troops.

The German army entered without opposition, and the path was cleared for Hitler to make his triumphant entrance. On March 13, an Anschluss law was drafted, and Hitler drove into Vienna the next day. A plebiscite on the Anschluss was scheduled to take place on April 10. By that time it had become obvious that there would be no interference from the Western European democracies. France's government had fallen on March 11, and the French were not able to re-form a ministry until the German takeover was complete. In Britain, Joachim von Ribbentrop worked to assuage the government of Prime Minister Neville Chamberlain, which was already committed to appeasement. In a March 14 speech to Parliament, Chamberlain announced his acceptance of what had transpired and his reluctance to resort to force. With the Gestapo arresting Austrian opponents of the Nazi regime and intimidating all dissenting voices, the results of the April 10 plebiscite were—as a foregone conclusion—overwhelmingly in support of the Anschluss.

SIGNIFICANCE

The Anschluss was a significant stepping-stone in Hitler's grand scheme to build German military strength and secure both domination over Western Europe and the destruction of the Soviet Union. The success of the Anschluss contributed to Hitler's delusory legend of invincibility, and it fore-

CHAMBERLAIN ON THE ANSCHLUSS

Most world leaders, including British prime minister Neville Chamberlain, displayed remarkably little reaction to the Anschluss. Chamberlain made the following remarks in a speech to the House of Commons on March 14, 1938.

In the first place, Great Britain and Austria are both members of the League [of Nations], and both were signatories, as was also the German Government, of treaties which provided that the independence of Austria was inalienable except with the consent of the Council of the League of Nations. Quite apart from this, His Majesty's Government are, and always must be, interested in developments in Central Europe, particularly events such as those which have just taken place, if only for the reason . . . that the object of all their policy has been to assist in the establishment of a sense of greater security and confidence in Europe. . . . Throughout these events His Majesty's Government have remained in the closest touch with the French Government who, I understand, also entered a strong protest in Berlin on similar lines to that lodged by His Majesty's Government. It seems to us that the methods adopted throughout these events call for the severest condemnation and have administered a profound shock to all who are interested in the preservation of European peace. . . .

In appraising recent events it is necessary to face facts, however we may judge them, however we may anticipate that they will react upon the international position as it exists to-day. The hard fact is—and of its truth every hon. Member can judge for himself—that nothing could have arrested this action by Germany unless we and others with us had been prepared to use force to prevent it.

I imagine that according to the temperament of the individual the events which are in our minds to-day will be the cause of regret, of sorrow, perhaps of indignation. They cannot be regarded by His Majesty's Government with indifference or equanimity. They are bound to have effects which cannot yet be measured. The immediate result must be to intensify the sense of uncertainty and insecurity in Europe. Unfortunately, while the policy of appeasement would lead to a relaxation of the economic pressure under which many countries are suffering to-day, what has just occurred must inevitably retard economic recovery and, indeed, increased care will be required to ensure that marked deterioration does not set in.

This is not a moment for hasty decisions or for careless words. We must consider the new situation quickly, but with cool judgment. . . . As regards our defense programs, we have always made it clear that they were flexible and that they would have to be reviewed from time to time in the light of any development in the international situation. It would be idle to pretend that recent events do not constitute a change of the kind that we had in mind. Accordingly we have decided to make a fresh review, and in due course we shall announce what further steps we may think it necessary to take.

1938

shadowed a pattern that would be repeated in nearly every formerly sovereign state that fell to Nazi influence. In each of these cases, Jewish populations were singled out for the persecution that would culminate in the Holocaust.

—*Raymond Pierre Hylton*

FURTHER READING

Bischof, Gunter, Anton Pelinka, and Alexander Lassner, eds. *The Dollfuss-Schuschnigg Era in Austria: A Reassessment.* New Brunswick, N.J.: Transaction, 2003. Emphasis in placed on the foreign policy miscalculations of the Schuschnigg regime, which the authors see as a major factor behind the implementation of the Anchluss in Austria.

Eimerl, Sarel. *Hitler over Europe: The Road to World War II.* Boston: Little, Brown, 1972. Falls somewhat short in its depiction of the role of the international community in this affair and views the implementation of the Anschluss as not being a smoothly run operation as much as it was a haphazard adventure that was carried to fruition through Hitler's brazen psychological ploys.

Kershaw, Ian. *Hitler, 1936-1945: Nemesis.* New York: W. W. Norton, 2000. Concludes that the key to the success of the Anschluss was Hitler's dexterity in steering the middle road between the extremist views of Göring and those of Papen.

Manchester, William. *The Last Lion: Winston Spencer Churchill; Alone, 1932-1940.* Boston: Little, Brown, 1988. Asserts that the plebiscite issue marked the critical point in Hitler's decision to annex Austria openly rather than maintain the sham of a puppet state.

Shirer, William L. *The Rise and Fall of the Third Reich: A History of Nazi Germany.* 30th anniversary ed. New York: Ballantine, 1991. Classic work presents one of the most complete accounts available of Hitler's browbeating of Schuschnigg and Schmidt at Berchtesgaden. As a foreign correspondent in Vienna, the author was witness to many events connected to the Anschluss.

SEE ALSO: Jan. 11, 1923-Aug. 16, 1924: France Occupies the Ruhr; Jan. 30, 1933: Hitler Comes to Power in Germany; Mar., 1933: Nazi Concentration Camps Begin Operating; Mar. 7, 1936: German Troops March into the Rhineland; Mar. 14, 1937: Pius XI Urges Resistance Against Nazism; July 6-15, 1938: Evian Conference; Sept. 29-30, 1938: Munich Conference; Nov. 9-10, 1938: Kristallnacht; Aug. 23-24, 1939: Nazi-Soviet Pact; Sept. 1, 1939: Germany Invades Poland.

March 3, 1938
RISE OF COMMERCIAL OIL INDUSTRY IN SAUDI ARABIA

In the early 1900's, oil was increasingly demanded for fuel. With the support of their governments, oil companies aggressively sought new sources of commercial oil, especially in the Middle East, where large sources of commercial oil were discovered in the Arabian Peninsula. The large oil fields of Saudi Arabia changed the country from a remote desert kingdom to an important player in world affairs.

ALSO KNOWN AS: Saudi Arabian Oil Company; Saudi Aramco

LOCALE: Saudi Arabia

CATEGORIES: Energy; natural resources; trade and commerce

KEY FIGURES

Ibn Saʿūd (c. 1880-1953), king of Hijaz and Najd, r. 1927-1932, and king of Saudi Arabia, r. 1932-1953

H. St. John B. Philby (1885-1960), British official and explorer who became a key adviser to Ibn Saʿūd

Karl Saben Twitchell (1885-1968), American mining engineer who first explored for water, minerals, and oil in Saudi Arabia

Charles R. Crane (1858-1939), American philanthropist

SUMMARY OF EVENT

The growing need for oil to fuel navies and new motorized vehicles in the early 1900's catalyzed the search for new commercial sources of oil. First discovered in Persia (modern-day Iran) in 1908, oil had also been found in 1927 near Kirkuk in modern-day Iraq, and exploration continued on the Arabian Peninsula. Calouste Sarkis Gulbenkian, an Armenian knowledgeable about the Russian Baku oil field, played an important role in the 1912 creation of the Turkish Petroleum Company (TPC), which sought to develop oil in the Ottoman Empire.

After World War I, the oil rights of the former Ottoman Empire were divided between the French and the

British. Political pressure forced the inclusion of American oil companies, too, and the issue became more important when a large commercial oil field was found near Kirkuk in 1927. Under an agreement signed in 1928, the TPC (later renamed the Iraq Petroleum Company) was to be owned by British Petroleum, Royal Dutch/Shell, the Compagnie Française des Petroles, the Near East Development Corporation (a group of five American oil companies), and Gulbenkian. All the companies involved signed the Red Line Agreement, which prevented them from seeking individual oil concessions in the former Ottoman Empire region (including all of the Arabian Peninsula except Kuwait).

After World War I, Major Frank Holmes of New Zealand became an agent for the Eastern and General Syndicate, which wanted to find business opportunities in the Middle East. During the 1920's, he obtained oil rights in eastern Saudi Arabia, the neutral zone between Saudi Arabia and Kuwait, and the island of Bahrain. The syndicate became short of money, however, and it decided to try to sell the oil concessions. Gulf Oil was interested in the oil concessions and bought them, but because the company had signed the Red Line Agreement—it was a member of the Near East Development Corporation—it was required to relinquish its purchase. Gulf Oil sold its concession in Bahrain to Standard Oil of California (called Socal and later Chevron), and the other concessions lapsed. Socal discovered a modest oil field in Bahrain on May 31, 1932.

Ibn Saʿūd was a formidable political and military leader who consolidated much of the Arabian Peninsula into a sovereign state under his rule. The British government formally recognized his kingdom—which was renamed Saudi Arabia in 1932—in the Treaty of Jiddah in 1927. The treaty had the important effect of replacing a previous treaty agreement with Ibn Saʿūd that had restricted his ability to negotiate commercial agreements with anyone but the British. The new treaty did not have this restriction.

H. St. John B. Philby was a British official and explorer who became deeply involved in the affairs of Ibn Saʿūd and his kingdom. He even converted to Islam in 1930 so that he could be a senior adviser to the king. King Ibn Saʿūd was in great need of money, and Philby believed that oil concessions were one possible solution. He was also concerned about the strong British influence in the region. Philby, who had a favorable opinion of the United States, decided to see if any American oil companies would be willing to pay for oil concessions in Saudi Arabia. A chance arose when King Ibn

Saʿūd was hosting a visit by Charles R. Crane, an American philanthropist with a strong interest in the Middle East. In response to the need for more irrigation in the kingdom, Crane offered the assistance of a mining engineer named Karl Saben Twitchell, who was under contract to Crane in Yemen. Twitchell began his work in 1932. His explorations in the country convinced him that there were commercial sources of gold and oil in the country, and he left to see if financing could be found in the United States.

Socal geologist Fred A. Davies believed that there might be a great deal of oil near Bahrain, and Socal immediately contracted Twitchell to help arrange an oil concession from King Ibn Saʿūd. Negotiations began in Jiddah in 1933. Socal was represented by Twitchell and lawyer Lloyd Hamilton with support from Philby. Saudi finance minister Abdullah Suleiman negotiated for the Saudi government, and Iraq Petroleum Company (IPC) also sent a negotiator, Stephen Longrigg, to Jiddah. However, IPC's reluctance to pay cash up front and Philby's hostility prevented IPC from being a serious competitor, and on May 29, 1933, an agreement was signed. Socal received the oil concession to eastern Saudi Arabia and preferential rights (which meant that it would be allowed to match any offer) to the rest of the kingdom for sixty years. Saudi Arabia received a loan (to be paid back from future royalties) in gold, a yearly fee, another loan if oil was found, and a royalty per ton of oil. Exploration and drilling began immediately.

The focus on exploration in eastern Saudi Arabia was at the Dammam Dome formation. Socal chose California Arabian Standard Oil Company (Casco), a subsidiary, to do the work, and drilling began in 1935. The Texas Company (Texaco) became a half owner in Casco in 1937 after it provided needed facilities and capital. The initial wells were not successful, and Socal began to consider closing its operations. On March 3, 1938, Dammam's well number seven hit significant oil at 4,727 feet. Other companies quickly showed interest in Saudi Arabia's oil, but the king was pleased with Casco and granted additional valuable oil concessions to the company. Casco and the later Arabian American Oil Company (Aramco) remained the chief producers of oil from Saudi Arabia, which gave American oil companies a strong position in Middle East oil production.

SIGNIFICANCE

Dammam's well number seven would operate until 1982 and produce 32.5 million barrels of oil. This well was just the start of oil production: By 1949, Saudi Arabian oil

1938

production was 500,000 barrels per day. In 2005, Saudi Arabia was producing more than 10 million barrels per day (8-9 percent of the world's use) and had one-fourth of the world's proven reserves. Iraq, which had only half as much in proven oil reserves, was second in the world. As the importance of the oil production in Saudi Arabia grew, its management changed. Casco became the Arabian American Oil Company (Aramco) in 1944, and Standard Oil of New Jersey (Exxon) and Socony-Vacuum Oil (Mobil) became partners in Aramco in 1948. The Saudi government gained 25 percent ownership of Aramco in 1973, 60 percent in 1974, and full ownership in 1980. The name was changed to the Saudi Arabian Oil Company (Saudi Aramco) in 1988. Oil accounted for approximately 75 percent of the Saudi Arabian government's revenue and 40 percent of its gross domestic product in 2005, and oil paid for the kingdom's economic development and modernization. The importance of the exported oil from Saudi Arabia and its neighbors in the Middle East made the political events of this part of the world of vital interest and concern to the world's most powerful nations.

—*Gary A. Campbell*

FURTHER READING

Brown, Anthony Cave. *Oil, God, and Gold*. New York: Houghton Mifflin, 1999. A very readable book about the details of the discovery and development of oil in Saudi Arabia.

Hamilton, Charles W. *Americans and Oil in the Middle East*. Houston: Gulf, 1962. An insider's view of U.S. involvement in the development of oil in the Middle East. Chapter 5 specifically deals with Saudi Arabia.

Lacey, Robert. *The Kingdom: Arabia and the House of Saud*. New York: Avon Books, 1981. A best-selling history of modern Saudi Arabia. Parts 4 and 5 deal with oil and petropower.

Mansfield, Peter, and Nicholas Pelham. *A History of the Middle East*. Rev. ed. New York: Penguin Books, 2004. Chapter 9 deals with the discovery of oil.

Sampson, Anthony. *The Seven Sisters: The Great Oil Companies and the World They Made*. New York: Viking Press, 1975. A best-selling history of the development of the international oil industry. The role of the Middle East is well covered.

Yergin, Daniel. *The Prize: The Epic Quest for Oil, Money, and Power*. New York: Simon & Schuster, 1992. A well-researched, best-selling history of the oil industry. Parts 2 and 3 cover the discovery and development of oil in the Middle East.

SEE ALSO: Jan. 10, 1901: Discovery of Oil at Spindletop; May 26, 1908: Oil Is Discovered in Persia; Apr. 26, 1920: Great Britain and France Sign the San Remo Agreement; Dec. 14, 1922: Oil Is Discovered in Venezuela; July 18, 1926: Treaty of Ankara; Sept. 17, 1928: Oil Companies Cooperate in a Cartel Covering the Middle East.

March 18, 1938
MEXICO NATIONALIZES FOREIGN OIL PROPERTIES

In order to keep hefty oil profits from going to foreign investors, the Mexican government seized control of all aspects of the Mexican petroleum industry. American and European oil companies complained about lost profits and wasted investments and pressured their governments to intervene, but Mexico refused to bow to diplomatic pressure and ultimately nationalized other industries in an effort to bolster the Mexican economy.

LOCALE: Mexico
CATEGORIES: Trade and commerce; diplomacy and international relations; government and politics; energy

KEY FIGURES

Lázaro Cárdenas (1895-1970), president of Mexico, 1934-1940

Franklin D. Roosevelt (1882-1945), president of the United States, 1933-1945
Cordell Hull (1871-1955), U.S. secretary of state, 1933-1944
Josephus Daniels (1862-1948), U.S. secretary of the Navy, 1913-1921, and ambassador to Mexico, 1933-1941

SUMMARY OF EVENT

In the 1920's, Mexico was the second-largest producer of petroleum in the world and the world's leading oil exporter. American and European business interests, however, controlled most aspects of the Mexican oil industry, and as a result Mexico's immense oil profits benefited foreign investors instead of the Mexican economy. Foreign companies made matters worse for Mexican unions by refusing to improve working conditions for Mexican oil workers. Tensions between workers and foreign managers gradually increased, and in May of 1937, an industrywide strike crippled the petroleum industry.

The Mexican government convinced union members to resume working while it attempted to negotiate a settlement, but oil companies claimed that financial difficulties prohibited them from fulfilling many of the workers' demands. As a result of this claim, President Lázaro Cárdenas ordered a full investigation of the oil industry. Although the study found that oil production had declined considerably due to the Great Depression of the 1930's, it also demonstrated that the Mexican oil industry produced more profits than the American oil industry.

More strikes and legal battles plagued Mexico's oil industry after this revelation. On March 18, 1938, in an effort to restore stability, Cárdenas announced that the Mexican government would assume sole control of production, refining, and distribution of petroleum and natural gas within Mexico, and the Mexican government quickly took control of all foreign oil properties within the country. The declaration affected seventeen foreign oil companies operating in Mexico, the largest of which were Mexican Eagle, operated by Royal Dutch/Shell, and Huasteca, operated by Standard Oil of New Jersey. The foreign companies estimated the value of lost property at more than $350 million.

The announcement of the creation of a state-owned monopoly was instantly popular in Mexico. Mexicans held spontaneous parades and took up collections to pay the foreign oil companies, which reacted with instant hostility. American-owned oil companies pleaded with the U.S. government to intervene, and Secretary of State Cordell Hull publicly condemned the action. The United States enacted a brief economic embargo against Mexico as a result, and the U.S. Treasury discontinued purchases of Mexican silver. Even so, the United States soon grudgingly followed Franklin D. Roosevelt's Good Neighbor Policy and urged American corporations to pursue all available legal avenues within Mexico before taking more extreme action. European nations reacted with similar bitterness: Great Britain demanded restoration of its oil properties and suspended diplomatic relations with Mexico when its demands were not met, and the Dutch government insisted on immediate and significant compensation. The dispossessed oil companies also started a massive public campaign to boycott Mexican petroleum products.

The American and European oil companies hoped

their actions would force Cárdenas to rescind his decree and return their property. Indeed, demands by the European and American governments did create hardships. The discontinuance of American silver purchases proved to be particularly burdensome. The United States purchased approximately thirty million dollars in silver each year from Mexico, and Mexico did not sell mass quantities of silver to any other nations. As a result of the halt in American silver purchases, Mexican silver soon appeared on the world market, and the price of silver fell rapidly. Furthermore, the silver profits that Mexico lost caused the value of the peso to plummet.

In order to manage the new national monopoly, Cárdenas soon created a state-run oil company called Petróleos Mexicanos (PEMEX), which received the exclusive right to extract, refine, and market oil within Mexico. Foreign oil companies had been rather successful in Mexico, but PEMEX had initial difficulties, particularly because foreign oil companies refused to sell PEMEX the chemicals it needed for refining. The foreign powers still hoped to force Mexico to relent and invite foreign companies into the country again. PEMEX persevered, however, and sought alternative methods of production. The company's experimentation led to a deadly explosion that killed a number of engineers, but ultimately PEMEX managed to produce the necessary chemicals. PEMEX faced difficulties also in obtaining equipment, and boycotts made foreign markets virtually impenetrable. As a result, Mexico began to sell increasingly large amounts of oil to the fascist regimes in Spain and Germany. In exchange, these nations provided PEMEX with machinery and technical assistance.

With the outbreak of World War II, Mexico found itself in an uncomfortable situation. It supplied oil products to Germany and the Axis Powers, but at the same time it tried to maintain a good relationship with the United States and the Allies. As a result of Mexico's position, the United States and Britain blocked Mexican oil shipments to their allies, and some American and British oil companies even advocated an invasion of Mexico. Finally, in 1943, American and British leaders realized that eliminating Nazi Germany's oil supply was more important than punishing Mexico. Further, as Ambassador Josephus Daniels had informed President Roosevelt, Cárdenas's position seemed secure, and Mexico was not likely to yield to foreign pressure. As a result, the American government persuaded dispossessed oil companies to settle, and the Mexican government paid the foreign oil companies twenty-four million dollars for seized properties, a small fraction of the value lost by the for-

1938

eign companies. Nevertheless, concessions led to a relaxation of restrictions against Mexico, and Mexican oil profits grew as World War II generated a high demand for oil.

SIGNIFICANCE

Generally, Mexicans saw the expropriation of their oil as an economic success. Indeed, the move was so popular that March 18 became an unofficial holiday in Mexico, and Lázaro Cárdenas ranked among Mexico's most popular presidents. Despite lost government revenues from silver sales, which caused the devaluation of the peso in the world economy, PEMEX ultimately generated tremendous profits for the Mexican government. On average, oil profits increased by 6 percent per year until the 1970's, when discoveries of new petroleum reserves further increased Mexican oil production.

Although nationalization provided the Mexican economy with increased oil revenue, the change damaged Mexico's economic relationships with the nations that lost property as a result of the expropriation. Fearful that the Mexican government could seize control of other industries, many businesses chose to keep their investments outside Mexico for several decades, and the lost revenue from the potential investments had an incalculable effect on the Mexican economy. Indeed, these businesses were correct in their suspicions: The oil expropriation laid the groundwork for the Mexican government to nationalize other industries that it judged essential public institutions. By then, however, a precedent of expropriation had been set, and other Mexican industries did not face the same level of international backlash when they were nationalized. The successful operation of PEMEX also encouraged the Mexican government to believe that government-owned monopolies could benefit the national economy. As a result, Mexico national-

ized its airline (Aeromexico) in 1950 and its telecommunications industry (TELMEX) in 1972.

—*John K. Franklin*

FURTHER READING

Dallek, Robert. *Franklin D. Roosevelt and American Foreign Policy, 1932-1945*. Rev. ed. New York: Oxford University Press, 1995. Places the Mexican oil expropriation into the context of American foreign policy during the Roosevelt administration. Includes a new afterword.

Jayne, Catherine E. *Oil, War, and Anglo-American Relations: American and British Reactions to Mexico's Expropriation of Foreign Oil Properties, 1937-1941*. Westport, Conn.: Greenwood Press, 2001. Examination of British and American reactions to the Mexican oil expropriation that demonstrates the inability of the United States and Britain to work together in their relationships with Mexico.

Schuler, Frederich. *Mexico Between Hitler and Roosevelt: Mexican Foreign Relations in the Age of Lázaro Cárdenas, 1934-1940*. Albuquerque: University of New Mexico Press, 1998. Examination of Mexico's foreign policy. Argues that the United States and Mexico had a good relationship during the covered period and that the oil expropriation stabilized the Mexican economy.

SEE ALSO: Mid-Oct., 1910-Dec. 1, 1920: Mexican Revolution; Dec. 31, 1911: Parliament Nationalizes the British Telephone System; Mar. 15, 1916-Feb. 5, 1917: Pershing Expedition; Jan. 31, 1917: Mexican Constitution Establishes an Advanced Labor Code; Dec. 14, 1922: Oil Is Discovered in Venezuela; 1936-1946: France Nationalizes Its Banking and Industrial Sectors.

March 21, 1938
WHEELER-LEA ACT BROADENS FTC CONTROL OVER ADVERTISING

By adding jurisdiction over "unfair or deceptive acts or practices in commerce" to section 5 of the 1914 Federal Trade Commission Act, the U.S. Congress broadened the Federal Trade Commission's power over deceptive advertisers with the Wheeler-Lea Act.

LOCALE: Washington, D.C.

CATEGORIES: Laws, acts, and legal history; marketing and advertising

KEY FIGURES

Burton Kendall Wheeler (1882-1975), U.S. senator from Montana, 1923-1946

Clarence Frederick Lea (1874-1964), U.S. congressman from California, 1917-1949

Woodrow Wilson (1856-1924), president of the United States, 1913-1921

SUMMARY OF EVENT

The first decade of the twentieth century witnessed numerous investigations by the U.S. Department of Commerce into alleged monopolistic business practices in the farm equipment, petroleum, steel, and tobacco industries, among others. Two groups had evolved with differing viewpoints concerning antimonopoly and antitrust legislation. One group believed that all trusts should be abolished, whereas the other thought that Congress should instead establish mechanisms to regulate monopolistic practices. The latter thinking prevailed and led Congress to enact the Federal Trade Commission Act in 1914. The Federal Trade Commission (FTC) was activated the following year.

Many analysts trace the origins of the Federal Trade Commission to the advertising industry association known in the twenty-first century as the American Advertising Federation (AAF). In 1905, several local advertising clubs (primarily in Chicago, Cincinnati, Cleveland, Detroit, Indianapolis, and St. Louis) formed what became the Associated Advertising Clubs of the World, one of the goals of which was to eliminate the false and deceptive advertising practices that were common at the time. The association's 1912 truth-in-advertising campaign is generally credited as being the first of its kind, and its lobbying efforts eventually led to President Woodrow Wilson's recommendations in 1914 that the Federal Trade Commission be formed. The vigilance committees set up by member clubs in many cities also resulted in the establishment of the Council of Better Business Bureaus.

The Federal Trade Commission Act focused on protecting businesses from unfair trade practices on the part of competitors. The act did not specifically define unfair competition, leaving that determination up to the FTC on a case-by-case basis. Legislators may not have intended the FTC to have strong punitive powers, but rather to serve as a barrier to protect weaker businesses from the predatory behavior of monopolies. The FTC grew to police the activities of business in general, not simply monopolistic practices, and developed strong punitive capabilities.

The power to regulate advertising was given to the FTC under section 5 of the 1914 act. The wording of this section originally prohibited only unfair methods of "competition." This led to a 1931 U.S. Supreme Court decision that held that the commission was without jurisdiction unless actual injury to competitors could be proved. The case before the Court involved a questionable weight-reduction product that could have been dangerous for some consumers. The Court's decision seriously limited the FTC's power to intervene in cases in which consumers, but not competitors, were injured. Congress subsequently amended the FTC Act in 1938, thereby closing the loophole opened by this decision. This amending legislation is commonly known as the Wheeler-Lea Act, named for its two cosponsors, Senator Burton Kendall Wheeler and Congressman Clarence Frederick Lea.

At the federal level, the Wheeler-Lea Act gave the government its most important control over false and deceptive advertising. Section 5 of the FTC Act was amended to read, "Unfair methods of competition in commerce and unfair or deceptive acts or practices in commerce are hereby declared unlawful." The intent behind the Wheeler-Lea Act was twofold. First, Congress wanted to expand the FTC's jurisdiction over unfair competition by extending it into commerce as well as industry. Second, Congress intended to give the commission more power to regulate false and deceptive advertising of food, drugs, therapeutic devices, and cosmetics. The first objective was accomplished through the modification of section 5 as previously discussed. The second goal was reached through section 12(a) of the amended act, which made it illegal to disseminate false information concerning foods, drugs, therapeutic devices, or cosmetics for the purpose of inducing their purchase. No matter how incidental a marketer's behavior seems, the FTC has the authority to act if a false advertisement is

1938

3101

sent through the U.S. mail or is concerned with commerce. False advertising that violates section 12(a) is by default unfair and deceptive under section 5.

The definition of false advertising in section 15 of the Wheeler-Lea Act was designed to be very inclusive. The intent to be false or deceptive was not specified as a necessary element; legislators wanted any materially misleading advertising to be subject to or cause for FTC action, regardless of the advertiser's intent. Media and advertising agencies were exempted from liability if they cooperated with the agency's investigation.

Aggrieved competitors who have, for example, been directly named in what they consider to be a false or deceptive comparative advertising campaign have several options for resolution of the problem. They can complain to industry arbitration organizations such as the Better Business Bureau's National Advertising Division (NAD) and appeal an NAD decision to the National Advertising Review Board (NARB). They can ask for assistance from the media in which the questionable ads are disseminated or take the issue directly to court under section 43(a) of the Lanham Act. They can resort to local and state regulatory bodies (such as the state attorney general) or file a complaint with the FTC. The commission is also capable of issuing its own complaint under section 5, even if no business or individual has lodged a complaint.

Advertisers usually consent to stop running advertisements disputed by the FTC. If the FTC believes that an advertisement is false or deceptive but the sponsor refuses to sign a consent decree and stop using the ad, the commission can issue a cease-and-desist order requiring the advertiser to stop running the questionable campaign. Under section 5, cease-and-desist orders become final in sixty days unless the advertiser requests a court review. If the advertiser requests a hearing, the cease-and-desist order cannot become final until an administrative law judge has reviewed the case. If the order is upheld by the judge, the sponsor can appeal to the full commission. Advertisers who violate final cease-and-desist orders are subject to substantial fines.

The FTC can seek court remedies under sections 13 and 14 of the amended act. These include injunctions to stop the campaign in question as well as fines or imprisonment for sponsors of the advertisement in severe cases that involve blatant intent to defraud or reckless endangerment of consumers. In some cases, even though the FTC believed that section 12 had been violated, the courts have disagreed with the commission and denied requests for injunctions to stop ad campaigns.

SIGNIFICANCE

Largely because of the Wheeler-Lea Act, the core of the FTC's regulatory mission became its efforts to end deceptive advertising, although antitrust concerns still influence FTC policy. The aggressiveness with which the FTC is able to carry out its mission depends heavily on the philosophy of the FTC chairperson as well as the presidential administration's relationship with business. In some periods, such as the late 1960's, the agency has been perceived as weak and ineffective. With the Wheeler-Lea Act as a foundation, the FTC underwent major reorganization and staffing changes during the 1970's that resulted in a more powerful and effective regulatory force. In the 1980's, President Ronald Reagan's administration sought to disarm the FTC. In contrast, President George H. W. Bush indicated soon after his election in 1988 that the FTC's inactivity concerning advertising practices would not continue under chairperson Janet Steiger. Steiger stated that the FTC would begin to hold both advertisers and their agencies responsible for false and deceptive advertising and that the commission would be especially interested in tobacco and alcohol advertising that encouraged underage persons to purchase those products as well as the practice of disguising commercial messages as thirty-minute or longer news or interview programs, commonly called infomercials.

In spite of these inconsistencies, the FTC developed into a more powerful regulator of advertising after the implementation of the Wheeler-Lea Act in 1938. Two areas in which this trend has been most apparent are the commission's requirement for substantiation of claims made in ads and its use of forced corrective advertising to help counter false advertising claims. In the years since passage of the Wheeler-Lea Act, the FTC has asked that sponsors of numerous disputed claims offer proof that their claims were true, particularly since 1970. Product claims that are literally untrue (that is, cannot be proven in laboratory tests) are considered to be inherently deceptive. Claims are also judged according to how the average "rational" consumer will perceive them. The FTC often admits as evidence the results of consumer surveys designed to determine the perceptions of average consumers to the claims in question.

In a move considered to be much more drastic than requiring claim substantiation, the FTC also began to force sponsors of deceptive advertising to pay for corrective advertising disclaiming previously made false statements. For example, in one of the first corrective advertising cases, the FTC required the makers of Listerine mouthwash to include in a ten-million-dollar advertising campaign a disclaimer stating that the product does not kill germs that cause the common cold, as advertisements had previously claimed. The commission members believed that the false claim of cold prevention was a major reason consumers selected the Listerine brand and that the corrective advertising campaign was the best method for eliminating this misperception.

At first, the FTC required sponsors whose original campaigns had been ruled false and deceptive to disclose that fact. This generated criticism from those who believed the requirement was beyond the FTC's scope of remedial authority. The FTC took heed and later required sponsors only to disclose that, contrary to what their previous advertising had stated, the claim in question was not true. In addition, the FTC's original requirement that 25 percent of the advertisement's space or time be devoted to the corrective message was changed to 25 percent of advertising expenditures during the same period when other advertisements were run.

The FTC's call for corrective advertising is probably the single most controversial activity ultimately derived from the expanded power given to the agency through the Wheeler-Lea Act. Had the language of the original act not been modified, the commission would not have obtained the authority to require sponsors to run corrective advertising for the sake of consumers who had acquired false information.

—William T. Neese

FURTHER READING

Clarkson, Kenneth W., and Timothy J. Muris, eds. *The Federal Trade Commission Since 1970: Economic Regulation and Bureaucratic Behavior.* New York: Cambridge University Press, 1981. Presents a comprehensive analysis of the FTC during the 1970's. Very informative.

Digges, Isaac W. *The Modern Law of Advertising and Marketing.* New York: Funk & Wagnalls/Printers' Ink, 1948. Although dated, provides a useful description of the legal environment surrounding the practice of marketing and advertising in the United States prior to 1948.

Dillon, Tom. "What Is Deceptive Advertising?" *Journal of Advertising Research* 13 (October, 1973): 9-12. Presents an interesting view that contrasts with criticisms that the FTC had been ineffective because of its focus on trivial issues and the unfair practices of small businesses instead of national advertisers.

Garon, Philip A., ed. *Advertising Law Anthology.* Washington, D.C.: International Library, 1974. Collection of articles related to all aspects of advertising law. Of particular relevance are "The FTC Ad Substantiation Program," by T. H. Hoppock, and "Corrective Advertising: Theory and Cases," by G. J. Thain.

Kintner, Earl W. *A Primer on the Law of Deceptive Practices: A Guide for Business.* 2d ed. New York: Macmillan, 1978. Discusses the foundations on which the U.S. laws concerning unfair and deceptive business practices are based.

Lane, W. Ronald, Karen Whitehill King, and J. Thomas Russell. *Kleppner's Advertising Procedure.* 16th ed. Upper Saddle River, N.J.: Prentice Hall, 2004. Well-established advertising textbook designed for undergraduate classes in the principles of advertising. Contains updated information concerning all aspects of advertising, including excellent coverage of legal and regulatory issues.

Maronick, Thomas J. "Copy Tests in FTC Deception Cases: Guidelines for Researchers." *Journal of Advertising Research* 31 (December, 1991): 9-17. Provides guidelines for research used in FTC deceptive advertising disputes, based on three decades of FTC case studies.

Moore, Roy L., Ronald T. Farrar, and Erik L. Collins. *Advertising and Public Relations Law.* Mahwah, N.J.: Lawrence Erlbaum, 1998. Text intended for advertising students and practitioners includes chapters on the FTC and on deceptive advertising practices. Features useful appendixes and index.

Ulanoff, Stanley M. *Advertising in America.* New York: Hastings House, 1977. Relatively strong historical orientation sets this book apart from others. Although somewhat dated, sections related to legal and regulatory issues will be of interest to historians.

SEE ALSO: 1903: Scott Publishes *The Theory of Advertising*; 1913: Fuller Brush Company Is Incorporated; Aug., 1913: Advertisers Adopt a Truth-in-Advertising Code; July, 1920: Procter & Gamble Announces Plans to Sell Directly to Retailers; 1923: A. C. Nielsen Company Pioneers in Marketing and Media Research; 1926-1927: Mail-Order Clubs Revolutionize Book Sales.

1938

April, 1938
CERLETTI AND BINI USE ELECTROSHOCK TO TREAT SCHIZOPHRENIA

Ugo Cerletti and Lucino Bini were the first to introduce the idea of inducing convulsions for therapeutic purposes by using electric currents rather than convulsive drugs.

LOCALE: Münsingen, Switzerland

CATEGORIES: Health and medicine; psychology and psychiatry

KEY FIGURES

Ugo Cerletti (1877-1963), Italian professor of neuropathology and psychiatry

Lucino Bini (b. 1908), Italian clinician

Ladislas J. Meduna (1896-1964), Hungarian psychiatrist

SUMMARY OF EVENT

The history of somatic treatment procedures in psychiatry (specifically, the use of electric currents for therapeutic purposes) has never followed a linear course of development. It is recorded that in 46 C.E. Scribonius Largus used the discharge of a torpedo fish to cure headaches and gout; Romans used electric eels for similar purposes. In the sixteenth century, Ethiopians applied electric catfish to mentally ill patients for the purpose of expelling "demons" from the human body. The element that all these diverse organic methods of treating mental illness have in common is that they are based on the belief that psychiatric conditions, particularly psychoses, can be influenced therapeutically through nonpsychological methods.

The invention of electroconvulsive therapy (ECT) by Ugo Cerletti and Lucino Bini in 1937 was entirely unrelated to earlier investigations on treating mental illness through the use of electric currents. The use of ECT as a treatment for mental illness, rather, must be credited to the Hungarian psychiatrist Ladislas J. Meduna, who first recognized the therapeutic effect of generalized seizures when he induced convulsions with pharmacologic agents.

Much of Meduna's research was in the neuropathology of schizophrenia, in a school that maintained that schizophrenia was an incurable, endogenous (originating internally), hereditary disease in which cerebral neurons were preferentially attacked. Other mental syndromes, particularly epilepsy, were considered exogenous (originating externally) in origin, and hence

curable. Meduna's attempt to induce seizures in schizophrenics resulted from his hypothesis that there is a biological antagonism between the process that produces epileptic attacks and the process that produces schizophrenia. The effect of the epileptic convulsion is that it changes the chemical constituents in the organism in a way suitable for the cure of schizophrenia.

Consequently, in January of 1934, Meduna treated his first patient with intramuscular camphor in oil, causing the patient to have a seizure fifteen to twenty minutes after the injection. Meduna obtained the first remissions in schizophrenics with camphor in oil. He soon realized, however, that this technique was inconvenient because the patients convulsed only after considerable time, sometimes had more than one seizure, or did not convulse at all. He therefore replaced the camphor injections with intravenous pentylenetetrazol (Metrazol). The pharmacologic convulsive treatment with Metrazol, and some other convulsive drugs, was immediately recognized as a valuable treatment for schizophrenia and, as reported several years later, also for depression.

In 1936, Cerletti, in the Rome Clinic, adopted the Sakel method (named for its inventor, Manfred Sakel) of treating schizophrenia by means of insulin coma (insulin shock treatment). The following year, Cerletti and Bini replaced the pharmacological induction of seizures with induction by means of an electric current. It was a logical sequence to Meduna's discovery. In 1870, electricity was used in animal experiments concerning epilepsy, and it was found that electrical shock was the simplest way to induce seizures. Cerletti's involvement in such research was not treatment directed; rather, it was aimed at investigating problems of epilepsy. It was reasonable, then, that when Cerletti heard about Meduna's treatment, he wondered why electricity had not been used.

Cerletti expressed the enthusiastic opinion that "shock treatments" with insulin coma and Metrazol had changed psychiatry from a morbid science into a therapeutically active field, and he immediately developed an extensive research program to investigate electroconvulsive therapy. In his previous research on experimental epilepsy, Cerletti had induced seizures by applying the electrodes to the mouth and anus of dogs. His considerable hesitation about attempting this procedure in humans resulted from the fact that half of the dogs treated in this manner had died. Bini, however, realized that death was caused by the current traveling through the heart. Consequently, when the investigators changed the location of the electrodes to the two temples of the dogs, the heart was no longer within the electric circuit, and no further animals were killed.

It was Bini who had first reported on Cerletti's studies, at the First International Congress on New Treatments of Schizophrenia, in Münsingen, Switzerland, in 1937, after he heard that electrical current was being used in a Rome slaughterhouse. Bini and Cerletti, however, delayed the clinical application of the treatment and visited the slaughterhouse, where they found that the animals were not killed by means of the electric current but were only stunned with electrodes applied to the head. The animals convulsed, and the actual killing was done before they regained consciousness. After spending two years performing experimental neuropathological studies to rule out brain damage and finding that neither the dogs nor other animals succumbed to the electrically induced convulsions, the researchers considered it safe to proceed with the first application of electroconvulsive therapy to human beings.

The first patient was treated in April, 1938, with a very primitive machine constructed by Bini. Cerletti's understandable fear of allowing Bini to proceed with the treatment explains why, at first, a minimal amount of eighty volts for one-tenth of a second was applied. Although the application of this voltage led to a short period of unconsciousness, no seizure resulted. A second stimulus of ninety volts for one-tenth of a second led to a somewhat longer "petit mal" (small seizure). After a minute, the patient awakened and began to sing a popular song. When the doctors discussed the prudence of a third stimulus, the patient unemotionally uttered something about dying but did not object to a third, stronger application, which led to a generalized seizure. The patient, a completely incoherent schizophrenic who had not been able to give his physicians any information about himself, received a total of nine treatments. During the two-year period of follow-up treatments, he was leading a normal life and maintained a job as a skilled worker.

After clinical application of electroconvulsive therapy had begun, Cerletti organized a detailed research program, giving assignments to the different members of his staff. Cerletti and Bini published the findings of this program in a monograph (in Italian) in 1942. In that publication, they answered many important questions concerning the procedure, but the monograph remained unknown in American psychiatric literature. Later, Cerletti gave two accounts of his work in English, in 1950 and 1956. These accounts, however, were partly distorted by Cerletti's belief that the injection of the brain substance of electroshocked animals into psychiatric patients would eliminate the need for convulsions. He assumed that repeated seizures in animals produced a substance in their brains that he called "acroagonine." Cerletti found that injections of such brain substances also increased the resistance of animals to certain infections. In psychotics, some improvement in affect (emotion) and anxiety was seen, but overall the results of this indirect method to reproduce the therapeutic effect of electroconvulsive therapy remained unsatisfactory.

Cerletti continued his research attempts to improve the electroconvulsive treatment techniques and to understand exactly how the treatment worked. He determined that the cerebral seizure was essential to the clinical results and that neither the currents used to elicit a seizure nor the motor aspects of the convulsion were significant. Anticipating some of the later interest in the hormonal effects of seizures, in 1956 Cerletti suggested that part of the vegetative syndrome induced by electroshock was localized in the diencephalic section of the cerebrospinal axis. Unfortunately, Cerletti never determined electroconvulsive therapy's exact mode of action.

SIGNIFICANCE

The development of electroconvulsive therapy had an immediate impact on the psychiatric community. In the late 1930's and early 1940's, the new therapy demonstrated by Cerletti and Bini largely replaced pharmacologic convulsive treatment. Moreover, following initial reports of the value of convulsive therapy in the treatment of affective disorders as well as schizophrenia, ECT became the most widely used organic therapy in psychiatry during the years immediately preceding and following World War II. Interest in the convulsive therapies increased with the demands of war. Many physicians were trained in clinical psychiatry by the military, and the convulsive therapies were a significant part of their education as well as their military clinical experience. When patients failed to respond to one therapy, insulin coma and seizure therapy were combined. Some physicians increased the number and frequency of seizure inductions and found positive results—particularly in schizophrenia—to be related to number and frequency of seizures.

The use of electroconvulsive therapy soon began to have a negative impact on some members of the psychiatric community, however. As the side effects of shock therapy as well as prefrontal lobotomy (another organic treatment developed at about the same time as shock therapy and largely used to treat the same disorders) came to be more and more recognized, many maintained that the cure did more harm than the disease. By 1946, accusations of random and/or indiscriminate use of these techniques on patients (to deal with anything from homosexuality to psoriasis) questioned the effectiveness of these organic methods. At that time, the American Group for the Advancement of Psychiatry issued a statement declaring that widespread and dangerous abuses in the use of ECT justified a campaign of professional education in the limitations of the technique and the institution of certain measures of control. In 1978, a task force of the American Psychiatric Association published a report of their findings on electroconvulsive therapy's effectiveness.

By the 1950's, psychotropic drugs had all but replaced electroconvulsive therapy in the treatment of schizophrenia. The efficacy of tricyclic antidepressant drugs, the monamine oxidase inhibitors, stimulants, and lithium in depressive and manic disorders further reduced the interest in and use of ECT. Consequently, many ECT facilities were closed, and it was only in the mid-1960's, as the limitations of the antidepressant drug therapies were recognized, that interest in this form of treatment was rekindled.

Once again, however, a gradual decline in the use of the convulsive therapies occurred, although some scientists continued their studies in reduced numbers. Much research was devoted to understanding the seizure process and improving its safety. The usefulness of intensive treatments in severely ill schizophrenics was reexamined, with follow-up studies finding that those who received intensive treatments exhibited better results in residual symptoms, work records, and rehospitalization rates than did those treated with pharmacotherapy alone.

Whereas insulin coma was virtually abandoned, electroconvulsive therapy continued to be used. Nevertheless, growing concern that ECT may cause irreparable damage to the brain and that its use may contravene or deny patients' rights to decide knowingly what is done to them led to judicial and legislative challenges to its use, as exemplified by the virtual ban the state of California placed on its use in 1974. Similar concerns voiced in England, Scandinavia, and Holland resulted in additional evaluations.

Ultimately, with improved equipment and techniques of treatment, clarification of the indications, and better education, the incidence of adverse reactions declined. Moreover, some researchers in the early twenty-first century believe that the legacy of this once-experimental psychiatric treatment may eventually lead to a better understanding of brain function and behavior.

—*Genevieve Slomski*

FURTHER READING

Abrams, Richard. *Electroconvulsive Therapy.* 4th ed. New York: Oxford University Press, 2002. Standard reference work on the subject covers the biological foundations and clinical applications of the procedure, reflecting state-of-the-art technology. Informative chapter on the history of convulsive therapy highlights the work of Cerletti and Bini. Includes bibliography.

Breggin, Peter R. *Electroshock: Its Brain-Disabling Effects.* New York: Springer, 1979. Informative work describes the adverse effects of electroconvulsive therapy (including brain damage) and notes the uses and potential abuses of this form of therapy. Accessible to lay readers as well as clinicians.

Cerletti, Ugo. "Old and New Information About Electroshock." *American Journal of Psychiatry* 107 (1950): 87-94. Article by one of the coinventors of electroshock therapy presents a history of the origin of this practice, offers a firsthand account of the invention, and discusses the first ten years of its application.

Fink, Max. *Electroshock: Restoring the Mind.* New York: Oxford University Press, 1999. Explains the use and efficacy of electroconvulsive therapy in the treatment of psychiatric disorders. Also presents a brief history of ECT. Includes comprehensive bibliography and index.

Kalinowsky, Lothar, and Paul H. Hoch. *Shock Treatments, Psychosurgery, and Other Somatic Treatments in Psychiatry.* 2d ed. New York: Grune & Stratton, 1952. Lengthy and rather dated work devoted to the organic treatment of psychiatric disorders includes a useful chapter on the historical development of treatment procedures that includes much information on Cerletti and Bini's work.

SEE ALSO: Nov.-Dec., 1935: Egas Moniz Develops the Prefrontal Lobotomy.

April 5, 1938
BALLET RUSSE DE MONTE CARLO DEBUTS

French critic René Blum and Russian impresario Sergei Denham joined in managing the new company Ballet Russe de Monte Carlo, which helped to popularize ballet in the United States through its frequent touring.

LOCALE: New York, New York
CATEGORY: Dance

KEY FIGURES
René Blum (1884-1944), French impresario and art critic who took over the management of Sergei Diaghilev's Ballets Russes, eventually renaming it the Ballet Russe de Monte Carlo
Sergei Denham (1897-1970), Russian impresario whose direction of the Ballet Russe de Monte Carlo helped to popularize ballet in the United States
Léonide Massine (1895-1979), French dancer originally from the Diaghilev company who served as the widely acclaimed choreographer for the Ballet Russe de Monte Carlo
Wassili de Basil (1888-1951), Cossack colonel who briefly joined Blum in leading the Ballet Russe de Monte Carlo
Michel Fokine (1880-1942), Russian choreographer whose revolutionary ideas about dance helped to modernize ballet
George Balanchine (1904-1983), Russian choreographer who contributed works to the Ballet Russe de Monte Carlo before beginning a long association with the New York City Ballet

SUMMARY OF EVENT
The Ballet Russe de Monte Carlo, aggressively promoted as "The One and Only," was synonymous with glamorous stars, sumptuous decor, and brilliant dancing for nearly a quarter of a century. An itinerant company with roots torn by war and internal intrigue, the Ballet Russe adopted an accessible approach in its dealings with the American public. Rather than being elitist, inapproachable bearers of high art, the company infiltrated remote corners of the United States, appearing in high school auditoriums as well as big-city opera houses. The Ballet Russe de Monte Carlo created a mass audience for ballet with success unmatched by fledgling American companies during the same period. Its contribution to the evolution of twentieth century theatrical dance is extremely significant.

Beginning in 1938, impresarios René Blum and Sergei Denham together guided the group's progress. Blum, formerly Monte Carlo Opera Ballet's director, managed the remains of Sergei Diaghilev's legendary Ballets Russes after Diaghilev's death in 1929. Denham, a Russian banker transplanted to New York, was vice president of a sponsoring organization called Universal Art (formerly known as World Art). This organization wished to assemble a new company for French choreographer Léonide Massine. Denham turned to Blum.

For roughly forty thousand dollars, Blum sold the rights to the valuable Monte Carlo name and elements of the Diaghilev repertory to Universal Art (which was backed by millionaire Julius Fleischmann). By arrangement, the Ballets Russes continued its annual spring season in Monte Carlo and its U.S. touring under Universal's management and financial support. Denham assumed the role of business director of the company—renamed Ballet Russe de Monte Carlo—while Blum remained its artistic director and Massine its choreographer and principal dancer. (In fact, to Blum's chagrin, the company was widely known as Massine's Ballet Russe.) The company's debut performance was given on April 5, 1938, in Monte Carlo, and on October 12, 1938, the company first appeared in New York City.

The Ballet Russe de Monte Carlo led by Blum, Denham, and Massine was one in a series of incarnations of the Ballet Russe name. The success of Blum and Denham's partnership followed the deterioration of Blum's earlier efforts to preserve the legendary company created by Diaghilev. Blum initially assumed direction of the Ballets Russes in the country of its patron, the prince of Monaco. In 1932, Russian Colonel Wassili de Basil joined him in his efforts to salvage the dissipated Diaghilev spirit. With new ballets by George Balanchine and Massine, this earlier company created a sensation during its tours of Europe and, in 1933, of the United States.

Blum and de Basil proved incompatible as partners, however. They split the group into two separate enterprises in 1936 with great hostility, dividing repertory, trademarks, costumes, and even dancers. Thriving on intrigue and confusion, de Basil changed the name of his reorganized company six times in less than eight years. Common appellations were "De Basil's Ballet Russe" and the "Original Ballet Russe." Litigation over rights of ownership to the ballets continued into the late 1940's, as did the rivalry between the two companies. These so-called Ballet Wars, often fought across continents, generated tremendous publicity. Newspapers from Europe to the Americas carried frequent updates on the squabbles and traced the dancers' shifting loyalties.

Indeed, in addition to the exotic company name, the star appeal of the dancers in Blum and Denham's company was crucial to its popularity. At its inception, the Ballet Russe de Monte Carlo took with it or hired such foreign favorites as Alexandra Danilova, Alicia Markova, Eugenie Delarova, Mia Slavenska, Tamara Toumanova, Serge Lifar, Michel Panieff, Marc Platoff, and Frederic Franklin. Among those lost to de Basil were premier danseur David Lichine and "baby ballerinas" (Balanchine's prodigies) Tatiana Riabouchinska and Irina Baronova.

Both Ballet Russe companies continued to tour Europe and North and South America with immense, if independent, success. The partnership undertaken by Blum and Denham ushered in golden years for the new Ballet Russe de Monte Carlo, and their travels took them from New York to Boston, Toronto, Los Angeles, Kansas City, and Seattle. The company was met by welcoming audiences, impressive box-office returns, and daily reviews. Many historians recall that theaters advertised "standing room only" as much as a month before the company's arrival in a given town.

Although the Ballet Russe was officially headquartered in Monte Carlo, the company became a permanent fixture at New York's Metropolitan Opera House as a result of the onset of World War II in 1939. With European tours impossible, the company performed frequently throughout the United States and Canada. Furthermore, when new Russian dancers became unavailable, Blum and Denham began to hire Americans. Many of them, seeking a share of the company's alluring image, at first adopted Russian stage names.

Although many of his previous works were retained by de Basil through court action, Massine created new choreographic masterpieces for the Ballet Russe de Monte Carlo. Favoring the avant-garde and the surreal, Massine often commissioned modern artists such as Henri Matisse and Salvador Dalí to create the decor for his ballets. The company came to be associated with colorful, flamboyant, even outrageous results. Blum and Denham employed the Diaghilev formula for an evening's concert: They presented three or four stylistically or thematically different ballets on one program. One critic compared the Ballet Russe to a three-ring circus in which an audience could pick its pleasure from a variety of interesting acts. Entertainment value aside, the com-

pany's repertoire was the subject of serious and intense scrutiny by patrons who were beginning to gain a critical understanding of ballet.

Despite its continued success, the Ballet Russe de Monte Carlo soon faced new political and artistic realities. The horrifying state of affairs in Europe dealt a severe blow to the dance company in the United States. Many dancers worried about family members overseas, and some even joined the armed forces. Most distressingly, while his company was touring the United States in 1943, Blum tragically decided to visit France instead. He was arrested by Nazi police in December and sent to the concentration camp at Auschwitz, where he died nine months later.

The prewar glamour of the Ballet Russe, replete with its images of Russian exoticism, started to fade. Indeed, external upheaval seemed to coincide with a change in the company's internal artistic philosophy. The new

Portrait of Léonide Massine by artist and theatrical designer Léon Bakst.

modern dance was rising to the forefront of American stages, as choreographers such as Martha Graham and Doris Humphrey sought to translate into movement the emotion of inherently national or personal themes. For example, dances were created about the Great Depression and unemployment, and about the American frontier, freedom, and equality. Denham responded to this outside impetus by inviting the young American dancer Agnes de Mille to create a work for the Ballet Russe in 1942. The result was *Rodeo*, a spirited depiction of ranch life in the American West.

Massine stayed with the group until 1943, when he left to form yet another offshoot company, Ballet Russe Highlights. Denham then appealed to Balanchine to rejuvenate his company. In contrast with the idiosyncratic ballets of Massine, Balanchine composed "neoclassic" ballets that were closely related to their music and structurally complex. He remained with the company until 1946, when he left to join Lincoln Kirstein in the formation of Ballet Society. These initial years of the Ballet Russe de Monte Carlo, guided by Blum and Denham with artistic direction by Massine and Balanchine, were profoundly instrumental in raising the American public's interest in the art of ballet.

SIGNIFICANCE

Blum and Denham's Ballet Russe de Monte Carlo made the United States excited about ballet. This was no small achievement, as the country was only slowly gaining an understanding of dance as legitimate entertainment and even art. The way had been paved by the frequent tours of Anna Pavlova's company and Diaghilev's Ballets Russes in the 1910's and 1920's. These dancers introduced the United States to the glamour and artistry of a European and Russian tradition that, until their visits, was mostly unfamiliar to Americans. The Ballet Russe de Monte Carlo capitalized on that earlier introduction, performing often enough to help a mass audience cultivate its tastes and emerging aesthetic values. The Ballet Russe's greatest asset was its familiarity to the public and its recognizable brand of showmanship.

Under Blum and Denham, the company preserved the Diaghilev mystique and kept the lauded Russian tradition before a starstruck public's eye. In so doing, however, it reinforced the notion that ballet was essentially a Russian art form. While some considered this a negative influence, it had the positive effect of elevating artistic standards for rising national and regional groups that struggled to compete with the Ballet Russe's established fame. Regardless of its international orientation, the Bal-

let Russe de Monte Carlo helped to establish ballet on a permanent, professional basis in the United States.

Probably the best-known choreographer of the decade, Massine created some of his finest pieces for the Ballet Russe de Monte Carlo. *Gaîté Parisienne*, which premiered in 1938, featured fun-loving cancan dancers and madcap waiters in a Paris music hall. Massine also produced a 1930's series of notable symphonic ballets set to the music of such composers as Hector Berlioz, Ludwig van Beethoven, and Johannes Brahms. *Rouge et Noir* (1939), with music by Dmitri Shostakovich, incorporated color-drenched settings and costumes by Matisse. Described as "a vast mural in motion," the ballet was a discordant allegory representing the forces of destiny in shaping a man's life.

De Mille made a different kind of contribution to the Ballet Russe de Monte Carlo, affecting both the company and its audiences. *Rodeo*, which premiered to dozens of curtain calls, was the Ballet Russe's first major attempt to incorporate American themes (although Massine had tried to do this on several occasions as well). *Rodeo* also employed an American composer, Aaron Copland, and American designer Oliver Smith.

Depicting a naïve cowgirl's fervent crush on a Kansas City cowboy, *Rodeo* was based on a realistic theme and believable characters—a true departure from the traditional ballet fantasies of swans, princes, and spirits. That this tribute to life in the United States could find success in the repertory of the Ballet Russe signified a new era in the company's history and the growing popularity of ballet as an American art form.

For his part, Balanchine brought an extensive repertory with him to the Ballet Russe de Monte Carlo. Among them were older works such as *Mozartiana* (1933) and *Serenade* (1935); recent works, including the 1941 *Concerto barocco* (created for another fledgling company, the American Ballet); and new works, such as *Danses concertantes* (1944), choreographed especially for the Ballet Russe. Over the next two decades, choreographers such as Frederick Ashton, Ruth Page, Ruthanna Boris, and Bronislava Nijinska added works to the repertory as well.

The Ballet Russe was certainly not the only group competing for audiences' attention. Often the company appeared in the same city or even the same theater with Kirstein's Ballet Caravan, a company that overtly attempted a nationalistic outlook. In other instances, the repertory of Blum and Denham's group overlapped with Colonel de Basil's Original Ballet. In their last parallel season, 1940-1941, the two companies both boasted versions of *Giselle*, *L'Après-midi d'un faune*, *Petrushka*, *Swan Lake*, and *Schéhérazade*. Presenter Sol Hurok, who then managed both Ballet Russe groups, ignored the coincidence because tickets continued to sell. Quite possibly, audiences did not distinguish between the two companies with similar names and repertoire; on the other hand, the presence and popularity of one company probably enhanced that of the other.

Under Denham's guidance, the Ballet Russe de Monte Carlo remained active until 1962 (roughly a decade longer than de Basil's group). During that time, it became an essentially American company, both in its travels and in its repertory. It partly preserved the spirit of the Diaghilev legend while absorbing some of the qualities of its new homeland in the process. Although after Massine's and then Balanchine's departure the company lacked definite artistic coherence, its very existence helped the American public to make (as one dancer remarked) "a habit out of art."

—Alecia C. Townsend

FURTHER READING

Amberg, George. *Ballet in America*. New York: Duell, Sloan & Pearce, 1949. An older publication that provides three detailed chapters on the succession of companies called the Ballet Russe. All are useful; Blum and Denham's group is discussed in a chapter titled "The Ballet Russe II: Massine's Ballet Russe." Appendix provides a comprehensive list of the company's repertoire.

Anderson, Jack. *The One and Only: The Ballet Russe de Monte Carlo*. New York: Hudson Hills Press, 2003. An excellent resource. Traces the company through birth, reorganization, and final performances. Contains well-researched information, extensive notes, rosters of repertoire and dancers, and important primary-source material.

Clarke, Mary, and Clement Crisp. "History of Ballet: Twentieth Century." In *The History of Dance*. New York: Crown, 1981. While this attempts to cover an obviously enormous topic in a comparatively small number of pages, it provides a helpful chronological sequence of developments in the art of ballet. The origins of the Ballet Russe and its implications are discussed in detail. Good for putting the company into the context of the history of dance.

Massine, Léonide. *My Life in Ballet*. Edited by Phyllis Hartnoll. New York: St. Martin's Press, 1968. A complex autobiography of the choreographer, with heavy emphasis on descriptions of works. The influence of Sergei Diaghilev on the author is stressed. Contains a catalog of ballets organized alphabetically.

Maynard, Olga. "The Companies: Ballet Russe de Monte Carlo." In *The American Ballet*. Philadelphia: Macrae Smith, 1959. A look at the evolution of theatrical dance in the United States, with a section devoted to Blum and Denham's Ballet Russe. Describes company history, repertory, and dancers in detail.

Stowitts, H. J., and Anne Holiday. *Najinski Dancing! From the Golden Age of the Ballet Russe*. Pacific Grove, Calif.: Park Place, 1996. A catalog from an art exhibition featuring images of Vaslav Najinski, one of the Ballet Russe's most famous dancers. No index.

SEE ALSO: Dec. 22, 1907: Pavlova Performs *The Dying Swan*; May 19, 1909: Diaghilev's Ballets Russes Astounds Paris; June 2, 1909: Fokine's *Les Sylphides* Introduces Abstract Ballet; June 25, 1910: *The Firebird* Premieres in Paris; Dec. 6, 1934: Balanchine's *Serenade* Inaugurates American Ballet.

May 26, 1938
HUAC IS ESTABLISHED

The House Un-American Activities Committee launched a crusade against subversive activity in the U.S. government, spreading its investigations to include unions, educational institutions, and the media. The committee came in later years to be a symbol of political intolerance, repression, and abuse of civil liberties by the government.

ALSO KNOWN AS: Dies Committee; House Special Committee on Un-American Activities; House Un-American Activities Committee
LOCALE: Washington, D.C.
CATEGORIES: Government and politics; civil rights and liberties; laws, acts, and legal history

KEY FIGURES

Martin Dies, Jr. (1900-1972), U.S. representative from Texas, 1931-1944, 1953-1958
J. Parnell Thomas (1895-1970), U.S. representative from New Jersey, 1937-1950
Samuel Dickstein (1885-1954), U.S. representative from New York, 1923-1946
J. Edgar Hoover (1895-1972), director of the Federal Bureau of Investigation, 1924-1972
Robert M. La Follette, Jr. (1895-1953), U.S. senator from Wisconsin, 1925-1946
John P. Frey (1871-1957), president of the Metal Trades Department of the American Federation of Labor
Harry Hopkins (1890-1946), adviser to President Franklin D. Roosevelt
Harold Ickes (1874-1952), U.S. secretary of the interior, 1933-1946
Frances Perkins (1882-1965), U.S. secretary of labor, 1933-1945

SUMMARY OF EVENT

Inspired by the failure of the country to emerge from the Great Depression, the ebbing of the New Deal, the reemergence of the Republican Party in the electoral process, the successful growth of trade unionism, and the uneasiness of international political affairs, loyalty probes by the U.S. Congress started to take center stage during the late 1930's in a delicate political process. Attempting to expose real and perceived conspiracies, a congressional committee was organized to investigate the affairs of individuals and groups who, it was alleged, were engaged in attempts to overthrow the existing so-

cial and political order of the nation. On May 26, 1938, the House Special Committee on Un-American Activities, popularly known as the House Un-American Activities Committee (HUAC), chaired by conservative Democrat Martin Dies, Jr., of Texas, was established. In June, the committee began hearings to seek out subversive activities against the government of the United States. Members of the committee included Democrats John J. Dempsey of New Mexico, Samuel Dickstein of New York, and Joe Starnes of Alabama and Republicans Noah M. Mason of Illinois, Harold G. Mosier of Ohio, and J. Parnell Thomas of New Jersey.

The committee was created for the purpose of uncovering fascist subversion, particularly Nazi spies and collaborators among the Ku Klux Klan, German American organizations, and other groups with pro-German, fascist, or Aryan leanings. HUAC did very little in this regard. Instead, the committee quickly changed its focus to the other end of the political spectrum, choosing to ferret out communist, rather than fascist, activity. In the light of this change of focus, first on HUAC's list for investigation were the Federal Theatre Project and the Federal Writers' Project. Born in New Deal legislation, these programs became early targets for Republican strategists in the congressional electoral campaigns of the late 1930's. Representative Thomas led the way, determining that evidence received from committee investigators clearly indicated that the Federal Theatre Project was a branch of the Communist Party. Actual evidence in support of the specific allegations against the project failed to materialize.

Next, HUAC investigated labor unions. Testifying before the committee, John P. Frey, president of the Metal Trades Department of the American Federation of Labor (AFL), accused all but one member of the leadership of the Congress of Industrial Organizations (CIO), a rival labor organization, of being either members of the Communist Party or sympathetic to its cause. Only John L. Lewis, president of the United Mine Workers, was exempted from this charge. Regardless of the accusations, no cross-examination of the witness took place and no subpoenas against those accused were issued. Charges were made in the presence of a supportive gallery of witnesses. Frey's indictment of the CIO leadership later was amended to state that the rank and file of the union were not being accused, only its leadership. Newspapers elaborated Frey's charges. By the end of his testimony, 280

1938

Martin Dies, Jr., chairman of the House Un-American Activities Committee, addresses the general conference of the Methodist Church in Atlantic City, New Jersey, in April, 1940. (AP/Wide World Photos)

CIO union leaders had been charged with Communist activity. In only a few cases was there any corroborating material to support the allegations.

Walter S. Steele of the *National Republic*, chairman of the American Coalition Committee on National Security, claimed to have documented evidence that more than 6.5 million Americans were engaged in conspiratorial activities against the government of the United States. Steele did not have to support his claim. By the end of the committee's first hearings, 640 separate groups, 483 newspapers, and 280 labor unions had been labeled as Communist organizations.

Included in the list of accused organizations was the American Civil Liberties Union (ACLU), which had recently been involved in the Senate Civil Liberties Committee hearings. The Senate's committee had been organized by Robert M. La Follette, Jr., to investigate official abuses of civil rights in trade union organizing activities during the decade. According to HUAC, both the Senate Committee and the ACLU had fallen under the influence of the Communist Party. Other groups receiving HUAC's ire were pacifist organizations, which were seen as dupes of the Communist conspiracy; the media, which, according to the committee, supported trade unionism at the ex-

pense of business; and institutions of higher education, which the committee said were rife with Communists and radicals encouraging racial strife and antifascist activities. The motion-picture industry received special attention; accusations against screen stars and writers such as James Cagney, Clark Gable, Dorothy Parker, Robert Taylor, and Shirley Temple were written into the records.

Despite HUAC's assurances that all those accused would be given a chance to clear their names, only a small number received that opportunity. Writer Heywood Broun read a prepared statement and then was asked to leave. Between June and October, witness after witness was paraded before the committee, supporting the idea that there were Communists in government positions, higher education, the media, and labor. By the November elections, public opinion had become divided on some of the committee's methods but not on the idea that there was a role for the committee in government.

Dies's attack on Communists eventually led to his attack on trade unionism, civil rights movements, and liberal agendas in general. He called for the resignation of government officials with whom he disagreed, such as Harry Hopkins, Harold Ickes, and Frances Perkins. His accusations that there were thousands upon thousands of Communists in the federal government conspired against New Deal programs and personalities alike. In his book *The Trojan Horse* (1940), Dies institutionalized the idea that Communism was an organized fifth column that had brought on the Great Depression and made President Franklin D. Roosevelt's New Deal its tool. He went on to accuse the president's wife, Eleanor, of being the Communist Party's most valuable asset in Washington, D.C. Once again, no evidence of these accusations ever materialized.

SIGNIFICANCE

HUAC's charges changed the nation's legislative agenda. The Republican Party's success in the 1938 election, its first major success in almost a decade, brought down New Dealers such as Michigan and Wisconsin governors Frank Murphy and Philip La Follette. At the national level, eight new Republican senators and eighty-eight new Republican members of the House of Representatives helped point to the facts not only that the New Deal was in trouble but also that there was a perceived need for government to ferret out subversives in the United States.

Despite Roosevelt's support, the Senate Civil Liberties Committee came to an end in 1940, after only four years in operation. On the other hand, HUAC went on for another thirty-five years. Dies's initial confrontation with those on the political left helped lay the groundwork for the killing of the Senate's committee by helping to elect those who would support the loss of its funding. Dies's committee also laid the foundation for the evolution of the McCarthy hearings of the 1950's and for government police operations such as the Counterintelligence Program (COINTELPRO) of the 1960's and 1970's.

Dies set up the rules for official government action that, in the end, ruined lives and careers, denied due process of law to those accused, and insinuated guilt by association. In the process, his committee produced a thorough challenge to the democracy it was attempting to protect. Although HUAC has a deeply entrenched reputation as being antidemocratic in itself, historians can now see that the underlying concern of the committee was not unfounded. More widespread scholarly access to Soviet-era documents became possible with the opening of the Soviet archives in the early 1990's, and evidence in those documents revealed that the Soviet Union had a substantial espionage program in the United States involving high-level U.S. government officials, including the cofounder and vice chairman of HUAC, Samuel Dickstein, who was paid $1,250 per month by the Soviet Union's People's Commissariat for Internal Affairs (NKVD) between 1937 and 1940. At the same time, it has since become an established principle of common law that the First Amendment right to assembly protects the right of American citizens to belong to the Communist Party, and persecuting citizens for their membership in the party is therefore unconstitutional.

—Thomas J. Edward Walker,
Cynthia Gwynne Yaudes, and Ruby L. Stoner

FURTHER READING

Bentley, Eric, ed. *Thirty Years of Treason: Excerpts from Hearings Before the House Committee on Un-American Activities, 1938-1968.* New York: Viking, 1971. At times hilarious and at other times sobering, this volume remains the best introduction to the things said and done in HUAC's name.

Dies, Martin. *Martin Dies' Story.* New York: Book-mailer, 1963. The memoir of the man who set the committee's tone and tact. Provides personal insight into Dies's life. Includes informative appendixes.

_____. *The Trojan Horse in America.* New York: Dodd, Mead, 1940. Dies's summary of the subversive threat posed by communists and native fascists.

Goodman, Walter. *The Committee: The Extraordinary Career of the House Committee on Un-American Activities.* New York: Farrar, Straus and Giroux, 1968. Written in a lively, journalistic style, this is the standard history of HUAC's first thirty years. Goodman criticizes both the committee, for its inquisitorial and sensationalist style, and the investigated, for their dissident politics and confrontational posturing.

Navasky, Victor. *Naming Names.* New York: Viking, 1980. This self-described moral detective story investigates HUAC in Hollywood and the difficult choices faced by those who received committee subpoenas.

Ogden, August Raymond. *The Dies Committee: A Study of the Special House Committee for the Investigation of Un-American Activities, 1938-1944.* Washington, D.C.: Catholic University of America Press, 1945. Discusses the antecedents of the committee, its formation, and its process of investigation.

O'Reilly, Kenneth. *Hoover and the Un-Americans: The FBI, HUAC, and the Red Menace.* Philadelphia: Temple University Press, 1983. Based on thousands of FBI and other government agency files obtained under the Freedom of Information Act, this book explores the on-again/off-again relationship between the FBI and HUAC. Particular emphasis is placed on the ways in which HUAC publicized information from FBI files on dissident individuals and groups.

Redish, Martin H. *The Logic of Persecution: Free Expression and the McCarthy Era.* Stanford, Calif.: Stanford University Press, 2005. An examination of the anti-Communist hysteria of the 1940's and 1950's. Includes a chapter on HUAC and the committee's investigation of Hollywood. Bibliographic references and index.

Schultz, Bud, and Ruth Schultz. *The Price of Dissent: Testimonies to Political Repression in America.* Berkeley: University of California Press, 2001. Includes two essays on HUAC by Dagmar Wilson and Abbie Hoffman, alongside many other essays on the history of the organized repression of dissent in the United States. Bibliographic references and index.

1938

Sexton, Patricia Cayo. *The War on Labor and the Left: Understanding America's Unique Conservatism.* Boulder, Colo.: Westview Press, 1991. Analyzes how the use of power has evolved in government and legal institutions, economic policies, and the media.

SEE ALSO: Jan. 19, 1920: American Civil Liberties Union Is Founded; Feb. 28, 1933: Perkins Becomes First Woman Secretary of Labor; Aug. 29, 1935-June 30, 1939: Federal Theatre Project Promotes Live Theater.

June 7, 1938
CHINESE FORCES BREAK YELLOW RIVER LEVEES

In an attempt to halt the Japanese invasion, Chinese forces breached levees along the Huang River (also known as the Yellow River). The resulting flood did not significantly aid the Chinese military, and although casualties from the flooding itself were not large, disease and famine afterward caused an estimated 890,000 deaths.

ALSO KNOWN AS: Huang River
LOCALE: Huang River, China
CATEGORIES: Disasters; military history; wars, uprisings, and civil unrest

KEY FIGURES

Chiang Kai-shek (1887-1975), leader of the Nationalist Chinese forces
Shang Chen (1887-1978), Chinese general whose troops carried out the breaching of the Huang levees
Hisaichi Terauchi (1879-1946), Japanese general who commanded advancing troops at the levees

SUMMARY OF EVENT

After oil pipelines were opened into the Persian Gulf and oil wells set on fire during the Persian Gulf War of 1991, many commentators asserted that a new kind of warfare had emerged: environmental warfare. On the contrary, however, environmental warfare is very ancient: Armies have modified the environment to achieve their own objectives or hinder the enemy for centuries. In the summer of 1938, the Chinese army committed perhaps the largest act of environmental warfare in history by breaching the levees of the Huang River (long known in the West as the Yellow River) to hinder the advancing Japanese army. The resulting floods slowed the Japanese and drowned some of their troops, but at the cost of hundreds of thousands of Chinese lives.

The Huang originates in west-central China. After it exits the highlands about 400 kilometers from the coast, it flows across a gently sloping, coastal plain to the sea. The Huang is the most sediment-laden large river in the

world, and the north China coastal plain is essentially like a vast alluvial fan; the Huang periodically jumps to a new path when its current channel becomes filled with silt. In the last twenty-five hundred years, historical records show dozens of diversions. In recent millennia, the river has followed two main courses. One, the present course, runs northeast and empties north of the Shandong Peninsula; the other empties south of the peninsula. Because the floodplain has a very gentle slope and is densely populated, floods throughout history have caused staggering loss of life. Many deaths were due to disease and starvation rather than drowning.

The war that caused the 1938 disaster was the result of a long-running campaign by Japan to expand its power at China's expense. Japan had occupied Korea, and following a short war (the First Sino-Japanese War, 1894-1895), China was forced to cede Taiwan to Japan in 1895. In 1931, following a bombing that many historians suspect was staged as a pretext for invasion, Japan invaded Manchuria and in 1932 set up the puppet state of Manchukuo. Over the next few years, the Japanese nibbled away at the frontiers of China, and by 1937, the limits of Japanese occupation hemmed in Beijing on the west, north, and east. In July, 1937, clashes at the only remaining bridge linking Beijing to the rest of China escalated into outright invasion, and the Second Sino-Japanese War began. Beijing was occupied on August 18. By the end of 1937, Japanese forces had occupied the coastal plain north of the Huang. In addition, Japan attacked Shanghai in mid-August, although it took until November to conquer the city. In December, Japanese forces moved inland and captured Nanjing as well.

In the spring of 1938, Japanese forces invaded the coastal plain south of the Huang and attacked the city of Xuzhou. Although at one point Chinese forces won their first major victory and forced a large Japanese force to retreat, the overall campaign was a victory for Japan, and Chinese forces retreated to the west. By June, Japanese forces commanded by Hisaichi Terauchi threatened to capture Zhengzhou, a strategic rail junction. His Chinese opponent Shang Chen was one of the ablest Chinese commanders, but he was unable to halt the Japanese advance. On June 8, press reports announced that Chiang Kai-shek had ordered the breaching of the levees along the Huang to impede the Japanese advance. The objectives of the diversion were to halt or at least slow the Japanese onslaught, cause casualties and damage to military equipment, and give the Chinese army time to withdraw and establish defenses.

Destruction of levees was not new in Chinese military history, and the upper part of the floodplain is especially vulnerable. The dikes were breached in 1128 and 1642 in nearly the same places as the 1938 breach. In 1937, the Chinese army had breached levees along the Grand Canal, which joins the Huang and Yangtze Rivers, to obstruct the Japanese, and Western journalists believed that the breaching of the levees in 1938 had been the subject of a great deal of planning.

Initial reports exaggerated the flooding. A week after the flooding, a Japanese report claimed 150,000 people had drowned, while a Chinese report claimed that 6,000 Japanese troops had also drowned. Some newspaper stories described a "wall of water," but later reports were more restrained. They stated that early estimates of death tolls were not credible, that most people were able to escape the flood, and that the floodwaters spread slowly and were generally shallow. There was widespread agreement that the flood had diverted almost the entire flow of the Huang and that the former course of the river below the breach had been reduced to a small stream. Most later reports stressed that the greatest danger to human life was from destruction of crops and famine, which was exacerbated by the war.

The floodwaters advanced southeast along tributaries to the Huai River and eventually entered the Yangtze. Reporters taken on an aerial survey of the flood area by the Japanese in early July reported that flooding had receded in many areas and was then concentrated on channels leading southeast. The summer of 1938 was described as both sweltering and unusually rainy, and natural flooding compounded the human disaster. Later that summer the Chinese also breached dikes along the Yangtze River, and natural flooding along the Yangtze caused additional damage and loss of life.

SIGNIFICANCE

Because Japan was at war only with China at the time of the flood, American and European journalists had access to both Chinese and Japanese sources. Japanese sources

reported that Japanese troops had been warned about the levees being mined but had been unable to locate the charges. They also claimed that Chinese troops fired on Japanese troops and local work parties who were attempting to repair the breaks. On June 16, a *New York Times* article reported that Chinese interviewed in Shanghai (then occupied by the Japanese) overwhelmingly favored breaching the dikes if it could halt the Japanese. A number of Western analysts also approved of the tactic. They noted that the flood created a huge humanitarian problem but that the war was a more serious cause for concern.

Although the flood delayed the Japanese and bought time for Chinese withdrawal, the Japanese eventually captured all the objectives they were striving for at the time of the flood. Most histories treat the flood as a minor episode in a much larger conflict, and very little detailed information is available in English. The most devastating loss of life occurred as a result of famine: Huge amounts of crops were destroyed, and the war prevented sufficient transportation of relief supplies. It is extremely hard to separate the effects of the flood from overall civilian loss of life in the war, but most published estimates claim half a million to one million lives lost. Official Chinese figures put the death toll at about 890,000. Bitterness over the flood may have been significant in causing many victims to reject the Nationalist cause in favor of the Communists. The Huang was diverted back to its present course in 1947.

—*Steven I. Dutch*

FURTHER READING

Dorn, Frank. *The Sino-Japanese War, 1937-1941: From Marco Polo Bridge to Pearl Harbor*. New York: Macmillan, 1974. Detailed account by a U.S. embassy officer stationed in China. Makes use of Japanese and Chinese sources. A brief account of the dike breaching can be found on pages 177-178. Map showing the new route of the river is on page 171.

Durdin, F. Tillman. "Chinese Attacking Japanese in Flood." *The New York Times*, June 13, 1938, p. 1. First major press account of the flood. Other significant *New York Times* accounts were published on June 8, 11, 15, 16, 17, 19, 26, and 28, and on July 4.

Elvin, Mark, and Liu Ts'ui-jung, eds. *Sediments of Time: Environment and Society in Chinese History*. New York: Cambridge University Press, 1998. Case studies of historical human environmental effects in China. One chapter deals with a military diversion in 1128 that was nearly identical to the 1938 event.

Lary, Diana. "Drowned Earth: The Strategic Breaching of the Yellow River Dyke, 1938." *War in History* 8, no. 2

1938

(April 1, 2001): 191-207. Deals more with the political setting and repercussions of the levee breach than the actual flood, but valuable because it contains the most detailed references to original Chinese sources.

Wilson, Dick. *When Tigers Fight: Story of the Sino-Japanese War, 1937-1945*. New York: Viking, 1982. The account of the flood is on pages 119-122 and includes a map. The account of the aftermath of the flood appears to be based on Dorn's account.

Zhao, Songqiao. *Geography of China: Environment, Re-*

sources, Population, and Development. New York: John Wiley & Sons, 1994. Includes general discussions of Huang floods but is especially noteworthy for a detailed map (on page 114) of changes in the river's course since 600 B.C.E.

SEE ALSO: 1926-1949: Chinese Civil War; July, 1931: Yellow River Flood; Feb. 24, 1933: Japan Withdraws from the League of Nations; Oct. 16, 1934-Oct. 18, 1935: Mao's Long March; Dec., 1937-Feb., 1938: Rape of Nanjing.

June 21, 1938
NATURAL GAS ACT

The Natural Gas Act mandated the Federal Power Commission to control gas prices in interstate commerce and to decide which pipelines could enter the interstate market.

LOCALE: Washington, D.C.

CATEGORIES: Environmental issues; natural resources; laws, acts, and legal history

KEY FIGURES

Clarence Frederick Lea (1874-1964), U.S. congressman from California

Sam Rayburn (1882-1961), U.S. congressman from Texas

Franklin D. Roosevelt (1882-1945), president of the United States, 1933-1945

SUMMARY OF EVENT

On June 21, 1938, Congress passed the Natural Gas Act (NGA), and seven days later, President Franklin D. Roosevelt signed it into law. The NGA provided the Federal Power Commission (FPC) much discretion in determining "just and reasonable" rates for the sale of natural gas in interstate commerce. The findings of the commission were to be "conclusive" so long as "supported by substantial evidence," but these findings could be challenged in court. The regulation of prices was not to apply to local sales or to intrastate deliveries; the state public-service commissions would continue to regulate these services. The FPC was given additional powers to regulate interstate pipelines and to award certificates of public convenience and necessity, meaning that no new pipeline could enter the interstate market without FPC approval. The major purpose of the law was to protect consumers from excessive prices; public safety and conservation of

a scarce resource were secondary considerations.

Since the late nineteenth century, the federal government had been regulating interstate business that was monopolistic or "affected with a public interest." Until the late 1920's, however, natural gas was generally an intrastate business, and it had been regulated by the state public-service commissions since the beginning of the twentieth century. The business changed as improvements in metals and welding made it possible for long seamless pipelines to cross state borders between areas of production and large urban centers in the North, and by 1936, thirty-five states had access to supplies of natural gas. The U.S. Supreme Court, in *Missouri v. Kansas Natural Gas* (1924), interrupted the status quo by ruling that the states could no longer regulate the prices of natural gas transported from one state to another, because the Constitution gave Congress exclusive power to regulate interstate commerce.

After the Court's decision, those suspicious of the large energy companies wanted the Congress to "fill in the gap" in the regulation of natural gas. In 1928, the Senate instructed the Federal Trade Commission to investigate the matter, and the commission's one-hundred-volume study recommended federal regulation of both electricity and natural gas. With the support of this study, the New Deal Congress passed the Federal Power Act of 1935, which enlarged the scope of the FPC and authorized it to regulate electricity sold between states. The FPC had both quasi-legislative and quasi-judicial functions, so that it could formulate rules with the force of law and interpret these rules in specific cases, subject to appeals in the federal courts.

After the passage of the Federal Power Act, Congressman Sam Rayburn, one of the strongest proponents of

New Deal regulations in the House of Representatives, instructed legislative drafters to take the law and use it as a model for similar legislation authorizing controls of natural gas sales. As Rayburn introduced the bill into the House, Burton Kendall Wheeler introduced the same bill into the Senate. Natural gas companies and state regulators, however, objected to some of the features of the Rayburn bill, and it failed to become law. The next year, Representative Clarence Frederick Lea, chairman of the appropriate commerce subcommittee, revised the bill with the assistance of Clyde Seavey, one of the members of the FPC. Lea introduced the new bill into the House that year, and although there was little opposition, there was not enough interest to get it to the floor for a vote.

Lea then turned to the natural gas companies for their views; after making some changes, he introduced the bill a second time in April, 1937. The companies had decided that regulation was in their interest. At this time, the companies' major problem was that oversupplies were driving down prices, and they were now happy to accept regulation in exchange for a guaranteed profit margin. In spite of a consensus in favor of regulation, the Senate was slower than the House to vote in favor of the bill, and the differences between the two chambers were not worked out until June 21, 1938. Compared with many innovative laws of the New Deal, the NGA was considered rather unexceptional, and the press at the time almost ignored the issue.

The NGA was vague and ambiguous in several key areas, and thus the implications of the law would evolve with judicial challenges. The most uncertain portion of the NGA was the statement that FPC regulation would not extend to "the production and gathering of natural gas." It was clear that the FPC would not have authority over the physical production of gas. Because the term "production and gathering" was not defined, however, it was unclear whether the FPC was authorized to regulate the sale of gas in the fields if the gas was destined for the interstate markets, or whether FPC regulations would apply only after the gas had been sold. This particular ambiguity would be the most controversial aspect of the history of the NGA. Over the years, interpreting this and similar provisions of the NGA would give employment to a large number of lawyers.

SIGNIFICANCE

The first major court battle of the NGA had to do with the method that the FPC was to use in determining "just and reasonable" rates. When the act was passed, regulatory bodies generally were following the fair-value standard that a probusiness Supreme Court had articulated in its 1897 *Smythe v. Ames* decision. According to this standard, regulated businesses were entitled to a rate of return based on the value of their capital investment. Beginning in 1942, a more aggressive FPC changed its standard to one of production investment costs, which meant a lower rate of return for gas businesses. The issue was tested in court in the case *Federal Power Commission v. Hope Natural Gas* (1944), in which the Supreme Court supported the FPC's position and overruled the *Smythe* precedent. The Court enunciated the principle that government regulators were no longer required to use the investment-value standard, but they could use any reasonable method or formula.

A more long-standing controversy was whether the FPC was authorized to regulate the price charged for natural gas in the fields (at the wellheads). The issue was complex, because although large companies were involved in both the production and the transmission of natural gas, some four thousand independent producers were not involved in interstate transmission. At first, the FPC did not regulate any sales in the fields, but in 1942, the commission began to regulate the large companies that both produced gas and controlled pipelines. The FPC decided against the regulation of the independent producers, but in the surprising landmark case *Phillips Petroleum Company v. Wisconsin* (1954), the Supreme Court ruled that the intent of Congress in 1938 had been to regulate the sale of natural gas in the fields when its destination was interstate commerce.

Because the *Phillips* decision required the FPC to regulate the sales of thousands of independents, the work of the FPC became much more extensive and complex. Lawyers and economists tended to view the *Phillips* decision as almost equal in importance to the NGA itself. Until 1960, the FPC made individual price determinations through a case-by-case approach. After a study pointed to the FPC as an example of the "breakdown of the administrative process," the commission changed to the area rate method, which was a determination of the reasonable requirements within each of twenty-three geographic regions. In the 1970's, the FPC changed to one standard rate to be used nationwide.

Until about 1968, large supplies of natural gas kept prices low, but by 1972, the FPC acknowledged that there actually were shortages in parts of the country. Because oil and gas are often substituted for each other, the increase in oil prices after the embargo of 1973 had a great impact on the market for natural gas. By about 1975, gas prices in the intrastate markets were about twice as high as those in the interstate market, and it was becoming apparent that

1938

price regulations were contributing to gas shortages in the interstate market. The situation became critical in the cold winter of 1976 and 1977, when a lack of supplies forced four thousand manufacturing plants to close and resulted in 1.2 million workers temporarily losing their jobs. Hundreds of schools had to close their doors in order to protect gas supplies for residential consumers.

President Jimmy Carter and his administration concluded that the only answer was to move to the deregulation of natural gas at the wellheads, and the result was the Natural Gas Policy Act (NGPA) of 1978. The NGPA was complex because it made distinctions among about twenty different categories of natural gas. The schedules provided that price controls for new gas and hard-to-get gas from deep wells would end by 1985, whereas the lifting of controls on old gas and gas in shallow wells would not end until 1987. President Ronald Reagan and his administration were committed to competitive markets, and they generally supported the principles of the NGPA of 1978. After the beginning of decontrols, prices did increase significantly by 1982, but adequate supplies ceased to be a problem. Thereafter, new discoveries of natural gas appeared to produce a satisfactory equilibrium and the public lost interest in the issue.

By the 1990's, the controversies of the Natural Gas Act of 1938 were a memory. Most economists tended to conclude that the NGPA of 1982 was a positive step, and few people wanted to return to the field regulations that began with the *Phillips* decision. It was not clear whether the Natural Gas Act had actually operated in the interest of the consumer, because evidence indicated that the realities of supply and demand had always influenced prices more than had price regulations.

With the growing concern for the environment, there was a new complexity about the implications of the term "conservation" in regard to the natural gas industry. Since the passage of the NGA in 1938, the justification for conserving natural gas had been to place a limit on how much gas was consumed so that supplies would last longer. Natural gas, however, is a clean-burning, environmentally friendly fuel, and efforts to decrease its use result in the increased use of other forms of energy that do more ecological damage. The limits of the obtainable reserves of this wonderful resource are as yet unknown.

—*Thomas Tandy Lewis*

FURTHER READING

Baum, Robert. *The Federal Power Commission and State Utility Regulation*. Washington, D.C.: American Council on Public Affairs, 1942. Presents a favorable interpretation of the early history of the FPC's regulation of natural gas.

Breyer, Stephen, and Paul W. MacAvoy. *Energy Regulation by the Federal Power Commission*. Washington, D.C.: Brookings Institution, 1974. Emphasizes the economics of regulation and argues that price regulation at the wellheads resulted in shortages.

Castaneda, Christopher James. *Invisible Fuel: Manufactured and Natural Gas in America, 1800-2000*. Boston: Twayne, 1999. History of the use of gas as an energy source in the United States includes discussion of the Natural Gas Act of 1938. Features chronology, selected bibliography, and index.

DeVane, Dozier. "Highlights of Legislative History of the Federal Power Act of 1935 and the Natural Gas Act of 1938." *George Washington Law Review* 14 (December, 1945): 30-41. Very informative account of how the act was passed, emphasizing the roles of Congressmen Rayburn and Lea.

Hawkins, Claud. *The Field Price Regulation of Natural Gas*. Tallahassee: Florida State University Press, 1969. Excellent, scholarly, and readable account of the passage of the act and of interpretations of the law by the courts.

Kohlmeier, Louis, Jr. *The Regulators: Watchdog Agencies and the Public Interest*. New York: Harper & Row, 1969. Interesting journalistic account is critical of the regulatory process. Includes substantial coverage of the regulation of natural gas.

MacAvoy, Paul W. *The Natural Gas Market: Sixty Years of Regulation and Deregulation*. New Haven, Conn.: Yale University Press, 2001. Argues that federal attempts to regulate natural gas have cost the United States billions of dollars and have encouraged intrusive involvement in the natural gas market on the part of regulatory agencies.

Sanders, M. Elizabeth. *The Regulation of Natural Gas: Policy and Politics, 1938-1978*. Philadelphia: Temple University Press, 1981. Excellent, informative study considers various theories of regulation. Concludes that legislators in 1938 were primarily influenced by local interests and that capture of the industry did not take place.

SEE ALSO: 1923: Federal Power Commission Disallows Kings River Dams; July 18, 1932: St. Lawrence Seaway Treaty.

June 25, 1938
FAIR LABOR STANDARDS ACT

The federal Fair Labor Standards Act, passed during the Great Depression, stipulated minimum wages and maximum hours of work for employees of firms engaged in interstate commerce in the United States.

LOCALE: Washington, D.C.

CATEGORIES: Laws, acts, and legal history; business and labor; social issues and reform

KEY FIGURES

Franklin D. Roosevelt (1882-1945), president of the United States, 1933-1945

Frances Perkins (1880-1965), U.S. secretary of labor, 1933-1945

Harlan Fiske Stone (1872-1946), associate justice of the United States, 1925-1941, and chief justice of the United States, 1941-1946

William Green (1873-1952), president of the American Federation of Labor

Thomas J. Walsh (1859-1933), U.S. senator from Montana

Hugo L. Black (1886-1971), U.S. senator from Alabama

SUMMARY OF EVENT

Enacted into federal law on June 25, 1938, the Fair Labor Standards Act (FLSA) was part of a package of reform legislation characterizing the so-called Second New Deal of President Franklin D. Roosevelt that began with his landslide reelection in 1936. It applied to all businesses that were engaged in or that affected interstate commerce. Article I, section 8 of the U.S. Constitution, the "commerce clause," provided the legal grounds granting federal jurisdiction to effectuate the act. Because the U.S. Supreme Court had begun giving broad construction to what was meant by interstate commerce (as it did in decisions regarding the Wagner Act, for example), the Roosevelt administration believed it would have wide latitude in applying the act.

The Fair Labor Standards Act placed a floor under wages and a ceiling over hours for those workers covered by the law. Initially, it established a minimum wage of forty cents an hour, with provisions for subsequent increases, and mandated a maximum forty-hour workweek. To smooth the act's implementation, the provisions for both wages and hours were to be phased into effect over eight years. The act also placed national authority behind the abolition of child labor. The labor of

children under sixteen years of age was forbidden, and persons under eighteen years of age were prohibited from working in hazardous occupations, including mining. In the act's original form, however, workers in a number of occupations were exempted from coverage, notably farm laborers, professional workers, and domestic servants, although these exemptions would be altered in time. The original bill before Congress envisaged a special board to administer the law. In subsequent years, however, oversight of the act fell to the Department of Labor's Employment Standards Administration.

President Roosevelt had given little thought to placing his political prestige behind a wages and hours bill until 1937. In efforts to combat the Depression, the National Industrial Recovery Act of 1933 (NIRA), sponsored by Roosevelt during his "First New Deal," sought to increase purchasing power by establishing minimum wages among the NIRA's participating businesses and industries. Along with several other major pieces of early New Deal legislation, however, the NIRA was declared unconstitutional by the Supreme Court in 1935.

By 1935, however, prolabor legislation and support for the incomes of disadvantaged groups were popular in Congress. The Guffey Coal Act of 1935 and the Merchant Marine Act of 1936, for example, each contained provisions to limit hours and raise wages. The institution of Social Security in 1935 was still another attempt to raise the incomes of disadvantaged groups. The National Labor Relations Act (Wagner Act) of 1935 threw federal protection around union organization and collective bargaining. The principles of a wages and hours bill were further vindicated in 1936 with congressional passage of the Walsh-Healy Act. Guided through Congress chiefly by Montana's Democratic senator Thomas J. Walsh, long an enemy of child labor, the act mandated that a prevailing minimum wage, as determined by the secretary of labor, was to be paid to workers on all jobs performed under federal contracts worth more than ten thousand dollars. Work hours were limited to eight per day, and the labor of boys under the age of sixteen and girls under the age of eighteen was prohibited.

Even with these enactments in the mid-1930's, the United States continued to differ from other advanced economies in regard to promulgating national standards for wages and hours. The American version of laissez-faire economics was deeply rooted in an endemic individualism coupled with a widespread fear of peacetime

1938

government intervention. Consequently, the Roosevelt administration faced serious difficulties in persuading Congress to pass the Fair Labor Standards Act.

These difficulties were compounded by Roosevelt's shift into a spirited campaign of reform following his 1936 reelection. The president was eager to defuse his growing popular opposition and restore the essence of several key programs of his first administration that had been held to be unconstitutional by the Supreme Court. He was also faced with a secondary economic depression that threatened to be as deep as the one he had inherited in 1933.

After initial rebuffs by Congress, the bill that became the Fair Labor Standards Act was introduced to the special congressional session called by Roosevelt in November, 1937. The bill was backed by the president's message to the nation that a self-respecting democracy "can plead no justification for . . . child labor, no economic reason for chiseling workers' wages or stretching workers' hours." Hugo L. Black, then a senator from Alabama and later a Supreme Court justice, had sponsored an earlier wages and hours bill. He chaired the joint congressional committees charged with conducting hearings on the bill. Backing his effort were socially conscious Progressives such as Secretary of Labor Frances Perkins, Leon Henderson, and White House aides Thomas Corcoran and Benjamin Cohen.

Opposition to the bill was intense. Critics branded the measure fascist, and the Chamber of Commerce and the National Association of Manufacturers (NAM) denounced the bill on both economic and constitutional grounds. Reflecting southern textile and lumber interests, congressmen from the South fought bitterly against prospective federal interference in or regulation of their industries. Nor was organized labor of one mind. The American Federation of Labor (AFL) and its president, William Green, seeking important changes in the bill, temporarily joined the NAM in opposition; the Congress of Industrial Organizations (CIO), under John L. Lewis, was split on the measure. A Gallup Poll indicated that most Americans, from the North and the South, favored the bill, as did many northern industries that competed with the low-wage, long-hour employment of southern workers. Amid such divisions, many of the bill's original features were dropped or amended. On June 13, 1938, the House passed the bill by a vote of 291 to 97. The Senate accepted it without a recorded vote. Roosevelt signed the FLSA on June 25, and it became effective on October 24.

SIGNIFICANCE

The FLSA reflected many debilitating and limiting congressional compromises, although over subsequent years amendments would remedy a number of these deficiencies. Leading economists in 1938 reckoned that in its original form the act covered fewer than eleven million workers, less than 25 percent of the employed labor force. Administration officials estimated that when the act took effect, nearly 300,000 workers covered by it were earning less than twenty-five cents an hour and 1.3 million workers normally labored more than forty-four hours a week. The national standard of a forty-hour workweek did not arrive until 1940.

The long battle to abolish child labor was also far from over. Entry into employment was restricted to those aged sixteen and over, and the act's administrators could raise that age to eighteen for work in hazardous or unhealthy industries. Administrators could lower the age of employment to fourteen, however, in industries other than manufacturing and mining in some cases. In addition, the act's coverage did not extend to agriculture, personal services, street trades, or retailing, which collectively were the largest employers of children.

The act proved to be the last of the Second New Deal's major reform measures. It was also a popular law. A 1939 Gallup Poll showed that 71 percent of the country favored it, and it therefore came as a political blessing to an embattled President Roosevelt. The president's own view of the measure was that it constituted "the most far-reaching and the most far-sighted program for the benefit of the workers ever adopted."

One purpose of the law was to secure better terms of employment for workers than they could secure acting alone. It undoubtedly raised wages for the lowest-paid employees, particularly in the South. These included workers in sawmills, canneries, cigar factories, and textile mills. Depending on the degree of enforcement of the act, which generally was low, it shortened the hours of work where abuses were greatest. Its general effects varied widely, from very positive to negative, depending on a variety of factors including product prices, the extent of unionization and collective bargaining, and the state of the economy. Unions eventually applauded it because it curtailed competition from underpaid workers. The act also excluded from legal employment many people who wished to work, by putting their wages above what employers were willing to pay.

The last word on the act was that of the Supreme Court. Until 1937, the Court had almost systematically eviscerated major New Deal programs. This had led

President Roosevelt to launch an attempt to pack the Court with his own appointees—a legal, if unpopular, method of changing the Court's conservative complexion by appointing additional justices. Politically, this unfolded as a battle that Roosevelt lost but a war—as a result of events beyond his control—that he won. Amid the controversy, five incumbent justices either died or retired before the constitutionality of the FLSA came before the Court in 1941, and Roosevelt had appointed five new, ostensibly liberal, justices to replace them. As a consequence, when redrafted, several major New Deal programs that earlier had been killed by the Court passed the test of constitutionality before the substantially reconstituted Court. Labor observers thought it a foregone conclusion that the FLSA would find Supreme Court approval, but at the time, the Roosevelt administration was not overly optimistic.

The test of the Fair Labor Standards Act came before the Supreme Court as *United States v. Darby Lumber Company* in 1941. The Darby Lumber Company bought timber, transported it to its mill, and manufactured it into finished lumber entirely within the state of Georgia. The finished lumber, however, was thereafter shipped out of state, thereby entering interstate commerce. By FLSA criteria, Darby's employees, who earned less than twenty-five cents per hour and who worked more than forty-four hours per week, were underpaid and overworked. Moreover, the company kept no records, as the Labor Department discovered when it tried to bring Darby into compliance with the FLSA. Darby's rejoinder was that the FLSA was unconstitutional insofar as it sought to regulate manufacturing taking place entirely inside Georgia. A Georgia district court agreed with this reasoning. On appeal, the case went before the U.S. Supreme Court.

At the request of Chief Justice Charles Evans Hughes, Associate Justice Harlan Fiske Stone wrote the Court's opinion, principally because Hughes deemed it to be a "great" case and because it involved issues that long had concerned Stone. In his opinion, Stone sought first to reassert the absolute nature of congressional power over interstate commerce. In effect, this was designed to return the Court to the sweeping mandate it received from Chief Justice John Marshall in *Gibbons v. Ogden* in 1824, a position that had been eroded by Supreme Court decisions such as *Hammer v. Dagenhart* in 1918 that separated actual manufacturing activities from the stream of interstate commerce. Stone declared that congressional authority over interstate commerce, on the contrary, was "complete in itself . . . and acknowledges no limitations

other than are prescribed by the Constitution." That power, he argued, was not susceptible to modification by states. He granted that although manufacturing was not commerce, the shipment of manufactured goods outside a state was commerce and thus fell under national authority.

In order to restore federal power over the regulation of child labor, Stone made his second assertion, namely, that congressional power to regulate child labor was "plenary." Such power was not limited to child labor in hazardous or unhealthy occupations. On both points and contrary to Darby's plea, the Supreme Court was unanimous. The Fair Labor Standards Act survived its constitutional test and gained additional strength from Stone's reaffirmation of Congress's complete authority over interstate commerce.

—Clifton K. Yearley

FURTHER READING

Babson, Steve. *The Unfinished Struggle: Turning Points in American Labor, 1877-Present.* Lanham, Md.: Rowman & Littlefield, 1999. Concise and comprehensive history of the American labor movement. Includes notes and index.

Bernstein, Irving. *A Caring Society: The New Deal, the Worker, and the Great Depression.* Boston: Houghton Mifflin, 1985. Examination of the New Deal by a leading labor historian maintains a critical balance despite a clear pro-New Deal bias. Chapter 5 presents an informative narrative history of the adoption of the FLSA.

Card, David, and Alan B. Krueger. *Myth and Measurement: The New Economics of the Minimum Wage.* Princeton, N.J.: Princeton University Press, 1995. Controversial study reports on data from interviews that suggest that increases in the minimum wage do not decrease employment. Includes references and index.

Douglas, Paul H., and Joseph Hackman. "The Fair Labor Standards Act of 1938 I." *Political Science Quarterly* 53 (December, 1938): 491-515.

_____. "The Fair Labor Standards Act of 1938 II." *Political Science Quarterly* 54 (March, 1939): 29-55. Two concise articles by a distinguished economist and a labor expert assess the immediate impact of the FLSA on the American workforce. Very informative.

Felt, Jeremy P. "The Child Labor Provision of the Fair Labor Standards Act." *Labor History* 11 (Fall, 1970): 477-481. Clear and concise scholarly assessment of the subject examines three decades of the FLSA's child labor provisions at work.

1938

Levin-Waldman, Oren M. *The Case of the Minimum Wage: Competing Policy Models.* Albany: State University of New York Press, 2001. Discusses the evolution of minimum wage policy and law in the United States, focusing on how the nature of arguments concerning a minimum wage has changed over time. Includes tables and figures, bibliography, and index.

Levitan, Sar A., and Richard S. Belous. *More than Subsistence: Minimum Wages for the Working Poor.* Baltimore: The Johns Hopkins University Press, 1979. Brief, clearly written work presents narrative, analysis, and advocacy concerning the minimum wage.

Nordlund, Willis J. *The Quest for a Living Wage: The History of the Federal Minimum Wage Program.* Westport, Conn.: Greenwood Press, 1997. Traces the process through which the U.S. government attempted to develop a fair method of ensuring that workers receive a living wage. Gives an overview of the first fifty years of the operation of the FLSA. Includes tables and figures, bibliography, and index.

Rauch, Basil. *The History of the New Deal.* New York: Capricorn Books, 1963. Fine summary of the New Deal by an important historian presents discussion of the work of Roosevelt's "Brain Trust" in writing and fighting for the president's legislation. Addresses the FLSA as part of a complex political picture in chapter 13.

Wilcox, Clair. *Public Policies Toward Business.* 3d ed. Homewood, Ill.: Richard D. Irwin, 1966. Excellent and authoritative work provides an overview of expanding government controls over American economic and social life. Chapter 32 deals with the FLSA in the context of previous domestic and foreign legislation on wages and hours.

SEE ALSO: Apr. 9, 1912: Children's Bureau Is Founded; June 4, 1912: Massachusetts Adopts the First Minimum Wage Law in the United States; Apr. 9, 1923: U.S. Supreme Court Rules Against Minimum Wage Laws; Oct. 29, 1929-1939: Great Depression; Feb. 5-July 22, 1937: Supreme Court-Packing Fight.

June 25, 1938
FEDERAL FOOD, DRUG, AND COSMETIC ACT

In response to growing concern about the inadequacy of regulations on food and drugs, the U.S. Congress passed the Federal Food, Drug, and Cosmetic Act, which required premarket safety clearance for certain products.

LOCALE: Washington, D.C.
CATEGORIES: Laws, acts, and legal history; trade and commerce

KEY FIGURES
Royal S. Copeland (1868-1938), U.S. senator from New York, 1923-1938, and chair of the Senate Commerce Committee, 1935-1938
Walter Gilbert Campbell (1877-1963), chief of the Food and Drug Administration
Rexford Guy Tugwell (1891-1979), assistant secretary of agriculture
Franklin D. Roosevelt (1882-1945), president of the United States, 1933-1945

SUMMARY OF EVENT

The Federal Food, Drug, and Cosmetic Act was passed in 1938 in response to growing concern that many parts of earlier legislation, such as the Pure Food and Drug Act of

1906, were either inadequate or outdated. A basic weakness of the regulative framework in the 1930's was the absence of proper public protection against food and drug products or advertisements that made fraudulent therapeutic claims. Furthermore, fraudulent claims were often made for cosmetic products, a category not addressed in the 1906 act or its subsequent amendments.

Following discussions between Walter Gilbert Campbell, chief of the Food and Drug Administration (FDA), and Rexford Guy Tugwell, the assistant secretary of agriculture, the FDA initiated a move to tighten the federal regulation of food, drugs, and cosmetics. When this legislative effort was later introduced in Congress by Senator Royal S. Copeland as Senate Resolution 1944 on June 12, 1933, it met with bitter opposition from business and advertising circles. This was partly because the bill's original sponsor, Tugwell, inspired suspicion and fear with his openly expressed belief in a planned economy.

To help assuage such resistance and to forestall passage of competing congressional measures introduced by powerful trade groups, Copeland modified several aspects of his earlier bill during 1934 and 1935. Nevertheless, business groups remained opposed to key parts of the Copeland bill such as the provision that the FDA would be responsible for regulating food, drug, and cosmetic advertising. Because the advertising regulation framework of the Federal Trade Commission (FTC) was relatively lenient, the business lobbyists wanted the FTC, rather than the FDA, to have such authority.

The likelihood of congressional passage of the modified Copeland bill appeared remote until two important developments occurred. First, the 1938 Wheeler-Lea Act reinforced FTC authority over food and drug products. Second, a drug tragedy emphasized the need for greater control over labeling and testing of products intended for public consumption: More than one hundred people died after consuming the drug Elixir of Sulfanilamide, which contained sulfanilamide dissolved in a potent poison called diethylene glycol. Apparently, this product was tested for flavor, appearance, and fragrance, but its safety was not evaluated before its market introduction. Clearly, if there had been stringent regulations to ensure safety tests of products intended for public consumption, this tragedy could have been averted.

These events created a political climate conducive to enactment of the Copeland bill. It was passed by the Senate on May 5, 1938, and by the House of Representatives on June 1, 1938. Finally, after more than five years of bitter legislative history since it was introduced in Congress, the Federal Food, Drug, and Cosmetic Act was signed into law by President Franklin D. Roosevelt on June 25, 1938.

The key provisions of the 1938 act were as follows: It prohibited traffic in new drugs unless they had been adequately tested for safe use under conditions prescribed on their labels. Drugs were required to carry warnings against habit formation (if any), to provide adequate directions for use, to bear warnings against unsafe use, and to have precautionary labeling if subject to deterioration over time. The Federal Food, Drug, and Cosmetic Act also prohibited traffic in foods and cosmetics that were injurious to health. The addition of any poison or other adulterant to food was prohibited; further, coal-tar dye products for hair were required to bear a warning label regarding use and preliminary testing.

The act contained several key innovations not offered by the amended version of its predecessor, the 1906 Pure Food and Drug Act. First, the 1938 act prohibited the production of food under unsanitary conditions that might contaminate it or render it injurious to public health. Second, foods considered harmful because of naturally contained poisons were subject to regulation. Third, the 1938 act empowered the imposition of emergency license restrictions whenever the dangers of

bacterial food contamination could not be addressed effectively by other statutory means. Fourth, label disclosure of artificial coloring, flavoring, or preservatives was specifically required, as was information on vitamin and mineral content and other characteristics of special dietary foods. Finally, greater authority and power were envisaged for agencies responsible for enforcing the law. Injunctive powers were added to other methods of enforcement previously available, and the penalties for noncompliance were increased. Furthermore, the 1938 act specifically allowed for factory inspections. It also provided for automatic premarket testing and approval of new drugs and coal-tar dyes.

SIGNIFICANCE

Compared to the 1906 act, the 1938 act was more comprehensive in scope and was better oriented to serving the public interest. It established the principle that food and drugs that were dangerous to the public should be prohibited, no matter what the source of the danger represented (for example, whether or not a poisonous agent was added artificially or occurred naturally). On the other hand, the act was criticized because, although it required drug manufacturers to establish that their products were safe, it did not mandate the establishment of product efficacy. Moreover, the act allowed for automatic clearance of drugs through time lapse if the FDA did not take any action. Both of these defects would be addressed in future legislation.

Additional aspects of the 1938 act merit special attention. Section 201 carefully defined what constituted a food or a drug. The statutory term "food" included all products that could be used as a food or drink by either humans or animals as well as all raw materials that do not have food value but enter into food products during manufacture. The term "drug" encompassed all substances that are recognized in the current official U.S. pharmacopoeia, recommended for use in a disease condition, or capable of affecting bodily structure or function.

Two aspects are worth noting. First, the statutory requirements that apply for a food are somewhat different from those that apply for a drug. Second, the definitions of what constitutes a "food" or a "drug" need not be mutually exclusive. That is, a given substance could satisfy the definition of both a food and a drug. Unless there is a clear statement concerning intended use as either a food or a drug, such a substance has to satisfy the statutory provisions that apply to both types of products. As one example, the manufacturer of a laxative in the form of a medicated candy or chewing gum could bring the product within the definition of the term "drug" and escape the rules concerning food. On the other hand, medicated foods (food products with added medicines) are considered to be adulterated foods. Unless such products can be justified as special dietary foods, as was done for the addition of iodine to table salt, the 1938 act banned the marketing of such products.

Another aspect of the 1938 act that led to some controversy was the congressional intent to allocate supervision of food advertising to the FTC and supervision of food labels and labeling to the FDA. This distinction remains unclear and has generated conflicting precedents. For example, the FTC has launched several proceedings on the basis of food labels. Although these proceedings appear legitimate given the agency's mandate to control unfair or deceptive acts in commerce, they may also be characterized as an encroachment on the FDA's authority. Moreover, the FDA and FTC decisions have not been consistent with regard to enforcing drug labeling requirements. A further complication is that some courts have ruled that the FDA's authority to proceed against a firm that misbrands products is not diminished by a prior proceeding against the same firm by the FTC, whereas other court decisions have implied just the opposite.

—*Siva Balasubramanian*

FURTHER READING

Anderson, Oscar E. *The Health of a Nation: Harvey W. Wiley and the Fight for Pure Food.* Chicago: University of Chicago Press, 1958. Wiley's biography; presents him as a crusader with a flair for publicity. An interesting look at the relationship between science and politics.

Curtis, Patricia A. *Guide to Food Laws and Regulations.* Ames, Iowa: Blackwell, 2005. Overview of all U.S. federal laws and regulations regarding the preparation, sale, and marketing of foodstuffs. Bibliographic references and index.

Herrick, Arthur D. *Food Regulation and Compliance.* 2 vols. New York: Revere, 1944-1947. Authoritative source on early food and drug laws in the United States. The 1906 act is compared with the 1938 act. Also reviews other federal food statutes. Despite being dated, this book offers a useful summary interpretation of the intent and scope of key sections of the 1938 act.

Hinich, Melvin J., and Richard Staelin. *Consumer Protection Legislation and the U.S. Food Industry.* New York: Pergamon Press, 1980. Examines enforcement procedures of the Food and Drug Administration, the Federal Trade Commission, and the Department of Agriculture. Explains the conflicts between federal, state, and local governmental food regulations.

Kay, Gwen. *Dying to Be Beautiful: The Fight for Safe Cosmetics.* Columbus: Ohio State University Press, 2005. Study of the history of safety regulation in the U.S. cosmetics industry. Part of the Women, Gender, and Health series. Bibliographic references and index.

Kleinfeld, Vincent A., and Alan H. Kaplan. *Federal Food, Drug, and Cosmetic Act: Judicial and Administrative Record, 1961-1964.* Chicago: Commerce Clearing House, 1965. This book belongs to the Food Law Institute Series and is a useful source of information on food, drug, and related laws. It contains details of the legislative and judicial activities initiated in connection with the Federal Food, Drug, and Cosmetic Act for the period 1961 through 1964. Several types of cases are described in detail.

Quirk, Paul J. "Food and Drug Administration." In *The Politics of Regulation*, edited by James Q. Wilson. New York: Basic Books, 1980. Focuses on the social and economic effects of drug regulation. Analyzes problems created by the food and drug laws and suggests various reforms. There is also a chapter in the book on the relationship between politics and government regulation.

Skinner, Karen. "Scientific Change and the Evolution of Regulation." In *Chemical Safety Regulation and Compliance*, edited by Freddy Homburger and Judith K. Marquis. Basel, Switzerland: S. Karger, 1985. Provides a good overview of the passage of the 1938 act and discusses its implications concerning food safety and food additives.

Temin, Peter. *Taking Your Medicine: Drug Regulation in the United States.* Cambridge, Mass.: Harvard University Press, 1980. A detailed history of food and drug regulation and its relationship to the development of new drugs and the therapeutic revolution. Relates this to economic behavior and the role of government in the drug market.

July 6-15, 1938
EVIAN CONFERENCE

The Evian meeting was an international conference, convened at President Franklin D. Roosevelt's initiative, to discuss comprehensive emigration policy in response to the rapidly accelerating numbers of Jewish refugees. The conference represented a critical turning point in the evolution of the Holocaust.

LOCALE: Evian, France

CATEGORIES: Atrocities and war crimes; diplomacy and international relations; human rights

KEY FIGURES

Franklin D. Roosevelt (1882-1945), president of the United States, 1933-1945

Adolf Hitler (1889-1945), chancellor of Germany, 1933-1945

Myron C. Taylor (1874-1959), chairman of the Evian Conference

George Rublee (1868-1957), director of the Intergovernmental Committee on Refugees

SUMMARY OF EVENT

The Evian Conference took place in the French resort community along Lake Geneva from July 6 through July 15, 1938. A climate of deep, ubiquitous anti-Semitism had been spreading throughout Nazi Germany, and it was unfolding with increasing viciousness. On September 15, 1935, Nazi Germany had legislated and begun the implementation of the Nuremberg Laws, racist statutes of the Third Reich that were critical to the marginalization, segregation, and dehumanization of German (and eventually Austrian) Jews. The Anschluss, which annexed Austria to Germany in March, 1938, provoked the administration of Franklin D. Roosevelt to respond to the proliferating crisis faced by European Jews.

The Anschluss made the situation of Jewish refugees much worse: It shattered the pattern of gradual German Jewish emigration. Prior to the Anschluss, Jewish emigration from Nazi Germany was slow, steady, and relatively small. The Jewish refugee crisis was deliberately and systematically precipitated by Nazi Germany's relentless attempts to eliminate "undesirables"; the Third Reich was eager to remove Jews from all its territories. The Evian Conference was a direct result of this urgent need for nations to deal with the Jewish refugee crisis.

Soon after the Anschluss, Roosevelt recommended that heads of state convene at an international meeting to negotiate a remedy to the plight of stateless Jewish émi-

grés. Although it is difficult to determine Roosevelt's exact motives for calling for such a meeting, it is clear that the president was responding to domestic political pressures, particularly from the isolationist forces in the United States and from groups of American Jews.

In the late 1930's, when the United States and most European countries were still attempting to emerge from the Great Depression, Roosevelt might have thought that the American public was unwilling to accept European Jewish refugees, given that the United States continued to have unemployment concerns for its own citizens. Strategically, the United States may have intentionally placed itself in a win-win situation: By calling for the conference, it communicated concern over the refugee crisis, but the country did not make any significant reforms to its own restrictive immigration policy. Instead, the Americans continued to maintain barriers that reduced the number of Jewish émigrés entering the United States. It appears that Roosevelt's strategy was to head off progressive immigration demands while circumventing any radical shift in immigration policy.

Representatives from thirty-two nations, including Australia, Belgium, Canada, Denmark, France, Great Britain, the Netherlands, New Zealand, Norway, Sweden, Switzerland, South Africa, the United States, and countries in Latin America, attended the meeting. Myron C. Taylor, former chairman of the United States Steel Corporation and a friend of Roosevelt, was charged with organizing the meeting at Evian and appointed as the conference chairman.

Throughout the meeting, a consensus of passivity and indifference in resolving the refugee crisis emerged among the delegates. At the conference's commencement, the U.S. delegation immediately assumed an apathetic and constrained posture by refusing to articulate a radical shift in its immigration policy or offer a systematic, comprehensive resolution to the crisis. Instead, the United States announced that it would honor its established immigration policy by merging the quotas for German and Austrian immigrants (which allowed for a combined annual maximum of 27,370 refugees). The British declared that Great Britain and its colonies were incapable of accepting any additional refugees and should be excluded from the absorption of any significant number of Jewish immigrants. In particular, Great Britain was reluctant to open its doors to greater numbers of Jewish refugees because of its resistance to ex-

1938

ternal pressures to greatly increase European Jewish immigration to Palestine.

The delegates of other countries responded to the reticence or reluctance of the United States and Great Britain to liberalize and expand their immigration policies by continuing their own restrictive immigration policies. As pretexts for their refusal to increase the number of refugees admitted to their respective countries, the delegates articulated a variety of claims, including that they were already saturated with such refugees and that their countries were suffering from profound economic problems.

The delegations did not discuss the reasons behind the massive immigration of European Jews or the Nazis' perpetration of anti-Semitic policies. Furthermore, the lack of public criticism of Nazi Germany's anti-Semitism was a manifestation of the countries' implicit recognition of Nazi Germany's sovereignty. By the end of the conference, the delegates of the thirty-two nation-states were virtually unanimous in their resistance to any liberalization or expansion of their respective immigration policies, with the sole exception of the Dominican Republic, which accepted a meager number of Jewish refugees supported by American Jewish philanthropic aid.

The conference also resulted in the creation of the Intergovernmental Committee on Refugees (IGCR), which sought to mitigate the problem of Jewish refugees by systematically facilitating global attempts to resettle émigrés. George Rublee was the chair of this committee, which was established in London. The Evian delegates gave the IGCR the power to negotiate with Nazi Germany to systematize the continuous emigration of Jewish refugees and to increase the flow of immigration, and to foster long-term assimilation of these immigrants in their newly adopted homelands. In essence, this committee's task was to serve as a global instrument to diplomatically resolve the Jewish refugee problem with Nazi Germany. However, the committee immediately faced the dilemma of solving the massive Jewish refugee problem without disrupting the current restrictive immigration policies of Evian's participants.

Although it is ironic that both the IGCR, under Rublee's leadership, and Nazi Germany shared a common objective of expediting the emigration of Jews, they disagreed about the logistics. The committee preferred that Jewish refugees emigrate with some of their possessions, while Nazi Germany wanted to receive compensation for Jews' departure. This impasse resulted in dire consequences for many of Germany's and Austria's remaining Jews. Furthermore, the nation-states represented by the IGCR contributed very little to efforts to resettle the European Jewish refugees, and this diminished the perception of the IGCR's potency and credibility. Ultimately, the IGCR did not have the support it needed to rescue Jewish refugees.

SIGNIFICANCE

Holocaust scholars widely regard the Evian Conference as a dismal failure and a watershed event in the history of the Holocaust. The inability of the proceedings at Evian to reform the participants' immigration policies resulted in a rapidly deteriorating situation for German Jews, and Jews desperate to escape Nazi Germany were hugely disappointed. This meeting signaled to Nazi Germany that the participants in the Evian Conference would respect the Nazis' sovereignty and domestic affairs. Furthermore, the delegates' reluctance to condemn the anti-Semitic policies of the Third Reich openly and officially was linked to Germany's accelerated path toward the "final solution": the extermination of the Jews. Adolf Hitler and the Nazis may have believed that the participants in the Evian Conference would also ignore or be bystanders to an accelerated German policy of genocide against European Jews.

Regrettably, at a critical moment for the fate of many European Jews, the ineptness and indifference of the states represented at Evian negated the potential to rescue a significant number of victims of the Holocaust. Organized attempts to rescue Jewish refugees for the duration of World War II remained inconsequential: The Bermuda Conference, which took place in April of 1943, was equally ineffective in its efforts to plan for the rescue of Jewish refugees.

—*Mitchel Gerber*

FURTHER READING

Bauer, Yehuda. *Jews for Sale? Nazi-Jewish Negotiations, 1933-1945*. New Haven, Conn.: Yale University Press, 1994. Intellectual historical investigation of the efforts to rescue Jews by negotiating with the Nazis.

_____. *Rethinking the Holocaust*. New Haven, Conn.: Yale University Press, 2001. Presents an analytical evaluation and articulates insights on a range of problematic topics of the Holocaust.

Feingold, Henry L. *The Politics of Rescue: The Roosevelt Administration and the Holocaust, 1938-1945*. New Brunswick, N.J.: Rutgers University Press, 1970. Classic historical study of the systematic efforts of the Roosevelt administration to assist European Jews threatened by Nazi Germany's plans for extermination.

Friedlander, Saul. *The Years of Persecution, 1933-1939.* Vol. 1 in *Nazi Germany and the Jews.* New York: HarperCollins, 1997. Meticulous study of the complex historical factors that led to the Holocaust.

Wyman, David S. *The Abandonment of the Jews: America and the Holocaust, 1941-1945.* New York: Pantheon Books, 1984. Historical study of the inadequate efforts of the United States to rescue European Jews.

SEE ALSO: Nov. 2, 1917: Balfour Declaration Supports a Jewish Homeland in Palestine; Jan. 30, 1933: Hitler Comes to Power in Germany; Mar., 1933: Nazi Concentration Camps Begin Operating; Mar. 14, 1937: Pius XI Urges Resistance Against Nazism; 1939-1945: Nazi Extermination of the Jews; Mar. 2, 1939: Pius XII Becomes Pope; Sept. 1, 1939: Germany Invades Poland; May 16, 1940-1944: Gypsies Are Exterminated in Nazi Death Camps.

1938

September 17, 1938
FIRST GRAND SLAM OF TENNIS

Don Budge became the first singles player in the history of tennis to win the grand slam—that is, he won all of the world's four major championship tournaments in the same calendar year. The grand-slam tournaments were the Australian, British, French, and U.S. amateur national championships.

LOCALE: Australia; France; England; United States
CATEGORY: Sports

KEY FIGURE
Don Budge (1915-2000), American tennis player and member of the International Tennis Hall of Fame

SUMMARY OF EVENT

In 1938, Don Budge from the United States became the first player ever to win the tennis grand slam when he won all four of the world's major tournaments in the same calendar year. The four grand-slam tournaments consisted of the national championships of Australia, France, England, and the United States. At that time, international competitive tennis was played only by amateurs, so Budge did not play against those who were playing on professional exhibition tours.

Budge's two finest years as an amateur player were 1937 and 1938. In both years, he was ranked as the world's number one player. In 1937, he won Wimbledon (the English championship) and the U.S. national championship, and he led the American team to its first Davis Cup victory in eleven years. In the semifinal round victory over Germany, Budge won the most thrilling singles victory in Davis Cup history. The team score was tied at two matches, and he lost the first two sets to Baron Gottfried von Cramm. Budge then came back to tie the match at two sets all and then fell behind four games to

one in the deciding fifth set before rallying to win. He was awarded the Sullivan Award as the top amateur athlete in the United States, and he was also named the Associated Press's Athlete of the Year.

In 1938, he defeated John Bromwich at the Australian finals, Roderich Menzel in France, Bunny Austin at Wimbledon, and Gene Mako in the United States. Budge helped the U.S. team win the Davis Cup again, and he repeated as the Associated Press Athelete of the Year. During 1938, Budge won six of the eight tournaments in which he played: He had a record of forty-three wins and two losses. In the period 1937-1938, he had a streak of wins in fourteen consecutive tournaments, winning ninety-two matches in a row. Budge also won the mixed doubles and the men's doubles titles at Wimbledon and in the U.S. national championship in 1938. In total, he won eight titles at the four grand-slam tournaments in 1938.

SIGNIFICANCE

Budge, who lived from June 13, 1915, to January 26, 2000, was more than six feet tall and was noted for his ability to use both power and finesse as his opponent and the court conditions dictated. He had a powerful serve and a smooth backhand that was considered one of the greatest ever. He played the game as a gentleman and almost never lost his temper.

The publicity that resulted from Budge's win increased tennis's recreational and competitive popularity, and tennis became a popular spectator sport throughout the world. Budge also had a positive effect on beliefs about exercise, fitness, and athletic competition. After 1938, Budge turned pro and played on the traveling tour against the world's top professionals, including Ellsworth Vines, Fred Perry, Bill Tilden, Bobby Riggs, and

Pancho Gonzales. He was elected to the International Tennis Hall of Fame in 1964. After the Don Budge slam in 1938, Rod Laver of Australia was the only player to duplicate the amateur slam (in 1962). Laver also won a professional slam in 1968; however, Budge remained the only American to have won the grand slam during the twentieth century. Women who have won a singles slam include Maureen Connolly in 1953, Margaret Smith Court in 1970, and Steffi Graf in 1988.

—*Alan Prescott Peterson*

FURTHER READING

Clerici, Gianni. *The Ultimate Tennis Book: Five Hundred Years of the Sport*. Chicago: Follett, 1975. Richly illustrated and thorough historical and cultural account of the evolution of tennis; also chronicles the economic growth of modern tennis as a participant and spectator sport.

Danzig, Allison. *The Fireside Book of Tennis*. New York: Simon & Schuster, 1972. A complete book on tennis history with very descriptive stories of great matches, including the one between Budge and von Cramm in 1937.

Gillmeister, Heiner. *Tennis: A Cultural History*. New York: New York University Press, 1998. Chronicles the evolution and development of tennis from the Middle Ages through the twentieth century.

Don Budge at Wimbledon in 1937, the year before his grand-slam victory. (AP/Wide World Photos)

SEE ALSO: July 1, 1903: First Tour de France; June, 1922: New Wimbledon Tennis Stadium Is Dedicated; Aug. 6, 1926: Ederle Swims the English Channel; Sept. 27, 1930: First Grand Slam of Golf.

September 29-30, 1938
MUNICH CONFERENCE

The Munich Conference formalized the capitulation of Prime Minister Neville Chamberlain and his French ally to Adolf Hitler's demands for the Sudetenland but failed to slake Hitler's thirst for power.

LOCALE: Munich, Germany
CATEGORIES: Diplomacy and international relations; expansion and land acquisition

KEY FIGURES
Edvard Beneš (1884-1948), president of Czechoslovakia, 1935-1938
Neville Chamberlain (1869-1940), prime minister of Great Britain, 1937-1940
Édouard Daladier (1884-1970), premier of France, 1938-1940
Emil Hácha (1872-1945), president of Czechoslovakia, 1938-1939
Adolf Hitler (1889-1945), chancellor of Germany, 1933-1945
Benito Mussolini (1883-1945), premier of Italy, 1922-1943
Walter Runciman (1870-1949), head of the British mission to Czechoslovakia

SUMMARY OF EVENT
As soon as Germany had annexed Austria in March, 1938, Adolf Hitler, chancellor of Germany, accelerated his political operations against the democracy of Czechoslovakia (now the Czech Republic and Slovakia). Although Czechoslovakia was stronger and more populous than Austria, it was also more divided internally as a result of the decision of the Paris Peace Conference in 1919 to draw its frontiers along economic and strategic rather than ethnic lines. Included in the new Czech state was the Sudetenland, a mountainous border area in western Czechoslovakia that was historically Austrian, linguistically German, and inhabited by more than three million people who were opposed to Czech domination. The region was strongly pro-Nazi.

The Anschluss (the German annexation of Austria) greatly intensified pan-German sentiment in the Sudetenland and correspondingly increased the power of the Sudeten German Party. Outwardly, the party worked for Sudeten autonomy within the Czech state, but during the summer months of 1938, Sudeten negotiators continually rejected proposals for settlements put forth by the Czech government in Prague. Secretly, the Sudeten German Party took orders from Hitler, who, unknown to the rest of the world, sought to dismember and ultimately destroy Czechoslovakia. As early as April, 1938, Hitler discussed with his cabinet plans to provide additional *Lebensraum* (living space) for the German people. This undisclosed plan, known to insiders as Operation Green, was the blueprint for the invasion of Czechoslovakia.

Since 1924, Czechoslovakia had been allied with France, an alliance that provided also for Soviet support, contingent on prior French support. By 1938, France had decided that it could not maintain its Eastern European alliances without the support of Great Britain. In the last analysis, support of Czechoslovakia against German aims depended on Great Britain. Neville Chamberlain, the British prime minister, was convinced that there were injustices in the treaties of 1919 that had to be removed if peace were to be preserved. He mistakenly believed that Hitler shared his abhorrence of war and that Hitler's objectives in Czechoslovakia were limited; he therefore favored a policy of appeasement. Instead of standing firmly behind Edvard Beneš, the president of Czechoslovakia, and his government in their efforts to resist German pressure, Chamberlain continually urged Beneš to make maximum concessions. In August, Chamberlain sent Walter Runciman, an English politician and millionaire shipbuilder, as an "impartial mediator" to investigate Czech-Sudeten differences at first hand. Runciman had no prior experience in such matters, and his pro-German sympathies were soon detected. The fact that Hitler was instructing the Sudeten leaders to keep increasing their demands remained hidden.

In September, when it became evident that Hitler was preparing an armed attack on Czechoslovakia and that the Czechs intended to resist, Chamberlain made three visits to Germany in the space of fourteen days. On September 15, at Hitler's mountain retreat near Berchtesgaden, Chamberlain conceded the right of self-determination to the Sudetens and promised to win acceptance of this point from the French and Czech governments. After this initial meeting, Chamberlain believed he had averted a general war, telling his sister, "I have no doubt whatever . . . that my visit alone prevented an invasion." He met Hitler again on September 22 at Bad Godesberg, a small town on the Rhine River, only to find that this concession was no longer enough. Hitler now demanded immediate Czech evacuation of the Sudetenland and German military occupation before the hold-

1938

ing of any plebiscite. Even Chamberlain balked at such bullying.

The outbreak of a general war seemed imminent, and on September 24 the Czechs mobilized in preparation for war, refusing to give in to Hitler. Chamberlain made a final effort to prevent hostilities, however, by proposing a four-power conference, which he asked Benito Mussolini, the Fascist dictator of Italy, to urge upon Hitler. On September 29, Chamberlain, Hitler, Mussolini, and the French premier, Édouard Daladier, met in Munich, at what became known as the Munich Conference. Together, without representatives of Czechoslovakia or its Soviet ally, they reached agreement on the Sudeten question. Relieved at the outcome of the Munich Conference, Chamberlain declared the settlement a "peace with honor." Abandoned by its allies, Czechoslovakia had no alternative but to relinquish the region to Hitler.

Significance

The Munich Agreement provided for the speedy and peaceful transfer of the Sudetenland to Germany and for an international guarantee of the reduced Czech state once the territorial demands of the Poles and Hungarians had been fulfilled. Chamberlain did prevent, at least temporarily, Hitler's military advance on the Czechs. He also secured Hitler's signature to an Anglo-German consultative pact, which he naïvely hoped would prevent the Nazi leader from acting unilaterally in the future. He paid an enormous price, however—soon the connotations of "sellout" and "peace at any price" would become attached to the terms "appeasement" and "Munich."

Czechoslovakia made its settlement with Poland, but difficulties with Hungary brought German and Italian intervention to determine the new Czech-Hungarian frontier. The British and French did not seem disturbed by the

British prime minister Neville Chamberlain (left) shakes hands with German chancellor Adolf Hitler at the signing of the Munich Agreement. (Library of Congress)

TEXT OF THE MUNICH AGREEMENT

Below is the agreement concluded at Munich, September 29, 1938, among Germany, Great Britain, France, and Italy.

GERMANY, the United Kingdom, France and Italy, taking into consideration the agreement, which has been already reached in principle for the cession to Germany of the Sudeten German territory, have agreed on the following terms and conditions governing the said cession and the measures consequent thereon, and by this agreement they each hold themselves responsible for the steps necessary to secure its fulfilment:

(1) The evacuation will begin on 1st October.

(2) The United Kingdom, France and Italy agree that the evacuation of the territory shall be completed by the 10th October, without any existing installations having been destroyed, and that the Czechoslovak Government will be held responsible for carrying out the evacuation without damage to the said installations.

(3) The conditions governing the evacuation will be laid down in detail by an international commission composed of representatives of Germany, the United Kingdom, France, Italy and Czechoslovakia.

(4) The occupation by stages of the predominantly German territory by German troops will begin on 1st October. The four territories marked on the attached map will be occupied by German troops in the following order:

The territory marked No. I on the 1st and 2nd of October; the territory marked No. II on the 2nd and 3rd of October; the territory marked No. III on the 3rd, 4th and 5th of October; the territory marked No. IV on the 6th and 7th of October. The remaining territory of preponderantly German character will be ascertained by the aforesaid international commission forthwith and be occupied by German troops by the 10th of October.

(5) The international commission referred to in paragraph 3 will determine the territories in which a plebiscite is to be held. These territories will be occupied by international bodies until the plebiscite has been completed. The same commission will fix the conditions in which the plebiscite is to be held, taking as a basis the conditions of the Saar plebiscite. The commission will also fix a date, not later than the end of November, on which the plebiscite will be held.

(6) The final determination of the frontiers will be carried out by the international commission. The commission will also be entitled to recommend to the four Powers, Germany, the United Kingdom, France and Italy, in certain exceptional cases, minor modifications in the strictly ethnographical determination of the zones which are to be transferred without plebiscite.

(7) There will be a right of option into and out of the transferred territories, the option to be exercised within six months from the date of this agreement. A German-Czechoslovak commission shall determine the details of the option, consider ways of facilitating the transfer of population and settle questions of principle arising out of the said transfer.

(8) The Czechoslovak Government will within a period of four weeks from the date of this agreement release from their military and police forces any Sudeten Germans who may wish to be released, and the Czechoslovak Government will within the same period release Sudeten German prisoners who are serving terms of imprisonment for political offences.

Munich, September 29, 1938.

ADOLF HITLER,
NEVILLE CHAMBERLAIN,
EDOUARD DALADIER,
BENITO MUSSOLINI.

---

fact that they were not consulted, and they did not press strongly for the promised guarantee of the remainder of the Czech state.

Hitler worked through the Slovak and Ruthenian nationalist groups to complete the destruction of the Czech state. Finally, in March of 1939, after brutally browbeating the new Czech president, Emil Hácha, in Berlin, Hitler forced the surrender of Bohemia and Moravia, established Slovakia as a German satellite, and assigned Ruthenia to Hungary. Thus, after months of negotiations and concessions to appease Hitler, the remainder of Czechoslovakia was finally occupied by Nazi troops, which had been Hitler's plan from the outset. These flagrant violations of the Munich Agreement belatedly awakened Chamberlain to the fact that Hitler was seeking not merely the self-determination of German-speaking people but also the domination of all Europe.

Among historians, the Munich Agreement has remained a source of debate. Although it is, as David Clay Large has put it, "one of the most widely condemned acts of diplomacy in modern history," defenders of the pact insist that even the slightest chance for peace warranted Chamberlain's decision to make the agreement with Germany. Moreover, Chamberlain's efforts allowed the Western powers a vital year to improve their armaments, strengthen their armed forces, plan their strategies, and prepare their countries psychologically for another war. Critics of the agreement contend the Germans actually improved their military position relative to the West in that same vital year, and that the agreement predisposed the Soviet Union toward an accommodation with Germany. Whatever the case, it is clear that Hitler's intention was not peace but war.

—*William Harrigan and Liesel Ashley Miller*

FURTHER READING

Adams, R. J. Q. *British Appeasement and the Origins of World War II*. Lexington, Mass.: D. C. Heath, 1994. Examines Britain's role in the lead-up to World War II. Sections titled "Variety of Opinion" and "The Search for Lessons" are especially informative on the topic of the Munich Conference.

Baumont, Maurice. *The Origins of the Second World War*. Translated by Simone de Couvreur Ferguson. New Haven, Conn.: Yale University Press, 1978. Concise yet thorough review of events leading up to and including the Munich Conference. Discusses also the Soviet response to the pact.

Dutton, David. *Neville Chamberlain*. London: Hodder Arnold, 2001. Focuses on Chamberlain's public life and how the events of his years as prime minister were perceived at the time and have been perceived since. Includes chronology.

Eubank, Keith. "The Road to War, 1938." In *The Origins of World War II*. 3d ed. Arlington Heights, Ill.: Harlan Davidson, 2004. Focuses on Czechoslovakia, negotiations between Hitler and Chamberlain, and the agreement among Germany, Britain, France, and Italy.

Jensen, Kenneth M., and David Hendrickson, eds. *The Meaning of Munich Fifty Years Later*. Washington, D.C.: United States Institute of Peace, 1990. Collection of essays provides a variety of viewpoints on the significance of the Munich pact.

Large, David Clay. "'Peace for Our Time': Appeasement and the Munich Conference." In *Between Two Fires: Europe's Path in the 1930's*. New York: W. W. Norton, 1990. Provides an insightful, detailed narrative of the process of appeasement, meetings between Hitler and Chamberlain, and the Munich Conference.

Taylor, Telford. *Munich: The Price of Peace*. Garden City, N.Y.: Doubleday, 1979. Lengthy and exhaustive study of every facet of the Munich Agreement, replete with details of the events leading to, during, and following the fateful conference.

Watt, Donald Cameron. *How War Came: The Immediate Origins of the Second World War, 1938-1939*. New York: Pantheon Books, 1989. Examines the final two years of peace and discusses the roles of appeasement and the Munich Conference in the onset of general war.

SEE ALSO: Jan. 11, 1923-Aug. 16, 1924: France Occupies the Ruhr; Nov. 8, 1923: Beer Hall Putsch; July 18, 1925-Dec. 11, 1926: *Mein Kampf* Outlines Nazi Thought; Jan. 30, 1933: Hitler Comes to Power in Germany; Mar., 1933: Nazi Concentration Camps Begin Operating; Mar. 7, 1936: German Troops March into the Rhineland; Feb. 12-Apr. 10, 1938: The Anschluss; Nov. 9-10, 1938: Kristallnacht; 1939-1945: Nazi Extermination of the Jews; Aug. 23-24, 1939: Nazi-Soviet Pact; Sept. 1, 1939: Germany Invades Poland.

October 5, 1938
DEATH OF MARIA FAUSTINA KOWALSKA

A humble nun and mystic, Kowalska left behind her diary Divine Mercy in My Soul, *which became a classic of Christian mysticism and spawned a devotion to the philosophy of divine mercy in the Catholic Church.*

LOCALE: Sisters of Our Lady of Mercy Convent, Kraków, Poland

CATEGORIES: Religion, theology, and ethics; publishing and journalism

KEY FIGURES

Maria Faustina Kowalska (Helena Kowalska; 1905-1938), author of *Divine Mercy in My Soul*, later canonized as Saint Maria Faustina Kowalska of the Most Blessed Sacrament

Michael Sopocko (fl. early twentieth century), Kowalska's spiritual adviser, who helped to propagate her message

John Paul II (Karol Józef Wojtyła; 1920-2005), Roman Catholic pope, 1978-2005, responsible for Kowalska's canonization

SUMMARY OF EVENT

Born August 25, 1905, Saint Maria Faustina Kowalska was the third of ten children in a very poor but devout family in Glogowiec, Poland. Although she lacked a proper education, her writings formed the basis of the Catholic philosophy of divine mercy, and she would become one of the most prominent Polish nuns in history. Her beginnings, however, were spartan. Stories about Kowalska's family recall that its members were so poor that Kowalska and her sisters had only one dress fit to wear to church and had to take turns wearing it, so the sisters all went to Mass at different times.

At an early age, Kowalska knew that she was destined for a holy life and asked her parents if she could join a convent. Her parents feared losing their favorite daughter, however, and they refused. The young woman became involved in dancing and other popular activities until one day she had a vision of God while she was at a dance. God asked her why she was wasting her life and not devoting herself to him, and he told her she should board a train for Warsaw and enter a convent.

She traveled to Warsaw and attempted to enter many convents, but none would allow her to stay. Finally Kowalska was accepted by the Sisters of Our Lady of Mercy, a group that worked with troubled young girls. After working for some time as a servant to pay the sum re-quired to join the convent, Kowalska entered as a postulant on August 1, 1925. A year later, she became a novice, and her name changed from Helena Kowalska to Sister Maria Faustina Kowalska of the Most Blessed Sacrament.

Jesus appeared to Kowalska on February 22, 1931, as a being of immense mercy who held one of his hands to his brilliant white robe and the other up in blessing. He revealed to her that she was to spread a message about the mercy of God and have an image painted of him exactly as he appeared to her. She was also instructed to found a Catholic congregation that would focus on the divine mercy of God. Kowalska's superiors balked at both ideas and forbade them.

Kowalska was saved, however, by her appointment to a new spiritual adviser, Father Michael Sopocko, who believed in her visions. Sopocko asked Kowalska to describe all her visions in a diary, and he commissioned a painter to portray Jesus according to Kowalska's description. At first Kowalska had a great deal of trouble writing, and her lack of education and frequent errors in spelling and grammar caused her to suspect that some of her thoughts might be heretical. She was also ostracized by nuns in the convent who thought that her visions were fictitious and that Jesus would not take an interest in a poor, lower-class nun.

In 1936, Kowalska became so sick that her superiors sent her to a sanatorium in Pradnik, Poland, where she began proselytizing to fellow patients, visitors, and anyone else who would listen. During the summer of 1938, Kowalska was so ill that she could not write in her diary, and she died in her convent on October 5, 1938. She had not been able to found a religious congregation based on the principle of divine mercy, but she had left behind her diary, which was eventually published as *Dzienniczek Sługi Bożzej S. M. Faustyny Kowalskiej: Profeski wieczystej zgromadzenia Matki Bożzej Miłosierdzia* (1981; *Divine Mercy in My Soul: The Diary of the Servant of God, Sister M. Faustina Kowalska*, 1987). The book served as a guidebook to divine mercy.

Kowalska's spiritual adviser, Father Sopocko, took over her heavenly mission and spread divine mercy's message. In 1941, a religious order was founded to celebrate and study divine mercy. However, disaster struck this community in 1958, when the Holy See (the government of the Roman Catholic Church) declared the teachings of divine mercy to be heretical. Theologians did not take into account Kowalska's lack of education, and as a result they interpreted some of her grammatical errors as arguments against the Church and as disloyal to the pope.

Devotion to divine mercy was declared heretical, but the archbishop of Kraków, Karol Józef Wojtyła, allowed the painting of Jesus that Father Sopocko had commissioned to remain on display so that petitioners could still pray to it. In 1965, Wojtyła, then cardinal of Kraków, launched an investigation into the life of Sister Maria Faustina Kowalska, and this investigation concluded that the teachings of divine mercy were not heretical. On April 18, 1993, Sister Maria Faustina Kowalska was beatified, and she was canonized on April 30, 2000, by Wojtyła, who by then was Pope John Paul II.

SIGNIFICANCE

For a large number of Catholics, Kowalska's writings spawned a new understanding of human beings' relationship with God. Her teachings also inspired Wojtyła, who became Pope John Paul II. Saint Faustina's work became one of the standard texts read by Catholics, and the diary of this uneducated nun took on an importance that rivaled works of popes and even other saints. Her book's popularity was especially amazing in the light of the vast difference in opportunities available to uneducated nuns from poor families and educated nuns from richer families.

The concept of divine mercy guided many in the Catholic Church during the twentieth century, and Saint Faustina became something of a national hero in Poland. Many of the quotations that she attributed to Jesus in her diary speak of Jesus' special love for that country, a very interesting notion that conflicted somewhat with Poland's especially horrific experiences during World War II, which began the year after Saint Faustina's death.

—*Josephine K. Portillo*

FURTHER READING

Kosiki, George W. *Study Guide to the Diary of Saint Faustina*. Toronto: Marian Press, 2003. A very good, directed study of Kowalska's writings.

Kowalska, Maria Faustina. *Diary of Sister M. Faustina Kowalska: Divine Mercy in My Soul*. Toronto: Marian Press, 2003. Saint Maria Faustina Kowalska's diaries, translated from Polish. An excellent resource. Spans more than six hundred pages.

Stackpole, Robert. *Pillars of Fire in My Soul: The Spirituality of Saint Faustina*. Toronto: Marian Press, 2003. Gives a good understanding of Faustina's connection to God and how that connection has been viewed by others.

SEE ALSO: May 16, 1920: Canonization of Joan of Arc; May 17, 1925: Thérèse of Lisieux Is Canonized; Dec. 8, 1933: Canonization of Bernadette Soubirous.

October 22, 1938
CARLSON AND KORNEI MAKE THE FIRST XEROGRAPHIC PHOTOCOPY

The technological breakthrough of xerographic photocopying created a revolution in the maintenance of records and the transmission of information.

LOCALE: Astoria, New York
CATEGORIES: Science and technology; inventions

KEY FIGURES

Chester F. Carlson (1906-1968), American physicist, inventor, and patent attorney
John H. Dessauer (1905-1993), director of research and engineering at the Haloid Company (later Xerox Corporation)
Otto Kornei (b. 1903), German American engineer
Roland Michael Schaffert (1905-1991), American scientist
Joseph C. Wilson (1909-1971), president of the Haloid Company (later Xerox Corporation)

SUMMARY OF EVENT

In Astoria, New York, stands an unpretentious building with a bronze plaque on a central wall commemorating an event that occurred on October 22, 1938, when Chester F. Carlson and Otto Kornei produced the first dim copy of an image by a process called "electrophotography." The text of the copy was simply "10-22-38 Astoria." Carlson patented the process and, after considerable additional work, also patented a working model of a copying machine based on electrophotography. Carlson had come to New York from California, where he had earned his bachelor's degree in physics at the California Institute of Technology in 1930. He was employed by the patent department of P. R. Mallory Company, and he carried out his experimental work in his spare time and entirely at his own expense. He hired Kornei, an unemployed engineer recently arrived from Germany, to assist him.

Carlson's invention may be contrasted with ordinary photography, in which an image is produced by the effect of light on a film or plate coated with a silver compound. In electrophotography, the light-sensitive element is a reusable plate of metal coated with a layer of sulfur and electrostatically charged before exposure. When the plate is exposed, electrical charge leaks away from the illuminated areas in proportion to the light that falls. The image is trapped as an invisible pattern of static charges, which may be rendered visible through the dusting of the plate with fine powder that adheres to the charged areas. The copying process ends when the powder pattern is transferred to paper and permanently bonded by heat or solvent vapors. In conventional photography, the image is developed through the bathing of the film in successive chemical liquids that darken the exposed areas and remove unexposed silver compounds. The advantage of electrophotography lies in the speed and convenience of dry developing and in the economy resulting from having a reusable plate, thus avoiding the consumption of expensive silver compounds.

In modern xerographic equipment, most of the technical details are different from the ones used by Carlson and Kornei, but the principles are essentially the same. The light-sensitive plate is usually coated with a thin layer of selenium, which is much more sensitive than the original sulfur, and electrostatic charging is accomplished by a corona discharge instead of through the rubbing of the plate with cloth or fur, as was the practice in 1938. The corona discharge is generated in a shielded wire maintained at a high voltage and moved across the selenium-coated plate prior to exposure. In 1938, the clinging powder image was transferred to paper by pressing, which caused the powder to stick to the paper. A more efficient method is now used in which the paper is given an electrical charge opposite to that of the powder, causing the image to be transferred as the powder clings preferentially to the paper.

For six years following his success in 1938, Carlson was unable to obtain financial backing for further research and development of his invention, despite repeated attempts. In 1944, he demonstrated his process in Columbus, Ohio, at the Battelle Memorial Institute. When asked for his opinion of the demonstration, Dr. Roland Michael Schaffert, then head of the Graphic Arts division at Battelle, wrote a memorandum favoring the new idea, and support was granted. In the years that followed, Battelle scientists, including William E. Bixby, L. E. Walkup, C. D. Oughton, J. F. Rheinfrank, and E. N.

Wise, improved the process and patented further inventions related to it. The work attracted additional support from the U.S. Signal Corps and from the Haloid Company of Rochester, New York, a small company that needed a new product to bolster earnings in the period following World War II. During this time many other companies were approached and offered a share in the new process in exchange for their support of the research at Battelle, but none was interested.

After 1947, research began to be directed toward the production of a practical copying device that could be sold commercially. In 1948, work had progressed far enough for a demonstration to be held at a meeting of the Optical Society of America in Detroit. The date was October 22, 1948, the tenth anniversary of Carlson's first copy, and for the occasion a new word, "xerography" (from the Greek, meaning "dry-writing"), was coined to replace the more technical term "electrophotography." The demonstration was a success, but Haloid could not immediately benefit from the publicity. Two more years of developmental work were necessary before the Model A copier, the first commercial xerographic copier, could be brought out in 1950. The Model A was successful mainly for preparation of multilith masters; it was not particularly successful as a document copier.

Not until 1960, after a long, expensive, and difficult period of development, did the Xerox Model 914 copier become available ("Xerox" and "914" are registered trademarks of the Xerox Corporation, Stamford, Connecticut). Many people contributed to the success of Model 914 (so called because it used 9-by-14-inch paper), but prominent mention should be made of Dr. John H. Dessauer, Haloid's vice president in charge of research and product development, and Joseph C. Wilson, the company president. Soon after the introduction of the new copier, Haloid adopted a new name: Xerox Corporation.

SIGNIFICANCE

Model 914 weighed about six hundred pounds and could make up to four hundred copies per hour. It was reliable and simple to operate. These virtues soon made it very popular, so much so that people began to speak and write of a "copying revolution." Many other companies began to develop and market competitive models, and in the latter part of the 1960's, smaller and faster copiers were available. By 1975 it was estimated that 2.3 million copying machines were in use in the United States, making a total of approximately seventy-

1938

eight million copies annually. Extrapolation from the growth of copying to that point led to the expectation that the volume would double within another five years, but that estimate proved to be short of actual figures. By the mid-1990's, the volume of xerographic copying in the United States soared beyond a billion copies annually.

By the end of the twentieth century, the technology of xerography had developed to the point where the process of making a single copy could be completed in less than a few seconds and at comparatively little expense. Advances from the early days of xerography included color copying as well as reduction and enlargement; in addition, copying machines were configured to accomplish such tasks as collating and even stapling.

The easy availability of a means to copy documents, periodicals, and books led to many benefits for businesses as well as for individuals. Communications of many kinds were speeded by the ability to produce perfect copies quickly, and informational, artistic, and other forms of the written word were able to reach audiences they may never otherwise have reached.

Along with the benefits of photocopying came some problems. For one thing, the excellent reproduction quality of many color copiers led to increased problems with the counterfeiting of currency and stock certificates. More widespread problems, however, came in the area of copyright infringement. In a 1976 government study of photocopying, 21,280 libraries were surveyed with regard to their copying practices. It was found that a total of 114 million copies were made, of which 54 million were of copyrighted materials. Authors and publishers became concerned about their rights, as libraries, always desirous of providing service at low cost, found copying irresistible. Eventually there were lawsuits, including the 1975 case of *Williams and Wilkins v. United States*. The U.S. Supreme Court reached a tie vote on the case, in which Williams and Wilkins, a publishing company, sought royalties from a library that had reproduced copyrighted materials. In 1976, President Gerald Ford signed into law a new copyright bill that went into effect on January 1, 1978. Under the new law, publishers would receive royalties for some of the copies made in libraries, but limited royalty-free "fair use" library copying was still allowed. During the next five years Congress amended the law four times, one of which was to align U.S. law with the provisions of the Berne Convention, a multinational copyright treaty of 1989.

—*Elizabeth Fee and P. Ann Peake*

FURTHER READING

Dessauer, John H. *My Years with Xerox: The Billions Nobody Wanted*. Garden City, N.Y.: Doubleday, 1971. Nontechnical account of the growth of Xerox Corporation by a scientist who worked there from 1935 to 1970. Includes material on the development of xerography and the people who made it possible, the farsighted business decisions that allowed the company to succeed, and the sociological implications of xerography.

Dessauer, John H., and Harold E. Clark, eds. *Xerography and Related Processes*. London: Focal Press, 1965. Collection includes a chapter that presents Carlson's account of the history of electrostatic recording. Features a picture of the first experimental copy and drawings from some of Carlson's earliest patents.

Golembeski, Dean J. "Struggling to Become an Inventor." *American Heritage of Invention and Technology* 4, no. 3 (1989): 8-15. Recounts the life and work of Chester F. Carlson, who developed xerography, and traces the subsequent commercial development of the process.

Gundlach, R. W. "Xerography from the Beginning." *Journal of Electrostatics* 24, no. 1 (November, 1989): 3-9. Surveys the history of xerography, emphasizing the contributions of Carlson and scientists at Battelle who made substantive improvements in the process. Also credits Xerox's business success to the uncommonly good management of Joseph C. Wilson.

Jacobson, Gary. "Carlson's Timeless Lessons on Innovation." *Management Review* 78 (February, 1989): 13-16. Brief review of the history of xerography on the occasion of its fiftieth anniversary. Draws on Carlson's notebooks for insights into his creativity.

Jacobson, Gary, and John Hillkirk. *Xerox: American Samurai*. New York: Macmillan, 1986. This history of Xerox has been praised as an inspirational story of American competitiveness against the Japanese and criticized for adulation of the corporation. Provides historical details about Carlson, Wilson, and the early days of Xerox. Includes a glossary of copier-related terms.

Owen, David. *Copies in Seconds: Chester Carlson and the Birth of the Xerox Machine*. New York: Simon & Schuster, 2004. Highly readable account of Carlson's invention, his struggle to have its potential recognized, and the work of all the other individuals, including scientists and corporate executives, who contributed to the development of photocopying technology.

Schaffert, Roland Michael. *electrophotography*. Rev. ed. New York: Focal Press, 1975. Devotes a chapter to a thorough discussion of the xerographic process. Includes charts, graphs, and photographs.

SEE ALSO: 1907: Lumières Develop Color Photography; Mar. 4, 1909: U.S. Congress Updates Copyright Law; 1930's: Invention of the Slug Rejector Spreads Use of Vending Machines.

October 30, 1938
WELLES BROADCASTS *THE WAR OF THE WORLDS*

Orson Welles terrified thousands with his radio broadcast of The War of the Worlds, *proving the power of the medium in the hands of a genius.*

LOCALE: New York, New York
CATEGORY: Radio and television

KEY FIGURES
Orson Welles (1915-1985), American actor and director
John Houseman (1902-1988), American actor, director, and acting teacher
Howard Koch (1902-1995), American scriptwriter and playwright

SUMMARY OF EVENT

On October 30, 1938, as newspaper headlines and radio news broadcasts carried threats of a coming world war, a Sunday-night radio drama sent thousands of Americans into panic, hysteria, and flight. The young Orson Welles and his Mercury Theatre had already acquired a reputation in New York for unusual productions either under the aegis of the Federal Theatre Project or begun while Welles worked for the project. Welles staged a modern-dress *Julius Caesar* with characters in uniforms resembling those of German and Italian soldiers and a memorable production of *Macbeth* with an African American cast. When Congress canceled funding for the Federal Theatre Project's production of Marc Blitzstein's political musical *The Cradle Will Rock* and the unpaid theater owners locked the doors, directors Welles and John Houseman led the cast and audience to a hastily rented theater down the street, making headlines and creating the first production of their new Mercury Theatre in 1937.

In the fall of 1938, Mercury Theatre had a radio broadcast spot on the Columbia Broadcasting System (CBS) opposite ventriloquist Edgar Bergen's popular program, featuring his dummy Charlie McCarthy, on the National Broadcasting Company (NBC) network. The Mercury Theatre company presented dramatic versions of classic stories, and Welles decided to present an update of H. G. Wells's 1898 novel *The War of the Worlds*

on the night before Halloween. As writer Howard Koch noted later, nothing much of the original story, set in England in the nineteenth century, could be used except the Martian invasion and the subsequent destruction wrought by the "alien beings."

Koch had only days to write the script. Welles told him to use the format of a news broadcast. To understand how listeners could have been so gullible as to be fooled by the program, it is helpful to have some knowledge of the format of radio in the 1930's. Radio airtime had to be filled with sounds. An easy way to fill "dead" time, particularly at night, was to broadcast live dance music from hotel ballrooms across the country. Listeners were conditioned to expect interruptions of these programs for news bulletins. In addition, commercial time slots were shorter and more flexible in their scheduling than later became the norm. Today, a viewer switching channels among major television networks during a commercial break simply finds more commercials. In 1938, a radio listener changing stations might have found another program in progress. The Mercury Theatre's fairly small audience was augmented during the first commercial break on Edgar Bergen's show as that show's listeners tuned in and found themselves in the midst of what seemed to be a Martian invasion.

These station switchers and other late arrivals missed the program's opening announcement: "The Columbia Broadcasting System and its affiliated stations present Orson Welles and the Mercury Theatre on the Air in a radio play by Howard Koch suggested by the H. G. Wells novel *The War of the Worlds*." This was followed by the show's musical theme and the introduction of the "director of the Mercury Theatre and star of these broadcasts, Orson Welles." Welles's lead-in to the script of "Invasion from Mars" was followed by a "weather report" and by what purported to be live dance orchestra music from downtown New York. The music was interrupted almost immediately by a bulletin announcing the "explosion of incandescent gas" on Mars, which was later connected to the takeoffs of the vehicles that would invade Earth.

1938

On October 31, 1938, Orson Welles (center) explains to reporters that he and his acting company meant no harm with their broadcast of The War of the Worlds. *(AP/ Wide World Photos)*

The time left for the presentation of the entire invasion, after commercials and the introduction, was only forty-five minutes. This included events from the take-offs from Mars to the spread of destruction across the United States and the ultimate destruction of the Martians, "slain, after all man's defenses had failed, by the humblest thing that God in His wisdom put upon this earth," to Orson Welles's closing line, "If your doorbell rings and nobody's there, that was no Martian . . . it's Halloween."

Of an estimated six million listeners, approximately one million believed that Martians had landed. Thousands did not wait to hear that the aliens had been destroyed by bacteria or that the broadcast was the "radio version of dressing up in a sheet and saying 'Boo!'" as Welles said at the end of the show. Some fled in their cars, some called friends and families to warn them, some rushed to churches, some guarded their property with guns, and some even headed for Grovers Mill, New Jersey, where "the Martians had landed," to lend a hand in the defense.

Meanwhile, at the CBS studio in New York, the actors were unaware of problems until the telephone rang as the closing theme played. Police officers entered and escorted the Mercury Theatre players out a back entrance. Although for several days it appeared that Welles, in par-

ticular, was in serious trouble, good sense prevailed at last. The show had been announced as an adaptation, and it was clear that no one connected with it had intended to create a panic or had dreamed that listeners would confuse it with reality. Dorothy Thompson, an important political newspaper columnist of the day, wrote a supportive column, helping to calm the overreaction.

Headlines in major newspapers on October 31 indicated the seriousness of the panic of the night before. The headline in the *New York Daily News* proclaimed "Fake Radio 'War' Stirs Terror Through U.S." *The New York Times* headed a front-page article "Radio Listeners in Panic, Taking War Drama as Fact." The accompanying piece was four columns in length, with four more columns on page 4 giving examples of reactions from all the New York City boroughs and upstate New York. The story ended with a statement from CBS "pointing out that the fictional character of the broadcast had been announced four times and had been previously publicized." Welles was quoted as expressing "profound regret" and commenting that he had "hesitated about presenting it . . . because 'it was our thought that perhaps people might be bored or annoyed at hearing a tale so improbable.'"

SIGNIFICANCE

At the end of the radio broadcast season, Welles and some of his company went to Hollywood. Welles directed and starred in the now highly respected film *Citizen Kane* (1941). He followed that success by directing *The Magnificent Ambersons* (1942), treasured by film buffs for its then-unusual camera angles. He was never to have such great success in Hollywood again, although he acted in a number of films and directed several more.

He directed *The Stranger* (1946), costarring Loretta Young and Edward G. Robinson, in which he also played a Nazi hiding under a false identity in a small American town. *The Lady from Shanghai* (1948), which he directed and in which he costarred with Rita Hayworth, is remembered for its climactic scene in a maze of mirrors. He both acted in and directed *Touch of Evil* (1958), which is considered to be cinematically innovative for its opening scene, shot in one long take as the camera takes the audience through the streets of the town in which the film is set. Later directors borrowed this "long take" opening on many occasions.

Welles acted in a number of later films, his most memorable performance perhaps being in *The Third Man* (1949), in which his presence was always announced by the film's distinctive theme song. Among the other films in which he had acting roles were *Compulsion* (1959), based on the Leopold and Loeb case; *Moby Dick* (1956), in which he played Father Mapple in a tour de force scene, preaching to the crew of the *Pequod* before they sailed; *The Long, Hot Summer* (1958); *Is Paris Burning?* (1966); *A Man for All Seasons* (1966); *Casino Royale* (1967); *Catch-22* (1970); and *Treasure Island* (1972). The version of *Macbeth* (1948) that he directed and in which he played the title role was a perhaps undeserved failure. Self-exiled to Europe, where he worked for a number of years, he was "forgiven" by Hollywood in 1970, when he received an Academy Award for "supreme artistry and versatility in the creation of motion pictures." He received a life achievement award from the American Film Institute in 1975. In the later part of his career, Welles appeared frequently on television, particularly on *The Tonight Show Starring Johnny Carson*, where he told interesting stories and performed magic tricks (he was a skilled magician), and in commercials for a winemaker in which he repeated the slogan "We will sell no wine before its time."

Houseman, who had been codirector of Mercury Theatre, followed Welles to Hollywood and produced a number of films, including *The Blue Dahlia* (1946), *Julius Caesar* (1953), *Executive Suite* (1954), *Lust for Life* (1956), and *This Property Is Condemned* (1966). He acted in several films during this period, and for a number of years he taught acting at Juilliard in New York City, training many students who became immensely successful. It was his role as a law professor in the film *The Paper Chase* (1973), however, followed by the same role in a popular television dramatic series based on the film, that made his face and voice so familiar to the general public that he was cast in a series of television commercials for an investment firm.

Through his work with the Federal Theatre Project, the Mercury Theatre, and his film work, both as director and actor, Orson Welles left a permanent creative mark on American theatrical entertainment. Ironically, what may live longest with the general public is his "panic broadcast." In the 1980's, a television docudrama re-created the broadcast, interwoven with the fictional stories of characters who listened to it. Woody Allen included the broadcast in his film *Radio Days* (1987). In 1970, scriptwriter Howard Koch published a book about the experience, *The Panic Broadcast: Portrait of an Event.*

Two years after the Mercury Theatre broadcast, Princeton professor Hadley Cantril, funded by the Rockefeller Foundation, studied the reaction of selected interviewees who had been frightened by it. He published the results in a volume titled *The Invasion from Mars* (1940). Cantril noted that the political and economic environment of the times was an element that should not be discounted in any consideration of the broadcast's effects. The radio pro-

---

INVADERS FROM MARS

In Howard Koch's 1938 radio play adaptation of H. G. Wells's The War of the Worlds, *an announcer makes this vivid report:*

Ladies and gentlemen, I have a grave announcement to make. Incredible as it may seem, both the observations of science and the evidence of our eyes lead to the inescapable assumption that those strange beings who landed in the Jersey farmlands tonight are the vanguard of an invading army from the planet Mars. The battle which took place tonight at Grovers Mill has ended in one of the most startling defeats ever suffered by any army in modern times; seven thousand men armed with rifles and machine guns pitted against a single fighting machine of the invaders from Mars. One hundred and twenty known survivors. The rest strewn over the battle area from Grovers Mill to Plainsboro, crushed and trampled to death under the metal feet of the monster, or burned to cinders by its heat ray. The monster is now in control of the middle section of New Jersey and has effectively cut the state through its center. Communication lines are down from Pennsylvania to the Atlantic Ocean. Railroad tracks are torn and service from New York to Philadelphia discontinued except routing some of the trains through Allentown and Phoenixville. Highways to the north, south, and west are clogged with frantic human traffic. Police and army reserves are unable to control the mad flight. By morning the fugitives will have swelled Philadelphia, Camden, and Trenton, it is estimated, to twice their normal population. Martial law prevails throughout New Jersey and eastern Pennsylvania. At this time we take you to Washington for a special broadcast on the National Emergency . . . the Secretary of the Interior . . .

gram took place during the last years of the Great Depression. On the eve of World War II, Americans were accustomed to listening to news broadcast from Europe; they heard Adolf Hitler himself speaking to the German people and their answering cry of "Sieg Heil!" In the movie theaters, they saw newsreels showing German troops. They had vicariously experienced the Spanish Civil War, in which the Fascist forces had "tested the guns" for the invasions of Poland, Czechoslovakia, Holland, Belgium, and France. Americans thus had reason to be apprehensive. Their hearts jumped when they heard the words "We interrupt this program" as they listened to their radios.

A wit said at the time that the panic happened because "all the intelligent people were listening to Charlie McCarthy." It was not that simple, however. The people who were taken in by the broadcast constituted a cross section of the American citizenry. Many of them missed the opening announcement and had swung into wild action before the repetition of the announcement at the commercial break. Many made some attempt to check on what was actually happening by calling neighbors or family members. If the callers got no answer, their fears were confirmed. If they could not get through to authorities because others were trying to make similar calls, the busy signal confirmed their fears. Some listeners did switch stations and realized the truth. Others who switched and heard nothing of the "invasion" reasoned that the other stations had simply not received word yet. Some of the more eschatological thought that the invasion was the justified end of the world. One man whom Cantril interviewed said that he had been pleased; he hoped his mother-in-law would be scared to death. Another interviewee said that when he was convinced of the reality of the invasion, he was struck by "how pretty all things on earth seemed."

Cantril concluded that anxiety about impending war was a less important cause of the panic than the "highly disturbed economic conditions many Americans have experienced for the past decade, the consequent unemployment, the prolonged discrepancies between family incomes, the inability of both young and old to plan for the future," all of which "engendered a widespread feeling of insecurity." He also noted that Americans had become highly suggestible.

—*Katherine Lederer*

FURTHER READING

Brady, Frank. *Citizen Welles: A Biography of Orson Welles*. New York: Scribner, 1989. Comprehensive biography devotes a large section to the broadcast of *The War of the Worlds* and its aftermath. Includes bibliographies and index.

Cantril, Hadley. *The Invasion from Mars: A Study in the Psychology of Panic*. 1940. Reprint. New Brunswick, N.J.: Transaction, 2005. Provides an account of the public panic followed by the findings of Cantril's funded study of some of the listeners and his conclusions. Includes the broadcast script.

Heyer, Paul. *The Medium and the Magician: Orson Welles, the Radio Years, 1934-1952*. Lanham, Md.: Rowman & Littlefield, 2005. Study of Welles focuses on his years in radio and his influence on the art of radio drama.

Holmsten, Brian, and Alex Lubertozzi, eds. *The Complete "War of the Worlds": Mars' Invasion of Earth from H. G. Wells to Orson Welles*. Naperville, Ill.: Sourcebooks MediaFusion, 2001. Illustrated volume includes the complete text of H. G. Wells's novel, Koch's script for the infamous radio program, and discussion of reactions to the program as well as two CDs featuring the original Mercury Theatre broadcast, interviews with Welles and Houseman, and more.

Houseman, John. *Run-Through*. New York: Simon & Schuster, 1972. Entertaining career memoir includes discussion of Houseman's work with Welles in the Federal Theatre Project and the Mercury Theatre, including the famous broadcast. Also recounts how the two actor-directors parted ways in Hollywood.

Koch, Howard. *As Time Goes By: Memoirs of a Writer*. New York: Harcourt Brace Jovanovich, 1979. Includes an account of Koch's involvement with Houseman, Welles, and the Mercury Theatre.

_____. *The Panic Broadcast: Portrait of an Event*. Boston: Little, Brown, 1970. The scriptwriter's account discusses the origin of the script, the night of the broadcast, and the results of the broadcast. Includes the full script, photographs of the studio performance, reproductions of news accounts, and cartoons about the broadcast.

SEE ALSO: Dec. 24, 1906: Fessenden Pioneers Radio Broadcasting; 1920's: Radio Develops as a Mass Broadcast Medium; Aug. 20-Nov. 2, 1920: Radio Broadcasting Begins; Nov. 28, 1925: WSM Launches *The Grand Ole Opry*; Sept. 9, 1926: National Broadcasting Company Is Founded; Mar. 19, 1928: *Amos 'n' Andy* Radio Show Goes on the Air; Aug. 29, 1935-June 30, 1939: Federal Theatre Project Promotes Live Theater; May 6, 1937: *Hindenburg* Dirigible Bursts into Flames.

November 9-10, 1938
KRISTALLNACHT

The night of violence dubbed Kristallnacht initiated the deliberate, government-sanctioned extermination of the Jews in Germany now known as the Holocaust. Subdued reaction to the anti-Semitic violence from both the international community and "ordinary" Germans opened the door to the Nazi policies of extermination that soon followed.

ALSO KNOWN AS: Night of Broken Glass; Imperial Crystal Night (Reichskristallnacht); Pogrom Night (Pogromnacht)

Locale: Berlin, Vienna, and other cities in Germany and Austria

CATEGORIES: Terrorism; atrocities and war crimes

KEY FIGURES

Herschel Grynszpan (1921-c. 1943/1945), a Polish-Jewish student living in Paris

Joseph Goebbels (1897-1945), chief propagandist for the Nazi Party in Germany

Hermann Göring (1893-1946), German field marshal and head of the armed forces

Adolf Hitler (1889-1945), chancellor of Germany, 1933-1945

SUMMARY OF EVENT

German anti-Semitism did not suddenly materialize with Adolf Hitler's rise to power in 1933; it was already entrenched among many in Germany's non-Jewish population. Hitler, however, fomented anti-ethnic sentiments and promulgated the myth of "Aryan" superiority to consolidate his power, establishing policies and laws against German Jews from the beginning of his rule. In 1933, he announced a daylong boycott against Jewish businesses, legislated against kosher butchering, and set in motion a policy prohibiting Jewish children from attending public schools. In 1935, the Nuremberg Laws declared that Jews were no longer German citizens. Soon afterward, Jews were relieved of their voting rights and outright hatred was exhibited throughout Germany on signs that read Jews Not Welcome. Laws passed in 1938 restricted Jewish enterprise and job opportunities and required that all Jews carry identification cards.

On November 7, 1938, a seventeen-year-old Polish-Jewish student, Herschel Grynszpan, assassinated German diplomat Ernst vom Rath in Paris in protest against the deportation of some twelve thousand Polish Jews living in Germany—including his own family—a week be-

fore, on October 28. The Polish government would not admit the homeless expatriates, who wandered near the border in pouring rain, without food or shelter, for several days. (The Polish government would eventually admit them to a concentration camp where conditions were generally worse.) Grynszpan received a letter from his mother on November 3 outlining their situation, and Grynszpan, a youth with few resources, appealed for help to the uncle and aunt with whom he was staying, but they could do little. Grynszpan, distraught, purchased a gun on November 7, walked into the German Embassy in Paris, and asked to see an official; vom Rath, a junior official, was on duty and Grynszpan was admitted to his office. He shot vom Rath three times in the stomach, reportedly cursing him and saying he was acting on behalf of the twelve thousand exiled Jews. Little did Grynszpan realize that he had provided the Nazi regime with an excuse to unleash unspeakable atrocities on Jews throughout Germany and Austria.

Propaganda minister Joseph Goebbels made the best of the opportunity, organizing "spontaneous" demonstrations against Jews that erupted in violence in cities and villages across the country. According to Goebbels, Hitler had received the news of vom Rath's death on November 9: "[T]he Führer," Goebbels reported in an address to the Nazi leadership, "has decided that . . . demonstrations should not be prepared or organized by the party, but insofar as they erupt spontaneously, they are not to be hampered."

In fact, the riots were initiated by members of the Gauleiters, the Sturm Abteilung (SA), and the Schutzstaffel (SS), who for the most part wore civilian garb. German citizens eventually joined them. What followed was a orgy of violence that lasted for two days. The rioters administered axes and sledgehammers to Jewish storefronts, shattering window panes—hence the name Kristallnacht, meaning "crystal night," in reference to the broken glass. The term was a euphemism, however. The destruction went well beyond the smashing of glass. Thousands of homes and stores were looted, damaged, or burned, and the destruction extended to more than fifteen hundred synagogues and several Jewish cemeteries. Police and firefighters stood idly by, their only mandate being to protect "Aryan" property.

Estimates vary on the number killed in the rioting, from as few as three dozen to as many as two hundred. The deaths were mainly the result of bludgeoning. In the after-

1938

math of the rioting, thirty thousand Jewish men were arrested and transported to concentration camps: Dachau, Buchenwald, Sachsenhausen, and elsewhere. The camps would be expanded to accommodate their new charges, and a means of systematic extermination began to emerge.

On November 11, Goebbels called for an end to the violence, which went unheeded in the camps. The number of deaths that followed as an immediate result of Kristallnacht—by suicide and in the camps—ran into the thousands. The London *News Chronicle* reported that at Sachsenhausen, for example, sixty-two men were beaten until they fell: "Twelve of the sixty-two were dead, their skulls smashed. The others were all unconscious. The eyes of some had been knocked out, their faces flattened and shapeless."

On November 12, a meeting of Nazi leaders was convened by Field Marshal Hermann Göring to hear the official anti-Jewish policy. As Göring put it: "I implore competent agencies to take all measures for the elimination of the Jew from the German economy, and to submit them to me." Göring concluded the meeting by noting that he "would not like to be a Jew in Germany."

SIGNIFICANCE

Incredibly, the Jews were seen as the instigators of the riots and were forced to clean the rubble of their ruined businesses and places of worship. Those who had survived the violence of the riots were now subjected to increasingly oppressive policies, fines, and restrictions on their movements—including the Judenvermoegersabgabe, a collective fine for the murder of vom Rath which today would be the equivalent of several billion U.S. dollars. The Nazis began to confiscate Jewish property as part of their program of "Aryanization." A mass exodus of Jews followed as many emigrated to the United States, Palestine, or sympathetic European nations. The assassin, Grynszpan, would remain in German custody awaiting a trial that never materialized; he was probably executed in 1944 or 1945.

Most striking, however, was the relatively mild reaction on the part of those Germans not directly in the path of Nazi violence. Even the international response—though outrage was expressed—was measured. Newspapers condemned the pogroms, but no immediate action was undertaken by the international community. In its November 11 issue, for example, *The New York Times* reported only that Goebbels had called a halt to the violence, not mentioning the undisguised fact that he had instigated it. The silence of the German people was tantamount to complicity: Whether they were cowed by fear,

shared the Nazis' ethnic hatreds, or simply were indifferent, their passivity in the face of the events of Kristallnacht made it clear to Nazi leaders that they faced little resistance. Hitler and his henchmen proceeded to excise the Jewish "threat" in the form of increasingly transparent atrocities that eventually constituted the Holocaust.

At the same time, Kristallnacht—to be followed four months later by the German invasion of Czechoslovakia (March 15, 1939)—made it clear to world leaders that the Nazi regime would stop at nothing to appropriate *Lebensraum* (living space) by incorporating central Eu-

---

GÖRING CALLS FOR THE REMOVAL OF JEWISH INFLUENCE

On November 12, Hermann Göring spoke before a meeting of the Nazi leadership to assess the Kristallnacht rioting, blaming the events on the Jews and calling for a series of laws that would remove the Jewish influence on the German economy:

Gentlemen! Today's meeting is of a decisive nature. I have received a letter written on the Führer's orders requesting that the Jewish question be now, once and for all, coordinated and solved one way or another.

Since the problem is mainly an economic one, it is from the economic angle it shall have to be tackled. Because, gentlemen, I have had enough of these demonstrations! They don't harm the Jew but me, who is the final authority for coordinating the German economy. If today a Jewish shop is destroyed, if goods are thrown into the street, the insurance companies will pay for the damages; and, furthermore, consumer goods belonging to the people are destroyed. If in the future, demonstrations which are necessary occur, then, I pray, that they be directed so as not to hurt us.

Because it's insane to clean out and burn a Jewish warehouse, then have a German insurance company make good the loss. And the goods which I need desperately, whole bales of clothing and whatnot, are being burned. And I miss them everywhere. I may as well burn the raw materials before they arrive.

I should not want to leave any doubt, gentlemen, as to the aim of today's meeting. We have not come together merely to talk again, but to make decisions, and I implore competent agencies to take all measures for the elimination of the Jew from the German economy, and to submit them to me.

Source: Transcript by Robert Conot in *Justice at Nuremberg* (New York: Harper and Row, 1983).

rope into an Aryan empire. Support for the policy of appeasement was coming to an end as visionary politicians began to foresee a second world war.

—*Christina J. Moose*

FURTHER READING

Gilbert, Martin. *Kristallnacht: Prelude to Destruction.* New York: HarperCollins, 2006. Prolific historian and Holocaust scholar Gilbert identifies Kristallnacht as the moment when the Nazi regime consolidated its momentum toward genocide. Eyewitness accounts from those in Berlin, Vienna, and other cities who endured the crime spree testify to the violence and personal terror experienced by the victims. Newspaper accounts and the reactions of ordinary people record the inadequate response. Photos and maps.

Hilberg, Raul. *The Destruction of the European Jews.* 3d ed. New Haven, Conn.: Yale University Press, 2003. Comprehensive account of the Nazi treatment of the Jews of Germany and Nazi-occupied Europe. Bibliography and index.

Johnson, Eric A., and Karl-Heinz Reuband. *What We Knew: Terror, Mass Murder, and Everyday Life in Nazi Germany—An Oral History.* Cambridge, Mass.: Basic Books, 2005. In answer to the conventional wisdom that the non-Jewish German public was unaware of the anti-Semitic atrocities growing in the Nazi state, Johnson and Reuband, using hundreds of interviews reproduced here, document that regime's popularity and the ease with which it took advantage of rampant anti-Semitism.

Laqueur, Walter, and Judith Tydor Baumel, eds. *The Holocaust Encyclopedia.* New Haven, Conn.: Yale University Press, 2001. Surveys all aspects of the Holocaust. Includes more than two hundred photos and many helpful research tools.

Read, Anthony. *Kristallnacht: Unleashing the Holocaust.* New York: Random House, 1989. Examines the Nazis' exploitation of German anti-Semitism on Kristallnacht and the international reaction, which the authors describe as "mere squeaks of indignation." A scholarly and complete examination of the Nazis' institutionalization of their policy of Jewish extermination. Photos.

Rubenstein, Richard L., and John K. Roth. *Approaches to Auschwitz: The Holocaust and Its Legacy.* Atlanta: John Knox Press, 1987. Analyzes the emergence and development of the concentration and death camps, focusing on both the victims and the perpetrators.

SEE ALSO: 1919-1933: Racist Theories Aid Nazi Rise to Political Power; Nov. 8, 1923: Beer Hall Putsch; July 18, 1925-Dec. 11, 1926: *Mein Kampf* Outlines Nazi Thought; Jan. 30, 1933: Hitler Comes to Power in Germany; Mar., 1933: Nazi Concentration Camps Begin Operating; June 30-July 2, 1934: Great Blood Purge; Mar. 14, 1937: Pius XI Urges Resistance Against Nazism; July 19-Nov. 30, 1937: Nazi Germany Hosts the *Degenerate Art Exhibition*; Feb. 12-Apr. 10, 1938: The Anschluss; 1939-1945: Nazi Extermination of the Jews; May 16, 1940-1944: Gypsies Are Exterminated in Nazi Death Camps.

1938

December, 1938
HAHN SPLITS THE URANIUM ATOM

Otto Hahn led the group that established uranium fission, an essential step toward the development of both nuclear power and nuclear weapons.

LOCALE: Kaiser Wilhelm Institute for Chemistry, Berlin, Germany

CATEGORIES: Science and technology; physics; chemistry

KEY FIGURES

Otto Hahn (1879-1968), German physical chemist
Lise Meitner (1878-1968), Austrian Swedish physicist
Fritz Strassmann (1902-1980), German chemist
Enrico Fermi (1901-1954), Italian American physicist
Irène Joliot-Curie (1897-1956), French physicist

Frédéric Joliot (1900-1958), French physicist
Pavle Petar Savić (1909-1994), Yugoslavian physical chemist
Otto Robert Frisch (1904-1979), Austrian English physicist

SUMMARY OF EVENT

When Adolf Hitler seized power in Germany on January 30, 1933, Otto Hahn did not think Hitler's regime would last. Hitler was still in power ten years later, however, and Hahn refused to work on military research for Hitler. In this the world was fortunate, for military research in Hahn's field led to the atomic bomb.

Hahn was a superb experimentalist; specifically, he

was a radiochemist. He headed the department of radioactivity of the Kaiser Wilhelm Institute for Chemistry in Berlin and had done so since the department's inception in 1912. Together with a colleague, Lise Meitner, he discovered a new element that they named protactinium. He enjoyed a modest fame that gave him some protection against Hitler's followers.

Much of Hahn's work lay in discovering the chain of decay products of the naturally occurring radioactive elements. Uranium, for example, is a natural element that is radioactive; that is, it emits radiation. Upon so doing, it changes or decays into a "daughter" element, thorium. Thorium, in turn, decays to radium, which decays to radon, and so forth, with the ultimate end product being a stable form of lead. As one element decays into another, three types of radiation may be emitted. British physicist Ernest Rutherford, under whom Hahn once studied,

Otto Hahn. (The Nobel Foundation)

named the three types for the first three letters of the Greek alphabet: alpha, beta, and gamma. Uranium, thorium, and radium all emit alpha particles when they decay. In 1909, Rutherford showed that alpha particles are actually helium nuclei, and, in fact, this is where the earth's helium originates. The helium used to fill balloons comes from gas wells drilled in the ground; it is found there because natural radioactive elements in the dirt and rocks emit alpha particles as they decay. Helium itself is stable and is not radioactive.

In trying to understand radioactive decay, some scientists pictured a uranium nucleus as composed of swarms of alpha particles. They imagined that alpha decay occurred when one of the alpha particles managed to break free and leave the swarm. In the uranium decay chain, there are eight steps in which alpha particles are emitted; there are six steps in which beta particles are emitted. Beta particles are the familiar electrons, but in this case they are emitted by the nucleus. One normally thinks of the nucleus as a ball of neutrons and protons, and it is not clear where the electron comes from. To envision a very crude model, suppose that a neutron is a proton (positive charge) and an electron (negative charge) somehow crammed together. In beta decay, a neutron must change into a proton and an electron. Thus, when the beta particle (electron) is ejected from the nucleus, the nucleus is left with one more proton (positive charge) than it formerly had.

Going beyond natural radioactivity, artificial radioactivity was discovered in 1934 by Irène Joliot-Curie and her husband, Frédéric Joliot. They showed that alpha particles striking the nuclei of light elements, such as aluminum, could make those elements radioactive, but alphas were ineffective at making heavy elements radioactive because alpha particles are composed of two protons bound together with two neutrons; heavy elements are composed of a large number of protons (92 for uranium) and a larger number of neutrons. The large positive charge of the heavy elements repels the positive charge of the alpha particle and keeps it from penetrating the nucleus.

When alpha particles were allowed to fall on the light element beryllium, a strange new particle was emitted. In 1932, James Chadwick showed that this new particle had zero charge; consequently, it was named the neutron. The neutron made a wonderful nuclear bullet because it was not repelled by the positively charged nuclei as the alpha particle had been. It became popular to bombard various elements with neutrons and look for interesting results. Enrico Fermi did exactly that. What usually oc-

THE DANGER AND PROMISE OF NUCLEAR FISSION

In his presentation speech on the occasion of Otto Hahn's receipt of the Nobel Prize in Chemistry on December 10, 1944, Professor A. Westgren, chairman of the Nobel Committee for Chemistry of the Royal Swedish Academy of Sciences, included these observations:

The discovery of nuclear fission is very momentous and indeed dangerous, but even more, it is full of promise. In autumn 1943, Hahn read a paper to the Swedish Academy of Sciences on his latest work in nuclear chemistry, and there referred to the possibility of splitting uranium by means of a chain reaction. In this process such enormous quantities of energy would be produced in a short instant that the effect would exceed any explosion phenomenon so far known. Hahn doubted however whether it was possible to surmount the technical difficulties involved. "Providence has not wanted the trees to reach to the sky," he said, and his hearers guessed from the passion in his voice that he wished that this conquest of atomic energy had been made at a much later date. He certainly shuddered at the thought that the atomic bomb was nearer at hand than the use of atomic energy for peaceful purposes.

Hahn's work has been inspired throughout by an invincible desire to solve the problems which he has encountered. Unlike Prometheus, who gave fire to Man, he has never dreamed of giving Man control over atomic energy. May humanity weigh deeply the responsibility which the gift of this discovery has imposed on it. Then this will be a blessing and a step towards the improvement of the conditions of human life.

Source: A. Westgren, "Presentation Speech," in *Nobel Lectures, Chemistry 1942-1962* (Amsterdam: Elsevier, 1964).

---

curred was that the target nucleus absorbed the incoming neutron, and then beta decayed into the element having one more proton. In a fateful experiment, Fermi bombarded uranium with neutrons. He expected to make a new element beyond uranium, a "transuranic" element. He made trace amounts of the elements that would come to be called neptunium and plutonium.

Because Hahn and Meitner were experts on the chemistry of the heavy radioactive elements, they repeated Fermi's experiment to analyze the results more carefully. Fritz Strassmann, a young German analytic chemist, joined their group in 1935. By early 1938, they had found ten different radioactive elements where Fermi had found only a few. Supposing the main ones to be beta decay daughters, Hahn, Meitner, and Strassmann proposed four transuranic elements, but they did so with reservations. Although they had seen evidence of their new elements, they had not been able to isolate them cleanly.

Pavle Petar Savić, a chemist from Yugoslavia, was now working with Joliot-Curie. They claimed to have found thorium after bombarding uranium with neutrons. Hahn's group thought it unlikely that one neutron could knock an alpha particle out of uranium and change it to thorium. They carefully checked for thorium but could find none. Savić and Joliot-Curie then claimed to have found a radioactive element that they could not separate from lanthanum. In a similar vein, Hahn's group found a radioactive product that they supposed was a type of radium, but they could not chemically separate it from barium.

In the waning weeks of 1938, Hahn and Strassmann conducted a remarkable series of complex experiments. The experiments were difficult because the researchers had to work with small samples. Hahn's group had only a weak neutron source; consequently, some of the daughter nuclei were produced only by the thousands. (It can be compared with the million billion atoms to be found in a pencil dot.) With Hahn's expertise, they used techniques such as fractional crystallization, wherein relatively pure crystals of various substances crystallize at different temperatures from a hot solution.

Hahn had pioneered the technique of tracing a substance by its radioactivity, in which case one does not need weighable quantities of the target substance. Daughter atoms are often created "glowing hot," which makes them stand out. Such nuclei are said to be in an excited state. Even if they could be seen with the naked eye, these nuclei would not look hot because they don't give off normal heat as they cool or "de-excite." Instead, they emit packets of energy called gamma rays. Hahn and Strassmann had sensitive Geiger-Müller counters with which to detect these gamma rays. From the number of rays detected, they could estimate the number of atoms in their sample.

In time, Hahn and Strassmann firmly established that the "radium" they thought they had formed, and that they had been unable to separate from barium, was in fact radioactive barium. As impossible as it seemed to them, a single neutron caused the uranium nucleus to split into two roughly equal parts. Their scientific paper announcing that humankind had split the atom was published on December 22, 1938.

1938

SIGNIFICANCE

Hahn asked Meitner to develop a theory that would make sense of his results. Meitner and her nephew Otto Robert Frisch became absorbed in the problem for some time. It seemed impossible to them that the nucleus should be brittle and seemingly split into two parts as if a neutron struck it along a cleavage line. In fact, Frisch recalled that Niels Bohr had suggested that the nucleus was not brittle, but was more like a drop of liquid. Frisch visualized the nucleus as a liquid drop struck by a neutron, causing it to vibrate. Oscillations could build up that would break the original drop into two drops. Because these smaller drops would both be positively charged, they would repel each other with tremendous force. Borrowing a term used to describe the splitting of cells in biology, Frisch later named the process "fission." Because of the strength of the electrical repulsion, the fission fragments should fly apart with millions of times the energy involved in chemical reactions. It took Frisch only a few hours to set up an experiment in his laboratory to detect the energetic fission fragments.

Another characteristic of fission was soon discovered: Each fission releases two or three neutrons. These neutrons can cause other fissions that cause still more fissions in what is called a chain reaction. If this reaction is controlled, one can build a nuclear reactor and use it for an energy source. If the reaction is allowed to proceed without control, a bomb can turn itself to incandescent vapor in less than one millionth of a second.

Hahn's work thus formed an essential link in the chain that led to both nuclear power and nuclear weapons. In 1944, Hahn received the Nobel Prize in Chemistry for his discovery of nuclear fission. As the power of the nucleus became available, some predicted that nuclear power would be so cheap, it would be provided free as a government service. Others saw in nuclear weapons a way to end World War II and to make future wars unthinkable. It can be argued that the use of the atomic bomb on Japan in 1945 ultimately saved many lives by making an Allied invasion of mainland Japan unnecessary. There is no doubt that the terrifying prospect of nuclear war was of prime importance in keeping the superpowers from directly attacking each other during the years of the Cold War.

Hahn's own life can be seen as a summary of the societal impact of his work. During World War I, Hahn worked with Fritz Haber to use poison gas as a weapon. When Hahn expressed reservations, Haber argued that gas could bring an early end to the war and thereby save lives. Later, Hahn was so upset when he saw the agony of Russian soldiers who had been gassed that he attempted

to use his own respirator to aid them. During World War II, although Hahn avoided direct military work, he did not actively speak out against government policies, but during the 1950's he became politically active and quite outspoken against the misuse of nuclear power and against the stockpiling of nuclear weapons.

—*Charles W. Rogers*

FURTHER READING

Hahn, Otto. *New Atoms: Progress and Some Memories*. New York: Elsevier, 1950. Collection of papers about the discovery of fission and related topics accessible to lay readers. Includes Hahn's Nobel lecture as well as some of his personal reminiscences from the history of natural radioactivity.

_____. *Otto Hahn: A Scientific Autobiography*. Edited and translated by Willy Ley. New York: Charles Scribner's Sons, 1966. Autobiography discusses Hahn's life in science and features three of his key scientific papers on discovering fission as well as biographical notes on other scientists. Includes photographs, a chronology of Hahn's life, a comprehensive bibliography of Hahn's publications, and many helpful footnotes by the editor/translator.

Hoffmann, Klaus. *Otto Hahn: Achievement and Responsibility*. New York: Springer-Verlag, 2001. Biographical work focuses on Hahn's contributions to science as well as his views on social and scientific responsibility. Includes index.

Irving, David. *The German Atomic Bomb*. New York: Simon & Schuster, 1967. Gripping account of the efforts of German scientists and the German government to develop the atomic bomb includes detailed discussion of Hahn's discovery of fission. Also addresses why the Germans failed despite their early start over the Allies' bomb programs.

Piel, Gerard. *The Age of Science: What Scientists Learned in the Twentieth Century*. New York: Basic Books, 2001. Overview of the scientific achievements of the twentieth century. Chapter 3 discusses the early days of nuclear physics, including Hahn's work. Includes many illustrations and index.

Rhodes, Richard. *The Making of the Atomic Bomb*. New York: Simon & Schuster, 1986. Comprehensive, highly detailed account of the making and use of the American atomic bomb, intended for general readers. Includes the story of Hahn's discovery of fission and places it within the context of the worldwide efforts then under way to develop the atomic bomb. Features extensive bibliography.

Shea, William R., ed. *Otto Hahn and the Rise of Nuclear Physics*. Boston: D. Reidel, 1983. Collection of copiously referenced papers on Hahn's discoveries of nuclear fission, nuclear isomerism, radiothorium (thorium-228), and related matters. Includes a fine chapter on Hahn and social responsibility. Accessible to the general reader, but somewhat technical at times.

SEE ALSO: Dec. 10, 1906: Thomson Wins the Nobel Prize for Discovering the Electron; 1912-1913: Bohr Uses Quantum Theory to Identify Atomic Structure; Mar. 7, 1912: Rutherford Describes the Atomic Nucleus; 1914: Rutherford Discovers the Proton; Feb., 1932: Chadwick Discovers the Neutron; Apr., 1932: Cockcroft and Walton Split the Atom.

December 10, 1938
BUCK RECEIVES THE NOBEL PRIZE IN LITERATURE

When Pearl S. Buck accepted the Nobel Prize in Literature in Stockholm, Sweden, on December 10, 1938, she became the first American woman to receive this honor.

LOCALE: Stockholm, Sweden
CATEGORY: Literature

KEY FIGURES
Pearl S. Buck (1892-1973), American author
Selma Lagerlöf (1858-1940), Swedish author and
    member of the Nobel Committee

SUMMARY OF EVENT
By the time the Swedish Academy's Nobel Committee met to consider candidates in 1938, Pearl S. Buck had already published seven novels and two biographies, including her first novel, *East Wind, West Wind* (1930), and the Pulitzer Prize-winning *The Good Earth* (1931). Although many of her books were renowned, the biographies became the decisive factor in the committee's decision. One of the biographies, *The Exile* (1936), was a memorial to Buck's mother, Caroline Sydenstricker, and had been been written soon after Buck's mother died; the other one, *Fighting Angel: Portrait of a Soul* (1936), commemorated her father's life.

The Nobel Prize was not for a given work. Instead, the Nobel Committee citation that accompanied the prize made it clear that Buck was being rewarded especially for the literary merit of the biographies of her parents and for the masterful way that she depicted Chinese peasant life in an area largely unknown to Western readers. (Buck's parents were missionaries, and she had grown up in China.) The committee also felt that the biographies would be of permanent interest to readers, which was one of the required criteria for the judges to consider in their deliberations.

It was with some uneasiness that Buck anticipated the

twentieth anniversary of the end of World War I. Little did she realize that on that day, November 11, 1938, the Swedish Academy would release the announcement of their choice of Pearl S. Buck for the 1938 Nobel Prize in Literature. Her first verbal reactions were in Chinese (she expressed disbelief) and then in English (she cited others who she thought deserved the prize more). While she described the four days spent in Stockholm as the happiest ones of her professional life, the days following the announcement were not without some misgivings: She felt herself to be an outsider in the American literary world, after living so much of her life in China, and although she was extraordinarily popular as a writer, she felt unappreciated by the predominantly male circle of American literary critics. Some American writers, too, made negative comments about her being selected, and this added to Buck's isolation.

There were others, however, who rallied around her in support, including S. J. Woolf, a writer for *The New York Times Magazine*, who wrote a flattering article about Buck. Sinclair Lewis, who had won the Nobel Prize in Literature in 1930 and had also received criticism, urged Buck to not let anyone take away from her the joy and satisfaction of receiving the prize. Dr. Selma Lagarlöf, the first woman to receive the Nobel Prize in Literature (in 1909), was one of Buck's main supporters; Lagarlöf sat on the selection committee. Henry Seidel Canby and Malcolm Cowley expressed their approval of the Nobel Committee's choice in published articles, and Dorothy Canfield Fisher, William Lyon Phelps, Edward Weeks, and Katherine Woods were also enthusiastic about her selection.

Many people assumed that the Swedish Academy had honored Buck in order to make a political statement, for she had already established herself as a powerful spokeswoman against totalitarianism and violence. Negative reaction to her selection ranged from unkind remarks to

Pearl S. Buck. (The Nobel Foundation)

outright hostility. One established critic complained about Buck's popularity; like some other literary critics, he believed that a novelist's success should come from discovery by a young critic who would foster the writer until, little by little, his or her reputation spread to the public, not the other way around.

Nonetheless, Buck's trip Stockholm was a joyous occasion. The Swedes were quite taken with her determination to follow custom by taking steps backward to her seat after receiving the prize rather than turn her back to King Gustav V. (Doing so was considerably more difficult for a woman in a long formal dress than for men wearing trousers.) For her Nobel lecture, Buck chose to revise an essay on the Chinese novel. In choosing this topic, she was able to accomplish at least two things: She provided the mostly European and American audience with an introduction to a rich literature that was largely unknown in the West, and she displayed her expertise in Chinese literature.

Regardless of any misgivings Buck or others may have had about her choice as a Nobel laureate, her return to the United States was filled with events and activities.

Requests and invitations poured in for speeches and interviews as well as for articles and reviews. The sheer volume of invitations meant that she could accept only those that interested her most and those that offered remuneration. Despite the pleasures that her celebrity provided, Buck became acutely aware of the difficulty that a woman had in sharing the attention with her husband. There were times when her husband was not invited to important occasions, and when declining these invitations was impossible, Buck was frustrated that she had to go alone or see her husband seated in the audience. Buck's experience made it clear that the United States was not yet completely prepared to include women in the circle of Nobel laureates.

SIGNIFICANCE

In addition to being the first American woman to be awarded the Nobel Prize in Literature, Buck was the third American and the fourth woman to be a Nobel laureate in any category. Writers from the United States had been conspicuously missing from award lists for more than thirty years, and when three Americans were honored during the 1930's, the message to American writers was that American writing was at last considered equal to European writing. The three women who preceded Buck were from Sweden, Norway, and Italy; recognition of an American woman was especially noteworthy.

It is important to note that Buck did not emerge from an elite circle of American writers. Instead, she gained popularity among the general population. Furthermore, Buck's writing had largely focused on Chinese culture, and she lived in China most of the time. Her selection as a Nobel laureate thus marked a new openness that had not been apparent in previous decades. The choice also indicated the Nobel Committee's recognition that there was more to good writing than aesthetics and that a book's universal appeal and comprehensibility could also be marks of excellence.

—Victoria Price

FURTHER READING

Conn, Peter. *Pearl S. Buck: A Cultural Biography.* New York: Cambridge University Press, 1996. A thorough account of Pearl S. Buck's life with a detailed chapter on her Nobel Prize.

Doyle, Paul A. *Pearl S. Buck.* Rev. ed. New York: Twayne, 1980. Provides a chronology of Buck's life and discusses her novels before and after receiving the Nobel Prize. Explains the factors that resulted in Buck's winning the prize.

Harris, Theodore F., and Pearl S. Buck. *Pearl S. Buck: A*

Biography. 2 vols. New York: John Day Company, 1969, 1971. In tracing Pearl Buck's life, this account gives a detailed account of Buck and her nomination for the Nobel Prize.

Sherby, Louise S. *The Who's Who of Nobel Prize Winners, 1901-2000*. 4th ed. Westport, Conn.: Oryx, 2002. Contains detailed information on Nobel Prize winners through 2000, organized chronologically by prize, as well as a brief history of the prizes. Entries include biographical details about recipients and lists of their relevant publications as well as summaries of their achievements. Features four indexes.

Thompson, Dody Weston. "Pearl Buck," in *American Winners of the Nobel Literary Prize*, edited by Warren G. French and Walter E. Kidd. Norman: University of Oklahoma Press, 1968. Discusses events and activities surrounding the awarding of the Nobel Prize to Pearl Buck.

SEE ALSO: Dec. 10, 1901: First Nobel Prizes Are Awarded; June, 1917: First Pulitzer Prizes Are Awarded; 1918: Cather's *My Ántonia* Promotes Regional Literature; Dec. 10, 1928: Undset Accepts the Nobel Prize in Literature.

1939
BOURBAKI GROUP PUBLISHES *ÉLÉMENTS DE MATHÉMATIQUE*

The "Bourbaki circle" of French mathematicians published the first of more than sixty monographs surveying and synthesizing the abstract structure of extant operational mathematics.

LOCALE: Paris, France
CATEGORY: Mathematics

KEY FIGURES
André Weil (1906-1998), French mathematician
Jean Dieudonné (1906-1992), French mathematician

SUMMARY OF EVENT

From the publications of Georg Cantor and Giuseppe Peano through the logicist work of Alfred North Whitehead and Bertrand Russell's *Principia Mathematica* (1910-1913), to the formal axiomatics of David Hilbert's *Grundlagen der Geometrie* (1899; *The Foundations of Geometry*, 1902) and *Grundzüge der Theoretischen Logik* (1928; *Principles of Mathematical Logic*, 1950), mathematics has evolved through several distinct phases in regard to its degree of abstraction, self-consistency, and unity. Notwithstanding the apparent limits of formalization attendant on Kurt Gödel's incompleteness theorems in 1931, in many areas of applied mathematics there remained numerous active followers of Hilbert's axiomatics. Axiomatics, for Hilbert, remained the means to provide and explain the deductive structure of logical and mathematical conceptual systems, isolating the general principles that serve as axioms from which all other key consequences can be deduced. Hilbert maintained that there are no innate differences in the degree and kind of rigor, clarity, and internal consistency between one

branch of mathematics and another, with axiomatics providing the language and method for unifying all mathematical specializations.

The modern ideas of Peano, Russell, Hilbert, and others have loosened many of the traditional connections of mathematics with specific ideas about "number" and "quantity," instead underscoring the general roles of abstract structures and axioms. As Hermann Weyl discusses in *Philosophie der Mathematik und Naturwissenschaft* (1927; *Philosophy of Mathematics and Natural Science*, 1949), key features of Hilbert's mathematical views that survived Gödel and intuitionist criticism include reliance on abstract deduction, an autonomous language and method continually concerned with solving outstanding practical problems and creation of new and more comprehensive and integrative concepts and methods.

In contrast to the practically inapplicable logicism of Gottlob Frege and Russell, and L. E. J. Brouwer's intuitionism, Hilbert's outlook was at least in part that of a working applications-oriented mathematician. Throughout the 1930's, the pragmatic counterbalance to formalist foundation studies included widespread use of Hilbert space representations in statistical and quantum mechanics, the efforts of Andrey Nikolayevich Kolmogorov on probability theory, and eventually the diverse effects of the composite French mathematical group known as Nicolas Bourbaki.

Notwithstanding a 1949 biographical note on "Professor Bourbaki" of the "Royal Poldavian Academy and Nancago University," the name "Bourbaki" designates a largely anonymous group of principally French mathematicians, first organized shortly before World War II. In a list that was never confirmed, André Deleachet in his text on mathematical analysis includes as key Bourbaki circle members noted mathematicians André Weil, Jean Dieudonné, Henri Cartan, Charles Chevalley, Jean Delsarte, and Samuel Erlenberg, most originally associated with the École Normal Supérieure in Paris.

Some have suggested that the pseudonym "Bourbaki" refers to the Greco-French general Charles Bourbaki, defeated in the Franco-Prussian War by unconventional German tactics, and thus obliquely to many French mathematicians responding to a perceived "germanic" onslaught of strict Hilbertian formalists. The nature of the Bourbaki group's systematic approach to and interpretation of mathematics was first presented in the initial volumes of the *Éléments de mathématique*, in 1939, then continued in several annual installments under the aegis of the Séminaire Bourbaki. As recounted by noted mathematician Laurent Schwartz, each of the Bourbaki volumes is the result of periodic group meetings, the resulting drafts of which involve lengthy criticism and revisions. Intended as high-level textbooks for "working mathematicians" at the postgraduate level and above, the *Éléments* are meant to serve as a perplexed mathematician's guide to the structural unity of all mathematics in the face of its apparent splintering into separate and noncommunicating specialisms.

Although in many respects incorporating the spirit and some of the technologies of Hilbert's formal axiomatics, as a prologue "Bourbaki" clearly distinguishes the latter's logical formalism from its own "structural axiomatics." In this structuralist approach, functions, operations, transformations, and substitutions are but different names for various types of fundamental relations. Bourbaki criticizes Hilbert's overemphasis on logico-deductive reasoning as the sole basis and unifying principle for mathematical relations, calling it the only external form and vehicle that the mathematician gives to his thought. What the Bourbakian method sets as its aim is exactly what it believes Hilbert's logical formalism cannot by itself supply—namely, the profound creativity and intelligibility of mathematics.

Taking a "naïve realist" approach, assuming mathematical theories as "given" and ignoring metamathematical questions on the nature and existence of mathematical objects or the connections between language and intuition, "structural relations" or structures are simply posited as the most fundamental points of common access for conceptually unifying the diversity of mathematical theories. Although never defined to the full satisfaction of many readers, mathematical structures are

characterized by Bourbaki as abstract common or generic concepts that can be applied to different sets of elements whose nature has been specified, common properties expressible in the same way in different mathematical theories, and the form of a possible system of related objects that ignores specific material features of the objects not relevant to their abstract interrelations. In contrast to premathematical givens or assumptions of Russell, Hilbert, or Brouwer, Bourbaki structures are described as practical and useful tools from which the global aspects of a mathematical problem or theory can be reconstructed from its local aspects.

As outlined in a number of ancillary journal publications in the *American Journal of Symbolic Logic* and the *American Mathematical Monthly*, the main Bourbakian structural principles propose a hierarchy and network of interrelations between mathematical subdisciplines and theories. Particular structures are thought of as inhering in specific sets, the fundamental mathematical entity of the Bourbaki system. As understood by Bourbaki, set theory is considered as the systematic study of a triadic hierarchy of structures, each structure characterized by a suitable set of axioms, and serving as a conceptual network or linkage between different theories of present-day mathematics. Bourbaki cites the most basic of the three levels as including three general families of mathematical structures from which all (sub)branches derive—namely, algebraic, ordinal, and topological structures.

The main structural features of the algebraic family are its forms of "reversibility," as best characterized by inversion and negation operators. Prototypical properties of ordinal or order structures are those networks, or lattices, defined via the predecessor/successor relation. The most abstract fundamental structure—the topological—is characterized by the basic concepts of neighborhood, continuity, and limit. Beyond the first structural level of parent structures are so-called multiple structures, involving combinations of two or more fundamental structures simultaneously. Bourbaki cites as examples of multistructures topological algebra (including topological entities and properties and algebraic composition rules) and algebraic topology (including algebraic entities and properties together with topological construction rules). Finally, the level of particular or special structures corresponds to the different theories and branches of contemporary mathematics, seen not as independent and separate areas, but as crossroads where several general and multiple structures intersect and meet. The legitimacy and plausibility of this structurally integrative approach in mathematics is for Bourbaki based on the closer, but largely unperceived, functional unity between different mathematical theories and departments arising from the internal evolution of mathematics since about 1860. In contrast to Hilbert's formal axiomatics, Bourbaki repeatedly states that the total number and interconnections between multiple and particular structures cannot be delimited or classified in advance. For Bourbaki, Hilbert's original program of complete axiomatization is possible only for certain "univalent" mathematical theories (such as relational logic and geometry), which are determined entirely by a finite system of explicit axioms. Although easier said than shown, Bourbaki repeatedly argues that it is necessary to identify and explicate parent and multistructures by working with the rich fields of particular structures in which higher-level abstractions are embedded.

SIGNIFICANCE

The subsequent impact and history of Bourbaki's initial publications has largely been continued contributions to structurally explicating other domains of pure and applied mathematics. As an example of three intersecting multistructures discussed in later volumes, the *Éléments* considers the theory of real numbers. If considered with regard to compositional rules such as addition and multiplication, the real numbers form an algebraic "group," which is a set or class of relations having a special characteristic property such as symmetry. If arranged according to their ordinal magnitudes, the real numbers encompass an ordered set. Finally, examining the theory of continuity and limits for real numbers in the most general fashion necessitates recourse to central connectivity and adjacency properties of a topological space. Thus in principle there are many advantages of a structuralist mathematics. Most notably, once a theorem is proven for a general abstract structure, it is applicable immediately for any specific realization of that structure. For example, developments in the theory of measure and integration can be structurally applicable to some aspects of probability theory, by virtue of the common parent set of structural axioms.

Bourbaki has subsequently endorsed the view that the most appropriate foundation for mathematics is a combination of axiomatic set theory and symbolic logic. In this view, mathematical entities (numbers, geometric figures, and the like) are never given in isolation, but only in and as part of parent and multistructures. Nevertheless, in contrast to Hilbert, Bourbaki replies that mathematicians cannot map out all structures by working mechanically with symbols, but require their own special "intuition" to inform but not eliminate symbolism, formalisms, and

axiomatics. What counts is not formal limits in themselves but whether a domain of mathematics is enlarged permanently by a study of its structural axioms.

The efforts of the Bourbaki circle to generalize axiomatically those (multiple and particular) mathematical structures in overlapping theories has continued in the more than sixty volumes and numerous journal papers appearing since 1939. To date, the order of publication of the *Éléments* has reflected only multistructures corresponding to particular extant areas of algebra, topology, topological vector space, integration theory, group theory, and Lie algebras. Not all the originally proposed topics of the Bourbaki circle have as yet been examined. In many cases, the Bourbakian structuralist approach has made it considerably more simple to see the general structures than the many previous hypotheses in areas such as the theory of fields, groups, lattices, and numbers. It is also true that in some classical areas of mathematics, it has not proven so simple to perceive and formulate mathematical theories in terms of axiomatized structures.

As the process of structural axiomatization continues, Bourbaki employs sometimes colorful idiosyncratic modifications of ordinary language whenever formal accuracy can be preserved along with intuitive perspicacity. This, among other aspects of the Bourbaki movement, motivated several other new approaches during the 1960's to reformulate elementary mathematics, in some cases contributing driving ideas behind the so-called new math. More particularly, the "structural" theory of mathematics by Bourbaki directly stimulated, and in some cases interacted with, the efforts of Jean Piaget and others to outline the structural genesis and psychological development of mathematical and logical abilities in children. Piaget and others have focused on the question of whether the mathematical architectures of the Bourbaki circle are simply arbitrary axioms or are in some manner actually innate and natural in respect of human cognition.

Some mathematicians and educators have reacted negatively to Bourbaki structuralism, fearing that its dream of all-inclusive axiomatics is too inflexible and too removed from specific content and examples. Many educators, in particular, emphasize that it is clearly possible to derive adequately and apply many aspects of classical mathematics without knowing their parent structures and their interconnections. Other more supportive developments in philosophy and critical theory, such as the diverse "structuralisms" of Claude Lévi-Strauss, Louis Althusser, Michel Foucault, Michel Serres, and others, bear a superficial resemblance to the jargon and rigor of the Bourbaki mathematics. Bourbaki structures should not be confused

1939

with Thomas S. Kuhn's *The Structure of Scientific Revolutions* (1962) or with other American philosophers' debates concerning how knowledge of abstract structures "matches" real structures of the physical world.

With the retirement of the Bourbaki group's original founders, it remains to be seen whether the colossal task of the project will be continued and completed beyond the roughly 25 percent now extant. Nevertheless, even the initial efforts of Bourbaki's structuralist mathematics have provided a stimulating and efficient method and model for organizing scientific as well as mathematical hypotheses in areas such as mathematical physics, linguistics, and economics, where there is adequate prior development and strong basic relationships that lend themselves to systematization.

—*Gerardo G. Tango*

FURTHER READING

Aczel, Amir D. *The Artist and the Mathematician: The Genius Mathematician Nicolas Bourbaki and How He Shaped Our World.* New York: Thunder's Mouth Press, 2006. Places the Bourbaki group's work in the context of its times and explores the revolution in mathematics associated with Bourbaki.

Beth, Evert Willem. *Formal Methods: An Introduction to Symbolic Logic and to the Study of Effective Operations in Arithmetic and Logic.* 1962. Reprint. New York: Springer-Verlag, 1970. Discusses typical influences of Bourbaki structuralism.

Beth, Evert Willem, and Jean Piaget. *Mathematical Epistemology and Psychology.* Translated by W. Mays. 1966. Reprint. New York: Springer-Verlag, 1974. The primary source for Piaget's structuralism.

Cartier, Pierre. "The Continuing Silence of Bourbaki: An Interview with Pierre Cartier, June 18, 1997." Interview by Marjorie Senechal. *Mathematical Intelligencer* 20, no. 1 (1998): 22-28. Discussion of the Bourbaki group by one of its members.

Fang, J., ed. *Towards a Philosophy of Modern Mathematics.* Hauppauge, N.Y.: Paideia Press, 1970. Excellent source for Bourbaki papers.

Geroch, Robert. *Mathematical Physics.* Chicago: University of Chicago Press, 1985. Discusses analyses influenced by Bourbaki and Piaget.

Kneebone, G. T. *Mathematical Logic and the Foundations of Mathematics: An Introductory Survey.* 1963. Reprint. Mineola, N.Y.: Dover, 2001. Provides a good introduction to the set theory, logical, and axiomatic methods of Bourbaki.

SEE ALSO: 1902: Levi Recognizes the Axiom of Choice in Set Theory; June 16, 1902: Russell Discovers the "Great Paradox"; 1904-1907: Brouwer Develops Intuitionist Foundations of Mathematics; 1904-1908: Zermelo Undertakes Comprehensive Axiomatization of Set Theory; 1906: Fréchet Introduces the Concept of Abstract Space; July, 1929-July, 1931: Gödel Proves Incompleteness-Inconsistency for Formal Systems.

1939
FORD DEFINES THE WESTERN IN *STAGECOACH*

John Ford's Stagecoach *combined realistic characterizations, dramatic special effects, and impressive location filming to define the Western as both popular culture and serious art form.*

LOCALE: United States
CATEGORIES: Motion pictures; entertainment

KEY FIGURES

John Ford (1895-1973), American director
John Wayne (1907-1979), American actor
Claire Trevor (1909-2000), American actor
Thomas Mitchell (1892-1962), American actor
Yakima Canutt (1895-1986), American rodeo cowboy, stuntman, and stunt director
Walter Wanger (1894-1968), American independent producer and sometime studio executive

SUMMARY OF EVENT

The camera seemed to jump forward toward the young cowboy standing by the roadside. The cowboy held a Winchester rifle in one hand and a saddle in the other, and his rugged face suddenly filled the screen with a compelling mixture of confidence and vulnerability. In this single shot, less than ten seconds in duration, director John Ford notified his audience and film critics that *Stagecoach* was no ordinary Western and that John Wayne was no ordinary film personality.

The film's content involved much more than cowboys, Apaches, chases, and shoot-outs. Dudley Nichols's screenplay was based on Ernest Haycox's short story "The Last Stage to Lordsburg," which appeared originally in *Collier's* magazine. Nichols placed the emphasis on both pathos and humor to underline the human feelings and personal struggles of his protagonists. An outlaw with a conscience and a prostitute with a yearning for respectability established a poignant ambiguity in the film's two main characters. Nichols's screenplay and Ford's direction stressed the interaction of nine people thrown together in a perilous journey from the frontier town of Tonto to Lordsburg. In their cramped quarters, the passengers were divided into two classes. The elite consisted of the pompous, overbearing banker Gatewood (Berton Churchill), the suave southern gentleman-gambler Hatfield (John Carradine), and the pregnant wife of an army officer, Lucy Mallory (Louise Platt). Of a lower social standing than this trio were the prostitute Dallas (Claire Trevor), the outlaw Ringo (John Wayne) in custody of Sheriff Wilcox (George Bancroft), the bumbling whiskey drummer Peacock (Donald Meek), and the buffoonish, verbose stage driver Buck (Andy Devine). Thomas Mitchell won an Academy Award for his performance as an alcoholic doctor, Doc Boone, fallen from the grace of professional respectability because of his drinking.

The story line had a strong populist bent. By the end of the film, the self-righteous Gatewood was arrested for embezzlement, Hatfield died in an Apache attack, and Lucy Mallory discovered her indebtedness to her social inferiors, as Doc Boone, Dallas, and Ringo helped her through childbirth. The wrongly accused Ringo revealed his physical prowess, strength of character, and sense of justice as he saved the stagecoach from the Apaches and then, with the blessing of Sheriff Wilcox, wreaked vengeance on the wastrel Plummer brothers, the murderers of his father and brother. The film thus upended the social pyramid. Right-minded Ringo and good-hearted Dallas, their characters redeemed, rode off together on a buckboard to his ranch in Mexico, while Gatewood went to jail.

In a time of autocratic studio bosses and meddlesome producers, Ford was fortunate to have Walter Wanger finance the film as an independent production through United Artists. Wanger allowed Ford considerable latitude as director, and Ford used this opportunity well. The visual imagery was impressive, as Ford captured the large vistas of Monument Valley with sweeping camera angles and deep-focus shots. In the confinements of the stagecoach and the way station, the camera helped to establish class distinctions through the physical and emotional distance between the characters. Except for the use of Monument Valley, however, none of these devices was original with *Stagecoach*. Therefore, many film critics and historians in recent decades have seen Ford's

work as less innovative than the contemporary critical and public response indicated. Within these limits, however, it must be noted that *Stagecoach* was an exceptional achievement in a specific set of circumstances. Ford's accomplishment was to bring so many new techniques into one film, which was, after all, a Western—a genre that had become a cliché-ridden, low-budget, mass-produced Hollywood staple during the years of the Great Depression. Ford's directorial virtuosity surprised and stimulated audiences and critics, who had come to expect little artistry in Westerns.

Ford had a good ear for folk and popular music and worked well with Richard Hageman, whose Academy Award-winning score offered carefully selected tunes drawn from American rural traditions. The film's songs varied from Stephen Foster's "Jeanie with the Light Brown Hair" to honky-tonk tunes typical of frontier saloons and bordellos. Hageman's music helped establish the film's sympathy for Dallas and Ringo and appealed to a broad public taste for symphonic versions of familiar tunes.

Stagecoach launched John Wayne to more than stardom; he became the archetypal Western hero whose film persona assumed mythic proportions in popular culture. Wayne had broken into motion pictures in 1926 as a stunt man and had made a series of generally unimpressive Westerns and other action-adventure films. By the mid-1930's, he had steady work as the lead in cowboy films for Monogram and Republic, two of Hollywood's minor studios. Fortunately for Wayne, he made a favorable impression on Ford, who sensed the lanky ex-collegiate football player's potential as a dominant screen personality. Wayne and Ford worked well together on *Stagecoach*. Even a casual viewer of the film will be aware that the actor's laconic voice and commanding presence somehow combined with a sincerity and an occasional suggestion of vulnerability to create a powerful personal image. Ford's camera captured all these qualities in Wayne's depiction of Johnny Ringo.

Few directors in motion-picture history have had the leeway granted to director Ford by producer Wanger, and even fewer have been able to translate an opportunity for creative expression into such a large financial and artistic success. The story itself was a reflection of Ford's sympathy for the common people, a perspective also brought to the screen in his films *The Grapes of Wrath* (1940) and *How Green Was My Valley* (1941). Ford's personal touch was especially visible in *Stagecoach*, a major event in his career and in the history of Hollywood Westerns.

1939

SIGNIFICANCE

Stagecoach rescued the Western from the wilderness of quickly made, often hackneyed B-films and the pristine Arcadia of music and dance inhabited by the singing cowboy. These two types of films had their strengths and their loyal fans, but the mix of cinematic creativity and social realism in *Stagecoach* set a standard for quality and box-office appeal that even the most profit-oriented studio could not ignore.

Ford's work was so different from other films of the time, however, that few producers and directors attempted to copy *Stagecoach*. Instead, they began to explore the genre with feature attractions as vehicles for established stars, proven directors, and the new technology of Technicolor. As film historian William K. Everson has observed, "Its enormous popularity was understandable. . . . What was surprising was that none of its immediate offspring even attempted to duplicate its artistic standards, but were content to be big 'shows.'" Examples abounded in the early 1940's. Director Raoul Walsh reunited Wayne and Trevor in *Dark Command* (1940) for Republic Pictures. William Wyler's *The Westerner* (1940) starred Gary Cooper and Walter Brennan for United Artists, and Fritz Lang's *Western Union* (1941) featured Robert Young, Randolph Scott, and Technicolor for Twentieth Century-Fox.

Ford's use of Monument Valley prodded other directors to film on location in the broad expanses of the American West. Among the many following in Ford's footsteps were Raoul Walsh, who placed Errol Flynn on the rolling plains to film George Custer's fatal blunders in *They Died with Their Boots On* (1941). King Vidor's *Duel in the Sun* (1946) presented the spectacle of a massive cattle drive, and George Stevens captured the grandeur of the Grand Tetons in *Shane* (1953).

Stuntman and second-unit director Yakima Canutt made a major contribution to *Stagecoach* in the film's exciting chase sequence, which also gave a major boost to his own career. Canutt was already a Hollywood veteran in 1939, but *Stagecoach* put his services in great demand. Westerns and other types of films as well began to use more complex and difficult stunts that called for the skills and experience of Canutt. He continued to be active as a stuntman into the 1940's and worked as a stunt director for many years thereafter. His later films included *Ben-Hur* (1959) and *El Cid* (1961).

In *Stagecoach*, Ford elicited a strong performance from John Wayne, at the time a little-known performer. From the release of *Stagecoach* when he was thirty-two until his death in 1979, Wayne projected the image of the iron-willed, two-fisted man of action with an unerring sense of justice. The hero of the common folk in *Stagecoach*, he starred as an army officer in Ford's cavalry trilogy and made a deep imprint on the public mind with his roles as courageous soldiers in several films about World War II. Because of his immense popularity over four decades, Wayne had a larger symbolic importance than most Hollywood stars. Known as a political conservative in his last years, Wayne also had another side to his image: the champion of the underdog, especially in his first major characterization as Johnny Ringo and in later Westerns such as *True Grit* (1969), *The Cowboys* (1972), and *The Shootist* (1976).

Stagecoach made John Ford the master of the mature Western. His direction of *My Darling Clementine* in 1946 brought the shootout at the O.K. Corral to the screen in impressive fashion, but he enjoyed even greater success with his cavalry trilogy *Fort Apache* (1948), *She Wore a Yellow Ribbon* (1949), and *Rio Grande* (1950). John Wayne appeared as the central character in all three films. In comparison with Wayne's roles in the B-Westerns of the 1930's, these characters were far from one-dimensional cowboys. In particular, *Rio Grande* explored the troubled relationship between professional commitment to military discipline and the importance of wife and family. In the end, the brutality of the frontier was decisive; the dominant male patriarch discovered that he needed his wife and that his son could stand on his own.

While critics and historians continue to debate the precise place of *Stagecoach* in the evolution of serious cinema, the film itself remains a durable and impressive contribution to American motion-picture history. Ford successfully combined popular culture with high culture through his creative use of camera, visual imagery, and character. Other directors such as Orson Welles, Akira Kurosawa, and Kihado Okamoto, as well as numerous film commentators, such as William K. Everson and Andrew Sarris, have testified to the lasting importance of *Stagecoach* as a serious achievement in motion-picture history.

—John A. Britton

FURTHER READING

Buscombe, Edward. *Stagecoach*. London: BFI, 1996. Brief monograph on Ford's film, including close formal reading of key scenes. Bibliographic references.

Edgerton, Gary. "A Reappraisal of John Wayne." *Films in Review* 37 (May, 1986): 282-289. Emphasizes Wayne's instinctive appeal to American audiences as the embodiment of the nineteenth century ideal of rugged honesty.

Everson, William K. *A Pictorial History of the Western Film*. New York: Citadel Press, 1969. Well-written general survey with carefully chosen illustrations from film stills and posters. Chapters 10 and 11 are especially helpful in assessing the Hollywood background for *Stagecoach* and the film's impact on the motion-picture industry of the 1940's and 1950's.

Fenin, George N., and William K. Everson. *The Western: from Silents to the Seventies*. Rev. ed. New York: Grossman, 1973. Greater factual detail and analytic depth than the Everson work cited above, with more text and fewer illustrations. Chapters 9 through 13 cover the period from 1920 to 1950, ranging from the big studio productions to the action B-Westerns and singing cowboy films that were typical of the 1930's.

Gallagher, Tag. *John Ford: The Man and His Films*. Berkeley: University of California Press, 1986. Thorough academic treatment of Ford and his work. Clearly written, although with some technical language. Contains an analysis of *Stagecoach*; Gallagher also discusses the film throughout the text in comparison with other Ford films. Covers Ford's private life as well as his Hollywood career. Careful research reflected in extensive and informative footnotes and filmography.

Grant, Barry Keith, ed. *John Ford's "Stagecoach."* New York: Cambridge University Press, 2003. Collection of essays on *Stagecoach* comprises work by major film scholars—including Leland Poague, Gaylyn Studlar, and William Rothman—as well as three newspaper reviews of the film from 1939. Bibliography, filmography, and index.

Parks, Rita. *The Western Hero in Film and Television: Mass Media Mythology*. Ann Arbor, Mich.: UMI Research Press, 1982. Broad, interpretive analysis of the cowboy hero that provides the literary and sociological setting for *Stagecoach* in American popular culture—from the frontier folk tales of the nineteenth century to the Hollywood films of the interwar years to the television Westerns of the 1950's and 1960's.

Place, J. A. *The Western Films of John Ford*. Secaucus, N.J.: Citadel Press, 1974. Useful compendium of Ford's Westerns, with descriptive commentary and representative illustrations.

Sarris, Andrew. *The John Ford Movie Mystery*. Bloomington: Indiana University Press, 1975. Incisive, stimulating overview of Ford's contributions as director and as social and political commentator.

Stowell, Peter. *John Ford*. Boston: Twayne, 1986. Sophisticated assessment of Ford's films within the context of American culture and history. Chapter 2 deals with *Stagecoach* in the development of the American frontier myth, and chapter 6 explores Ford's use of narrative structure in that film and in *The Searchers* (1956).

Zolotow, Maurice. *Shooting Star: A Biography of John Wayne*. New York: Simon & Schuster, 1974. Detailed, pioneering biography based on interviews and some private archives. Nicely written; includes anecdotes and insights into Wayne's personality. Much material on the Wayne-Ford relationship, including the production of *Stagecoach*.

SEE ALSO: 1930's-1940's: Studio System Dominates Hollywood Filmmaking; Aug. 17, 1939: *The Wizard of Oz* Premieres; Dec. 15, 1939: *Gone with the Wind* Premieres.

1939

1939
MÜLLER DISCOVERS THE INSECTICIDAL PROPERTIES OF DDT

Paul Hermann Müller's discovery that the chlorinated organic compound dichloro-diphenyl-trichloroethane is an effective insecticide led to its widespread use for controlling vectors of disease and causes of devegetation.

LOCALE: Switzerland

CATEGORIES: Science and technology; chemistry; agriculture; health and medicine; environmental issues

KEY FIGURES
Paul Hermann Müller (1899-1965), Swiss chemist
Othmar Zeidler (d. 1911), German chemist

SUMMARY OF EVENT
It has been known for centuries that numerous species of insects are vectors of human diseases and causative agents of agricultural devegetation. The scientific community recognized this problem, and numerous researchers attempted to discover insecticides that were potent to insects yet relatively innocuous to humans, animals, and vegetation. Prior to the discovery of the insecticidal property of DDT in 1939 by Paul Hermann Müller, inorganic, arsenic-based insecticides were most commonly developed because of their effectiveness in controlling insects. These insecticides, which were initially used during the latter half of the 1800's, however, were found to be very toxic to humans and other mammals. Other common insecticides utilized prior to the 1940's were the inorganic fluorinated compounds plus organic-based nicotine, pyrethrum, and derris compounds. These substances, however, had limited application and insufficient permanent effect because of their instability in the environment.

Müller, a Swiss chemist, worked on developing an alternative to the most widely used inorganic arsenic-based insecticides while he was employed by the Swiss firm J. R. Geigy during the mid-1930's. He thus did not concentrate on modifying the noncarbonaceous "inorganic" compounds consisting of the metal arsenic and other elements, which, when combined, produce arsenic salts, oxides, or hydrides depending on the elemental composition. Instead, he focused on carbon-containing "organic" compounds, which, when combined with the element chlorine, produce organochlorine compounds.

Müller's task was to synthesize an original compound or to discover an existing one that would be not only an effective and safe insecticide but also economical and inoffensive in odor. Müller had determined from a review of the published scientific literature regarding patented insecticides that the most effective mode of inducing insecticidal activity was through direct contact of the compound with the insect. This meant that it was not necessary for the insects to consume the insecticides in order for a toxic effect (that is, death) to occur. He also concluded that for an insecticide to be effective, especially for agricultural use, it needed to be chemically stable and, accordingly, relatively resistant to decay or inactivation in the environment.

As a result of his conclusions drawn from the literature, Müller decided to study organochlorine compounds. Many compounds in this class were already known to be relatively chemically stable under ambient conditions. In addition, an organochlorine compound called chloroform was already known to exhibit insecticidal properties. Accordingly, Müller focused on studying organochlorine compounds that contained a chemical group similar to the chloroform molecule. He eventually discovered an organochlorine molecule that exhibited potent insecticidal activity.

In 1939, Müller and his research group at J. R. Geigy developed an insecticide product that they named Gesarol. Müller had discovered that the active ingredient in Gesarol was insecticidal when tested against beetles and moths. The active ingredient was the organochlorine compound dichloro-diphenyl-trichloroethane (DDT), which was originally synthesized in the laboratory of Othmar Zeidler, a German chemist, in 1874. Zeidler's intention was not to develop an insecticide but to determine the substitution reactions involving chlorine atoms and aromatic organic compounds. Zeidler discovered the compound DDT as one of many products of such reactions, but its insecticidal property was unknown to anyone until years later.

Although Müller discovered the insecticidal properties of DDT in 1939 and the Swiss government put the compound to use almost immediately to control the devastating Colorado beetle, U.S. government approval of DDT for use as an insecticide was not initiated to any degree until 1944. The American government, through several federal health agencies, conducted tests during 1942 and 1943 to determine the effectiveness of DDT. In addition, tests were conducted also to determine potential long-term (chronic) and immediate (acute) health effects to

THE WORK OF THE SCIENTIST

In 1948, Paul Hermann Müller received the Nobel Prize in Physiology or Medicine for his discovery of the insecticidal properties of DDT. In his presentation speech at the awards ceremony, Professor G. Fischer spoke of the nature of scientific discovery:

The story of DDT illustrates the often wondrous ways of science when a major discovery has been made. A scientist, working with flies and Colorado beetles, discovers a substance that proves itself effective in the battle against the most serious diseases in the world. Many there are who will say he was lucky, and so he was. Without a reasonable slice of luck hardly any discoveries whatever would be made. But the results are not simply based on luck. The discovery of DDT was made in the course of industrious and certainly sometimes monotonous labour; the real scientist is he who possesses the capacity to understand, interpret and evaluate the meaning of what at first sight may seem to be an unimportant discovery.

Source: G. Fischer, "Presentation Speech," in Nobel Lectures, Physiology or Medicine 1942-1962 (Amsterdam: Elsevier, 1964).

humans. Based on the results of the governmental tests, it was concluded that DDT was indeed effective for terminating insect pests, yet relatively innocuous to human health. The product Gesarol with its active ingredient, DDT, was suggested by the J. R. Geigy company for possible use to combat the insect vectors confronted by the American troops engaged in World War II and stationed in Europe, Africa, and the South Pacific, where they were exposed to typhus-carrying lice and mosquitoes that transmitted malaria. The idea was derived from historical documentation of the use of the insecticide pyrethrum during 1900 in Cuba and 1904 in Panama to destroy the species of mosquitoes that transmitted yellow fever (*Aëdes*) and malaria (*Anopheles*) to humans. Although pyrethrum did not exhibit permanent activities, its use and the resulting benefits to soldiers in Cuba and workers in Panama demonstrated an effective application of an insecticide in order to decrease the outbreak of human diseases resulting from insect vectors. As a consequence of this historical account, the effectiveness of DDT, and the perceived innocuous impact to humans, the insecticide was selected by the U.S. government in 1944 as the optimal insecticide for use to protect American troops from the insect vectors that transmitted typhus and malaria. Later, the insecticide was released for agricultural and general commercial purposes following the war.

SIGNIFICANCE

The impact of using DDT as an insecticide can be viewed both positively and negatively. From a positive perspective, the insecticide proved to be instrumental in controlling insect pests and, in turn, preventing outbreaks of disease and destruction of vegetation. On the negative side, DDT was eventually shown to exhibit greater toxicity and potential for adverse environmental impact than originally reported.

It was documented that the use of DDT in Italy and Japan during World War II resulted in the cessation of outbreaks of typhus through the decimation of lice. The use of DDT in Naples during early 1944 to delouse clothing, the native inhabitants, and American and English troops marked the first reported time in which human beings were able to end a typhus epidemic at will. Equally as important, delousing programs using DDT helped to prevent future outbreaks of typhus in epidemic proportions.

Outbreaks of malaria, a disease transmitted by mosquitoes, which was endemic in the South Pacific islands during the war, were also decreased as a result of the use of DDT. The chemical insecticide was discharged from airplanes and sprayed liberally over the islands to control the proliferation of mosquitoes, without reported cases of toxicity to humans. As a result of the reported effectiveness of DDT in decreasing outbreaks of typhus and malaria among military personnel and its use to end and prevent typhus epidemics during the World War II era, Müller was awarded the 1948 Nobel Prize in Physiology or Medicine.

Following the U.S. government's approval of the use of DDT for agricultural and commercial purposes, the insecticide was used extensively on American farms and in residential areas. Although it was effective and appreciated for protecting crops and combating insect infestations, concerns began to arise regarding the compound's toxicity. Evidently, the initial toxicity testing conducted by the U.S. government during the early 1940's and the lack of reported cases of illness among exposed troops during World War II were not accurate indicators of potential long-term or chronic health effects in humans.

Indiscriminate use of DDT during the postwar years resulted in reported contamination of food, water, and soil. In turn, the insecticide passed through the food chain, and DDT residues were detected in humans and other animals. It was discovered later that DDT has the propensity to absorb into and through biological tissue and accumulate in body fat. In addition, excessive exposure to DDT was determined to increase the risk of damaging the nervous system in humans and other mammals. These findings resulted in the eventual ban of DDT for use in the United States approximately thirty years following the discovery of its insecticidal property. It should be noted that although the insecticide is stable in the environment, tends to accumulate in fat tissue, and has the potential to induce adverse environmental impact, DDT did not cause any reported fatalities to humans. Indeed, in comparison with the alternatives available at the time, DDT was relatively safe. Unfortunately, the misuse and overuse of DDT led to excessive environmental contamination and, subsequently, to an end of its legal use.

—*Michael S. Bisesi*

FURTHER READING

Asimov, Isaac. *Asimov's Biographical Encyclopedia of Science and Technology.* 2d rev. ed. Garden City, N.Y.: Doubleday, 1982. Presents biographical sketches of more than one thousand great scientists, including Müller. Müller's biography presents an overview of his discovery of the insecticidal property of DDT.

Berenbaum, May R. *Bugs in the System: Insects and Their Impact on Human Affairs.* Boston: Addison-Wesley, 1995. Survey of the life and evolution of insects around the world, with emphasis on how insects have affected and continue to affect human beings and their societies. Chapter 9 is devoted to humans' development of ways to eradicate insects. Includes index.

Dunlap, Thomas R. *DDT: Scientists, Citizens, and Public Policy.* Princeton, N.J.: Princeton University Press, 1981. Provides a historical perspective on DDT, with detailed descriptions of its uses and impacts. Includes bibliography and index.

Jukes, Thomas H., et al. *Effects of DDT on Man and Other Mammals.* New York: Irvington, 1973. Collection of scientific papers provides detailed information regarding the effectiveness and toxicity of DDT.

Steinberg, Ted. *Down to Earth: Nature's Role in American History.* New York: Oxford University Press, 2002. An examination by an environmental historian of how geography, plants, animals, and natural resources have shaped the economic, political, and cultural institutions of the United States. Includes brief discussion of the impact of agricultural use of pesticides.

Taton, René. *Science in the Twentieth Century.* Translated by A. J. Pomerans. New York: Basic Books, 1966. Provides an overview of the historical sequences of events that influenced the development of various scientific disciplines and applications.

Whorton, James. *Before "Silent Spring": Pesticides and Public Health in Pre-DDT America.* Princeton, N.J.: Princeton University Press, 1974. Focuses on the history and evolution of the development of insecticides in response to the need to control insects that affect agriculture and public health. Includes index.

SEE ALSO: 1917: American Farmers Increase Insecticide Use; 1930: Dutch Elm Disease Arrives in the United States; Feb. 4, 1936: Darling Founds the National Wildlife Federation; June 25, 1938: Federal Food, Drug, and Cosmetic Act.

1939-1945

NAZI EXTERMINATION OF THE JEWS

The Nazis began extermination of the Jews in an effort to achieve Hitler's goal of eradicating the Jewish race. The Nazi program resulted in the deaths of six million Jews from Germany and from areas of Europe occupied by the German armed forces.

ALSO KNOWN AS: The Holocaust
LOCALE: Europe
CATEGORIES: Atrocities and war crimes; World War II; wars, uprisings, and civil unrest; human rights

KEY FIGURES

Adolf Hitler (1889-1945), chancellor of Germany, 1933-1945
Adolf Eichmann (1906-1962), head of the Austrian Central Immigration Office and chief of the German deportation system during World War II
Heinrich Himmler (1900-1945), commander of the SS and chief of the German Gestapo
Reinhard Heydrich (1904-1942), second in command of the SS and commander of the Sicherdienst (SD), or security service
Josef Mengele (1911-1979), chief physician of Auschwitz

SUMMARY OF EVENT

The extermination of European Jews during World War II, which has come to be known as the Holocaust, was the outgrowth of Adolf Hitler's violent persecution of Germany's Jews through tactics that began with his ascent to power in 1933. Systematically deprived of their political rights, occupations, and property, the Jews in Germany suffered physical violence, mental anguish, exile, and death at the hands of the National Socialist German Workers' Party (the Nazi Party). On January 30, 1939, Hitler predicted that the coming world war would bring "the annihilation of the Jewish race throughout Europe." World War II began seven months later, on September 1, when Hitler's armed forces invaded Poland. Simultaneously, Hitler and his henchmen, including Adolf Eichmann and Heinrich Himmler (commander of the Schutzstaffel, or SS, the Nazi secret police), initiated policies and programs they hoped would bring about the extermination of the Jews.

At the time of the Nazi invasion of Poland, Reinhard Heydrich was placed in charge of German actions affecting the Jews in Poland, who constituted about two million of the Polish population in 1939. During medieval and early modern times, many Jews had been driven to Poland by persecution and expulsion from Western Europe. Moreover, when the Polish borders were redrawn after World War I, the nation gained areas that included many Jews. Heydrich first began to deal with the Polish Jews in a directive dated September 21, 1939. This order was issued to the heads of the *Einsatzgruppen*, or mobile killing squads. First, Jewish property was to be "Aryanized," or expropriated. Second, Jews were to be forced into ghettos in the large cities. In each ghetto, Jews were required to establish a Council of Elders, or *Judenrat*, which was to administer the ghetto in conformity with Nazi orders. Historians regard Heydrich's directive as the preliminary step to the so-called final solution, which eventually accomplished the near destruction of European Jewry.

In addition to ghettoization, another of Hitler's policies toward the Jews in 1939 was murder. The *Einsatzgruppen* that accompanied the German armies in Poland and elsewhere were given orders to massacre Polish civilians, especially Jews. Eventually, members of the *Einsatzgruppen* operated throughout Eastern Europe and, with the assistance of some two hundred thousand collaborators, tortured and murdered about one and one-half million Jews by the end of World War II. Two difficulties arose, however, with the *Einsatzgruppen*. First, as diligent as they were in murdering Jews, they could not possibly accomplish the destruction of all of Europe's Jews. In only two days at Babi Yar in Russia, the *Einsatzgruppen* shot thirty-five thousand Jews, but the Russian Jewish population numbered four to five million. Second, there was some concern about the ability of members of this Nazi elite to retain their sanity as they went about their duties. "The unlimited brutalization and moral depravity," wrote German general Johannes Blaskowitz, "will spread like an epidemic through the most valuable German human material" and "brutal men will soon reign supreme."

In order to help solve these two problems, the Nazis devised a more efficient means of murder that was expected to have a less brutalizing effect on the murderers. Ghettoization had concentrated the Jews into rather small areas—including the central Polish cities of Radom, Lwów, Lublin, Warsaw, and Kraków—that were then sealed. Jews from throughout Europe, including Germany, were deported to the Polish ghettos. Concentrated in the worst parts of cities and required to subsist on a few calories per day, many Jews fell ill or starved to death. The Nazis found starvation too slow, however, and so prepared other means of extermination. In the meantime, they exploited the Jews as a natural resource.

The largest form of exploitation involved using Jews as forced laborers for various large-scale projects. Many Jews were literally worked to death during the construction of concentration and labor camps. Once the labor camps were in operation, major German industrial corporations, such as Krupp and I. G. Farben, continued the brutal process of killing Jewish laborers with overwork. At the I. G. Farben synthetic rubber works at Auschwitz, the estimated life expectancy of workers was three to four months. The ghettos were also centers of labor where Jews were required to produce a variety of manufactured goods for the Nazis. Although the Jews were, by

their labor, contributing significantly to the German war effort, Hitler's implacable objective remained the destruction of their race, regardless of the impact on the German economy or the war.

By the winter of 1942, rumors of the Nazi determination to destroy all Jews began to circulate. Actually, that decision had already been made, and efforts to implement the decision were being carried out. Because the mass shootings of the *Einsatzgruppen* had certain drawbacks, as had the program of starvation, German technical skills were used to devise an orderly technology of murder. Facilities for mass extermination by gas were constructed at six camps: Auschwitz-Birkenau, Treblinka, Sobibór, Majdanek, Belżec, and Chełmno. At the same time, the Nazi bureaucracy organized to undertake mass murder and to process the corpses as effi-

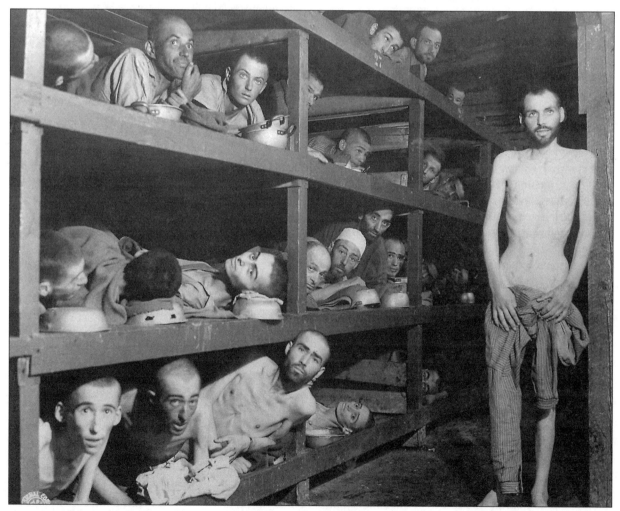

Prisoners in Buchenwald concentration camp near Jena, Germany, in April, 1945. (Library of Congress)

ciently as possible. Top Nazi officials coordinated the entire procedure at the Wannsee Conference held near Berlin on January 20, 1942. As a result of the decisions made at that conference, the Nazis began to transport Jews from all over Europe by rail to the extermination camps.

The camps were very efficient; for example, in two months of the summer of 1942, three hundred thousand Jews from the ghetto of Warsaw were gassed at Treblinka, and the *Judenrat* of the Warsaw ghetto was forced to furnish six thousand Jews per day for transportation to Treblinka. Throughout German-occupied Europe, Jews were sent to extermination camps in Poland and Germany until one and three-quarter million had been exterminated at Auschwitz, one and one-half million had died at Majdanek, and hundreds of thousands had been killed elsewhere by 1944.

About fifty thousand people were engaged in carrying out the extermination process in the camps. Two types of gas were used: carbon monoxide and hydrogen cyanide (Zyklon B), which was considered to be much quicker than carbon monoxide. The procedure was much the same in the various death camps. Jews would arrive jammed into railroad boxcars. Forced out of the cars, they were sent to barbershops, where their heads were shaved and the hair was carefully retained for various manufacturing purposes. They were then required to surrender all their clothing, valuables, eyeglasses, and everything else they possessed—even artificial limbs. Those Jews not spared to be used for forced labor were then marched to large open areas in front of gas chambers, where they were forced to wait, often for hours, while smaller groups

were "processed." These smaller groups were marched into the gas chambers, which were filled with so many people that there was no room even to fall down. The doors were sealed, and, while the remainder waited, the gas was turned on for about half an hour. When all inside were dead, doors at the opposite end from the entrances were opened and the corpses were removed. Gold fillings and valuable dental bridges were salvaged, and the bodies were cremated while the next group entered the chamber. By 1944, this process had become so efficient that tens of thousands of Jews were being slaughtered

HEYDRICH AND THE GESTAPO

Those who gather information gather power. Furthermore, those who misuse information condemn themselves. Reinhard Heydrich was the chief gatherer of information for the Nazi Party from 1936 to 1941, and he did not hesitate to use it to intimidate, distort, murder, and organize genocide.

In 1931, Heinrich Himmler organized the Sicherheitsdienst (SD, or security service) as the autonomous intelligence branch of the Schutzstaffel (SS). Heydrich was put in charge of the SD. His authority expanded greatly when Adolf Hitler became chancellor in 1933, and even greater power came to him in 1936 when he was given control of the Geheime Staatspolizei (Secret State Police, better known by its abbreviation, Gestapo) as well as the SD in the newly organized Reichssicherheitshauptamt (RSHA, Reich Department of Security), which also controlled the criminal police (Kripo).

In 1936, a new law essentially freed Heydrich and his Gestapo from any judicial oversight. He could use any means whatsoever to do the bidding of Himmler and Hitler. While the SD watched all political opponents (or Nazi Party rivals) and collected information on them, the Gestapo tracked, bullied, tortured, and killed anyone detected in any activity deemed subversive to National Socialism. The Gestapo also took over the duties of border police in order to catch spies and saboteurs.

In September, 1939, the functions of the security police and SD were combined, and groups of officers were transferred to each occupied country. They formed Einsatzgruppen (mobile task forces), which sought out Jews and political enemies for *schutzha*ft (protective custody), a euphemism for imprisonment without trial. Eventually, these task forces simply murdered any Jews and "undesirables" that they found. The Gestapo was also charged with establishing the system of concentration camps, where murder was later carried out with efficiency on an industrial scale.

To cover these extensive duties, RSHA had some forty-five thousand Gestapo officers during World War II. After the war, the International Military Tribunal at Nuremberg declared the Gestapo and SD to be criminal organizations. Its members were thereafter candidates for prosecution as war criminals. Had Heydrich survived that long, he would certainly have been executed along with the other chief Nazis.

1939

daily. Auschwitz held the record: In July of 1944, thirty-four thousand people were killed there in a single day.

In addition to their extermination efforts, the Nazis undertook medical experiments on the Jews. Regarding Jews as potential research animals, the Nazis were ready to test literally any drug or attempt any type of experiment on them, as Dr. Josef Mengele—known as the "Angel of Death"—demonstrated. All segments of the German scientific community took part in these experiments, for reasons that were frequently obscene and sadistic as well as scientific. Almost all of the experiments involved torture and resulted in the deformity or death of the victims. In short, such "research" was little more than one aspect of the extermination process, as Mengele himself performed the daily selection of experimental subjects at Auschwitz. By the end of World War II, the combined activities of the *Einsatzgruppen*, the medical experimenters, and the extermination camps had brought death to approximately six million Jews. Some of the Jews who died in the camps did not reach the gas chambers or become the subjects of experimenters; they died of typhus, cholera, or dysentery.

SIGNIFICANCE

Hitler's program of extermination was not limited to Jews. The Nazis also attempted to exterminate all intellectuals, priests, deformed persons, Gypsies, homosexuals, and other "undesirables," bringing the total number exterminated to between ten million and twelve million.

Despite his determination, Hitler failed to decimate the Jewish race or even to eliminate Jews from Europe. In many countries, brave individuals stepped forward to protect Jews, often claiming them as their own relatives and providing them with food and lodging. One example is Swedish diplomat Raoul Wallenberg, who used his position to save many Jews. Hitler underestimated the human nature of many of the Germans in his employ, not to mention people in Poland, Lithuania, and France who did not support the mass extermination. Hitler's plan was highly mechanistic, relying on a cold, unfeeling bureaucracy, and this bureaucracy was sometimes circumvented.

In their sufferings under the Nazis, many Jews lost their faith in God and therefore in the world. Nevertheless, Jewish resistance, as some scholars have noted, was not unknown. The Warsaw ghetto uprising drew thousands of German troops away from the front, and minor events within the camps distracted the camp commanders each day. The Jews fought back when and as they could.

To "choose life" under the conditions of the concentration camp had to have been one of the hardest things an individual could do. Author Elie Wiesel, who received the Nobel Peace Prize in 1986, made that choice, but it was an internal pact—one that he has written about in most of his books, most notably his memoir *Un di Velt hot geshvign* (1956; *Night*, 1960) and his novella *Le Jour* (1961; *The Accident*, 1962). Many of those who survived the camps confronted terrible feelings of guilt, and it was not uncommon for survivors to commit suicide decades later, as did Italian author Primo Levi. Other survivors

believed it to be their duty to bear witness to the Holocaust, so that such mass destruction of human life could never again happen and so that those responsible could be brought to justice.

—Saul Lerner and John Jacob

FURTHER READING

Browning, Christopher R. *The Origins of the Final Solution: The Evolution of Nazi Jewish Policy, September 1939-March 1942*. Lincoln: University of Nebraska Press, 2004. Highly detailed and well-documented work focuses on the beginnings of the Holocaust.

Des Pres, Terrence. *The Survivor: An Anatomy of Life in the Death Camps*. New York: Oxford University Press, 1976. Describes well how those in the camps had to live one day at a time—as though they had no past, history, or future—in order to survive.

Friedlander, Henry. *The Origins of Nazi Genocide: From Euthanasia to the Final Solution*. Chapel Hill: University of North Carolina Press, 1995. Examines the intentions of the Nazis and traces each step along the way to the "final solution."

Greene, Joshua M., and Shiva Kumar, eds. *Witness: Voices from the Holocaust*. New York: Free Press, 2000. Companion volume to a documentary film collects the remembrances of twenty-seven Holocaust witnesses, including camp survivors, American prisoners of war, and resistance fighters.

Hilberg, Raul. *Perpetrators, Victims, Bystanders: The Jewish Catastrophe, 1933-1945*. New York: HarperCollins, 1992. Explains early German interest in eradication of the Jews and discusses the roles played by various individuals.

Langer, Lawrence L. *Admitting the Holocaust: Collected Essays*. New York: Oxford University Press, 1995. Attacks the misguided revisionism of those who argue that the Holocaust did not happen and aims to force the German people to admit their complicity in the acts.

Levi, Primo. *"Survival in Auschwitz" and "The Reawakening": Two Memoirs*. New York: Summit Books, 1986. Two visceral commentaries on camp life by a survivor who later killed himself.

Marrus, Michael R., ed. *The Nazi Holocaust: Historical Articles on the Destruction of European Jews*. 9 vols. Westport, Conn.: Meckler, 1989. Multivolume work collects decades of writings to present the definitive study of the Nazi execution of European Jews.

SEE ALSO: 1919-1933: Racist Theories Aid Nazi Rise to Political Power; July 18, 1925-Dec. 11, 1926: *Mein*

Kampf Outlines Nazi Thought; Jan. 30, 1933: Hitler Comes to Power in Germany; Mar., 1933: Nazi Concentration Camps Begin Operating; Mar. 7, 1936: German Troops March into the Rhineland; July 6-15, 1938: Evian Conference; Nov. 9-10, 1938: Kristallnacht; Sept. 1, 1939: Germany Invades Poland; May 16, 1940-1944: Gypsies Are Exterminated in Nazi Death Camps.

1939-1949
BILL MONROE AND THE BLUE GRASS BOYS DEFINE BLUEGRASS MUSIC

The innovative playing style of Bill Monroe and the Blue Grass Boys led to the development of a new musical genre, bluegrass, which combines the "high lonesome" sound of Appalachian vocal performance with blistering speed in instrumentals.

LOCALE: Nashville, Tennessee
CATEGORY: Music

KEY FIGURES
Bill Monroe (1911-1996), American country and bluegrass singer-songwriter
Charlie Monroe (1903-1975), Bill's older brother and early performing partner
Lester Flatt (1914-1979), American singer, songwriter, guitarist, and emcee
Earl Scruggs (b. 1924), American banjo player

SUMMARY OF EVENT
In October of 1939, George D. "Judge" Hay, the creator and producer of *The Grand Ole Opry*, invited Bill Monroe and the Blue Grass Boys to audition for a spot on the prestigious radio broadcast. Although Monroe lacked the experience and name recognition of such *Opry* stars as Roy Acuff, he was confident that his Blue Grass Boys were ready for the task. His opinion was proved correct, when, at the conclusion of the band's audition, the *Opry*'s representatives, Judge Hay and David Stone, offered Monroe what was in essence a lifetime appointment to the Opry's slate of performers.

Insight into the unique Monroe sound is best obtained by examining one of the audition numbers performed by the Blue Grass Boys, "Mule Skinner Blues." This popular Jimmie Rodgers song, which became one of Monroe's top showpieces, provides excellent commentary on the innovator's musical ingenuity. Monroe took Rodgers's newfangled "blue yodel" and rhythmically reshaped it by increasing the tempo to a fiery speed and significantly elevating the vocal pitch to fit his high tenor voice. In short, Bill Monroe fused a popular hill-billy song with the older string-band sound, and in the process, he created a new style of music.

After his successful audition for Judge Hay, Monroe selected "Mule Skinner Blues" as his inaugural piece for *The Grand Ole Opry*. According to observers, when the curtain went up, the audience and *Opry* regulars alike, including stars such as Roy Acuff, Uncle Dave Macon, and Pee Wee King, were awed by the furious tempo of the Blue Grass Boys. Band member Cleo Davis later observed that the audience "couldn't think as fast as we played."

Without question, Bill Monroe and the Blue Grass Boys were perceived by their contemporaries as being new, unique, and exciting, but it would be erroneous to credit any single individual with having been the inventor of a genre of music. Does Bill Monroe merit the title "father of bluegrass music"? Yes, but the story is complex, and there were several plateaus and numerous personages involved in the evolution of the music. The Monroe Brothers, Bill and Charlie, performed as a duo in the mid-1930's; the Monroe Brothers were followed in 1939 by Bill's first group of Blue Grass Boys, who awed folks at *The Grand Ole Opry*. In 1945, Monroe put together his most celebrated band, including Lester Flatt, Earl Scruggs, Chubby Wise, and Cedric Rainwater. The new band provided increased refinement and new instrumentation for Monroe's creation. Although bluegrass evolved through several stages and involved a host of contributors, through it all, Bill Monroe remained the guiding and inspirational force.

Born on September 13, 1911, near Rosine, Kentucky, William Smith Monroe was the youngest child in a musical family of six. From his earliest youth, Bill loved the fiddle and guitar, but he was relegated to the mandolin in the family band, as his older brothers, Birch and Charlie, had prior claims to Bill's instruments of choice. One of the greatest musical influences in Bill's early life was his uncle, Pendleton Vandiver, a fiddler who played at dances in the area. As a boy, Bill provided guitar rhythm

1939

for his uncle and, in the process, gained valuable insight into the capabilities of the fiddle. Monroe also acknowledged the virtuosity of black guitarist and fiddler Arnold Schultz as being one of the molding forces in his music. As a result of the influences of Vandiver, Schultz, and, later, Clayton McMichen, Monroe kept his mandolin in tune with his bands' fiddles—an important ingredient in the ultimate development of the Monroe sound.

When Bill turned eighteen, he moved north to join brothers Birch and Charlie, who were working in oil refineries in East Chicago. The brothers supplemented their income by performing as an acoustic trio for the WLS-Chicago radio station's National Barn Dance road show. Although the Depression years were extremely difficult for the Monroe brothers, in 1933 Charlie and Bill decided to leave their day jobs to become full-time musicians. The Monroe Brothers, as they were billed, worked for the southern-based "Crazy Water Crystal Barn Dance," and they developed a considerable following in the South and Midwest. The duo began their recording career in February, 1936, and by 1938, they had recorded sixty songs for Victor Records that were released on the Bluebird label. Perhaps the most significant accomplishment of Bill Monroe during his tenure with Charlie was the proficiency he gained on the mandolin, transforming it into a popular solo instrument.

After six years of performing with the Monroe Brothers, Bill left the family band in 1938 in the hope of perfecting his own musical ideas, something he could not do with his older brother as boss. In search of a new partner, Bill ran an advertisement in an Atlanta newspaper that resulted in the hiring of Cleo Davis as his new guitarist and lead singer. As the duo's repertoire expanded beyond the songs of the Monroe Brothers, Bill advertised for additional band members, and he eventually hired bassist Amos Garen and fiddler Art Wooten. Monroe named the expanded band Bill Monroe and the Blue Grass Boys in honor of his home state of Kentucky. Throughout 1939, Monroe labored endlessly, tutoring Cleo Davis on how to do his guitar runs and Wooten on how to bow his fiddle. In addition to his emphasis on speed and clarity, Monroe forced his members to play in unconventional keys. His band was the first to play in B-flat, B-natural, and E, and when Monroe moved up to a B-flat or B, he went beyond the capabilities of most fiddlers and guitarists. In the process of perfecting his new sound, Monroe also established higher standards of professionalism for acoustic musicians.

Another contribution of Monroe's 1939 band was the utilization of the string bass, an instrument popularized by jazz musicians, in country music. Although Monroe was not the first to use a string bass in his band—Roy Acuff and a few others were experimenting with the integration of the bass into their music—after the grand success of the Blue Grass Boys at the *Opry* in 1939, the bass became a mainstay in all bluegrass and country bands.

Perhaps the most significant new Blue Grass Boy was Art Wooten, the first in a long line of Monroe's world-class fiddlers that included Tony Magness, Gordon Terry, Chubby Wise, Kenny Baker, Bobby Hicks, Charlie Cline, Howdy Forrester, Benny Martin, and "Tater" Tate. The fiddle was not only critical to the new instrumentals he was perfecting, but it also influenced Monroe's unique vocal quality, which is often described as the "high lonesome sound." This sound became another characteristic that helped to define bluegrass music.

Guitarist Cleo Davis proved to be an able replacement for Charlie Monroe. He worked with the band through their first appearance on *The Grand Ole Opry*, but he departed before their first recording session in 1940. Davis had a worthy list of successors that included Clyde Moody, Pete Pyle, Lester Flatt, Jimmy Martin, Edd Mayfield, Del McCoury, Wayne Lewis, Tom Ewing, and others. By October of 1939, Monroe had fused his hard-driving tempo with the high lonesome sound, and the result was the style that proved so successful on *The Grand Ole Opry*.

Although Bill experienced great success following his debut at the *Opry*, the World War II years were difficult for all bands. Not only did the military draft make retaining a band quite difficult, but the implementation of gas rationing and other federal restrictions also greatly reduced the size of audiences. In an attempt to carry the music to the people, Bill organized his own traveling tent show in 1943, and it proved to be a major success. The tent show was a combined minstrel and vaudeville show that included comedy, jug players, harmonica players, and even a baseball team. Using such unorthodox techniques, Monroe, an ingenious businessman, attracted record crowds, kept his music alive, and weathered the war years in good financial shape.

In the postwar era, Monroe assembled his most renowned band, which included the five-string banjo wizard Earl Scruggs; Scruggs added the final ingredient that was to distinguish bluegrass as a unique form of music. Scruggs, a native of Cleveland County, North Carolina, who had played for Lost John Miller and the Allied Kentuckians, was encouraged by Jim Shumate, a Monroe band fiddler, to audition for a position with the Blue Grass Boys. Fearful of losing his regular job, Scruggs was reluctant, but Shumate arranged for the audition. There was also doubt among the Blue Grass Boys as to whether or not a banjo should be added to the band; Monroe had already experimented with a banjo player, David "Stringbean" Akeman, in 1942, but Akeman's old-time style of play was incompatible with the band's rapid-fire tempo. Scruggs appeared for his audition and played an old standard, "Sally Goodin," which he followed with a new song titled "Dear Old Dixie." Lester Flatt, who had opposed the addition of a banjoist, was so dumbfounded that he recommended to Monroe that Scruggs be hired whatever the cost.

Scruggs utilized a three-fingered (thumb, index, middle) picking style that was indigenous to western North Carolina. Although he did not invent the three-fingered technique, Scruggs certainly refined and revolutionized the style. His banjo solos at the *Opry* made him an instant star, and his style of banjo playing became a permanent part of the Monroe sound.

It would be hard to exaggerate the impact of Earl Scruggs on Bill Monroe's band, but it is a mistake to conclude, as some critics have, that the banjo is the first requirement of bluegrass. Clearly, Monroe assigned a greater importance to the fiddle and mandolin. It would also be a mistake to minimize the importance of singer, songwriter, and guitarist Lester Flatt, who sang lead on many Monroe recordings and who contributed a number of hit songs to the band's repertoire, including "Why Did You Wander?" and "Will You Be Loving Another Man?" Fiddler Chubby Wise was also important to this model bluegrass band, as he perpetuated the extremely high standards set by his predecessors for bluegrass fiddling. It is also clear that bassist Howard Watts (who used the stage name Cedric Rainwater) complemented the virtuosity of the other band members.

SIGNIFICANCE

By 1948, Monroe's innovation was clearly being transformed from the "Monroe sound" into the musical genre of bluegrass. This transformation was signaled by an ever-increasing number of Monroesque bands appearing across the country. Rather than being flattered by this newly emerging school of imitators, however, Monroe was enraged; he considered the copying to be equivalent to theft. He was understandably disturbed in 1948 when three of his Blue Grass Boys—Flatt, Scruggs, and Rainwater—left to form their own band, Lester Flatt, Earl Scruggs, and the Foggy Mountain Boys.

Monroe had lost numerous band members since 1939, but this was the first time a group had left to go into direct competition with him. Their sound, as well as much of their repertoire, was without question the creation of Bill Monroe. Other imitators included Ralph and Carter Stanley (the Stanley Brothers), who had a singer and mandolin player, Darrell "Pee Wee" Lambert, who was a Bill Monroe clone. When the Stanley Brothers were signed by Columbia Records in 1948, Monroe moved from Columbia to Decca, being totally intolerant of his imitators. Other bands imitating the Monroe sound were Wilma Lee and Stoney Cooper, the Bailey Brothers, the Briarhoppers, and the Blue River Boys.

Although some of Monroe's resentment was justified—as when Wilma Lee and Stoney Cooper recorded and released Monroe's "Wicked Path of Sin" before he could release it himself—with the increasing number of bands aping his music, bluegrass was becoming more than a personalized sound. Bluegrass was becoming a musical genre, and the future of the music was becoming more secure. By 1965, Bill Monroe came to realize the significance of his contribution, and the resentment he formerly expressed for his competitors ended. Formal recognition of Bill Monroe's contribution to bluegrass music came in September, 1991, when he was selected by his peers and fans to be one of the first three inductees into the International Bluegrass Music Association's Hall of Honor.

—Wayne M. Bledsoe

FURTHER READING

Black, Bob. *Come Hither to Go Yonder: Playing Bluegrass with Bill Monroe*. Foreword by Neil V. Rosenberg. Chicago: University of Illinois Press, 2005. Part of the Music in American Life series, this memoir of one of Monroe's banjo players focuses on his experiences as part of Monroe's band. Bibliographic references and index.

Kochman, Marilyn, ed. *The Big Book of Bluegrass*. New York: Quill, 1984. A heavily illustrated text with historical notes, artist interviews, and personal notes. Special attention is given to the patriarchs of bluegrass and current innovators. Should be used with caution; contains errors.

Malone, Bill C. *Country Music U.S.A.: A Fifty-Year History*. Austin: University of Texas Press, 1968. A scholarly book that is useful for placing Monroe's work in a larger context.

Rinzler, Ralph. "Bill Monroe: 'The Daddy of Blue Grass Music.'" *Sing Out* 13 (February/March, 1963): 5-8. The first work to call for Bill Monroe's recognition as the "father of bluegrass."

1939

Rosenberg, Neil V. *Bluegrass: A History*. Urbana: University of Illinois Press, 1985. The definitive work on bluegrass music, written by the leading authority. The best first source for anyone desiring to know more about bluegrass. Contains extensive bibliography as well as discography.

_____. "From Sound to Style: The Emergence of Bluegrass." *Journal of American Folklore* 80 (April, 1967): 143-150. Special emphasis given to the transformation of the Bill Monroe sound into a genre.

Smirth, Richard D. *Can't You Hear Me Callin': The Life of Bill Monroe, Father of Bluegrass*. Boston: Little, Brown, 2000. Lengthy, authoritative biography of Bill Monroe, including a discography and a videography of video recordings of Monroe's performances. Bibliographic references and index.

SEE ALSO: 1910's: Handy Ushers in the Commercial Blues Era; Nov. 28, 1925: WSM Launches *The Grand Ole Opry*; Aug. 4, 1927: Rodgers Cuts His First Record for RCA Victor.

January 2, 1939

MARIAN ANDERSON IS BARRED FROM CONSTITUTION HALL

When the Daughters of the American Revolution refused to allow contralto Marian Anderson to sing at Constitution Hall, Anderson rescheduled her appearance and sang outside the Lincoln Memorial.

LOCALE: Constitution Hall, Washington, D.C.
CATEGORIES: Civil rights and liberties; social issues and reform; music

KEY FIGURES

Marian Anderson (1897-1993), first leading African American singer of classical and operatic roles
Eleanor Roosevelt (1884-1962), American social activist, author, and chair of the United Nations Commission on Human Rights
Solomon Hurok (1888-1974), Russian American concert manager

SUMMARY OF EVENT

Even with her rich, warm, evocative contralto, Marian Anderson, the first African American to perform with New York's Metropolitan Opera Company, did not arrive easily at fame and acceptance, particularly among prejudiced whites. The daughter of a poor Philadelphia widow, she got what training she could afford, then evolved an expanded vocal repertoire that included material ranging from spirituals to folk songs and grand opera. She developed a significant following among classical music fans. In 1939, however, when she requested the use of Washington's Constitution Hall from its owners, the Daughters of the American Revolution (DAR), she was humiliated by a flat rejection.

Marian, the first of three daughters of John and Annie Anderson, was born at her grandmother's house in Philadelphia on February 27, 1897. Her father, a coal and ice seller, died of brain cancer when Marian was a girl, leaving his wife, a schoolteacher, to support the family by taking in laundry and working in Wanamaker's Department Store. Anderson, who progressed from the Union Baptist Church junior choir to public performances of duets and solos, also learned to play the piano and violin. She concentrated on a business curriculum at William Penn High School, then transferred to South Philadelphia High for music training and studied privately under voice coach Mary Patterson.

Public response to Anderson's extensive range and expressive talents brought invitations to a variety of public musical forums and Negro colleges as well as membership in the Philadelphia Choral Society. White philanthropists often donated funds to assist her obviously promising future in music. Despite the beneficence of a few, segregation laws and local custom required her to travel to her singing engagements on separate train cars from white passengers, to ride in service elevators, and to eat in substandard dining areas maintained for nonwhite patrons. Overnight accommodations in hotels proved so difficult to obtain that she usually stayed in private residences.

In 1921, Anderson received a church-sponsored scholarship for voice lessons with Giuseppe Boghetti, who strengthened her technique and stage presence and taught her operatic roles. With the help of her African American piano accompanist and manager William "Billy" King, she gained the stature to demand a fee of one hundred dollars per performance. A period of low self-esteem arising from unfavorable reviews deflated her enthusiasm temporarily, but the expertise she gained from learning foreign languages to augment her vocal talent, in addition to the backing of her mother, sisters, coach, and manager, restored her to her earlier levels of confidence.

In 1925, after defeating three hundred contenders in a local singing competition, Anderson won the privilege of appearing with the New York Philharmonic at Lewisohn Stadium under the direction of Eugene Ormandy. Good reviews bolstered her competitiveness. As a result, in 1930, on a scholarship from the National Association of Negro Musicians, she traveled to Europe to study. While sailing on the ocean liner *Ile de France*, she sang for distinguished passengers. The experience proved beneficial to her career, encouraging her to return to Berlin to immerse herself in the German language. Back in the United States, she demonstrated her cosmopolitan training with a cross-country tour.

It was in the midst of this increasing professional success, on January 2, 1939, that Anderson was refused by the Daughters of the American Revolution when she attempted to book the use of Constitution Hall in Washington, D.C., for a concert to be performed on Easter Sunday. The refusal was based solely on Anderson's race. At the time the rejection came, Anderson was on tour in California. She met with interviewers to voice her sadness and shame. In characteristic low-key, nonjudgmental style, she refused to affix blame and noted, by way of explanation, that crusading for racial equality was foreign to her nature. She did, however, alter her personal criteria for performance sites and refused to sing where nonwhites were refused admittance.

The refusal to let Anderson sing proved embarrassing to the two hundred thousand members of the DAR, an elite women's historical society founded in 1890 to honor descent from patriots, encourage patriotism and activities related to teaching history, foster genealogical research, honor the American flag and Constitution, found citizenship clubs, award scholarships and medals, assist disabled veterans, and generally further Americanism. To save face in response to press stories about the organization's action, the DAR's leaders cited a Washington, D.C., law restricting integrated performances. They insisted that the DAR had in fact challenged bigotry by publicizing the local restrictions that forbade Anderson's performance. This story proved to be false.

Other entertainers and leaders came to Anderson's defense and protested the obvious attempt to hide racial discrimination. As a conciliatory gesture, Eleanor Roosevelt resigned from and broke all ties with the DAR and persuaded Anderson to sing a free Easter concert at the steps of the Lincoln Memorial. The Sunday performance, attended by more than seventy-five thousand

people, including government dignitaries, representatives from Howard University, and the secretary of the National Association for the Advancement of Colored People (NAACP), showed Anderson's sincere response to the racist action of an elitist clique. Choked with tears at the sight of so many supporters, Anderson faltered on the words to the national anthem. She drew on her professional training and years of onstage experience to help complete her usual repertoire of hymns, classical arias, and national favorites. She closed with a simple rendition of "America."

Anderson's performance at the Lincoln Memorial became the focal point of her career. To commemorate her public triumph, the U.S. Department of the Interior commissioned a mural. Fellow entertainers of all races boycotted future performances scheduled for Constitution Hall. For her self-control and positive attitude, Anderson accepted honors from Eleanor Roosevelt and from the king and queen of England. In subsequent years, she entertained at the White House for the inaugural galas of Dwight D. Eisenhower and John F. Kennedy. The policy at Constitution Hall eventually changed in regard to use by nonwhites, and Anderson subsequently performed there on several occasions.

SIGNIFICANCE

The nationwide notoriety that resulted from the DAR's rejection and its triumphant aftermath brought Anderson a deluge of opportunities to travel, perform, study, and record. Reluctant to release many of her RCA recordings, she reworked studio performances until they reached her high standards. Her most popular recording, a soulful, intense rendering of "Ave Maria" marked by her characteristic vibrato and amplitude, sold a quarter of a million copies.

Twice Anderson toured Denmark, Sweden, Norway, and Finland, impressing Finns by singing in their language. The admiration of royalty, local fans, and notable musicians, especially composer Jean Sibelius, escalated her Scandinavian appearances from mere acclaim to "Marian fever." European and Asian audiences, particularly Russians and those in other nations under communist regimes, demanded encores of her spirituals, claiming "Deep River" and "Heaven, Heaven" as their favorites. Konstantin Stanislavsky carried a bouquet of lilacs to entice her to sing *Carmen*.

Returning to the United States in triumph, Anderson came under the management of Russian American impresario Solomon Hurok. Under his direction she accepted new challenges, touring in Japan, Africa, and

At the U.S. Department of the Interior in 1943, Marian Anderson greets audience members after singing at the dedication ceremony for a mural commemorating Anderson's 1939 Lincoln Memorial concert. (Library of Congress)

South America. She gave concerts before standing-room-only crowds at New York City's Town Hall and Carnegie Hall and at the Philadelphia Forum. Far from her original rewards of fifty cents per performance, she earned hefty fees commensurate with her talents. Fans poured out their response to her compassion, which brought them comfort in times of personal crisis. Critics acknowledged her maturing grace, range, control, and musical technique. She performed more than seventy-five concerts per year and had many other opportunities she could not accept without overextending her voice and sapping her energies.

Even with increased audience rapport, racism continued to crop up in correspondence, reviews, and public treatment, especially after Anderson was invited to sing before Nazis in the 1940's. Following her reply to their questions about race, Hitler's staff dropped their request for a concert. In the United States, she was presented

with the key to Atlantic City, but white hotels refused her requests for reservations. These unsettling public insults were somewhat offset by awards and honoraria from fifty universities, including Howard, Temple, Smith, Carlisle, Moravian, and Dickinson.

At the age of thirty-seven, Anderson received the Springarn Medal, awarded annually by the NAACP to an African American achiever. A year later, in 1940, she earned the Bok Award, an annual prize accorded to a native Philadelphian. She used the ten thousand dollars that accompanied the award to endow the Marian Anderson Scholarship for students of the arts. To ensure unprejudiced administration of the annual scholarship, she placed her sister Alyce in charge.

In 1943, Anderson left the Philadelphia home she shared with her mother and married architect Orpheus Fisher of Wilmington, Delaware, whom she had met during her school years. The couple built Mariana Farm in a rural setting outside Danbury, Connecticut. Often absent from home on tour, she reserved the summer months for domestic pleasures, particularly sewing, cooking, and gardening. Her particular delight was the success of her strawberry patch. By choice, she had no children so that she could avoid the problem of separation from family while she devoted her life to music. To fill the gap left by voluntary childlessness, she immersed herself in the activities of her sisters' children, who were frequent visitors to her home.

In middle age, Marian Anderson continued to achieve renown. At the bidding of German fans, she returned to post-Nazi Berlin to perform. In 1955, New York impresario Rudolf Bing organized her debut as Ulrica, the aged sorceress in Giuseppe Verdi's *Un ballo in maschera* (1857-1858; *The Masked Ball*). This performance at the Metropolitan Opera House was the first ever by an African American performer. It made extra demands on her limited stage experience, which she met by practicing her acting role and deliberately subduing stage fright. She reprised her part in the opera on tour in Philadelphia, where black fans mobbed the performance. Continuing to refine the role of Ulrica in later appearances, she commented that she felt that perfection of the small character part was an essential part of her training for the operatic stage.

At the age of fifty-four, Anderson wrote her autobiography, *My Lord, What a Morning* (1956), in which she revealed personal reflections on poverty and longing in her childhood, when performing before distinguished audiences lay far outside the grasp of a black singer. Late in her career, having toured Europe and the United States once more, she was named in 1958 as an alternate delegate to the United Nations for her support of human rights. In 1959, two years before her formal retirement, she accepted from President Dwight D. Eisenhower the Presidential Medal of Freedom. At the age of seventy-six, she appeared at the Kennedy Center and, as the sole woman among fellow honorees George Balanchine, Arthur Rubinstein, Richard Rodgers, and Fred Astaire, received a national award.

The famed singer returned to the spotlight long after the end of her stage career. At the age of eighty-seven, to raise scholarship funds, Anderson, still regal and gracious, presided over a concert at Danbury's Charles Ives Center. Feted by admirers including Jessye Norman, Isaac Stern, William Warfield, Cicely Tyson, Phylicia

Rashad, Connecticut governor William A. O'Neil, and President George Bush, she graciously accepted the national acclaim that well-wishers extended. She later became more reclusive but remained a symbol of African American achievement and grace under pressure.

—Mary Ellen Snodgrass

FURTHER READING

Anderson, Marian. *My Lord, What a Morning: An Autobiography*. 1956. Reprint. Urbana: University of Illinois Press, 2002. Presents the most factual information available on Anderson's childhood and developing career. Somewhat sentimentalized, but avoids bitterness in recounting events related to racial prejudice. Includes photographs and index.

Keiler, Allan. *Marian Anderson: A Singer's Journey*. New York: Scribner, 2000. Comprehensive biography places the better-known events of Anderson's life within the context of her larger life and the times in which she lived. Includes discography, bibliography, and index.

Sweeley, Michael. "The First Lady." *National Review* 41 (September 29, 1989): 65-66. Brief, articulate summary of Anderson's life and career focuses in particular on the open-air concert at the Charles Ives Center.

"A Tribute to Marian Anderson: Famed Contralto Is Honored at Gala Concert in Connecticut." *Ebony* 45 (November, 1989): 182-185. Article serves as a tribute to Anderson's concert at the Charles Ives Center and fills in information about her retirement and widowhood. Includes photographs.

Trotter, Joe William, Jr. "From a Raw Deal to a New Deal? 1929-1945." In *To Make Our World Anew: A History of African Americans*, edited by Robin D. G. Kelley and Earl Lewis. New York: Oxford University Press, 2000. Addresses the position of African Americans in the United States during the period when Anderson was prevented from singing at Constitution Hall, providing some historical context for the incident.

SEE ALSO: 1910's: Handy Ushers in the Commercial Blues Era; Feb. 15, 1923: Bessie Smith Records "Downhearted Blues"; Nov., 1925: Armstrong Records with the Hot Five; Dec. 4, 1927: Ellington Begins Performing at the Cotton Club; 1933: Billie Holiday Begins Her Recording Career; Oct. 10, 1935: Gershwin's *Porgy and Bess* Opens in New York.

1939

February 15, 1939
OPPENHEIMER CALCULATES THE NATURE OF BLACK HOLES

J. Robert Oppenheimer calculated that stellar matter could collapse under intense gravitational pressure to form what would later become known as a black hole.

LOCALE: Berkeley, California
CATEGORIES: Astronomy; physics; science and technology

KEY FIGURES
J. Robert Oppenheimer (1904-1967), American physicist
George Michael Volkoff (1914-2000), Canadian physicist and student of Oppenheimer
Karl Schwarzschild (1873-1916), German physicist
Lev Davidovich Landau (1908-1968), Soviet physicist
Hartland S. Snyder (1913-1962), American physicist and student of Oppenheimer

SUMMARY OF EVENT

Sir Isaac Newton first formulated the mathematical nature of gravity and its relationship to mass in 1692, when he theorized that the more massive an object, the more gravity it possesses. Such a relationship is true for all objects with mass, including a child's marble, the earth, and massive stars. Shortly after Newton's brilliant philosophical and mathematical treatment of gravity, scientists began to consider the limits of mass and gravity. In 1796, Pierre-Simon Laplace used the eighteenth century notion that light was made of microscopic particles, or corpuscles, and reasoned that if there were a sufficiently massive body somewhere in the universe, these light corpuscles could not escape from its surface. Laplace's reasoning, however, was nothing more than armchair musings on the limits of Newtonian gravity.

In 1915, German physicist Albert Einstein reconsidered Newton's description of gravity with profound effect in a treatment he called the general theory of relativity. Einstein's theory united such seemingly disparate ideas as light, energy, time, space, matter, and gravity into a single formulation, enabling all these concepts to be treated as unified elements of single conditions for the first time.

Later that year, German physicist Karl Schwarzschild considered the new philosophy of gravity proposed by Einstein. Schwarzschild began to ponder the relativistic mathematical implications of a point in space emanating an intense gravitational field and what an observer would see as that point in space was approached. He was contemplating Einstein's notion that light is affected, or bent, when traveling through a gravitational field, a concept substantiated in 1913 when the light of a star was apparently bent while traveling through the gravitational field of the Sun.

Schwarzschild's mathematics were designed to establish the limits of relativity and the degree of the bending effect on light, not to define what would later become known as a "black hole." The significance of Schwarzschild's work was not only that he had uncovered some extremely interesting concepts based on relativity but also that some remarkable effects were mathematically allowed by relativity that seemed to violate even common sense.

Schwarzschild discovered that as one approaches his theoretical focal point of intense gravity (such as Earth's mass concentrated in a single point), space literally curves in on itself, and relativity dictates that not even light can escape such a point. More significantly, Schwarzschild discovered that the intense gravitational field need not be confined to a single point in space. His calculations demonstrated that such effects could be observed if one compressed the planet Earth to a sphere with a diameter of 1 centimeter. This relationship of mass to diameter has become known as the Schwarzschild radius.

In 1939, American physicist J. Robert Oppenheimer and his student George Michael Volkoff were doing calculations on the nature of extremely massive star cores at the University of California, Berkeley. They were contemplating the theory of Soviet physicist Lev Davidovich Landau, who had used Newton's theory of gravity in the previous decade. Landau created the first theoretical treatment of the center of very dense stars known as neutron stars. Landau believed that if a star were massive enough, the core would contract and be composed of densely packed neutrons.

The discussion of stellar densities continued, and it was suggested to Landau that if the density were great enough, the core of the star would continue to collapse even beyond the neutron state to a single point. Landau dismissed this suggestion as ridiculous, insisting that his calculations demonstrated that this could never happen. However, Oppenheimer and Volkoff reasoned that there was nothing in the relativistic calculations that would prevent collapse beyond the neutron star state and added that Landau had used Newtonian concepts that had been superseded by relativistic concepts.

On February 15, 1939, Oppenheimer and Volkoff published a paper making these points in the *Physical Review*. The two scientists continued to speculate even after their paper was published: They teamed up with another one of Oppenheimer's graduate students, mathematics prodigy Hartland S. Snyder, and formulated a more refined mathematical picture of such a hypothetical stellar collapse. In this treatment, published less than a year after the Oppenheimer-Volkoff paper, Oppenheimer and Snyder described in detail the effects of such a stellar collapse. They discussed the effects that would prevent such a collapse, including a rapid spin rate, stellar explosions, and internal pressure that would act to resist the collapse. Still, they speculated that a truly massive star could not help but collapse in on itself. Eventually, light would bend back into the star, as would any other form of radiation, until it could no longer escape. As they described it, "The star thus tends to close itself off from any communication with a distant observer; only its gravitational field persists."

In these two papers, Oppenheimer and his students were the first to address the idea of a black hole as more than an academic exercise. They both introduced the idea of such an object and also related it to stellar concepts. Furthermore, they went on to mathematically define the limits of such an object. At no time during any of these discussions did the term "black hole" ever arise. Indeed, even Oppenheimer had no idea that such an object really existed, and if it did, he did not know it might ever be detected; by his own definition, the object would tend to cut itself off from any outside communication. The person credited with first using the term "black hole" (in 1967) was Princeton physicist John Archibald Wheeler.

In late 1963, a group of scientists convened in Dallas, Texas, for a meeting titled "An International Symposium on Gravitational Collapse and Other Topics in Relativistic Astrophysics." Scientists discussed the relationship of very strong, high-energy point sources emanating from space, and most strongly suspected that these point sources of extraordinary energy could well be caused by the collapse of very massive stars up to or beyond the Schwarzschild radius. The meeting was chaired by Oppenheimer and was also attended by Martin Schwarzschild (son of Karl) and by Wheeler, who contributed his long-held convictions that black holes did in fact exist. Although no black hole has ever been directly observed, strong indirect evidence points to their existence.

SIGNIFICANCE

The Oppenheimer-Volkoff paper was an important early use of Einstein's relativity because it deliberately challenged Landau's use of classical Newtonian physics within the same predictive environment. It clearly demonstrated the superiority of relativistic physics compared with classical physics, which became a practically useless measure of predicting stellar conditions. Oppenheimer employed relativistic physics—and made its superiority obvious—in his now-famous discussion of the core of neutron stars.

Oppenheimer's paper made an important comparison between Newtonian and classical physics and justified his view of neutron stars, but it also gave rise to a wildly conjectural concept. It proposed that there could be a class of star so dense that it devoured itself and became, in essence, a hole in space and time, where space literally curved in on itself. In his follow-up paper, Oppenheimer used Snyder's mathematical genius to further refine the concept of a black hole to the point that it became a well-defined physical entity. It was Oppenheimer's refinement of the idea that took the concept of black holes from a physical abstraction to a physical entity.

The Oppenheimer-Snyder work defined the black hole in terms that are still used. Twenty years after their paper was published, scholars determined that a class of bizarre stellar objects emitted prodigious quantities of energy, and Oppenheimer's studies were applied to further understand these objects' strange environment and makeup. Oppenheimer's work discussed the relativistic concepts of observing a black hole from nearby space and even within the direct physical influence of a black hole. Today, his work remains an important tool for explaining the extremes of relativistic physics.

Black holes are a vital piece of the universe's vast puzzle, and ideas about black holes are widely used in a variety of cosmological and astrophysical theories. They are blamed for everything from hot jets of matter seen ejected from the center of some galaxies to energetic X-ray pulses emitted from star groups. There may be a black hole lurking at the heart of nearly every galaxy, and black holes may hide a significant portion of the universe's mass. The knowledge gained in studying these ideas is vital to predicting whether the universe will continue expanding indefinitely or will ultimately collapse on itself. The science and theory of these enigmatic objects remain some of the most startling and interesting ideas in science in the late twentieth century.

—*Dennis Chamberland*

1939

FURTHER READING

Asimov, Isaac. *The Collapsing Universe*. New York: Walker, 1977. Asimov provides an easy-to-grasp look at the story of black holes as seen from the layperson's perspective. In his readable style, Asimov attacks the discussion from both the historical and scientific points of view.

Crease, Robert P., and Charles C. Mann. *The Second Creation: Makers of the Revolution in Twentieth Century Physics*. 1986. Reprint. New Brunswick, N.J.: Rutgers University Press, 1996. In this book, Crease and Mann follow the making of twentieth century physics from its nineteenth century roots to the most enigmatic mysteries of the late 1980's. Examines characters and personalities as well as the issues of physics. Although this work makes little mention of Oppenheimer's famous black hole paper of 1939, it offers a unique and fascinating glimpse into his character and personality.

Harwit, Martin. *Cosmic Discovery*. New York: Basic Books, 1981. This book offers a readable style and approach that details the development of the black hole concept and Oppenheimer's contribution. The book is written somewhat stiffly from the lay perspective, and it contains valuable information, photographs, and illustrations.

Miller, Arthur I. *Empire of the Stars: Obsession, Friendship, and Betrayal in the Quest for Black Holes*. Boston: Houghton Mifflin, 2005. Provides background on the history of the idea of black holes and describes the debate concerning the nature of black holes as well as the implications of that debate for science.

Shipman, Harry L. *Black Holes, Quasars, and the Universe*. New York: Houghton Mifflin, 1976. In this excellent book, black holes are covered extensively in a readable style and related to their cosmic cousins, the pulsars and quasars. The book relates how Oppenheimer's work with pulsars dovetailed into the black hole theory and how both are related to quasars. The book is thoroughly illustrated and is quite readable by those with a good background in the sciences.

Sullivan, Walter. *Black Holes: The Edge of Space, the End of Time*. Garden City, N.Y.: Doubleday, 1979. This excellent book is well illustrated and easy to read, offering a clear picture of the revolution in physics that led to the theoretical discovery of black holes by Oppenheimer and his colleagues. It details the pioneering efforts of Einstein and Schwarzschild and describes the historic 1963 Dallas conference, where the concept of black holes was first announced to the public.

Susskind, Leonard, and James Lindesay. *An Introduction to Black Holes, Information, and the String Theory Revolution: The Holographic Universe*. Hackensack, N.J.: World Scientific, 2004. Explains concepts that physicists of the early twenty-first century have developed in relation to black holes and thinking about space, time, matter, and information.

Wheeler, John A. *A Journey into Gravity and Spacetime*. New York: W. H. Freeman, 1990. Wheeler, the Princeton physicist who coined the term "black hole," depicts gravity from its simplest forms to the black hole. The book is written for the armchair scientist but is full of interesting stories and is lavishly illustrated in color so that anyone can enjoy it piecemeal or in its entirety.

SEE ALSO: Nov. 25, 1915: Einstein Completes His Theory of General Relativity; 1916: Schwarzschild Solves the Equations of General Relativity; Nov. 6, 1919: Einstein's Theory of Gravitation Is Confirmed over Newton's Theory; 1927: Lemaître Proposes the Big Bang Theory; 1931-1935: Chandrasekhar Calculates the Upper Limit of a White Dwarf Star's Mass; 1934: Zwicky and Baade Propose a Theory of Neutron Stars.

March 2, 1939
PIUS XII BECOMES POPE

Pius XII became Pope six months before Hitler's invasion of Poland officially began World War II. Prewar attempts at avoiding large-scale conflict were not productive, and throughout the war Pius XII was concerned with maintaining an independent role for the Vatican and the Church in the face of German domination. Accusations that Pius XII was anti-Semitic and supported Hitler's Germany were later refuted by scholars.

LOCALE: Vatican City

CATEGORIES: Religion, theology, and ethics; World War II; diplomacy and international relations; wars, uprisings, and civil unrest

KEY FIGURES

Pius XII (Eugenio Maria Giuseppe Giovanni Pacelli; 1876-1958), Roman Catholic pope, 1939-1958

Pius XI (Ambrogio Damiano Achille Ratti; 1857-1939), Roman Catholic pope, 1922-1939

SUMMARY OF EVENT

Before he assumed the papacy and became Pius XII, Cardinal Maria Giuseppe Giovanni Pacelli served as secretary of state for Pope Pius XI, a capacity in which he continued his diplomatic work, focusing particularly on the position and interests of the Church in Germany. In 1917, he had served as an archbishop and was nuncio to Bavaria, where he developed a concordat between the provincial Bavarian government and the Vatican. In 1925, he was assigned to Berlin to work on a similar treaty with the German government, and he remained there until 1929, when Pius XI appointed him secretary of state of the Vatican and elevated his rank to cardinal.

The future Pius XII was aware of the fragility of the German Weimar Republic and witnessed the rise of Adolf Hitler's Nazi Party in the wake of the impact of the Great Depression. As papal secretary of state he traveled widely: He visited the United States and many other nations in North and South America. During his travels, he developed an appreciation of the extent of Catholicism's reach and of the Church's different, often region-specific problems. Later, Pius XII played a particularly important role in developing the concordat with Hitler's Third Reich on July 20, 1933. Fearing the loss of extensive Church property, the closure of Catholic schools and seminaries, and restrictions on the clergy and on chuchgoers, Rome entered into the agreement with Hitler. The terms, however, were not in the Vatican's favor: The agreement subordinated the Church to the state, silenced German Catholic opposition to Hitler, and gave credibility to Hitler's regime.

From 1933 to 1939, Roman Catholic interests in Germany suffered: After the outbreak of the war, the Church and its priests were ignored or subject to persecution. As the war neared, Cardinal Pacelli played a crucial role in the drafting of the encyclical *Mit brennender Sorge*, which denounced Nazism and fascism, used diplomacy to indicate Vatican displeasure with German policies, and reprimanded Catholic bishops for not adequately denouncing German aggression and authoritarianism. When Pius XII was elected pope on March 2, 1939—on the first and only ballot—the Germans condemned his elevation, and they blocked his efforts at mediation. Throughout the late spring and summer of 1939, Pius XII called for a conference to resolve the differences among European powers, but his efforts were unsuccessful.

1939

Pope Pius XII. (Library of Congress)

SUMMI PONTIFICATUS

Pope Pius XII's first encyclical condemned the rise of totalitarianism around the world:

Venerable Brethren, as We write these lines the terrible news comes to Us that the dread tempest of war is already raging despite all Our efforts to avert it. When We think of the wave of suffering that has come on countless people who but yesterday enjoyed in the environment of their homes some little degree of well-being, We are tempted to lay down Our pen. Our paternal heart is torn by anguish as We look ahead to all that will yet come forth from the baneful seed of violence and of hatred for which the sword today ploughs the blood-drenched furrow.

But precisely because of this apocalyptic foresight of disaster, imminent and remote, We feel We have a duty to raise with still greater insistence the eyes and hearts of those in whom there yet remains good will to the One from Whom alone comes the salvation of the world—to One Whose almighty and merciful Hand can alone calm this tempest—to the One Whose truth and Whose love can enlighten the intellects and inflame the hearts of so great a section of mankind plunged in error, selfishness, strife and struggle, so as to give it a new orientation in the spirit of the Kingship of Christ.

Perhaps—God grant it—one may hope that this hour of direct need may bring a change of outlook and sentiment to those many who, till now, have walked with blind faith along the path of popular modern errors unconscious of the treacherous and insecure ground on which they trod. Perhaps the many who have not grasped the importance of the educational and pastoral mission of the Church will now understand better her warnings, scouted in the false security of the past. No defense of Christianity could be more effective than the present straits. From the immense vortex of error and anti-Christian movements there has come forth a crop of such poignant disasters as to constitute a condemnation surpassing in its conclusiveness any merely theoretical refutation.

Source: Pope Pius XII, *Summi Pontificatus*, Encyclical of Pope Pius XII on the Unity of Human Society to Our Venerable Brethren: The Patriarchs, Primates, Archbishops, Bishops, and Other Ordinaries in Peace and Communion with the Apostolic See. Given at Castel Gondolfo, near Rome, on October 20, 1939.

Although Pius XII opposed the unconditional surrender required by the Allies, Vatican attempts to alleviate hunger in Rome and its vicinity reached more than 3.6 million individuals each month. Pius XII also supported efforts to identify missing persons and return displaced persons to their homes.

Scholars have been concerned about claims that Pius XII was an anti-Semite and that he could have been more attentive to the plight of European Jews during the war, but study of the documentary evidence indicates that these accusations are largely without merit. Pius XII directly intervened to save Jews in the Vatican and supported a wide range of actions to alleviate the distress and horrors they experienced during the Nazi regime. The papacy provided more than four million dollars in relief to Jews during the war and, on two occasions, December 24, 1942, and June 2, 1943, Pius XII denounced the German plan to exterminate the Jews. The papacy was also actively involved in attempts to address the many factors inherent in Europe's refugee crisis.

After the defeat of Germany and Japan in 1945, Pius XII appointed a new generation of cardinals, worked to support the United Nations and other institutions that were focused on maintaining peace, and expanded his anticommunist policies and programs throughout the world. Pius XII viewed Russian communism's atheistic and material core as the next threat to Christianity and organized religion, and in 1949 he proclaimed that any Catholic who was aligned with communism was automatically excommunicated from the Church. Theologically, Pius XII declared the Assumption of Mary into Heaven as a dogma of faith in his encyclical *Munificentissimus Deus* (1950), and he declared 1954 as the Marian Year to commemorate the doctrine of the Immaculate Conception of Mary. Pius XII's health declined during the 1950's, and he died on October 9, 1958. He was succeeded by Pope John XXIII.

Despite the German invasion of Poland on September 1, 1939, and the outbreak of World War II, Pius XII continued his diplomatic efforts. While he was unable to bring the conflict to a close, Pius XII served as a conduit between the internal German resistance to the war and the Allied Powers, especially Britain and the United States. After Italy entered the war in June, 1940, as a German ally, Pius XII strove to keep Rome out of the battle: He sought—but failed—to have Rome recognized as an international city. Only once during the war did a bomb hit the Vatican; that incident occurred on March 1, 1943, when Italian members of the Fascist Party caused the explosion. (Rome, however, was not spared, and a July 19, 1943, attack destroyed parts of the San Lorenzo quarter.)

SIGNIFICANCE

The nineteen years of Pope Pius XII's pontificate saw the turbulent outbreak of World War II, the subsequent defeat of the Axis Powers (Germany, Japan, and Italy), the postwar diplomacy that led to the Cold War between the United States and the Soviet Union, and the mounting concern that the Roman Catholic Church was detached from the world and its needs. Pius XII defended the interests of the Vatican and the Roman Church while advancing the cause of human rights, and his actions resulted in the rescue of many Jews from the horrors of the Holocaust. His postwar years focused on the recovery of the Church in Europe and on combating forms of Marxist communism that denounced God and religion and sacrificed individual rights and liberties in the name of collectivist values.

Pius XII was consistently opposed to statism, fascism, communism, and all other variations of totalitarianism. Theologically, he was a conservative who produced many encyclicals that reinforced traditional Church doctrine; his most notable doctrinal and liturgical achievements were his declaration of the Assumption of Mary into Heaven as a dogma of faith and his establishment of the Marian Year in 1954. His conservatism tended to stifle those who desired greater freedom from the dictates of the Church hierarchy, and his succession by the more liberal Pope John XXIII resulted in the creation of the Second Vatican Council, which John XXIII hoped would "let light shine into the church."

—*William T. Walker*

FURTHER READING

Blet, Pierre. *Pius XII and World War II: According to the Archives of the Vatican*. Translated by Lawrence J. Johnson. New York: Paulist Press, 1999. A study of Pius XII's role as defender of the Vatican, the Church, and human rights during World War II.

Bottum, Joseph, and David G. Dalin, eds. *The Pius War: Responses to the Critics of Pius XII*. Lanham, Md.: Lexington Books, 2004. A response to and defense of the interpretations of John Cornwell and other scholars who advanced criticisms of Pius XII's actions and failures during World War II.

Cornwell, John. *Hitler's Pope: The Secret History of Pius XII*. New York: Viking Penguin, 1999. Cornwell's critique of Pius XII is the most widely cited; he argued that Pius XII failed to take a stand against Hitler and the horrors of the Holocaust.

Dalin, David G. *The Myth of Hitler's Pope*. Washington, D.C.: Regnery, 2005. A defense of Pius XII and his actions during World War II; Dalin attempts to dismantle the Cornwell thesis.

Friedländer, Saul. *Pius XII and the Third Reich: A Documentation*. Translated by Charles Fullman. New York: Alfred A. Knopf, 1966. An examination of primary sources that raise questions about the relationship between the Vatican and Hitler's Germany during World War II.

Sánchez, José M. *Pius XII and the Holocaust: Understanding the Controversy*. Washington, D.C.: Catholic University of America, 2002. An important, valuable, and balanced study that examines the multitude of factors that emerged in the controversy of Pius XII's actions toward the Jews during World War II.

SEE ALSO: Aug. 9, 1903: Pius X Becomes Pope; June 7, 1912: Pope Pius X Condemns Slavery; Jan. 30, 1933: Hitler Comes to Power in Germany; Mar. 14, 1937: Pius XI Urges Resistance Against Nazism.

1939

March 31, 1939
SHERLOCK HOLMES FILM SERIES BEGINS

Basil Rathbone starred in the first of fourteen films that made him the most popular Sherlock Holmes in cinema history.

LOCALE: United States
CATEGORIES: Motion pictures; entertainment

KEY FIGURES

Basil Rathbone (1892-1967), successful and respected stage and film actor who achieved his greatest popularity in the film role of Sherlock Holmes

Nigel Bruce (1895-1953), venerable character actor who played Holmes's bumbling sidekick, Dr. Watson

Darryl F. Zanuck (1902-1979), executive producer for Twentieth Century-Fox who signed Rathbone and Bruce for their roles and oversaw the production of the first two films of the series

Sidney Lanfield (1898-1972), director of *The Hound of the Baskervilles*

Mary Gordon (1882-1963), character actor who played Holmes's landlady, Mrs. Hudson, throughout the series

SUMMARY OF EVENT

In the spring of 1939, American moviegoers of all ages were familiar with Sherlock Holmes as a film character. First popularized in the late 1880's and early 1890's through the novels and short stories of Sir Arthur Conan Doyle, Sherlock Holmes had been represented on silent film in Europe and the United States since the beginning of the twentieth century. After talking pictures were introduced in the late 1920's, a number of Holmes films followed, the most popular of which was a highly successful five-film series starring British actor Arthur Wontner. By 1939, Sherlock Holmes was still popular in print, had been represented successfully on stage, and had been portrayed in numerous radio versions. Basil Rathbone's portrayal of the Baker Street sleuth was certainly no novelty.

One of the most popular of the Holmes stories, *The Hound of the Baskervilles*, was familiar to many. Twentieth Century-Fox made the story into a film that stuck fairly closely to its source (unlike later movies in the Rathbone series). The plot begins with the mysterious death of Sir Charles Baskerville of Baskerville Hall. It is rumored on the Dartmoor marshland that Sir Charles was killed by a supernatural hound that for centuries has been

avenging the brutal murder of a young peasant woman by Sir Charles's wicked seventeenth century ancestor Sir Hugo Baskerville. Upon the death of Sir Charles, young Sir Henry Baskerville inherits his uncle's estate, and Holmes is called to investigate the danger that the avenging hound might present to Sir Henry. Holmes eventually discovers that the hound is merely a mortal beast trained by John Stapleton, a neighbor and distant Baskerville relative who had hoped to kill Sir Henry and claim the estate for himself. After Holmes solves the mystery, young Sir Henry is able to marry Stapleton's stepsister Beryl, and the two are presumed to live quietly and happily forever.

Ultimately, the Doyle stories were designed to showcase the deductive powers of Sherlock Holmes and to tantalize the audience with mystery and suspense. By highlighting the vicious canine, however, *The Hound of the Baskervilles* adds a touch of horror and the macabre to the detective mixture. The 1939 film version of Doyle's classic emphasized the horror element. Twentieth Century-Fox advertised the film as "literature's most shocking, spine-chilling mystery story," pitting Holmes "against the giant, unearthly Beast from Hell that roams the fog-swept moor . . . terrorizing the countryside . . . striking horror into the hearts of two young lovers!" As the opening credits roll, the misty Dartmoor setting prepares the audience for what Watson later calls "the dreadful eeriness of this place." Insert titles announce that "in all England there is no district more dismal than that vast expanse of primitive wasteland, the moors of Dartmoor in Devonshire," and the action begins at night on the boggy Grimpen Mire with the terrified Sir Charles fleeing the howling of the hound. Then, when Sir Charles collapses from heart failure, a horrific, wild-eyed man scurries from the bushes to steal Sir Charles's pocket watch. Although the film was shot entirely at the Twentieth Century-Fox studios, the atmosphere of the moors is genuinely eerie; when the audience finally sees the hound, however, it appears to be of normal size and is not sufficiently frightening.

Twentieth Century-Fox also emphasized the romantic element of Doyle's story. In the end, Sir Henry Baskerville wins the heart of his beautiful neighbor, Miss Beryl Stapleton, and in advertisements for the film, the studio gave the lovers as much prominence as Holmes and Watson. Two actors known for playing romantic leads, Richard Greene and Wendy Barrie, were cast to play Sir Henry and Miss Stapleton, and the opening credits gave

Greene top billing, followed by Rathbone and Barrie, with Nigel Bruce (as Dr. Watson) receiving secondary billing and separated in the credits from Rathbone. Emphasis on the romantic element was also reflected in Cyril Mockridge's music for the opening credits. The music began by suggesting horror—ominous measures featuring brass instruments—then segued into several bars of sweeping, romantic violins before returning to the opening mood, which continued into the first scene on the moor.

Richard Greene's romantic Sir Henry failed to dominate the screen. Instead, it was Rathbone's brisk, electric, intense characterization of Holmes and Bruce's languid, good-natured characterization of Watson that carried the picture, along with striking portrayals of numerous minor characters. For example, Lionel Atwill, who in *Sherlock Holmes and the Secret Weapon* (1942) would make a very effective Professor Moriarty, here created an effectively mysterious Dr. Mortimer. The slim and gravel-voiced John Carradine played the Baskervilles' servant with a compelling and taciturn quality, and in a typically brief appearance, Mary Gordon created the role of Mrs. Hudson, which she would play

Basil Rathbone as he appeared in the role of Sherlock Holmes in The Hound of the Baskervilles. *(AP/Wide World Photos)*

throughout the series. The result was a rich fictive world dominated by the Rathbone/Bruce tandem and especially by the intensity of Rathbone as Holmes.

Five months later, in September, 1939, Twentieth Century-Fox capitalized on Rathbone and Bruce's success by releasing a second Holmes film, *The Adventures of Sherlock Holmes*. The two character actors were well on their way to becoming the most popular Holmes and Watson in cinema history. In this and subsequent films, Rathbone and Bruce received top billing and were featured as the stars; their personal status was emphasized even more than their roles as Holmes and Watson.

In October, 1939, Rathbone and Bruce began solidifying their new fame by repeating their roles for radio, and they went on to act in more than two hundred radio

performances from 1939 through 1946. In September, 1942, Universal Pictures purchased the film rights to the Doyle short stories and began a series of twelve more Rathbone/Bruce films. The last of these was *Dressed to Kill*, and after it was released in 1946, Rathbone quit the series to return to New York and his first love, the stage. Although Rathbone had initially felt challenged by the Holmes role, he eventually tired of it, feeling that he was simply repeating himself rather than growing as an actor. Unfortunately, he had become so identified with the role that his career as an effective character actor was essentially destroyed. Children asking him for his autograph would often not know that Sherlock Holmes was a fictional character and that the man they addressed was really the actor Basil Rathbone, and Rathbone could not appear on screen without reminding audiences of Sherlock Holmes. In the late 1940's in New York, Rathbone worked on stage, radio, and television with some success but without offsetting his typecasting as Holmes, and he even returned to the role in 1953 in a play and a television pilot, both of which were unsuccessful. He did not appear again in film until the middle 1950's, and then with little success. By the early 1960's, he was acting in cheap thrillers for American International Pictures, and he ended his film career by appearing in a pair of obscure films, *Autopsy of a Ghost* (1967) and *Hillbillies in a Haunted House* (1967). Although Rathbone achieved international fame as Sherlock Holmes, his acting career was finally severely limited by his phenomenal success in that role.

SIGNIFICANCE

There had been many successful and popular portrayals of Sherlock Holmes before Rathbone's appearance in *The Hound of the Baskervilles* in 1939. William Gillette, H. A. Saintsbury, Eille Norwood, John Barrymore, Clive Brook, Raymond Massey, Arthur Wontner, and others had given significant performances as the great detective. Gillette, who acted until 1935, had played Holmes on stage, in film, and on radio for more than thirteen hundred performances and was considered by many in his heyday to be the definitive Sherlock Holmes. The British actor Eille Norwood had made forty-seven short, silent films in the early 1920's as Holmes. By 1946, however, Rathbone's performance in the series of fourteen Sherlock Holmes films had eclipsed all other portrayals.

In the decades following Rathbone's 1946 departure from the Universal series, many other actors portrayed Holmes. Actors such as Peter Cushing, Christopher Lee, Douglas Wilmer, Fritz Weaver, John Neville, Stewart Granger, John Wood, Nicol Williamson, Christopher Plummer, Roger Moore, Frank Langella, Ian Richardson, and others played Holmes on film, stage, and television. For forty years, however, no one threatened to dislodge Rathbone as the image of Sherlock Holmes until Jeremy Brett began his long and effective series of Holmes tales for England's Granada Television in the mid-1980's. For nearly half a century, Rathbone reigned supreme as the popular image of Sherlock Holmes.

Some of Rathbone's popularity in the role must be attributed to his appearance. Tall and slender, with a strong nose, dark hair, piercing eyes, and a slightly receding hairline, Rathbone bore a striking resemblance to the image of Holmes created by the most famous and most influential of Doyle's illustrators, Sidney Paget, who es-

tablished the initial and most abiding portrait of Holmes in his many drawings for the original publication of Doyle's stories in the *Strand Magazine*. As an excellent and experienced character actor, Rathbone also brought to the role an intensity coupled with a thoughtful intelligence and an aristocratic manner that perfectly suited the character.

Rathbone's height, intense eyes, angular features, and lack of muscularity all suggested brains rather than brawn, and he brought to his portrayal of Holmes an aristocratic demeanor that had been honed in earlier roles, beginning with his portrayal of the stern Mr. Murdstone in *David Copperfield* (1935) and including a bravura performance as the oily Guy of Gisbourne in *The Adventures of Robin Hood* (1938). Also of no small consequence was Rathbone's precise, deep, and crisp speaking voice, which seemed to capture the very sound of clear thinking. Rathbone's aristocratic manner, so essential to the Sherlock Holmes character, would not be sufficiently recaptured until the advent of Jeremy Brett's Holmes in the mid-1980's. As Rathbone had become the definitive Sherlock Holmes for movies, Brett promised finally to eclipse him by becoming the definitive Holmes in the next dominant popular medium—television.

In addition, Rathbone had an advantage over all previous and subsequent screen Sherlocks when he was paired with Nigel Bruce's incomparable Dr. Watson, whose good-natured bumbling served as the perfect foil to Rathbone's characterization. The Watson character has always proved deceptively difficult to play: A companion and contrast to Holmes, Watson tends to be sycophantic, prosaic, even dull, and many actors cannot bring any meaningful liveliness to the role. Bruce, however, managed to create a richly sentimental warmth in Watson that complemented a genuinely close relationship with Holmes, and in some respects Nigel Bruce's Watson proved an even more indelible screen image than Rathbone's Holmes.

Another factor contributing to Rathbone's enormous popularity was the timing of the series, which coincided with U.S. involvement in World War II. Many of the films in the Universal series exploited the war consciousness, creating un-Doyle-like tales that set Holmes against Nazi spies, and a number of the films in the series ended with uplifting, jingoistic speeches such as the one that caps *Sherlock Holmes in Washington* (1943), in which Holmes quotes Winston Churchill: "In the days to come, the British and American people for their own safety and the good of all will walk together in majesty and justice and in peace." Finally, the timing of the

Rathbone series coincided perfectly with the advent of television as a powerful cultural force in the United States. As local stations sought films for their afternoon and late-night movie slots, the Rathbone series proved both useful and popular. Given that all the pre-1929 Holmes films were silent and thus not commercially viable, and because most of the pre-Rathbone sound versions were either lost or not readily available, the Rathbone series enjoyed a virtual monopoly. Consequently, the fourteen Rathbone/Bruce films became the most popular series of feature films ever shown on American television.

The Rathbone Holmes series is not generally thought of as cinematically innovative or daring, but in one way two of the films are almost shocking for their time. When Doyle created his detective hero at the end of the nineteenth century, he had made Holmes a narcotics addict who injected cocaine, heroin, morphine, and other drugs to combat the monotony of his daily routine. Only when challenged by a particularly difficult case did Holmes find life stimulating enough to make drugs unnecessary. At the end of *The Hound of the Baskervilles*, Holmes has solved all the mysteries, trapped the murderer, and brought peace and justice to Baskerville Hall; he has declared it "a very interesting case for your annals, Watson." Announcing that he has had a strenuous day and will now turn in, Holmes pauses at the door and, turning back to Watson, says, "Oh, Watson, the needle!" This was a startling line, given the conservatism and heavily censored nature of the film industry of the 1940's. Holmes's addiction would not be dealt with openly on film until the mid-1970's, when *The Seven Percent Solution* (1976) unabashedly focused on Holmes's drug use. There is another veiled reference to Holmes's addiction in *Sherlock Holmes and the Secret Weapon* (1942), the second film in the Universal series. Near the end of the film, the evil Professor Moriarty has captured Holmes and has strapped him to an operating table; Moriarty plans to kill Holmes by draining his blood, drop by agonizing drop. Smiling, Moriarty says, "The needle till the end, eh?"

Edgar Allan Poe invented the detective genre in the 1840's, and before the century was finished, Sir Arthur Conan Doyle had made Sherlock Holmes the most compelling of all detective characters. As a kind of popular romantic hero, the detective character entertains audiences by surpassing the limits felt by ordinary people, but Sherlock Holmes's intelligence made him especially appealing to popular audiences. Unlike such heroes as the cowboy of the American Western or the usual police detective, Holmes does not resort to weapons, violence, or physical prowess. He wins by using deductive reasoning that permits him to cull meaning from what seems prosaic and meaningless to everyone else.

—*Terry Nienhuis*

FURTHER READING

Barnes, Alan. *Sherlock Holmes on Screen: The Complete Film and TV History*. London: Reynolds & Hearn, 2004. Wonderfully illustrated history of Holmes's portrayals on screen. Breaks down the performances by category and provides some interesting analyses.

Davies, David Stuart. *Holmes of the Movies: The Screen Career of Sherlock Holmes*. New York: Bramhall House, 1968. Very readable survey of Holmes literature covers Doyle and the major actors who have portrayed Holmes. Devotes three chapters to Rathbone. Includes photographs and filmography but no index.

Eyles, Allen. *Sherlock Holmes: A Centenary Celebration*. New York: Harper & Row, 1986. A sumptuously illustrated coffee-table book covering Holmes in all popular forms, including radio. One Rathbone chapter and a very useful chapter on recent Holmes figures. Includes index, academically slanted bibliography, chronological list of Doyle stories, and a valuable chronological list of performances. Eleven chapters, 144 pages.

Haydock, Ron. *Deerstalker! Holmes and Watson on Screen*. Metuchen, N.J.: Scarecrow Press, 1978. Sixteen-chapter survey devotes nearly three chapters to Rathbone and Bruce. Written in a very personal, chatty style; its main strength is its wealth of detail. Includes photographs, annotated bibliography, and index.

Pohle, Robert W., Jr., and Douglas C. Hart. *Sherlock Holmes on the Screen: The Motion Picture Adventures of the World's Most Popular Detective*. South Brunswick, N.J.: A. S. Barnes, 1977. Although dated, still very useful. Provides unusually thorough and specific details on scores of films. Features a long chapter on the Rathbone series. Includes many photographs, a list of Doyle stories, bibliography, and index.

Rathbone, Basil. *In and Out of Character*. Garden City, N.Y.: Doubleday, 1962. Autobiography of eighteen chapters and 278 pages, in which, amazingly, Rathbone covers the Holmes series in a single ten-page chapter. This chapter, however, is essential reading, as it bristles with deep feeling. Includes an incisive analysis of the Sherlock phenomenon and reveals

1939

Rathbone's ultimate disappointment that the series so seriously damaged his acting career.

Richardson, Ian, and David Stuart Davies. *Starring Sherlock Holmes*. London: Titan Books, 2003. An attractive and generally well-researched volume on all the Holmes performances. Pays special attention to those by Rathbone, Brett, and Peter Cushing.

Steinbrunner, Chris, and Norman Michaels. *The Films of Sherlock Holmes*. Secaucus, N.J.: Citadel Press, 1991. Excellent lengthy survey includes many illustrations. Devotes a full chapter to each Rathbone/Bruce film. One of the best books of its kind; unusu-

ally detailed, informative, and well written. However, it provides no index, bibliography, or other scholarly aids.

SEE ALSO: 1930's: Hollywood Enters Its Golden Age; 1930's-1940's: Studio System Dominates Hollywood Filmmaking; 1931-1932: Gangster Films Become Popular; 1934-1935: Hitchcock Becomes Synonymous with Suspense; 1939: Ford Defines the Western in *Stagecoach*; Aug. 17, 1939: *The Wizard of Oz* Premieres; Dec. 15, 1939: *Gone with the Wind* Premieres.

April, 1939
THE GRAPES OF WRATH PORTRAYS DEPRESSION-ERA AMERICA

John Steinbeck's use of journalistic exposé, documentary style, and experimental fiction in The Grapes of Wrath, *a critique of modern inhumanity, produced one of the most controversial novels of the century.*

LOCALE: New York, New York
CATEGORY: Literature·

KEY FIGURES

John Steinbeck (1902-1968), American novelist
Carol Henning Steinbeck (1906-1983), Steinbeck's wife, typist, and editor and an activist for migrant workers
Tom Collins (1897?-1961), U.S. government camp worker
Pascal Covici (1885-1964), Steinbeck's editor and literary confidant
Edward F. Ricketts (1896-1948), American amateur biologist

SUMMARY OF EVENT

The man who would come to write the quintessential American novel of the Great Depression began the 1930's in obscurity and with uneven literary success. John Steinbeck had rejected his middle-class upbringing in Salinas, California, and the pretensions of college (Stanford University) for the life of an itinerant laborer and aspiring writer. His efforts of the early 1930's were regarded by most critics as florid and vague renditions of humanity's encounter with a mystical nature. In *Tortilla Flat* (1935), however, he began to restrain his style and to construct richer, more detailed portraits of the folkways

of people on the social margins. With *In Dubious Battle* (1936) and *Of Mice and Men* (1937), Steinbeck established himself as a sensitive chronicler of the vanishing rural communities of the United States and the persistent underclass. These novels also confronted the Great Depression more bluntly than most popular authors dared.

By 1936, waves of destitute farmers ("Okies") were fleeing the Dust Bowl to Salinas and Monterey, California, where Steinbeck saw them victimized by nature and by other human beings. He began researching their plight for a series of journalistic exposés. As the intricacy of the farmers' experience emerged, however, he decided to expand his work into a fictional treatment of the migrant quandary as an emblem for the Depression itself. The situation also invited Steinbeck to make better use of his maturing style and social concerns. His careful attention to regional dialects and folkways, the relationship between political struggle and human need, and the use of innovative narrative techniques all came together in what was to be his greatest novel. After several false starts, Steinbeck began serious writing in May, 1938. His wife, Carol Henning Steinbeck, typing and editing throughout, also provided the book's title, a phrase from the lyrics of "The Battle Hymn of the Republic."

The Grapes of Wrath (1939) recounts the suffering and human endurance of the Joad family as they abandon their bankrupt farm in Oklahoma for the promise of work in California. Eldest son Tom jumps parole (stemming from a questionable manslaughter conviction) to help lead the family westward. Ma Joad, an intuitive genius of human nature and a noble sufferer, struggles to keep her extended family whole amid their despondence. A fallen preacher, Casey, accompanies them as a mouthpiece for the author's folk philosophy and the source of Christian imagery throughout the tale. As the family traverses the legendary Route 66, Steinbeck exposes a litany of American sins: exploitative banks and agribusiness, the xenophobic defensiveness of the middle class, and a socioeconomic order that seems perversely distant from human morality and needs. The Joads and Steinbeck find temporary solace within a "government camp," a utopian model of participatory democracy, altruism, and cooperation. In the end, however, the Joads move on to an exploitative farm camp where Casey is killed (crucified); Tom must then flee after he murders again in retaliation.

Steinbeck's migrants are not unambiguous heroes, nor are their oppressors simplistic villains. All of his characters' good and bad natures are complicated by circumstance. Material scarcity, social disarray, and an inhuman economic machine cause men to violate their own heartfelt sense of morality. Steinbeck's concept of humankind was deeply influenced by his close friend, amateur biologist Edward F. Ricketts. Partly through

interactions with Ricketts, Steinbeck developed the quasi-scientific notion of the "phalanx": He believed that individuals in groups were able to locate transcendent elements of human nature, evil, and morality that were not apparent to individuals alone. "Maybe all men got one big soul ever'body's a part of," Casey preaches. Such primal themes pervade the novel through allusions to Christianity, Jeffersonian agrarianism, American Transcendentalism, and tribal social organization. The thread of hope for American renewal in the face of relentless tragedy courses through Ma and Tom Joad and their ability to locate the common morality of "human spirit." The literary merits and sophistication of the novel remain controversial, but it is inarguable that Steinbeck offered his general readers a compelling depiction of modern society as diseased and beyond human control.

Beyond the more apparent social and philosophical messages, Steinbeck wanted to construct a monument to the American "common man." His spare, descriptive writing called attention to the details of human relations, rather than to his own literary artistry. Descriptions of physical gestures, dialect and inflection, and quick dialogic exchanges constitute much of the narrative. Such elements were intended to underscore the profundity of common struggles and to suggest the rich meanings within everyday relationships. Steinbeck's most daring literary innovation, however, came in his punctuating of the main plot with numerous "interchapters." These passages wrenched the reader out of the Joads' story and into more general and often more prosaic ruminations on the migrants' plight.

Steinbeck intended to disorient and permanently change his readers. Many critics, however, have argued that *The Grapes of Wrath* had a similar effect on its creator. He suddenly became the most discussed novelist in the United States; he was elected to the National Institute of Arts and Letters and was awarded the Pulitzer Prize. His book became a best seller and produced a firestorm of debate, both political and aesthetic. Critics often dismissed Steinbeck as a mawkish sentimentalist of limited skill. Questions about his place within the literary pantheon were renewed in 1962, when Steinbeck received the Nobel Prize. While he continued to write at a decent pace after 1939, *East of Eden* (1952) was the only subsequent novel that approached his earlier work in its ambition. Steinbeck never again invested in his writing the level of passion, social conscience, and literary experimentation that made *The Grapes of Wrath* a landmark of American cultural history.

THE CAUSES OF REVOLT

In The Grapes of Wrath, *Steinbeck included "interchapters" in which he ruminated on the migrants' plight in order to distance readers from the main plot and allow a longer perspective on the social machinery that drove it. One famous passage concerns the evolution of farming from a family occupation to an industry to which the Joads were clearly in thrall:*

And the great owners, who must lose their land in an upheaval, the great owners with access to history, with eyes to read history and to know the great fact: when property accumulates in too few hands it is taken away. And that companion fact: when a majority of the people are hungry and cold they will take by force what they need. And the little screaming fact that sounds through all history: repression works only to strengthen and knit the repressed. The great owners ignored the three cries of history . . . and every effort of the great owners was directed at repression. The money was spent for arms, for gas to protect the great holdings, and spies were sent to catch the murmurings of revolt so that it might be stamped out. The changing economy was ignored, plans for the change ignored; and only means to destroy revolt were considered, while the causes of revolt went on.

Source: John Steinbeck, *The Grapes of Wrath* (New York: Random House, 1939).

1939

SIGNIFICANCE

The publication of *The Grapes of Wrath* was among a handful of literary events that reverberated into the larger political and social arenas of American culture. Steinbeck anticipated some controversy, and he had the lyrics to the "The Battle Hymn of the Republic" printed on the hardcover edition's endpapers as a sign of his patriotism. The strategy failed; the book has been among the most banned, burned, and censored literary works of modern times. Steinbeck himself was accused variously of instigating worker unrest, of betraying the dignity of the migrants themselves, and simply of being a mediocre writer. Nevertheless, *The Grapes of Wrath* has remained one of the most widely read works of serious American fiction of the century and an influential example of the activist novel.

The political Right first attacked the book as inaccurate, biased propaganda, neither fair nor artistic. Steinbeck was called an outright liar and anti-American by some newspapers and many farm owners' organizations around the country. His blistering depictions of brutality by landowners were challenged in all manner of publications. *Collier's* spoke for many when it branded the book subversive propaganda. Still, Steinbeck enjoyed no less a fan than Eleanor Roosevelt, who praised the book's disturbing images of the American underbelly as a call to action. Senator Robert M. La Follette, Jr., initiated an official inquiry into the work conditions of California farms. The Supreme Court declared unconstitutional a California law that had been used against migrant workers. The growing momentum for reform faded, however, as World War II provided new opportunities for the itinerant and unemployed.

Controversy over the novel quickly shifted from politics to taste and morality. Most bannings and burnings were responses to the characters' earthy dialogue and occasional mentions of sexuality. Charges of obscenity have maintained the book's dubious place on the list of most-censored works; it has often been removed from school reading lists and libraries. From the time of publication, however, attempts to ban or abridge the novel for reasons of propriety have been challenged as excuses for suppressing its political ideas. Moreover, few authors have enjoyed Steinbeck's broad readership and popular esteem. Although hardly resolved, persistent controversies over who should read *The Grapes of Wrath* often raise deeper questions about the motives and intentions of censorship. Nevertheless, Steinbeck's use of a more frank and naturalistic style may have helped accustom American readers to the more explicit content of postwar popular fiction.

The deeper cultural impact of *The Grapes of Wrath* was more subtle and enduring than the immediate response it garnered in 1939. Although the book did not have the same demonstrable social influence as Harriet Beecher Stowe's *Uncle Tom's Cabin* (1852), Edward Bellamy's *Looking Backward: 2000-1887* (1888), or Upton Sinclair's *The Jungle* (1906), controversy generated by the novel foreshadowed persistent arguments about the role of social issues and ideology in an age of mass communications. Even journalists who were sympathetic to Steinbeck's cause at the time pondered the consequences of his blending of reportage with literary license in a popular novel. The question of art's duty to fact and impartiality would become all the more pressing after World War II. As film and television gained authority in American life, the social responsibilities, even politics, of popular artists were more carefully scrutinized; some artists were "blacklisted" for their views. Steinbeck's novel suggested the power of socially committed novelists to redirect political agendas and to influence public opinion. This memory of the radical art of the 1930's certainly informed later attacks on alleged Communists in the film and television industries.

To the chagrin of many critics, *The Grapes of Wrath* has been regarded by general readers as one of the great American novels and continues to be a standard text in secondary school English classes. Like James T. Farrell, John Dos Passos, and even film actor and director Charles Chaplin, Steinbeck strove to engage art with immediate social issues without sacrificing the artist's unique qualities of vision and experimentation. These artists argued that a radically changed modern society required new forms of narrative. Farrell and Dos Passos were more dogged—some say more talented—in their pursuit of this goal. *The Grapes of Wrath* thus is probably taught more as history than as literature. Nevertheless, Steinbeck helped to advance the art of the social-issue novel beyond the didacticism of nineteenth century efforts and the often leaden style of much proletarian fiction by the radical Left. After World War II, issue-oriented fiction became more often the purview of film and television than of literature. *The Grapes of Wrath* suggested a palatable recipe for mixing social activism and fiction. Much of such fiction has humanized social issues, dramatizing the ways in which abstract debates affect common lives. Still, the more provocative blends of literary innovation and social exposé have continued to flourish, especially among African American novelists such as Ralph Ellison, James Baldwin, Alice Walker, and Toni Morrison. Whatever form the book's legacy has taken, however, the events surrounding *The Grapes of Wrath* have dramatized the ways in which art matters.

—*Steven Smith*

FURTHER READING

Astro, Richard. *John Steinbeck and Edward F. Ricketts: The Shaping of a Novelist.* Minneapolis: University of Minnesota Press, 1973. A detailed chronicle of Steinbeck's relationship with Ricketts. Explores the place of biological science in the author's thought about human behavior and society. Of special importance to *The Grapes of Wrath* is a chapter on Steinbeck's "phalanx" theory of society as a biological organism. Photographs of both men are included.

Benson, Jackson J. *The True Adventures of John Steinbeck, Writer.* New York: Viking Press, 1984. A biography of Steinbeck that emphasizes his life over his works.

Bloom, Harold, ed. *John Steinbeck's "The Grapes of Wrath."* Philadelphia: Chelsea House, 2005. Anthology of evaluations of the novel by leading Americanists and literary critics, including Harold Bloom, Howard Levant, Donald Pizer, and Frederic I. Carpenter.

Donohue, Agnes McNeill, comp. *A Casebook on "The Grapes of Wrath."* New York: Thomas Y. Crowell, 1968. An anthology of commentary on the novel and Steinbeck. Contemporaneous articles about the book's accuracy, literary quality, and general reception are included from sources throughout American culture. Also includes material on the controversy surrounding Steinbeck's winning of the Nobel Prize in 1962.

Heavilin, Barbara A., ed. *The Critical Response to John Steinbeck's "The Grapes of Wrath."* Westport, Conn.: Greenwood Press, 2000. Collection of critical essays on the novel, including a selection of criticism from the first fifty years of its publication, as well as a section devoted to the criticism of the 1990's.

Steinbeck, John. *"The Grapes of Wrath": Text and Criticism.* Edited by Peter Lisca. New York: Penguin Books, 1977. This critical edition provides the most reliable version of the original novel and includes selected evaluations of the book from the time of publication into the 1970's. Also includes a selected bibliography of Steinbeck and scholarship on his work.

_____. *Steinbeck: A Life in Letters.* Edited by Elaine Steinbeck and Robert Wallsten. New York: Viking Press, 1975. An indispensable collection of Steinbeck's correspondence. Regarding *The Grapes of Wrath*, there are revealing letters to friends that recount Steinbeck's experiences in migrant farmer camps. Moreover, there are important exchanges with Pascal Covici, Steinbeck's editor, about the novel's form and its controversial ending.

_____. *Working Days: The Journals of "The Grapes of Wrath," 1938-1941.* Edited by Robert DeMott. New York: Viking Press, 1989. An account of Steinbeck's writing of the novel through his own journal entries. DeMott's extensive annotations and supportive material are helpful in establishing the social setting in which the book was created.

SEE ALSO: Feb., 1906: Sinclair Publishes *The Jungle*; Oct. 29, 1929-1939: Great Depression; 1930's: Guthrie's Populist Songs Reflect the Depression-Era United States; 1934-1939: Dust Bowl Devastates the Great Plains.

1939

April 7, 1939
ITALY INVADES AND ANNEXES ALBANIA

Italy's successful invasion of Albania in 1939 emboldened dictator Benito Mussolini and brought about an annexation of Albania that lasted for four years.

LOCALE: Albania; Italy

CATEGORIES: Military history; diplomacy and international relations; expansion and land acquisition

KEY FIGURES

Zog I (1895-1961), king of Albania, r. 1928-1939

Benito Mussolini (1883-1945), Italian fascist dictator, 1922-1943

Enver Hoxha (1908-1985), leader of Albanian Communist Party and dictator, 1944-1985

Galeazzo Ciano (1903-1944), Italian count, Fascist, and foreign minister under Mussolini

SUMMARY OF EVENT

The forces of the Fascist dictator Benito Mussolini attacked Albania, which had been a close ally, on April 7, 1939, and easily added that country to Italy's growing empire. Albanian resistance gradually grew, however, and by 1943, when Italy left the war and Nazi troops showed up to hold Albania, three main resistance forces and the Yugoslav Partisans were all vying for control. The Italian invasion created the power vacuum that ultimately allowed the communist forces of the brutal Enver Hoxha to come to power in Albania.

For more than a decade in interwar Europe, the young state of Albania had increasingly fallen under Italian influence. In 1924, when Zog I came to power for the second time, he did so with the backing of the Yugoslav government. When Zog had himself crowned king in 1928, relations with Yugoslavia rapidly soured. He courted Italian economic and military aid, especially after a spy scandal with the Yugoslavs. The poor relations between Belgrade and Rome left Yugoslavia suspicious that Albania would become Mussolini's minion. Furthermore, in the face of Serbia's blatant anti-Albanian measures in Kosovo, Zog took the title "king of the Albanians," not simply "king of Albania." This name promised future conflict over Kosovo.

Italy's grab for Albania was conditioned by two trends. First was the well-known fascist desire to turn the Mediterranean into an "Italian sea," a concept that invoked the grandeur of the Roman Empire. This impulse

gave rise not only to the desire to conquer Albania, but also to engage in massive, and often brutal, adventurism in Libya, Ethiopia, Egypt, and Greece. Less well known but equally important to Italy's immediate geopolitical strategy was mistrust of Hitler and the Nazis and the desire to expand Italian influence at a rate proportionate to that of the Third Reich. In the aggressive style of the day—which was not unique to fascism but was rooted in older, elitist practices of the major world powers—the Italians craved compensation for recent Nazi successes in taking over Austria and Czechoslovakia. Albania was to suffer the consequences for this rivalry between Rome and Berlin.

Over a week before the invasion, the Italians had presented King Zog with a capitulation agreement, which he delayed signing. Then, early in the morning of April 7, 1939, Italian forces landed at four cities on the Albanian coast. On paper, this major amphibious assault was a riotous success. It involved about twenty-two thousand soldiers, four hundred airplanes, three hundred tanks, and a large number of warships. The day before, as King

ALBANIA, 1939

3184

Zog had appealed for succor to other countries, the Italians had evacuated their civilians and dropped leaflets by air into the Albanian capital, Tirana, explaining that they only intended to restore order and justice.

According to historian Bernd Fischer, the Albanian defense forces, which consisted of around four thousand effective soldiers and three thousand British-trained gendarmes, offered almost no resistance, but if they had, the poorly trained Italian forces, with their disorganized tactics and shoddy equipment, would probably have met with an embarrassing defeat. The Italians landed at Durrës, Vlorë, Shëngjin, and Sarandë. King Zog headed for exile in Greece with his wife, Queen Geraldine (née Apponyi) and two-day-old son, Leka, that same day. At midmorning the next day, Italian trooops were already in Tirana. Only at the coastal city of Durrës did the Italians meet significant resistance. Estimates of casualties are sketchy, but several hundred people probably died on each side during the takeover.

Although Italian control never really extended beyond the coast and the cities, Albania and Italy were united in a "personal union" headed by King Victor Emmanuel III in Rome. This amounted to an annexation: Albanians technically became Italian citizens, the populous and hotly disputed Kosovo region was attached to Albania, and a free trade zone made Albania's economic situation somewhat better. Nonetheless, Albanians bristled at their loss of sovereignty and realized that their local government was nothing but a pawn of Mussolini. Galeazzo Ciano rewrote the Albanian constitution in 1939 and abolished Tirana's foreign ministry, and Italy tried to cement its control further by founding a local Fascist Party, Italianizing the educational system, and absorbing Albania's security forces into Italy's.

The war heightened tensions between the Gegs of northern Albania and the southern Tosks, the country's main two linguistic and cultural groups. Most of King Zog's support had come from the north, and a monarchist resistance group called Legaliteti was formed by Abaz Kupi, hero of the defense of Durrës. A separate resistance movement known as the Balli Kombëtar also emerged with a strong nationalist platform. Both groups came into conflict with the Communist-dominated Partisan movement. This latter group, which was officially known as the National Liberation Front, was greatly influenced by the Yugoslav Communists and would ultimately triumph by mobilizing as many as seventy thousand men and women as fighters, especially in the Tosk areas. These sectional rivalries and disputes over Yugoslav influence and Kosovo continued to manifest themselves after the war.

SIGNIFICANCE

With the Italian invasion of 1939, Albania was dragged into World War II. For Italy, the glory of adding another Mediterranean colony was soon overshadowed by the rash move that followed: the failed invasion of Greece in late 1940, which largely proceeded from bases in Albania and showed that the Italian military had not fixed its fatal flaws. World War II brought many changes. As the famous Albanian novelist Ismail Kadare said in testimony before the U.S. Congress in 1991, the war was ultimately responsible for bringing the long-lived Stalinist dictatorship to Albania, since Hoxha's rule emerged from the mobilization and military success of the antifascist forces of national liberation. The fact that King Zog fled ignominiously into exile undercut his efforts to create a legitimate government in exile; this in turn aided the Communists in their eventual rise to power.

The destruction wrought by the war itself was light when compared to some European states such as Poland, Russia, and Yugoslavia. Approximately thirty thousand Albanians died, but the extensive losses of livestock, transportation infrastructure, and housing made postwar recovery difficult for Europe's poorest state. The invasion of southern Albania by the Greek army at the end of the war added to existing resentments over border demarcation and minority rights on both sides of the frontier.

At first, the war induced cooperation between Yugoslav and Albanian Communists, and the former provided the latter with organizational and military support. Ultimately, however, the war's legacy heightened the rivalry between the two states over the Kosovo region. The area was returned to Yugoslavia after the war, which for most Albanians meant that more than a million of their conationals were returned to Serbian domination. The Kosovar Albanians responded with a major rebellion against Yugoslav rule that lasted from November, 1944, to May, 1945. The promises of Yugoslav leader Tito (Josip Broz) to return the region to Albania once Serbian nationalism had been diluted within the new socialist Yugoslavia came to naught, in part because of the Tito-Stalin split of 1948 that left Albania vehemently pro-Moscow and anti-Belgrade. As the 1999 conflict and continuing United Nations occupation of the province demonstrates, the future of Kosovo remained very contested.

The long, harsh decades of Hoxha's communism in Albania ensured that postwar relations with Italy would be cold. Through the media and through contacts with the five-hundred-year-old Italo-Albanian, or Arbëresh, populations of Calabria and Sicily, Italy gradually reemerged as the most accessible land of plenty; thou-

1939

sands of Albanians emigrated there in the 1990's. Italy became Albania's leading trading partner and leading donor of aid, and the Italian government sent armed forces—which were welcomed by the Albanian government—to help restore stability after the economic and governmental crisis of 1997.

—*John K. Cox*

FURTHER READING

Ciano, Count Galeazzo. *Diary, 1937-1943*. New York: Enigma Books, 2002. One of the most important political diaries of the twentieth century, smuggled out of Italy by Ciano's widow after his execution by the forces of Mussolini and Hitler.

Elsie, Robert. *Historical Dictionary of Albania*. Lanham, Md.: Scarecrow Press, 2004. Entries on all key figures in the eras of Zog and Hoxha.

Fischer, Bernd. *Albania at War, 1939-1945*. West Lafayette, Ind.: Purdue University Press, 1999. One of the most extensive works available in English on this period, based on excellent archival sleuthing and interviews.

Kadare, Ismail. *The General of the Dead Army*. New York: New Amsterdam, 1991. Path-breaking novel by one of Europe's greatest writers, recalling the resistance struggle and commenting on postwar Albanian-Italian relations.

Tomes, Jason. *King Zog of Albania: Europe's Self-Made Muslim Monarch*. New York: New York University Press, 2004. Detailed study of the regime that came to depend very heavily on Mussolini even before the invasion of 1939.

Vickers, Miranda. *The Albanians: A Modern History*. London: I. B. Tauris, 1995. A balanced and erudite study that emphasizes both what is unique about Albania and how the country fits into the European context.

SEE ALSO: 1911-1912: Italy Annexes Libya; Oct. 24-30, 1922: Mussolini's "March on Rome"; Oct. 11, 1935-July 15, 1936: League of Nations Applies Economic Sanctions Against Italy; Aug. 3, 1940-Mar., 1941: Italy Invades British Somaliland; Sept. 13, 1940: Italy Invades Egypt.

April 30, 1939
AMERICAN TELEVISION DEBUTS AT THE WORLD'S FAIR

At the New York World's Fair, television was displayed to the American public for the first time, NBC announced the start of regularly scheduled television broadcasting in the United States, and David Sarnoff gave a prophetic address about the new industry of television.

LOCALE: Long Island, New York
CATEGORIES: Radio and television; communications and media; science and technology; inventions

KEY FIGURES
David Sarnoff (1891-1971), founder and president of the Radio Corporation of America
Vladimir Zworykin (1889-1982), Russian American inventor
Philo T. Farnsworth (1906-1971), American inventor
Franklin D. Roosevelt (1882-1945), president of the United States, 1933-1945

SUMMARY OF EVENT

The 1939 New York World's Fair was a technology showcase, but its most significant innovation went largely unnoticed at the time. On the opening day of the

fair, television was displayed to the American public for the very first time. On that day also, the National Broadcasting Company (NBC) announced plans to begin regularly scheduled television broadcasting. That afternoon, David Sarnoff, the founder and president of the Radio Corporation of America (RCA), NBC's parent company, made several truly visionary pronouncements about the industry he was about to launch.

Sarnoff was born in Russia in 1891 and moved to the United States with his family at the age of nine. As a young man, Sarnoff gained national celebrity working for Marconi Radio when he manned a Morse code receiver for seventy-two hours after the *Titanic* sank in 1912, taking down the names of survivors. Sarnoff rose quickly in the Marconi company and eventually struck out on his own in the 1920's, founding RCA. A decade of diligent planning and hard work produced the most successful commercial radio company—manufacturer and broadcaster—of the period. The millions of dollars that RCA made with its NBC radio subsidiary (the Red and Blue Networks) and its sales of console radios provided the seed money needed to make television a reality.

The term "television" first appeared in a 1907 issue of

Scientific American; however, experiments in video transmission actually began in the 1880's. Early on, there was a difference of opinion whether mechanical or electronic systems would work best. In the 1920's and early 1930's, Britain's Television, Ltd., developed a cumbersome, clattering contraption that could send a watery image eight miles through the air. Vertically mounted spinning wheels with glass lenses set into their perimeters were used in both the camera and the receiver to transduce light. As the wheels spun, they created a sound similar to a film projector, and the image was likewise displayed on a wall screen. The British Broadcasting Company initially showed a great deal of interest in this system; however, it was never able to send a clear, flicker-free picture, and it eventually was scrapped in favor of the fast-developing electronic television system.

Another U.S. immigrant from Russia, Vladimir Zworykin, invented the "iconoscope" in 1923. His employer, Westinghouse, showed no interest in the device, so Zworykin sought out his fellow Russian émigré, David Sarnoff. Sarnoff recognized that, crude as it was, the iconoscope represented the basis of an effective electronic television process. The iconoscope used light-sensitive materials to transduce light. Coupled with another new invention, the cathode-ray tube (CRT), electronic television was born. During the early 1930's, Zworykin perfected electronic television while Sarnoff went about gathering up all the television-related patents he could get his hands on. In addition to the iconoscope, Zworykin invented the "kinescope," a receiver for iconoscope signals.

Many television components were designed at RCA, but several significant elements were invented by other companies and by independent inventors. Prominent among these inventors was San Francisco-based Philo T. Farnsworth. He created an "image dissector" in 1927. This apparatus was essential to high-quality electronic television, and RCA initially infringed on his patent. Farnsworth, in his early twenties and with no formal college-level science training, sued RCA. When the court finally found in his favor, RCA was forced to pay ongoing royalties to his Philco, Inc. for use of the image dissector.

With an acceptable electronic television system completed, and with all legal questions settled, NBC began experimental television broadcasting from Camden, New Jersey, on July 7, 1936. The initial day's programming consisted of Sarnoff and his senior executives welcoming viewers, of which there were next to none, from his office on the fifty-third floor of Radio City. The

broadcast continued with actors from the Broadway play *Tobacco Road*, a singing act, and dancers from Radio City Music Hall. The United States was on the air, but it was losing the international race for television.

Both Germany and England already had regularly scheduled television services. Although picture quality was poor, Germany went on the air in 1935, broadcasting daily to eleven public viewing rooms around Berlin. England, having finally settled the issue of electronic versus mechanical television, began its regular service early in 1936. Britain's pioneering efforts in television design had an enormous beneficial side effect, the invention of radar. This technology, closely related to television, proved lifesaving to the English during the Battle of Britain in the summer of 1940.

In the United States, Zworykin had estimated that it would cost $100,000 to get television operational, but Sarnoff ended up spending $20 million by 1938. After several years of testing, Zworykin's system was ready, and RCA began distribution of its first television set, the TRK 660. This was a $660 console unit that stood four and one-half feet tall and had a flip-up, mirrored lid. The picture tube sat vertically, pointing upward inside the cabinet, and the image was reflected and reversed in the mirror so that people sitting around the console could view it. Because of the high price, only about one hundred sets were sold, most of them to RCA and NBC executives, with a few going to New York City bars.

Sarnoff, known to have a flair for the dramatic, chose the World's Fair for his big announcement. The fair opened on April 30, 1939, in Flushing Meadows, Long Island. A gigantic camera tethered to a mobile broadcast van was set up for the opening ceremonies. Franklin D. Roosevelt became the nation's first "television president" as he described the fair as "a beacon of progress and hope." His speech, along with that of New York mayor Fiorello La Guardia, was carried by cables to monitors inside the RCA exhibit. It was then relayed to NBC's transmitter for broadcast to monitors in NBC's Radio City headquarters and to the one hundred or more sets around the city. Tens of thousands of people were at the fair that day, but it is estimated that, at most, two thousand people watched these events on television.

NBC broadcast pictures featuring the fair's symbols, including the Trylon and Perisphere, in the background. Its camera swept across the Court of Peace, panned the gathering throng, and captured the arrival of the president's motorcade. Mayor La Guardia recorded the first close-up when he walked up to the camera and stared into it. After televising Roosevelt's initial address, the cam-

1939

SARNOFF ANNOUNCES THE BIRTH OF AN INDUSTRY

The following is an excerpt from the speech that David Sarnoff presented at the opening of the RCA pavilion at the 1939 World's Fair, in which he made a number of hopeful predictions about the new technology of television.

Today we are on the eve of launching a new industry, based on imagination, research and accomplishment. We are now ready to fulfill the promise made to the public last October, when, after years of research, laboratory experiments and tests in the field costing millions of dollars, the Radio Corporation of America announced that television program service and commercial television receivers would be made available to the public with the opening of the New York World's Fair. . . .

And now we add radio sight to sound. It is with a feeling of humbleness that I come to this moment of announcing the birth in this country of a new art so important in its implications that it is bound to affect all society. It is an art which shines like a torch of hope in a troubled world. It is a creative force which we must learn to utilize for the benefit of all mankind.

era was moved to the RCA Pavilion for Sarnoff's dedication. Fairgoers could step inside and watch the "show" on black-and-white monitors, then step outside to prove to themselves that what they were seeing was indeed real.

Sarnoff, in his speech, promised a new industry for the United States. NBC began regularly scheduled television broadcasts the same day, and receiving sets began to be made more widely available. Fairgoers also felt a sense of destiny of another sort. Clouds of war were already forming over Europe. Commercial television was interrupted by World War II just as people were learning of its existence, and the war meant a further delay of almost eight years before television sets were in anything but very limited use. That only a few thousand people actually watched the World's Fair on television that day is ironic, because television grew into an industry that prided itself on covering memorable events and broadcasting shared experiences. Still, Sarnoff and NBC were the first to bring the United States commercial television, an industry for which economic, social, and political effects are still evolving—and being debated—today.

SIGNIFICANCE

In retrospect, Sarnoff's presentation was a relatively inconsequential television milestone. Almost nobody saw the broadcast. England and Germany were already "on the air," and the coming world war put American television broadcasting on hold for several more years. The

World's Fair broadcast is significant because Sarnoff made several indisputably accurate predictions about what television would be like. He believed that television would bring Americans together as a nation, that it would spawn new industries, and that it would change the American political system. At the time, however, Sarnoff was focusing on a more immediate effect of his announcement.

In the 1930's, the U.S. Federal Communications Commission (FCC) was faced with the task of selecting a national video transmission standard. RCA, Philco, and Dumont each had invested heavily in research on and development of such systems. All were capable of transmitting pictures, but each was totally incompatible with the others. Sarnoff was certain that if he could get his system to market first, a wave of public support (similar to that of early radio listeners) would propel the RCA system to the forefront, forcing the FCC to select it as the national standard. Sarnoff's plan suffered from poor timing, however. With the United States just coming out of the Depression, few Americans had the money to buy a TRK 660. The world war brought television development to a standstill, so the great outpouring of support that Sarnoff hoped for never materialized. Nevertheless, Sarnoff's ploy had the desired effect. The FCC settled on RCA's system, with only minor modifications, as the American video standard in 1941.

Although this rush to market was in RCA's best interest, it proved less than optimal for American television viewers. The American video standard—the picture seen on American television sets—is of lower quality than the standards required in all other major industrial nations. The image is fuzzier and less true to life than television images in Britain, France, Germany, and Japan. These nations, with their researchers free from the pressure of private enterprise, took the time to perfect their broadcasting systems before presenting them to the public.

Sarnoff's loftier predictions of things to come were indeed precise. Television brought viewers together to witness and be a part of all major national events. The first half century of television history yielded hundreds of common shared experiences, among them President John F. Kennedy's assassination, the Apollo 11 Moon landing, the Vietnam War, the Watergate hearings and the resignation of President Nixon, and the space shuttle

Challenger disaster. Less notable, but still important in American culture, are the many beauty pageants, Rose Parades, football bowl games, and World Series that viewers have watched. As time passed and television audiences grew, the producers of such events modified their presentation to make them easier and more profitable for television to broadcast.

Just as Sarnoff promised, the growth of television produced many new industries. Prominent among these were the manufacture of broadcast and reception equipment as well as the production of programs. In addition, many parallel and ancillary businesses owe their existence to television. Radar, satellite communications, and computers, for instance, all share elements of television technology. Other businesses emerged to support the television industry, including ratings services (such as the A. C. Nielsen Company) and cable television providers.

Sarnoff also believed that showmanship would replace thoughtful expression on the part of politicians once they were exposed to television, a prediction that has arguably been proved correct. It is true that television has had its noteworthy political moments, such as Edward R. Murrow's *See It Now* episode in 1954 that took on communist-hunting Senator Joseph McCarthy, the 1960 Kennedy-Nixon presidential campaign debates, and the combined use of live television and nationwide telephone call-ins that allowed access to the candidates during the 1992 presidential election. For the most part, however, the political discourse that has appeared on television has been one-sided, taking the form of campaign advertising. The process of packaging a candidate's ideology in an advertiser's format, with only thirty seconds or a minute for most messages, offers little to voters to allow them to gauge accurately a candidate's plans, goals, or abilities. Sarnoff was right—the more evocative the picture, the more influenced the voter.

Sarnoff envisioned greatness for television, yet even he might not have believed that fifty years after television service began in New York City in 1939, 98 percent of all American homes would be receiving it. Delivered through direct broadcast, cable, and satellite dish, television reached approximately ninety million American households in 1989, and American households watched an average of seven hours of programming per day. Sarnoff lived into the 1970's, long enough to see his product mature. As a businessman, he understood something that the American public took much longer to realize: The entertainment programs on television are not what is important—they are just filler between the commercials.

—*Thomas C. Breslin*

FURTHER READING

Abramson, Albert. *The History of Television, 1880 to 1941*. Jefferson, N.C.: McFarland, 1987. Early chapters present, in language generally accessible to lay readers, a comprehensive discussion of the technological developments between 1671 and 1900 that led to television; later chapters are more technical. Includes developments outside the United States that are often ignored in American television histories, such as the 1930's development of television in Japan and London television service between 1936 and 1939.

Barnouw, Eric. *The Golden Web: 1933-1953*. Vol. 2 in *A History of Broadcasting in the United States*. New York: Oxford University Press, 1968. Covers the development of radio through its ascendancy in the 1930's and begins the history of the development of commercial television. Well documented.

_____. *Tube of Plenty: The Evolution of American Television*. 2d rev. ed. New York: Oxford University Press, 1990. Condensed, updated version of the material in Barnouw's three-volume set *A History of Broadcasting in the United States*, published between 1966 and 1970. Very readable general survey of television development.

Bilby, Kenneth. *The General: David Sarnoff and the Rise of the Communications Industry*. New York: Harper & Row, 1986. Comprehensive biography focuses on Sarnoff in the context of his industry. Relatively unbiased account by a former RCA executive and associate of Sarnoff covers the full range of Sarnoff's career. Includes bibliography.

DeFleur, Melvin L., and Everette E. Dennis. *Understanding Mass Communication*. 7th ed. Boston: Houghton Mifflin, 2001. College-level text provides both technical and historical information about television's development. Includes pictures and diagrams.

Everson, George. *The Story of Television: The Life of Philo T. Farnsworth*. New York: W. W. Norton, 1949. Uncritical biography by a man who recognized the young Farnsworth's ability and helped him find funding for his research laboratory. Emphasizes the rags-to-riches odyssey of Farnsworth from farm boy to internationally known inventor. Includes material unavailable elsewhere.

Gross, Lynne S. *Telecommunications: Radio, Television, and Movies in the Digital Age*. 8th ed. New York: McGraw-Hill, 2002. College-level text provides a good overview of electronic mass media, including the history of radio and television.

1939

Head, Sydney W., Thomas Spann, and Michael A. McGregor. *Broadcasting in America: A Survey of Electronic Media.* 9th ed. Boston: Houghton Mifflin, 2000. The standard introduction to the institutions of radio and television in the United States.

Lyons, Eugene. *David Sarnoff.* New York: Harper & Row, 1966. Biography by Sarnoff's cousin is uncritical but provides considerable material about Sarnoff's family, his early poverty and pursuit of a career, and his rise from office boy to executive.

Ritchie, Michael. *Please Stand By: A Prehistory of Television.* Woodstock, N.Y.: Overlook Press, 1994. Covers the period of television broadcasting before 1948. Includes interesting appendixes, bibliography, and index.

Sterling, Christopher H., and John Michael Kittross. *Stay Tuned: A History of American Broadcasting.* 3d ed. Mahwah, N.J.: Lawrence Erlbaum, 2001. Comprehensive one-volume history of radio and television in the United States.

Udelson, Joseph H. *The Great Television Race: A History of the American Television Industry, 1925-1941.* Tuscaloosa: University of Alabama Press, 1989. Chronicles the people, inventions, and events important to the development of commercial television worldwide.

SEE ALSO: Aug. 20-Nov. 2, 1920: Radio Broadcasting Begins; Dec. 29, 1923: Zworykin Applies for Patent on an Early Type of Television; Sept. 9, 1926: National Broadcasting Company Is Founded; June 10, 1934: Federal Communications Commission Is Established by Congress; Nov. 2, 1936: BBC Airs the First High-Definition Television Program; Sept. 1, 1940: First Color Television Broadcast.

May 16, 1939
FIRST U.S. FOOD STAMP PROGRAM BEGINS

The first food stamp plan established by the U.S. Department of Agriculture began as an experiment in Rochester, New York.

LOCALE: Rochester, New York

CATEGORIES: Social issues and reform; government and politics; health and medicine

KEY FIGURES

George D. Aiken (1892-1984), U.S. senator from Vermont

Christian Archibald Herter (1895-1966), U.S. congressman from Massachusetts

Robert M. La Follette, Jr. (1895-1953), U.S. senator from Wisconsin

Henry A. Wallace (1888-1965), U.S. secretary of agriculture, 1933-1940

SUMMARY OF EVENT

In May, 1939, eleven million people in the United States were receiving federal food assistance through direct donations of commodities. At that time, various groups were searching for methods of increasing consumption of grapefruit and other surplus foods. In January, 1939, at the National-American Wholesale Grocers Convention in Chicago, a plan developed by the grocers had been presented that proposed the issuance of "scrip" vouchers to unemployed people and those with low incomes. The vouchers would permit recipients to purchase designated foods and foodstuffs at retail grocery stores at prices 50 percent below normal. The federal government would make up to grocers the difference between the amount actually charged and the normal price. The plan's cost to the government was estimated at $1.4 billion. In addition to providing food to the needy at reduced prices, the plan would help wipe out agricultural surpluses.

The plan was submitted to the National Food and Grocery Conference Committee, which was composed of representatives from all areas of the food industry, from manufacturers to retailers. The U.S. Department of Agriculture explored the proposal, and at a meeting of the committee on March 13, 1939, department representatives announced an experimental food stamp plan that would distribute certain surplus food items through regular channels of trade. The plan was to be tried out in six cities with populations of more than fifty thousand. This represented a relatively cautious approach to the paradoxical dual problems of hunger and food surpluses. During the early years of the New Deal and the Great Depression, such a program might have been rushed into operation on a nationwide scale.

The decision to try a food stamp or coupon approach in lieu of direct distribution of commodities was based on the following factors. First, the food stamp approach reflected a desire to match more closely the kinds, varieties, and amounts of foods being made available to low-income families to the actual needs of such families. Second, such a plan was thought to provide more assurance that federal subsidies would actually increase food consumption rather than partially replace previous food expenditures. Third, planners believed that there were inherent advantages in utilizing regular commercial food-distribution channels rather than food banks or charities.

The plan called for the issuance of food stamps to needy persons receiving or certified for public aid. Each such client would be permitted to purchase a minimum value (varying according to size of family) of one type of stamp that could be used to purchase any food product. In addition, clients would receive, free of charge, another type of stamp in an amount equal to 50 percent of the value of the stamps purchased. These supplemental stamps would be redeemable only for certain food commodities. This feature of the plan was intended to guarantee that the free stamps would increase consumption, especially of surplus commodities. According to Secretary of Agriculture Henry A. Wallace, who addressed a meeting of the National Food and Grocery Conference Committee in Washington, D.C., on March 13, 1939, the plan aimed to increase the domestic consumption of surplus food commodities. Issuance of the stamps would create demand for commodities that were surplus not because the need for them did not exist but because the persons who needed them most could not afford them.

Records of various public health services and studies by the Bureau of Home Economics indicated that malnutrition and undernourishment, particularly of children, were widespread in every U.S. state at that time. These same studies estimated that millions of people in the United States spent an average of $1.00 or less per week for food. Such low expenditures translated into low prices and surpluses for farmers and into diets for low-income families that were less than the minimum necessary to maintain adequate standards of health. The proposed plan was designed to raise average spending on food to $1.50 per week per person for those eligible to participate in the program. The plan was heartily endorsed by the National Food and Grocery Conference Committee.

The first food stamp plan established by the U.S. Department of Agriculture began as an experiment on May 16, 1939, in Rochester, New York, and was subsequently extended to five additional experimental areas: Montgomery County, Ohio; King County, Washington; Jefferson County, Alabama; Pottawatomie County, Okla-

homa; and Des Moines, Iowa. Secretary of Agriculture Wallace stated that the stamp plan would apply at first only to food but that it might be extended to other goods, cotton products in particular, if it proved to be successful and if satisfactory arrangements could be made with retailers. Wallace also stated that measures such as the stamp plan, with the government subsidizing expanded consumption, were not the most desirable solution to the problem of making abundance work for the American people; he hoped that other solutions ultimately would be found.

The first food stamp program was established through the broad authority contained in Section 32 of Public Law 74-320, passed in 1935. Section 32 permanently appropriated an amount equal to 30 percent of U.S. Customs receipts from all sources each year for the secretary of agriculture, to be spent on three purposes: encouragement of agricultural exports, encouragement of domestic consumption of agricultural commodities, and reestablishment of farmers' purchasing power. Specifically, Section 32 provided that the funds were to be used "to encourage the domestic consumption" of agricultural commodities or products. The secretary of agriculture was given authority to pay benefits to low-income people to further the three stated purposes.

The food stamp plan was first administered by the Federal Surplus Commodities Corporation and later by the Surplus Marketing Administration and its successor organizations, the Agricultural Marketing Administration and the Food Distribution Administration of the U.S. Department of Agriculture. The United States was divided into four regions, each with a regional director who was given considerable discretionary powers to carry out program policy and procedures.

A two-color stamp plan was formulated in an attempt to ensure that the federal subsidy actually was used for additional food purchases and to control the kinds of food participants could purchase with the free additional coupons. Participating families were required to exchange an amount of money representing estimated normal food expenditures for orange stamps of the same monetary value. Along with these orange stamps, participants were provided, without cost, additional blue stamps, which they could use to buy designated surplus foods. In this manner, the plan attempted to concentrate the additional purchasing power on surplus foods—that is, foods for which there were marketing difficulties. In 1939, a significant portion of the nation's food supply could be classified in the surplus category. When the program was first begun, the surplus commodities on the

1939

blue stamp list were butter, eggs, white and grain flour, cornmeal, oranges, grapefruit, dried prunes, and dried beans. At one time or another the list also included rice, hominy grits, peaches, pears, apples, raisins, peas, tomatoes, snap beans, cabbage, onions, pork, and lard.

Foods were designated as blue-stamp (surplus) food each month by the secretary of agriculture, and a list of the foods designated was sent to participating retail merchants. Participating retailers were required to post notices of these monthly designations in their stores as a means of informing participants of the foods that could be purchased with the blue stamps. It was intended that this posting also would bring these foods to the attention of other customers and thereby encourage increased purchases of the surplus foods among higher-income families not participating in the plan.

Both the orange and the blue stamps were printed in two denominations—twenty-five cents and one dollar—and resembled postage stamps in design. In fact, an engraver's plate for an old postage stamp was redesigned and used for food stamp purposes. The stamps were issued in books. Participating areas were required to use public funds to establish a revolving fund to purchase the orange stamps from the Department of Agriculture. The revolving fund was subsequently replenished from the proceeds received from the sale of these orange stamps to participants.

SIGNIFICANCE

As measured by the number of participants, the food stamp plan reached its peak in May, 1941, when approximately four million people participated. New geographic areas were brought into the plan after 1941, but it never operated on a nationwide basis. As measured by the number of geographic areas served by the plan, the peak was reached in August, 1942, when 1,741 counties—about half of the counties in the nation—and eighty-eight cities were included. These areas contained almost two-thirds of the population of the United States, according to the 1940 census. During the forty-six months that the plan was in operation, the additional food purchasing power provided to participants by the federal government was $260 million.

Surveys and studies indicated that the plan did increase food consumption levels among participating groups. The early plan, however, was believed to have been greatly abused. The Department of Agriculture estimated that 25 percent of all benefits were misused. Some of the same types of abuse were repeated in later food stamp programs. For instance, some stamps reportedly

were traded for liquor and tobacco, and some grocers would buy them for cash at a discount, an activity now known as trafficking.

The plan was discontinued in early 1943, when World War II wartime conditions had greatly reduced unemployment and greatly increased demands on U.S. food supplies, thereby removing part of the rationale for the program. Inasmuch as the program was predicated on the existence of surplus foods, the program was terminated as such surpluses turned to scarcity during the early years of U.S. involvement in World War II. The program had been established administratively and never had been explicitly authorized by Congress.

Immediately following termination of the plan, two bills were introduced to establish a food stamp, or food allotment, program legislatively: House Resolution 2997, by Representative Christian Archibald Herter (Republican of Massachusetts), on June 18, 1943, and Senate Bill 1331, by Senators George D. Aiken (Republican of Vermont) and Robert M. La Follette, Jr. (Progressive of Wisconsin), on July 8, 1943. An amendment to establish a food stamp program, incorporating the thrust of the Senate bill, was proposed in the Senate on February 10 and 11, 1944, by Senators Aiken and La Follette. The amendment was defeated by a vote of forty-six to twenty-nine. Hearings on the bill itself had been concluded on January 26, 1944, by a subcommittee of the Senate Committee on Agriculture and Forestry.

The U.S. government did not institute another food stamp program until 1961, when a pilot program was undertaken. That program became permanent with the passage of the Food Stamp Act of 1964, but it underwent a number of changes in the latter part of the twentieth century. In May, 2002, the Food Security and Rural Investment Act reauthorized the federal government's food stamp program.

—Gregory P. Rabb

FURTHER READING

Batchelder, Alan B. *The Economics of Poverty.* New York: John Wiley & Sons, 1971. Discussion of poverty in the United States includes a chapter titled "Transfer Programs Now Operating," which contains a short discussion of the food stamp program that was created in the early 1960's.

Gaus, John M., and Leon O. Wolcott. *Public Administration and the United States Department of Agriculture.* 1940. Reprint. New York: Da Capo Press, 1975. Presents an excellent brief description of the first food stamp plan and how the plan evolved out of a proposal developed by the National-American Wholesale Grocers.

Harrington, Michael. *The New American Poverty*. New York: Holt, Rinehart and Winston, 1984. Examines poverty in the United States and praises the food stamp program for establishing uniform national levels of nutritional assistance. Asserts that "food stamps have been a triumph."

Haveman, Robert. *Starting Even: An Equal Opportunity Program to Combat the Nation's New Poverty*. New York: Simon & Schuster, 1988. Discusses the impacts of programs intended to address the problem of poverty in the United States, including food stamps. Presents statistics and examines proposed reforms for the food stamp program.

Katz, Michael B. *In the Shadow of the Poorhouse: A Social History of Welfare in America*. Rev. ed. New York: Basic Books, 1996. History of the development of social programs aimed at relieving the plight of the poor in the United States. Includes notes and indexes.

King, Ronald F. *Budgeting Entitlements: The Politics of Food Stamps*. Washington, D.C.: Georgetown University Press, 2000. Discusses the political and governmental budgeting issues related to the federal food stamp program since the 1960's. Includes index.

U.S. Congress. Senate. Committee on Agriculture, Nutrition, and Forestry. *The Food Stamp Program: History, Description, Issues, and Options*. Washington, D.C.: Government Printing Office, 1985. Includes an excellent description of the first food stamp plan, with details on how the program was administered, the problems it encountered, and evaluations of its successes and failures.

SEE ALSO: Apr. 9, 1912: Children's Bureau Is Founded; June 4, 1912: Massachusetts Adopts the First Minimum Wage Law in the United States; Nov. 23, 1921-June 30, 1929: Sheppard-Towner Act; Oct. 29, 1929-1939: Great Depression; Aug. 14, 1935: Roosevelt Signs the Social Security Act.

1939

June 12, 1939
DEDICATION OF THE BASEBALL HALL OF FAME

According to the "romantic" version of the origins of the game of baseball, in 1839 Abner Doubleday, then a West Point cadet, set up the first baseball diamond in Cooperstown, New York, and thereby invented the game. As that event's one hundredth anniversary approached, baseball promoters attempted to increase interest in the sport by establishing a baseball hall of fame and museum, which was formally dedicated in 1939.

ALSO KNOWN AS: National Baseball Hall of Fame and Museum

LOCALE: Cooperstown, New York

CATEGORIES: Sports; organizations and institutions

KEY FIGURES

Abner Doubleday (1819-1893), army officer reputed to be the inventor of baseball

A. G. Mills (1844-1929), head of the 1907 commission that named Doubleday as the inventor of baseball

Abner Graves (1834-1926), former Cooperstown resident who allegedly witnessed Doubleday's invention of baseball in 1839

Albert Goodwill Spalding (1850-1915), early baseball pitcher and a force behind the Mills Commission

Ford Christopher Frick (1894-1978), sportswriter and National League president who proposed a hall of fame

Kenesaw Mountain Landis (1866-1944), commissioner of baseball

Henry Chadwick (1824-1908), writer who established many of baseball's early rules

SUMMARY OF EVENT

Baseball's origins have always been controversial, but the prevailing belief is that it evolved from the British game of rounders. Henry Chadwick, the New York sportswriter noted for establishing both the first box score and the rules of the game in the mid-nineteenth century, was among the most noted advocates of this theory. However, in the early 1900's, Albert Goodwill Spalding, former player and founder of one of the early sporting businesses, argued that baseball was a purely American sport. His notoriety, combined with the forcefulness of his argument, resulted in the creation of a commission to determine baseball's origin. In 1905, a commission of seven men under the direction of A. G. Mills, former league president and officer in the Civil War, spent three years on the study.

Using primarily the testimony of Abner Graves, a retired Denver mining engineer and a former resident of

Cooperstown, New York, the commission concluded that baseball had originated in Cooperstown. Graves testified that he had been present when, in 1839, a schoolmate named Abner Doubleday laid out the game on a local field. The commission reported its findings on December 30, 1907, concluding that Doubleday had invented baseball in Cooperstown in 1839. The discovery of an aged baseball hidden in an old trunk in a nearby town in 1934 lent credence to the earlier report. The "Doubleday ball" was implied to have been one of the first baseballs used by Doubleday.

The Mills Commission's report was immediately controversial, particularly in view of the evidence that games similar to baseball had been played much earlier than 1839. It was also noteworthy that Graves would have been only five years old at the time he allegedly observed Doubleday, and that the two could not have been schoolmates. At the least, however, the Mills Commission set in motion events that resulted in excitement and public awareness of the game.

In 1935, with the one hundredth anniversary of the game approaching, baseball's most powerful leaders began to discuss a way to commemorate the game. Ford Christopher Frick, president of the National League, proposed to Commissioner Kenesaw Mountain Landis that a hall of fame be established to honor the game's outstanding participants.

Cooperstown was the logical choice for the hall's site. In 1932, the significance of the Mills report led the people of Cooperstown to purchase the alleged site on which Doubleday played, and they built a grandstand and fence in the area. The field was dedicated in 1935. Since the town now owned the Doubleday ball, the town's trustees convinced Frick that land adjacent to the field should be the site of the new hall of fame and museum. At the time, the Doubleday ball was stored at the National Baseball Museum, Inc., which was directed by Alexander Cleland and was little more than an upstairs room in the local Village Club. In addition to the ball, the museum contained a number of trophies and artifacts donated by various notable figures.

In 1936, organized baseball donated $100,000 to begin building a larger and more suitable headquarters for the hall and the library that would accompany it. A Cooperstown architect, Frank Whiting, was selected to design the building. The chosen site, adjacent to Doubleday Field, was the former Leo Block building on Main Street, right in the middle of downtown. Plans were completed by July, 1937.

The first election, held in 1936, utilized members of the Baseball Writers Association of America (BBWAA), a professional association of baseball journalists, as voters. A total of 226 votes were cast, and 75 percent approval was required for an individual's election to the hall. The outcome of the voting, which was announced January 29, 1936, resulted in the induction of five retired players: Ty Cobb, Babe Ruth, Honus Wagner, Walter Johnson, and Christy Mathewson (who had died in 1925). Plaques commemorating all of these players were hung in the hall. Subsequent elections prior to the hall's dedication created a Veterans Committee, which in 1937 consisted of Commissioner Landis, the two league presidents, and three others. The committee members elected five "builders of baseball" to the hall: George Wright, Morgan Bulkeley, Ban Johnson, John McGraw, and Connie Mack. Although the original idea was that election would be determined by baseball writers, complaints that the game's early pioneers and players were being overlooked resulted in a semipermanent Veterans Committee.

The new hall's dedication was not the only event held to commemorate the anniversary of baseball in 1939. Ball games around the country were played according to 1839 rules, although ballplayers dressed in contemporary uniforms. In Cooperstown alone, twenty-seven baseball days were staged, and players from various colleges and organizations played on Doubleday Field.

The hall's official dedication took place on June 12, 1939. Landis, Frick, American League president Will Harridge, and the National Association (for minor-league teams) president William Branham cut a ribbon that officially opened the building to the public. Of the twenty-five inductees, the eleven who were still living all attended the ceremony, and all but Ty Cobb posed for what became a famous photograph (Cobb arrived too late to be included in the picture). In commemoration of the event, a postage stamp was also issued; it depicted a painting of children playing baseball. In addition to the induction ceremonies, retired players were divided into teams and played an exhibition game for fans, many of whom had never had the opportunity to see those players in their prime. The Hall of Fame game became an annual ritual, with major-league teams playing an exhibition game each year on the day of induction.

SIGNIFICANCE

In reality, baseball did not originate with Doubleday, and the rules were not first established in Cooperstown. If any single person could be labeled the "father of baseball," it would be Henry Chadwick. As a writer and promoter of the sport, Chadwick established many of the early rules by which the game was played. For his contributions, Chadwick himself was inducted into the Hall of Fame in 1938.

Nevertheless, Cooperstown became the ultimate destination for baseball fans. The Hall of Fame founders certainly achieved their two primary goals: placing Cooperstown on the map and honoring those who elevated baseball to the status of the "national pastime." The National Baseball Hall of Fame and Museum was not only the first such sporting commemorative site, but it also remains the most well known. Most major sports now have their own halls of fame, but few of the locations of these halls are as familiar to sports fans as Cooperstown.

The size and goals of the National Baseball Hall of Fame and Museum have evolved over the decades, as the histories of women's baseball, the Negro Leagues, and esoteric memorabilia have been recognized. Arguments have persisted concerning who should be inducted and, sometimes, who should not have been. Each year, fans await the list of new inductees that is announced in early winter, and thousands attend the induction ceremonies to honor their heroes.

—Richard Adler

FURTHER READING

James, Bill. *Whatever Happened to the Hall of Fame?* New York: Simon & Schuster, 1995. Noted for his use of statistics in analysis of baseball strategy, the author compares the pros and cons of hall members as well as recounts the history of the museum.

Levine, Peter. *A. G. Spalding and the Rise of Baseball.* New York: Oxford University Press, 1985. Spalding was one of the founders of modern baseball. Establishment of the Mills Commission was due in large part to his arguments for the American origin of the game.

Smith, Ken. *Baseball's Hall of Fame.* New York: Grosset & Dunlap, 1977. One of the first books written on the subject of the early history of the hall. Somewhat dated, but still provides insight into the history.

Vail, James. *The Road to Cooperstown.* Jefferson, N.C.: McFarland, 2001. The author discusses the mechanisms for induction into the hall, as well as a comparison of those who have been selected.

SEE ALSO: Jan. 1, 1902: First Rose Bowl Game; Oct. 1-13, 1903: Baseball Holds Its First World Series; Jan. 12, 1906: American College Football Allows the Forward Pass; Oct. 1-9, 1919: Black Sox Scandal; Jan. 3, 1920: New York Yankees Acquire Babe Ruth; Aug. 20-Sept. 17, 1920: Formation of the American Professional Football Association; July 6, 1933: First Major League Baseball All-Star Game.

1939

Summer, 1939
STALIN SUPPRESSES THE RUSSIAN ORTHODOX CHURCH

The long Bolshevik campaign against religious practice and belief in the Soviet Union reduced the Russian Orthodox Church nearly to institutional extinction by the late summer of 1939.

LOCALE: Soviet Union
CATEGORIES: Atrocities and war crimes; religion, theology, and ethics; organizations and institutions

KEY FIGURES
Joseph Stalin (Joseph Vissarionovich Dzhugashvili; 1878-1953), general secretary of the Communist Party of the Soviet Union, 1922-1953
Adolf Hitler (1889-1945), chancellor of Germany, 1933-1945
Sergius (1867-1944), senior prelate of the Russian Orthodox Church, 1927-1944
Aleksi (1877-1970), metropolitan of Leningrad, 1933- 1944, and head of the Russian Orthodox Church, 1945-1970

SUMMARY OF EVENT
When the Bolsheviks came to power in Russia in 1917, they began to act on their atheist convictions, which held that all religion is an opiate, a spiritual gin that capitalist exploiters use to drug the workers into submission. They decreed the separation of church and state, nationalized church lands and assets, canceled the status of the Russian Orthodox Church as a legal entity, discontinued state subsidies to religious bodies, deprived church marriages and baptisms of official standing, and banned organized religious education of the young. In 1922, in the midst of famine, the Bolshevik regime ordered the church treasures confiscated, ostensibly to finance relief for the starving. Believers and international religious

bodies, among them the Holy See, offered to ransom the Russian Orthodox Church's sacramental objects, but the Bolshevik regime moved ahead. Soviet press accounts reported some fourteen thousand bloody fights as priests and parishioners tried to guard their churches. Many churches were closed and priests and hierarchs arrested. Vasily Belavin Tikhon, the patriarch (religious leader) of Moscow, was placed under house arrest. With government support, a Renovationist, or Living Church, movement was organized and split the church for a time.

When Patriarch Tikhon died on April 7, 1925, his death plunged the Russian Orthodox Church into a rolling crisis of leadership. By 1927, ten out of eleven prelates successively named to act as head of the church were in prison or in exile, and most of the bishops were in similar straits. The man who emerged as acting head of the church was Metropolitan Sergius. Arrested more than once, Sergius was released from prison in March of 1927 and issued a declaration of loyalty to the Soviet Union on July 24 of that year. Sergius's action in support of a godless and hostile state outraged many believing Orthodox people in the Soviet Union as well as many Soviet exiles abroad. Sergius justified his declaration as necessary to preserve the church.

The forced industrialization and collectivization drives launched under the leadership of Joseph Stalin in 1928 led to another crisis for the church. Troops and Communist Party workers fanned out into the countryside. Peasant resistance to them produced violence, the slaughtering of livestock, and the destruction of food stores. More than five million people were said to have died in this human-made famine. Peasants defended their churches and priests with scythes and pitchforks against soldiers and communist militants determined to deal harshly with the vestiges of Orthodox reaction. The campaign changed the face of the Russian countryside, which later became dotted with the shells of churches serving as granaries, overcrowded dwellings, storehouses, and workshops, their rusting and disintegrating cupolas standing hollow against the sky.

A third great wave of church closings began in 1936 and gathered momentum over the next three years. This was the period of the great purges. The terror of the prison camp complex of the Gulag Archipelago in Siberia was felt in every corner of the land. An estimated nineteen million Soviet citizens died in the purges, and the police (the NKVD—Narodnyi Komissariat Vnutrennikh Del, or the People's Commissariat of Internal Affairs) became the largest employer in the Soviet Union, responsible for one-sixth of all new construction. With

restraint and normal living swept away, church closings on a large scale resumed, and the arrest of priests and the incarceration of bishops accelerated.

By mid-1939, Metropolitan Sergius lived in Moscow virtually alone, cut off from any regular contact with the churches still functioning in the country. Only four active bishops remained in all of Russia: Metropolitan Aleksi of Leningrad was the second; Aleksi's suffragan, Nikolai of Peterhof, was the third; and Metropolitan Sergi, who later defected to the Germans, was the fourth. All four prelates lived from day to day in the expectation of arrest.

The numbers of open churches and functioning priests were very small. Soviet official sources and foreign scholars confirm that there were no open churches at all in more than one-third of the provinces of the Russian federated republic. One-third of the provinces of the Ukraine had no functioning churches, and an additional three Ukrainian provinces had only one open church each. According to Friedrich Heyer, the German troops that occupied Kiev in 1941 found only two churches in that diocese; sixteen hundred churches had been functioning before the 1917 Revolution. Three priests were serving in those two churches, one at the edge of the city of Kiev and one in the countryside. In the Ukrainian province of Kamenets-Podolski, the Germans found one aged priest holding services. A mission team that followed German troops into the area south of Leningrad found two priests reduced to complete impoverishment. It is probably a fair estimate that in 1939 two hundred to three hundred churches were functioning in the Soviet Union, and no more than three hundred to four hundred priests were conducting services.

Describing the situation through the 1930's in the diocese of Rostov-on-Don, Nikita Struve observed that the archbishop, Serafin, was exiled to the far north, where he soon died. His vicar, Nicholas Ammasisky, was sent to the steppes to graze a flock of sheep. He was arrested a second time and shot, but miraculously recovered from his wounds. The former cathedral was transformed into a zoo.

According to historian Dimitry Pospielovsky, in Odessa, where there had once been forty-eight churches, Stalin allowed only one to remain open, apparently as a favor to a great eye doctor in that city who had treated him. Stalin, however, made no promise to spare the priests. Each Sunday, and later just at Easter, a priest would appear from the congregation in the Odessa church and celebrate the liturgy, only to disappear into the NKVD dungeons the following day. After all the priests who dared martyrdom had disappeared, there remained a few deacons who could perform the entire rite except for the Eucharist. They likewise disappeared and were replaced by psalmists, who in turn were liquidated. There remained only the laity, who prayed as best they could in the church. In the summer of 1939, then, the Russian Orthodox Church teetered on the edge of institutional destruction.

SIGNIFICANCE

In the late summer of 1939, an event occurred that was unrelated to Stalin's repression of the Russian Orthodox Church but that profoundly affected its situation. Signed on August 23, 1939, the Molotov-Ribbentrop Pact opened the door to Soviet annexation of Eastern Poland in September of 1939 and of the Baltic states and Romanian Bessarabia and Northern Bubovina in 1940. The annexations brought the Russian Orthodox Church millions of faithful parishioners and thousands of active parishes, functioning churches, and priests. The church also acquired monasteries, nunneries, seminaries, and other resources.

On June 22, 1941, Adolf Hitler's armies attacked the Soviet Union and swept forward on a thousand-mile front stretching from the Baltic Sea to the Black Sea. Behind German lines, thousands more Orthodox churches were able to open their doors and start serving believers living in pre-1939 Soviet territories, most of whom had long been denied the opportunity to worship in a functioning church.

As soon as Hitler attacked, Metropolitan Sergius publicly rallied believers to the defense of the Motherland. When German forces were advancing on Moscow, however, Stalin ordered Sergius evacuated, and the head of the Russian church was sent by train to Ulyanovsk, a small provincial city about 435 miles (700 kilometers) east of the capital. Sergius was able to open some churches in that region and consecrated a few bishops, thereby reconstituting diocesan life along the Volga. By the spring of 1942, there were about a dozen Orthodox prelates of episcopal rank.

On September 4, 1943, Stalin received Sergius and two other metropolitans in the Kremlin. Stalin authorized the opening of more churches, convents, seminaries, and theological academies, as well as allowing more bishops and the elevation of a new patriarch. Four days later, nineteen bishops assembled and elected Sergius as patriarch. By this time, Red Army forces were pushing the Germans back, and Stalin's motives in his more supportive religious policy probably revolved around the need for reliable leadership over the thousands of Orthodox parishes that had been established under the German occupation. Stalin probably also perceived an advantage in tapping Russian pride and religious patriotism as Soviet rule was being reestablished in the lands overrun by Hitler. The Russian Orthodox Church emerged from the war with about fourteen thousand churches.

The travails of Orthodox believers in the Soviet Union did not end with the country's victory in World War II. Nikita S. Khrushchev launched another antireligious assault in the 1959-1964 period, but even Khrushchev's onslaught did not reduce the Russian Orthodox Church to the desperate straits of 1939. Under Soviet leader Mikhail Gorbachev, late in the twentieth century the church was permitted to reopen thousands of parishes, scores of monasteries and nunneries, and a substantial number of seminaries and theological training schools. During that period, a new law of freedom of conscience was promulgated. Although religious believers continued to encounter problems and difficulties of various kinds, Soviet people found the opportunity to worship, teach children religion, engage in charitable work, and perform other religious functions and duties to an extent not witnessed since the Bolshevik Revolution of 1917.

—*Nathaniel Davis*

1939

FURTHER READING

Alekseev, Wasilli, and Theofanis G. Stavrou. *The Great Revival: The Russian Church Under German Occupation*. Minneapolis, Minn.: Burgess, 1976. In specialized publications written in Russian and French, Alekseev presented firsthand and eyewitness accounts of the desperate straits through which the Russian Orthodox Church was passing in 1939 and the church revival experienced in German-occupied territories during World War II. These and other valuable materials are presented here in English.

Anderson, Paul B. *People, Church, and State in Modern Russia*. 1944. Reprint. New York: Hyperion, 1980. Classic, insightful work by the dean of American scholars on religion in the Soviet Union. Anderson played a central role in drawing the Russian Orthodox Church into ecumenical cooperation after World War II. Includes index.

Davis, Nathaniel. *A Long Walk to Church: A Contemporary History of Russian Orthodoxy*. 2d ed. Boulder, Colo.: Westview Press, 2003. Wide-ranging and statistically detailed account of the history of the Russian Orthodox Church. Includes tables and figures, selected bibliography, and index.

Ellis, Jane. *The Russian Orthodox Church: A Contemporary History*. London: Croom Helm, 1986. Focuses on the situation of the Russian Orthodox Church in the late twentieth century and the rise and repression of Orthodox dissent. Provides comprehensive description of churches, clergy, convents, theological education, and other aspects of Orthodox church life during the period covered. Includes bibliography and index.

Fletcher, William C. *A Study in Survival: The Church in Russia, 1927-1943*. New York: Macmillan, 1965. Highly respected American scholar of religion in the Soviet Union traces the story of the Russian Orthodox Church's travails through the turnaround that followed Stalin's reception of Metropolitan Sergius in 1943. Includes bibliography and index.

Pospielovsky, Dimitry. *The Orthodox Church in the History of Russia*. Crestwood, N.Y.: St. Vladimir's Seminary Press, 1998. Comprehensive account of the history of the Russian Orthodox Church from prehistory to current times.

_____. *The Russian Church Under the Soviet Regime, 1917-1982*. 2 vols. Crestwood, N.Y.: St. Vladimir's Seminary Press, 1984. Analyzes the experience of the church under Soviet rule, drawing on published and unpublished documents as well as interviews. Includes extensive footnotes and bibliography.

Struve, Nikita. *Christians in Contemporary Russia*. Translated by Lancelot Sheppard and A. Manson. New York: Charles Scribner's Sons, 1967. Highly sensitive and deeply informed account presents poignant and illuminating vignettes of religious life in the Soviet Union in 1939. Also provides coverage of later periods. Includes index.

Timasheff, Nicholas S. *Religion in Soviet Russia, 1917-1942*. 1942. Reprint. Westport, Conn.: Greenwood Press, 1980. Classic work conveys the realities of the situation of the Russian Orthodox Church before and during World War II.

SEE ALSO: 1903-1906: Pogroms in Imperial Russia; Jan. 22, 1905: Bloody Sunday; Oct. 30, 1905: October Manifesto; 1917-1918: Bolsheviks Suppress the Russian Orthodox Church; 1917-1924: Russian Communists Inaugurate the Red Terror.

August, 1939
UNITED STATES BEGINS MOBILIZATION FOR WORLD WAR II

The prospect of involvement in war prompted the United States to convert domestic production to meet military needs. The result was a huge increase in U.S. industry's production but very little change to the American economy's basic structure.

LOCALE: United States

CATEGORIES: Business and labor; economics; World War II; wars, uprisings, and civil unrest

KEY FIGURES

Franklin D. Roosevelt (1882-1945), president of the United States, 1933-1945

Harry S. Truman (1884-1972), U.S. senator from Missouri and chairman of the committee investigating defense spending

James F. Byrnes (1879-1972), director of the Office of Economic Stabilization

Donald Marr Nelson (1888-1959), head of the War Production Board

William Signius Knudsen (1879-1948), head of the Office of Production Management

William Martin Jeffers (1876-1953), head of the Government Rubber Board

Emory Scott Land (1879-1971), head of the U.S. Maritime Commission

SUMMARY OF EVENT

In June, 1940, German forces overran France, and the British military placed large orders for military supplies from the United States. These orders helped spur U.S. industrial mobilization, but events in Europe also aided President Franklin D. Roosevelt's administration in passing a number of military appropriations bills. Although more money was becoming available for wartime production, U.S. industry was reluctant to exploit this market. Conditioned by the static economic situation of the Depression, many capitalists expected such conditions to return after the war.

Expanding plants for wartime production was seen as a risky, short-term investment, and the Roosevelt administration tried in various ways to persuade industrialists that this was not true. For example, the federal government offered to finance expansion through low-interest loans from the Reconstruction Finance Corporation. The Revenue Act of 1940 provided an incentive in the form of a depreciation of new defense plants of 20 percent per year, instead of the former 5 percent tax write-off. Most important, however, was the "cost-plus" provision incorporated into government defense contracts. Private industry was guaranteed the cost of producing particular military hardware plus a profit of a certain percentage of the cost. This plan proved lucrative to industry but led to excessive waste in production. Eventually, Senator Harry S. Truman of Missouri led a special investigation into the waste and corruption in defense work, and the resulting revelations resulted in improved efficiency.

Roosevelt wrestled desperately with the problem of centralizing control of industrial mobilization. Drawing on his experiences during World War I, he first established the War Resources Board (WRB) in August, 1939. The WRB drew up a plan of mobilization providing for rigid government controls, but Roosevelt rejected this plan for political and personal reasons, and he permitted the WRB to be dissolved in October, 1939, after organized labor accused it of being prejudiced in favor of big business. A pattern of establishing an agency with a vague mandate and then reorganizing it when its attempts to operate provoked criticism was repeated during succeeding years.

The next attempt at central direction was the establishment of the National Defense Advisory Commission on May 28, 1940. Composed of representatives of labor, industry, the armed services, and the consuming public, the commission was under the direction of a former General Motors executive named William Signius Knudsen, who was expected to balance these various interests. The most vexing problem was the assignment of priorities to the various manufacturers for the acquisition of scarce materials. Ideally, such materials ought to have gone to factories in proportion to the relative importance of their finished products to the health of the economy as a whole. Knudsen never solved this problem; instead, he permitted the Army-Navy Munitions Board to gain great power in acquiring scarce materials.

On January 7, 1941, Roosevelt tried another reorganization. The Office of Production Management (OPM) was created with Knudsen and labor leader Sidney Hillman of the Congress of Industrial Organizations (CIO) as joint directors. The OPM did succeed in beginning the

Members of the U.S. Office of Production Management, including Edward Reilly Stettinius, Jr. (third from left), and William Signius Knudsen (second from right), meet with British minister of supply Lord Beaverbrook (center) in August, 1941. (Library of Congress)

1939

shift toward a war economy, but it placed strains on domestic needs and shortages developed in the electric power, aluminum, steel, and railroad-equipment industries. By August 28, 1941, Roosevelt was ready for another change. At first, a slight adjustment was made with the creation of the Supplies Priorities and Allocation Board, headed by Sears, Roebuck executive Donald Marr Nelson. Within a few months, the OPM had gone the way of the WRB, and Nelson was called to the White House to head an entirely new organization called the War Production Board (WPB).

Established on January 16, 1942, the WPB was to have supreme command over the entire economy. Nelson, however, proved inadequate for the job; he permitted the military to regain control over priorities and seemed to favor big corporations in the allocation of contracts. He also permitted the economy to develop unevenly. Ship factories were built at a pace far exceeding the ability of the steel industry to supply material for ship construction. Nelson remained as head of the WPB until 1944, but long before then control of economic mobilization had been assigned to yet another agency.

Recognizing that problems were developing under the WPB, Roosevelt asked Supreme Court associate justice James F. Byrnes to head the new Office of Economic Stabilization (OES). This new office replaced the WPB as supreme arbiter of the economy. Byrnes did solve the problems of priorities and brought order to the entire mobilization scheme. He seemed to have the political astuteness required to make the OES work. In May, 1943, his agency's official title was changed to Office of War Mobilization, and in October, 1944, it became the Office of War Mobilization and Reconversion.

SIGNIFICANCE

Despite such frequent reorganization of the government's regulatory bodies, U.S. industry performed fantastic feats of production during the war years. Statistics tell part of the story. In 1941, the United States produced approximately $8.5 billion worth of military equipment. Using the same dollar value, in 1944 the sum was $60 billion. Included in these gross figures was an increase in the annual production of planes from 5,865 in 1939 to almost 100,000 in 1944. Ship tonnage rose from one million tons in 1941 to nineteen million in 1943. Certain parts of the economy performed miracles. As public director of WPB, William Martin Jeffers, president of the Union Pacific Railroad, directed the creation of a great synthetic rubber industry, and Admiral Emory Scott Land, head of the U.S. Maritime Commission, prodded the shipbuilding industry to the point that a ship could be produced in fewer than ten days. Comparable production feats were achieved by other industries.

In the long run, the most significant fact of this remarkable production was that it was accomplished with little effect on the basic corporate structure of the U.S. economy. Of course, shortages existed in the civilian community during World War II, and rationing was introduced for foodstuffs, including meat and sugar. Although restraints were imposed on free enterprise, however, outright government seizure of private industry was never attempted. For the most part, government gave business exceptional freedom in choosing what it could produce and how; the only requirement was that national goals were met. In fact, the government let contracts for a wide variety of experimental or unusual projects, such as the famous *Spruce Goose* developed by Howard Hughes's engineers. Government allowed exceptional industrialists, such as Andrew Jackson Higgins, Preston Tucker, and Henry Kaiser, to mass-produce patrol torpedo (PT) boats and landing craft, gun turrets, and ships with little interference and almost no concern for cost. Kaiser, for example, cut the production time for a Liberty Ship (a basic freighter crucial to the war effort) from 120 days to 4.5 days. As British historian Paul Johnson has observed, the war "put back on his pedestal the American capitalist folk-hero."

The War Production Board's efforts increased busi

nesses' involvement in planning future economic activities, and many were persuaded that government could and should play a role in economic planning. The size of government has never returned to its pre-Depression levels, and only in the administration of Ronald Reagan did the military's share of the gross national product remain at less than 6 percent for more than a year. Ironically, many business leaders took from the war the exact opposite message from what it had taught. Rather than reaffirming the phenomenal productive capacity of the United States, business left the war expecting special favors and government considerations.

—George Q. Flynn and Larry Schweikart

FURTHER READING

Catton, Bruce. *The War Lords of Washington.* New York: Harcourt, Brace & World, 1948. Argues that the war failed to produce the social revolution that started with the New Deal, because putting industrialists in charge ended the opportunity for social reform. Given the extraordinary production of the system, Catton's thesis does not convince.

Civilian Production Administration. *Industrial Mobilization for War, 1940-1945.* Washington, D.C.: Government Printing Office, 1947. The official government record of mobilization.

Divine, Robert A. *The Reluctant Belligerent: American Entry into World War II.* 2d ed. New York: John Wiley & Sons, 1979. A valuable source of information about the political climate in the United States at the dawn of World War II.

Higgs, Robert. *Crisis and Leviathan: Critical Episodes in the Growth of American Government.* New York: Oxford University Press, 1987. Examines the War Production Board and dozens of other government agencies as agents of government expansion during wartime. Hypothesizes that wars and other critical episodes created a ratchet effect that caused government power and scope to increase.

Janeway, Eliot. *The Struggle for Survival.* New Haven, Conn.: Yale University Press, 1951. This brief volume in the Chronicles of America series is a convenient treatment of the economic mobilization for the general reader.

Johnson, Paul. *Modern Times: A History of the World from the Twenties to the Nineties.* Rev. ed. New York: HarperCollins, 1991. Vast interpretive history of the modern world devotes more than two chapters to World War II and spends several pages celebrating the efforts of U.S. business.

Kennedy, David M. *Freedom from Fear: The American People in Depression and War, 1929-1945.* New York: Oxford University Press, 1999. Describes how Americans responded to the deprivations of the Great Depression, the recovery period of the New Deal, and the country's entrance into World War II. Includes maps and index.

Nelson, Donald M. *Arsenal of Democracy: The Story of American War Production.* New York: Harcourt, Brace & World, 1946. A personal account of the WPB's achievements by its director. Depicts the difficult decisions about strategy that the WPB had to make and praises the free enterprise system for its efficiency and productivity.

Novick, David, Melvin Anshen, and W. C. Truppner. *Wartime Production Controls.* New York: Columbia University Press, 1949. An older but useful study of the problems faced by Nelson and his associates in allocating priorities.

Rhodes, Benjamin D. *United States Foreign Policy in the Interwar Period, 1918-1941: The Golden Age of American Diplomatic and Military Complacency.* Westport, Conn.: Praeger, 2001. In-depth examination of American diplomacy during the period covered. Features selected bibliography and index.

Rockhoff, Hugh. *Drastic Measures: A History of Wage and Price Controls in the United States.* New York: Cambridge University Press, 1984. Argues that controls kept inflation under wraps during the war, a tactic that only postponed its effects.

SEE ALSO: Jan. 30, 1933: Hitler Comes to Power in Germany; Aug. 23-24, 1939: Nazi-Soviet Pact; Sept. 1, 1939: Germany Invades Poland; Sept. 10, 1939: Canada Enters World War II; May, 1940: Roosevelt Uses Business Leaders for World War II Planning; May 10-June 22, 1940: Collapse of France; June 14, 1940: United States Begins Building a Two-Ocean Navy.

1939

August 17, 1939
THE WIZARD OF OZ PREMIERES

The Wizard of Oz catapulted Judy Garland into stardom and set a new standard for cinematic design in musical fantasy. Acclaimed and beloved by generations of audiences, it has become one of the most famous films of all time.

LOCALE: United States
CATEGORIES: Motion pictures; entertainment

KEY FIGURES

Mervyn LeRoy (1900-1987), American film director and producer
Arthur Freed (1894-1973), American producer and songwriter
Victor Fleming (1883-1949), American director
Judy Garland (1922-1969), American singer and actor
Ray Bolger (1904-1987), American song-and-dance man
Jack Haley (1899-1979), American actor
Bert Lahr (1895-1967), American actor and vaudevillian

SUMMARY OF EVENT

Samuel Goldwyn sold the film rights to L. Frank Baum's classic 1900 children's book *The Wizard of Oz* to Metro-Goldwyn-Mayer (MGM) for $75,000 on June 3, 1938.

The studio had, however, been preparing to film the story for several months prior to the sale. As early as January, 1938, Mervyn LeRoy had entrusted William Cannon with the task of preparing the story for the screen. The first of the twelve screenwriters who worked on the script was Irving Brecher; others included Herman Mankiewicz, Ogden Nash, Noel Langley, Herbert Fields, Samuel Hoffenstein, Florence Ryerson, and Edgar Allan Woolf. Langley, Ryerson, and Woolf received screen credit. Harold Arlen and Edgar Harburg wrote the music and lyrics; they had been hired in May. The model for both the writers and the composers was Walt Disney's animated film *Snow White and the Seven Dwarfs* (1937), which had been extremely successful just a year earlier. From the beginning, however, MGM did not apparently expect to make much money on the live-action fantasy. Instead, this was to be the studio's "prestige picture" for the year.

When the film began production, Norman Taurog was the director, but he left within a short time to direct the Mickey Rooney vehicle *The Adventures of Huckleberry Finn* (1939). Richard Thorpe, director of a few Tarzan films, followed briefly, then—for seven days—came George Cukor. Cukor, like his successor Victor Fleming, left *The Wizard of Oz* to work on *Gone with the Wind*

(1939). Finally, King Vidor completed the sequences in Kansas that would begin and end the film. On-screen directorial credit went to Victor Fleming, and it seems clear that he did the lion's share of the director's work. The many writers, directors, producers, and assorted others who worked on the film, however, show just how much of a collaborative effort filmmaking was in the large studios of the 1930's and 1940's.

Much of the film's appeal stemmed from the performances of its stars, but these, too, changed before the final version was cut. At the outset, Louis B. Mayer attempted to borrow Shirley Temple from Twentieth Century-Fox to play the role of Dorothy, but Fox head Darryl F. Zanuck refused. The alternative was Judy Garland, the choice of both LeRoy and his assistant Arthur Freed. Garland was sixteen years old and more mature than the Dorothy of the book, but with a tight-fitting brassiere and pigtails, she began to look the part. At first, the Scarecrow and the Tin Woodman were to be played by Buddy Ebsen and Ray Bolger, respectively, but after much complaining by Bolger, the two actors changed roles. Before long, Ebsen developed an allergy to the makeup needed to play the Tin Woodman, and he was replaced by Jack Haley.

The part of the Cowardly Lion was apparently always intended for Bert Lahr. Gale Sondergaard tested for the part of the Wicked Witch, but the role eventually went to Margaret Hamilton. A number of actors were considered for the role of the Wizard. LeRoy wanted Ed Wynn, but he turned the part down because he thought it was too small (Wynn based his decision on an early version of the script in which the Wizard's part was considerably smaller than in the final version). Others mentioned for the part included Wallace Beery, W. C. Fields, Hugh Herbert, and Charles Winninger. The final choice was Frank Morgan.

Production began in the fall of 1938 and was completed in the spring of 1939. Several features of the final film were noteworthy, including the wardrobe and makeup, the special effects, and the music. The head of the MGM wardrobe department was Gilbert Adrian, and his counterpart in makeup was Jack Dawn. To give the effect of a straw man, the makeup people fashioned a light mask of baked rubber made to simulate burlap. For the Tin Woodman, a suit of buckram covered over with metallic cloth painted silver served to give the illusion of a tin man. Bert Lahr wore fifty pounds of genuine lion skins.

Virtually all the characters endured many changes in costume and makeup. For example, the witch's costume at various times included sequins and cowled headdress, fright wig and false nose, several hairstyles, and green skin. For the diminutive Munchkins who populated the land of Oz, Adrian and Dawn concocted costumes and makeup that would make the already small actors cast in the roles appear even smaller than they were. Oversized belts, hats, buttons, and so on accentuated the smallness of the Munchkins. The Munchkin makeup required wigs, prosthetic items, and skullcaps. Dawn organized an assembly line to manage the makeup of the Munchkins, a kind of real-life echo of the sprucing up of the Cowardly Lion, Scarecrow, Tin Woodman, and Dorothy that took place within the film in Emerald City.

Equally complex were the special effects. The film contained many fantastic effects: a tornado that swept Dorothy and her dog Toto into the land of Oz, a good witch who traveled in a bubble, flying monkeys, talking and apple-throwing trees, a flying witch, a huge, spectral appearance by the Wizard, and a melting witch. In charge of special effects for the picture was A. Arnold "Buddy" Gillespie, and he and his cohorts used five of the six types of special effects available at the time: miniatures, back projection, optical effects, matte painting, and full-scale mechanical effects.

Some of the flying monkeys were full-scale effects; various types of rear and front projection created the effects of the Wizard's disembodied head and the head of the witch in her large crystal ball. The witch on her broomstick writing in the sky was a miniature; the witch was, in reality, three-eighths of an inch high, and her broomstick was a hypodermic needle filled with milk and dye. Matte painting was used to create the panorama of Emerald City and parts of the witch's castle. Other effects included the Cowardly Lion's swishing tail, which was controlled by a man on a catwalk with a fishing pole, the line of which was attached to the tail; dry ice and an elevator simulated the melting witch. Elevators proved dangerous, and Margaret Hamilton, the wicked witch, was injured using one in her departure from Munchkinland near the beginning of the film. On the second take, the flames that accompanied her departure set alight her hat and broom, and her face and right hand were burned. She left the set for six weeks.

Perhaps the most complicated effect in the film was the tornado. The tornado was a muslin sock connected to a slot in a floor and to a steel gantry at the top of a stage. The gantry had a small car that could zigzag horizontally. From the bottom, fuller's earth and compressed air were fed into the tornado to create the illusion of a great wind whipping up dust as it crossed the prairie. Eight-by-four panels of glass with cotton balls pasted on them served to heighten the effect of a stormy sky. Once photographed, the film of the tornado was projected to form a backdrop for the actors scurrying to shelter.

In addition to its effects, *The Wizard of Oz* contained a stunning musical score. From romantic ballads to jaunty dance numbers to ebullient celebratory choruses, the music and songs were various and vibrant. The score was the creation of Harold Arlen (music) and Edgar Harburg (lyrics), and their genius provided not only memorable songs and tunes but also songs that were integrated with the plot development. "Somewhere over the Rainbow," for example, clearly sets the wistful tone for a young girl whose life is as uneventful as the sepia-colored print of the scene indicates. The lyrics prepare viewers for Oz as a dreamworld ("a land that I heard of once in a lullaby") and a land of color ("skies are blue," "troubles melt like lemon drops," "bluebirds," and, of course, the rainbow image itself). Dorothy's longing for color, adventure, and release finds expression in the song. In a similar way, the songs of the Scarecrow, Tin Woodman, and Cowardly Lion fill in their personalities. Unlike other musicals of the 1930's, *The Wizard of Oz* contained no large-scale production numbers that existed merely for their own sake. The closest the film came to such a scene was in the Lion's "King of the Forest" number; even that song, however, indicates the Cowardly Lion's inner goodness. The scene also serves to provide a playful interlude before the climactic encounter with the Wizard.

Such lively music and words deserved equally lively choreography, and in this, too, the film excelled. LeRoy wanted Busby Berkeley to handle the dance numbers, but Bobby Connolly came from Warner Bros. to take over as dance director. His dance numbers were visually imaginative. The sprightly nursery-rhyme effect of "The Wicked Witch Is Dead" sequence far outshone similar sequences in Laurel and Hardy's *Babes in Toyland* (1934), and Ray Bolger's floppy footwork as the Scarecrow became justly famous. It is interesting to note that much of Bolger's first dance was cut to keep the film from running too long.

The completed film was a triumph of cinematic art that demonstrated how the collaboration of many people could produce a serendipitous masterpiece. It premiered first in Wisconsin on August 12, 1939, and three days later in Hollywood. The film opened in general release on August 17. *The Wizard of Oz* sums up much of what went on in the films of the 1930's: The Depression-weary lives of middle Americans are visible in the open-

ing and closing sequences in Kansas, and the lavish worlds of escape that Hollywood was famous for producing in the decade appear in the colorful Oz sequences. Both the fantasy and the "reality" in the film express the need for self-reliance and cooperation; all one needs to succeed, the film implies, are a little ingenuity and pluck. In a year in which high romance was the order of the day—witness such 1939 productions as *Gone with the Wind*, *Stagecoach*, *Ninotchka*, *Destry Rides Again*, *Only Angels Have Wings*, and *Mr. Smith Goes to Washington*—*The Wizard of Oz* provided romance enough for everyone.

SIGNIFICANCE

The Wizard of Oz was more successful than anyone involved with its making expected. Shortly after its release, the market was flooded with memorabilia related to the film: party masks, rag dolls, wooden dolls, rubber dolls, Valentine cards, stationery, and dart games. Such merchandise continued to sell decades later; clearly, the public, in North America and around the world, took the film to its heart. It also took Judy Garland to its heart, and the film had a profound impact on her career. She had signed her first contract with MGM on September 27, 1935, only three months after her thirteenth birthday. *The Wizard of Oz* was her eighth film and the one that catapulted her to worldwide fame.

For her role in the film, Garland won a special Academy Award as the best juvenile performer of the year. The honor was well deserved; Garland played her part with a conviction and a depth of feeling that struck a chord in audiences. MGM knew it had a star on its hands, and the studio's story department set about finding musical properties for her. In the next two years, she starred in seven films. As late as 1968 (six months before she died), Garland guest-hosted a television talk show on which Margaret Hamilton made a surprise appearance. Garland asked her wicked witch adversary from *The Wizard of Oz* to "Laugh! Just do that wicked, mean laugh!" Hamilton did as she was asked, and the audience went wild.

The Wizard of Oz is among the most familiar films in history. It has enjoyed a long life on network television (it was the first film MGM sold to network television in 1956), and its release to the home video market has ensured that many households own a copy of the musical. Released in 1939, popularly referred to as the single greatest year of the Hollywood studio system, *The Wizard of Oz* is one of the central films supporting that title. Moreover, what MGM referred to in 1939 as the film's "kindly philosophy" has not gone out of fashion. Audi-

1939

ences young and old continue to seek escape to fantastic worlds in motion pictures, looking for places where good always triumphs over evil and people get what they desire.

—*Roderick McGillis*

FURTHER READING

Billman, Carol. "'I've Seen the Movie': Oz Revisited." In *Children's Novels and the Movies*, edited by Douglas Street. New York: Frederick Ungar, 1983. A comparison of the book with the film. Argues that the film reduces the clutter of the book and simplifies the plot and that the visual splendor of the film helps it to surpass the book, despite the fact that both are moralistic. Notes that the artificiality of the effects adds to the film's (and Oz's) fantastic quality.

Fricke, John, Jay Scarfone, and William Stillman. *"The Wizard of Oz": The Official Fiftieth Anniversary Pictorial History*. New York: Warner Books, 1989. A detailed account of the making of *The Wizard of Oz* and its subsequent impact. Filled with rare photographs of the players and professionals associated with MGM, of Oz memorabilia and merchandise, and of memos and letters related to the film and its creation. Bibliography.

Harmetz, Aljean. *The Making of "The Wizard of Oz."* New York: Alfred A. Knopf, 1977. A detailed account of how a major studio worked in the heyday of the Hollywood studio system. Many interviews with the people who worked on the film, and many behind-the-scenes photographs. A more complete account of the special effects than in the Fricke, Scarfone, and Stillman volume. Index and bibliography.

Langley, Noel, Florence Ryerson, and Edgar Allan Woolf. *"The Wizard of Oz": The Screenplay*. New York: Delta, 1989. The first publication of the entire film script, including the addition of scenes and songs cut from the final version. Introduction and notes by Michael Patrick Hearne. Contains film stills and other photographs. Hearne's introduction chronicles, in brief, the making of the film.

McClelland, Doug. *Down the Yellow Brick Road*. New York: Pyramid Books, 1976. Recounts the legends behind the making of the film. For a general audience rather than for aficionados. Many film stills.

Scarfone, Jay, and William Stillman. *The Wizardry of Oz: The Artistry and Magic of the 1939 M-G-M Classic*. New York: Applause, 2004. Lengthy study of the makeup, special effects, set design, props, and costumes employed in the film. Bibliographic references and index.

Swartz, Mark Evan. *Oz Before the Rainbow: L. Frank Baum's "The Wonderful Wizard of Oz" on Stage and Screen to 1939*. Baltimore: The Johns Hopkins University Press, 2000. Recounts the history of Oz adaptations up to the 1939 film, comparing them to the version that since 1939 has been definitive. Bibliographic references and index.

SEE ALSO: 1929: *Hallelujah* Is the First Important Black Musical Film; 1933: *Forty-Second Street* Defines 1930's Film Musicals; 1934: Lubitsch's *The Merry Widow* Opens New Vistas for Film Musicals; 1939: Ford Defines the Western in *Stagecoach*; Dec. 15, 1939: *Gone with the Wind* Premieres.

August 23-24, 1939
NAZI-SOVIET PACT

The Nazi-Soviet Pact freed Adolf Hitler from the immediate possibility of a two-front war, allowing him to attack Poland and trigger the beginning of World War II hostilities.

ALSO KNOWN AS: Molotov-Ribbentrop Pact; Ribbentrop-Molotov Pact
LOCALE: Moscow, Soviet Union (now Russia)
CATEGORIES: World War II; wars, uprisings, and civil unrest; military history; diplomacy and international relations

KEY FIGURES
Neville Chamberlain (1869-1940), prime minister of Great Britain, 1937-1940
Édouard Daladier (1884-1970), premier of France, 1938-1940
Adolf Hitler (1889-1945), chancellor of Germany, 1933-1945
Maksim Maksimovich Litvinov (Meier Moiseevich Wallach; 1876-1951), Soviet commissar for foreign affairs, 1930-1939
Vyacheslav Mikhailovich Molotov (Vyacheslav Mikhailovich Skryabin; 1890-1986), Soviet commissar for foreign affairs, 1939-1949
Joachim von Ribbentrop (1893-1946), German foreign minister, 1938-1945
Joseph Stalin (Joseph Vissarionovich Dzhugashvili; 1878-1953), dictator of the Soviet Union, 1929-1953

SUMMARY OF EVENT
The signing of a treaty of nonaggression between Nazi Germany and Communist Russia in August, 1939, surprised most European observers, who believed that a rapprochement between the diametrically opposed dictatorships was impossible. Relations between the Soviet Union and Germany had declined substantially since 1933, when the National Socialist regime under Adolf Hitler had assumed power in Germany. Before 1933, Hitler had frequently denounced Bolshevism; in his political autobiography, *Mein Kampf* (1925-1926; English translation, 1939), he had stressed the need for Germany to acquire living space (*Lebensraum*) in Eastern Europe at the expense of the Soviet Union. Hitler's genuine interest in Eastern Europe was demonstrated in January, 1934, when he signed a nonaggression treaty with Poland, which had traditionally been Russia's enemy.

Soviet leader Joseph Stalin viewed this pact as a potential threat to Russia's security, and he concluded that sooner or later Hitler would start a war somewhere in Europe. Beginning with a successful bid for membership in the League of Nations in September, 1934, Stalin and his foreign minister Maksim Maksimovich Litvinov became the leading champions of "collective security," the concert of European governments against Hitler, and the "Popular Front," the cooperative effort of European moderate leftists and Communist Parties against fascism. During Italy's invasion of Ethiopia (which began in 1940), the Soviet Union made a staunch defense of the covenant only to find this an irritant rather than an aid in warming up to the West. When the Popular Front coalition in republican Spain came under assault, the Soviets provided critical military supplies while the Western forces avoided participating in the Spanish Civil War (1936-1939).

The activities of the world revolutionary Communist International, or Comintern, which was supported and sustained by Moscow, were now sharply curtailed. In May, 1935, the Soviet government took major steps to encircle Germany by concluding pacts of mutual assistance with France and Czechoslovakia; the agreement with the latter, however, was to bind the Soviet Union only if France made the first move toward extending aid to the Czechs in the event of a German attack. Hitler used these treaties as an excuse to occupy the Rhineland in 1936, and in the fall of that year he countered them by signing an agreement with Italy and the Anti-Comintern Pact with Japan; the pact was directed against the Soviet Union.

Meanwhile, the Stalinist purge trials and the execution of numerous army officers did nothing to strengthen Western confidence in the Soviet Union as a viable military ally against Hitler. By 1937, the attitude toward the Soviet military posture contributed to the genesis of the appeasement policy in the French and British governments, led at that time by Édouard Daladier and Neville Chamberlain, respectively. The fruit of this policy was Hitler's bloodless conquest of Austria and Czechoslovakia during 1938 and 1939. The Soviets were prepared to come to Czechoslovakia's defense in 1938, but Western appeasement doomed such a move. As a result, in 1939 Stalin was driven to accept a policy of "Fortress Russia." In response, the collective security coalition collapsed, and Stalin set about reexamining all available options in the conduct of his foreign affairs.

1939

Vyacheslav Mikhailovich Molotov signs the Nazi-Soviet agreement while Joachim von Ribbentrop (left) and Joseph Stalin (right) stand behind him. (NARA)

Stalin's subsequent exercise of one of these options—namely, the conclusion of a nonaggression pact with Germany—was the result of the last prewar crisis involving Nazi demands on Poland. Shortly after the Nazi occupation of Prague in mid-March, 1939, the German foreign minister, Joachim von Ribbentrop, submitted a series of demands to Poland that were categorically refused. Although he was furious, Hitler could not undertake an immediate solution of the Polish question for a number of reasons. First, in the light of Anglo-French promises to aid the Poles if attacked by Germany (made in late March and early April, 1939), Hitler appeared to suspect that the Western powers might fight back if he attacked Poland. Second, both Hitler and the Western powers were uncertain about the role that the Soviet Union might play in the event of a German attack on Poland. If the Soviet Union joined the Western powers in an alliance, Hitler would be caught in a two-front war. If he

could engage the Soviets in a pact of nonaggression, however, Hitler might be able to force Great Britain and France to back down, as they had in the past. If this pattern were not repeated, Hitler reasoned, he would at least be in a better position to dispose of a military thrust from the West. Hitler also delayed aggression because he had to draft extensive military plans that would provide the operational details for both the invasion of Poland and the defense of the Reich from an attack by the Western powers.

On April 3, Hitler ordered his military commanders to draw up such plans; those for the Polish campaign, known by the code name Operation White, were to be ready by September 1, 1939, the scheduled date of their implementation. By the end of April of 1939, Hitler was beginning to give serious consideration to rapprochement with the Soviet Union. Stalin, too, was anxious to prevent his country from becoming isolated if Hitler invaded Poland. Because the Soviet leader was still uncommitted regarding the Polish question, however, the diplomacy surrounding it assumed the character of a contest between the Western powers and the German Reich for the prize of Russia's favor. From mid-April to mid-August, 1939, the British and French governments made several clumsy attempts to negotiate a common defense against Hitler's designs on Poland. Neither Chamberlain nor Daladier relished the idea of negotiating with the hated Bolsheviks. Consequently, they carried on talks with the Soviet Union at a slow pace through second-rank officials. When they finally dispatched a joint Anglo-French military mission to Moscow in the critical days of August, it traveled by boat rather than by airplane.

Apart from these problems, a Soviet-Western pact foundered almost immediately on traditional Russo-Polish animosity. Russian leaders insisted that a Soviet-Polish military agreement would have to be arranged before the Soviet Union would conclude any pact with Great Britain and France. Poland, however, adamantly rejected any such agreement with the Soviet Union. The prospects for accord between the West and the Soviet Union were not promising.

During the often-overlooked British and German talks, Neville Chamberlain clearly expressed his preference for appeasing Hitler rather than forming a grand alliance with the Soviet Union. Chamberlain's proposals to the Third Reich were quite generous. They included an enormous loan to Germany and settlement of colonial problems as well as the Polish crisis on terms favorable to Hitler. In addition, the British offered Germany an Anglo-German condominium over Europe, and all Hitler had to do was promise that he would not invade Poland. For the moment, however, Hitler preferred the destruction of Poland in a short, local war to another Munich Agreement.

The Anglo-French-Russian negotiations, carried on with considerable publicity, were closely watched by the German Foreign Office. By the end of April, Berlin had decided to explore the possibilities of a Russo-German rapprochement to which the Soviet ambassador had alluded earlier in the month. In his April 28 speech before the Reichstag, Hitler formally renounced Germany's nonaggression pact with Poland. Surprisingly, his address was devoid of his usual invective against Bolshevism and the Soviet Union.

Initially, Stalin pursued a cautious policy designed to avoid Soviet isolation in an increasingly dangerous international environment. By early 1939, however, increasing Soviet economic and military strength gave him sufficient confidence to take the diplomatic offensive. Stalin believed that Germany was far weaker than the Western powers and would be more likely to meet his demands. In response to Germany's apparent interest in better relations, on May 3 the Soviet Union announced the dismissal of Litvinov, a pro-Western Jew with a British wife, as Soviet commissar for foreign affairs. He was replaced by Vyacheslav Mikhailovich Molotov, a determined negotiator who was Stalin's oldest and closest associate. Although the two dictatorships negotiated in an atmosphere of deep distrust, the Russo-German talks made steady progress in contrast to the negotiations between the Soviet Union and the other Western powers. Finally, at the end of July, Molotov used his negotiators to indicate the Soviet Union's willingness to enter into a commercial treaty with Germany that would be followed later by a political agreement.

By this time, however, Germany was desperate for a political pact, as the planned date for the invasion of Poland was only a month away. The Soviet-German trade talks were more than a mere preliminary to the pact. Because economically strapped Germany needed Soviet-supplied raw materials, Soviet negotiators extracted German agreement to deliver Germany's most up-to-date weapons and vast quantities of strategic goods. Now the arch appeaser, Stalin gained additional time to build up the Red Army by buying off Hitler with fresh trade deals. The signing of a commercial agreement on August 19 only served to intensify the impatience of Hitler and Ribbentrop for an immediate political arrangement with the Soviet Union.

Apparently, Stalin wanted to be sure that Germany would become embroiled in war with the West over Poland. He was fearful that Great Britain might back down on its support to Poland, thus containing Hitler's aggression in Eastern Europe to the Soviet frontier. Therefore, in trying to attain an essential goal of Soviet foreign policy—namely, the escape from isolation—Stalin had to take the risk that he might actually deepen his country's isolation. When he decided that Great Britain would fight, when his mistrust of the West outweighed his suspicion of the Nazis, and when he became convinced that there were real advantages to be gained from a bargain with Hitler, then and only then did Stalin approve the signing of the nonaggression pact so desperately sought by his German counterparts.

Stalin decided to go ahead, and Ribbentrop was received in Moscow on August 23. As signed by Ribbentrop and Molotov early on August 24, the treaty contained a mutual promise of neutrality and nonaggression. A "Secret Additional Protocol" attached to the treaty divided Eastern Europe into German and Soviet spheres of interest. Poland was to be partitioned between the two powers, Germany was allowed influence over Lithuania, and the Soviet Union was given a free hand in Estonia, Latvia, and Finland. The Soviet Union also declared its interest in Romania's Bessarabia.

SIGNIFICANCE

The Nazi-Soviet Pact had several important results. The immediate effect was to precipitate World War II. Assured of Russian neutrality, Hitler launched his invasion of Poland as originally planned on September 1; the British and French declared war on Germany two days later when Hitler failed to respond to their demand for immediate withdrawal from Poland. Meanwhile, Stalin gained at least temporary immunity from German attack, and he proceeded to build up Soviet armed forces. The sphere of interest granted to Stalin in Eastern Europe appeared to provide him with a strong forward defensive zone against possible German attack.

Russia attacked Finland on November 30, 1939, after the Finns refused to grant territorial and naval base concessions. Led by Carl Gustaf Mannerheim, the Finns resisted with astonishing strength, annihilating five Soviet divisions. However, a Soviet offensive in February, 1940, succeeded, and Stalin then dictated peace terms that were more severe than the original Soviet demands. He later absorbed the Baltic states, including Lithuania, which Hitler conceded to him in a readjustment of their pact. Simultaneously in the Far East, the Nazi-Soviet

1939

Pact enabled Stalin to relieve the pressure that Japan had been exerting on the Soviet Union's Asian frontier since the outbreak of an undeclared Russo-Japanese war in 1938. Nominally an ally of Nazi Germany, Japan terminated the conflict in April, 1939, and signed a mutual agreement on September 15, 1939.

Intermediately, however, the alliance nearly proved disastrous for Stalin. Hitler got the better of the pact because he was able to conquer most of Europe and turn on the Soviet Union at a time of his choosing. Stalin assumed that he was dealing with Hitler from a position of unassailable strength, and so he was able to secure the favorable revision of the secret protocol of the Soviet-Nazi pact on several occasions. Stalin was preparing to do so again in late 1940; he thought that Hitler could not do without the Soviet Union's political and economic support in Germany's continuing war with Great Britain and that this dependence would increase with time. Refusing to believe mounting evidence that Hitler was preparing to attack, Stalin was genuinely shocked by Operation Barbarossa (Germany's World War II invasion of the Soviet Union). For Hitler, Stalin's misplaced trust in him almost spelled a German victory over Russia in 1941 and 1942. Viewed in wider perspective, however, the Nazi-Soviet Pact added considerably to Hitler's overconfident attitude toward Russia. The ultimate failure of Hitler's military campaign against Russia and his loss of the war brought about an extension of Soviet influence into central Europe that existed into the 1990's.

Many historians have considered the Nazi-Soviet Pact's possible ramifications. How would the course of World War II have changed if Hitler had maintained the pact against Britain before the United States launched its all-out intervention? Britain might have surrendered. Even after Barbarossa began, the possibility of a Nazi-Soviet truce on the eastern front would have stiffened considerably German resistance against Allied forces. A negotiated armistice to World War II could have occurred in Europe because British intelligence learned that Heinrich Himmler made overtures to an interested Stalin about a Russian front truce.

—*Edward P. Keleher and Douglas W. Richmond*

FURTHER READING

Bullock, Alan. *Hitler: A Study in Tyranny.* Rev. ed. New York: Harper Perennial, 1991. A detailed account, from the German vantage point, of how the development of the Polish crisis led to the Nazi-Soviet accord in August, 1939.

Carr, E. H. *German-Soviet Relations Between the Two Wars, 1919-1939.* Westport, Conn.: Greenwood Press, 1983. Contains a discussion of the 1939 Nazi-Soviet Pact.

Churchill, Winston S. *The Gathering Storm.* Vol. 1 in *The Second World War.* 1948. Reprint. Tampa, Fla.: Mariner Books, 1986. Chapters 20 and 21 trace the course of the Polish crisis and the rapprochement between Germany and Russia.

Haslam, Jonathan. *The Soviet Union and the Struggle for Collective Security in Europe, 1933-39.* New York: St. Martin's Press, 1984. Haslam defends the sincerity of Soviet attempts to ensure collective security.

Kershaw, Ian. *Hitler, 1936-1945: Nemesis.* New York: W. W. Norton, 2000. The second volume of Kershaw's acclaimed biography of Hitler (the first was *Hitler, 1889-1936: Hubris*). Accords Ribbentrop a central role in establishing an alternative foreign policy that found favor with Hitler.

Read, Anthony, and David Fisher. *The Deadly Embrace: Hitler, Stalin, and the Nazi-Soviet Pact, 1939-1941.* New York: W. W. Norton, 1989. A skillful correlation of concurrent sets of secret negotiations that outline the British and German talks.

Rossi, Angelo. *The Russo-German Alliance, August 1939-June 1941.* Translated by John and Micheline Cullen. Boston: Beacon Press, 1951. This study deals with the uneasy relations between Nazi Germany and Soviet Russia after the negotiation of their nonaggression pact in August, 1939.

Shirer, William L. *The Rise and Fall of the Third Reich: A History of Nazi Germany.* 30th anniversary ed. New York: Ballantine, 1991. Classic work is still one of the most readable and informative histories of the Third Reich. Although Shirer's research has been superseded in some respects, this remains one of the best introductions to the Nazi era, especially given that the author witnessed many of Hitler's actions while serving as a foreign correspondent in Berlin.

Ulam, Adam B. *Expansion and Coexistence: The History of Soviet Foreign Policy, 1917-67.* New York: Frederick A. Praeger, 1968. Ulam's study offers a controversial evaluation of the diplomatic background of the Nazi-Soviet Pact from the Russian vantage point.

SEE ALSO: Nov. 25, 1936: Germany and Japan Sign the Anti-Comintern Pact; Feb. 12-Apr. 10, 1938: The Anschluss; Nov. 9-10, 1938: Kristallnacht; Sept. 1, 1939: Germany Invades Poland.

September 1, 1939
GERMANY INVADES POLAND

Germany's invasion of Poland initiated the first fighting in World War II, demonstrated to the Western powers that a policy of appeasement was untenable, as the Nazis had come to seem insatiable, and launched the German policies that would result in the Holocaust.

LOCALE: Poland

CATEGORIES: World War II; colonialism and occupation; wars, uprisings, and civil unrest

KEY FIGURES

Adolf Hitler (1889-1945), German dictator, 1933-1945

Joachim von Ribbentrop (1893-1946), German foreign minister, 1938-1945

Józef Beck (1894-1944), Polish foreign minister, 1932-1939

Neville Chamberlain (1869-1940), prime minister of Great Britain, 1937-1940

Lord Halifax (Edward Frederick Lindley Wood; 1881-1959), British foreign secretary, 1938-1940

Joseph Stalin (Joseph Vissarionovich Dzhugashvili; 1878-1953), general secretary of the Central Committee of the Communist Party of the Soviet Union, 1922-1953

Maksim Maksimovich Litvinov (Meier Moiseevich Wallach; 1876-1951), Soviet commissar for foreign affairs, 1930-1939

Vyacheslav Mikhailovich Molotov (Vyacheslav Mikhailovich Skryabin; 1890-1986), Soviet commissar for foreign affairs, 1939-1949

Benito Mussolini (1883-1945), Fascist premier of Italy, 1922-1943

Galeazzo Ciano (1903-1944), Italian foreign minister, 1936-1943, and son-in-law of Benito Mussolini

Édouard Daladier (1884-1970), premier of France, 1938-1940

SUMMARY OF EVENT

On March 15, 1939, after the Nazis had staged a bogus crisis, German troops marched into Czechoslovakia and occupied Prague, thus completing the annexation of the Czech state that Adolf Hitler had planned in 1938. Hitler and his henchmen then turned their attention to Poland. On March 21, Joachim von Ribbentrop, foreign minister of Germany, summoned Józef Beck, the foreign minister of Poland, to Berlin and gave him a list of German demands. Danzig, a free city administered under the super-

vision of the League of Nations, in which Poland had certain economic rights, was to revert to German control; Germany would receive an extraterritorial road and railway across the Polish Corridor, a strip of Polish territory separating East Prussia from the remainder of the German Reich; and Poland would agree to associate itself with Germany in an anti-Russian policy. Colonel Beck rejected these demands.

In the meantime, alarmed by the seizure of Prague, Great Britain and France guaranteed Poland's independence and territorial integrity. On March 31, Prime Minister Neville Chamberlain announced that if Germany invaded Poland, Great Britain and France would give Poland all the support in their power. London and Paris could not, however, give effective direct assistance to Warsaw because Poland was separated from them geographically by Germany. Poland's best help could come only from the Soviet Union, and in the weeks following the Anglo-French guarantee, Moscow became the center of European diplomacy.

Soviet dictator Joseph Stalin was worried about Hitler's rising power, especially because the Red Army was undergoing reorganization in the wake of the executions of so many of its high officers in 1937. Stalin decided to explore the feelings of both the Allies and the Nazis. On April 16, 1939, Maksim Maksimovich Litvinov, the Soviet commissar for foreign affairs, who was believed to be friendly toward the West, approached the Allies with an offer to conclude a mutual assistance pact. The next day, the Soviet ambassador in Berlin inquired of the Reich foreign ministry whether Russo-German relations might be improved. The Germans made some noncommittal answers at once. The Allies made no answer at all until, after a delay of three weeks, Chamberlain and his Conservative cabinet, with their inveterate suspicion of Russian motives, virtually rejected Litvinov's advances. Meanwhile, Litvinov had been replaced by the iron-willed opportunist Vyacheslav Mikhailovich Molotov.

Hitler now scored a success in another quarter. On May 22, he made the Pact of Steel with Italy, in which the two powers pledged themselves to fight as allies in the event one of them went to war. Benito Mussolini, the Fascist dictator of Italy, was anxious for gain and, over the protest of his son-in-law and foreign minister, Galeazzo Ciano, committed his country to war on Hitler's terms. This alliance strengthened Hitler's position, and on May 23, he told his generals that war with Poland was inevitable. Hoping to prevent the Soviet Union from helping Poland, the Nazis opened serious talks with the Russians on May 30.

During the next two months, the situation did not develop rapidly. The Russian and German negotiators hesitated to commit their countries to a clearly defined pact. By now, the West had also sent delegates to Moscow, but they also acted slowly, unable to carry the strongly anti-communist and anti-Russian Colonel Beck with them. Because most of their country had been occupied by Russia for more than a century prior to 1918, the Poles were understandably reluctant to readmit the Red Army in 1939. On the other side, Stalin distrusted the West. With the events in Munich still in mind, he doubted their determination to resist Hitler and suspected them of wishing to embroil him in war with Germany. In August, it became apparent that Stalin had chosen Hitler because Hitler could give more and ask for less than Chamberlain or French premier Édouard Daladier. In the early hours of August 24, the Soviet-German nonaggression pact was signed; a secret protocol spelled out the share of Poland that each power would take.

Poland's situation was now critical. On August 23, believing that his pact with Stalin would convince Chamberlain and Daladier that helping Poland would be futile,

Hitler ordered his attack to begin at dawn on August 26. The British, however, were determined to honor their guarantee, and they signed a formal treaty with Poland on August 25. The same day, facing the prospect of war with less than ten fully equipped divisions, Mussolini informed Hitler that he would remain neutral in the event of a conflict. At this point, Hitler paused; in the evening, he ordered the invasion, then only twelve hours away, to be postponed.

Hitler attempted to separate the Poles from their allies. Daladier and Chamberlain stood firm, however, and when it became apparent that his efforts to shake them had failed, Hitler unleashed his army and air force on Poland. On September 1, at 4:45 A.M., six armored divisions (panzers) rolled forward while the pilots of the German Luftwaffe struck at the Polish airfields. The Germans had developed a new kind of warfare based on the rapid advance of tanks and mobile artillery, closely supported by aircraft. This so-called Blitzkrieg (literally, lightning war) was launched with devastating success.

The Luftwaffe smashed the Polish railway system, with the result that Polish attempts to mobilize effectively failed. Air strikes against Polish troops attempting to defend Warsaw were so successful that Polish forces collapsed completely in that area. Heavy air attacks also

THE GERMAN INVASION OF POLAND

occurred against military targets inside Warsaw once the Germans realized that their armor could not operate effectively in the narrow streets. Considerable collateral damage and casualties among the civilian populace also resulted from air attacks. Having hoped that, with good luck and bad weather, Poland could resist for six months, the West watched the Polish army become torn to pieces within two weeks.

On September 3, the British and French government fulfilled their commitment to Poland by declaring war. Nevertheless, they were unable to do anything to avert Poland's fate, and the Poles found themselves in an impossible strategic situation. Their entire country was a flat plain; the only defensible feature was the Bug River. It lay so far to the east, however, that a defense along it would have forced the Poles to surrender all their economic assets and political centers. Nevertheless, by placing most of their troops in the Polish corridor and between Warsaw and the industrial city of Ladz, the rest of the Polish army was stretched dangerously thin. German armored forces quickly broke through Poland's border defenses and penetrated deep into the interior. On September 17, the Russians hastily invaded Poland from the east to secure their portion of the spoils; by October 2, 1939, all organized Polish resistance had ceased.

Adolf Hitler salutes his troops as they march toward a wooden bridge constructed by the Germans across the San River near Jarosław, Poland, in September, 1939. (Hulton Archive/Getty Images)

1939

SIGNIFICANCE

Following the German occupation of Czechoslovakia, the Allies had realized that allowing Hitler to annex territory until he was satisfied was not going to be an effective means to prevent war. Germany's forces would keep expanding until they were too powerful to be resisted should the nation desire to add western Europe to its territories. France and England therefore made Poland their "line in the sand." Should the Nazis invade, war would result. The ultimatum gave Hitler momentary pause, but only momentary, and with the invasion of Poland, he crossed the line. Two days later, with the French and English declarations of war, World War II began.

The process by which the Wehrmacht (the German armed forces) analyzed its performance after the Polish invasion explains why the German army did so well on World War II battlefields. By early October, the high command obtained reports from units down to the regimental level. The army then established a rigorous training program throughout to correct mistakes. Thereafter the army trained for sixteen hours a day and six to seven days a week. When the Wehrmacht streamed west in May, 1940, few armies of the twentieth century had been as well trained or disciplined.

From the beginning, the German invaders embarked on Hitler's racial and ideological crusade. Atrocities fell immediately on Jews as well as Poles. Hitler ordered that Poland's ruling and intellectual elites be liquidated. Stalin's secret police also wiped out large numbers of army officers and the Polish intelligentsia. An even deadlier fate devastated the Jews. There were 3.25 million Jews in Poland in 1939; less than 10 percent survived to 1945. The largest number were exterminated in various death camps, of which Treblinka, Sobibór, and Auschwitz have become particular symbols of the Holocaust. The Jewish partisan movement began in the summer of 1942 as a result of the German action to liquidate the ghettos by transporting the Jews to the death camps. The nightmare lasted only a few years, but wounds of the German invasion lingered long after the fighting ended.

—*Samuel K. Eddy and Douglas W. Richmond*

FURTHER READING

Bullock, Alan. *Hitler: A Study in Tyranny*. Rev. ed. New York: Harper & Row, 1964. This definitive biography tells the story of Hitler's career, which culminated in the outbreak of World War II.

Chodakiewicz, Marek Jan. *Between Nazis and Soviets: Occupation Politics in Poland, 1939-1947*. Lanham, Md.: Lexington Books, 2004. Study of the internal politics of Poland during German occupation during World War II, as well as during the Soviet occupation that occurred in the war's aftermath. Maps, bibliographic references, index.

Colvin, Ian. *Vansittart in Office*. London: Victor Gollancz, 1965. Fills in details of British diplomatic activity behind the Chamberlain administration.

Garliński, Jozef. *Poland in the Second World War*. New York: Hippocrene Books, 1985. Concludes that despite the mistakes it committed, the Polish government could not have avoided confrontation with Germany and the Soviet Union.

Gross, Jan. *Polish Society Under German Occupation: The General Government, 1939-1944*. Princeton, N.J.: Princeton University Press, 1979. The longest and most severe occupation by Germany of any European country receives detailed consideration here.

Krakowski, Shmuel. *The War of the Damned: Jewish Armed Resistance in Poland, 1942-1944*. New York: Holmes & Meier, 1984. Krakowski describes the conflict in Poland between Hitler's forces and the Jews, who were determined to resist the Third Reich even at the cost of their lives.

Namier, Lewis B. *Europe in Decay: A Study of Disintegration, 1936-1940*. London: Macmillan, 1949. Reprint. Gloucester, Mass.: Peter Smith, 1963. A series of well-written, analytic reviews of the memoirs of some of the principal leaders who participated in the diplomatic prelude to the war—a series of pictures of demoralized and debased European ministers of state.

Reynaud, Paul. *In the Thick of the Fight*. Translated by J. D. Lambert. New York: Simon & Schuster, 1955. A personal memoir by the French statesman and cabinet minister.

Taylor, A. J. P. *The Origins of the Second World War*. London: Hamish Hamilton, 1961. An interpretation of the events leading up to the invasion of Poland that blames Britain and France for causing the war.

Toynbee, Arnold, and Veronica M. Toynbee, eds. *Survey of International Affairs, 1939-1946. The Eve of War, 1939*. London: Oxford University Press, 1959. A detailed study, country by country, of the events of the summer of 1939, written by experts.

Trzcinska-Croydon, Lilka. *The Labyrinth of Dangerous Hours: A Memoir of the Second World War*. Toronto: University of Toronto Press, 2004. Personal memoir of a Polish fighter in the underground resistance who was eventually captured and sent to Auschwitz.

SEE ALSO: Oct., 1925: Germany Attempts to Restructure the Versailles Treaty; Jan. 30, 1933: Hitler Comes to Power in Germany; Mar., 1933: Nazi Concentration Camps Begin Operating; Mar. 7, 1936: German Troops March into the Rhineland; Feb. 12-Apr. 10, 1938: The Anschluss; Nov. 9-10, 1938: Kristallnacht; 1939-1945: Nazi Extermination of the Jews; Aug. 23-24, 1939: Nazi-Soviet Pact; Apr. 9, 1940: Germany Invades Norway; May 16, 1940-1944: Gypsies Are Exterminated in Nazi Death Camps.

September 10, 1939
CANADA ENTERS WORLD WAR II

Canadian soldiers proved to be tough, battle-hardy fighters capable of major contributions to the Allied war effort. Troops from Canada were on the front lines of some of the war's most dangerous campaigns.

LOCALE: Canada; France; Italy; England

CATEGORIES: Diplomacy and international relations; government and politics; wars, uprisings, and civil unrest; World War II

KEY FIGURES

William Lyon Mackenzie King (1874-1950), prime minister of Canada, 1921-1926, 1926-1930, and 1935-1948

Winston Churchill (1874-1965), prime minister of Great Britain, 1940-1945

Adolf Hitler (1889-1945), chancellor of Germany, 1933-1945

Benito Mussolini (1883-1945), prime minister and dictator of Italy, 1922-1943

SUMMARY OF EVENT

When Great Britain declared war against Germany on September 3, 1939, Canada was expected to do the same. In a show of independence, Canada waited one week before declaring war on September 10, 1939. With the nation's experience during World War I still fresh, Canadian prime minister William Lyon Mackenzie King had promised the people of Canada that conscription would be instituted only for domestic military service and that Canadian citizens would not be forced to fight a foreign war. By 1942, however, it became clear that conscription for foreign military service could not be avoided. King decided to put the matter to a vote of the people, and on April 27, 1942, the Canadians voted three to one for conscription.

The Canadian troops' first engagement in battle during World War II occurred not in Europe but in Hong Kong. In October of 1941, when troops were ordered to prepare for deployment in the Pacific, the threat of war with Japan was not yet imminent. The Canadian troops were not well prepared for battle engagements: The 1,975 Canadian soldiers assigned to the British Crown Colony of Hong Kong had expected to see only garrison duties.

On December 18, 1941, the Japanese launched a surprise attack on Hong Kong. The Canadians fought gallantly, holding out until Great Britain surrendered Hong Kong to the Japanese on Christmas Day. Of the 1,975 Canadian troops defending Hong Kong, approximately 550 died either in battle or as prisoners of war, and about 500 Canadian troops were wounded. The total casualty rate amounted to more than 50 percent, one of the highest in all of Canada's wartime theaters.

The first Canadian battle on the European continent came on August 19, 1942, at Dieppe, France. Intended as a test for a large-scale invasion of Europe, the exercise was ultimately a huge disaster for the Canadians, who lost the element of surprise and were forced to surrender. Nearly 5,000 Canadian troops were committed to the one-day-long Battle of Dieppe; of these, approximately 2,000 were taken prisoner and nearly 1,000 were killed. In this battle, the Canadian air force lost 13 aircraft and 10 pilots, and the British air force lost 106 planes and 81 crew members. These combined losses made August 19, 1942, the day of the Allied air forces' greatest losses.

The Canadians' next major effort took place in Italy. After recovering from the Battle of Dieppe, the First Canadian Army trained extensively in England and numbered 250,000 troops. The First Infantry Division and a tank brigade participated in the invasion of Sicily on July 10, 1943, but the four-week campaign took its toll on the Canadians. On September 3, 1943, Canada's First Infantry Division and British soldiers landed at Italy's southern tip. Benito Mussolini, Italy's Fascist dictator, had already been removed from power, and the Italians had signed a secret armistice with the Allies. The Germans were still determined to defend Italy, however, and they posed a formidable threat to the Allies.

The most notable clash between the Canadians and Germans in Italy was known as Little Stalingrad, and it occurred in Ortona, Italy, in December of 1943. The Canadians fought fiercely and helped to clear the way for the liberation of Rome on June 4, 1944, but at heavy cost. Approximately 93,000 Canadians fought in Italy, and the casualty rate there topped 25 percent casualties, including almost 6,000 killed in action.

While the Italian campaign occupied twenty divisions of German forces, the Allies were preparing for the massive invasion of Western Europe. Two days after the Allied liberation of Rome, the D-day invasion began in France. For several months, the Royal Canadian Air Force had been bombing the area they planned

CANADA JOINS THE ALLIED WAR EFFORT

Following Great Britain's declaration of war on Germany on September 3, 1939, Canadian prime minister William Lyon Mackenzie King addressed the people of Canada to inform them of the steps their country would take next. He concluded his address with these words:

In what manner and to what extent Canada may most effectively be able to co-operate in the common cause is . . . something which Parliament itself will decide. All I need to add at the moment is that Canada, as a free nation of the British Commonwealth, is bringing her cooperation voluntarily. Our effort will be voluntary.

The people of Canada will, I know, face the days of stress and strain which lie ahead with calm and resolute courage. There is no home in Canada, no family, and no individual whose fortunes and freedom are not bound up in the present struggle. I appeal to my fellow-Canadians to unite in a national effort to save from destruction all that makes life itself worth living, and to preserve for future generations those liberties and institutions which others have bequeathed to us.

to invade, preparing it for the Allied offensive. The Royal Canadian Navy contributed 110 ships and more than 10,000 sailors to the invasion effort. Canadian minesweepers cleared a path across the English Channel for the invading fleet, and Canadian destroyers pounded German beach fortifications while armed merchant cruisers ferried soldiers to the beach and later carried the wounded back to England.

The Canadian infantry and tanks that landed at Juno Beach in Normandy worked to eliminate the German fortifications that had escaped damage from the naval bombardment. The Canadian troops again proved themselves in battle, and by the end of the day they had destroyed the German fortifications covering the beach and were moving inland. Canadian losses at Juno Beach numbered approximately 340 dead, 600 wounded, and 50 prisoners of war.

The ensuing Battle of Normandy was costly for both the Axis and the Allied powers. More than 300,000 Axis soldiers were killed, and they lost most of their equipment, including more than 2,000 tanks. The Canadians' casualties numbered around 18,500, with more than 5,000 dead. Although these high casualty rates were partly due to misguided command decisions and lack of training, they were also the result of the particularly dan-

gerous tasks to which the Canadians were assigned. Canadian troops were placed at the spearhead of the attacking forces and therefore suffered more casualties than others. Some scholars have claimed that the Canadians often volunteered for the more difficult tasks and so naturally suffered especially high casualty rates.

On July 25, 1944, the second-bloodiest day for the Canadians occurred near Caen, where the British and Canadians were to keep German forces contained while the Americans prepared an attack. The Americans were delayed by bad weather, and the Canadians were ordered to carry out an attack on their own. The Germans had laid many traps, and the Canadians paid a heavy price: The Black Watch regiment, for example, had 300 men at the start of the day and only 15 at its end. In total, the attack cost more than 1,500 Canadian lives.

After the invasion at Normandy, the Canadians were largely responsible for defending northwestern Europe. Their most notable concerns included clearing northern coastal France and capturing the rocket-launching sites that were still sending rockets toward England. The Canadians also reopened the Schelde Estuary to the Belgian port of Antwerp.

SIGNIFICANCE

The Canadian military forces played a vital and effective role in all theaters of operation during and especially after World War II. Canadian troops—like the forces from other Allied nations—were ill prepared for the fighting, but they quickly became battle hardened. In places such as Dieppe and Caen, the Canadians' willingness to meet the challenges posed by their experienced adversaries proved the soldiers' bravery and constitution. Their active participation in operations from the Pacific to the Netherlands ensured their place in the top echelon of the Allied fighters.

In addition to its wartime sacrifices, Canada made some gains during World War II. The Canadians began the war with fewer than a dozen naval vessels and left it with well over a hundred. Moreover, Canada's economic recovery after the Great Depression occurred very rapidly because of the war, and the nation established many social programs and support systems for war veterans.

—*Glenn S. Hamilton*

FURTHER READING

French, David. *Raising Churchill's Army: The British Army and the War Against Germany, 1919-1945.* New York: Oxford University Press, 2000. Details the assembly of the Allied forces that fought against the Axis countries during World War II.

Gilbert, Adrian. *Germany's Lightning War: The Campaigns of World War II*. Newton Abbot, England: David and Charles, 2000. Provides a vast amount of tactical information, some of which centers on Canadian involvement in World War II.

Townshend, Charles, ed. *Oxford Illustrated History of Modern War*. New York: Oxford University Press, 1997. Presents extensive discussion and photographs concerning the Canadian involvement in World War II.

SEE ALSO: July 10, 1920-Sept., 1926: Meighen Era in Canada; 1921-1948: King Era in Canada; Aug., 1930-1935: Bennett Era in Canada; Aug. 1, 1932: Canada's First Major Socialist Movement; Oct. 23, 1935-Nov. 15, 1948: King Returns to Power in Canada; Aug., 1939: United States Begins Mobilization for World War II; May, 1940: Roosevelt Uses Business Leaders for World War II Planning; Aug. 16, 1940: Ogdensburg Agreement.

November 1, 1939
ROCKEFELLER CENTER IS COMPLETED

The completion of Rockefeller Center, the first planned complex of city office buildings and public spaces in the United States, influenced urban planning and provided a symbolic focus for Depression-era New York City.

LOCALE: New York, New York
CATEGORIES: Architecture; urban planning

KEY FIGURES

John D. Rockefeller, Jr. (1874-1960), American financier, real estate developer, and philanthropist
Raymond Hood (1881-1934), American architect
Nelson A. Rockefeller (1908-1979), president of Rockefeller Center, Incorporated
David Sarnoff (1891-1971), founder and president of the Radio Corporation of America

SUMMARY OF EVENT

On November 1, 1939, John D. Rockefeller, Jr., drove the last rivet on Rockefeller Center during a ceremony marking the official completion of the New York City commercial and entertainment complex. The building program, which for ten years had symbolized corporate optimism in the face of the Great Depression, consisted at the time of thirteen structures and a plaza that would become famous. Speaking at the completion ceremony were Nicholas Murray Butler, president of Columbia University, which held the lucrative land lease on the property; David Sarnoff, president of the Radio Corporation of America (RCA), which was the anchor tenant in the project's main building; Thomas A. Murray, president of the Building and Construction Trades Council, who extolled the project as a model of corporate and union cooperation; New York mayor Fiorello H. La

Guardia; and Nelson A. Rockefeller, the president of Rockefeller Center, Incorporated, who served as the master of ceremonies.

Rockefeller Center held both short-term and long-term significance to the institutions and constituencies represented by the speakers. Columbia University saw its income from the land on which the complex was built increase more than tenfold, from $300,000 per year to $3.3 million. RCA received a corporate home of unsurpassed prestige, almost immediate and universal name recognition, and the most modern facilities in which to create and showcase its productions. The ten-year construction period had provided 75,000 jobs at union wages during the height of the Depression, and had created an estimated 150,000 jobs in support industries. New York City found in Rockefeller Center—in addition to the benefits of employment and tax revenue—a focal point and landmark that became synonymous with the city itself.

For John D. Rockefeller, Jr., the complex that bore his name would become the most famous and enduring monument and legacy of his career. The son of the oil industrialist John D. Rockefeller, Sr., he had focused his interests on real estate development and the philanthropic charities that his father had established. At the same time that he was building Rockefeller Center, he was also organizing and financing the restoration of colonial Williamsburg, Virginia. His intentions for Rockefeller Center were impressively fulfilled. He wanted good design, profitable returns on investment, and international tenants who would help to stimulate foreign trade. The center also symbolized his optimism in the nation's future and his belief in civic-minded corporatism.

The completion of Rockefeller Center was the final result of an idea that had originally been relatively traditional and modest. Ten years earlier, the Metropolitan Opera had been looking to build a new theater. Rockefeller became involved and collected rights to the leases on Columbia University's land and neighboring properties in midtown Manhattan, and he helped to implement a plan that would include a new opera house supported by rents from surrounding commercial buildings. He set up the Metropolitan Square Corporation, headed by Arthur Woods, to oversee the property. Todd, Robertson, Todd Engineering was named first as developers and later as managers of the project. L. Andrew Reinhard and Henry Hofmeister were appointed as architects, with Benjamin Morris, Raymond Hood, and Harvey Corbett as consultants. Initially, Rockefeller's involvement was to end with the development of the property and his donation of the public plaza. The stock market crash of October 29, 1929, forced the Metropolitan Opera to withdraw from the project, however, and Rockefeller assumed full financial responsibility.

The overall plan for the center evolved over the next several years. The architectural team of Reinhard and Hofmeister was expanded to include a consortium of firms, including Corbett, Harrison, and MacMurray and Hood, Godley, and Foulihoux, which called itself the Associated Architects. Of this group, Reinhard, Hofmeister, Harrison, and Hood were most active in the design. All the architects had in common a background in the Beaux-Arts tradition of architecture and an interest in and familiarity with modern styles and practices. Their approaches to design and construction might best be described as conservative modernism.

In consideration of the state of the nation's economy, the architects were instructed to maximize the income potential of the land but still to design a complex that would be humane and modern. The central position previously allocated to the Metropolitan Opera House was replaced with a towering skyscraper, the RCA building. Massed around it in an abstract angular composition were other skyscrapers of varying heights that became the corporate centers of such major companies as the Time-Life Corporation, Eastern Airlines, the Associated Press, and the American Rubber Company. Lower buildings, serving as trade centers for foreign countries, flanked a promenade that funneled pedestrians from Fifth Avenue to the plaza at the center of the complex. By the time Rockefeller drove the last rivet, Rockefeller Center, symbol of the metropolis of the future, encompassed more than five million square feet of office space.

Although the shapes and proportions of the buildings were to a certain extent predetermined by zoning restric-

tions and tenants' needs, architect Raymond Hood is credited with dominating the final style of the center. Hood had won the *Chicago Tribune* building design competition in 1922; since then, his skyscraper style had shown an evolving abstraction and simplification of the stepped-back gothic tower popular with architects in the 1920's and 1930's. For Hood and other architects of the period, the setbacks, originally imposed by zoning laws to permit light penetration to the streets, were not merely practical necessities; they were design elements that gave skyscrapers upward movement, energy, and visual variety. Hood's incorporation of setbacks to relieve the monolithic nature of the RCA Building thus tied the design of the structure firmly to the more conservative, historically derived forces of early twentieth century architecture, in contrast to the more radical abstract modernism that had developed in Europe by the late 1920's.

Rockefeller Center's unity of design extended beyond related building styles and materials. The interior decoration of the structures was developed according to a theme, the progress of civilization, in order to give the complex spiritual content. Murals and sculptures were sought from the most prominent artists of the day. At times, as in the case of Pablo Picasso, the commissions were refused because artists were either unsympathetic to corporate interests or resistant to dictated content. On one occasion, the management received more than it expected. In 1934, the Mexican painter Diego Rivera's mural *Man at the Crossroads* caused a scandal when communist iconography was identified in it; Rivera's mural was eventually removed and reconstituted in Mexico City. Throughout the complex, the dominant stylistic influence on the decorative program was Art Deco.

Even before its official completion, Rockefeller Center became a magnet for visitors. Its soaring edifices and open spaces seemed to represent the best that a city could be and encouraged hope in a future of prosperity during the dark years of the Depression.

SIGNIFICANCE

Rockefeller Center marked a turning point in urban planning and development in the United States. It was the first time that a complex of stylistically related commercial buildings had been planned in the middle of a city. Its public plaza was unprecedented both for being privately built and supported and for being urban rather than rural or agrarian in design and ambience. The mixture of skyscrapers and low buildings, all visually unified but each one surrounded by light and air, became a benchmark for corporate urbanism and a model for subsequent developments in other cities after World War II. Prior to the construction of Rockefeller Center, the large-scale planning and design of large sections of city property had been the domain of city governments, especially through the "cities beautiful" movement at the turn of the century. Subsequently, the private sector would lead the way, although frequently with municipal aid and encouragement. Not all of these developments would be as successful as Rockefeller Center, and certain practices, such as the wholesale destruction of older buildings and homes to make way for redevelopment, would become controversial legacies of the Rockefeller program.

Part of Rockefeller Center's success and influence stemmed from its designers' attempts to incorporate features that would relieve the potential for urban congestion inherent in a project of its size. The center featured the first integral garage in an urban commercial building. Underground roadways permitted trucks to make deliveries, and at the completion ceremony, it was noted that eight hundred trucks serviced the center daily without disrupting traffic on neighboring streets. Underground walkways connected the buildings as well. Shops and restaurants helped to service the office workers' practical needs.

Although the primary function of Rockefeller Center was commercial, public use was not only permitted but also encouraged. The famous skating rink in the plaza was added specifically to increase pedestrian traffic in the complex's central area. Visitors were allowed access to terrace and rooftop gardens. Shops and exhibitions invited strolling and browsing. Extravagant displays of flags and seasonal decorations evoked a festive mood. The emphasis on the center as an integrated focal point of the urban fabric of the city, a self-contained community tied to the larger metropolis, reflected the designers' attempt to adapt contemporary European theories of social urban planning to an emphatically capitalistic, profit-motivated enter-

prise. This integrated approach was to add a new dimension to corporate building in the following decades.

The center's influence was felt not only in the area of corporate urbanism but also in the development of New York City itself. Through its location between Fifth and Sixth Avenues, Rockefeller Center anchored and stabilized the shopping district on the first street and helped to revitalize the second. It inaugurated a midtown business district that expanded after World War II as other office towers clustered in its vicinity, borrowing its prestige

Rockefeller Center's RCA Building in 1933, six years before the entire complex was completed. (Library of Congress)

1939

and, at times, even its designs. Radio City Music Hall became a center of popular entertainment and a main tourist attraction for the area, and the plaza, with its seasonal decorations and skating rink frequently featured in television programs and motion pictures, became one of the most recognized urban sites in the country.

—*Madeline C. Archer*

FURTHER READING

Balfour, Alan. *Rockefeller Center: Architecture as Theater*. New York: McGraw-Hill, 1978. Descriptive, condensed history of the project presents detailed analysis of the buildings themselves, the architects, and the theoretical and historical influences on the designs. Features more than two hundred photographs, including views of the property before construction and of the subsequent development in the area. Includes notes, brief annotated bibliography, and index.

Jordy, William. "Rockefeller Center and Corporate Urbanism." In *The Impact of European Modernism in the Mid-Twentieth Century*. Vol. 5 in *American Buildings and Their Architects*. 1972. Reprint. New York: Oxford University Press, 1986. Informative, considered analysis of the successes and failures of Rockefeller Center's architecture and public spaces. Places the plan within the historical context of urban design and planning, thus explaining its conservative and innovative features. Includes photographs and footnotes.

Kilham, Walter H., Jr. *Raymond Hood, Architect: Form Through Function in the American Skyscraper*. 1974. Reprint. New York: Architectural Book Publishing, 1999. Subjective, first-person account by a member of Hood's architectural firm provides a behind-the-scenes view of architectural practices, Hood's personality and attitudes, and the problems attendant on various commissions, including Rockefeller Center. Includes bibliography and index.

Krinsky, Carol H. *Rockefeller Center*. New York: Oxford University Press, 1978. Comprehensive, scholarly contextual history of the project, including later developments through the 1970's. Examines the center's impacts and influences as well as its art and decorative program. Includes photographs, illustrations, extensive bibliography, and index.

Loth, David. *The City Within a City*. New York: William Morrow, 1966. Anecdotal, accessible account of Rockefeller Center's history and development. Provides background on the principal participants and recounts colorful episodes.

Okrent, Daniel. *Great Fortune: The Epic of Rockefeller Center*. New York: Viking Press, 2003. Entertaining account by a journalist traces the events surrounding the creation of the center and places the accomplishment in the context of its times. Includes illustrations, bibliography, and index.

Reynolds, Donald Martin. *The Architecture of New York City: Histories and Views of Important Structures, Sites, and Symbols*. Rev. ed. New York: Macmillan, 1994. Interesting and informative chronological survey of New York City architecture from the seventeenth century to the end of the twentieth century. Provides details about a wide range of significant buildings and structures. Chapter 13 is devoted to Rockefeller Center. Includes glossary, bibliography, and index.

Rockefeller Center, Incorporated. *The Last Rivet: The Story of Rockefeller Center, a City Within a City, as Told at the Ceremony in Which John D. Rockefeller, Jr., Drove the Last Rivet of the Last Building, November 1, 1939*. New York: Columbia University Press, 1940. Essentially a transcript of the ceremony that marked the official completion of Rockefeller Center. Includes texts of speeches describing the history of the property and project. Notably absent are any references to the designers or architects. Especially interesting for comparative reasons, as researchers have found certain details of the history recollected in the speeches of some major participants to be erroneous. Includes photographs of the property before, during, and after construction.

Roth, Leland M. *American Architecture: A History*. 2d ed. Boulder, Colo.: Westview Press, 2003. Discussion of the history of architecture in the United States examines the many different forces that have influenced styles and trends. Places the design of the urban skyscraper within the larger national context. Includes many illustrations, chronology, glossary, and index.

SEE ALSO: May-June, 1925: Paris Exhibition Defines Art Deco; Spring, 1931: Le Corbusier's Villa Savoye Exemplifies Functionalist Architecture; May 1, 1931: Empire State Building Opens; Oct., 1932: Wright Founds the Taliesin Fellowship; Feb., 1934: Rivera's Rockefeller Center Mural Is Destroyed; 1937-1938: Aalto Designs Villa Mairea; May 27, 1937: Golden Gate Bridge Opens.

November 30, 1939-March 12, 1940
RUSSO-FINNISH WAR

When the Soviet Union forcibly annexed Finnish territory, emulating recent German expansion, the Finns resisted, launching the Russo-Finnish War. Staunch fighting by Finnish soldiers allowed Finland to retain its independence, albeit with a significant loss of territory.

ALSO KNOWN AS: Winter War; Soviet-Finnish War
LOCALE: Finland; Soviet Union
CATEGORIES: Wars, uprisings, and civil unrest; expansion and land acquisition

KEY FIGURES
Carl Gustaf Mannerheim (1867-1951), Finnish commander in chief and later president of Finland, 1944-1946
Kirill Meretskov (1897-1968), commander of Russian forces on the Finnish front, 1939
Vyacheslav Mikhailovich Molotov (Vyacheslav Mikhailovich Skryabin; 1890-1986), Russian foreign minister
Joseph Stalin (Joseph Vissarionovich Dzhugashvili; 1878-1953), general secretary of the Central Committee of the Communist Party of the Soviet Union, 1922-1953
Kliment Voroshilov (1881-1969), commander of Russian forces on the Finnish front, January-March, 1940

SUMMARY OF EVENT
On November 30, 1939, the armed forces of the Soviet Union launched an invasion of Finnish territory. While the Soviet air force bombed Finnish cities, Soviet troops advanced into Finland on two fronts. Some units advanced eastward on a front bordered by the White Sea on the north and Lake Ladoga on the south, while a larger Soviet force advanced northward into the Karelian Isthmus between Lake Ladoga and the Gulf of Bothnia. The Soviets deployed 470,000 troops, supported by 2,200 tanks and more than 2,000 aircraft against a Finnish force of 295,000 men with virtually no aircraft or tanks. This invasion resulted from a number of factors in the tumultuous history of the two nations.

The czars of Russia and the kings of Sweden long battled for domination of the area that later became Finland. Peter I of Russia (r. 1682-1725) incorporated most of Finland into his empire at the conclusion of the Great Northern War in 1721. During the Napoleonic wars, Al-

exander I of Russia (r. 1801-1825) declared Finland to be a grand duchy with himself as its grand duke. Although many Finns were unhappy with Russian rule, no opportunity presented itself to them to break away until the Russian Revolution of 1905.

With Czar Nicholas II (r. 1894-1917), the last Russian czar, distracted by revolt in his far-flung dominions, Finnish students led a revolt against the Russian ruler. Two revolutionary military forces, the Red Guard and the Nationalists, led armed assaults on Russian military garrisons. When the revolutionaries fell out among themselves over political issues, Nicholas managed to regain control of the grand duchy by granting its people nearly complete autonomy and the world's first parliament elected by universal suffrage.

When the great Russian Revolution of 1917 came, many Finns opted for complete independence. Taking advantage of Russian preoccupation with civil war between the Communists and White (royalist and non-Communist) forces and the concurrent foreign intervention in Russia, Finnish nationalists declared Finland's independence on July 18, 1917, and suppressed the Finnish Bolsheviks. The Red Army of the Soviet Union attempted to suppress the Finnish government, but was defeated by German troops and a Finnish army commanded by Carl Gustaf Mannerheim in May, 1918. Finnish and Soviet representatives confirmed Finland's independence and settled the borders between their countries in the Treaty of Dorpat in 1922. Relations between the Finnish and Soviet governments remained stable and friendly until the beginnings of German rearmament and territorial expansion in the mid-1930's.

German dictator Adolf Hitler made it plain in his book *Mein Kampf* (1925-1927; partial English translation, 1933) that he planned to destroy communism and acquire living space for Germany's excess population in the Ukraine. Soviet dictator Joseph Stalin realized that Hitler could accomplish his ambitions only through a successful war against the Soviet Union. Stalin became increasingly anxious to strengthen Soviet defenses as Hitler became more aggressive in throwing off the territorial and military terms of the Treaty of Versailles. In planning the defense of their nation, Soviet leaders decided that they must garrison troops and ships in areas belonging to Finland. In 1937, Soviet emissaries proposed a military alliance between the two countries. The Finns turned down the Russian proposals because they wanted to remain neutral in the event of a new European war, which seemed likely.

By 1939, the Soviet proposals for an alliance turned into demands for military bases for their troops in Finnish territory. The Finnish government resisted these demands, thinking that the rivalry between Germany and the Soviet Union would guarantee their own continued neutrality. The Nazi-Soviet nonaggression pact of August, 1939, shattered the Finnish hope that they could continue to walk a tightrope between the two great-power antagonists. Secret protocols of the pact divided Europe into German and Soviet spheres of influence. The Soviet sphere included Finland and the small Baltic republics of Estonia, Latvia, and Lithuania, as well as eastern Poland.

When the German army invaded Poland and defeated its armed forces in September of 1939, the Soviets occupied the eastern part of the country. The German invasion brought Great Britain and France into the war, which quickly escalated into a global conflict. While the

European countries confronted each other, Stalin occupied and annexed the Baltic republics during October and November, 1939. On October 5, Stalin summoned Finnish emissaries to Moscow. The Finnish government sent the emissaries, but at the same time ordered the mobilization of the Finnish army. The Soviet foreign minister, Vyacheslav Mikhailovich Molotov, demanded of the emissaries that their government allow Soviet troops to establish bases on Finnish territory. As the Finnish representatives continued to resist Soviet demands, Stalin ordered a massive military buildup on the Russo-Finnish border. He also ordered general Kirill Meretskov to plan an invasion of Finland.

When Molotov reported to Stalin that the Finns would never accept the Soviet demands, the dictator ordered an invasion of Finland. On November 26, the Soviet government claimed Finnish troops had shelled the border village of Mainila. Using this supposed aggression as an excuse, the Soviet government broke off relations with the Finns on November 29 and invaded Finland the next day. Concurrently, Soviet bombers launched attacks against Finnish cities, including Helsinki.

Mannerheim, the hero of the Finnish war of independence in 1918, assumed command of the Finnish army. A career soldier who had risen to the rank of general in the imperial Russian army during World War I, Mannerheim was an able commander who well understood the rigors of a winter war. Mannerheim and the Finnish General Staff had long planned for the possibility of a Soviet invasion of their country. Their plan called for the small Finnish army to hold the Russians at bay in the Karelian Isthmus while reserves could be called to active service. Both in the isthmus and on a front north of Lake Ladoga the Finns fought the Red Army to a standstill in November and December.

During the fighting, the Finnish government tried to secure military aid from abroad. The Germans held fast to their nonaggression pact with the Soviet Union. The French and the British seemed willing to send military aid if the Finns would grant

RUSSO-FINNISH WAR

MANNERHEIM'S SPEECH TO FINNISH SOLDIERS

On March 14, 1940, Carl Gustaf Mannerheim thanked his troops for their enormous efforts and tried to explain the terms of the Treaty of Moscow. Although Mannerheim voiced appreciation for the help given by the Western powers, he also acknowledged that the Finnish army was severely hampered by the West's refusal to grant the troops the right of transit.

Soldiers of the glorious Finnish army!

Peace has been concluded between our country and the Soviet Union, an exacting peace which has ceded to Soviet Russia nearly every battlefield on which you have shed your blood on behalf of everything we hold dear and sacred.

You did not want war; you loved peace, work and progress; but you were forced into a struggle in which you have done great deeds, deeds that will shine for centuries in the pages of history. More than fifteen thousand of you who took the field will never again see your homes, and how many those are who have lost for ever their ability to work. But you have also dealt hard blows, and if two hundred thousand of our enemies now lie on the snowdrifts, gazing with broken eyes at our starry sky, the fault is not yours. You did not hate them or wish them evil; you merely followed the stern law of war: kill or be killed.

Soldiers: I have fought on many battlefields, but never have I seen your like as warriors. I am as proud of you as though you were my own children; l am as proud of the man from the Northern fells as of the son of Ostrobothnia's plains, of the Carelian forests, the hills of Savo, the fertile fields of Häme and Satakunta, the leafy copses of Uusimaa and Varsinais-Suomi. I am as proud of the sacrifice tendered by the child of a lowly cottage as of those of the wealthy. . . .

In spite of all bravery and spirit of sacrifice, the Government has been compelled to conclude peace on severe terms, which however are explicable. Our Army was small and its reserves and cadres inadequate. We were not prepared for war with a Great Power. While our brave soldiers were defending our frontiers we had by insuperable efforts to procure what we lacked. We had to construct lines of defense where there were none. We had to try to obtain help, which failed to come. We had to find arms and equipment at a time when all the nations were feverishly arming against the storm which sweeps over the world. Your heroic deeds have aroused the admiration of the world, but after three and a half months of war we are still almost alone. We have not obtained more foreign help than two reinforced battalions equipped with artillery and aircraft for our fronts, where our own men, fighting day and night without the possibility of being relieved, have had to meet the attacks of ever fresh enemy forces, straining their physical and moral powers beyond all limits.

Source: Carl Gustaf Mannerheim, "His Commander in Chief's Order of the Day, Nr. 34," in *Invasion in the Snow: A Study of Mechanized War*, edited by John Langdon-Davies (Boston: Houghton Mifflin, 1941).

1939

them bases for their armed forces on Finnish territory. U.S. president Franklin D. Roosevelt publicly denounced Soviet actions, but he was not inclined to send military aid. The Finns were no more willing to have French and British bases on their soil than they were to have Soviet bases, so the appeal of Finnish representatives did not succeed.

The Soviet troops at the front proved to be poorly led and ill equipped for war in conditions where the temperature often reached forty degrees below zero and lower. Their offensive halted, the Red Army found itself constantly harassed by the Finns and without supplies. Thousands were killed in the fighting and thousands more froze or starved to death. Even while his troops were dying, Stalin was planning a new offensive.

In December, the Soviet dictator replaced most of the generals on the Finnish front. General Kliment Voroshilov became the commander of Soviet forces and launched a new offensive against the Finns in February of 1940 with overwhelming force. The Finnish army gave up a considerable amount of territory but managed to fight the Russians to a standstill once again. By this time, Mannerheim had given up on aid from the French or British, and he advised the Finnish government to make peace on any terms short of unconditional surrender.

The Finns negotiated an armistice on February 13. Peace was finalized in the Treaty of Moscow, signed on March 12, 1940. The Finns had lost 22,425 men killed, 43,557 wounded, and 1,434 missing in action. The Russians had lost 53,500 killed, 176,000 wounded, and 16,000 missing in action. The exact numbers of civilian casualties are unknown, but hundreds of Finnish civilians died in the Russian bombings, which intensified during January and February, 1940.

SIGNIFICANCE

The terms of the Treaty of Moscow forced the Finns to give up more than thirty-five thousand square kilometers of their territory. The Finns also agreed to the establishment of Russian military bases in their territory and signed a mutual assistance pact with the Soviets. Harsh as these terms were, the Finns kept their independence and did not suffer the fate of the Baltic republics, which were annexed outright into the Soviet Union. Through the sacrifice of their soldiers in the face of overwhelming odds, the Finns managed to keep their freedom. The mutual assistance pact proved useless, as rather than aid the Soviet Union against Germany, Finland accepted German military support when it launched the Continuation War against the Soviets in June of 1941.

Perhaps the greatest significance of the Winter War lay in its effects on the stature of the Soviet Union and the Red Army in the eyes of the world. In response to the illegal invasion of Finland, the Soviet Union was ejected from the League of Nations, and despite their victory, their losses were so great as to make the Red Army look vulnerable. This perception of vulnerability may have contributed to Hitler's decision to invade the Soviet Union. Ironically, the Soviets' losses could also have been interpreted as an indication of the extreme difficulty of staging an invasion in wintertime, a lesson Hitler famously learned himself when he did invade the Soviet Union.

—Paul Madden

FURTHER READING

Engle, Eloise, and Lauri Paananen. *The Winter War: The Soviet Attack on Finland, 1939-1940.* Harrisburg, Pa.: Stackpole Books, 1973. Written for a popular audience, concentrates primarily on the soldiers and battles on the front lines.

Jakobson, Max. *Finland Survived: An Account of the Finnish-Soviet Winter War, 1939-1940.* Helsinki, Finland: Otava, 1961. Pro-Finnish account of origins and course of the war suitable for general readers. Written by a Finn, the language is sometimes confusing and the book reveals some obvious biases.

Tillotson, H. M. *Finland at Peace and War, 1918-1993.* Wilby Hall, England: Michael Russell, 1993. Heavily weighted toward military history, contains an account of Finnish history that puts the 1939-1940 war into a broader perspective of Finnish history.

Trotter, William R. *A Frozen Hell: The Russo-Finnish Winter War of 1939-1940.* Chapel Hill, N.C.: Algonquin Books, 2000. Surveys the origins, course, and results of the war in language accessible to most readers. Bibliographic references and index.

Upton, Anthony F. *Finland, 1939-1940.* Newark: University of Delaware Press, 1974. A concise overview of the origins of the war, the battles of the war, and the war's results. Recommended for high school audiences and above.

Van Dyke, Carl. *The Soviet Invasion of Finland, 1939-1940.* Portland, Oreg.: F. Cass, 2001. A volume in F. Cass's series on Soviet military experience: Recounts the war from the Soviet perspective and places it in the context of Soviet history. Bibliographic references.

SEE ALSO: Dec. 6, 1917-Oct. 14, 1920: Finland Gains Independence; Mar. 7, 1936: German Troops March into the Rhineland; 1937-1938: Aalto Designs Villa Mairea; Aug. 23-24, 1939: Nazi-Soviet Pact; Apr. 9, 1940: Germany Invades Norway.

December 15, 1939
GONE WITH THE WIND PREMIERES

Following its premiere, Gone with the Wind, *independently produced by David O. Selznick, received a then-record ten Academy Awards and became the biggest blockbuster in motion-picture history to that time.*

LOCALE: Atlanta, Georgia
CATEGORIES: Motion pictures; entertainment

KEY FIGURES

David O. Selznick (1902-1965), American independent film producer
Margaret Mitchell (1900-1949), American novelist
Vivien Leigh (1913-1967), British film actor
Clark Gable (1901-1960), American film actor
Olivia de Havilland (b. 1916), American film actor
Leslie Howard (1893-1943), British film actor
Hattie McDaniel (1895-1952), African American film actor
Victor Fleming (1883-1949), American film director
William Cameron Menzies (1896-1957), American film production designer

SUMMARY OF EVENT

In 1935, David O. Selznick left Metro-Goldwyn-Mayer (MGM), the premiere Hollywood studio of the time, to form Selznick International Pictures. As an independent producer, Selznick made films that were in keeping with his preference for adaptations of classical novels, often with central roles for women. Early in 1936, at the urging of his East Coast story editor Kay Brown, Selznick read a synopsis of an as-yet-unpublished Civil War melodrama by Margaret Mitchell. Worried about the box-office failure of other Civil War stories and the length of the novel, Selznick initially refused to pay the asking price of sixty-five thousand dollars for the book's film rights. Just a week after the book's official publication in July, 1936, Selznick reconsidered and made an offer of fifty thousand dollars, which was accepted. The novel immediately became a runaway best seller, and the *Gone with the Wind* phenomenon began.

Selznick was obsessive about his role in film production. No detail was too small for his involvement, and no price was too high to achieve the quality he sought. These facts are partially responsible for the cost and length of the production of *Gone with the Wind*. In addition, Selznick had a contract with United Artists to distribute the films he produced through 1938. Popular opinion,

however, demanded that Clark Gable, who was under contract to MGM, play the role of Rhett Butler. Louis B. Mayer, the head of MGM, agreed to lend Gable and to provide one-half of the film's financing (estimated then at $2.5 million) in return for world distribution rights and half the total profits. Because he had other films then in various stages of production and because of his typically extravagant methods, Selznick did not have enough capital to make *Gone with the Wind* on his own. In order to get Gable and financial backing, Selznick eventually accepted Mayer's offer.

In early 1937, Selznick commissioned Sidney Howard, a Pulitzer Prize-winning playwright, to write the screenplay. In six weeks, Howard completed a four-hundred-page script that translated into six hours of screen time. To get the script to a more manageable length, Selznick and Howard worked on three subsequent drafts in early 1938. Still not satisfied with the script, Selznick put it aside while he returned to the unresolved casting problems.

During this time, as a means of focusing public attention on *Gone with the Wind* while stalling production until the contract with United Artists expired, Selznick's publicity director, Russell Birdwell, orchestrated a nationwide "search for Scarlett," seeking an actress to play Scarlett O'Hara. Selznick was never convinced that an inexperienced or unknown actress should play the central character, who would be on screen in nearly every shot of the film, but he relished the publicity that the search provided. He considered a number of established Hollywood stars for the role of Scarlett, including Bette Davis, Miriam Hopkins, Paulette Goddard, Norma Shearer, Jean Arthur, Joan Bennett, and Katharine Hepburn, but none was felt to be quite right. Selznick signed with MGM for the use of Gable in August, 1938, and production was scheduled to begin in December, 1938, even though there was still no finished script and the roles of Scarlett and of many of the supporting characters had not yet been cast. The "burning of Atlanta," in which old movie sets on Selznick International's backlot were set ablaze while doubles for Rhett and Scarlett fled, initiated the production of the film.

Rewrites on the script continued and employed a number of writers, including Jo Swerling, Oliver H. P. Garrett, Charles MacArthur, F. Scott Fitzgerald, and Ben Hecht. Selznick insisted that the writers use only dialogue from the novel and respect the narrative structure

On January 26, 1939, production of *Gone with the Wind* began in earnest, with George Cukor as director. After only a few weeks of filming, Cukor left the production, in part because of his refusal to comply with Selznick's demand for approval of every camera setup. In addition, Cukor was widely known as a "woman's director," and Clark Gable felt that his role was being diminished at the expense of the female characters. Victor Fleming, with whom Gable felt comfortable, was chosen to replace Cukor.

The removal of Cukor set a tone of upheaval that was to characterize the remainder of the production. Selznick demonstrated that, with the exception of the stars, all personnel were expendable parts and that he was the dominant creative force of the production. At least five different directors, three cinematographers, and countless writers were involved in the production of *Gone with the Wind*—a fact that had surprisingly little effect on the film's look, as it was Selznick, and to a lesser extent production designer William Cameron Menzies, whose vision shaped the film.

Filming officially ended on June 27, 1939, although work on retakes and process shots continued. Postproduction was only slightly less chaotic than the other stages of the film's creation, but Selznick showed a four-hour version to MGM executives in late August and received an enthusiastic response. The completion of the music track, intertitles, additional editing, and the largest main title ever designed resulted in a final version running three hours and forty minutes. Two sneak previews in September received overwhelmingly positive response, although some criticism was leveled at the amount of kissing in the film and at Rhett's final line, "Frankly, my dear, I don't give a damn." The use of any profanity, and specifically the word "damn," was forbidden by the Motion Picture Production Code of 1930. Selznick eventually received permission to use the word, although he was fined five thousand dollars for violating the code.

Gone with the Wind premiered in Atlanta on December 15, 1939, and the occasion delivered all the glamour and spectacle of Hollywood during its heyday. Huge

Searchlights frame the "Tara" facade of Loew's Grand Theater in Atlanta, Georgia, for the premiere of Gone with the Wind. *(AP/Wide World Photos)*

of the original as closely as possible. None of the writers who followed Howard was allowed to work without Selznick's constant interference, and script revisions continued throughout the film's production.

Casting decisions for principal roles were finally announced on January 13, 1939. Olivia de Havilland landed the role of Melanie, which she had actively pursued, and Leslie Howard reluctantly consented to play Ashley as part of a deal that allowed him to produce his next film. Vivien Leigh was chosen to play Scarlett, and although she had been a serious contender for several months, Selznick preferred to have her arrival in Hollywood seem the result of happenstance rather than deliberate planning in order to avoid the wrath of rejected actresses.

crowds thronged the spotlit theater, women fainted when Clark Gable arrived, and many of the country's most wealthy and powerful people attended. The film went on to garner ten Academy Awards, including the Irving G. Thalberg Memorial Award, for outstanding achievement in motion-picture production, for Selznick. The first Oscar awarded to an African American performer went to Hattie McDaniel, who played Mammy and who would remain the only black to win an Oscar for another twenty-four years.

SIGNIFICANCE

The total production cost of *Gone with the Wind*, including prints and publicity, ran to $4.25 million, more than twice the average cost for a prestige picture of the time. The length of the film and the inclusion of an intermission were extremely rare practices. *Gone with the Wind*'s production eventually utilized 59 leading and supporting cast members, 2,400 extras, 1,100 horses, 375 pigs, mules, oxen, cows, dogs, and other animals, 450 vehicles, including wagons, ambulances, and gun caissons, 90 sets built using 1 million feet of lumber, 5,500 wardrobe items, and 449,512 feet of film shot in Technicolor, a relatively new process at the time. All of these elements added up to the biggest film spectacle ever produced, one that many industry insiders predicted would fail to return a profit.

The popularity and profitability of *Gone with the Wind* signaled both the height and the beginning of the end of the Hollywood studio system. The year 1939 was a banner year for Hollywood, producing such films as *Dark Victory, Stagecoach, The Wizard of Oz, Wuthering Heights,* and *Mr. Smith Goes to Washington,* and profits increased through the war years. However, the Hollywood system of "vertical integration," in which production, distribution, and exhibition were controlled by the major Hollywood studios, was under attack as a monopolistic practice. In 1948, a court decision put an end to block booking, blind bidding, price fixing, and other unfair business practices, and the major studios were ordered to divest themselves of their theater holdings. The decision spelled the beginning of the end for the studio-based production system.

As an independent producer, Selznick already worked outside the studio system, although he relied on the cooperation and financial support of the major studios to produce the top-quality "blockbuster" films that were his goal. The phenomenal success of *Gone with the Wind* marked the arrival of the independent producer as a dominant force in the industry, and Selznick served as a model for the production approach that eventually replaced the studio system in the new Hollywood. Selznick's filmmaking method was not marked by the assembly-line efficiency and economy often equated with the studio system but was both extravagant and painstaking. He believed that the public would pay increased ticket prices to see high-quality film spectaculars, and the reception of *Gone with the Wind* proved him correct.

The marketing strategy employed for the release of *Gone with the Wind* became a model for later blockbuster films. Exhibitors charged seventy cents at the door, two to three times the going rate for a movie ticket. Loew's Incorporated, MGM's parent company, charged exhibitors 70 percent of the box-office revenues, twice the usual fee for a top feature, which Loew's then split with Selznick. Initially, the film opened only in large cities in premiere movie theaters; subsequently (nearly two years later, in some cases), it was released to second-run theaters. *Gone with the Wind* was reissued four times by 1948 and continued to reap profits with each new release.

In 1940, Selznick International Pictures had only three films in release, but the company netted $10 million in profits that year. Only MGM, with profits of $8.7 million, was even close, and half its profits came from its distribution of *Gone with the Wind*. The film became the biggest blockbuster in movie history and was not dislodged from its number one position until 1965 and *The Sound of Music.*

—*Toni A. Perrine*

FURTHER READING

Behlmer, Rudy, ed. *Memo from David O. Selznick: The Creation of "Gone with the Wind" and Other Motion-Picture Classics, as Revealed in the Producer's Private Letters, Telegrams, Memorandums, and Autobiographical Remarks.* Introduction by Roger Ebert. Massive compendium of Selznick's personal papers and official and unofficial correspondence, revealing much about his contributions to his films and his manner in collaborating with and managing others. Filmography and index.

Bridges, Herb, and Terryl C. Boodman. *"Gone with the Wind": The Definitive Illustrated History of the Book, the Movie, and the Legend.* New York: Simon & Schuster, 1989. Published to coincide with the fiftieth anniversary of the film. Contains hundreds of stills, many in color. Brief history of the film, from preproduction to premiere. No index.

Cameron, Judy, and Paul J. Christman. *The Art of "Gone with the Wind": The Making of a Legend.* Englewood

1939

Cliffs, N.J.: Prentice Hall, 1989. Introduction by Daniel Mayer Selznick. Another oversized anniversary edition, with full-page photos and more production information than the Bridges book. Includes limited index, original memos, and telegrams related to the film's production.

Flamini, Roland. *Scarlett, Rhett, and a Cast of Thousands*. New York: Macmillan, 1975. Numerous photos from the collection of the author and others. Includes detailed history of the film's production and a good index.

Lambert, Gavin. *GWTW: The Making of "Gone with the Wind."* Boston: Little, Brown, 1973. The author knew Vivien Leigh, George Cukor, and David O. Selznick. Provides interesting information regarding the psychological disposition of the key people involved. Includes bibliography and index.

Schatz, Thomas. *The Genius of the System: Hollywood Filmmaking in the Studio Era*. New York: Pantheon Books, 1988. Explores the Hollywood studio system with close analysis of representative companies, including Selznick International Pictures. Provides insightful historical context for production of *Gone with the Wind*. Includes notes on sources and index.

Taylor, Helen. *Circling Dixie: Contemporary Southern Culture Through a Transatlantic Lens*. New Brunswick, N.J.: Rutgers University Press, 2001. This study of the transatlantic reception of representations of the American South includes a chapter devoted to sequels and revisions of *Gone with the Wind*, attesting to the lasting popularity and influence of the work on both sides of the Atlantic. Bibliographic references and index.

SEE ALSO: May 16, 1929: First Academy Awards Honor Film Achievement; 1930's-1940's: Studio System Dominates Hollywood Filmmaking; 1931-1932: Gangster Films Become Popular; 1934-1938: Production Code Gives Birth to Screwball Comedy; 1939: Ford Defines the Western in *Stagecoach*; Aug. 17, 1939: *The Wizard of Oz* Premieres.

1940
GARCÍA LORCA'S *POET IN NEW YORK* IS PUBLISHED

In Poet in New York, *Federico García Lorca described his feelings of attraction to and repulsion by white urban American civilization from the perspective of an Old World outsider.*

LOCALE: Mexico
CATEGORY: Literature

KEY FIGURES
Federico García Lorca (1898-1936), Spanish poet and playwright whose travels to New York City inspired the volume *Poet in New York*
Salvador Dalí (1904-1989), Spanish Surrealist painter and close friend of García Lorca who had a strong personal and artistic impact on the writer
Luis Buñuel (1900-1983), Spanish Surrealist film director who belonged to García Lorca's circle of close friends
Walt Whitman (1819-1892), American poet whose work influenced the style and content of García Lorca's poetry in general and *Poet in New York* in particular
Pedro Calderón de la Barca (1600-1681), Spanish playwright whose work is echoed in *Poet in New York*

SUMMARY OF EVENT
Federico García Lorca is widely regarded as Spain's most distinguished twentieth century writer of poetry and drama. García Lorca was a major participant in the flowering of Spanish literature that occurred in the years between World War I (1914-1918) and the Spanish Civil War (1936-1939), an era of richness and diversity that has been compared to the sixteenth and seventeenth century Spanish Golden Age.

Having already published numerous volumes of poetry, in 1929 García Lorca found himself at an artistic and personal impasse. Early that year, García Lorca had received inquiries regarding the possibility of giving a series of lectures in the United States, and at the urging of his family he embarked on his first trip outside Spain in the summer of 1929. The trip led him, via France and England, to Columbia University in New York City. Although they stimulated his literary output, the new and completely different surroundings also proved to be overwhelming and shocking.

Written in 1929 and 1930 while the poet was living in New York City and published after his death, *Poeta in Nueva York* (1940; *Poet in New York*) belongs to García Lorca's mature period of artistic evolution. It is, in fact, part of a new stage in his development as a poet, both stylistically and thematically. In this volume of poetry, a new vision of modern civilization is expressed, yet it is a vision that originates from some of the same emotional responses to the world that gave rise to his earlier volumes: *Libro de poemas* (1921; book of poems), *Poema del cante jondo* (1931; *Poem of the Deep Song*, 1987), and *Romancero gitano* (1928; *The Gypsy Ballads of García Lorca*, 1951, 1953). The themes underlying the poems of these early volumes—desire for the unattainable, nostalgia for a lost Eden, and the sterility of self-consciousness—reappear in *Poet in New York* with larger social implications. García Lorca's volume also explores the themes of materialism, dehumanization, violence, and racism.

The poet-persona (although the book contains autobiographical elements, the speaker in each of the poems in the volume cannot be identified with the poet) of *Poet in New York* becomes outraged against the empire of office buildings, the river drunk on oil, and the suits of clothing empty of humanity—all of which are the tangible results of humankind's intellectual endeavors. In the midst of this teeming humanity, the speaker of the poems desires a moment of peace and fulfillment (which is unattainable); his nostalgia for childhood grows stronger as Eden grows more inaccessible.

Near the beginning of the volume, García Lorca's persona identifies with a tree that cannot bear fruit because of its self-consciousness. By the end of the volume, however, the speaker identifies with nature and with the blood and human vitality of natural violence. He sides with the blacks of Harlem, and he experiences all the pain of consciousness. Rendered passive by the impact of this harsh world on his suffering sensibility, he can only name the objects of his nightmare vision. In his outrage, however, when he has sufficient strength to react against this world, he calls for a revolution that will flood the streets with blood and destroy the bloodless suits of Wall Street.

Thus, although some thematic similarities to his earlier poetry exist in *Poet in New York*, the manner in which García Lorca confronts the New World (New York City) radically differs from his manner of expression prior to his departure from Spain (the Old World). García Lorca moves from a state of participation in nature and in his community, manifested in the rhythmic, frequently dramatic poetry of imagery drawn from the natural world of southern Spain, to a state of extreme estrangement and dislocation from his familiar universe. This alienation manifests itself in the dissonant, subjective, and violent imagery drawn from the technological world of New York City. *Poet in New York*, then, reflects García Lorca's experience of depression and alienation in a foreign reality he perceives to be hostile, yet it is also an account of his psychological journey from alienation and disorientation to reintegration into the natural world.

Poet in New York marks the first appearance in García Lorca's work of poems that seriously address the topic of homosexuality—notably in "Tu infancia en Menton" (your childhood in Menton) and "Oda a Walt Whitman" (ode to Walt Whitman). Under the aegis of the noble American poet Walt Whitman, García Lorca ventures to introduce and defend homosexual love. The poem is an ode both to Whitman and to the agonized individuals whose homosexuality brings them only the pain of frustrated love. They are alienated human beings for whom there is no place in the world and who know the anguish of unfulfilled desire.

Transcending the poet's private vision of modern civilization, *Poet in New York* also reflects a metaphysical dimension; modern man recognizes the spiritual wasteland in which he lives. He discovers that he is alone, empty, without roots, and without belief in a divine being. Locked in a prison of subjectivity, he no longer belongs to the world or the cosmos. Now he is conscious, and his vision separates him from the world and his gods; he is fallen. The myth of the Fall expresses both the state of man's alienation from God and nature, resulting from consciousness, and the state of modern civilization's alienation from any unifying reality that might have held society together as a community.

SIGNIFICANCE

In the 1920's, Surrealism exploded onto the artistic horizon with the publication of French poet André Breton's *Manifeste du surréalisme* (*Manifesto of Surrealism*, 1969) in 1924 and the publication of the journal *La Révolution surréaliste* (the Surrealist revolution). Breton described Surrealism as the poet's surrendering to a state of pure psychic automatism, a state in which the poet could express—by means of the written word—the actual functioning of thought. Poetry, then, was dictated by thought, without any control exercised by reason. Consequently, it was exempt from any aesthetic or moral concerns. García Lorca himself had participated actively in the propagation of the ideas of Surrealism in 1928 by founding and editing *Gallo*, an avant-garde magazine that acknowledged the influence of many prominent Surrealist poets, painters, and musicians of the day.

Because García Lorca's New York poetry was indeed

1940

a startling departure from his earlier poetry in its tone of alienation and violent imagery, and because of its surface resemblance to some French Surrealist poetry written by Breton and Paul Éluard, *Poet in New York* was generally labeled as Surrealist at the time of its publication. Although *Poet in New York* does reflect the influence of Surrealism in both its use of language and its imagery, however, there is a basic difference between Breton's Surrealist poetry and García Lorca's symbolic poetry. García Lorca's New York poetry functions symbolically and metaphorically. The irrational, illogical, surrealistic (but not Surrealist) images, considered together, compose an organic whole expressive of a feeling or idea in the poet's mind; these images come into being by their relation to the subject rather than by their relation to each other. In other words, the notion of automatism or chance, which is at the root of Surrealist creation, is not an active force in García Lorca's New York poetry.

The critical reception of *Poet in New York* has been extremely varied. When the poems started to appear, many Spanish critics, certain that García Lorca was a popular poet, tended to regard the poetry from the New York period as a temporary aberration on his part. It was considered a strange, impenetrable work, apparently Surrealist in origin. To many, the New York poems represented a rejection of the traditional style of his earlier poetry and an embarkation on a new experiment in poetic creation. García Lorca's "experiment" was regarded by many as a failure: In their opinion the poetry somehow did not measure up to the greatness of his earlier work.

The issue of García Lorca's influence is complex. In Spain, García Lorca's New York poetry did have an effect on his younger contemporaries, but this influence is difficult to isolate from the influence García Lorca himself was receiving. García Lorca certainly influenced the poet Luis Cernuda, a poet of similar but more refined temperament; Cernuda followed García Lorca in the note of rebellion that finally broke out openly in the former's poetry. Other prominent Spanish poets never accepted García Lorca's Surrealist manner. They were unable to accept the iconoclastic aspects of his work—both in form and content—specifically those aspects that clashed with Spanish tradition. After the Spanish Civil War ended in 1939, Spanish poets returned to formalism and tranquillity, to simple human expression, and even to religion under the varied influence of many poets, including the modern poet Antonio Machado. Aside from evoking an appreciation of its rebelliousness and prohibited themes, García Lorca's New York poetry had little direct impact on later Spanish poets.

In Latin America, however, the situation proved different. Among the many Latin American poets influenced by García Lorca were Carlos Correa in Chile, Miguel Otero Silva in Venezuela, Jorge Zalamea in Colombia, Claudia Lars in Central America, and Manuel José Lira in Mexico. To them, García Lorca was a spokesman not only for his native Spain but also for the twentieth century Western world. García Lorca's work presented a new spiritual insight. Tormented and mutilated, but still sensually realistic, the New York poems carried a peculiarly important message to the modern age. They were not viewed as the fabrications of a mind that had lost touch with reality, as the outpourings of a Surrealist creating a gruesome antihuman nightmare world. Although they were regarded as García Lorca's most difficult poems—musically discordant, disrupted in meter, poured into arbitrary autonomous form, cascading with the fragments of exploded metaphor—their secret was that a new world of imagery had been created to embody the intense spiritual effort that informs them. The intricate imagistic and metaphoric language of *Poet in New York* proceeds from a vision of the world that, finding no expressive instrument in the traditions of any literary medium, demanded of the poet a new imaginative invention.

Poet in New York, an intensely personal yet strikingly universal work, is an example of modern alienation from self, family, society, and religion. The work has been regarded as an apocalyptic vision of the United States. On the social level, García Lorca denounces the poverty and exploitation he sees around him, criticizes Wall Street (which was in the midst of the 1929 stock market crash) and its materialism and capitalism, hurls invectives against the pope and much of organized religion, and even looks forward to the day when a cataclysmic upheaval is envisioned as overtaking the city.

—Genevieve Slomski

FURTHER READING

Allen, Rupert C. *The Symbolic World of Federico García Lorca*. Albuquerque: University of New Mexico Press, 1972. In this original study of García Lorca's poetic and dramatic use of symbolism, the author discusses *Poet in New York* as a volcanic eruption of symbols of personal as well as social destruction, disease, and disintegration. Contains bibliography.

Barea, Arturo. *Lorca: The Poet and His People*. Translated by Ilsa Barea. London: Faber & Faber, 1954. Although somewhat dated, Barea's study argues that, above all, García Lorca's work is "popular" in the sense that it touched a generation, speaking to the emotional and revolutionary forces that were beginning to take shape. In addition, the author discusses the themes of sex and death in García Lorca's poetry and drama. Includes appendix of Spanish quotations from García Lorca's works.

Cobb, Carl W. *Federico García Lorca*. New York: Twayne, 1967. The aim of this perceptive, well-written work is to give a general overview of some of García Lorca's representative works. Cobb devotes an entire chapter to *Poet in New York* and discusses the prophetically tragic outlook that infuses García Lorca's work with the turbulence, rebellion, and frustration of spirit of the modern age. Chronology, bibliography.

Craige, Betty Jean. *Lorca's "Poet in New York": The Fall into Consciousness*. Lexington: University Press of Kentucky, 1977. This brief scholarly study focuses on the Fall as the thematic center of *Poet in New York*. The nostalgia for a lost Eden and the sterility of self-consciousness, according to Craige, are the driving forces of the volume. Discusses the work in the context of García Lorca's earlier poetry. Contains a brief bibliography.

Dalí, Salvador, et al. *Sebastian's Arrows: Letters and Mementos of Salvador Dalí and Federico García Lorca*. Translated by Christopher Maurer. Chicago: Swan Isle Press, 2005. A careful and fascinating study of the friendship between these two men. Includes an excellent introduction by Maurer, a Spanish professor at Boston University.

Gibson, Ian. *Federico García Lorca: A Life*. New York: Pantheon Books, 1997. An essential work by a noted scholar. Thoroughly analyzes García Lorca's literary and political activity.

Londre, Felicia Hardison. *Federico García Lorca*. New York: Frederick Ungar, 1984. This perceptive work discusses the personal and artistic influences in García Lorca's life, his major plays, the musicality of his early poetry, and the folk ballads, paintings, and stories. It also analyzes the new directions in his more mature poetry. Useful bibliography.

Maurer, Christopher. Introduction to *Poet in New York*. Translated by Greg Simon and Steven F. White. New York: Farrar, Straus and Giroux, 1988. In this brief but excellent essay, Maurer points out the many reasons why he considers *Poet in New York* to have been a turning point in the poet's work. Also discusses the volume in the context of the poet's life.

Predmore, Richard L. *Lorca's New York Poetry: Social Injustice, Dark Love, Lost Faith*. Durham, N.C.: Duke University Press, 1980. The aim of this original study is to explore and elucidate the poetic symbolism and thematic structure of García Lorca's New York poetry. Predmore measures the poetic language of the work in the light of the ambiguous symbolism already developed in earlier works. Contains a brief bibliography.

SEE ALSO: 1922: Eliot Publishes *The Waste Land*; Oct., 1924: Surrealism Is Born; Feb., 1930: Crane Publishes *The Bridge*; July 17, 1936: Spanish Civil War Begins; Apr. 26, 1937: Raids on Guernica; July, 1937: Picasso Exhibits *Guernica*.

1940

1940
WRIGHT'S *NATIVE SON* DEPICTS RACISM IN AMERICA

Richard Wright's Native Son *shocked white Americans with its graphic depiction of the rage and violence engendered by racism in the hearts of African Americans.*

LOCALE: Chicago, Illinois
CATEGORIES: Literature; social issues and reform

KEY FIGURE
Richard Wright (1908-1960), African American writer

SUMMARY OF EVENT
In 1939, Richard Wright completed work on *Native Son*, his second work of fiction and his first full-length novel. The book's publication in 1940 immediately established Wright as an important author and a spokesman on conditions facing African Americans. Earlier, Wright had published a collection of four novellas titled *Uncle Tom's Children* (1938), which gained him the attention of some literary critics and helped him to win a Guggenheim Fellowship. The fellowship enabled Wright to devote all his time to writing.

Native Son, published by Harper's, was unlike any book by an African American writer ever published up to that time. Speaking of *Uncle Tom's Children*, Wright had said, "I had written a book which even bankers' daughters could read and weep over and feel good. I swore to myself that if I ever wrote another book, no one would weep over it; that it would be so hard and deep that they would have to face it without the consolation of tears." *Native Son* was indeed such a book. To avoid the unfocused sympathy of those who wished to avoid the hard realities of life for African Americans, Wright created for his protagonist a violent young black man in Chicago, Bigger Thomas, who murders two women, one black and one white, and who is then condemned to death, which he faces unrepentantly. Bigger and all his friends are resentful, frustrated by racism, and both fearful of the white world and inclined to violence toward it.

Harper's was somewhat concerned about the graphic nature of some of the book, but the publisher insisted on only limited changes. Just before publication, however, the Book-of-the-Month Club expressed interest in including *Native Son* as one of its selections if several sexually explicit scenes were removed and if Bigger Thomas did not show such obvious sexual interest in the white character, Mary Dalton. Wright agreed to these changes.

Upon publication in 1940, *Native Son* became an immediate hit. In less than six months, a quarter of a million copies had been sold at five dollars a copy—at a time when the minimum wage in the United States was thirty-five cents an hour. The first edition sold out in only three hours. Virtually every major newspaper and magazine in the nation reviewed the book. *Native Son* was on the best seller list for nearly four months. No other African American writer had ever achieved such fame and financial success. Moreover, no other African American writer had ever focused such attention on the conditions of life in black ghettos before. In the introduction to the first edition, Dorothy Canfield wrote: "*Native Son* is the first report in fiction we have had from those who succumb to . . . crosscurrents of contradictory nerve impulses, from those whose behavior patterns give evidence of the same bewildering, senseless tangle of abnormal nerve-reactions studied in animals in laboratory experiments." For many white Americans, Bigger Thomas became a symbol of the entire black community.

Prior to the publication of *Native Son*, Wright had worked at a variety of jobs to support himself, his invalid mother, a number of relatives, and a wife. These jobs had included janitorial work, selling burial insurance, employment on the Federal Writers' Project of the Works Progress Administration, and occasional writing for left-wing and Communist Party publications. Wright had joined the Communist Party in 1935, but he resigned his membership in 1944. With the financial security brought by the success of *Native Son*, Wright could devote himself to literary pursuits, and he spent the rest of his life writing.

The first impact of *Native Son* on Wright's writing was to encourage him to produce an autobiography, *Black Boy: A Record of Childhood and Youth* (1945), which described his life growing up in the South. Wright was born near Natchez, Mississippi, in 1908, and his parents then took the family to Memphis, where Wright's father abandoned them. There followed an itinerant existence in Tennessee, Arkansas, and Mississippi that entailed rough and bruising contact with Jim Crow segregation laws and the heavy-handed demands for obsequious behavior made by the racial etiquette of the place and time. *Black Boy* ended with Wright's migration to Chicago and the vaguely expressed hope that life would be better there. This book also became a matter of national debate and helped to establish Wright as a commentator on current racial conditions, not just a writer of fiction. More than four hundred thousand copies of the book were sold within a few weeks.

The financial independence delivered by *Native Son* also allowed Wright to make some personal changes. He divorced his first wife, to whom he had been married for less than a year, and married Ellen Poplar, a Jewish woman, in 1942. The couple had one child, a daughter named Julia.

The African American community recognized the accomplishment represented by *Native Son* when the National Association for the Advancement of Colored People (NAACP) awarded Wright its prestigious Spingarn Medal in 1940.

Native Son launched Wright's career as a writer. He went on to produce nineteen major fiction and nonfiction works, screenplays, and stage plays, and he became the first of the modern generation of African American writers.

SIGNIFICANCE

Since its publication in 1940, Richard Wright's *Native Son* has never been out of print. Orson Welles produced a Broadway play based on the book, and film versions were released in 1950 and 1986. The book and its author have been the subject of numerous scholarly and popular investigations from literary, historical, and sociological perspectives.

Although the author was a Mississippian who set his story in Chicago and wrote it while living in New York, the plot of *Native Son* has continued to be a metaphor for much of the black experience throughout the United States. The book explores individuals, their environments, and the ways in which environments shape people. In an essay titled "How Bigger Was Born," Wright wrote of his character:

> He is a product of a dislocated society; he is a dispossessed and disinherited man; he is all of this and he lives amid the greatest possible plenty on earth and he is looking and feeling for a way out. . . . He was an American because he was also a native son; but he was also a Negro nationalist in a vague sense because he was not allowed to live as an American. Such was his way of life and mine; neither Bigger nor I resided fully in either camp.

In 1940, most white Americans were unaware of such feelings on the part of African Americans. There was little contact between the races. In a survey taken in 1942, less than half of all white Americans approved of integrated transportation facilities, and only about one in three approved of integrated schools or neighborhoods. Most whites, however, seemed to feel that blacks were satisfied with existing conditions. The usual white concept of African Americans was bifurcated. On one hand were the happy-go-lucky "darkies," who were obviously poor and socially unequal but who did not worry about their situation at all; on the other were the fearful, downtrodden victims of southern bigotry. *Native Son* confronted the United States with the fact that the first of these stereotypes was false and the second was a national, not a regional, problem.

The growing urban ghettos of the North and West were not lands of opportunity but instead festering wounds in which people lived and died largely without hope. On a broad scale, Wright brought into the open the hatred, fear, and violence that he saw as characterizing American race relations. After *Native Son*, literary critic Irving Howe asserted, "American culture was changed forever." Quaintness and idealized folksiness disappeared from black literature, and the way was opened for later African American writers to emphasize their own ethnic culture. Later black writers could repudiate white culture and could celebrate black identity and even mili-

Richard Wright. (Library of Congress)

1940

tancy. Wright's message in *Native Son*, variations of which have appeared frequently since, is that African Americans may wish to destroy the symbols of white cultural dominance and control. Trickery, when directed toward the dominant culture, is acceptable, as is militancy. These ideas have become widespread since the publication of *Native Son*.

This does not mean that the influence of *Native Son* has been seen as all positive, even by blacks. James Baldwin commented that the book was "the most powerful and celebrated statement we have yet had of what it means to be a Negro in America." Baldwin, however, did not think Wright dealt adequately with the psychological and social conditions of Bigger Thomas's life, and he argued that this failure prevented Wright from conveying any sense of black life as a complex group reality. In a 1949 essay titled "Everybody's Protest Novel," Baldwin wrote that *Native Son* was in its own way as simpleminded as Harriet Beecher Stowe's *Uncle Tom's Cabin: Or, Life Among the Lowly* (1852). In "Many Thousands Gone," an essay published in 1951, Baldwin remarked that Wright wrote as if racism were a social problem that could not be cured but could be checked.

Although Wright's reputation as a writer and as a spokesman for African Americans ebbed during the 1950's, as younger black writers such as Baldwin and Ralph Ellison rejected Wright's naturalistic style of writing as well as the Marxist overtones of *Native Son*, Wright's influence was revived in the 1960's. With the growth of the militant black consciousness movement, there came a resurgence of interest in Wright's work. It is generally agreed that Wright's influence in *Native Son* is not a matter of literary style or technique. The novel's impact, rather, comes from ideas and attitudes, and Wright's work became a force in the social and intellectual history of the United States in the last half of the twentieth century. A part of this impact developed from Wright's work after *Native Son*. Wright described Bigger as "vaguely a Negro nationalist." During the years Wright spent in France, from 1947 to his death in 1960, he spent much of his time supporting nationalist movements in Africa.

Wright wrote with a mixture of fearlessness and brilliance. He said he wanted to move black writing beyond the servile depiction of stereotyped "colored people." With *Native Son* he accomplished that while at the same time showing how little black Americans and white Americans really knew about one another.

—*Michael R. Bradley*

FURTHER READING

Abcarian, Richard. *Richard Wright's "Native Son": A Critical Handbook*. Belmont, Calif.: Wadsworth, 1970. Collection of reviews, critical essays, and chapters on topics related to *Native Son*. Insights presented are informed by the context of the book's publication in the aftermath of the racial unrest of the 1960's.

Bone, Robert. *Richard Wright*. Minneapolis: University of Minnesota Press, 1969. Brief sketch of Wright's life provides a good source of information on the author for general readers. Includes some analysis of his work.

Butler, Robert J., ed. *The Critical Response to Richard Wright*. Westport, Conn.: Greenwood Press, 1995. Collection of critical essays discussing *Native Son*, *Black Boy*, and two other major Wright works. Includes commentary by the editor on how critical responses to Wright have changed in the years since *Native Son* was first published.

Fabre, Michael. *The World of Richard Wright*. Jackson: University of Mississippi Press, 1985. Collection of essays written over a period of twenty years by one of Wright's most prominent biographers. Considers many aspects of Wright's art and interests.

Felgar, Robert. *Richard Wright*. Boston: Twayne, 1980. Brief biography focuses on the facts of Wright's life and devotes little discussion to critical analysis of his work.

Gayle, Addison. *Richard Wright: Ordeal of a Native Son*. Gloucester, Mass.: Peter Smith, 1983. Biography presents an informative account of Wright's life, especially his years in France. Examines the issue of whether or not Wright was the target of special scrutiny by the U.S. government.

Hakutani, Yoshinobu, ed. *Critical Essays on Richard Wright*. Boston: G. K. Hall, 1982. Collection of essays on Wright's work by various writers and critics includes important essays by James Baldwin and Irving Howe.

Rowley, Hazel. *Richard Wright: The Life and Times*. New York: Henry Holt, 2001. Comprehensive, indepth biography places Wright's work in the larger context of American society and the era in which he wrote.

SEE ALSO: 1910-1930: Great Northern Migration; 1920's: Harlem Renaissance; 1926-1927: Mail-Order Clubs Revolutionize Book Sales; Oct. 7, 1929: *The Sound and the Fury* Launches Faulkner's Career.

1940-1941
MOORE'S SUBWAY SKETCHES RECORD WAR IMAGES

Sculptor Henry Moore accepted a wartime assignment to make a series of sketches as a record of England at war after he was inspired by the huddled shapes of Londoners using subway stations as air-raid shelters.

LOCALE: London, England
CATEGORY: Arts

KEY FIGURES
Henry Moore (1898-1986), English artist
Kenneth Clark (1903-1983), retired director of the
　　London Museum and chairman of the War Artists'
　　Advisory Committee
Herbert Read (1893-1968), English art historian and
　　author

SUMMARY OF EVENT
Henry Moore first became known as a sculptor of some repute in 1928. He usually is identified as the sculptor of massive stone architectural or landscape figures, of more or less human shape, perforated in their centers and with heads that are often mere protuberances.

Moore's travel in France and Italy in 1925 was a strong catalyst for his art. His *Mother and Child* (1924-1925) shows the influence of Masaccio and a remarkable boldness and austere strength. His cubist works from this period manifest the influence of monumental Mexican Chac Mool statues. Moore's *Seated Woman* (1928), the culmination of his early drawings from life, was the first piece that forecast his lifelong sculptural style. Moore's first major commission was the monumental relief *North Wind* (1928-1929) on the headquarters of the London Transport Board. The first of Moore's characteristic reclining figures, that in Leeds, England, was done in 1929.

The years from 1929 to 1939 represent Moore's experimental period. Stephen Spender, a poet and friend of Moore, wrote about the prewar meetings of friends at Henry and Irina Moore's studio, where discussions ranged over such topics as abstract art, representationalism, Surrealism, and functionalism. Writing about Moore's drawings, art historian Kenneth Clark noted that in the period 1932 to 1934 the sketches of reclining figures and mother-and-child groups show Moore moving in the direction of more abstract human shapes and the use of holes. The Moores moved to a new home in Kingston in 1934. It had a field that fulfilled Moore's ideal setting for sculpture as a "monumental art standing freely on the ground, under the sky."

The world of Henry Moore, like that of all Europeans, came apart in 1939 with the intrusion of World War II. The Chelsea School of Art, where Moore taught, was evacuated from London, and Moore became essentially an unemployed artist. His successive studios were destroyed by bombs. *Recumbent Figure* (1938) was Moore's last large piece before the interruption of war. His next major sculpture would be the Northampton *Madonna and Child* in 1943.

From 1939 to 1943, Moore primarily recorded ideas in notebooks. His drawings, however, were not insignificant, and many later bore sculptural fruit. Clark called *Two Women: Drawing for Sculpture Combining Wood and Metal* (1939) one of Moore's greatest drawings, the colors adding drama and creating space. Similarly, Moore's 1939 lithograph *Spanish Prisoner* first articulated Moore's interest in the perceptual relationship between internal and external form. From this piece evolved his helmet-head sculptures (1939-1940 and early 1950's).

A drawing of 1940 titled *September 3, 1939*, ominously depicted a group of women bathing near Dover, gazing seaward toward France. In the same year came a series of sketches of upright oval "cocoons" within which are inserted abstract "embryos." These were realized in wood as *Internal and External Forms* (1953-1954). Moore referred to them as "a mother and child idea, something young and growing being protected by a shell."

The *Shelter Drawings* of 1940-1941 are without doubt Moore's most famous. According to art historian Herbert Read, Moore's drawings can be placed in two categories: those made as rehearsal of ideas for sculpture, including the life drawings of his student days, and drawings done for their own sake, both actual scenes (*Shelter Drawings*) and imaginary scenes such as his most famous drawing, *Crowd Looking at a Tied-Up Object* (1942).

The Nazi bombing of London began in earnest in September of 1940 and ended in May of 1941. When Moore and his wife were confined in the subway during an air raid, Moore got his first sight of people lying in an underground station with their blankets, pillows, and necessities. He later recalled, "I had never seen so many reclining figures. Even the train tunnels seemed like holes in my sculpture!" When Kenneth Clark, chairman of the newly formed War Artists' Advisory Committee, saw Moore's sketches of that experience, he persuaded the sculptor to accept a commission.

The project had its problems. Rather than intrude on

1940

3233

what was left of the privacy of the shelterers, Moore made only quick sketches accompanied by mnemonic notes. He then worked from memory at his Parkhill Road studio and later, after his studio was bombed, at his house at Much Hadham, outside London.

Some of the figures he sketched are seated on benches; some sketches are street scenes of buildings collapsing, such as *Head Made Up of Devastated Buildings* and *Morning After the Blitz*. The series includes the well-known *Sleeping Child Covered with Blanket* and *Pink and Green Sleepers*, which Moore's friend Stephen Spender favored as Moore's most famous shelter drawing.

Given Moore's penchant for reclining figures, the sight of the huddled and sleeping denizens of the London tube was for him a moving revelation of meaning: the reclining figure as a suffering human being. The drawing *Tube Shelter Perspective* depicts long rows of figures reclining along the receding length of a subway tunnel.

For many, the *Shelter Drawings* appear to be impressionistic studies. Eric Newton, a critic for the London *Sunday Times*, wrote of "Moore's unearthly studies of a white, grub-like race of troglodytes swathed in protective blankets in underground shelters." Moore himself saw them as poetic symbols of the Blitz, comparing them to "the bowels of slave ships from Africa." Read observed Moore's ability to capture the fear, boredom, and protective love expressed in the bodily attitudes of the people. Clark noted that "the stoicism and dignity of the shelterers" inspired several classical renderings, such as the *Two Seated Figures*, which are "like late Roman patricians, awaiting the coming of the barbarians."

As one might expect, in Moore's drawings the human body is given sculptural weight and substance, as if occupying three-dimensional space. When, well after the last air raid in May of 1941, Moore revised his exactly recorded drawings into more imaginative finished forms, the results were drawings of monumental power and among the finest graphic works of his career. Moore filled two sketchbooks with groups. Clark later described these sketches as "among the most precious works of art" of the twentieth century.

SIGNIFICANCE

Wishing to keep Moore under contract, the War Artists' Advisory Committee offered him several unappealing projects. Moore was a son of miners and farmers. When, in 1941, Herbert Read suggested that he make a series of drawings of miners, both Moore and the committee were amenable. Moore decided to work in the Wheldale colliery in his hometown of Castleford, the very mines in

which his father had worked. He thus had a great sympathy for the project. In every sense, Moore's *Studies of Miners at Work* was a direct result of his work in the subway shelters. To him, the mines resembled the tube tunnels and the miners recalled the shelter figures "imprisoned in claustrophobic space." This time the drawings were made on the spot, with the coal dust and dimly lit atmosphere producing certain distorting and tenebrist effects that were compatible with the mind of the artist.

When Moore arrived in Castleford, he was given a tour of the tunnels that verified his early memory of the harshness of life and work in the mines. He later recorded his profound impressions of crawling on hands and knees deep into the mine, in "a dense darkness you could touch," the thick coal dust impervious to miners' lamps, under "a mile's weight of rock."

For a week at a time, Moore made sketches by day and refined them in the evening. Finally, his on-site notebook sketches became two sketchbooks and twenty finished drawings in crayon, chalk, watercolor, and india ink. Although Moore was not as emotionally moved by the miners as he had been by the shelterers, his drawings are powerful. Some imbue the miners with an idealized dignity. Moore's studies of miners working on their backs provided him with a rich variety of new ideas for his famous reclining figure sculptures, in particular his *Falling Warrior* (1956-1957) and his *King and Queen* (1952-1953).

Moore was glad to see the end of the miners project in 1942, because it allowed him to return to his first love, sculpture. Although the *Shelter Drawings* were intended as documents of the war and not as studies for generating ideas for sculpture, they nevertheless inspired, by their humanizing force, other drawings of groups of draped figures, often with resultant statues. Moore's work in the 1940's seemed preoccupied with an almost classical concern for human destiny. His drawing *Women Winding Wool* suggests the Three Fates; *Group of Draped Standing Figures* (1942) seems to depict characters in a Greek drama, as does *Crowd Looking at a Tied-Up Object*. His drawing *Three Standing Figures* (1947-1948) grew into the stone ladies of Battersea Park, London.

The shelter studies promoted Moore's international fame. Many of them were among the drawings that, with one reclining figure sculpture, composed Moore's first-ever exhibit in the United States, in May of 1943, at Curt Valentin's Buchholz Gallery in New York City. Valentin, who purchased all the pieces himself, disseminated many of them at a profit to major museums such as New York's Museum of Modern Art and Chicago's Art

Institute. The exhibit also traveled to Los Angeles.

Moore's commission to make *Madonna and Child* (1943) for the fiftieth anniversary of St. Matthew's Church in Northampton also resulted from the *Shelter Drawings*. Seeking to make the anniversary a magnificent artistic occasion, Walter Hussey, the vicar, commissioned a Benjamin Britten cantata. Hussey was impressed with Moore's work in the war artists' exhibit in London's National Gallery in 1942 and urged the hesitant sculptor to accept the commission. The public reaction to the finished work was either love or hate—nothing in between. Moore became notorious as thousands visited the church just to see what the fuss was all about. Some years later, *Madonna and Child* ceased to raise eyebrows and came to be considered one of Moore's more realistic sculptures.

It is possible to find unarguable echoes of the *Shelter Drawings* in Moore's subsequent output. The year 1950 saw *Helmet Heads No. 1* in lead and bronze and his abstract *Double Standing Figure* for Vassar College (for which Moore made pages of studies in 1948). His bronze *Draped Reclining Figure* and an abstract stone screen adorned the Time-Life Building in London (1952), his *Warrior with Shield* (1953-1954) resides in Toronto, the United Nations Educational, Scientific, and Cultural Organization (UNESCO) Building in Paris commissioned *Reclining Figure* (1957-1958), and in 1961 the St. Louis, Missouri, airport purchased two bronze figures.

In choosing for his archetypal models the imposing sculptural creations of ancient Egypt and Mexico, Moore asserted his ties to tradition. Although Moore showed his work in Surrealist exhibitions (1933-1939) with Alberto Giacometti, Jean Arp, and Joan Miró, he nevertheless felt apart from that school. He saw roles for both the unconscious, emphasized by the Surrealists, and the conscious. As he explained to Spender, however hard he tried to produce a nonrepresentational piece, even his most abstract work seemed like something real.

Three criteria can be used to judge the greatness of an artist: prolific output, absolute mastery of a medium, and universal representativeness of the art, with relevance for later ages. All three apply to Moore. Moore is representative of the artistic tradition of Western civilization. His work recalls the great art and artists of the past but was modern in its day. In view of his expanding power and clarity of purpose through the years, Moore will doubtless become a model and point of departure for artists of the future.

—*Daniel C. Scavone*

FURTHER READING

Andrews, Julian. *London's War: The "Shelter Drawings" of Henry Moore*. Burlington, Vt.: Lund Humphries, 2002. Presents the *Shelter Drawings* along with explanations and commentary. Includes comparisons of some drawings to photographs of the locations.

Berthoud, Roger. *The Life of Henry Moore*. 2d rev. ed. London: Giles de la Mare, 2003. Comprehensive biography is filled with detailed anecdotes that intimately present the mind and heart of Henry Moore. Includes many black-and-white illustrations.

FitzGibbon, Constantine. *The Winter of the Bombs*. New York: W. W. Norton, 1958. Vivid description of the Nazi Blitz of London provides excellent background on the context in which Moore produced his *Shelter Drawings*.

Lichtenstern, Christa. "Henry Moore and Surrealism." Translated by Sally Arnold-Seibert. *Burlington Magazine* 113 (November, 1981): 645-658. Intends to demonstrate through a few examples that Surrealist impulses shaped Moore's art, particularly from 1930 to 1940 and to a certain extent throughout his career.

Moore, Henry. *Henry Moore Drawings*. New York: Harper & Row, 1974. Survey of the development of Moore's art presents a study of the relationship between his drawings and his sculpture. Copiously illustrated with 304 plates of Moore's graphic art, 40 in color.

_____. *Shelter Sketch Book*. London: Editions Poetry London, 1940. Small volume reproduces beautifully the *Shelter Drawings* on eighty-one leaves, in their original colors. Contains no text.

Read, Herbert. *Henry Moore: A Study of His Life and Work*. New York: Praeger, 1965. Authoritative biography and critique of Moore's work by a great art historian and friend of the artist. Illustrated with 245 photographs of Moore's art.

Spender, Stephen. "Realism's Blitz." *Art and Antiques* 9 (January, 1992): 75-77, 97-98. Interesting personal recollection, by a close friend of Moore, of times spent together with other friends and artistic discussions that took place in the decade before World War II.

SEE ALSO: Oct., 1924: Surrealism Is Born; Sept. 1, 1939: Germany Invades Poland; July 10-Oct. 31, 1940: Battle of Britain.

1940

April-May, 1940
SOVIETS MASSACRE POLISH PRISONERS OF WAR

When the Soviets executed more than four thousand Polish prisoners of war in the Katyn Forest in the early spring of 1940, German propagandists attempted to use the event to influence public opinion in Poland and to split the Allied cause.

LOCALE: Katyn Forest, near Smolensk, Soviet Union (now Russia)

CATEGORIES: Atrocities and war crimes; human rights; World War II; wars, uprisings, and civil unrest

KEY FIGURES

Winston Churchill (1874-1965), prime minister of Great Britain, 1940-1945 and 1951-1955

Franklin D. Roosevelt (1882-1945), president of the United States, 1933-1945

Joseph Stalin (Joseph Vissarionovich Dzhugashvili; 1878-1953), first secretary of the Communist Party of the Soviet Union, 1922-1953

Joseph Goebbels (1897-1945), minister of propaganda for Nazi Germany

SUMMARY OF EVENT

On August 23, 1939, the Soviet Union and Nazi Germany signed an agreement that set the stage for the outbreak of World War II in Europe. The agreement, in part, provided the basis for the dismemberment of Poland. Shortly thereafter, on September 1, 1939, German armed forces attacked Poland, and on September 17, the Soviet army moved into eastern Poland and occupied its assigned portion of Polish territory. Under the weight of the German onslaught and the Soviet invasion, Polish resistance collapsed, and the remnants of Poland's government fled the country.

Immediately after the termination of hostilities in Soviet-occupied Poland, Soviet authorities began the forced deportation of approximately 1.2 million Poles to areas within the Soviet Union. In addition, the Soviets captured more than 200,000 members of the Polish armed forces. These prisoners were joined by thousands of Polish reservists arrested at home as well as by soldiers who had initially escaped to Lithuania and Estonia only to be taken by the Soviets after the Baltic states fell under Soviet control. In the final count, approximately 250,000 members of the Polish armed forces, including about 10,000 officers, were placed in more than one hundred major Soviet prison and labor camps.

The international situation changed dramatically on June 22, 1941, when Germany launched a surprise attack on the Soviet Union. Soon thereafter, the Soviets and the Polish government in exile, located in London, reestablished diplomatic relations and agreed that the Soviets would grant amnesty to those Poles being held in the Soviet Union. Simultaneously, the new Polish embassy in the Soviet Union took steps to organize a Polish army on Soviet soil composed of those members of the Polish armed forces who were being held as prisoners of war by the Soviets.

Eventually, after these former prisoners had been assembled by the new Polish military command in the Soviet Union, it became clear that approximately 15,000 soldiers remained missing, including some 8,000 officers. Moreover, it was not just professional officers who were missing: Hundreds of reservists, including doctors, lawyers, educators, and journalists, were also missing. Investigations by Polish authorities revealed that the missing individuals had been held at three camps: approximately 6,500 men at Ostashkov, 4,000 at Starobelsk, and 5,000 at Kozelsk. In late April and early May, 1940, troops from the Soviet Union's People's Commissariat of Internal Affairs, known as the NKVD (Narodnyi Komissariat Vnutrennikh Del), had removed in small groups all but 448 of the prisoners from the three camps. Investigations revealed that the men from Kozelsk had been taken by rail to a point immediately west of Smolensk, but there they had disappeared. Indeed, of the approximately 15,000 men originally held in these three camps, only the 448 survived. Polish requests for information concerning the missing soldiers were addressed to Soviet officials but were met with evasive and contradictory responses. Nevertheless, between the summer of 1941 and the spring of 1943, the Poles continued to attempt to ascertain the fate of the missing soldiers.

Meanwhile, in late February, 1943, German field police discovered the mass graves of several thousand individuals, apparently Polish officers, in the Katyn Forest about ten miles west of Smolensk. Prior to the German capture of the area in 1941, the Katyn Forest had been controlled by the NKVD. This information was transmitted to Berlin, where Nazi officials recognized the propaganda value of this discovery and moved to capitalize on the opportunity. Consequently, on April 13, 1943, German radio announced that Soviet authorities had executed thousands of Polish prisoners of war. The Germans

Germans conduct exhumation of bodies from the mass graves found in the Katyn Forest.

quickly followed this announcement by inviting a series of specially chartered international groups to examine the site and report their conclusions.

Three investigatory commissions were formed under German sponsorship. First, an international commission was formed, drawing distinguished specialists in the field of forensic medicine from twelve European countries other than Nazi Germany. On April 28, 1943, the members of this commission began a three-day investigation of the grave sites in the Katyn Forest. While there, they examined 982 corpses already exhumed by German authorities and 9 that had been previously untouched and were randomly selected by the commission. During their investigation, the members of the group had complete freedom to move throughout the area and enjoyed the full cooperation of the Germans at the site. Simultaneously, the Germans invited a medical delegation from the Polish Red Cross in German-occupied Poland to conduct a second investigation in the Katyn Forest. Without the knowledge of the German authorities, the Polish underground infiltrated the Polish Red Cross group. The Polish team remained at the site for five weeks, during which it, like the international commission, was given full German support as well as freedom of movement around the site, including authority to photograph whatever the team members wished. Finally, a specially formed German medical team was sent to Katyn. In addition to these three teams, journalists from Germany, German-

occupied Europe, and neutral European states visited the Katyn Forest, as did German-sponsored Polish and Allied prisoner-of-war delegations.

The German authorities, the various medical commissions, and the other visitors to the area found more than 4,000 corpses buried in eight mass graves that were six to eleven feet deep. In addition to the bodies actually found, some analysts have speculated that more than 300 more undiscovered Polish corpses may remain in the forest. In any case, all but 22 of the bodies found were clad in Polish uniforms and were piled face down in the graves in layers. Many, especially the younger men, had had their greatcoats tied over their heads with ropes connected tightly to their hands, which were tightly bound behind their backs. As a result, any movement of the hands would serve to tighten the ropes that secured the greatcoats at the neck. In addition, many bore bayonet wounds. All, however, had been shot through the head in a similar manner. Finally, the individual graves of two Polish general officers, in uniform, were also located in the forest.

Based on a variety of evidence collected at the site, the three German-sponsored commissions independently reached similar conclusions. They agreed that the Polish prisoners had been executed and buried about three years prior to their exhumation. In other words, they had been murdered in the spring of 1940. Given that this was more than a year prior to the German invasion of the Soviet Union in June, 1941, and given that the Katyn Forest was under the control of the NKVD at the time of the killings, the conclusion of the commissions was that Soviet authorities had killed the Polish prisoners. The conclusions of the three commissions were confirmed and further supplemented by additional evidence supplied by the families of the dead soldiers and by the survivors of Camp Kozelsk. This additional material clearly established that the Polish soldiers found in the forest were the missing prisoners from Camp Kozelsk. Finally, the fact that the Germans fully cooperated with the investigators at the Katyn Forest site and subsequently attempted to preserve the evidence of the atrocity suggested that the Nazis were not the murderers.

Meanwhile, the Soviet Union denied the German accusations and charged that the Nazis had themselves

1940

committed the crime. On April 15, 1943, two days after the initial German radio broadcast announcing the discovery of the mass graves, the Soviets stated that the Polish prisoners had been seized by invading Nazis during the summer of 1941 and, subsequently, the Nazis had executed them. After the capture of the Smolensk region, the Soviet authorities organized a special Soviet commission to investigate the Katyn Forest murders. The Soviet team was composed exclusively of Soviet medical experts; no international medical experts were asked to participate. Predictably, given the official title of the Soviet investigatory team, the "Special Commission for Ascertaining and Investigating the Circumstances of the Shooting of Polish Officer Prisoners by the German-Fascist Invaders in the Katyn Forest," the Soviet team concluded that the Germans had murdered the Poles between September and December of 1941. The Soviets claimed to have found nine documents on the bodies bearing dates after May, 1940. In view of the fact that most of the bodies had been previously and extremely carefully searched by the German-sponsored commissions, most observers discounted these so-called finds as fabrications.

Following World War II, the Katyn Forest atrocity was inconclusively examined at the Nuremberg Trials, and later, in considerable detail, in 1951-1952 by a committee of the U.S. House of Representatives. Notwithstanding continued Soviet denials of guilt and assertions that the Germans were responsible, virtually all analysts outside the Communist countries concluded that the Soviets had killed the Polish prisoners found in the Katyn Forest. Finally, in 1990, fifty years after committing the atrocity, the Soviets acknowledged that the NKVD had murdered the men.

Two questions remained, however, even after the establishment of Soviet guilt for the Katyn atrocity. First, what happened to the more than 10,000 Poles held at Camps Starobelsk and Ostashkov? Apparently these men were also killed by the NKVD, although their exact fate remained unclear. Second, why were 448 men from Kozelsk, Ostashkov, and Starobelsk allowed to live? It would seem that the NKVD selected those individuals who appeared to be pro-Communist, who were susceptible to Soviet propaganda, or who, by virtue of their backgrounds, were deemed worthy of selection for survival.

SIGNIFICANCE

Nazi propaganda minister Joseph Goebbels immediately recognized the significance of the Katyn Forest discovery and took special pains to make certain that Germany derived the fullest propaganda dividends from the Soviet atrocity. For example, the German-controlled media in Poland provided extensive coverage of the Katyn Forest investigations and argued that Jewish Bolshevism was responsible for the atrocity. The Poles were told that they must look to the Germans for protection against the ruthless Soviets. Moreover, the extensive daily coverage, extending from April 14 to August 4, 1943, coincided with the Nazi massacre of the Warsaw ghetto, which took place from mid-April to mid-May, 1943.

In addition to attempting to influence Polish public opinion, the Germans intended to use the atrocity to split the Allied cause. There, however, the Germans unwittingly assisted Moscow in the latter's policy objectives. Immediately following the German announcement of the discovery of the mass graves in the Katyn Forest, on April 15, 1943, the Polish government in exile in London decided to call on the International Red Cross to conduct a full investigation. The following day, the British press reported this decision. On April 17, a spokesperson for the Polish government in exile confirmed the decision, and, that same day, the Poles formally made their request to officials of the International Red Cross in Geneva, Switzerland. Meanwhile, in Berlin, acting on a British press story predicting the Polish request to the Red Cross, but prior to the formal request itself, Goebbels decided to embarrass the Poles by issuing a second German request to the International Red Cross to investigate the atrocity. The timing of the German request was designed to coincide with the Polish request, thereby making it appear that the London Poles and Berlin were acting in concert. The German request was thus handed to the representatives of the International Red Cross in Geneva less than one hour prior to the Polish appeal. For its part, the International Red Cross responded that it would conduct an investigation provided that the Soviet Union joined with the Poles and Germany in requesting such an investigation. The Soviet Union, of course, did not agree to join in the request.

The appearance of Polish-German cooperation in requesting the investigation provided Soviet leader Joseph Stalin with an opportunity to cut his ties with the London Poles in favor of his own Moscow-sponsored Union of Polish Patriots. Thus not only did the Soviets fail to request an investigation by the International Red Cross, but on April 19, 1943, the Soviet media also denounced members of the Polish government in exile for collusion with the Nazis in perpetuating the so-called Nazi-fabricated allegations that the Soviet Union was responsible for the Katyn atrocity. This theme was in turn repeated by the pro-Soviet media outside the Soviet Union. The free Polish media responded that the Polish government in exile was merely seeking answers to questions as to what had happened in Katyn Forest.

Nevertheless, on April 21, 1943, Stalin informed British prime minister Winston Churchill and U.S. president Franklin D. Roosevelt that the Soviets had decided to sever relations with the Polish government in exile in London. Churchill and Roosevelt responded by appealing to Stalin not to risk the unity of the Allies by breaking relations with the London Poles, and Churchill appealed to the Polish leaders in London to drop the entire matter. Notwithstanding British and American appeals, however, on April 26, 1943, the Soviets notified the Polish ambassador in Moscow of the Soviet government's decision to break relations with the Polish government in exile in London. Subsequently, despite the fact that the London Poles, under pressure from the British, withdrew their request to the International Red Cross for a neutral investigation the day after the severance of Soviet-Polish relations, the Soviet Union remained firm in its decision to break relations.

Clearly, Stalin had decided to use the Polish government in exile's response to the German announcement of the Katyn discovery as his excuse to dispose of the independent Polish authorities in London in favor of the Soviet-backed Poles. Indeed, the latter would ultimately serve as a central component in the satellite regime erected by the Soviet Union in postwar Poland. Thus the massacre of more than four thousand Polish prisoners of war by the Soviet NKVD in the Katyn Forest and the disappearance and presumed execution of another ten thousand Polish prisoners not only deprived Poland of a significant element of the prewar Polish elite but also ultimately was used to advance Soviet objectives in postwar Eastern Europe.

—*Howard M. Hensel*

FURTHER READING

Abarinov, Vladimir. *The Murderers of Katyn*. New York: Hippocrene Books, 1993. Account by a Soviet journalist is one of the most in-depth discussions of the massacre available.

Lauck, John H. *Katyn Killings: In the Record*. Clifton, N.J.: Kingston Press, 1988. Comprehensive overview of the events leading up to the massacre and the various investigations that followed, especially the hearings of the select committee of the U.S. House of Representatives.

Mackiewicz, Jozef. *The Katyn Wood Murders*. London: World Affairs Book Club, 1951. Early examination of the atrocity is presented in a somewhat personalized manner.

Paul, Allen. *Katyn: The Untold Story of Stalin's Polish Massacre*. New York: Scribner, 1991. Presents vivid forensic details in recounting the 1940 Katyn Forest massacre and its precursors. Includes illustrations.

Sanford, George. *Katyn and the Soviet Massacre of 1940: Truth, Justice, and Memory*. New York: Routledge, 2005. Detailed study draws on Soviet documentation released in the 1990's to examine the factors that led to the Soviets' use of mass murder in the Katyn Forest.

Tucker, Robert C. *Stalin in Power: The Revolution from Above, 1928-1941*. New York: W. W. Norton, 1990. Informative work offers insight into Stalin and his regime. Includes brief but significant discussion of the Katyn Forest massacre.

Zawodny, J. K. *Death in the Forest: The Story of the Katyn Forest Massacre*. 1962. Reprint. New York: Hippocrene Books, 1988. Readable account provides a detailed and balanced examination of the Katyn Forest massacre and its implications.

SEE ALSO: Apr. 13, 1919: British Soldiers Massacre Indians at Amritsar; Jan.-Feb., 1932: El Salvador's Military Massacres Civilians; Aug. 11-13, 1933: Iraqi Army Slaughters Assyrian Christians; Summer, 1939: Stalin Suppresses the Russian Orthodox Church; Aug. 23-24, 1939: Nazi-Soviet Pact; Sept. 1, 1939: Germany Invades Poland; Dec., 1940: Koestler Examines the Dark Side of Communism.

1940

April 9, 1940
GERMANY INVADES NORWAY

The German invasion of Norway began with a successful surprise attack by land, sea, and air and challenged the traditional dominance of British sea power in Europe. It secured valuable resources for Germany for the remainder of the war, but at the expense of committing the Germans to maintaining an occupation force of 300,000 troops that would come to be needed elsewhere.

LOCALE: Norway

CATEGORIES: Wars, uprisings, and civil unrest; World War II; colonialism and occupation

KEY FIGURES

Adolf Hitler (1889-1945), German dictator, 1933-1945

Vidkun Quisling (1887-1945),
    Norwegian politician

Winston Churchill (1874-1965), first
    lord of the British Admiralty,
    1939-1940, and later prime
    minister, 1940-1945, 1951-1955

Otto Ruge (1882-1961), Norwegian
    army commander

Nikolaus von Falkenhorst (1885-
    1968), commander of German
    infantry and later governor-
    general of Norway, 1940-1944

Haakon VII (1872-1957), king of
    Norway, r. 1905-1957

Carl Joachim Hambro (1885-1964),
    president of the Norwegian
    Storting

Neville Chamberlain (1869-1940),
    prime minister of Great Britain,
    1937-1940

SUMMARY OF EVENT

Soon after the outbreak of World War II, Grand Admiral Erich Raeder, commander in chief of the German navy, drew Adolf Hitler's attention to the importance of Norway's coast for Germany's submarines, surface raiders, and blockade runners. He emphasized that an Allied capture of the ice-free port of Narvik in northern Norway would prevent Germany from importing vital Swedish iron ore. Hit-

ler did not show much interest in Scandinavia until he received reports that Britain was in fact considering a descent on Norway, spurred on by Winston Churchill, the first lord of the Admiralty. The Russo-Finnish War, which began on November 30, 1939, also prompted Allied agitation for sending troops to Finland via Narvik and northern Sweden.

On December 10, 1939, Vidkun Quisling, a Norwegian nationalist with Nazi sympathies, came to Berlin to propose to Hitler a Norwegian coup d'état to forestall the British, and Hitler appointed a staff to study ways of intervening. When Churchill, on February 16, 1940, sent the destroyer *Cossack* into Norwegian territorial waters to rescue British prisoners from the supply ship *Altmark*,

German soldiers make their way up a snowy slope during the invasion of Norway. (NARA)

Hitler accelerated preparations for a German invasion, code-named Operation Weserubung (exercise on the Weser). A British cabinet decision on March 12 for landing troops at Narvik was reversed that same day by the end of the Russo-Finnish War, but Hitler decided not to risk further delay. Britain started mining Norway's shipping channels on April 8, but by then German invasion forces were on their way—most of the navy, twelve hundred aircraft, and the vanguard of six reinforced army divisions under the capable command of General Nikolaus von Falkenhorst—moving toward an April 9 surprise dawn attack on Denmark and Norway.

Thus the Norwegian cabinet, after discussing British minelaying into the evening of April 8, had to reconvene in the early hours of April 9 to face reports of an approaching German threat. Norwegian mobilization orders were delayed and muddled. The army, short on rifles, artillery, and ammunition and without tanks, was also between drafts, with almost no men in barracks. Norway's planes were obsolete, and most of the navy's ships were museum pieces. Soldiers and civilians alike were surprised and confused, and the unexpected German dawn attack quickly seized most of its objectives—seaports and air fields at Narvik, Trondheim, Bergen, Stavanger, and Kristiansand.

The most important opposition occurred at the narrows of the Oslofjord, where the fortress at Oskarsborg sank a German heavy cruiser (*Blucher*), damaged a pocket battleship (*Lutzow*), and delayed the invasion flotilla by more than twelve hours. This enabled King Haakon VII, the cabinet, and the Storting (parliament) to escape the German plan for their capture, taking a special train north at 7:23 A.M., followed by commandeered trucks carrying the nation's gold reserves. Six German airborne companies seized Fornebu airport on the morning of April 9 and occupied Oslo that afternoon, followed the next day by reinforcements from Falken-

horst's main army. The seizure of Oslo had the effect of isolating Norwegian troops in Ostfold, southern Norway, and Telemark from the Norwegian forces retreating northward.

On the evening of April 9, Storting president Carl Joachim Hambro persuaded that assembly to grant full emergency powers to the king and cabinet for the duration of the war. Ongoing attempts to capture the king or persuade him to name Nazi puppet Quisling prime minister failed, as did an air raid intended to kill the Norwegian leaders. By evening on April 9, however, the Germans held all the main ports and airfields, and by April 10 strong squadrons of fighters and bombers were already operating from them. The new commander in chief of Norway's army, Otto Ruge, retreating northward, relied chiefly on help from Britain, whose Prime Minister Neville Chamberlain assured him, "We are coming as soon as possible, and in great strength."

Indeed, on the morning of April 9, the British Home Fleet under Admiral Sir Charles Forbes was in a position to sail into Bergen after the Germans with a far superior naval force. Strong German air attacks on his fleet that afternoon, however, persuaded Forbes to abandon his planned attack. A British cabinet project for a naval attack on Trondheim was also canceled because of the threat of German air power. Instead, from April 14-17, Britain landed an Allied expedition in the region of Narvik and sent smaller contingents to the west coast ports of Andalsnes and Namsos in the hope of converging on Trondheim and linking up with Norwegians in the Gudbrandsdal. The Allied soldiers arrived too late, however, and were too few in number. Without armored vehicles, field artillery, or effective aircraft, the British were no match for the well-equipped and fast-moving Germans. Defeated in the Gudbrandsdal and Trondheim areas, the Allies on May 28 drove the isolated German garrison out of the port of Narvik, but by then defeat in France forced the Allies to abandon Norway. The Allied evacuation of June 5-8 carried the Norwegian king and political leaders to England as a government in exile, while General Ruge remained behind to surrender his troops on June 10.

SIGNIFICANCE

In the Norway campaign, the Germans had and employed superior forces, took the offensive, and achieved surprise. The Luftwaffe (German air force) outmatched British naval power in ways that seemed to threaten the security of Britain itself. The Norway invasion also marked the first major combined operation of the three service branches, demonstrating the necessity for cooperation among air, land, and sea forces in future campaigns. Allied weaponry and methods were exposed in Norway as outmoded, and the Allied intelligence system ineffective.

The German capture of Norway had wartime consequences for both sides. Germany gained secure access to Sweden's iron ore, Trondheim became an important German submarine base, and other air and naval bases in the far north were used for attacks on Allied ship convoys to Russia between 1941 and 1945. Britain, although beaten in the struggle for Norway, avoided significant losses while inflicting enough damage on the German navy to reduce its importance during the 1940 Battle of Britain. Another significant benefit for Great Britain was the fall of Chamberlain's ineffectual administration, and its replacement by the national coalition government headed by Churchill.

The Norwegian population of less than three million could not be a major factor in the war, but their large merchant marine helped the Allies, and their example of continuing underground resistance was a moral asset and also tied down 300,000 German occupation troops until 1945, preventing those troops from participating on the fronts of the European theater. At the end of the war, King Haakon VII and the government returned to Oslo, Falkenhorst and Raeder went on trial as war criminals, and Vidkun Quisling was convicted of treason and shot.

—*Samuel K. Eddy and K. Fred Gillum*

FURTHER READING

Churchill, Winston S. *The Gathering Storm.* Vol. 1 in *The Second World War.* London: Cassell, 1948. An indispensable account of the author's role.

Derry, T. K. *The Campaign in Norway.* London: Her Majesty's Stationery Office, 1952. The official history of British army operations.

Gray, Edwyn. *Hitler's Battleships.* London: Leo Cooper, 1992. Includes an account of German landing operations taken largely from Walther Hubatsch's untranslated history of the 1940 Scandinavian wars.

Høiback, Harald. *Command and Control in Military Crisis: Devious Decisions.* Portland, Oreg.: F. Cass, 2003. Case studies comparing the command and control systems employed in Norway in 1940 with those on the western front in World War I. Bibliographic references and index.

Kersaudy, François. *Norway, 1940.* New York: St. Martin's Press, 1991. Brief, balanced, broadly researched account that is also well translated. Includes the clearest account of Norwegian operations so far available in English.

Kynoch, Joseph. *Norway, 1940: The Forgotten Fiasco.* Shrewsbury, Shropshire, England: Airlife, 2002. Personal account of a British soldier's experiences in the Norwegian invasion. Bibliographic references and index.

Moulton, J. L. *The Norwegian Campaign of 1940: A Study of Warfare in Three Dimensions.* London: Eyre and Spottiswode, 1966. Analytic critique of the British campaign, with a few references to German and Norwegian sources.

Ruge, Friedrich. *Der Seekrieg*. Annapolis, Md.: U.S. Naval Institute, 1957. Chapter 5 gives a decidedly German perspective on the campaign.

SEE ALSO: 1929-1940: Maginot Line Is Built; Mar. 7, 1936: German Troops March into the Rhineland; Feb. 12-Apr. 10, 1938: The Anschluss; Sept. 29-30, 1938: Munich Conference; Nov. 9-10, 1938: Kristallnacht; Sept. 1, 1939: Germany Invades Poland; 1940-1941: Moore's Subway Sketches Record War Images; May 10-June 22, 1940: Collapse of France; May 26-June 4, 1940: Evacuation of Dunkirk; July 10-Oct. 31, 1940: Battle of Britain.

May, 1940
FLOREY AND CHAIN DEVELOP PENICILLIN AS AN ANTIBIOTIC

Baron Florey and Ernst Boris Chain concentrated and clinically tested penicillin, the first successful and widely used antibiotic drug.

LOCALE: Oxford, England
CATEGORY: Health and medicine

KEY FIGURES
Baron Florey (1898-1968), Australian pathologist
Ernst Boris Chain (1906-1979), British biochemist
Alexander Fleming (1881-1955), Scottish
    bacteriologist

SUMMARY OF EVENT

During the early twentieth century, scientists were aware of antibacterial substances but did not know how to make full use of them in the treatment of diseases. Sir Alexander Fleming discovered penicillin in 1928, but he was unable to duplicate his laboratory results of its antibiotic properties in clinical tests. As a result, he did not recognize the medical potential of penicillin.

Between 1935 and 1940, penicillin was purified, concentrated, and clinically tested by pathologist Baron Florey, biochemist Ernst Boris Chain, and members of their Oxford research group. Their achievement has since been regarded as one of the greatest medical discoveries of the twentieth century. Florey was a professor at Oxford University in charge of the Sir William Dunn School of Pathology. Chain had worked for two years at Cambridge University in the laboratory of Frederick Hopkins, an eminent chemist and discoverer of vitamins. Hopkins recommended Chain to Florey, who was searching for a candidate to lead a new biochemical unit in the Dunn School of Pathology.

In 1938, Florey and Chain formed a research group to investigate the phenomenon of antibiosis, or the antagonistic association between different forms of life. The union of Florey's medical knowledge and Chain's biochemical expertise proved to be an ideal combination for exploring the antibiosis potential of penicillin. Florey and Chain began their investigation with a literature search in which Chain came across Fleming's work and added penicillin to their list of potential antibiotics.

Their first task was to isolate pure penicillin from a crude liquid extract. A culture of Fleming's original *Penicillium notatum* was maintained at Oxford and was used by the Oxford group for penicillin production. Extracting large quantities of penicillin from the medium was a painstaking task, as the solution contained only one part of the antibiotic in ten million. When enough of the raw juice was collected, the Oxford group focused on eliminating impurities and concentrating the penicillin. The concentrated liquid was then freeze-dried, leaving a soluble brown powder.

In May, 1940, Florey's clinical tests of the crude penicillin proved its value as an antibiotic. Following extensive controlled experiments with mice, the Oxford group concluded that they had discovered an antibiotic that was nontoxic and far more effective against pathogenic bacteria than any of the known sulfa drugs. Furthermore, penicillin was not inactivated after injection into the bloodstream but was excreted unchanged in the urine. Continued tests showed that penicillin did not interfere with white blood cells and had no adverse effect on living cells. Bacteria susceptible to the antibiotic included those responsible for gas gangrene, pneumonia, meningitis, diphtheria, and gonorrhea. American researchers later proved that penicillin was also effective against syphilis.

In January, 1941, Florey injected a volunteer with penicillin and found that there were no side effects to treatment with the antibiotic. In February, the group began treatment of Albert Alexander, a forty-three-year-old policeman with a serious staphylococci and streptococci infection that was resisting massive doses of sulfa drugs. Alexander had been hospitalized for two months after an infection in the corner of his mouth had spread to

1940

his face, shoulder, and lungs. After receiving an injection of 200 milligrams of penicillin, Alexander showed remarkable progress, and for the next ten days his condition improved. Unfortunately, the Oxford production facility was unable to generate enough penicillin to overcome Alexander's advanced infection completely, and he died on March 15.

A later case involving a fourteen-year-old boy with staphylococcal septicemia and osteomyelitis had a more spectacular result: The patient made a complete recovery in two months. In all the early clinical treatments, patients showed vast improvement, and most recovered completely from infections that resisted all other treatment.

TEAM "WONDER DRUG"

Penicillin was a bacteriological curiosity when Sir Alexander Fleming isolated it in 1928—at best a possible local antiseptic. No one realized that this chemical would become a potent, systemic antibacterial "wonder drug."

It would be more than a decade before the monumental applications of penicillin were investigated by Baron Florey and Ernest Chain, marked by the exciting observation that its injection into mice killed disease-causing staphylcocci and gangrene-causing bacteria. In these experiments, all the untreated mice injected with the disease bacteria died, whereas virtually all the penicillin-treated animals survived. Florey began to direct the great scientific resources of Oxford's School of Pathology toward full-scale study of the drug. By virtue of much work, carried out by numerous gifted Oxford scientists, the basic project proceeded quickly. First, the wide range of microbes killed by penicillin was identified. Then the pharmacology and the toxicology of the drug were delineated in animals and in humans.

A major initial stumbling block to human studies was the fact that successful treatment of a single human being required administration of the entire "yield" of penicillin, isolated from hundreds of gallons of culture medium. The efforts of another of Florey's colleagues, Norman Heatley, led to development of the laboratory equipment that allowed the production of enough penicillin for wider human testing. Production of penicillin was soon increased enough to allow successful treatment of ten cases of human bacterial infection.

Exciting though this was, Britain—in the throes of World War II—did not have the resources to produce enough penicillin for widespread use. Therefore, Florey traveled to the United States and convinced the American Office of Scientific Research to fund the effort. Thanks to this massive American funding and the collaborative efforts by American industry, enough penicillin was produced to allow its widespread use in treatment of war casualties after the 1944 Normandy invasion. With large-scale production of penicillin now well in hand, Florey next identified the best methods for testing the efficacy of the drug and effecting the most appropriate ways to administer it to patients. In 1945, Florey, Chain, and Fleming shared the Nobel Prize in Physiology or Medicine "for the discovery of penicillin and its curative effect in various infectious diseases."

SIGNIFICANCE

Penicillin is among the greatest medical discoveries of the twentieth century. Florey and Chain's chemical and clinical research brought about a revolution in the treatment of infectious disease. Almost every organ in the body is vulnerable to bacteria. Before penicillin, the only antimicrobial drugs available were quinine, arsenic, and sulfa drugs. Of these, only the sulfa drugs were useful for treatment of bacterial infection, but their high toxicity often limited their use. With this small arsenal, doctors were helpless to treat thousands of patients with bacterial infections.

The work of Florey and Chain achieved particular attention because of World War II and the need for treatments of such scourges as gas gangrene, which had infected the wounds of numerous World War I soldiers. With the help of Florey and Chain's Oxford group, scientists at the U.S. Department of Agriculture's Northern Regional Research Laboratory developed a highly efficient method for producing penicillin using fermentation. After an extended search, scientists were also able to isolate a more productive penicillin strain, *Penicillium chrysogenum*. By 1945, a strain was developed that produced five hundred times more penicillin than Fleming's original mold had.

Penicillin, the first of the "wonder drugs," remains one of the most powerful antibiotics in existence. Diseases such as pneumonia, meningitis, and syphilis are still treated with penicillin. Penicillin and other antibiotics also had a broad impact on other fields of medicine, as major operations such as heart surgery, organ transplants, and management of severe burns became possible once the threat of bacterial infection was minimized.

Florey and Chain received numerous awards for their achievement, the greatest of which was the 1945 Nobel Prize in Physiology or Medicine, which they shared with Fleming for his original discovery. Florey was among the most effective medical scientists of his generation, and Chain earned simi-

THE ACTION OF ANTIBIOTICS

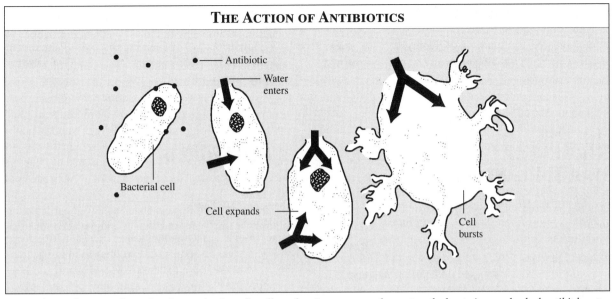

An antibiotic destroys a bacterium by causing its cell walls to deteriorate; water then enters the bacterium unchecked until it bursts.

lar accolades in the science of biochemistry. This combination of outstanding medical and chemical expertise made possible one of the greatest discoveries in human history.

—*Peter Neushul*

FURTHER READING

Bickel, Lennard. *Florey: The Man Who Made Penicillin.* Carlton South, Vic.: Melbourne University Press, 1995. Relates how the brilliant and ambitious Florey pursued the testing and production of penicillin. Places the work of Florey and Chain in the context of their times.

Clark, Ronald W. *The Life of Ernst Chain: Penicillin and Beyond.* New York: St. Martin's Press, 1985. Biography provides a complete examination of Chain's career, including four chapters on his penicillin work. Draws on Chain's papers, which are housed at the Contemporary Medical Archives Center of the Welcome Institute for the History of Medicine in London.

Hare, Ronald. *The Birth of Penicillin, and the Disarming of Microbes.* London: George Allen & Unwin, 1970. Excellent firsthand description of Alexander Fleming's early work with penicillin by an author who was among those who witnessed that work. A brief but very informative account of Fleming's work that provides the reader with a perspective on the state of penicillin research before Florey and Chain.

Hobby, Gladys L. *Penicillin: Meeting the Challenge.* New Haven, Conn.: Yale University Press, 1985. One of the best overall descriptions available of the roles played by Fleming, Florey, Chain, and numerous other scientists in the discovery, development, and eventual mass production of penicillin. Benefits from the author's extensive personal work with penicillin as a scientist employed by the Pfizer Corporation. Includes extensive footnotes.

Lax, Eric. *The Mold in Dr. Florey's Coat: The Story of the Penicillin Miracle.* New York: Henry Holt, 2004. Relates the story of the discovery of penicillin and its development into a useful drug. Sheds light on the personalities of the scientists involved. Includes bibliography and index.

Macfarlane, Gwyn. *Howard Florey: The Making of a Great Scientist.* Oxford, England: Oxford University Press, 1979. Excellent biography of Florey blends both personal and archival data. The author worked at Oxford and was an acquaintance of Florey's for twenty years. Makes extensive use of the Florey archives at the Royal Society.

Mateles, Richard I., ed. *Penicillin: A Paradigm for Biotechnology.* Chicago: Canadida Corporation, 1998. Volume reprints *The History of Penicillin Production,* a classic work first published in 1970, along with new chapters that address advances in penicillin research since that time. Also discusses the status of penicillin and its derivatives at the end of the twentieth century.

1940

Williams, Trevor I. *Howard Florey: Penicillin and After.* New York: Oxford University Press, 1985. A well-documented examination of Florey's entire scientific career, including both penicillin and his postwar work.

SEE ALSO: 1907: Plague Kills 1.2 Million in India; Apr., 1910: Ehrlich Introduces Salvarsan as a Cure for Syphilis; Sept., 1928: Fleming Discovers Penicillin in Molds; 1932-1935: Domagk Discovers That Sulfonamides Can Save Lives.

May, 1940

ROOSEVELT USES BUSINESS LEADERS FOR WORLD WAR II PLANNING

President Franklin D. Roosevelt's appointment of William Signius Knudsen of General Motors Corporation to take charge of the manufacturing aspect of military supply marked a turning point in U.S. military preparation and anticipated the later development of the military-industrial complex.

LOCALE: Washington, D.C.

CATEGORIES: World War II; wars, uprisings, and civil unrest; government and politics; manufacturing and industry

KEY FIGURES

Franklin D. Roosevelt (1882-1945), president of the United States, 1933-1945

William Signius Knudsen (1879-1948), president of General Motors Corporation

Louis A. Johnson (1891-1966), U.S. assistant secretary of war, 1937-1940, and secretary of defense, 1949-1950

Edward Reilly Stettinius, Jr. (1900-1949), chairman of the board of the United States Steel Corporation and chairman of the War Resources Board

Sidney Hillman (1887-1946), president of the Amalgamated Clothing Workers union and associate director-general of the Office of Production Management

Leon Henderson (1895-1986), administrator of the Office of Price Administration and Civilian Supply, 1941-1942

Donald Marr Nelson (1888-1959), former executive vice president of Sears, Roebuck and Company

James F. Byrnes (1879-1972), U.S. senator from South Carolina, 1931-1941, associate justice of the U.S. Supreme Court, 1941-1942, and head of the Office of Economic Stabilization, 1942-1943, and the Office of War Mobilization, 1943-1945

SUMMARY OF EVENT

Modern war involves the conflict of rival industrial complexes as much as it involves armed combat between opposing armies. The crux of the problem of industrial mobilization of the United States for World War II was how to supply the war materials required by U.S. and Allied military forces while meeting the needs of the country's civilian population. Complicating that task were three fundamental difficulties of war production. The first difficulty involved the technical and engineering problems of large-scale manufacture of new and complex military equipment that had to meet exacting specifications. The second was the shortage of many critical resources, given the magnitude of military demands. The third—which aggravated the other two—was the pressure to meet the goals of war production as rapidly as possible. Overcoming those difficulties required a degree of centralized control, or national planning, that was anathema to most Americans in peacetime. The exercise of such control was sensitive politically because decisions concerning industrial mobilization inevitably affected people's lives and interests.

During World War I, mobilization of the American economy took place through hasty improvisation rather than planning and preparation. Congress, in the National Defense Act of 1920, assigned to the assistant secretary of war responsibility for planning how to shift the economy from a peace to a war basis in a future emergency. The upshot was a series of industrial mobilization—or M-Day—plans by the War Department in the 1930's. Although the details varied, the keystone of those plans was the establishment of a new agency, referred to from 1936 on as the War Resources Administration, to assume control over the nation's resources so as to meet war production requirements.

In the aftermath of the triumph of German dictator Adolf Hitler in the Munich crisis in the fall of 1938, President Franklin D. Roosevelt moved to strengthen the

United States militarily to meet what he saw as the threat of German aggression in Europe and Japanese expansionism in the Far East. In the summer of 1939, Assistant Secretary of War Louis A. Johnson, a strong champion of preparedness, induced Roosevelt to allow him to appoint a National Resources Board. That board, made up of top business executives headed by Edward Reilly Stettinius, Jr., chairman of the United States Steel Corporation, reviewed the War Department's industrial mobilization plans. Johnson hoped that the National Resources Board would become the nucleus of the War Resources Administration envisaged by the War Department's M-Day plans. Roosevelt, however, shied away from a superagency to handle industrial mobilization as draining too much power from his office, and worse, transferring that power to businesspeople hostile to the New Deal. He thus ignored the board, refusing even to make public its recommendation for economic authority to be held by a single administrator in the event of war.

In the wake of the German Blitzkrieg (lightning war) that swept over Western Europe in the spring of 1940, Roosevelt successfully asked Congress for a special appropriation of $1.1 billion for rearmament and publicly called for the production of fifty thousand airplanes per year. In late May, 1940, he appointed, under a World War I congressional authorization, a seven-member Advisory Commission to the Council of National Defense (popularly known as the National Defense Advisory Commission, or NDAC). The NDAC represented a broader cross section of interests than the War Resources Board had and was firmly under Roosevelt's authority.

Stettinius was the NDAC commissioner for materials; Sidney Hillman, the president of the Amalgamated Clothing Workers union and a founder of the Congress of Industrial Organizations (CIO), was commissioner for employment; Chester C. Davis, a former administrator of the Agricultural Adjustment Administration, was commissioner for food products; Ralph Budd, president of the Association of American Railroads, was commissioner for transportation; Leon Henderson, a New Deal economist, was commissioner for price stabilization; and Harriet Elliott, dean of women at the University of North Carolina, was commissioner for consumer protection. In June, 1940, Donald Marr Nelson, former executive vice president of Sears, Roebuck and Company, was made a de facto NDAC member as coordinator of national defense purchases. The key member, however, and expected driving force of the NDAC was William Signius Knudsen, the commissioner for industrial production.

Born in Denmark in 1879, Knudsen immigrated to the United States in 1900 and worked for a bicycle manufacturer that turned to the manufacture of automobile parts. After the firm was purchased by the Ford Motor Company, Knudsen rose to production manager of the giant Ford plant at Highland Park, Michigan. While there, he made his mark applying and improving the techniques of mass production associated with the moving assembly line. After he was fired in 1921 by an increasingly erratic and eccentric Henry Ford, he became vice president in charge of operations and then president and general manager of the Chevrolet division of the General Motors Corporation (GM). By 1927, he had pushed Chevrolet ahead of Ford as the best-selling automobile brand.

Thanks to Knudsen's cost cutting through continuous improvement of the techniques of mass production, Chevrolet continued to show a profit even during the worst of the Great Depression. In 1933, Knudsen became executive vice president of General Motors in charge of all car, truck, and body operations in the United States and Canada. In 1937, he succeeded Alfred P. Sloan, Jr., as GM president. Knudsen was attractive to Roosevelt for many reasons. Although not a supporter of the New Deal, he was not identified with the more extreme antiadministration wing of the business community. His role in negotiations ending the 1937 sitdown strike at GM and opening the door for unionization of GM made him acceptable to organized labor. The German invasion of Denmark had made him strongly anti-Axis. Most important was his reputation as a production wizard.

Knudsen achieved no more than mixed results in his efforts during the summer and fall of 1940 to overcome bottlenecks in the production of such critical items as machine tools, airplane engines, and tanks. He was handicapped by his lack of experience in Washington politics and by the ramshackle administrative structure of the NDAC. The major problem was that the NDAC lacked the power to force manufacturers to switch to military production. Most personally embarrassing to Knudsen was continued noncompliance by the automobile industry.

By late 1940, complaints about the effectiveness of Knudsen's leadership were growing. Critics found him too willing to cater to the estimates of military needs of the U.S. armed services, thereby neglecting American civilian and allied military needs. Owners of small businesses grumbled that the bulk of defense contracts were going to a relatively few giant corporations. Liberals and

1940

leaders of organized labor were unhappy with the generous financial inducements—such as cost-plus contracts, under which the contracting firm received the cost of production plus a fixed fee or guaranteed profit—offered to businesses to win their cooperation. The loudest complaints came from those, such as Secretary of War Henry L. Stimson, calling for a more aggressive program to expand the country's industrial capacity. Knudsen shared the Depression-fed anxiety of many corporation executives that adding new plants would aggravate the problem of overproduction in peacetime. The attacks by "all-outers" against what they charged was Knudsen's "business as usual" approach were heightened when he brushed aside in the fall of 1940 a proposal advanced by Walter Reuther of the United Auto Workers union for large-scale conversion of the automobile industry to airplane production.

In January, 1941, Roosevelt reshuffled the industrial mobilization machinery to meet expected new demands from the planned lend-lease program. He replaced the NDAC with the Office of Production Management (OPM), keeping Knudsen on as director-general of the new agency. In a bow to organized labor, Sidney Hillman was named associate director-general. Knudsen soon lost the confidence of the White House. Roosevelt was dissatisfied with an agreement Knudsen reached with the automobile industry in the spring of 1941. That agreement called for a 20 percent reduction in civilian car production, less than Roosevelt wanted. His unhappiness was heightened by the public conflict between Knudsen and Leon Henderson, the administrator of the new Office of Price Administration and Civilian Supply (established on April 11 to protect consumer interests) for control over the allocation of materials such as steel, building supplies, and copper that were in short supply.

The upshot was that Roosevelt, in late August, 1941, established the Supply Priorities and Allocations Board (SPAB), with Donald Marr Nelson, the head of the OPM's division of purchases, as executive director. The SPAB would be the policy-making and coordinating agency for the entire defense program. The OPM was relegated to implementing the policies laid down by the SPAB.

On January 16, 1942, soon after the Japanese attack on Pearl Harbor, Roosevelt created the War Production Board (WPB), with Nelson at its head, to replace the OPM and SPAB. Knudsen was assigned to expedite production in plants under War Department control, given an army commission as a lieutenant general, and made special adviser to Undersecretary of War Robert P.

Patterson. In September, 1944, he was appointed director of the Air Technical Service command, with the responsibility of purchasing, distributing, and maintaining the aircraft and other equipment of the Army Air Force. Although Hillman remained head of the WPB's labor division, he no longer played a major role in the war mobilization effort. The focus of his interest shifted to the CIO's political action committee.

Under the War Powers Act of March, 1942, the WPB was given broad authority over all aspects of production and procurement. Nelson was only partially successful in overcoming the obstacles of full war production. Adoption of the Controlled Materials Plan in November, 1942, resolved the problem of allocating scarce raw materials by dividing the available supplies among the different government purchasing agencies, which then made allocations to their prime contractors. Roosevelt's appointment of special "czars" to deal with the problems of petroleum, rubber, and manpower, however, diluted the WPB's overall authority.

Although the WPB at its first meeting prohibited the manufacture of civilian automobiles after January 31, 1942, Nelson generally shied away from compulsion except as a last resort. Like Knudsen, he preferred to win business cooperation by offering generous financial inducements. Liberals were unhappy with the possible conflicts of interest resulting from the WPB's reliance on so-called dollar-a-year men, business executives on temporary leave from their firms to work for the WPB while still drawing their regular salaries from those firms. Most important, Nelson allowed the armed services to handle procurement, or contracting for equipment and supplies.

As a practical matter, Nelson probably had no alternative except to allow the military service to handle procurement. The services had established purchasing offices that would be difficult and time-consuming to duplicate, and Nelson thought it best to defer to military expertise in the laying down of specifications for equipment and supplies. Still, the decision had far-reaching consequences. The services' heavy demands threatened to leave the Allies and the civilian economy with shortages. The result was the so-called feasibility dispute that climaxed in the fall of 1942, when many civilian officials, including Nelson, questioned the ability of the economy to meet military demands.

The immediate conflict was resolved by a compromise whereby the military program was scaled back through extending scheduled delivery dates farther into the future. Keeping military demands within realistic

　　　Roosevelt Uses Business Leaders for World War II Planning

limits remained a continuing source of friction. An additional problem was that the services suspended the peacetime requirement of competitive bidding for most contracts because of time constraints. Because procurement officers preferred to deal with a small number of suppliers, the bulk of wartime contracts went to a relatively few large corporations. Cozy relationships often developed between procurement officers and the firms with which they dealt.

In October, 1942, Roosevelt appointed James F. Byrnes, a former senator from South Carolina and Supreme Court justice, to head the new Office of Economic Stabilization. Although the agency was set up to coordinate the government's wartime price and wage stabilization efforts, Byrnes gradually extended his control over all aspects of the economy. That control was formalized by the creation in May, 1943, of the Office of War Mobilization, or OWM (later renamed the Office of War Mobilization and Reconversion, or OWMR), headed by Byrnes. The WPB was placed under supervision of the OWM. Byrnes was successful in ironing out most of the remaining difficulties in the government's direction of war production.

By early 1944, the military situation appeared so promising that Nelson wanted to begin a gradual reconversion to civilian production. His idea was to assist the smaller firms that had been largely left out of the war contract bonanza by giving them a head start in the postwar civilian market. The plan faced strong resistance from big business. The military services were similarly hostile, warning that Nelson was too optimistic. In the controversy that followed, Byrnes sided against the gradual reconversion plan. Nelson was eased out as head of the WPB in August, 1944, and sent on a fact-finding mission to China.

SIGNIFICANCE

Even under the strains and redirections caused by the government's mobilization efforts, American industry during World War II was extremely productive. The gross national product (in constant dollars) rose from $91.3 billion in 1939 to $166 billion in 1945. The index of manufacturing production rose 96 percent, that of agricultural production 22 percent, and that of transportation services 109 percent. By 1942, American war production equaled that of Germany, Italy, and Japan combined. By 1944, American factories were producing twice the volume of the Axis powers. The WPB began to loosen its controls over the economy in the spring of 1945. The issuance of "spot authorizations" allowing

manufacturers to resume civilian production began in April; orders prohibiting civilian use of critical materials were rescinded soon after the German surrender in early May. The WPB was terminated on October 4, 1945.

　　　　　　　　　　　　　　　—*John Braeman*

FURTHER READING

Catton, Bruce. *The War Lords of Washington.* New York: Harcourt, Brace, 1948. An indictment of big business domination of the war mobilization program, by an associate and admirer of War Production Board head Donald M. Nelson.

Chandler, Lester V., and Donald H. Wallace, eds. *Economic Mobilization and Stabilization: Selected Materials on the Economics of War and Defense.* New York: Henry Holt, 1951. An anthology of materials treating the problems of economic stabilization during wartime that draws heavily on the experience of the United States in World War II. Part 2 focuses on the machinery of World War II economic mobilization.

Koistinen, Paul A. C. *Arsenal of World War II: The Political Economy of American Warfare, 1940-1945.* Lawrence: University Press of Kansas, 2004. Massive, comprehensive study of U.S. production and industrial and economic mobilization during World War II. Bibliographic references and index.

Nelson, Donald M. *Arsenal of Democracy: The Story of American War Production.* New York: Harcourt, Brace, 1946. Nelson's account, and defense, of his role in the war mobilization effort.

Polenberg, Richard. *War and Society: The United States, 1941-1945.* Philadelphia: J. B. Lippincott, 1972. An excellent survey of all aspects of the American home front during World War II. Includes a brief but perceptive treatment of the problem of industrial mobilization.

Smith, Ralph Elberton. *The Army and Economic Mobilization.* Washington, D.C.: Office of Military History, U.S. Army, 1959. A balanced and judicious history of War Department planning for and involvement in World War II economic mobilization.

Somers, Herman M. *Presidential Agency: OWMR, the Office of War Mobilization and Reconversion.* Cambridge, Mass.: Harvard University Press, 1950. An excellent account of James F. Byrnes's coordination and direction of the government's wartime management of the economy.

U.S. Bureau of the Budget. *The United States at War.* Washington, D.C.: Government Printing Office,

1940

1946. This official history is a comprehensive survey of the administrative machinery for wartime government management of the economy.

U.S. Civilian Production Administration. *Industrial Mobilization for War: History of the War Production Board and Predecessory Agencies, 1940-1945.* Washington, D.C.: Government Printing Office, 1947. The in-depth official history of the administrative problems and techniques involved in the mobilization of American industry during World War II.

SEE ALSO: Nov. 16, 1933: United States Recognizes Russia's Bolshevik Regime; Oct. 11, 1935-July 15, 1936: League of Nations Applies Economic Sanctions Against Italy; Mar. 7, 1936: German Troops March into the Rhineland; Aug., 1939: United States Begins Mobilization for World War II; Sept. 1, 1939: Germany Invades Poland; Sept. 10, 1939: Canada Enters World War II; May 10-June 22, 1940: Collapse of France; June 14, 1940: United States Begins Building a Two-Ocean Navy.

May 10-June 22, 1940
COLLAPSE OF FRANCE

The collapse of France occurred after German forces breached the Maginot line and overwhelmed the combined French and British military forces, eliminating France as a serious opponent to Germany for the remainder of World War II.

LOCALE: France
CATEGORIES: World War II; colonialism and occupation; wars, uprisings, and civil unrest

KEY FIGURES
Adolf Hitler (1889-1945), German dictator, 1933-1945
Gerd von Rundstedt (1875-1953), German commander in France
Erich von Manstein (Erich von Lewinksi; 1887-1973), Rundstedt's chief of staff
Maurice Gamelin (1872-1958), inspector general of the French army and vice president of Higher Council of War, 1935-1940
Maxime Weygand (1867-1965), French general and successor to Gamelin in 1940
Philippe Pétain (1856-1951), premier of Vichy France
Paul Reynaud (1878-1966), premier of France, March-June, 1940
Winston Churchill (1874-1965), prime minister of Great Britain, 1940-1945, 1951-1955
Benito Mussolini (1883-1945), Fascist premier of Italy, 1922-1943

SUMMARY OF EVENT
When World War II broke out in September, 1939, France was weak and demoralized. Unable to face a resurgent Germany alone and unaided, French leaders had followed the British in appeasing the aggressions of Adolf Hitler, the chancellor of Germany. France's domestic political problems had worsened during the interwar years, and there was a feeling of disillusionment with the politicians of the Third French Republic. Finally, France's military establishment, ostensibly strong, was actually weak in both planning and practice. Hidden behind the daunting series of fortifications known as the Maginot line, the French army waited for the Germans to attack and did not go to the aid of Poland when the Germans invaded it. From September, 1939, to May, 1940, the border between France and Germany was characterized by inactivity, for the French were reluctant to move out of their defenses. What mobile forces the French had were concentrated on the Belgian border, prepared to go to that country's aid should the Germans invade.

Meanwhile, following his successes in the east, Hitler made plans to invade France. In the winter of 1939-1940, he appointed General Gerd von Rundstedt as commander of Army Group A and approved a modified Schlieffen Plan that would call for the Germans to sweep through Belgium and attack northern France. It was clear from the concentration of French mobile forces along the Belgian border that the French expected such an attack. Rundstedt's chief of staff, General Erich von Manstein, a strong proponent of the utility of the armored division, proposed instead that the German armies concentrate on a push through the Ardennes forest, outflanking both the Maginot line and the French mobile forces. The French considered the Ardennes impassable to armor, and the area was lightly defended. Hitler approved of Manstein's plan, and following his Blitzkrieg invasion of Norway and Denmark in April, 1940, he prepared to attack France.

The British and French were totally unprepared militarily and psychologically for the German assault. During the 1930's, France had focused on the building of the Maginot line. Military preparedness lagged behind that of Germany, which, after 1936, had concentrated on building mobile, armored forces along with new aircraft such as the Stuka divebomber. The lessons of the successful, rapid German campaign in Poland in September, 1939, were also lost on the French high command. The senior French leadership was basically very old. For example, General Maurice Gamelin, overall commander of Allied forces in France, was sixty-eight years old in 1940. Very few senior French generals grasped the fact that new battlefield technology had changed the face of combat since 1918. The French and British General Staffs made few substantive inspections of the front and remained dangerously ignorant of the poor state of training of the armies or of the low state of morale of the troops.

On May 10, 1940, the German armies invaded Belgium, and Army Group A struck through the Ardennes, achieving an immediate breakthrough. The French cabinet, led by Premier Paul Reynaud, removed General Gamelin from command because he had committed all his armored forces to the fighting in Belgium and held none in reserve. General Maxime Weygand was appointed to replace Gamelin. To bolster the French cabinet and increase its prestige, Reynaud took over the Ministry of War himself and recalled Marshal Philippe Pétain, the aged hero of World War I, to act as his deputy.

Weygand could not contain the German forces, and they swept close to Paris, encircling and trapping the French troops against the back of the Maginot line. Reynaud appealed to Great Britain for additional aid, particularly fighter planes, but Winston Churchill, the British prime minister, refused the request because he foresaw that he would need them to protect England. Reynaud's cabinet was in a state of indecision and confusion over the obviously deteriorating military and political situation. Word reached Paris that the roads from northern and eastern France were jammed with hundreds of thousands of fleeing, terrified refugees. German tanks were moving with no significant opposition from the defeated and demoralized Allied armies.

There were obvious signs of panic in Paris, where the train stations were overwhelmed with citizens and government officials who were trying to evacuate the city before the Germans arrived. To spare the historic city and its population, Paris was declared to be an open city. That is, the government announced that it would not defend Paris: The Germans would be allowed to occupy it, in the hope that it would be spared from a devastating bombing campaign.

On June 11, the French cabinet withdrew to Tours, as the German armies approached Paris. Churchill implored the French not to surrender but to retreat to North Africa and carry on the fight from there. Although Reynaud agreed, the French military saw no reason to carry

Adolf Hitler (center) poses in front of the Eiffel Tower in June, 1940, after taking France. (Library of Congress)

DE GAULLE'S APPEAL OF JUNE 18

With the rise of the Nazi-installed Vichy government, led by Philippe Pétain, François Darlan, Joseph Darnand, and others, the commander of the French Free Forces, General Charles de Gaulle, issued his famous "Appeal of June 18," aired by the British Broadcasing Corporation on that date in 1940. De Gaulle's words prompted the French Resistance, the struggle against Nazi occupation that would last through World War II:

The leaders who, for many years, were at the head of French armies, have formed a government. This government, alleging our armies to be undone, agreed with the enemy to stop fighting. Of course, we were subdued by the mechanical, ground and air forces of the enemy. Infinitely more than their number, it was the tanks, the airplanes, the tactics of the Germans which made us retreat. It was the tanks, the airplanes, the tactics of the Germans that surprised our leaders to the point to bring them there where they are today.

But has the last word been said? Must hope disappear? Is defeat final? No!

Believe me, I speak to you with full knowledge of the facts and tell you that nothing is lost for France. The same means that overcame us can bring us to a day of victory. For France is not alone! She is not alone! She is not alone! She has a vast Empire behind her. She can align with the British Empire that holds the sea and continues the fight. She can, like England, use without limit the immense industry of United States.

This war is not limited to the unfortunate territory of our country. This war is not finished by the battle of France. This war is a world-wide war. All the faults, all the delays, all the suffering, do not prevent there to be, in the world, all the necessary means to one day crush our enemies. Vanquished today by mechanical force, we will be able to overcome in the future by a superior mechanical force.

The destiny of the world is here. I, General de Gaulle, currently in London, invite the officers and the French soldiers who are located in British territory or who would come there, with their weapons or without their weapons, I invite the engineers and the special workers of armament industries who are located in British territory or who would come there, to put themselves in contact with me.

Whatever happens, the flame of the French resistance must not be extinguished and will not be extinguished. Tomorrow, as today, I will speak on Radio London.

Source: Charles de Gaulle, *The Speeches of General de Gaulle* (New York: Oxford University Press, 1944).

on the fight, especially after Benito Mussolini, the Fascist dictator of Italy, declared war and sent Italian troops into southern France. On June 16, in the face of almost certain defeat, Reynaud resigned his cabinet positions, and because the majority of the government wanted to conclude an armistice with Germany, Pétain was named premier with full powers. He appealed to Hitler, and on June 22, 1940, the French surrendered to Germany.

SIGNIFICANCE

France's surrender did not mark the end of all French resistance to the Germans: When it became clear that the French government was no longer able or willing to fight, Brigadier General Charles de Gaulle, serving as an undersecretary of state for war, fled to England. On June 18, 1940, de Gaulle broadcast from London his first appeal for France to continue the struggle against Nazi Germany. Eventually, a signficant French resistance movement would develop. In June of 1940, however, few Frenchmen had the will to resist any further.

According to the terms of the surrender, France was divided into two parts; northern France was to be under German occupation, and southern France was to be nominally independent. The French fleet was to be interned in its home ports and was not to be used for the duration of the war. Pétain formed a government at the small southern town of Vichy, and in July formally abolished the constitution of the Third French Republic and established himself as virtual dictator. It was France's most inglorious moment and Germany's greatest, for Hitler had captured in one month what the German armies of 1914 had failed to take in four years of fighting.

—*José M. Sánchez and James J. Cooke*

FURTHER READING

Corum, James S. *The Roots of Blitzkrieg: Hans von Seeckt and German Military Reform*. Lawrence: University of Kansas Press, 1992. A fine study of the rebuilding of the German army that eventually defeated France and Britain in 1940.

Diamond, Hanna, and Simon Kitson, eds. *Vichy, Resistance, Liberation: New Perspectives on Wartime France*. New York: Berg, 2005. Collection of essays reconsidering many aspects of France's occupation during World War II. Bibliographic references and index.

Doughty, Robert A. *The Breaking Point: Sedan and the Fall of France*. Hamden, Conn.: Archon Books, 1992. An analysis of the German breakthrough at Sedan, a battle that destroyed Allied defensive plans.

_____. *The Seeds of Disaster: The Development of French Army Doctrine, 1919-1939*. Hamden, Conn.: Archon Books, 1985. Discusses the decisions and the doctrine that brought France to the disaster of 1940.

Footitt, Hilary. *War and Liberation in France: Living with the Liberators*. New York: Palgrave Macmillan, 2004. In addition to discussing France's brief defense, occupation, and liberation, this study looks at the long-term effects of the occupation and liberation on French culture and politics. Bibliographic references and index.

Horne, Alistair. *To Lose a Battle: France, 1940*. Rev. ed. Boston: Little, Brown, 1990. Horne's classic work remains an excellent, detailed account of the French military disaster in 1940.

Weygand, Maxime. *Recalled to Service*. London: William Hinemann, 1952. These memoirs by a key player shed much light on the lost battles of 1940.

SEE ALSO: 1929-1940: Maginot Line Is Built; Nov. 16, 1933: United States Recognizes Russia's Bolshevik Regime; Feb. 6, 1934: Stavisky Riots; Oct. 11, 1935-July 15, 1936: League of Nations Applies Economic Sanctions Against Italy; Mar. 7, 1936: German Troops March into the Rhineland; Aug., 1939: United States Begins Mobilization for World War II; Sept. 1, 1939: Germany Invades Poland; Sept. 10, 1939: Canada Enters World War II; Apr. 9, 1940: Germany Invades Norway; June 14, 1940: United States Begins Building a Two-Ocean Navy.

May 16, 1940-1944
GYPSIES ARE EXTERMINATED IN NAZI DEATH CAMPS

Gypsies were transported from Nazi-occupied Europe to the Nazis' death camps, where they were exterminated along with Jews and other ethnic groups in an effort to "purify" the Aryan race.

ALSO KNOWN AS: Porajmos

LOCALE: German-occupied Europe, especially modern Poland

CATEGORIES: Atrocities and war crimes; wars, uprisings, and civil unrest; World War II

KEY FIGURES

Reinhard Heydrich (1904-1942), commander of the German secret service and the concentration camp system

Heinrich Himmler (1900-1945), commander of the SS and overseer of the Nazi "final solution"

Ernst Zindel (fl. mid-twentieth century), German senior councilor and bureaucratic coordinator of government policies concerning the Gypsies

Adolf Hitler (1889-1945), German dictator, 1933-1945

Robert Ritter (1901-1951), anthropologist and leading German expert on the "Gypsy problem"

Eugen Fischer (1874-1967), German professor of anthropology

SUMMARY OF EVENT

On May 16, 1940, German police rounded up almost three thousand Gypsies living in western and northwestern Germany and put them on trains bound for German-occupied Poland. These deportations initiated a more radical phase of the attempt by the German government to solve what they called the "Gypsy problem." The solution to the "problem" resulted in tens of thousands of Gypsy deaths over the next five years. Although the total number of Gypsies who died during what Gypsies call the Porajmos (the Gypsy holocaust) remains unknown, some estimates range as high as one-half million. Four distinct but related factors in European history contributed to this massive destruction of human lives: the lifestyle of the Gypsies and their reputation in European folklore, the eugenics movement, the euthanasia movement, and the Nazi seizure of power in Germany.

According to ethnologists, ancestors of the modern Gypsies began emigrating from northwestern India around 1000 C.E. They developed a nomadic lifestyle, never staying in one area for long. They retained their own distinct language. They earned money by fortune-telling, entertaining audiences with their unique music and dancing, and by theft and chicanery. Arriving in Europe sometime during the fourteenth century, they were often viewed as criminals and pests. Many European monarchs decreed laws limiting their mobility and contact with their own settled populations. By the twentieth century, many Europeans viewed the Gypsies as nomadic criminals who were a danger to the public welfare. Even the European scientific community began to denounce the Gypsies in the late nineteenth century with the advent of the "science" of eugenics.

Sir Francis Galton, a first cousin to Charles Darwin, founded eugenics in the 1870's. In several influential

1940

books, Galton argued that governments should encourage the genetically well-endowed members of their countries to reproduce in order to improve the human race. He also maintained that persons with congenital diseases and deformities should not be allowed to pass on their flawed genes to future generations. A number of scientists and laypersons around the world took up Galton's cause and began to push their lawmakers to implement eugenics laws. The eugenics societies that soon emerged in most of the European nations and in the United States began to demand that their governments adopt laws for the mandatory sterilization of people they identified as genetically deficient.

Some, if not all, of these eugenics societies adopted distinctly racist agendas, identifying blacks, Jews, Gypsies, and other "people of color" as being genetically inferior to the "white" races. In Germany, Eugen Fischer and Ernst Ruedin emerged as the most outspoken advocates of eugenics. Both were professors and both warned of an impending "biological crisis" that could irreparably damage the German race. Adolf Hitler, leader of the Nazi Party, read one of Fischer's books while imprisoned after his failed attempt to overthrow the German government in 1923. Hitler was so impressed by Fischer's arguments that he incorporated many of them into his own semiautobiographical book *Mein Kampf* (1925-1927; partial English translation, 1933).

When Hitler became chancellor of Germany in 1933, the eugenicists realized they had a powerful ally in the highest position of the German government. Although many of the leading eugenicists never joined the Nazi Party, they worked closely with Nazis in the German government to develop a racial policy for the German people. The Nazis created a number of government agencies such as the Reich Office for Research on Race Hygiene and Population Biology to identify and solve the racial problems of Germany. They also established university chairs of Racial Hygiene in many of the most prestigious institutions of higher learning to study the racial problem.

By 1935, the racial experts proposed that allegedly undesirable elements (homosexuals, carriers of hereditary diseases, the terminally insane, and others) be excluded from German society through incarceration. The eugenicists also proposed that "alien" minorities in Germany (particularly the Jews and the Gypsies) be excluded as well and forbidden to intermarry with Germans. The German parliament responded by passing the infamous Nuremberg laws that deprived Jews and Gypsies of German citizenship and provided stiff penal-

ties for sexual relations between Germans and non-Germans. The government also established bureaus to deal with the several racially undesirable elements in Germany. To deal with the Gypsies, the government established the Zentralstelle zur Bekaempfung des Ziguenerunwesen (ZBZ; the Central Office to Combat the Gypsy Pest).

One career bureaucrat of the ZBZ, Senior Council Ernst Zindel, recommended in 1935 that the Gypsies be identified and placed on reservations under close supervision. Accordingly, Reinhard Heydrich, head of the Sicherheitdienst (SD; the secret service) and the ZBZ, commissioned a young scientist named Robert Ritter to study and identify all Gypsies living in Germany. Ritter performed a number of tests on more than twenty thousand German Gypsies over the next ten years, including blood types, cranial and skeletal measurements, and eye, hair, and skin pigmentation. As Ritter's work progressed, Heydrich adopted ever more restrictive legislation concerning the Gypsies.

In 1935, Heydrich ordered that all municipal governments establish Gypsy camps. By law, nomadic Gypsies could stay only in these camps. After 1937, Gypsies could leave these camps only during the day. Also in 1937, Heydrich adopted a regulation that permitted "preventive arrest" of anyone his police deemed likely to commit a crime. The police in German cities often used this law to arrest Gypsies and send them to concentration camps. In 1938, Heydrich ordered that all Gypsies must register with the local police whenever they entered a new district. In January of 1940, Ritter issued a report to Heydrich recommending that all pure and "mixed-blood" Gypsies be sent to work camps and completely isolated from German society. The May, 1940, deportations represented Heydrich's first step in implementing Ritter's recommendation. The mass deportation of Gypsies from the rest of occupied Europe did not begin until November of 1941, when members of the German government apparently decided on an even more radical solution to the Gypsy problem.

The so-called final solution to the racial problems as defined by the Nazis owed much to a movement in the German medical profession related to but distinct from the eugenics movement. Beginning shortly after World War I, some German doctors advocated the medical termination of "lives unworthy to be lived." These doctors, including many eugenicists, argued that the terminally ill, the hopelessly insane, and persons incapable of thought, be granted mercy deaths—euthanasia. A number of doctors began to practice euthanasia illegally and without authorization. After the outbreak of World War II, Hitler personally authorized the implementation of euthanasia under the strict surveillance of competent doctors. Between 1939 and 1945, German doctors killed many thousands of their own citizens without the consent of the patients or their relatives. Some estimates put the number of "mercy deaths" as high as seventy thousand. A special group of German medical personnel called T-4 usually carried out the actual killing of patients.

The T-4 group worked out several methods for killing large numbers of people at one time, including the use of carbon monoxide gas. Sometime in 1940 or 1941 (the exact date is uncertain, given that no written order exists), Hitler apparently made the decision to apply the methods of mass euthanasia to solve the Jewish and Gypsy problems. Heydrich and Himmler entrusted the deportation of Jews and Gypsies living in the German-occupied territories to Adolf Eichmann. In 1942, Eichmann began the mass transport of Jews and Gypsies to concentration camps and ghettos in Poland, where the T-4 group had set up mass extermination centers in January, 1942. In camps such as Auschwitz, Chełmno, Sobibór, Belżec, Majdanek, and Treblinka, Schutzstaffel (SS) personnel began the systematic murder of millions of Jews, Gypsies, Slavs, and other racially undesirable or asocial persons. According to some Polish sources, the SS also began to murder Gypsies wherever they found them in the occupied territories without bothering to ship them to the camps in Poland. According to witnesses, at least twenty thousand Gypsies perished in Auschwitz alone, many dying from malnutrition or typhus.

SIGNIFICANCE

By the time the death camps halted operations in late 1944, tens of thousands of Gypsies had died from various causes directly related to their incarceration. One historian puts the Gypsy death toll at 500,000, although the actual number may be significantly higher or lower. Like the Jews, the Gypsies were a people long used by Europeans to stand for the "Other" and thereby to define themselves. The extermination of the Gypsies, then, like that of the Jews, merely took to a horrific extreme a racist logic that was at the heart of European history and of the self-understanding of many European races. Moreover, like the larger Holocaust of which it is a part, the Gypsy extermination had effects on both European and Gypsy history that are impossible to describe or measure adequately.

—*Paul Madden*

FURTHER READING

Crowe, David M. *A History of the Gypsies of Eastern Europe and Russia*. New York: St. Martin's Press, 1994. Surveys the Gypsy communities of all the Eastern European and Russian areas during the Holocaust.

Editors of Time-Life Books. *The Apparatus of Death*. Alexandria, Va.: Time-Life Books, 1991. A brief account of the Gypsy holocaust, along with a number of rare photographs of the deportation of Gypsies from occupied Europe and the death camps.

Friedlander, Henry. *The Origins of Nazi Genocide: From Euthanasia to the Final Solution*. Chapel Hill: University of North Carolina Press, 1995. Incorporates accounts of Nazi policies toward the Gypsies throughout the book.

Milton, Sybil. "Holocaust: The Gypsies." In *Century of Genocide: Critical Essays and Eyewitness Accounts*, edited by Samuel Totten, William S. Parsons, and Israel W. Charny. 2d ed. New York: Routledge, 2004. An account of the Gypsy Holocaust, appearing in a collection that also discusses the Nazi exterminations of the Jews and the disabled. Bibliographic references and index.

Mueller-Hill, Benno. *Murderous Science: Elimination by Scientific Selection of Jews, Gypsies, and Others—Germany, 1933-1945*. New York: Oxford University Press, 1988. Shows the complicity of the non-Nazi German scientific community in the "final solution."

SEE ALSO: Apr. 24, 1915: Armenian Genocide Begins; 1919-1933: Racist Theories Aid Nazi Rise to Political Power; Mar., 1933: Nazi Concentration Camps Begin Operating; Mar. 14, 1937: Pius XI Urges Resistance Against Nazism; 1939-1945: Nazi Extermination of the Jews; Sept. 1, 1939: Germany Invades Poland.

1940

May 26-June 4, 1940
EVACUATION OF DUNKIRK

The British Expeditionary Force in France and Belgium was cornered by the German Blitzkrieg invasion of those countries. In a massive evacuation, the force was transported across the English Channel to the relative safety of England. Although it lost a great many supplies, the preservation of its troops enabled the British army to continue in the war, and the evacuation of French troops to England formed the foundation for a Free French armed force.

LOCALE: Dunkirk, France; English Channel
CATEGORIES: Wars, uprisings, and civil unrest; World War II; military history

KEY FIGURES

Lord Gort (John Standish Surtees Prendergast Vereker; 1886-1946), commander in chief of the British Expeditionary Force

Jean-Marie Charles Abrial (1879-1962), commander of French naval forces at Dunkirk

Sir Bertram H. Ramsay (1883-1945), British flag officer at Dover

Gerd von Rundstedt (1875-1953), German commander in France

Winston Churchill (1874-1965), prime minister of Great Britain, 1940-1945, 1951-1955

Adolf Hitler (1889-1945), chancellor of Germany, 1933-1945

Anthony Eden (1897-1977), secretary of war of Great Britain, 1940

Hermann Göring (1893-1946), commander of the German Luftwaffe

SUMMARY OF EVENT

When the Germans invaded Poland in 1939, the British sent an expeditionary force to France. By May of 1940, it had risen to a strength of ten infantry divisions. In the meantime, Adolf Hitler, the chancellor of Germany, had issued orders for a general offensive, planned by General Erich von Manstein, against France, Belgium, and Holland. At dawn on May

10, the German army and air force struck. In accordance with Allied plans, two French armies and nine divisions of the British Expeditionary Force advanced into Belgium, to confront the German attack there. On May 13, six German divisions broke through the French defenses farther south along the Meuse River and struck northwestward toward the English Channel. On May 20, German forces reached the English Channel coast at the mouth of the Somme near Abbeyville, trapping the Allied forces in Belgium and northern France.

The progress of the Germans toward the coast had seriously alarmed General Lord Gort, the commander in chief of the British Expeditionary Force, and as early as May 19, he informed the British government that he was considering withdrawing his nine divisions to the English Channel for possible evacuation. The British Admiralty, the War Office, and Admiral Sir Bertram H. Ramsay, the flag officer commanding Dover, began to improvise plans for such an evacuation under the code name Dynamo.

The prospects for a successful evacuation did not appear promising, as German forces moved northeastward along the coast. Boulogne and Calais were quickly surrounded, and a German force moved toward Dunkirk, the

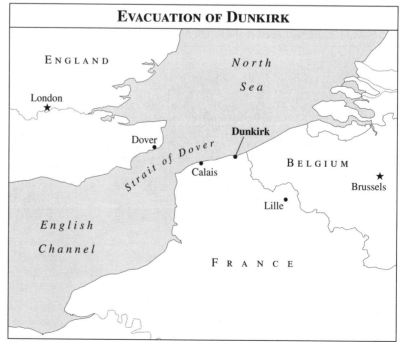

EVACUATION OF DUNKIRK

last port through which an Allied evacuation could take place. On May 24, however, Gerd von Rundstedt ordered the German armor to halt, less than fifteen miles from Dunkirk. This decision became one of the most controversial of the entire war. After the war, German generals singled out Hitler as responsible for the failure to finish off the Allied forces. In fact, a number of senior generals shared the blame.

The halt, however, allowed the British and French to establish a defense line around Dunkirk and provided them time to put Operation Dynamo into motion. Hermann Göring, the German Luftwaffe commander, told Hitler that if the Allies left Dunkirk by sea, the German air force could stop them by bombing alone. Evacuation of the British began during the night of May 26. The French continued to consider defending Dunkirk as a fortress; it was not until May 28 that they decided to withdraw their troops and issued orders to Admiral Jean-Marie Charles Abrial, in command of their forces at Dunkirk, to cooperate with the British. The Royal Navy recruited hundreds of small civilian pleasure craft to ferry troops from the beaches to the larger naval ships waiting offshore. The Luftwaffe's attempt to stop the evacuation proved much more difficult than Göring had imagined. German fighters, still operating from bases in western Germany, were farther from Dunkirk than British fighters operating from England. Although the British could not gain control of the air over Dunkirk, the British did hamper the German air attacks, destroying 240 German aircraft while losing 177 planes.

On May 26, Hitler rescinded the halt order, but problems in the German command structure slowed the German advance, and it was not until May 30 that they even realized that the British were evacuating their troops. In the early morning hours of June 4, the last British ship left Dunkirk. The evacuation was over, a feat of heroism and great organizational skill on the part of the Royal Navy and Ramsay. Altogether, the British, with some French assistance, rescued 338,000 men, 224,000 of them British—many more than anticipated. The cost was heavy, however. The British used 760 ships, of which 228, mostly small craft, were sunk by air attack, and the French had about 300, of which 60 were lost.

SIGNIFICANCE

The evacuation of the British Expeditionary Force from Dunkirk ensured that the British army could continue in the war. Although the British had been forced to leave behind all their heavy equipment, tanks, artillery, and transport, their trained men were rescued, and they

British soldiers taken prisoner at Dunkirk, June, 1940. (NARA)

1940

formed the nucleus of the British army of the future. The loss of their equipment, however, meant that Britain had no effective land-based defense against a German invasion. It thus set the terms for the Battle of Britain, in which the Royal Air Force became the primary defenders of the island.

—Samuel K. Eddy and Donald L. Layton

FURTHER READING

Atkin, Ronald. *Pillar of Fire: Dunkirk, 1940.* Edinburgh: Birlinn, 2000. First-person narrative of the Dunkirk invasion by a British soldier. Includes bibliographic references and index.

Carse, Robert. *Dunkirk, 1940: A History.* Englewood Cliffs, N.J.: Prentice-Hall, 1970. Captures the horror, shock, and excitement that surrounded the withdrawal at Dunkirk, but does not present a detailed analysis of the event.

Collier, Richard. *The Sands of Dunkirk*. New York: E. P. Dutton, 1961. An attempt to reconstruct the fighting at Dunkirk, this book's greatest strengths are its full tables of units and ships.

Divine, A. D. *Dunkirk*. New York: E. P. Dutton, 1948. Informative, although dated, account of the evacuation based on the logs of small boat masters and Admiralty reports.

Gelb, Norman. *Dunkirk: The Complete Story of the First Step in the Defeat of Hitler*. New York: William Morrow, 1989. An anecdotal reprise of the Dunkirk story based mostly on the standard secondary sources.

Harman, Nicholas. *Dunkirk, the Necessary Myth*. London: Hodder & Stoughton, 1989. Revisionist account of the evacuation emphasizes British manipulation of the press at home.

Lord, Walter. *The Miracle of Dunkirk*. New York: Viking, 1982. One of the best accounts of the Dunkirk evacuation available. Presents interpretations of major issues that are soundly based on scholarship.

SEE ALSO: 1929-1940: Maginot Line Is Built; Mar. 7, 1936: German Troops March into the Rhineland; Sept. 29-30, 1938: Munich Conference; Sept. 1, 1939: Germany Invades Poland; Sept. 10, 1939: Canada Enters World War II; Apr. 9, 1940: Germany Invades Norway; May 10-June 22, 1940: Collapse of France; July 10-Oct. 31, 1940: Battle of Britain.

June 14, 1940
UNITED STATES BEGINS BUILDING A TWO-OCEAN NAVY

On the eve of World War II, the U.S. government began construction of warships that would come to dominate both the Atlantic and the Pacific.

LOCALE: United States

CATEGORIES: Government and politics; wars, uprisings, and civil unrest; military history; World War II

KEY FIGURES

Franklin D. Roosevelt (1882-1945), president of the United States, 1933-1945

Carl Vinson (1883-1981), U.S. congressman from Georgia

Park Trammel (1876-1936), U.S. senator from Florida

Harold Raynsford Stark (1880-1972), chief of U.S. naval operations

SUMMARY OF EVENT

The goal of establishing a two-ocean fleet was a powerful, if elusive, force in determining the nature of the U.S. Navy before the Japanese attack on Pearl Harbor plunged the United States into war in 1941. In the late 1930's, the two-ocean standard became the latest in a succession of rallying cries designed to gain support for naval expansion among the American public. Its appeal originated in a growing recognition that vital U.S. interests were being threatened simultaneously by Germany and Japan. This two-ocean focus was an extension of threat perceptions and arguments dating back to the 1890's and made more pressing with the Anglo-Japanese alliance of 1902 and

Japan's victory over Russia in the 1904-1905 Russo-Japanese War. With the collapse of naval arms limitations in 1936, the rearmament of National Socialist (Nazi) Germany, and the naval buildup and military adventurism of Japan, the necessity of creating fleets capable of fighting independently in widely separated theaters seemed evident. The U.S. Congress, responding to the change in popular attitude, passed legislation between 1938 and 1941 designed to translate the ideal of a two-ocean fleet into reality.

U.S. naval policy in general has mirrored national ambition. In the 1890's, and especially after the Spanish-American War, the horizon of that ambition increased measurably. At a single stroke, the United States became both a Caribbean and a Pacific power. U.S. control of the Philippines was perplexing for many people in the United States but exciting for navalists and imperialists. Together with Hawaii, which was annexed in 1898, the Philippines provided U.S. commerce with a toehold in the fabled China trade. Distant possessions seemed to mandate an increased fleet, and an increased fleet required overseas bases, setting the foundation for a self-perpetuating expansion of the military and naval establishment.

For better or worse, expanded interests called for expanded responsibilities, and President Theodore Roosevelt, an enthusiastic convert to U.S. imperialism, led the movement to secure those interests. Between 1905 and 1909, Congress authorized the construction of sixteen new battleships of the all-big-gun, dreadnought style by which international naval power was measured. Meanwhile, work on the Panama Canal, which was intended to provide much-needed flexibility for the fleet, continued toward its completion in 1914.

By the time of Theodore Roosevelt's presidency, Japan and especially Germany were seen as the most important potential threats to U.S. commerce and possessions. Tension caused by the treatment of Japanese nationals living in the United States was the primary reason for congressional approval of the last six new battleships authorized during Roosevelt's administration. The attention of most U.S. naval experts was fixed on Germany, where an ambitious twenty-year naval construction program had been announced in 1900. Whereas the German fleet law was intended as a challenge to British naval supremacy, it was also perceived as a threat to U.S. interests by a host of U.S. congressmen and naval authorities. That traditional German concerns were continental and that the German navy had a nearer rival in Great Britain seemed to make no difference. Those guiding U.S. naval policy believed that it would be a mistake for the United States to allow itself to be surpassed in naval power by any nation that also maintained a great standing army. This growing American fear of Germany was also reflected in the concentration of the fleet. Long a dictum of the most distinguished U.S. naval strategic synthesizer, Captain A. T. Mahan, the concentration of naval forces was adopted by Roosevelt as a cardinal principle of fleet deployment. Throughout his presidency, and that of William Howard Taft as well, the main fleet remained posted in the Atlantic Ocean.

After 1914, the prewar desire to improve the U.S. Navy to second place behind the British fleet was replaced by a determination to build a navy second to none. This challenge to British naval superiority, the first ever by the United States, was engendered by British arrogance toward neutral U.S. shipping and a fear of the naval landscape in the postwar world. President Woodrow Wilson and Congress joined in the $588 million naval construction act of 1916, which mandated ten new super-dreadnought battleships and six battle cruisers. Wilson called for a similar program in 1918 to strengthen the U.S. bargaining position at the upcoming Paris Peace Conference.

By 1924, the U.S. Navy would be the most powerful in the world, a dismaying prospect to the British government. U.S. naval ascension was delayed by the decision to shift battleship construction assets to the production of antisubmarine warships, such as destroyers, and to merchant ships to counter losses to German submarines. In

the three years that followed the signing of the armistice ending World War I, the United States built more warships than all the rest of the world combined. In taking dead aim at British naval superiority, the United States also revealed apprehension concerning Japan's being linked to Britain by the ten-year renewal of the Anglo-Japanese alliance in 1911. Between 1917 and 1921, Japanese naval appropriations tripled, undoubtedly affected by the upsurge in U.S. construction. It is not surprising that with the demise of German naval power in 1919, concern in the United States shifted from the Atlantic to the Pacific. In the summer of that year, the battle fleet was divided, with the newer and heavier units being sent to the West Coast.

Fear of a costly, all-out naval race in the immediate postwar period served to induce a certain amount of moderation. In Washington, D.C., in 1921-1922, the five leading naval powers adopted a system of restrictions on individual capital ships (battleships and battle cruisers) and aircraft carriers as well as on the aggregate tonnages of capital war fleets. By the terms of the Five-Power Treaty, Great Britain and the United States were to share the first rank of naval power, Japan was assigned the second rank (approximately 60 percent of capital ship parity with the first-rank powers), and France and Italy were relegated to the third rank. In 1930, this agreement was augmented by the London Treaty, which established similar kinds of restrictions on the noncapital construction (cruisers, destroyers, and submarines) of Great Britain, the United States, and Japan. Thus from 1922 through 1936, the size and nature of the U.S. war fleet were restricted by international agreement.

Domination of the Imperial Japanese Navy by the hardliners of the so-called Fleet Faction, who chafed at Japan's second-rank status under the treaties, resulted in significant pressure on the Japanese government to demand equal status with the United States and Great Britain at the London Naval Conference of 1935. When Great Britain and the United States demurred, the Japanese government provided the requisite notice that it would no longer abide by the naval treaties after December, 1936. Japan's subsequent penetration of China in 1937 and Hitler's annexation of Austria and absorption of the Sudetenland in 1938 seemed to provide ample proof for the proposition that unilateral restraint by the United States was a dangerous policy. The issue of naval preparedness became correspondingly less controversial.

In 1932, U.S. naval officers applauded the election of navalist Franklin D. Roosevelt to the presidency after the lean years of Republican naval and military expendi-

A newly completed ship at the Bethlehem-Fairfield shipyards in Baltimore, Maryland, in 1943. (Library of Congress)

tures. They were not disappointed. On the same day he signed the National Industrial Recovery Act (NIRA) into law in June, 1933, Roosevelt signed an executive order using $238 million of NIRA public works funds for construction of new warships. This first step in building the U.S. Navy up to "treaty limits" was followed by congressional moves to improve the status of the war fleet. Spearheaded by the navalist chairman of the House Naval Affairs Committee, Carl Vinson, and the aging chairman of the Senate Naval Affairs Committee, Park Trammel, this movement's objective was the replacement of all the fleet's obsolete warships, or "floating coffins," to use Vinson's words. The resulting Vinson-Trammel Act, also known as the Vinson Naval Parity Act, which became law in March, 1934, envisioned the replacement of almost one-third of the existing tonnage of the U.S. Navy, including practically all the destroyers and submarines. The act did not appropriate funds for construction

but served as a blueprint for U.S. naval policy. The clear intention of this action was the establishment of a fighting force that would be the equal of any in the world. Both the NIRA-funded ships and the Vinson-Trammel Act exacerbated strategic concerns in Japan, which was approaching its warship treaty limits and now faced new, qualitatively superior, U.S. warships.

By 1938, many isolationists, hemispherists, and internationalists were in agreement that a powerful navy was an indispensable adjunct to a free United States, and so another authorization bill swiftly passed through Congress. The second Vinson-Trammel bill, the Naval Expansion Act, or Vinson Naval Act, sought the creation of a navy 20 percent larger than that permitted by the former limitation treaties. As Europe plunged into war, the last restraints on full-scale naval construction disappeared. On June 14, 1940, the day that Paris fell to the German Blitzkrieg, President Roosevelt signed into law a naval expansion bill that authorized an 11 percent increase in appropriations. Three days later, Admiral Harold Raynsford Stark, chief of naval operations, asked Congress for an additional four billion dollars in order to bring the fleet up to the two-ocean standard. This bill, which was passed the following month, was the largest single naval construction program ever undertaken by any country. It provided for a 70 percent increase in combat tonnage to be constructed over a period of six years.

SIGNIFICANCE

President Roosevelt, who largely acted as his own secretary of the Navy, shared most admirals' perception that the battleship defined naval power. Although additional aircraft carriers were authorized in the late 1930's, the main focus of the Roosevelt naval buildup was the production of the seventeen new battleships authorized prior to U.S. entry into World War II.

Despite the flurry of construction authorizations, U.S. naval power was insufficient to protect the Atlantic and Pacific interests of the United States in the wake of Pearl Harbor. A full year prior to that catastrophe, the Navy, pressured by the president, had been forced to shift its strategic focus from an offensive action against Japan to a position that in any future war would include both Germany and Japan; the fleet would take the offensive in the Atlantic while assuming a defensive posture in the Pacific. Even this severe modification of the strategy implicit in the two-ocean standard did not achieve satisfactory results for a disconcertingly long period of time.

Although the success of Japan's surprise attack on Pearl Harbor might well be considered the result of a failure of specific rather than general preparedness, the inability of U.S. naval resources to provide adequate protection against the onslaught of Germany's U-boat attack during all of 1942 provides convincing evidence that the Atlantic fleet had not achieved even a one-ocean capability at that time. This was an outgrowth of the myopic battleship strategic paradigm that restricted movement toward true capabilities in air, surface, and subsurface warfare. It was not until early 1943 that U.S. naval forces began to gain the upper hand in the Atlantic and Pacific theaters of the war.

—*Meredith William Berg and William M. McBride*

FURTHER READING

Baer, George W. *One Hundred Years of Sea Power: The U.S. Navy, 1890-1990.* Stanford, Calif.: Stanford University Press, 1994. Detailed history of the modern U.S. Navy examines how naval policy has been formulated. The Navy's readiness for World War II is discussed in chapter 8.

Davis, George T. *A Navy Second to None: The Development of Modern American Naval Policy.* 1940. Reprint. Westport, Conn.: Greenwood Press, 1971. Informative scholarly study of U.S. naval policy and armaments as well as the relation of naval power to commerce.

Hagan, Kenneth J. *This People's Navy: The Making of American Sea Power.* New York: Free Press, 1991. Excellent concise history of the U.S. Navy examines the service's military, political, and technological evolution.

O'Connell, Robert. *Sacred Vessels: The Cult of the Battleship and the Rise of the U.S. Navy.* Boulder, Colo.: Westview Press, 1991. Readable cautionary account of naval strategic weapons and the profession in which they evolved.

Pelz, Stephen E. *Race to Pearl Harbor: The Failure of the Second London Naval Conference and the Onset of World War II.* Cambridge, Mass.: Harvard University Press, 1974. Excellent examination of the naval policies of the great sea powers from the end of arms limitations to Pearl Harbor. Draws on American, Japanese, and British sources.

Tuleja, Thaddeus V. *Statesmen and Admirals: Quest for a Far Eastern Naval Policy.* New York: W. W. Norton, 1963. Provides informative discussion of the interwar relationship between the naval policies of the United States and Japan.

Wheeler, Gerald. *Prelude to Pearl Harbor: The United States Navy and the Far East, 1921-1931.* Columbia: University of Missouri Press, 1963. Presents clear discussion of the attitudes of senior naval officers, Congress, the executive branch, and the U.S. public during an important period of naval limitation.

SEE ALSO: Nov. 8, 1932: Franklin D. Roosevelt Is Elected U.S. President; Aug. 31, 1935-Nov. 4, 1939: Neutrality Acts; Dec., 1936: Inter-American Conference for the Maintenance of Peace; Aug., 1939: United States Begins Mobilization for World War II; May, 1940: Roosevelt Uses Business Leaders for World War II Planning; Aug. 16, 1940: Ogdensburg Agreement.

1940

June 30, 1940
CONGRESS CENTRALIZES REGULATION OF U.S. COMMERCIAL AIR TRAFFIC

The Civil Aeronautics Act of 1938 brought organized regulation of the domestic civil aviation industry and presaged the development of the Civil Aeronautics Board in 1940 and the Federal Aviation Administration in 1958.

LOCALE: Washington, D.C.
CATEGORIES: Space and aviation; transportation; trade and commerce

KEY FIGURES

Clarence Frederick Lea (1874-1964), U.S. congressman from California, 1917-1949
Patrick Anthony McCarran (1876-1954), U.S. senator from Nevada, 1933-1954
Franklin D. Roosevelt (1882-1945), president of the United States, 1933-1945

SUMMARY OF EVENT

Several landmark regulatory efforts helped to shape commercial aviation in the United States. First, the Air Mail Act of 1925 relieved the government from the responsibility of carrying airmail and allowed contracts to be given to commercial airlines through competitive bidding. Second, the Air Commerce Act of 1926 placed responsibility for the development of the airways, aids to navigation, and safety regulation squarely with the federal government. The Federal Aviation Administration had its roots in the Air Commerce Act of 1926. Third, the Civil Aeronautics Act of 1938 laid foundations for centralized federal control. The act came to subject commercial air transportation to regulation of entry and exit from the industry, routes, and fares.

By the mid-1930's, the growth of airmail and air passenger operations had firmly established the U.S. airline industry. After the disastrous years of the Great Depression, aircraft manufacturers began providing more aircraft to airlines for air passenger service. The advent of World War II put even greater emphasis on the development of military and eventually commercial aviation. Progress and acceptance of new technology were substantial, and the future appeared bright for the industry.

As motor carriers' popularity and dominant positions as movers of domestic passengers grew, comparisons between the nation's airways and railroads began to be made. Because both railroads and major carriers had been substantially regulated by the mid-1930's, some

thought was given to the potential for regulation of the domestic airline industry. Economic regulation, furthermore, was precipitated by uneconomic duplications of routes or substantial signs of exercise of market power. The Interstate Commerce Commission regulated railroads and motor carriers, but airlines were judged to be in a substantially different industry from their surface-oriented counterparts.

Airlines approached the federal government to suggest working out a basic set of guiding principles, and the fact that the legislation was initiated by the airlines rather than by the government made it unique. The Air Mail Act of 1934 had created three agencies that overlapped in authority, bringing confusion and hardship for the airlines. After several months of study by industry leaders and government officials, a completely new and all-encompassing law was passed affecting civil aviation in the United States. The new law found its base in Article 1, section 8 of the U.S. Constitution, the same foundation used for the Interstate Commerce Act of 1887 and the Motor Carrier Act of 1935. The Civil Aeronautics Act was introduced into Congress by Senator Patrick Anthony McCarran and Congressman Clarence Frederick Lea and was passed by Congress on June 23, 1938.

The Civil Aeronautics Act (also known as the McCarran-Lea Act) amended or repealed all major previous legislation related to aviation, and in doing so it prepared the setting for regulation of a growing industry. Air transportation was judged to be substantially different from previously regulated forms of surface transportation. Issues of competition, monopoly, public service, passenger focus, and safety were all in the minds of regulators. This law and its counterparts for surface transportation found their basis in the industry's public-service nature. Government officials believed that they should regulate industries or organizations that were concerned with the public interest and were important to the economy. Public-service regulations were destined to ensure that rates charged were equitable, services offered were reasonable and nondiscriminatory, and the public interest was protected.

The 1938 act was in many ways more advanced than the industry it was designed to serve, as it was based on regulatory provisions of the Interstate Commerce Act that had proved effective. Many provisions in the 1938 act were taken almost verbatim from the Interstate Commerce Act. Other provisions were refined to reflect the half century of experience with the regulation of rail transportation. The mechanics of the Civil Aeronautics Act were based on the argument that regulation of air transportation, both economic and safety aspects, should be administered by three separate agencies. The original three agencies were the Civil Aeronautics Authority (CAA), composed of five members who were to establish policies for regulation of safety and economics, an administrator of aviation appointed to carry out the CAA's safety policies and economic regulations, and an air safety board, which was formed as an independent group of three persons responsible for the investigation of aircraft accidents.

At first, the three agencies' jurisdictions overlapped, and adjustments had to be made to the authority structures. In April and June of 1940, President Franklin D. Roosevelt proposed changes that became effective on June 30, 1940. The organizational changes, known as the 1940 amendments to the Civil Aeronautics Act, led to the reorganization of the three agencies into two. The first agency, the Civil Aeronautics Board (CAB), was set up as an independent group of five persons who reported to the president. This board exercised legislative and judicial authority over civil aviation as well as executive control of the economic regulations that governed airmail carriers. The investigation of aircraft accidents also became the responsibility of the CAB. The second agency created by the 1940 amendments was the Civil Aeronautics Administration, headed by an administrator who would focus on the execution of safety regulations. The Civil Aeronautics Administration was placed under the Department of Commerce.

The Roosevelt plans submitted to Congress in 1940 led to reorganization in which the five-member Civil Aeronautics Authority became the independent CAB; the Office of the Administrator of Civil Aeronautics was renamed the Civil Aeronautics Administration and placed under the Department of Commerce, wholly separate from the CAB; the three-person air safety board was abolished, with its procedures and personnel absorbed into a bureau of safety within the CAB. The CAB, however, retained the responsibility for prescribing safety regulation and suspending or revoking certain aircraft or airmen certificates. The president's belief was that reorganization would reduce the number of administrative agencies and simplify the task of executive management while drawing a more practical separation between the functions of the administrator and the functions of the CAB.

Significance

The CAB had specific definitions and interpretations of regulations unique to the air transport field. Although there were parallels to surface transportation in economic regulation, safety regulation was much different. In the decades following World War II, there was a tremendous increase in the speed of aircraft and rapid growth in the number of daily flights. These factors, coupled with the increasing inadequacy of aviation navigation facilities, created serious congestion and danger. The problem was graphically illustrated in May, 1958, by the collision of a military jet trainer and a civilian transport plane, the third major disaster in less than four months. The worst civil aviation tragedy in the nation's history to that date occurred in 1956, when two airliners collided over the Grand Canyon, with a combined loss of 128 lives. The mounting number of air accidents gave rise to the demand for a single aviation agency to conduct the operation and development of aviation facilities and services related to air traffic control.

The Federal Aviation Act of 1958 brought no major changes to economic regulations, but it did establish the Federal Aviation Agency, which was directed by a civilian administrator. This agency in effect replaced the Civil Aeronautics Administration, which had previously been charged with safety regulation. The administrator was given the power to regulate the use of navigable air space, to establish and operate air navigation facilities, to prescribe air traffic rules for all aircraft, to conduct research and development, and to suspend or revoke safety certificates, subject to review by the CAB. In addition, the administrator retained all authority previously granted to the Civil Aeronautics Administration.

The 1958 act also created the federal government's policy toward several aviation-related issues. The CAB was to encourage and develop an air transportation system properly adapted to the present and future needs of the foreign and domestic commerce of the United States, the postal service, and national defense. Air transportation was to be regulated in a manner that would recognize and preserve its inherent advantages, assure the highest degree of safety, and foster sound economic conditions. Economic regulation would include the promotion of adequate, economical, and efficient service by air carriers at reasonable charges, without unjust discrimination, undue preferences and advantages, or unfair or destructive competitive practices. Competition would be encouraged to the extent necessary to ensure the sound development of an air transportation system that would serve the public interest. Finally, federal policy would promote safety in air commerce as well as promoting, encouraging, and developing civil aeronautics.

On October 15, 1966, Congress created the Department of Transportation. The department became operational in April, 1967, and the Federal Aviation Agency was placed in the new department, with its name changed to the Federal Aviation Administration. The act also transferred the CAB's accident investigation and related safety functions to the Department of Transportation and delegated them to an independent agency, the National Transportation Safety Board. In all other respects, the CAB's function remained unchanged.

Airlines continued to grow and prosper. The airlines' share of domestic intercity common carrier passenger miles rose from less than 1 percent in 1930 to more than 77 percent in 1974. U.S. airlines carried 94 percent of overseas travelers in 1974, and airlines also became carriers of diverse types of freight. In 1974, air-freight revenues totaled more than $1.2 billion, which amounted to about 9 percent of air carrier revenues and more than 1 percent of freight revenues for all modes of transport.

Regulation consistently focused on industry development. The acts passed in the middle of the twentieth century proved that the federal government was paying close attention to the stabilization and organization of the commercial aviation industry and to the regulations that ensured its operation and safety. Existing U.S.-based carriers continued to enjoy protection in market share and stability through careful regulatory activities, and it was not until the late 1970's and the 1980's that the industry turned its attention to deregulation and a return to free-market control.

The efficacy of deregulation was vigorously debated. Many argued that the new freedoms given to aviation departed substantially from the direction of early economic regulation and made it difficult for the domestic system to operate effectively. Although safety issues were not deregulated, they were affected by increased competitive pressures in the commercial aviation industry. Debates will likely continue on deregulation and on the efficacy of economic regulatory tools. Lending further urgency to the debate over airline safety were attacks by hijackers and terrorists during the last three decades of the twentieth century and the beginning of the twenty-first century, highlighted most dramatically by terrorists' use of airplanes to hit the World Trade Center's twin towers in New York City and the Pentagon in Washington, D.C.,

on September 11, 2001. Outrage over these attacks and fears of more attempts prompted the tightening of airport security and the bulletproofing of cockpit doors; cockpit crews were issued weapons, and the deployment of air marshals on airplanes increased. In the wake of the 2001 attacks, Congress also established the Transportation Security Administration, which succeeded the FAA as the primary agency responsible for security in civil aviation.

—*Theodore O. Wallin*

FURTHER READING

Davis, Grant M. *Transportation Regulation: A Pragmatic Assessment.* Danville, Ill.: Interstate Printers and Publishers, 1976. Discusses various pieces of regulation concerning various transportation industries.

Harper, Donald V. *Transportation: Users, Carriers, Government.* 2d ed. Englewood Cliffs, N.J.: Prentice-Hall, 1982. Discusses the interactions among the users and providers of transportation services as well as government involvement in the transportation industries.

Hazard, John L. *Transportation: Management, Economics, Policy.* Cambridge, Md.: Cornell Maritime Press, 1977. A good foundation for the economics of transportation, with references to regulatory actions. Specific sections deal with aviation regulation.

Kane, Robert M. *Air Transportation.* 14th ed. Dubuque, Iowa: Kendall/Hunt, 2002. Undergraduate textbook provides a section on history that includes excellent coverage of the early airmail days and the Kelly Act's ramifications. Material on subsequent aviation legislation nicely supplements earlier coverage.

Wells, Alexander T., and John G. Wensveen. *Air Transportation: A Management Perspective.* 5th ed. Monterey, Calif.: Brooks/Cole, 2003. Textbook aimed at undergraduates includes a brief but thorough discussion of contract airmail service and the original twelve contract airmail routes.

July 1, 1940
U.S. FISH AND WILDLIFE SERVICE IS FORMED

As part of an effort to organize the federal government more efficiently, the U.S. Congress merged the Bureau of Fisheries and the Bureau of Biological Survey to form the Fish and Wildlife Service in the U.S. Department of the Interior.

LOCALE: United States
CATEGORIES: Organizations and institutions; environmental issues; government and politics

KEY FIGURES
Spencer Fullerton Baird (1823-1887), first commissioner of the U.S. Fish Commission
Clinton Hart Merriam (1855-1942), first chief of the U.S. Bureau of Biological Survey

SUMMARY OF EVENT
In an effort to organize the government more efficiently according to functions, the U.S. Congress on July 1, 1940, merged the Bureau of Fisheries from the Department of Commerce and the Bureau of Biological Survey from the Department of Agriculture into the Fish and Wildlife Service in the Interior Department. This was somewhat unusual, because the trend had long been to divide and expand government bureaucracies instead of consolidating them for greater efficiency and less duplication of effort. The work done in the field by the agencies involved continued almost exactly as it had before consolidation.

The Bureau of Fisheries originated as the U.S. Fish Commission by act of Congress in 1871. Spencer Fullerton Baird, director of the National Museum and assistant secretary of the Smithsonian Institution, was the key person behind the creation of the Fish Commission and served as its first commissioner. Baird was in the habit of spending his summers along the New England coast, where he noticed a pattern of gradual decrease in the number of the fish he was accustomed to catching. Inquiries among local fishermen confirmed what he had suspected.

It was decided that a commission would be appointed to discover the cause of the problem and attempt to correct it in an expedient manner. No money was available for the commission, so Baird agreed to serve without salary and furnished office space in his own home. The chairman of the appropriations committee refused Baird's request for money to rent offices for fear that a new government bureaucracy would get started. Never-

theless, the commissionership eventually became a salaried position, and in 1903 the U.S. Fish Commission was renamed the Bureau of Fisheries in the Department of Commerce. Its duties included the systematic investigation of reasons for the decrease of commercial food fish in the coastal and inland waters of the United States. The bureau studied fish migratory patterns and investigated the effects of pollution on the fishing industry.

The bureau also established federally operated fish hatcheries and began propagating freshwater food fish in the lakes and rivers of the United States. This project was later expanded to the coastal areas to include marine fish, shellfish, and lobsters. Methods of storing and processing fish were compared, and improvements in fishing methods and equipment were suggested. In 1906, responsibility for Alaskan salmon fisheries and fur seals was transferred from the Treasury Department to the

Spencer Fullerton Baird. (National Oceanic and Atmospheric Administration/Department of Commerce)

Bureau of Fisheries. The bureau protected certain Alaskan fur-bearing animals, sea lions, and walruses and also collected whaling data.

The Bureau of Biological Survey began as the Division of Entomology, later called Economic Ornithology and Mammalogy, in the U.S. Department of Agriculture in 1885. Headed by Clinton Hart Merriam, the survey investigated the interrelationships of birds and agriculture and the relationship of mammals to agriculture and forestry. The work was subdivided into four areas: wildlife research, regulation of game laws, refuge management, and predator and rodent control.

The Biological Survey introduced new techniques for studying wildlife based on the use of the cyclone trap, which soon demonstrated that there were many more animal species in North America than anyone had imagined. The bureau also began mapping the United States according to flora and fauna. It studied the relationship between the geographic distribution of specific plants and animals and the climates of given regions. In addition, the bureau operated the federal bird refuge system and large game preserves, a responsibility eventually transferred to the U.S. Forest Service. The government purchased marshlands for bird refuges. Farmers and ranchers welcomed the bureau's work in controlling rodents and predators that destroyed their crops and livestock. The bureau also sought to control rabies.

SIGNIFICANCE

The 1940 merger of the two bureaus into the U.S. Fish and Wildlife Service continued and enlarged the work of conservation begun by the bureaus' founding leaders, and the importance of the Fish and Wildlife Service has grown steadily ever since. One vehicle for the organization's growth has been the federal grants-in-aid program to the states for wildlife and fish restoration projects.

Soon after World War II, the service's Office of Foreign Activities became involved in international fishery projects, working with the State Department to help negotiate and administer international fishery agreements. Members of the Fish and Wildlife Service began attending international conferences on fisheries and serving on international fishery commissions. Members also administered educational programs in foreign countries to share the results of their experience and research.

Eventually, an organizational distinction was made between commercial fisheries and sport fish and game. In 1970, the Bureau of Commercial Fisheries was transferred to the Commerce Department under the name of the National Marine Fisheries Service. The Bureau of

Sport Fisheries and Wildlife remained in the Interior Department under the name of the Fish and Wildlife Service. The basic goals of the service remained what they had always been: to ensure that the population of the fisheries is high enough to fulfill the needs of the human population and to protect the fisheries from the destruction that overuse can cause.

Under the Endangered Species Acts of 1966 and 1973, the Fish and Wildlife Service became responsible for implementing the acts' provisions. The service acquired habitats for endangered species and sought to restore them. In 1975, the service began evaluating the impacts on fish and wildlife of offshore development and oil spills. The service also conducts aerial and ground surveys of migratory birds and seeks to protect waterfowl production areas, sometimes setting up nets and barriers to prevent human incursions during mating and birthing seasons.

In addition to its programs for conservation and preservation, the service has produced many valuable studies of American natural history.

—William H. Burnside

FURTHER READING

Cameron, Jenks. *The Bureau of Biological Survey: Its History, Activities, and Organization.* 1929. Reprint. New York: Arno Press, 1974. Detailed history of the Bureau of Biological Survey and how it conducted its work in the early twentieth century. Includes the texts of key laws relating to birds and wildlife in an appendix.

Clarke, Jeanne Nienaber, and Daniel C. McCool. *Staking Out the Terrain: Power and Performance Among Natural Resource Agencies.* 2d ed. Albany: State University of New York Press, 1996. Well-developed assessment of the rise and fall of natural resource bureaucracies in the United States, including the Fish and Wildlife Service.

Clepper, Henry. *Origins of American Conservation.* New York: Ronald Press, 1966. Brief survey of the history of conservation in the United States includes chapters on wildlife regulation and restoration, forests and forestry, fisheries, and water conservation.

Dolan, Edward F. *The American Wilderness and Its Future: Conservation Versus Use.* New York: Franklin Watts, 1992. Discussion of the attempt to balance the need for conservation with the need to use natural resources. Includes information on the role of the U.S. Fish and Wildlife Service in the enforcement of laws under the Endangered Species Act.

Dupree, A. Hunter. *Science in the Federal Government: A History of Policies and Activities to 1940.* Cambridge, Mass.: Belknap Press, 1957. Classic, well-documented study of the relationship between the development of science in the United States and national politics. Discusses the Fish and Wildlife Service as part of the effort to use the tools of science in the work of conservation.

Jaussaud, Renee M. "United States Fish and Wildlife Service." In *Government Agencies*, edited by Donald R. Whitnah. Westport, Conn.: Greenwood Press, 1983. Provides a brief history of the bureaus that were part of the U.S. Fish and Wildlife Service from 1871 to 1976.

Merchant, Carolyn. *The Columbia Guide to American Environmental History.* New York: Columbia University Press, 2002. Discusses how humans and environment have interacted throughout American history, including human impacts on animal species. Includes an environmental history time line and an extensive guide to resources.

SEE ALSO: Mar. 14, 1903: First U.S. National Wildlife Refuge Is Established; Mar. 4, 1913: Migratory Bird Act; Sept. 1, 1914: Last Passenger Pigeon Dies; Aug. 25, 1916: National Park Service Is Created; June 3, 1924: Gila Wilderness Area Is Designated; Mar. 16, 1934: Migratory Bird Hunting and Conservation Stamp Act.

July 10-October 31, 1940
BATTLE OF BRITAIN

Germany launched an aerial attack on Great Britain in an attempt to clear the way for a land invasion. The Royal Air Force, however, successfully defended the island, and the Germans were forced to postpone the invasion of Britain and to turn instead toward the Soviet Union.

LOCALE: England; English Channel
CATEGORIES: Wars, uprisings, and civil unrest; World War II; military history

KEY FIGURES
Sir Alan Francis Brooke (1883-1963), British general officer and commander in chief of the Southern Command
Winston Churchill (1874-1965), prime minister of Great Britain, 1940-1945, 1951-1955
Sir Hugh Dowding (1882-1970), commander in chief of the Fighter Command with the Royal Air Force
Hermann Göring (1893-1946), commander in chief of the German Luftwaffe
Albert Kesselring (1885-1960), commander of Luftwaffe Luftflotte 2
Keith Park (1892-1975), commander of Royal Air Force Number 11 Group
Erich Raeder (1876-1960), commander in chief of the German navy
Hugo Sperrle (1885-1953), commander of Luftwaffe Luftflotte 3

SUMMARY OF EVENT
With the German conquests of the Low Countries and France completed by June of 1940, Britain stood alone in Western Europe to confront Adolf Hitler's forces. Winston Churchill spoke to his countrymen: "Hitler knows he will have to break us on this island or lose the war." British military leaders assumed that a German invasion of Britain from across the English Channel was likely to begin in the near future.

Although the British Royal Navy controlled the seas immediately around Britain, its forces were strained by the need to protect the Atlantic supply routes used by American supply ships against German U-boat attacks. Some fifty-five army divisions could be mustered to defend the island, but many of those divisions were only at half strength. Prospects of defending against a German ground attack were further complicated by the fact that British forces fleeing Dunkirk earlier in June were forced to abandon most of their supplies while retreating from German forces.

An army general observed at the time that the defense of Britain would fall primarily on the Royal Air Force (RAF), particularly on the Fighter Command planes. Since 1936, Sir Hugh Dowding, head of the Fighter Command, had tried to convince the cabinet and the Air Council that, in the next war, Britain would be on the defensive. For that reason, priority in aircraft planning and production should be given to a buildup of fighter plane strength, not bombers as the Air Council wanted. Dowding also stressed the need for improved detection and

1940

early warning of enemy aircraft. Over much opposition and after much delay, Dowding's warnings persuaded the Air Council to alter its contingency plans. In 1939, the Air Council ordered stepped-up production of more fighters, as well as the construction of an early warning system.

British designers developed two types of improved fighter planes: the Hurricane and the Spitfire. Both flew at maximum speeds of three hundred miles per hour (fast for the time), had heavy armor, constant speed propellers, self-sealing fuel tanks, and eight machine guns. The innovative design of these planes had a major impact on the course of Britain's air battle with the German Luftwaffe (air force).

During 1937, British physicists had worked on air-craft detection by means of radio wave signals, and what would later be known as radar was quickly developed. Work began on building a linked system of radar stations, ground observation units, and Fighter Command sector control bases that would enable the Fighter Command to anticipate and intercept enemy bombers. Hundreds of barrage balloons and antiaircraft artillery added to the British defensive shield.

Since the German invasion of France, Hitler had sought to persuade the British to negotiate a settlement and end the fighting between their nations. His peace overtures were rejected out of hand by Churchill. Although he believed the mission "technically unfeasible," Hitler approved Operation Sea Lion, the military plan for the German invasion of England, in July of 1940. The invasion was tentatively set to begin on September 21, some two months later. Ninety thousand German troops would make up the initial assault force, building to ten divisions within two weeks. Preparations for Operation Sea Lion went forward rapidly. More than twelve hundred boats and barges were assembled at French ports across the Channel from England. Troops were trained in landing procedures, and bases were built for the aircraft that were to provide air cover during the landing. A central element in the plan was to neutralize Britain's air force before German troops crossed the English Channel.

Serious disagreements then arose between the German naval and army high commands as to whether the landings should be made along a broad front in southern and eastern England as the army wanted, or on a more concentrated front in Kent and Sussex. Admiral Erich Raeder insisted that his ships could not assure protection of the assault forces over the broad front, and the generals feared that the narrow front would enable the British to place their full force in one locality and so more effectively contest the invasion. Raeder finally won his point, and the narrow front plan was adopted; but the delay

The Luftwaffe's field marshal, Hermann Göring (left), discusses plans with chief of staff Major General Hans Jechonnek in 1940. (Hulton Archive/Getty Images)

had further shortened the time margin for implementation. Logistic revisions had to be made with dangerous haste to get Operation Sea Lion under way before autumn storms closed the Channel.

Across the Channel, British ground and air defense preparations were also proceeding. Under General Sir Alan Francis Brooke, the Home Guard was increased to five hundred thousand men; mobile field guns, antitank weapons, and small arms were provided in ever larger amounts; more than two million bomb shelters were built and distributed; and plans to resist German landings from the sea or by parachutes from the air were developed.

It was increasingly apparent to both sides that control of the air over southern England would be the critical factor in determining the success or failure of a German invasion. The Luftwaffe's commander in chief, Hermann Göring, had no doubt that his pilots could gain that control. Indeed, he believed that his bombers would so pulverize British defenses within a month's time that they would have to surrender, and a cross-Channel invasion would be unnecessary. Göring had cause for optimism. With more than thirteen hundred bombers and twelve hundred fighter planes, the Luftwaffe in Western Europe greatly overmatched the Royal Air Force. The Luftwaffe squadrons were organized into three air groups (Luftflotten); of these, the latest was Luftflotte 2, commanded by Albert Kesselring, and Luftflotte 3, commanded by Hugo Sperrle. The air groups were stationed in France and the Netherlands, from whence they would spearhead the German air offensive.

To confront the German air power, Dowding's Fighter Command had only about 700 front line fighter aircraft, with another 350 in reserve. They were, of necessity, deployed all over the island. Even the heaviest concentration of fighter planes—those in Park's Number 11 Group in the southeast—would probably be outnumbered by as much as ten to one by the attacking German planes. Dowding's most serious shortage, however, was of men to fly the planes. There were only a few more than fourteen hundred fully trained fighter pilots and almost no reserves available to replace them if they were disabled or killed.

Assigning precise beginning and ending dates to the Battle of Britain is a somewhat arbitrary proposition: There were German attacks on the British Isles before the "battle" is thought to have begun, and the fighting continued for quite a while after the most intense phase—which defines the battle proper—ended. Indeed, the Battle of Britain was followed immediately by what is known as the Blitz, a period of German bombing of En-

glish cities that lasted until May of 1941. Most historians place the decisive period of the battle between July 10 and October 31, 1940. The fighting during that period consisted of a number of bomber attacks and fighter plane encounters, increasing in size and intensity. During July and into early August, the Luftwaffe carried out intermittent strikes, mostly on British shipping in the Channel and on the port of Dover. Some 150 civilians were killed and twenty ships were sunk in these strikes, but dozens of Luftwaffe planes were downed by RAF fighters and antiaircraft fire. On August 1, Hitler ordered the Luftwaffe to destroy the Royal Air Force and establish air superiority. "The German air force is to overcome the British air force with all means at its disposal, and as soon as possible," Hitler ordered.

The next phase of the German air offensive was directed at the radar stations and airfields in the southeastern counties of England. British losses of men and machine were heavy, and the prospects of clearing the area for the Sea Lion landings were enhanced. The airfields were quickly repaired, radar stations were rebuilt, and the Fighter Command was able to complete most of its operations by mid-August. As a result of the energetic efforts of Lord Beaverbrook, the minister of aircraft production, Britain more than made up its losses in fighter aircraft. The pilot shortage was partly rectified through increased graduation from training schools, the retraining of bomber pilots, and shifting pilots from other branches of the military, as well as recruitment of foreign pilots then in Britain.

Meanwhile, Göring had been planning Operation Eagle, a massive saturation bombing of Britain's southern ports and airfields. Operation Eagle had to be postponed several times in early August because of bad weather. Then on August 13, designated "eagle day" by the German Command, British radar stations picked up signals of very large formations of approaching aircraft: Operation Eagle had begun. The German attackers came in several waves, and Park's fighters rose to meet them. Some of the German bombers penetrated British defenses and did further damage, but the Hurricanes and Spitfires shot down forty-seven of the enemy planes at the cost of thirteen British craft.

Bad flying weather returned, causing a two-day suspension of the operation. By August 15, favorable weather prompted Göring to order a renewal of the bombings. He declared that the objective was to obliterate the Royal Air Force planes and facilities. On that day, and into August 16, four successive waves came across the Channel and across the North Sea from bases in Nor-

1940

way. Luftflotte 2 and Luftflotte 3 bombers eluded Park's fighters and the antiaircraft guns in sufficient numbers to destroy four aircraft factories and five airfields around London. The bombers from Norway had been sent with insufficient fighter escort and they were brought down in large numbers. In those two days, the Luftwaffe had seventy-six planes shot down, the worst damage in a short period the German air force would ever suffer.

In all, between August 8 and August 26, the British fighters destroyed 602 German aircraft—mostly bombers, especially the Stuka dive bombers, which proved very vulnerable to British defenses. In that same period, 259 British fighters were shot down during these daylight raids. Under intense bombardment, Britain refused to yield to German air power. Churchill praised the efforts of the Royal Air Force and the British military in his famous speech to the House of Commons on August 20, 1940. "Never in the field of human conflict has so much been owed by so many to so few," Churchill observed.

Despite the growing German losses, the Luftwaffe attacks intensified. Göring was convinced that, weather permitting, Britain could be brought to its knees in approximately two weeks. During the last week of August and the first week of September, 1940, there were more than thirty major attacks averaging more than one thousand planes per raid. Most of the bombs were directed at the airfields and sector stations of Number 11 Group. Vice Marshal Park admitted that the damage was extensive and that the fighting efficiency of his command was being seriously impaired. Dowding saw the mounting loss of fighter pilots as critical: In those two weeks, 103 RAF pilots were killed or declared missing. By September 6, the Fighter Command (and therefore all of Britain) appeared on the verge of defeat. Across the Channel, Operation Sea Lion preparations were stepped up with the news of the Luftwaffe successes.

Then, in early September, Göring made a serious tactical error. He ordered the Luftwaffe to shift its attacks from RAF facilities toward massive attacks on London and other population centers. Göring had received intelligence reports that the Fighter Command had been neutralized and no longer had sufficient strength to defend against German bombers. Those reports were wrong, as the events of the following week would illustrate. If Göring had pursued his objective of destroying the Fighter Command, Germany might have won the Battle of Britain.

On September 7, the British government sent out the code signal "Cromwell," signifying that the expected invasion was now at hand. On that same day, nearly two hundred German bombers hit East London, killing more than three hundred civilians and inflicting extensive damage to houses, docks, and warehouses. That night, another 250 bombers, guided by the light of the extensive fires, did more damage to the British capital. Park sent up his fighters to intercept. In the air battles that ensued, another thirty-eight German planes were shot down, as were twenty-eight British aircraft. Most important, Park had demonstrated that the Fighter Command was still functioning and lethal. London was again bombed on September 9, but with less effect than on September 7, because only about half of the attacking planes were able to penetrate and attack their targets. As the attacks continued, nearly one thousand civilians per week were dying in raids on London. Churchill, fearing any show of weakness, ordered the Royal Navy and the RAF Bomber Command to attack French port facilities that could be used by Germany in a cross-Channel invasion. It was increasingly obvious that the Germans did not yet control the Channel or the air space over England. Faced with that knowledge, Hitler postponed Operation Sea Lion to the spring of 1941.

What proved to be Göring's last major effort to clear the way for the invasion came on September 15, 1940. He threw everything he had into the day's fighting. Some 123 bombers with 5 fighter escorts each went out from the continental bases. Park's squadrons, reinforced by planes from other British air groups, went to meet the Luftwaffe. The air battle began about noon and lasted until late in the evening. When the day ended, sixty German planes had been destroyed, with British losses of only twenty-six aircraft. September 15, 1940, would later be identified by many as the turning point in the Battle of Britain. "We still keep this day, and I hope we will always keep it," Harold Macmillan would write, "in commemoration of our victory."

SIGNIFICANCE

German air attacks on England would continue for the better part of a year, as the Battle of Britain evolved into the Blitz sometime around October 31. In many ways, however, British victory was achieved on September 15. Two days afterward, realizing that the Luftwaffe could not gain air supremacy and that it was too late for weather favorable to further attacks, Hitler ordered the indefinite postponement of Operation Sea Lion. His interest turned eastward instead, and German plans for the invasion of Russia (Operation Barbarossa) began. Britain would still have to endure repeated pounding by German bombers in the Blitz, but in the summer of 1940, the "gallant few" of the RAF Command had saved Britain from invasion. Adding up the final cost, more than forty thousand British civilians were killed. In addition, more than forty-six thousand were injured and more than one million homes were destroyed. Six to seven hundred British military aircraft had been destroyed, as against some fourteen hundred German aircraft of all types.

In addition to preserving England from invasion, occupation, and defeat, the Battle of Britain was a turning point in American perception of the war. It demonstrated that Britain was capable of resisting the Nazis' aggression—something that no other country had yet accomplished and that many Americans thought beyond British power. Moreover, the radio broadcasts of Edward R. Murrow from the rooftops of London during the battle—with the sound of bombs falling all around him—brought the stakes of the conflict home to Americans by bringing the visceral experience of enduring a Nazi bombing attack into their living rooms. It weakened somewhat—albeit only somewhat—the isolationist mood of the nation, and it ensured that most would see the British as allies and the Germans as enemies.

—*James W. Pringle and Lawrence I. Clark*

FURTHER READING

Bickers, Richard Townsend, ed. *The Battle of Britain: The Greatest Battle in the History of Air Warfare.* Englewood Cliffs, N.J.: Prentice Hall, 1990. A detailed examination of the Battle of Britain written by a former RAF pilot and British military historian. Contains photographs, detailed information on military aircraft, day-to-day analysis of the air battles, index, and chapter on "RAF Heroes" killed during the Battle of Britain.

Fisher, David E. *A Summer Bright and Terrible: Winston Churchill, Lord Dowding, Radar, and the Impossible Triumph of the Battle of Britain.* Washington, D.C.: Shoemaker & Hoard, 2005. History of the Battle of Britain, focusing on the importance of Churchill's moral leadership and Dowding's military strategy to the British victory. Bibliographic references and index.

Franks, Norman. *Battle of Britain.* New York: Gallery Books, 1990. A useful general intro-

"NEVER . . . WAS SO MUCH OWED BY SO MANY TO SO FEW"

In his August 20, 1940, speech to Parliament, Winston Churchill attempted to dispel fears of an impending Nazi invasion by noting that the Allied soldiers' recent sacrifices had done much to strengthen Britain's position.

The gratitude of every home in our Island, in our Empire, and indeed throughout the world, except in the abodes of the guilty, goes out to the British airmen who, undaunted by odds, unwearied in their constant challenge and mortal danger, are turning the tide of the World War by their prowess and by their devotion. Never in the field of human conflict was so much owed by so many to so few. All hearts go out to the fighter pilots, whose brilliant actions we see with our own eyes day after day. . . .

A good many people have written to me to ask me to make on this occasion a fuller statement of our war aims, and of the kind of peace we wish to make after the war, than is contained in the very considerable declaration which was made early in the autumn. . . . I do not think it would be wise at this moment, while the battle rages and the war is still perhaps only in its earlier stage, to embark upon elaborate speculations about the future shape which should be given to Europe. . . . But before we can undertake the task of rebuilding we have not only to be convinced ourselves, but we have to convince all other countries that the Nazi tyranny is going to be finally broken. The right to guide the course of world history is the noblest prize of victory. We are still toiling up the hill; we have not yet reached the crest-line of it; we cannot survey the landscape or even imagine what its condition will be when that longed-for morning comes. The task which lies before us immediately is at once more practical, more simple and more stern. . . . For the rest, we have to gain the victory. That is our task.

. . . Some months ago we came to the conclusion that the interests of the United States and of the British Empire both required that the United States should have facilities for the naval and air defense of the Western Hemisphere against the attack of a Nazi power. . . . We had therefore decided spontaneously, and without being asked or offered any inducement, to inform the Government of the United States that we would be glad to place such defense facilities at their disposal by leasing suitable sites in our Transatlantic possessions for their greater security against the unmeasured dangers of the future. . . . His Majesty's Government are entirely willing to accord defense facilities to the United States on a 99 years' leasehold basis. . . . Undoubtedly this process means that these two great organizations of the English-speaking democracies, the British Empire and the United States, will have to be somewhat mixed up together in some of their affairs for mutual and general advantage. For my own part, looking out upon the future, I do not view the process with any misgivings. I could not stop it if I wished; no one can stop it. Like the Mississippi, it just keeps rolling along. Let it roll. Let it roll on full flood, inexorable, irresistible, benignant, to broader lands and better days.

duction to the Battle of Britain by a British aviation writer. Includes photographs, appendix, and index.

Gilbert, Martin. "France's Agony, Britain's Resolve" and "The Battle for Britain." In *The Second World War: A Complete History*. New York: Henry Holt, 1989. In this widely acclaimed book, the official biographer of Winston Churchill provides a valuable history of German strategy and the defiance of the British people.

Hough, Richard, and Denis Richards. *The Battle of Britain: The Greatest Air Battle of World War II*. New York: W. W. Norton, 1989. Richards, the coauthor of the official history of the Royal Air Force, and Hough, a former RAF pilot, draw heavily on official sources in this detailed military history. Includes photographs, illustrations, maps, detailed appendix, index, and day-to-day chronology of the fighting.

Robinson, Derek. *Invasion, 1940: The Truth About the Battle of Britain and What Stopped Hitler*. New York: Carroll & Graf, 2005. A reconsideration of the role of the RAF in preserving Britain from invasion: Emphasizes the weather and the ability of the Royal Navy to protect the island by staging night attacks on German ships in the Channel. Bibliographic references and index.

SEE ALSO: 1929-1940: Maginot Line Is Built; Mar. 7, 1936: German Troops March into the Rhineland; Feb. 12-Apr. 10, 1938: The Anschluss; Sept. 29-30, 1938: Munich Conference; Sept. 1, 1939: Germany Invades Poland; 1940-1941: Moore's Subway Sketches Record War Images; Apr. 9, 1940: Germany Invades Norway; May 10-June 22, 1940: Collapse of France; May 26-June 4, 1940: Evacuation of Dunkirk.

August, 1940
JAPAN ANNOUNCES THE GREATER EAST ASIA COPROSPERITY SPHERE

The empire of Japan sought to lead a bloc of Asian nations that would establish its political, economic, and cultural independence from the Western group of nations—including the United States, Great Britain, France, and the Netherlands—that had colonies in East Asia.

LOCALE: Japan
CATEGORIES: Diplomacy and international relations; colonialism and occupation

KEY FIGURES
Hachirō Arita (1884-1965), general in the Japanese Army and minister of foreign affairs
Nobuhiro Satō (1769-1850), originator of the greater East Asia concept
Hideki Tojo (1884-1948), war minister, 1940-1941, and prime minister of Japan during World War II, 1941-1944
Subhas Chandra Bose (1897-1945), Indian revolutionary

SUMMARY OF EVENT
The Japanese government faced a crisis of monumental proportions in 1940. The major Western powers—the United States and Great Britain—demanded that Japan abandon its claims on and occupation of China. The

Americans and the British also insisted that Japan withdraw from French Indochina, a colony that the Japanese had seized from the Vichy government in France. Failure to comply, the Western governments announced, would result in the adoption of severe economic sanctions against the Japanese. At this point, control of the Japanese government lay in the hands of the Imperial Japanese Army and Navy. A surrender of the holdings that it had already taken in China and a withdrawal from French Indochina would be in complete contravention of the military's long-range plans for expansion.

Accordingly, in August of 1940, the Japanese government proclaimed the creation of the Greater East Asia Coprosperity Sphere, which would incorporate Japan, Manchuria, Korea, and China into an independent economic and political entity composed solely of Asian peoples. The sphere would ultimately include French Indochina, the Dutch East Indies, the Philippine Islands, and Burma, and extremists even considered both India and Australia as possible additions.

The concept of a cooperative agreement among Asian peoples had long been a dream of the Japanese leadership. As early as the latter part of the eighteenth century and in the first half of the nineteenth century, Japanese scholar Nobuhiro Satō introduced the concept of a greater East Asia. He argued that Japan should aggressively expand its territory by seizing the Ryikyu Island group, Luzon (in the Philippines), and ultimately Java (in the Dutch East Indies) as part of what he called the "southward advance" strategy. If Japan were to achieve a leadership position in Asia, it would have to dominate a number of its neighbors.

Hachirō Arita, a professional diplomat who had served as foreign minister in a number of Japanese cabinets in the twentieth century, rationalized that the Coprosperity Sphere was not an attempt by Japan to monopolize economic and political power in Southeast Asia. Instead, he argued, it was designed to promote mutual opportunities for its members through support of independence movements, trade agreements, loans of capital, and exchanges of ideas.

The Japanese government announced the implementation of the new concept with great fanfare. The idea, however, was largely a piece of propaganda: No carefully delineated master plan for its implementation had been devised by the civilian leadership. The government left the mechanics of its application to the military governor in each conquered territory, which resulted in a wide variety of different economic and political approaches among jurisdictions, depending on the needs of the troops stationed in each area and the availability of goods. In November of 1942, Premier Hideki Tojo called representatives from all of the conquered countries to Tokyo for a conference on the goals of the Coprosperity Sphere. In his opening speech, he attacked the United States and Britain for their exploitation of Asian peoples and promised that Japan would lead the East Asian nations in a program of mutually beneficial economic development, racial harmony, and independence.

Japan, however, had already established a reputation for brutality in its relationship with its neighbors. In 1937, it received worldwide condemnation for the widely publicized destruction of the Chinese city of Nanjing. According to records developed during the postwar Tokyo War Crimes Tribunal, soldiers of the Tenth Japanese Imperial Army and the Sixteenth Division were responsible for the murders of more than two hundred thousand Chinese soldiers and civilians. The army was also accused of some twenty thousand rapes of Chinese women. Equally devastating records were uncovered in the final days of the Japanese army's occupation in Manila, where thousands of Filipinos were slaughtered by the Japanese as they retreated from Manila's walled city in early 1945.

Included in the list of politicians invited by Tojo was

Subhas Chandra Bose, the head of the provisional government in India, which wanted to overthrow British rule in the subcontinent. The Japanese established and trained the Indian National Army as well as the Burma Area Army with the intention of using the help of these two groups in a planned invasion of British India. Such an invasion never progressed past its initial planning stages, however, because the Japanese troops stationed on the Indian border lacked the supplies and equipment necessary to undertake such a campaign.

SIGNIFICANCE

Although Japan's promotion of the Greater East Asia Coprosperity Sphere seemed to be a shrewd propaganda move to secure the cooperation of Asians in countries colonized by Europe, in practice the movement was a failure. Despite pronouncements made by Japan's central government on the benefits that the new organization would provide to the colonial peoples of Southeast Asia, the Japanese military proved to be substantially more oppressive in its relationships with the colonial peoples than the Europeans and Americans had been.

The Japanese conquerors stripped the colonies of all the wealth they could find and cruelly abused the peoples under their control. Many of the local economies were devastated by these actions, which often left members of the native populations without enough food and equipment to support themselves. Moreover, the occupiers slaughtered members of the local population who objected to Japanese rule.

As World War II progressed in countries such as the Philippines and Burma, locals joined guerrilla groups and undermined the Japanese military administrations wherever they could, even though the latter were ruthless in their efforts to end such opposition. As the Allied forces gradually defeated the Japanese, local peoples took revenge on both retreating Japanese soldiers and the native citizens who had aided them. For example, Japanese colonies such as those established on the island of Mindanao in the Philippines were wiped out by members of the Filipino resistance.

—*Carl Henry Marcoux*

FURTHER READING

Harries, Meirion, and Susie Harries. *Soldiers of the Sun: The Rise and Fall of the Imperial Japanese Army.* New York: Random House, 1991. A detailed report on the activities of the Japanese army in the conquered countries under their control.

Ienaga, Saburo. *The Pacific War, 1931-1945.* New York: Pantheon Books, 1978. Chronicle of the events of the

1940

war in the Pacific by an outstanding Japanese historian. Explains the failure of the Japanese civil authorities to curb action by the military that led to the war's disastrous outcome.

Lebra, Joyce C. *Japan's Greater East Asia Co-prosperity Sphere in World War II*. New York: Oxford University Press, 1975. A collection of individual reports by Japanese military and political leaders. Also includes contributions by writers from other countries.

Tanaka, Yuki. *Hidden Horrors: Japanese War Crimes in World War II*. Boulder, Colo.: Westview Press, 1998.

A detailed study by a Japanese researcher into the motivation for the crimes committed by the Japanese military.

SEE ALSO: Aug. 22, 1910: Japanese Annexation of Korea; Jan. 7, 1932: Stimson Doctrine; Feb. 24, 1933: Japan Withdraws from the League of Nations; Dec. 29, 1934: Japan Renounces Disarmament Treaties; July 7, 1937: China Declares War on Japan; Dec., 1937-Feb., 1938: Rape of Nanjing; Sept., 1940: Japan Occupies Indochinese Ports.

August 3, 1940-March, 1941
ITALY INVADES BRITISH SOMALILAND

After a search for battle sites that they would be able to conquer, Italian forces struck British Somaliland. Although the Italians achieved their basic objective—to complicate British access to Ethiopia—their victory in the area was temporary.

ALSO KNOWN AS: East African Campaign; Abyssinian Campaign

LOCALE: British Somaliland (now in Somalia); Italian Somaliland (now in Somalia); French Somaliland (now Djibouti)

CATEGORIES: Military history; colonialism and occupation; World War II; wars, uprisings, and civil unrest

KEY FIGURES

Benito Mussolini (1883-1945), prime minister and dictator of Italy, 1922-1943

Winston Churchill (1874-1965), prime minister of Great Britain, 1940-1945

Amadeo (1898-1942), third duke of Aosta and commander of the Italian forces in British Somaliland

Guglielmo Nasi (1879-1971), commander of the native African troops of the Italian army

Alfred Godwin-Austen (1889-1963), commander of British defensive forces in British Somaliland

Archibald Wavell (1883-1950), commander of the British Middle East command

SUMMARY OF EVENT

Of all the Italian campaigns during World War II, the invasion and occupation of British Somaliland was counted as the sole Italian success in an independent

operation. The purpose of the invasion was to deny the British access to French Somaliland and its port city of Djibouti, which would cut off access to Ethiopia. On August 3, 1940, Amadeo, a field marshal, and General Guglielmo Nasi led the invasion forces into British Somaliland. The invading force of approximately 175,000 troops consisted of nearly 70 percent native African troops who had been enlisted as members of the Italian army and were gathered mostly from the Italian colony of Italian Somaliland.

On June 10, 1940, after witnessing Nazi Germany's massive territorial gains during its early victories and after the fall of France, Benito Mussolini, the Fascist Italian dictator, decided to join World War II on the side of the Axis forces, which had previously consisted of Germany and Japan. On June 10, 1940, Italy formally declared war on Great Britain, but it was slow to initiate any action against its new enemy. After surveying the strength of various Allied forces around the world, Mussolini decided to launch his first offensive action in Africa, since a campaign there was likely to end in an Italian victory.

The British army had approximately thirty-six thousand troops in Africa. On the other hand, the Italians had nearly one million troops in the same area. Britain's success as a colonial power was largely dependent on its impressive navy, and the Italians realized that they could defeat the British on land if not at sea. When Italy's army confronted the British in Africa in 1940, the vast Italian forces quickly overwhelmed the few battalions of British defenders stationed in British Somaliland.

Both the Axis and Allied Powers were extremely interested in the control of the Suez Canal and in the Middle East's vast oil supplies. Throughout World War II,

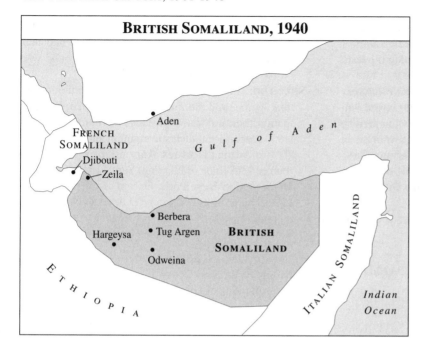

BRITISH SOMALILAND, 1940

French Somaliland
Aden
Gulf of Aden
Djibouti
Zeila
Berbera
Hargeysa
Tug Argen
BRITISH SOMALILAND
Odweina
ETHIOPIA
ITALIAN SOMALILAND
Indian Ocean

When the total size of the initial invading and defending forces are considered, a careful analysis of these numbers shows that the British were able to conduct an extremely skillful and orderly withdrawal while inflicting maximum casualties on the Italians. At first Winston Churchill criticized General Archibald Wavell, head of the Middle East command, for practically giving away British Somaliland without a fight, but later, after analyzing the numbers carefully, Churchill withdrew any criticisms of Wavell's tactics; Churchill realized that the alternative could have cost Britain its entire defensive force.

The Italians had little interest in gaining natural resources or territory in British Somaliland. Instead, Italian interests were based entirely on denying access to Ethiopia via British Somaliland. While British Somaliland had no direct access to Ethiopia, it could access the area through French Somaliland and its port of Djibouti. However, by preventing Great Britain from contact with the border between British Somaliland and French Somaliland, the Italians were able to keep the British away from Ethiopia.

SIGNIFICANCE

The Italian invasion of British Somaliland was successful largely due to the fact that the invading Italian troops overwhelmingly outnumbered the defending British troops. The main objective of the invasion—to deny Great Britain access to Ethiopia through the French Somaliland port of Djibouti—was also met. This victory, however, came at significant human cost to the Italians, particularly in light of the imbalance in numbers of troops. The British inflicted more than 2,000 casualties and lost only 260 of their own troops. Also, in the face of huge numbers of Italian troops, the British successfully evacuated most of their assets. In other words, the British defeat was not a total defeat, and it was not long before they regained their strength.

The Italian occupation of British Somaliland was very short-lived. In March of 1941, Great Britain launched a successful military expedition from Aden to retake British Somaliland from the Italians. This expedition was just a part of a multipronged and successful Allied offen-

the Allies maintained the upper hand in the Middle East. The Axis forces had several victories, although many of these were short-lived, including the Italian invasion and occupation of British Somaliland. In this campaign, the four battalions of British defenders were vastly outnumbered by the attacking Italians, who formed three separate columns to take the western cites of Zeila, Hargeisa, and Odweina. Zeila and Hargeisa both fell to the Italians on the second day of the invasion, and Odweina fell on the third day.

The British defending forces fell east to Tug Argan, where their main positions were located. Two of the three Italian columns joined forces for the attack on Tug Argan and moved into position, while the third column moved on toward the capital city Berbera. The British, realizing their desperate straits, received a few reinforcements and a new commander, General Alfred Godwin-Austen, but they were still only able to hold Tug Argan for a few days. The British defenders then retreated to the north coast city of Berbera, the capital of British Somaliland. On August 19, 1940, the British troops were successfully evacuated across the Gulf of Aden to the city of Aden in southern Yemen, leaving British Somaliland to the victorious Italians.

Defense of British Somaliland cost the British 38 deaths, 111 wounded, and 111 missing soldiers. The Italians fared significantly worse: Their losses included approximately 465 deaths, 1,530 wounded, and 34 missing.

1940

sive military operation into North Africa, known as the North African Campaign. The Italians' success was at least partly based on use of modern technology. Italian forces did an excellent job of coordinating by radio as they split into three separate columns in the western cities of Zeila, Hargeisa, and Odweina. In addition, the Italians were able to force the British troops out of British Somaliland with remarkable speed: In a little more than two weeks, the Italians controlled the British Somaliland capital city of Berbera and had driven all the defending British troops off the continent and into the British protectorate of Aden.

—*Glenn S. Hamilton*

FURTHER READING

French, David. *Raising Churchill's Army: The British Army and the War Against Germany, 1919-1945.* New York: Oxford University Press, 2000. This work contains a detailed accounting of the military tactics and equipment utilized by Great Britain's troops during World War II.

Gilbert, Adrian. *Germany's Lightning War: The Cam-*

paigns of World War II. Newton Abbot, England: David and Charles, 2000. This book conveys a great deal of information concerning the tactics of ground war utilized by the Axis countries.

Goda, Norman J. W. *Tomorrow the World: Hitler, Northwest Africa, and the Path Toward America.* College Station: Texas A & M University Press, 1998. This work contains detailed information on Axis tactics utilized during the African campaign.

Townshend, Charles, ed. *Oxford Illustrated History of Modern War.* New York: Oxford University Press, 1997. This work contains a great deal of text and photographs that fully cover the African campaign of World War II as well as many other conflicts.

SEE ALSO: 1911-1912: Italy Annexes Libya; Early 1920: Britain Represses Somali Rebellion; 1925-1926: Mussolini Seizes Dictatorial Powers in Italy; Oct. 11, 1935-July 15, 1936: League of Nations Applies Economic Sanctions Against Italy; Apr. 7, 1939: Italy Invades and Annexes Albania; Sept. 13, 1940: Italy Invades Egypt.

August 16, 1940
OGDENSBURG AGREEMENT

The United States and Canada entered into an agreement on hemispheric defense.

LOCALE: Ogdensburg, New York
CATEGORY: Diplomacy and international relations

KEY FIGURES

Winston Churchill (1874-1965), prime minister of Great Britain, 1940-1945

William Lyon Mackenzie King (1874-1950), prime minister of Canada, 1921-1926, 1926-1930, and 1935-1948

James Layton Ralston (1881-1948), Canadian defense minister

Franklin D. Roosevelt (1882-1945), president of the United States, 1933-1945

SUMMARY OF EVENT

After only slight hesitation, Canada followed the mother country, Great Britain, in going to war against Germany in 1939. Canada's southern neighbor, the United States, was sympathetic to Great Britain and its allies but vowed to remain neutral.

The situation changed drastically after the Germans

conquered France in June, 1940. The German armies seemed invincible, and there was a real threat that they might cross the English Channel and conquer Great Britain. The United States, realizing the gravity of the world situation, became more concerned about its security and that of the Western Hemisphere. The prime minister of Great Britain, Winston Churchill, developed a contingency plan to have the British royal family, in the event of a German takeover, flee Britain and take sanctuary in Canada. Clearly, the Atlantic Ocean was no longer a barrier to world conflict.

Franklin D. Roosevelt, the president of the United States, was worried about both Western Hemisphere security and Great Britain's ability to stay in the war. He wanted to help Great Britain and prepare his own country for the war he knew it would one day enter, but he believed that the U.S. public was not ready for full-fledged participation. Roosevelt therefore conceived the lend-lease policy to address both issues. Under lend-lease, Great Britain would lease certain military bases in the Western Hemisphere (in Newfoundland, Bermuda, and elsewhere) to the United States for ninety-nine years. In return, the United States would lend surplus aircraft and other military equipment to Great Britain. Thus the British military would be strengthened and the United States would gain control of bases that would help it defend the Western Hemisphere against potential German aggression.

Canada was not consulted under this agreement. Although a close ally and associate of Great Britain, Canada had been a sovereign nation since the Statute of Westminster in 1931. The Canadian prime minister, William Lyon Mackenzie King, had been slow to recognize the threat posed by Nazi Germany. King, indeed, was ambivalent about his country's entry into the European war until the very last moment. There were many political pressures on King not to enter the war; the voices raised in opposition ranged from those of Francophones in Quebec, whose fierce opposition to Britain made them reluctant to enter the war even though their own mother country, France, was on the British side, to those of isolationist farmers in the Prairie Provinces who saw no apparent need for Canada to intervene in foreign disputes. Most Canadians, however, supported King when he decided to commit Canada to the war effort at the side of Great Britain.

Once engaged in the war, King shared the concerns of Roosevelt and Churchill regarding Western Hemisphere security. He was heartened by the lend-lease agreement, but he was concerned about Canadian national sovereignty as affected by the accord, especially in the case of Newfoundland. Newfoundland's close geographic proximity to Canada put it in the natural Canadian sphere of influence. Newfoundland had been an independent, self-governing dominion for sixty years, until the 1930's, when, because of its inability to handle the economic depression of that era, it had been taken over by Great Britain. King and the majority of the Canadian public expected that one day Newfoundland would join the rest of Canada (as, in fact, it did in 1949). King was thus unwilling to accept the permanent transfer of bases in Newfoundland to U.S. sovereignty.

Roosevelt was friendly toward Canada and knew the country well from his summer visits to the Canadian island of Campobello. Recognizing King's concern over the situation, Roosevelt advised the Canadian leader that he would be reviewing troops in the town of Ogdensburg, located in northern New York State, close to the Canadian border, on August 16, 1940. King decided that

President Franklin D. Roosevelt (left), Prime Minister William Lyon Mackenzie King (center), and Secretary of War Henry L. Stimson in Ogdensburg, New York, two days after Roosevelt and King signed the Ogdensburg Agreement. (AP/Wide World Photos)

it would be to Canada's advantage for him to meet Roosevelt at Ogdensburg. In deference to Canadian public opinion, he made no public announcement of the visit, fearing that it would be seen as an act of submission or surrender to the United States.

King did his best to keep the meeting a secret. Even James Layton Ralston, the Canadian minister of defense, whose responsibilities were vitally concerned with the situation, learned of the meeting only through reading the next day's newspapers. On the morning of August 16, Roosevelt arrived in Ogdensburg, accompanied by the U.S. ambassador to Canada, J. Pierrepont Moffat. Roosevelt met King, and the two men together reviewed U.S. troops. Roosevelt and King then repaired to a railway carriage, where the substantive discussions were held. The two men were very different. King was a mystic who regularly attended séances in order to communicate with the spirit of his dead mother. Roosevelt, on the other hand, was regarded by many as the ultimate political opportunist, although his fierce commitment to democracy and liberalism never wavered. Nevertheless, the two men, who knew each other from previous meetings, established a good working rapport, and they quickly reached a broad consensus.

The centerpiece of this consensus was the so-called Continental System, which provided that Canada and the United States would regularly consult each other about military conditions. It also stipulated that the two countries would prepare themselves to mount a common defense of the Western Hemisphere. It even allowed for the possibility of temporary establishment of U.S. bases on Canadian soil. This was the aspect of the Continental System most disagreeable to Canadian nationalists. The U.S. bases, however, were only in the context of Canadian involvement in the lend-lease policy. Although King and Canada had not been involved in the formulation of this policy, Roosevelt's briefing apprised the Canadian prime minister of the lend-lease initiative, of which King wholeheartedly approved. King and Roosevelt also reached agreement on the status of Newfoundland. Roosevelt abjured any possible U.S. intent to control or annex Newfoundland permanently and stated that the future status of Newfoundland was up to the inhabitants of the island themselves, in consultation with the Canadian and British governments.

SIGNIFICANCE

The most important achievements of the Ogdensburg meeting were not in the precise terms hammered out between Roosevelt and King but in the general spirit of un-

derstanding and mutual support built between the two men. Canada and the United States had enjoyed friendly relations for many years, but the two countries had never really been allies. The Ogdensburg Agreement prepared Canada and the United States for the alliance that would exist between them when the United States entered World War II in 1941 and that would continue through the postwar years.

The Ogdensburg Agreement also represented a shift on the part of Canadian military and defense policy from a primary orientation toward Great Britain to a similar orientation toward the United States. By 1940, Canadian independence had been fully achieved. Canada, large in area but small in population, would inevitably have to engage in cooperation and alliance with another, more powerful country. Canada previously had been wary of the United States because the latter country was so much larger in population. The dominance of the United States on the North American continent had caused observers periodically to wonder if Canada might eventually be annexed by the United States. Although the Ogdensburg Agreement might have seemed to subordinate Canada to U.S. defense policy, it had the countervailing effect of firmly enshrining the interests of an independent Canada within a North American defense context. This reaffirmation of Canadian independence substantially assisted U.S.-Canadian cooperation after the United States entered the war. It also smoothed the way for eventual Canadian participation in two postwar defense alliances led by the United States: the North Atlantic Treaty Organization (NATO) and the North American Air Defense Pact (NORAD).

Predictably, King faced considerable outcry in the Canadian nationalist press once he returned to Ottawa and his meeting with Roosevelt was revealed to the public. However, his achievement in the Ogdensburg meeting was considerable, helping to cement Allied cooperation in the long and determined struggle against Nazi Germany and its threat to democracy and freedom.

—*Nicholas Birns*

FURTHER READING

Gibson, Frederick, and Jonathan G. Rossie, eds. *The Road to Ogdensburg*. East Lansing: Michigan State University Press, 1993. Collection of essays on developments in Canadian-U.S. relations leading up to the Ogdensburg Agreement.

Kimball, W. F. *The Most Unsordid Act: Lend-Lease, 1939-1941*. Baltimore: The Johns Hopkins University Press, 1969. Provides background on British-U.S.

relations in the period when the Ogdensburg Agreement was formulated.

Perras, Galen Roger. *Franklin Roosevelt and the Origins of the Canadian-American Security Alliance, 1933-1945: Necessary, but Not Necessary Enough*. Westport, Conn.: Praeger, 1998. Focuses on Roosevelt's role in encouraging Canada to establish a defense pact with the United States.

Pickersgill, J. W. *The Mackenzie King Record*. Toronto: University of Toronto Press, 1960. A comprehensive archive of the events of King's tenure as prime minister.

Riendeau, Roger. *A Brief History of Canada*. 2d rev. ed. New York: Facts On File, 2006. Concise history includes discussion of King's government and the World War II years in Canada.

Sokolsky, Joel J., and Joseph T. Jockel, eds. *Fifty Years of Canada-United States Defense Cooperation: The Road from Ogdensburg*. Lewiston, N.Y.: Edwin Mellen Press, 1992. Collection of essays by noted American and Canadian scholars discusses cooperation between the two nations in the years following the Ogdensburg Agreement.

Stacey, C. P. *Arms, Men, and Governments: The War Policies of Canada, 1939-1945*. Ottawa: Queen's Printers, 1970. Discusses Canadian defense policy in the World War II period.

Teatero, William. *Mackenzie King: Man of Mission*. Don Mills, Ont.: Nelson, 1979. Brief biography of the prime minister.

SEE ALSO: 1921-1948: King Era in Canada; Oct. 21, 1924: Halibut Treaty; Dec. 11, 1931: Formation of the British Commonwealth of Nations; July 18, 1932: St. Lawrence Seaway Treaty; Oct. 23, 1935-Nov. 15, 1948: King Returns to Power in Canada; Sept. 10, 1939: Canada Enters World War II.

September, 1940
JAPAN OCCUPIES INDOCHINESE PORTS

The Japanese Imperial Army, in the midst of an invasion of China, determined that an occupation of French Indochina was critical to the success of that endeavor as well as to its plans for Japanese military expansion into Southeast Asia generally. The Japanese government convinced the Vichy French government to allow it to occupy Indochina, thereby solidifying its hold on the region.

LOCALE: French Indochina (now in Vietnam, Cambodia, and Laos)

CATEGORIES: Colonialism and occupation; diplomacy and international relations; World War II; wars, uprisings, and civil unrest

KEY FIGURES

Yōsuke Matsuoka (1880-1946), Japanese foreign minister

Hideki Tojo (1884-1948), Japanese general and prime minister of Japan, 1941-1944

Hachirō Arita (1884-1965), Japanese general and minister of foreign affairs

SUMMARY OF EVENT

The Japanese military establishment seized control of its country's government during the 1930's. Through the use of both assassination and intimidation, the Imperial Japanese Army, claiming that its policies reflected the will of Emperor Hirohito, established itself as the main political force in the island nation. The army planned to strengthen its hold on power by expanding the empire through the conquest of neighboring countries and exploiting their resources. The concept of empire, however, was not new to Japan. Just before the turn of the twentieth century, the military had seized control of Korea, described as "a dagger pointed at the heart of the empire." In late 1931 and early 1932, the army overran Manchuria, established a puppet emperor, Puyi, and began a major exploitation of the newly conquered territory's natural resources.

The Japanese army invaded China proper in July of 1937. The army was committed to conquering China, and it engaged in a tremendous expenditure of men and equipment. Despite a series of impressive victories against the opposition Chinese Nationalist and Communist forces in the field, however, the Japanese high command never succeeded in gaining complete control of China's vast territory. In 1940, the Japanese high command considered the occupation of French Indochina's ports critical to the success of its long-range plans for the military, political, and economic domination of Southeast Asia. In order to proceed with the planned invasions of Malaya and the Dutch East Indies, as well as to cut off

1940

supplies to Chiang Kai-shek's Chinese forces from the French colony's key cities of Haiphong and Hanoi, French Indochina had to be neutralized.

In 1887, the French, after interfering in the local politics of the area for decades, had seized control of what were then the territories of Cochinchina, Annam, Tonkin, Cambodia, and Laos, and named the new political entity the Indochinese Union. For the next five decades, they exploited the area, establishing mines and rubber and rice plantations. As was common for European colonial regimes, the French authorities organized (or compelled) cheap local labor to run these operations. Their trade was forced to stop by the advent of World War II.

Yōsuke Matsuoka, Japan's foreign minister, began negotiations with France's Vichy government to cooperate with Japan with reference to the Indochina question. Japan had joined Germany and Italy in the Tripartite Pact of September 27, 1940. Certainly, this new ally of the victorious Germans influenced the thinking of the recently defeated French. Japanese General Issaku Nishihara arrived in Hanoi to negotiate with the French leader, Admiral Jean Decoux.

After some procrastination on its part, Vichy agreed to allow the Japanese army to occupy southern Indochina. The Japanese needed at least twelve weeks of full access to the country in order to build the additional bases necessary to launch their impending planned attacks on surrounding military targets such as the Dutch East Indies. The Japanese also succeeded in preventing Chiang Kai-shek's Nationalist forces from receiving any more supplies through northern Indochina. The Japanese, citing their policy of "Asia for the Asians," sought to gain support from the local population for their occupation of the country once they gained control.

The U.S. government regarded the Japanese action as tantamount to an invasion and demanded that the Japanese army withdraw from the French colony, as well as from China itself. Despite the restrictions that the United States imposed on exports to Japan, however, the island nation's military hierarchy had no intention of giving up its recent conquests. On December 7, 1941, Japan launched an all-out attack on Allied bases in Hawaii, the Philippines, Singapore, Malaysia, and the Dutch East Indies.

The bases that the Japanese army and navy acquired in the Indochina agreement with Vichy France served as critical launching pads for the invasion of the Dutch colonial possessions to the south. The quick surrender of Singapore allowed the army to advance their timetable for the invasion of the Dutch East Indies, which

Hideki Tojo. (AP/Wide World Photos)

quickly fell to a determined combined Japanese army and navy campaign. Once the Japanese military succeeded in conquering French Indochina, the Dutch East Indies, Malaysia, Singapore, and the Philippines, the Japanese government launched what proved to be a largely propagandistic campaign designed to regulate the politics and the economies of those countries. Called the Greater East Asia Coprosperity Sphere, the plan called for the eventual independence of all of its participants, as well as the integration of their economies into a master plan headed by Japan itself. The Japanese called for an end to colonialism in the area, repeating the slogan of "Asia for the Asians."

In practice, the central Japanese government left the implementation of the program to the military governments of each conquered country. As was the case in Indochina, the military simply confiscated any goods they thought of value and shipped them to the Japanese home islands, leaving the local populations in desperate economic shape. It was only after the U.S. Navy successfully interdicted Japan's supply lines from Burma, the Dutch East Indies, and Indochina to its home islands that these critical raw materials were lost to the Japanese war effort.

SIGNIFICANCE

Although the Japanese military profited initially from the acquisition of French Indochina, its long-term goal of incorporating the former French colonial possession into its master economic plan failed miserably. Not only did the United States and its allies defeat the Japanese in the field, but also the behavior of the Japanese occupiers toward the indigenous peoples in the lands that they conquered turned out to be so brutal and rapacious that they received little if any support when World War II began to turn against them. While it was true that the colonial peoples of Burma, India, Malaysia, the Philippines, and the Dutch East Indies sought independence, they quickly realized that with the Japanese they had only exchanged one colonial master for another. In most of the former European and American colonies, the local population aided their former masters to overthrow the Japanese occupiers.

All these nations would achieve their independence shortly after the conclusion of World War II in one manner or another. French Indochina was split up into three independent countries—Vietnam, Cambodia, and Laos. Meanwhile, Hideki Tojo, Japan's prime minister, and Yosuke Matsuoke, its foreign minister—both of whom had played prominent roles in the adoption of the country's plans of aggression—were charged as major war criminals by the Allied Forces at the conclusion of the war. Foreign Minister Matsuoke died June 26, 1946, before he could be tried. Prime Minister Tojo, however, was found guilty of seven major counts, sentenced to death, and executed.

—*Carl Henry Marcoux*

FURTHER READING

Harries, Meirion, and Susie Harries. *Soldiers of the Sun: The Rise and Fall of the Imperial Japanese Army*. New York: Random House, 1991. A detailed description of the operations of the Japanese army and its development, from its beginnings in 1890 until its dissolution in 1945.

Hoyt, Edwin P. *Japan's War: The Great Pacific Conflict*. New York: Cooper Square Press, 2001. Hoyt used the 101-volume offical Japanese-language history of World War II, never previously thoroughly examined by a Western scholar. He has made excellent use of these documents to give some insight to Japanese thinking about the war.

Ienaga, Saburo. *The Pacific War, 1931-1945: A Critical Perspective of Japan's Role in World War II*. New York: Pantheon Books, 1978. Prominent Japanese historian and university professor questions what the Japanese people could have done to avoid their nation's participation in World War II.

Toland, John. *The Rising Sun: The Decline and Fall of the Japanese Empire, 1936-1945*. New York: Random House, 1970. This is the work of an American historian, but his work was ably assisted by his Japanese wife and her family, which greatly facilitated his face-to-face interviews of Japanese who had held key positions during the war. His family connections also aided him in his extensive review of the records of the Japanese Ministry of Foreign Affairs and the Military History Archives of the Japan Defense Agency.

SEE ALSO: 1926-1949: Chinese Civil War; Jan. 7, 1932: Stimson Doctrine; Dec. 29, 1934: Japan Renounces Disarmament Treaties; July 7, 1937: China Declares War on Japan; Dec., 1937-Feb., 1938: Rape of Nanjing; Aug., 1940: Japan Announces the Greater East Asia Coprosperity Sphere.

1940

September 1, 1940
FIRST COLOR TELEVISION BROADCAST

The Radio Corporation of America and the Columbia Broadcasting System both demonstrated color television systems in 1940, although the RCA system was not adopted until 1953.

LOCALE: New York, New York
CATEGORIES: Science and technology; radio and television; communications and media

KEY FIGURES
Peter Carl Goldmark (1906-1977), head of the Columbia Broadcasting System's research and development laboratory
William S. Paley (1901-1990), founder and head of the Columbia Broadcasting System
David Sarnoff (1891-1971), founder and head of the Radio Corporation of America

SUMMARY OF EVENT
Although color television had been demonstrated in Scotland in 1928 (by engineer John Logie Baird), 1940 serves as the benchmark for the invention of a medium that would come to dominate television technology during the latter third of the twentieth century. Two events in 1940 denote that year as the beginning of color television. First, on February 12, 1940, RCA demonstrated its color television system privately, including to members of the Federal Communications Commission (FCC), an administrative body that had the authority to set standards for an electronic color system in the United States. The demonstration did not go well; indeed, David-Sarnoff, head of the Radio Corporation of America (RCA), canceled a planned public demonstration and had his engineers return to the Princeton, New Jersey, headquarters of RCA's laboratories.

On September 1, 1940, CBS struck its blow for a competition to determine the color system that would become the standard for the United States. On that late-summer day, CBS demonstrated to the public a sequential color system that was based on the research of engineer Peter Carl Goldmark. CBS's color technology was the superior of the two systems demonstrated in 1940. Goldmark's system broke the television image down into three primary colors through a set of spinning filters in front of black and white, causing the video to be viewed in color. This was known as additive color.

Although Goldmark had been at work as a research engineer at CBS since January, 1936, he did not attempt to develop a color television system until March, 1940, after he had witnessed the spectacle of the Technicolor motion picture *Gone with the Wind* (1939). Inspired, Goldmark began to tinker in his tiny CBS laboratory in the headquarters building in New York City.

If a decision had been made in 1940, the CBS color standard would have been accepted as the national standard. At that time, however, the FCC was trying to establish a black-and-white standard; color television seemed decades away. A 1941 decision by the FCC to adopt standards only for black-and-white television left the issue of color unresolved. This standards recommendation was based on the advice of the National Television Standards Committee, which represented electronics manufacturers and leading research scientists.

The two leading broadcasting companies in the United States did not simply accept the FCC's decision. Control of a potentially lucrative market as well as personal rivalry threw William S. Paley, head of CBS, and Sarnoff into a race for the control of color television. Both companies would pay dearly in terms of money and time in developing the technology for color television, and it would not be until the 1960's that color television would become common in the United States.

RCA's leadership in the development of the accepted black-and-white television system gave the National Broadcasting Company (NBC), a subsidiary of RCA, a head start over CBS. Once black and white became the standard in the late 1940's, however, CBS saw the creation of a workable color system as a potential weapon to counter the advantage long held by NBC.

CBS took a far different approach from that of RCA. Goldmark alone did the work for the CBS Laboratories. In contrast, RCA relied on a corporate laboratory staffed by highly skilled but largely anonymous scientists. Sarnoff ran RCA laboratories as a true corporate monolith; no scientists at RCA ever became as famous as Sarnoff.

The CBS color system was incompatible with the RCA standard for black-and-white television. In other words, viewers would need one set to watch black-and-white programming and one for color. Moreover, because the CBS color system needed more spectrum space than the National Television Standards Committee black-and-white system in use, CBS was forced to request that the FCC allocate new channel space in the ultrahigh frequency (UHF) band, which was then not being used. In contrast, RCA scientists labored to fashion a compatible color system that required no additional spectrum space.

Not surprisingly, in the early 1940's, CBS received little encouragement from the FCC, even though roughly one hundred scientists were trying to perfect the color system. Indeed, the leaders of CBS were not able to convince the FCC to do anything about color television before the end of World War II. This meant that, although CBS had a workable color system, it faced a world lining up to purchase RCA's black-and-white television sets in 1945.

The suburbanites who populated new communities in American cities sought television immediately; they did not want to wait for governmental bodies to decide on a color standard and then for manufacturers to redesign assembly lines to make color sets. Americans, rich with savings accumulated during the prosperity of the war years, wanted to spend immediately, not wait as they had through the Great Depression. After the war, the FCC saw no reason to open up proceedings about color.

CBS founder William S. Paley (left) with CBS executive Frank Stanton in 1951. (Hulton Archive/Getty Images)

1940

Black-and-white television was operational; customers were waiting in line for the new electronic marvel. To give its engineers time to create a compatible system, RCA skillfully lobbied the members of the FCC to take no action.

There were legitimate problems with the CBS mechanical color television technology. Not only was it incompatible with the millions of new black-and-white television sets being sold, but it also was noisy and bulky, and it did not always maintain the color balance. Demonstrations often went poorly. CBS proclaimed that through further engineering work it would improve the actual sets, but RCA was able to convince other manufacturers to support it in preference to CBS principally because of its proven manufacturing track record.

In 1946, RCA demonstrated a new electronic color receiver with three picture tubes, one for each of the primary colors. The color was fairly true; there was little flicker, but any movement on the screen caused color blurring. This was an all-electronic system, in contrast to the mechanical system of CBS. It was also compatible with the

standard for black-and-white television. Thus ended the invention phase of color television begun in 1940. The race for standardization would require seven years of corporate struggle before one system would win out.

SIGNIFICANCE

The inventions of CBS and RCA set off the race toward a standard for color television. Each company would pour millions of dollars into convincing the FCC to select its system as the standard. The winner of the first round was RCA when, in 1946, the FCC again rejected the color technology of CBS as the standard. CBS had tried to convince the world it was time to adopt color; officials of RCA argued that black and white was here, whereas color was still five years away.

In 1950, the FCC reversed its decision and accepted the mechanical scanning system after a convincing demonstration. RCA countered with a lawsuit seeking to overturn the commission's decision. In 1951, RCA lost this suit, and it seemed that the CBS color system would become the national standard. CBS began to manufacture color television sets while RCA worked to reverse the official rulings. According to one source, RCA poured about $150 million more into research and tendered many more millions to Washington, D.C., lobbyists and lawyers.

In the end, few of CBS's color sets were made, because American involvement in the Korean War caused the company to cease production in October, 1951. This gave the opposing forces time to convince the National Television Standards Committee that any color system ought to be compatible with the millions of black-and-white sets Americans had already purchased—as was RCA's system.

So lobbied, the FCC rescinded its 1950 ruling approving the CBS color television system. On December 17, 1953, it reapproved the compatible RCA system. Seeing what the delay caused by the Korean War cost CBS, RCA moved quickly. In 1954, in eighteen cities in the United States, the Rose Parade held in Pasadena, California, on New Year's Day was broadcast in color on NBC. Few viewers had color sets at that time, but owners of black-and-white-compatible sets could receive the signal and see the parade in black and white.

Through the 1950's, black-and-white television remained the order of the day. Five years after the 1953 adoption of the National Television Standards Committee, only the NBC television network was regularly airing programs in color. Full production and presentation of programming in color during prime time would not come until the mid-1960's; most industry observers acknowledge 1972 as the date of the true arrival of color television. By 1972, more than one-half the homes in the United States owned color sets. At that point, *TV Guide* stopped tagging color program listings with a special symbol and instead tagged black-and-white shows. Gradually, only cheap portable sets were made for black and white, whereas color sets came in all varieties, from tiny handheld pocket models to mammoth projection televisions.

It should be noted that, despite RCA's victory in the race to have its color system become the standard, specialized uses of closed-circuit television in medical settings used the high-quality color rendition of the CBS system for many years. Indeed, the pictures from the Moon transmitted by American astronauts were sent on CBS cameras—built by RCA.

—Douglas Gomery

FURTHER READING

Barnouw, Erik. *A History of Broadcasting in the United States*. 3 vols. New York: Oxford University Press, 1966-1970. Massive work still stands as among the most important histories of broadcasting in the United States. The coming of color television is covered in the second and third volumes.

Bilby, Kenneth. *The General: David Sarnoff and the Rise of the Communications Industry*. New York: Harper & Row, 1986. Biography by a longtime associate of Sarnoff presents a balanced account of his life. Provides a detailed history of RCA's contribution to the invention and innovation of color television.

Dreher, Carl. *Sarnoff: An American Success*. New York: Quadrangle, 1977. Comprehensive work on the activities of RCA and its founder presents a detailed history of the invention and innovation of color television.

Fink, Donald G., and David M. Lutyens. *The Physics of Television*. Garden City, N.Y.: Doubleday, 1960. Compact volume gives an excellent explanation of how television works in nontechnical language accessible to readers with only modest science background. Explains color systems in the final chapter.

Goldmark, Peter C., and Lee Edson. *Maverick Inventor: My Turbulent Years at CBS*. New York: Saturday Review Press, 1973. Autobiography of the key inventor at CBS includes three chapters that detail the development of color television. Provides a rare look into the world of corporate technological research and development.

Head, Sydney W., Thomas Spann, and Michael A. McGregor. *Broadcasting in America: A Survey of Electronic Media*. 9th ed. Boston: Houghton Mifflin, 2000. Comprehensive introduction to the institutions of radio and television in the United States. Includes discussion of the invention and innovation of color television technology.

Lichty, Lawrence W., and Malachi C. Topping, comps. *American Broadcasting: A Source Book on the History of Radio and Television*. New York: Hastings House, 1975. Collection of articles and documents covering the history of radio and television. Informative concerning the history of all forms of television technology, including color television, as well as the changing economics and social impact of this mass entertainment industry.

Metz, Robert. *CBS: Reflections in a Bloodshot Eye*. New York: Playboy Press, 1975. A history of one of the most important broadcasting institutions in the United States.

Smith, Sally Bedell. *In All His Glory: The Life of William S. Paley*. New York: Simon & Schuster, 1990. Biography includes detailed examination of the history of the Columbia Broadcasting System and explains why CBS developed color television technology.

Sterling, Christopher H., and John M. Kittross. *Stay Tuned: A History of American Broadcasting*. 3d ed. Mahwah, N.J.: Lawrence Erlbaum, 2001. Comprehensive history of radio and television in the United States provides excellent coverage of the development of color television technology.

SEE ALSO: Aug. 20-Nov. 2, 1920: Radio Broadcasting Begins; Dec. 29, 1923: Zworykin Applies for Patent on an Early Type of Television; Sept. 9, 1926: National Broadcasting Company Is Founded; June 10, 1934: Federal Communications Commission Is Established by Congress; Nov. 2, 1936: BBC Airs the First High-Definition Television Program; Apr. 30, 1939: American Television Debuts at the World's Fair.

September 12, 1940
LASCAUX CAVE PAINTINGS ARE DISCOVERED

Discovery of the cave paintings at Lascaux enabled archaeologists to elaborate on the historical evolution of prehistoric art techniques and to determine that such techniques originated further back in the chronological record of human cultures than had previously been believed.

LOCALE: Near Montignac, Dordogne, France
CATEGORIES: Archaeology; arts; prehistory and ancient cultures

KEY FIGURES
Henri-Édouard-Prosper Breuil (1877-1961), French archaeologist
Marcel Ravidat (fl. mid-twentieth century), French youth who was the first to enter Lascaux Cave

SUMMARY OF EVENT

For several generations after its discovery in 1868, the cavern at Altamira in Spain, along with a few discoveries made in the Levantine (southeastern) regions of Spain and in southwestern France, represented the richest archaeological remains of paintings by prehistoric man in Europe. Then, quite by accident, a new, exceptionally rich find in the region of Dordogne in France occurred shortly after the outbreak of World War II.

On September 12, 1940, five boys—three local youths named Ravidat, Marsal, and Queroy, accompanied by two refugees, Coencas and Estréguil, who had fled the German occupied northwestern zone of France—were roaming through fields belonging to the ruins of a dwelling referred to locally as the Chateau Lascaux. The muffled yelping of their lost dog, who had fallen into a narrow opening at the base of an upturned tree, drew their attention to what appeared to be the mouth of a large cavern or grotto. Seventeen-year-old

Marcel Ravidat entered the hole and slid down 7.6 meters (about 25 feet) to a sandy floor in a vaulted oval subterranean hall 18 meters by 9 meters (approximately 59 feet by 29.5 feet) in size. When he lit matches to illuminate his surroundings, he became the first person in fifteen thousand years to gaze upon the wondrous prehistoric polychromatic cave paintings of Lascaux.

Although they had no way of realizing it, what they had discovered resembled the famous Altamira paintings in northern Spain. The latter had been discovered seventy years before. The Lascaux cavern walls were covered with paintings of wild beasts: horses and stags, oxenlike creatures with strangely elongated bodies, and especially prominent and dominating, bulls with strange spotted patterns covering portions of their bodies. Scattered among the animals in this prehistoric scene were a series of symbols or emblems: checkers and marks resembling sprigs of grass or leaves. The first graphic impressions of what the cave contained were drawn by Estréguil.

The second, more technically perfected, set of sketches came a few days later, when the youths had informed the local schoolmaster of their discovery. Qualified archaeologists were brought to view the site. Abbé Amédée Bouyssonie was one of the archaeologists who was notified; he had discovered the famous Neanderthal man skeleton in 1908. Bouyssonie was aware that Henri-Édouard-Prosper Breuil of the College of France, a well-known archaeologist who had been involved in a number of excavations connected with Neanderthal remains and Mousterian-period prehistoric cultures, had come to Dordogne in June, 1940. Together with M. Peyrony, director of the famous local museum of prehistoric cultures at Les Eyzies, the two archaeologists undertook a more systematic exploration of the Lascaux cavern. For

1940

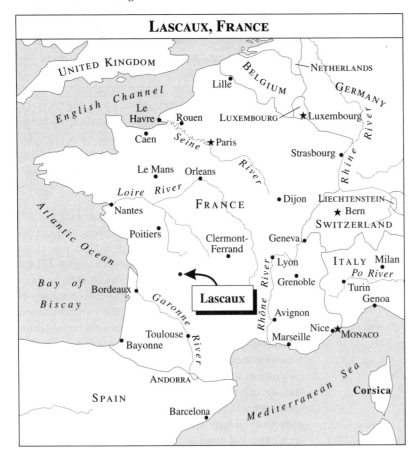

LASCAUX, FRANCE

role in attempts to re-create the cultural conditions of human existence in prehistoric times: the presence of a drawing of what Breuil called a "half-conventionalized man" lying beside what were obviously his hunting tools (a javelin and a throwing stick). This human figure, presumed to be fatally wounded, faces the prominently outlined figure of a bison. The latter, his entrails disemboweled by the hunter's spear, appears to be gazing at its stalker.

Those who first entered Lascaux Cave were astounded to find a number of other unique forms of artistic expression. Perhaps the most impressive was an outline of a child's hand and forearm. Although such primitive techniques of representing the "artists" themselves were not uncommon in prehistoric cave sites, archaeologists were impressed particularly by this tiny reminder of the community of painters who executed the frescos at Lascaux, simply because it was the only such hand to be found among such a large number and variety of representations of animals.

Breuil, the opportunity was particularly important because, as a specialist interested in establishing a general theory covering the chronological evolution of prehistoric art, he knew that Lascaux held a great potential for a new archaeological breakthrough.

The first survey revealed more than eighty pictures, both in the main hall and in a side gallery attached to it. Most of these were found on blocks of stone that had fallen from the cavern roof above. It would take some time before more complex theories concerning the age and content of the paintings would emerge. Almost immediately, however, Breuil wrote a preliminary report on the findings and submitted it to the prestigious English scientific journal *Nature*.

The sizes of the primitive paintings varied from small proportions (about 30 centimeters, or roughly 12 inches) to very large drawings (some 5 meters, or about 16 feet, long). It was evident immediately that a number of different techniques had been used to create artistic effects, and that many paintings had been retouched or restored. Breuil noticed something that would play an important

Indeed, the number and variety of animals found depicted at Lascaux were not the only things that impressed those who found them; the uniqueness of (apparent) symbolism was equally striking. Some paintings contain simple symbols to tell a "practical" story. This is the case of what later came to be called the "falling horses," which are depicted in chaotic disorder, often upside down, to represent primitive man's common method of hunting such prey by driving them off the edges of precipices. Other scenes contain elements that were much too complex for the first observers of the paintings to comprehend beyond the mere state of wonder they engendered. This is the case with the so-called Apocalyptic Beast, which appears prominently in the main hall of the cavern. This animal figure may have represented an ox or a prehistoric rhinoceros. The body is massive and sagging, as if in a late state of pregnancy, and spotted with curious oval-shaped rings. Other features appear to be grossly distorted, such as the tiny head and neck on the otherwise massive beast. Most perplexing for the first observers, who could not even begin to interpret the meaning of what they had found, were the "horns" of the unidentifiable Apocalyptic Beast. These appear as straight, rigid sticks capped by peculiar "tufts" that bear no resemblance even to now-extinct animals known to have existed in this prehistoric period.

In addition to these visually impressive features of the Lascaux paintings, an announcement came from Breuil immediately after his first viewing of the site that would alter the theoretical bases for scientific observation of prehistoric cave paintings. Drawing on his previous experience nearby at Font de Gaume (Les Eyzies), where he had identified partial remains of paintings that had been painted over in the Magdalenian archaeological period (c. 15,000 B.C.E. to 10,000 B.C.E.), Breuil hypothesized that the Lascaux paintings were considerably older than the Magdalenian period. Although the archaeologists who found the Lascaux paintings retained full respect for the previously unequaled paintings at Altamira, Spain, which many called the "Sistine Chapel of Magdalenian art," specialists looking at this new discovery in 1940 were nearly certain that they would be able to push the origins of prehistoric art back to a much earlier age, christened by Breuil with the name "Perigordian."

SIGNIFICANCE

Although from the early nineteenth century archaeologists had studied a fairly wide range of artifacts left behind in Paleolithic human settlements in various areas of Western Europe, it was the discovery, in 1868, of the now famous Cantabrian site at Altamira that provided the first evidence that prehistoric Aurignacian and Magdalenian human cultures (dating from about 25,000 to 15,000, and 15,000 to 10,000 years ago, respectively) practiced painting on the interior walls of subterranean caverns. On the ceilings of the caverns at Altamira was an extraordinary panorama of polychrome paintings of animals, mainly gigantic bisons, together with pictographs that some thought represented huts and roofs, or, possibly symbolic figures. Some were made up of checkers, squares, and dots. There were also some engraved (not painted) "semihuman" forms. Later, specialists studying the Altamira site suggested that such pictographs held a key to ritual practices carried out by late Paleolithic human communities.

The main disappointments associated with the Altamira site, somewhat in contrast to several other important, if less spectacular, discoveries made a few years later in the Gironde and Dordogne departments of France (specifically at Pair-non-Pair and at La Mouthe, respectively), involved chronological dating. If archaeologists were in general agreement that the first forms of human art as archaeologists understand it appeared in the Aurignacian period (c. 25,000 B.C.E. to 15,000 B.C.E.), they seemed to be at a loss for making any finer distinctions concerning stages of artistic development leading to a "crossover" into the relatively sophisticated Magdalenian period (15,000 B.C.E. to 10,000 B.C.E.).

Both the Pair-non-Pair and La Mouthe sites, partially because of the more primitive techniques used to paint much less finished figures, but also because of archaeological artifacts found in them, were considered to be of Aurignacian origin. For some time, however, no one knew how to tie these earliest known paintings to the very considerable number of more "advanced" works associated with the Magdalenian period.

1940

In 1900, Breuil began to build a chronological scheme at La Mouthe to evaluate cave art that would establish a major reputation for him. Breuil's theory for dating cave art was based on comparative techniques more than on styles (which seemed to change very little over several millennia). Between his first publication on the subject in 1902 and 1934, when he published *L'Evolution de l'art pariétal dans les cavernes et abris ornées de France* (the evolution of rock art in the caves of France), Breuil worked out a scheme that would be retained in its major essentials in his capstone monograph *Quatre cents siècles d'art pariétal* (1952; *Four Hundred Centuries of Cave Art*, 1952), published some twelve

Painting in the Great Hall of the Bulls, Lascaux Cave.

years after the Lascaux discoveries. This scheme held that the passage from the primitive technique of the earliest human artists (handprints and finger meanders, sometimes referred to as "macaroni style") to the "classical" style of the "high" Magdalenian was marked by a "two-cycle" or "repeat-development" system. The crux of this view was that Aurignacian artists, the work of some of whom Breuil was able to identify at Lascaux, had already mastered a series of technical methods of painting that would be "remastered" and altered during the period of passage from Aurignacian to Magdalenian times.

The complete first cycle, which Breuil claimed could be detected in different Aurignacian sites, included use of the following techniques: introduction of color pigments, first yellow, then red; use of fine lines of color, then bolder lines, with flat shading, usually in red; and finally, black linear drawings. These characteristic methods could be expected in cave paintings predating 15,000 B.C.E. For later, classical Magdalenian-period painting, Breuil posited the following cycle of techniques: use of simple black line drawings, some hatched and then stumped; plain, flat brown paintings followed by polychromes, partially and then entirely outlined in black; and finally, red linear drawings.

Although professional archaeologists continued to debate the "final" accuracy of Breuil's method of dating primitive cave art according to evolutionary stages in techniques employed, the fact that many Lascaux paintings were composed of superimposed "layers" (reflecting the application of later techniques to existing "base" paintings) lent considerable weight to Breuil's thesis that they were much older than Altamira's classical Magdalenian compositions. His "proof" of this thesis was important not only for establishing the relative ages of different examples of primitive cave art but also for "unscrambling" the symbols mixed together in complex scenes in prehistoric cultural landmarks, particularly at Lascaux.

—*Byron D. Cannon*

FURTHER READING

Breuil, Henri. *Four Hundred Centuries of Cave Art.* Translated by Mary E. Boyle. 1952. Reprint. New York: Hacker Art Books, 1979. General work includes discussion of the place of the Lascaux paintings in the overall framework of prehistoric art.

_____. "A Remarkable Painted Cave on the Estate of Lescaux (Montignac, Dordogne)." *Nature* 147 (1941): 12-13. The earliest written description of the Lascaux paintings prepared by a well-known professor at the College of France who was among the first

people to enter the caverns in 1940.

Conkey, Margaret W. "On the Origins of Paleolithic Art: A Review and Some Critical Thoughts." In *The Mousterian Legacy: Human Biocultural Change in the Upper Pleistocene*, edited by Erik Trinkhaus. Oxford, England: British Archaeological Reports, 1983. Scholarly work focuses on prehistoric artistic products recovered by archaeologists in the southwestern regions of Europe. Reviews theories that have been put forth by a number of prominent commentators and compares early interpretations with more recent approaches.

Curtis, Gregory. *The Cave Painters: Probing the Mysteries of the World's First Artists.* New York: Alfred A. Knopf, 2006. Focuses on what archaeologists have been able to understand about the lives of the creators of prehistoric cave art.

Fagan, Brian. *From Black Land to Fifth Sun: The Science of Sacred Sites.* New York: Perseus Books, 1998. Approaches the scientific examination of various ancient sites and artifacts, including prehistoric cave art, from the perspective of their possible sacred or spiritual meanings. Discusses how archaeologists' interpretations of such sites and artifacts have changed over time.

Laming-Emperaire, Annette. *Lascaux: Paintings and Engravings.* Translated by Eleanore Frances Armstrong. Harmondsworth, Middlesex, England: Penguin Books, 1959. Comprehensive work by a well-known French archaeologist draws on the wide variety of literature on the Dordogne cave paintings that accumulated over the first two decades after their discovery. Discusses methods used to date the paintings and especially to interpret the possible meanings behind the prehistoric artists' work.

Sieveking, Ann. *The Cave Artists.* London: Thames and Hudson, 1979. Beautifully illustrated volume covers cave art in the southwestern region of Europe, concentrating on the area spanning southwestern France and northeastern Spain. Objectively reviews Breuil's theory on the prehistoric cultural stages reflected in cave paintings, pointing out both its strengths and apparent weaknesses.

SEE ALSO: Dec., 1908: Boule Reconstructs the First Neanderthal Skeleton; Summer, 1923: Zdansky Discovers Peking Man; Summer, 1924: Dart Discovers the First Australopithecine Fossil; Fall, 1937-Winter, 1938: Weidenreich Reconstructs the Face of Peking Man.

September 13, 1940
ITALY INVADES EGYPT

Italy's African empire nearly disappeared in 1940. Poor preparation, bad morale, and obsolete weapons spelled disaster for the Desert War, which began when Italy invaded Egypt. This disaster was only averted by the British decision to transfer troops from North Africa to Greece and the subsequent timely arrival of the German Afrika Korps, which allowed the Axis to preserve its presence in North Africa through 1943.

ALSO KNOWN AS: Desert War
LOCALE: Libya; Egypt; Sudan; Ethiopia; Somalia
CATEGORIES: Wars, uprisings, and civil unrest; World War II; colonialism and occupation

KEY FIGURES
Rodolfo Graziani (1882-1955), Italian field marshal and governor-general of Libya
Archibald Wavell (1883-1950), British commander in chief in the Middle East
Richard O'Connor (1889-1981), British commander of the Western Desert Force
Benito Mussolini (1883-1945), Italian dictator, 1925-1943
Winston Churchill (1874-1965), prime minister of Great Britain, 1940-1945, 1951-1955

SUMMARY OF EVENT
General Archibald Wavell, commander in chief for British imperial and Commonwealth forces in the Middle East, faced a daunting task in the summer of 1940. Italy declared war on France and England on June 10, and Wavell had only sixty-threee thousand men to protect Egypt, Palestine, Trans-Jordan, and Iraq. There were an additional ten thousand troops in the Sudan, Kenya, and British Somaliland. Some of these troops were needed for internal security roles, which made the odds even worse for a successful showdown with the Italians.

Under the dynamic Air Marshal Italo Balbo, Italy maintained 250,000 men in Libya. A separate command in Italian East Africa contained 300,000 troops. Like the forces of the United Kingdom, some of the Italian troops were needed to maintain internal security, especially in East Africa, where Ethiopian guerillas known as the Patriots maintained an armed resistance to Italian authority. Still, Italian forces in the region greatly outnumbered their British counterparts. This was also true in the air, where Italy could deploy 500 aircraft vs. 370 for Great Britain. On water, the odds also favored Italy, although

only by a small margin. These numbers were formidable, and considering that England faced a possible invasion by the German Wehrmacht, reinforcements for Africa and the Middle East were unlikely. Italy's bombastic dictator, Benito Mussolini, recognized this, and he ordered his proconsuls to advance on all fronts. This aggressive strategy paid its first dividend in August, 1940, when Italian forces overran British Somaliland.

Friction, poor planning, and failed leadership intervened, however, to end any possibility of an Italian "blitzkrieg" in North Africa. First, Balbo died in a friendly fire incident on June 28. This slowed Italian plans to invade Egypt until he was replaced by Marshal Rodolfo Graziani, whose experience was mainly in counterinsurgency warfare. Finally, on September 13, Italian units crossed the Libyan-Egyptian frontier, initiating phase one of World War II's famous Desert War. Graziani directed the Tenth Army, a force of six infantry divisions. Although unfamiliar with the fine points of armored and mechanized warfare, he was worried his desert flank allowed the British armored divisions numerous opportunities to attack. Graziani also had a very long supply line stretching back to Tripoli, nearly twelve hundred miles west of the Egyptian frontier.

The marshal had good reasons to worry. Although Italy had more troops, these soldiers were poorly prepared for modern warfare. From small arms to heavy artillery, most Italian weapons were obsolete, underpowered, or unreliable. For instance, the tiny M-13 tankette was so poorly protected, it could be destroyed even by British antitank rifles, which were ineffective against German armor. In contrast, the formidable "Matilda" tank employed by some British units was nearly impervious to any Italian weapon. These handicaps ended Italian thrusts into the Anglo-Egyptian Sudan, Kenya, and Egypt. In the latter, Graziani started a march toward Alexandria, but halted after crossing only sixty miles. At this point, arguing "one can not break a steel door with fingernails," he ordered his troops to dig in and await a British counterattack. Graziani deployed soldiers in six fortified outposts, but poor staff work created gaps that a daring enemy might slip through to hit these positions from the flank or the rear.

General Richard O'Connor was just the man to take advantage of this flaw. Commander of the British Western Desert Force, he was directed by Wavell to disrupt the Italian forces, exploiting any possibility to drive them out of Egypt. Next, Prime Minister Winston Churchill delivered on a gutsy plan that sent additional tanks, including the deadly Matildas, to Egypt, rather than keep them for home defense. Churchill knew that if the Royal Air Force was defeated by the German Luftwaffe, England would stand no chance against a German infantry invasion, so the tanks would do more good elsewhere. This decision allowed O'Connor to direct a mechanized force of tanks and truck-mounted infantry, providing his Western Desert Force with a massive advantage in mobility.

Dubbed Operation Compass, the British attack began on December 9. Hitting the Nibeiwa fortified camp at daybreak, O'Connor's men produced a textbook example for the combined arms attack: Artillery, armor, and infantry attacked in perfect order, overwhelming the surprised defenders. Although the Italians fought for several hours, Nibeiwa demonstrated the great advantage the British gained from their Matilda tanks. Attacked with grenades, antitank guns, and even medium artillery, the tank's armor was thick enough to stop all but the most lucky of shots. A captured Italian officer described rampaging Matildas, shells bouncing off their armor plates with impunity, as "the nearest thing to hell I ever saw."

This happened in nearly every battle of Operation Compass, and the seeming invincibility of the British tanks was a tremendous blow to Italian morale.

Nibeiwa opened up the Italian front, and as Graziani's troops were on foot, many could not escape. By January 1, 1941, he lost 30,000 men and vast quantities of equipment, while British losses totaled just 810 killed or wounded. Four days later, the fortress of Bardia fell, netting an additional 38,000 Italian prisoners, plus supplies of food, ammunition, fuel, and, most important, trucks. The latter were quickly employed to replace British losses from desert wear and tear. Bardia's capture caused Anthony Eden, Britain's foreign secretary, to quip, "Never has so much been surrendered by so many to so few."

On January 6, the Australian Sixth Infantry Division laid siege to Tobruk. A major fortress and key port for eastern Libya, Tobruk was defended by 32,000 men, 220 guns, and 70 tanks. The Australians, who had just captured Bardia, conducted skillful assaults that overwhelmed one position after another. Resistance ended on January 22, with another 27,000 men lost by the Italian army. Australian casualties totaled 500.

With the fall of Tobruk, Wavell faced difficult choices. Italian forces had invaded Greece on October 28, 1940, but quickly bogged down in difficult mountain terrain. Greek counterattacks pushed the invaders back into Albania, which induced German support for their Axis partner. Churchill saw this as a golden opportunity to widen the war and ordered Wavell to form an expeditionary force to aid the Greeks. Simultaneously, Wavell was conducting an offensive into Italian East Africa, which began on January 19, 1941. This was a three-pronged attack, featuring Allied columns advancing into Eritrea, Ethiopia, and Somalia. Combined with the attrition to men and machines from the Western Desert Force—due mainly to poor roads and the harsh desert climate—Wavell had very few troops capable of offensive action. It was therefore unclear what he could do about the Italian army retreating into western Libya.

O'Connor convinced his superior that it was still possible to destroy this force. Sending what little armor

EGYPT, 1940

and mechanized troops were still functional, he managed to outflank the Italians again at Beda Fom. Despite hard fighting between February 6 and 9, 1941, this battle marked the end of the Tenth Army. Italian losses included 150,000 men killed, wounded, or captured; while British forces suffered 2,000 casualties.

Beda Fom demonstrated beyond a doubt that successful desert warfare required tanks and motorized vehicles. It also destroyed most of the Italian garrison holding Libya. O'Connor was poised to eliminate the remnants and end Italy's presence in North Africa. Churchill intervened, however, ordering more British forces dispatched to Greece in March, 1941. Doing so gave the Italians breathing space and allowed General Erwin Rommel to organize his newly arrived Afrika Korps. As a result, the Desert War continued for two more years.

SIGNIFICANCE

Italy's 1940-1941 debacles greatly influenced the course of World War II. First, they revealed grave flaws in the Italian armed forces, flaws that could not easily be fixed. Despite Fascist boasts to the contrary, Italy's economy could not gear up quickly to produce improved weapons. Thus Italian soldiers employed out-of-date tanks, such as the lightly armored yet slow M-13, or underpowered 47mm antitank guns, the shells of which bounced off most Allied tanks made in 1941-1943. Italy's insufficient armaments guaranteed more humiliating defeats by a British opposing force with weapons systems even better than those of 1940. Nor was a technology gap the only problem—the Italian Army also failed to recover from its North African disaster because the officer corps was riddled with incompetence. It never produced leaders who could inspire their men to pick up their obsolete weapons and fight in their despite.

Second, Italy's loss of East Africa and western Libya significantly enhanced Great Britain's geopolitical position in North Africa. The British conquest of Eritrea and Somalia ended any Italian threat to the Red Sea—the back door to the Suez Canal. Liberating Ethiopia not only played well—as the first occupied nation freed from Axis tyranny—but also secured another back door into Egypt. Also, the string of Italian defeats, especially those in Libya, destroyed Italy's home front morale and began the process that culminated in the overthrow of Mussolini in 1943. Finally, Italy's 1940 debacles forced German intervention into the Balkans and North Africa. U.S. general George C. Marshall claimed this was "one of the principal factors in Germany's defeat."

—*John P. Dunn*

FURTHER READING

Latimer, Jon. *Operation Compass, 1940: Wavell's Whirlwind Offensive*. Westport, Conn.: Praeger, 2004. Excellent, brief account based mainly on British sources.

Moorehead, Alan. *Desert War*. 1941. Reprint. London: Penguin Books, 2001. Very good presentation from the Commonwealth perspective.

Pitt, Barrie. *The Crucible of War: Western Desert*. 1940. Reprint. London: Jonathan Cape, 1980. Good overview that examines both Libyan and Ethiopian campaigns of 1940 and 1941.

Walker, Ian J. *Iron Hulls, Iron Hearts: Mussolini's Elite Armored Divisions in North Africa*. Marlborough, Wiltshire, England: Crowood Press, 2003. Important English-language effort to explain the many problems facing the 1940 Italian army.

SEE ALSO: Apr. 2, 1930: Haile Selassie Is Crowned Emperor of Ethiopia; May 26, 1937: Egypt Joins the League of Nations; Apr. 7, 1939: Italy Invades and Annexes Albania; Aug. 3, 1940-Mar., 1941: Italy Invades British Somaliland.

1940

November 7, 1940
TACOMA NARROWS BRIDGE COLLAPSES

Strong winds forced the Tacoma Narrows Bridge to oscillate in an unexpected, twisting fashion that ripped the bridge asunder and dumped the central span, a car, and a dog into the sea. Studies of the collapse led to the development of the science of bridge aerodynamics.

LOCALE: Tacoma Narrows, Puget Sound, Washington
CATEGORIES: Engineering; physics; urban planning

KEY FIGURES

Clark Eldridge (1896-1990), original designer and chief engineer of the Tacoma Narrows Bridge
Frederick B. Farquharson (1895-1970), engineer who tried to save the bridge and whose pioneering studies of bridge aerodynamics led to the designing of safer suspension bridges
Leon Moisseiff (1872-1943), world-famous bridge designer who made fatal changes in Eldridge's original design

SUMMARY OF EVENT

When it was built, the Tacoma Narrows Bridge was the third-longest suspension bridge in the world (the Golden Gate Bridge was the longest, and the George Washington Bridge was the second longest). Leon Moisseiff had participated as a consulting engineer in the design of nearly every major suspension bridge built during the previous twenty years, and he intended the Tacoma Narrows Bridge to be the most beautiful bridge in the world and the capstone of his career. Indeed, the bridge was breathtaking: a thin ribbon of roadway suspended from cables gracefully draped from two towers that soared 436 feet above the water. More than a mile long, it connected Tacoma with the peninsula across a narrow arm of Puget Sound. The nature of the seafloor dictated where the two support towers could be placed, and once they were established, engineers determined that the length of the central span would be nearly 2,800 feet. The fast tidal surges that flowed through the channel four times a day at a depth of nearly 200 feet made the construction of the towers' foundations even more complicated. However, after only nineteen months of construction, the bridge officially opened on July 1. It was in use for only four months.

As Clark Eldridge, the bridge's original designer and chief engineer, drove across the bridge at 8:30 A.M. on November 7, 1940, the wind was blowing at 38 miles per

hour. Eldridge experienced the notorious undulating motion of the roadbed as it rose and fell, making humps and valleys like the body of a sea serpent. When the wave motion was at its worst, cars in different valleys actually lost sight of each other. The bridge's history of sinuous dancing in the wind led to its being referred to as "Galloping Gertie," a nickname also used for the Wheeling Suspension Bridge in West Virginia, which shook apart on May 17, 1854. Eldridge was not overly concerned by the Tacoma bridge's movement on that morning: The bridge had already survived a storm with winds of 50 miles per hour and had been designed to withstand the push of winds at 120 miles per hour. Eldridge calmly returned to his office.

Frederick B. Farquharson, professor of civil engineering at the University of Washington, drove onto the bridge around 9:30 A.M. that same day. He was responsible for designing mechanisms to reduce the bridge's motion, so he began filming and measuring the roadbed's waves. He had already had strong anchor cables attached between the roadbed and the shore, and other cables with dynamic dampers (piston-in-cylinder mechanisms similar to automobile shock absorbers) attached between the roadbed and the suspension towers. When the anchor cables snapped, the dampers could do nothing because their seals had been breached when the bridge was sandblasted prior to painting. Farquharson's recommendation to attach wind-deflector panels to the sides of the roadbed had only just been approved; these panels would have given the bridge a more streamlined profile in order to reduce wind effects.

About 10:00 A.M., Leonard Coatsworth, a news editor for the *Tacoma News Tribune*, drove onto the bridge with his family's dog, Tubby. The wind had increased to 42 miles per hour, and the deck rose and fell 3 feet every 90 seconds. Suddenly the bridge began to twist about its center line, a type of motion that had never before occurred. Although at first the twisting motion was small, within minutes it grew so large that the roadbed tilted at a 45-degree angle, pushing the left sidewalk about 28 feet below the right sidewalk. Then the left sidewalk rose and the right sidewalk fell, and so on, in 5-second intervals. Coatsworth's car was thrown against the curb in the opposite lane. Coatsworth crawled out a window, but the terrified dog would not come with him.

Not able to stay on his feet, Coatsworth clung to the curb as he crawled toward the east tower, nearly 400 feet

A large section of the roadway collapses in the center span of the Tacoma Narrows Bridge. (AP/Wide World Photos)

1940

away. As he neared the tower, he met Winfield Brown, a college student who had earlier walked across the bridge to experience the roller-coaster effect. As they neared the tower, they were able to stagger the 1,575 feet from the tower to the toll plaza at the eastern end of the bridge. At about the same time, near the west tower, the driver and passenger of a Rapid Transfer Company van were able to jump out of the vehicle just before it tipped. With the help of some workmen, the van's occupants reached the western end of the bridge safely.

At 10:30 A.M., a large chunk of concrete dropped from the bridge's central span. The wind subsided, and the bridge steadied somewhat. Howard Clifford, one of several photographers who had arrived, tried to rescue the dog, Tubby, but could not reach him. Farquharson was able to reach Tubby, but the dog bit him on the finger. As Farquharson struggled to safety, the air was filled with

the shriek of twisting steel girders, the sharp gunshot sounds of breaking cables and popping bolts, and the grinding of concrete against concrete. One of the two suspension cables slipped from its saddle atop a tower, and at 11:02 A.M., a 650-foot-long section of the roadway tore loose from the central span and dropped 210 feet into Puget Sound. Other segments fell soon after, as did Coatsworth's car (with Tubby still inside). By 11:10 A.M., most of the central span was gone, and the bridge was quiet.

SIGNIFICANCE

The basic principles of bridge building seem simple enough: Each segment of the bridge must be able to sustain its own weight plus the weight of any load it might carry. Further, the forces on a bridge segment must be passed on to support towers or to the shore, but for a long suspension bridge it is difficult to calculate these forces accurately. As a substitute, engineers use an accepted design theory that incorporates both assumptions and experimental measurements in order to create estimates for the unknown forces.

Eldridge's original design cost $11 million and called for 25-foot open-grid-work trusses that would stiffen the roadbed, but eastern financiers would not lend construction money unless a suitable engineer was allowed to review and change the plans. Moisseiff was selected to do this, and he used the relatively new deflection theory to guide his calculations. He proposed using solid-plate trusses that were only 8 feet high because this allowed him to design a more visually appealing bridge that used less steel and therefore cost less. His design was accepted. The bridge was built with a $6.4 million loan plus $1.6 million in toll revenues. Unfortunately, Moisseiff had pushed deflection theory into untested territory, as the shallow trusses and narrow roadway made the Tacoma Narrows Bridge three times more flexible than the Golden Gate Bridge, which had been the most flexible bridge up to that point.

Farquharson's wind-tunnel tests of a carefully constructed scale model of the bridge and his measurements during the final hours before the bridge's collapse showed that the structure's failure was due to torsional flutter. When the wind rammed into the plate truss on the bridge's side, the wind current divided, blowing over and under the bridge in unequal amounts. This caused the roadway to tilt, and that tilt caused the winds to be even more unequal, which caused more tilt, and so forth, until finally the weight of the roadway pulled it back to a horizontal level. The roadway's momentum then carried it through the horizontal plane, tilting the roadbed the opposite way, and so on. The model showed that this cycle repeated every five seconds, just as Farquharson had measured. In order for a bridge to be safe, the bridge's

dynamic response had to be taken into account. Farquharson helped develop the tools to do that, and ten years later a new and successful Tacoma Narrows Bridge was opened.

—Charles W. Rogers

FURTHER READING

Billah, K. Yusuf, and Robert H. Scanlan. "Resonance, Tacoma Narrows Bridge Failure, and Undergraduate Physics Textbooks." *American Journal of Physics* 59 (February, 1991): 118-124. Shows that physics texts focus on the wrong mechanism for failure and gives the correct mechanism. Includes numerous references. Article is rather technical; see Feldman reference below.

Feldman, Bernard J. "What to Say About the Tacoma Narrows Bridge to Your Introductory Physics Class." *Physics Teacher* 41 (February, 2003): 92-96. A simplified version of the Billah and Scanlan article cited above.

Freiman, Fran Locher, and Neil Schlager. *Failed Technology: True Stories of Technological Disasters*. Vol. 2. New York: Gale Research International, 1995. Investigative reports of technological disasters, including the Tacoma Narrows Bridge failure and the loss of the *Challenger* space shuttle in 1986. Very interesting and easy to read.

Scott, Richard. *In the Wake of Tacoma: Suspension Bridges and the Quest for Aerodynamic Stability*. Reston, Va.: American Society of Civil Engineers, 2001. Uses nontechnical language to trace the development of suspension bridges from the failure of the Tacoma Narrows Bridge to a possible bridge spanning the Strait of Gibralter.

SEE ALSO: Mar. 19, 1932: Dedication of the Sydney Harbour Bridge; May 27, 1937: Golden Gate Bridge Opens.

November 13, 1940
DISNEY'S *FANTASIA* PREMIERES

Although Fantasia *drew fire from critics and was not a commercial success in its first release, the film advanced the art of animation by freeing it from strict plot and character limits.*

LOCALE: Broadway Theater, New York, New York
CATEGORIES: Motion pictures; entertainment

KEY FIGURES

Walt Disney (1901-1966), American entrepreneur and film producer
Leopold Stokowski (1882-1977), British-born American conductor

SUMMARY OF EVENT

Walt Disney had few nay-saying critics left when *Fantasia* appeared in 1940. Less than three years earlier, he had silenced most of those who had said that a feature-length cartoon was an absurdity by releasing *Snow White and the Seven Dwarfs* (1937), which was an instant critical and financial success, as was Disney's second animated feature, *Pinocchio* (1940). Even while those two features were being released, however, Disney was working on what would become the most ambitious and controversial animation project of his career: *Fantasia.*

Throughout the 1930's, Disney had been pushing his animators toward continual improvement of their already highly developed painting skills. Many of the artists who worked for Disney feared that the goal of such refinement was a photographic, representational realism that would, they felt, take the heart out of animation. There was no lack of grounds for such fears. The 1934 Disney short *The Goddess of Spring* was intended to train animators in realistic animation of human figures; the 1937 short *The Old Mill* was a test run of the multiplane camera, which gave animation a three-dimensional look (a feature that helped to win the short an Academy Award). *Snow White* combined both techniques, and *Pinocchio* improved them, to the extent that reviewers voiced the very fears of the animators: Was Disney headed toward photorealism?

The opening sequence of *Fantasia* removed such fears when the film premiered at New York's Broadway Theater on November 13, 1940. Unlike the other sequences in the film, this visual interpretation of Johann Sebastian Bach's Toccata and Fugue in D Minor developed no story and created no characters. Instead, an abstract movement of line and color grew out of the music. The closest the

segment came to any representation was a sequence showing a brief dance of strings and bows, but even this was short-lived. No amount of abstraction in the animation could protect Disney, however, from the charge of some music critics—such as Dorothy Thompson of the *New York Herald Tribune*—that the pure abstraction of music was tainted by any visualization. From the standpoint of animation, however, Disney had proved that the art could succeed without story or character.

Another anxiety about the premiere of *Fantasia* was the technical innovation the Disney studio called Fantasound. Decades before the appearance of commercial stereo recording, Disney engineers had pioneered a multitrack recording process, and they envisioned showing *Fantasia* only in theaters equipped to be compatible with the process. The music was recorded on nine sound cameras (through thirty-three microphones) and was played back by an expensive synchronized unit developed by engineers at the Radio Corporation of America (RCA) and installed in the Broadway Theater. Neither Disney nor the Broadway was a stranger to sound technology; Disney himself had developed a technique for synchronizing music with cartoon action in the first sound cartoon, *Steamboat Willie* (1928), which had premiered in the same theater.

The Fantasound unit was itself a source of controversy. Because the unit was a piece of stage equipment, the stage employees' union members argued that they should operate the new toy; because it was electronic, the electricians' union members argued that it should be theirs. By the time a compromise was worked out, allowing both unions a piece of the installation, technicians had to work twenty-four-hour shifts (at overtime rates) to be ready for the premiere. Reviewer Sam Robins of *The New York Times* raved about the sound system. "When the waters hurl Mickey Mouse down a flight of stairs," he enthused, "the music pours out of one corner of the theatre and floods the auditorium."

The sequence Robins referred to was the film's version of *The Sorcerer's Apprentice* by composer Paul Dukas. Unlike Bach's music, the Dukas piece begs visual and narrative interpretation: It is intended to tell a story (and is in fact based on one by Johann Wolfgang von Goethe). In fact, Disney's treatment of the piece was the kernel around which *Fantasia* grew. In 1938, Disney met conductor Leopold Stokowski at a Hollywood party and mentioned his idea of animating a Mickey Mouse version of

THE MUSIC OF *FANTASIA*

Fantasia *includes several major works of Western music, two of which—Bach's Toccata and Fugue in D Minor and Mussorgsky's* Night on Bald Mountain—*were adapted for the film by Leopold Stokowski.*

- Johann Sebastian Bach, Toccata and Fugue in D Minor, BWV 565 (1703-1707): Stokowski adapted this piece for performance by an orchestra; in the film, this music accompanies a series of abstract images.
- Peter Ilich Tchaikovsky, *Nutcracker Suite*, Op. 71a (1816): In the film, this music frames a series of dances performed by characters such as fairies, mushrooms, and fish.
- Paul Dukas, *L'Apprenti sorcier* (1897): In the famous "sorcerer's apprentice" sequence, Mickey Mouse plays the role of the apprentice.
- Igor Stravinsky, *The Rite of Spring* (1912-1913): This music accompanies a depiction of Earth's history, including the extinction of the dinosaurs.
- Ludwig van Beethoven, Sixth Symphony in F, *Pastorale*, Op. 68 (1808): In this memorable scene, centaurs, fauns, and other mythological creatures relax and play together.
- Amilcare Ponchielli, *La Gioconda: Dance of the Hours* (1876): As it was originally, this piece is performed as a ballet, but here the dancers are elephants, ostriches, hippos, and alligators.
- Modest Mussorgsky, *Night on Bald Mountain* (1867): In one of the film's final scenes, the demon Chernabog and other malevolent creatures wreak havoc until Franz Schubert's "Ave Maria" (1825) signals the breaking of day and the entrance of monks.

The Sorcerer's Apprentice. Stokowski not only approved but also offered to conduct the piece and suggested expanding the film to include other classical works.

In celebrating the ways in which *Fantasia* broke new ground, critics have not always acknowledged the extent to which it grew out of Disney's previous work. From the beginning, Disney's sound cartoons had incorporated music written to augment the action. In 1929, after only six Mickey Mouse sound shorts had been made, Disney and his musical director, Carl Stalling, adapted screen animation to a classical melody, Edvard Grieg's *March of the Dwarfs*. To do so, Stalling had to rewrite the music to fit the action, just as Stokowski later did for *Fantasia*. The finished cartoon, *Skeleton Dance*, launched a new series for Disney: He called them Silly Symphonies. Although the term "symphony" was obvious tongue-in-cheek hyperbole, it indicated that music would dominate these shorts rather than merely punctuate the action, as the music did in the Mickey Mouse shorts. Most of the

Silly Symphonies were developed musically, without dialogue. It was as a Silly Symphony, at first, that Disney intended *The Sorcerer's Apprentice*; with Stokowski's collaboration, it became the embryo of *Fantasia*.

SIGNIFICANCE
If *Fantasia* can be considered Disney's greatest success, it can also be called his biggest failure. In attempting to bring together the audiences of animated films and classical music, he succeeded, at first, in alienating a goodly percentage of both. Although his studio finally made back its investment after the film was rereleased, Disney never lived to see *Fantasia* find the popular acceptance it finally reached. In an interview conducted for a television special celebrating the fiftieth anniversary of *Fantasia*, Walt's nephew Roy E. Disney recalled that his uncle never got over the popular and critical neglect of what he considered his masterpiece; his audience, he felt, did not understand. "I don't regret it," Walt Disney said in 1961. "But if we had it to do all over again, I don't think we'd do it."

The biggest misunderstanding, perhaps, was Disney's motive. Music critics feared he was trying to turn masterpieces into bits of kitsch; average theatergoers felt he was trying to "elevate" them, and justifiably resented the condescension. According to film critic and historian Neil Sinyard, "Actually, nothing was farther from Disney's mind. What he was attempting in *Fantasia* was the same as in his other cartoons—to extend the boundaries of animation." Extend them he did. Even though *Fantasia*'s box-office doldrums caused Disney to back away from both the animation of classical music and purely abstract animation, other animators were inspired by *Fantasia* to expand the art of animation in several directions. Carl Stalling, cocreator of Disney's Silly Symphonies, had left Disney before the *Fantasia* project, yet in his work for Warner Bros. he began working classical melodies into greater and greater roles in Looney Tunes and Merrie Melodies shorts. *A Corny Concerto* (1943), directed by Bob Clampett and written by Frank Tashlin, is a parody of *Fantasia* that features Elmer Fudd introducing two short segments of pantomime comedy involving Daffy Duck, Porky Pig, and Bugs Bunny, set to Stalling's adaptation of two well-known waltzes by Johann Strauss.

Stalling and animator Chuck Jones had Bugs Bunny

tackle opera; Gioacchino Rossini's *Barber of Seville* was parodied in *The Rabbit of Seville* (1950), and Richard Wagner's work provided the basis for *What's Opera, Doc?* (1957). Jones, who had animated his first short only two years before the premiere of *Fantasia*, described the segment performed to Tchaikovsky's *Nutcracker Suite* segment as the "happiest, most perfect single sequence ever done in animated cartoons, perhaps in motion pictures." The scene's influence on Jones's animation is obvious in his work.

Even though the box-office disappointment of *Fantasia* caused Disney to be more cautious in many ways, he and his animators still followed through on two of the artistic implications of *Fantasia*. First, although they never again came close to the level of abstraction found in the film's opening piece, they did experiment with Surrealism in the "Pink Elephants on Parade" sequence in *Dumbo* (1941), and the expressionistic play of light and color in the stag fight scene in *Bambi* (1942) provided further evidence that Disney features were not attempts at photorealism. The entire design of *Alice in Wonderland* (1951) militates against realism, as do the "Never Land" scenes in *Peter Pan* (1953). After the 1950's, any carp about realism became moot, as the new economics of animation forced animators to develop the more linear, stylized approach that would dominate cartoons for two decades, until computer animation and bigger budgets once more made the creation of realistic detail and shading economically feasible.

The second artistic legacy of *Fantasia*, the visualization of music through animation, showed the influence of the film's negative criticism. Several Disney features of the 1940's stitched together musical narratives, but the musical originals were more popular in nature. *Make Mine Music* (1946) was a pastiche of ten songs in various styles, their stories told by animation. Stokowski was involved in this film at the outset, although by the time it was in production he was no longer with the project. Similar patchworks were *Fun and Fancy Free* (1947) and *Melody Time* (1948). Furthermore, all Disney cartoon features continued to combine music and action, as the studio's Academy Award nominations for music attested.

Fantasia continued to influence the art of animated film for decades after its release, in part because of its unusual availability after 1969. Disney established an ingenious cyclical rerelease practice that kept public interest in the films high; the practice began with *Snow White*'s second release in 1943. Eventually, the studio settled on a seven-year cycle for most features. *Fantasia*'s profits

had been so dismal, however, that Disney waited only a little more than three years before rereleasing it in 1944; it was released again only two years later. After three more releases (1953, 1956, 1963), the studio took a chance on leaving prints in permanent circulation beginning in 1969. The popular reaction was extraordinary, especially among young audiences. The "psychedelic" subculture saw *Fantasia* as "mind-expanding" and enjoyed watching it again and again, often enhancing the experience with the use of drugs. Many college film series included *Fantasia* on a yearly basis, with no apparent loss in the film's popularity from overexposure. When advanced stereo systems were installed in many theaters in the late 1970's, the multitrack experience of the original 1940 premiere was re-created—although many mistakenly believed that the stereo version was new; few remembered the elaborate sound system used for the original release.

For the fiftieth-anniversary release of *Fantasia* in 1990, the Disney studio undertook a full-scale restoration project, cleaning up the negatives frame by frame and releasing the "new" prints for the Christmas season. For the following Christmas, 1991, the Disney studio at last released the film on videotape for home use.

—John R. Holmes

FURTHER READING

Finch, Christopher. *The Art of Walt Disney*. Rev. ed. New York: Harry N. Abrams, 2004. Highly illustrated volume provides brief, descriptive commentaries on Disney films, including *Fantasia*.

Maltin, Leonard. *The Disney Films*. 4th ed. New York: Disney Editions, 2000. Comprehensive guide to all Disney films through the end of the twentieth century by an accomplished film critic. Excellent criticism reveals Maltin's love and admiration for Disney without devolving into blind praise. Section on *Fantasia* is generous in scope and balanced in analysis.

Schickel, Richard. *The Disney Version: The Life, Times, Art, and Commerce of Walt Disney*. 3d ed. Chicago: Ivan R. Dee, 1997. History of the man and his studio offers a corrective to the excessive praise of the studio-controlled books that preceded it—although it sometimes goes too far in the other direction. Chapter on *Fantasia* provides a good balance of information and excellent film criticism.

Sinyard, Neil. *The Best of Disney*. Greenwich, Conn.: Twin Books, 1988. Provides insightful commentary from a respected film critic along with full-color blowups of frames from Disney films. Briefly dis-

1940

cusses controversies about *Fantasia* not mentioned in "official" Disney-sponsored sources.

Taylor, Deems. *Walt Disney's "Fantasia."* New York: Simon & Schuster, 1940. Mostly a promotion piece, this profusely illustrated account of the film is nevertheless valuable for musicologist Taylor's contemporary comments about the project. Most of the text sim-

ply describes the film, but the opening chapter gives interesting behind-the-scenes background.

SEE ALSO: Sept., 1911: Der Blaue Reiter Abandons Representation in Art; Mar. 31, 1924: Formation of the Blue Four Advances Abstract Painting; Dec. 21, 1937: Disney Releases *Snow White and the Seven Dwarfs.*

December, 1940
KOESTLER EXAMINES THE DARK SIDE OF COMMUNISM

Arthur Koestler, a former member of the German Communist Party, published Darkness at Noon, *a novel that revealed the evils of the totalitarian regime in the Soviet Union. The work became a best seller in several countries and influenced attitudes toward the Soviet Union and communist movements worldwide.*

ALSO KNOWN AS: *Darkness at Noon*
LOCALE: England
CATEGORIES: Literature; government and politics

KEY FIGURES
Arthur Koestler (1905-1983), Hungarian-born novelist and essayist
Daphne Hardy (1917-2003), artist and British translator of Koestler's work
Joseph Stalin (Joseph Vissarionovich Dzhugashvili; 1878-1953), general secretary of the Communist Party in Russia and dictator of the Soviet Union, 1929-1953
Nikolay Ivanovich Bukharin (1888-1938), Russian revolutionary and leader in the Communist Party

SUMMARY OF EVENT
Arthur Koestler, born in Hungary and raised in Austria, joined the German Communist Party as a young man. After a trip to Stalinist Russia during 1932-1933, however, Koestler became disillusioned with communism and left the party in 1938. His participation in the Spanish Civil War (1936-1939) provided materials for *Spanish Testament* (1937), a work that established his reputation in England and on the Continent as a critic of both communism and fascism. *The Gladiators*, his first novel, was published in 1939. When the Nazis invaded France in 1940, Koestler was living in Paris with his mistress, Daphne Hardy, and they escaped to England through Portugal. They managed to bring the English translation she had made of Koestler's second novel, for which Hardy had

suggested the title *Darkness at Noon*, and the book was published by Jonathan Cape in December of 1940.

In *Darkness at Noon*, Koestler was careful not to identify either the specific country or the leaders who inspired the work. Instead, the fictional hero of the novel, Nicholas Salmanovitch Rubashov, is described as one of a group of revolutionaries who helped establish communism in his country. The leader who had spearheaded the revolution is dead, and his successor, referred to as No. 1, has systematically eliminated all of the old guard. Koestler describes Rubashov's interrogations, in which he is interviewed first by one of his old comrades and later by

Arthur Koestler. (NARA)

one of the newly minted revolutionaries. Although Koestler uses these men to highlight the differences between the first and second generations of the revolution, his account of Rubashov's imprisonment makes it clear that the protagonist has no alternative but to confess that he has been engaged in counterrevolutionary activities for years.

The incarceration of his main character was a convenient way for Koestler to create an opportunity for internal monologue, in which the imprisoned leader could think about communism's philosophical and ethical roots. Rubashov's thoughts reveal communism to be a system in which the ends, however brutal, justify the means, and it is also one in which the individual counts for nothing, while the community—represented by the party—was of paramount importance. In the conversations between Rubashov and his interrogators, Koestler exposes the methods the party uses to build an ingenious case against Rubashov for crimes he did not commit. Through the protagonist's confession at a public trial to trumped-up charges, Koestler shows that even the most dedicated communists are being made into sacrificial figures to advance party leaders' revolutionary agenda.

Although Koestler did not mention any real persons by name, readers were able to see that *Darkness at Noon* was on one level a thinly disguised roman à clef that fictionalized the Moscow show trials of 1935-1936. In these sham trials, a number of prominent Communist leaders were called upon to confess crimes against the state and the people. Among these supposed counterrevolutionaries was Nikolay Ivanovich Bukharin, on whom the character of Rubashov was loosely based.

Bukharin was one of the original Communist leaders who had been in Vladimir Lenin's inner circle when the Communists came to power in Russia in 1917. After Lenin's death, Bukharin had sided with Leon Trotsky during the power struggle in which Joseph Stalin eventually secured power in Soviet Russia. Although he was briefly reconciled with the new dictator, in the mid-1930's Bukharin was one of several prominent figures identified for elimination by Stalin. People in Western countries had received some information about these trials prior to 1940, but Koestler's novel vividly dramatized the nature of the proceedings, the megalomania that drove Stalin's

---

THE TEMPTATIONS OF GOD

While imprisoned, the protagonist of Darkness at Noon, *the former commissar Nikolai Rubashov, hears this pronouncement from the disillusioned and half-drunk Soviet official Ivanov, a former comrade who has become his interrogator:*

The temptations of God were always more dangerous for mankind than those of Satan. As long as chaos dominates the world, God is an anachronism; and every compromise with one's own conscience is perfidy. When the accursed inner voice speaks to you, hold your hands over your ears....

The greatest criminals in history are not of the type Nero and Fouché, but of the type Gandhi and Tolstoy. Gandhi's inner voice has done more to prevent the liberation of India than the British guns. To sell oneself for thirty pieces of silver is an honest transaction; but to sell oneself to one's own conscience is to abandon mankind. History is a priori amoral; it has no conscience. To want to conduct history according to the maxims of the Sunday school means to leave everything as it is. You know that as well as I do. You know the stakes in this game....

Source: Arthur Koestler, *Darkness at Noon* (New York: Macmillan, 1940).

---

actions, and the moral bankruptcy of communism.

The novel achieved only modest initial sales in Britain, but it was picked up as a selection by the American Book-of-the-Month Club, and a wide audience became aware of the ideology behind the Soviet experiment in government. Many former Communists in the West saw in *Darkness at Noon* a vindication of their decision to leave the party. At the same time, the novel prompted strong reaction against loyal Communists.

The book's popularity eventually forced members of the party to take action to refute Koestler's accusations. In 1945, two members of the British Communist Party published a pamphlet titled *The Philosophy of Betrayal*, which cataloged the propagandistic nature of Koestler's work. The strongest reaction, however, came from the French Communists after a French translation of the novel was published in 1945. Party leaders directed members to buy and destroy all copies of the novel; perhaps because of this notoriety, sales in France reached a quarter million. Important French intellectuals such as Jean-Paul Sartre and Maurice Merlau-Ponty felt compelled to write strident attacks against *Darkness at Noon*, defending not only Marxist theory but also the practice of communism under Stalin.

SIGNIFICANCE

In the first decade following its publication, *Darkness at Noon* brought home to Western readers the philosophical

1940

underpinnings of what was becoming not only an important alternative system of government but also a radically different view of human nature. Claims by Soviet leaders, especially Stalin, that they were creating a workers' paradise were undermined by Koestler's portrait of the ruthless methods being employed by the revolutionaries against citizens who dared challenge any action by the party or its leader. Koestler's novel made it clear that under the Soviet system, there was no respect for individual freedoms or even for individual lives. In contrast, the party's power was so far-reaching that any action taken by party leaders was automatically deemed appropriate and justified.

This chilling portrait of communism's effects was influential in shaping the French elections of 1946. Although the French Communist Party was the largest party in the country at that time, it was unable to exert its will in the elections the following year, when France's bicameral legislature was created. Several commentators attributed this failure to the campaign mounted by conservatives and socialists that used *Darkness at Noon* to illustrate communism's evils. The novel played a part in shaping attitudes in other countries as well, including the United States, so that by 1946, when former British prime minister Winston Churchill spoke about the Iron Curtain that had descended over much of Eastern Europe, citizens in the West were predisposed to approve their governments' moves toward the Cold War.

—*Laurence W. Mazzeno*

FURTHER READING

Bloom, Harold, ed. *Arthur Koestler: Darkness at Noon.* Philadelphia: Chelsea House, 2004. Collection of previously published works includes an essay on Cold War discourse and one on the novel's reception in France.

Calder, Jenni. *Chronicles of Conscience: A Study of George Orwell and Arthur Koestler.* Pittsburgh: University of Pittsburgh Press, 1968. Examines the careers of two writers whose political novels had significant impacts in building awareness of and revulsion for totalitarian systems of government.

Cesarani, David. *Arthur Koestler: The Homeless Mind.* New York: Free Press, 1998. Comprehensive biography attempts to place *Darkness at Noon* within the framework of Koestler's development as a novelist and essayist. Also explains the novel's importance as a political statement.

Harns, Harold, ed. *Astride Two Cultures: Arthur Koestler at Seventy.* London: Hutchinson, 1975. Collection of essays about Koestler's work includes a perceptive analysis by Growny Rees of *Darkness at Noon*, outlining the political events on which Koestler draws for his fiction and discussing the impact the novel had in the decades immediately after its publication.

Levene, Mark. *Arthur Koestler.* New York: Frederick Ungar, 1984. Chronicles Koestler's career and discusses his works in their social, political, and historical contexts.

Merrill, Reed, and Thomas Frazier. *Arthur Koestler: An International Bibliography.* Ann Arbor, Mich.: Ardis, 1979. Includes an introduction that provides insight into Koestler's intellectual development, helping to explain the ideology that lies at the heart of his political fiction.

Pearson, Sidney A., Jr. *Arthur Koestler.* Boston: Twayne, 1978. Features a chapter that outlines the plot and themes of *Darkness at Noon*. Includes a separate discussion of the novel's influence in shaping attitudes about communism in Western democracies.

Sperber, Murray A., ed. *Arthur Koestler: A Collection of Critical Essays.* Englewood Cliffs, N.J.: Prentice Hall, 1977. Collection of essays includes several that focus on Koestler's political novels and the reception that *Darkness at Noon* met in England, the United States, and France.

SEE ALSO: 1917-1924: Russian Communists Inaugurate the Red Terror; Mar. 2-6, 1919: Lenin Establishes the Comintern; Aug., 1919-May, 1920: Red Scare; May 18, 1928: Shakhty Case Debuts Show Trials in Moscow; Oct. 1, 1928: Stalin Introduces Central Planning; Jan., 1929: Trotsky Is Sent into Exile; Dec., 1934: Stalin Begins the Purge Trials.

December 30, 1940
ARROYO SECO FREEWAY OPENS IN LOS ANGELES

The Arroyo Seco Freeway, the first part of the Los Angeles freeway system, began the development of a system of superhighways that would affect nearly every facet of life and culture in the United States.

LOCALE: Los Angeles, California
CATEGORIES: Transportation; travel and recreation; environmental issues; urban planning

SUMMARY OF EVENT

The Arroyo Seco Freeway, the first freeway constructed in Southern California, was built to help solve a serious transportation problem that had developed in the greater Los Angeles area. Its success led to the construction of many other freeways in the region, which in turn eventually led to new problems.

In the early part of the twentieth century, when Los Angeles was growing fast, trains and streetcars provided the principal forms of transportation. Investors could make phenomenal profits by buying rural real estate, extending railway or streetcar lines through the area, and then selling the land at a much higher price. Companies and individuals engaging in such speculation set fares that encouraged people to buy land out in the suburbs but that were too low to sustain operating costs for the trains and streetcars. After all the land had been bought, transportation costs could no longer be offset by profits from real estate sales. Existing services soon became overcrowded, and few additional lines were built. Links were not established between suburbs, either—to reach a given suburb from a neighboring one, an individual had to make a trip in to the city and then out again. Railroad and streetcar companies often used campaign contributions and other financial inducements to ensure that the city government would ignore the complaints of citizens about the poor state of transportation in the region.

One solution—at least for a while—was the automobile, and with increases in auto traffic, new roads were built. Usually these were thoroughfares, intended to connect suburbs to one another or to the central business district. These thoroughfares, however, provided frontage for merchants, who gradually lined the new roads with stores and other businesses. As shoppers began visiting the new establishments, the resulting congestion interfered with traffic flow. Soon a new road was needed, and the process would repeat itself. It thus became necessary to limit access to the new highways. As

California passed laws to limit such access, engineers began to study highways that had already been built or that were being built. These included the Bronx River Parkway in New York, completed in 1923, and the autobahns in Germany, constructed at Adolf Hitler's direction beginning in 1933.

The Bronx River Parkway, like many parkways to follow, was built to accommodate automobile traffic only. Because the cars of the day were slow, sharp curves that limited speeds to 35 miles per hour were not a problem. Only fifteen miles long, the parkway's significance lay in the fact that access to it was limited and that it had been artfully designed as a long, narrow park with a road through it.

Hitler's autobahns had an entirely different purpose. During World War I, railroads had been used to transport troops, rations, and munitions to railheads, where they were transferred to trucks and horse-drawn carts. Because roads connecting the front with the railheads had been intended for the occasional farm vehicle, not for sustained use by major armies, they soon deteriorated into muddy ruts. Hitler wanted a highway system that could withstand continued use by heavy vehicles. The resulting design included shoulders for disabled vehicles and curves that permitted safe passage at speeds up to 120 miles per hour.

The engineers who designed the Arroyo Seco Freeway drew on these and other examples. The land chosen for the purpose provided only a narrow strip for two roadways, each thirty-five feet in width, separated by a curbed median strip six feet wide. Funding was provided by the state of California, which for the first time agreed to fund highway construction within a metropolitan area.

Reaction to the first two freeways (another was built at about the same time through the nearby Cahuenga Pass) was positive. City planners believed that the new roads would halt the decline of the city's central business district. Downtown merchants considered the freeways essential to bringing shoppers to their stores. The people living in outlying areas considered the freeways a tremendous improvement over the congested roads and expensive, crowded public mass-transit systems they had endured before. The consensus was that additional freeways were needed, and the Los Angeles City Planning Department and the Los Angeles County Regional Planning Commission soon developed a com-

The recently opened Arroyo Seco Freeway in 1940. (Caltrans)

prehensive master plan with that aim. Before any additional freeways could be built, however, World War II intervened. The war effort brought many defense-related industries to Southern California, and the limitations of the highway system impeded the movement of both workers and materials, underscoring the need for improved roads.

After the war, freeway construction took off. In the eastern United States, toll roads were built with the expectation that the bonds issued to finance them would be paid off by the tolls. In contrast, California paid for its freeways with state taxes on gasoline and motor-vehicle registration, the same method later used by the federal government to fund the interstate highway system.

SIGNIFICANCE

The Arroyo Seco Freeway showed that superhighways worked. In many ways, the freeway laid the groundwork for the National System of Interstate and Defense Highways, proposed in 1944 but not funded until 1956.

This system, largely completed by 1981, eventually consisted of some 41,000 miles of high-speed, limited-access highways linking all major cities in the contiguous United States. The federal government covered 90 percent of the costs of construction, with state governments responsible for the remaining 10 percent. The National Highway Trust Fund was established in 1956 to pay for this system, with a tax of three cents levied on each gallon of motor fuel (the tax was raised to four cents in 1959).

The system as a whole proved successful and not particularly controversial. In rural areas, the new superhighways were generally seen as beneficial. In the early 1960's, however, it was found that fatal accidents occurred eight times more often on the interstate system than on other roads. Research showed that the primary cause was poor rural emergency medical care; ambulance personnel at the time had little medical training, and because the interstate highways were often far from towns, response times tended to be lengthy. The U.S. Department of Transportation responded by setting up programs to train emergency medical technicians to serve rural areas.

The entire country benefited from the interstate highway system in that it brought American citizens closer together. Long-distance driving times and expenses were reduced, as were many of the risks, irritations, and inconveniences of travel. Easier access to what previously were considered to be remote locations improved the sense of national community and reduced the effects of geographic barriers. On rural interstate roads, cars generally carried multiple passengers, rest areas functioned well, and business spurs whisked motorists in and out of small communities for services.

The story changed, however, and became more controversial, where the interstate system entered cities. In the cities, nearly all the benefits of superhighways went to local commuters, so it was more difficult to justify federal funding. At the same time, the costs were much higher than in rural areas. Apart from land acquisition and construction costs, which are always greater in metropolitan areas, there were other, more subtle, costs. For instance, interstate highways competed with mass transit. In the case of the Arroyo Seco Freeway, local mass transit was seriously deficient, and there was little local interest in improving it. Many cities, however, particularly in the East, originally developed with walking as the principal means of transportation. These cities had sufficiently high population densities to allow for efficient mass-transit systems. In such areas, competition from freeways sometimes resulted in decreased mass-transit ridership and accompanying financial stress to mass-transit systems.

Another cost of building freeways through cities came in the form of the barriers the freeways erected, often dividing areas within cities. A freeway may save commuting time, but it may also split the neighborhood it traverses and force residents to spend more time getting to places that were formerly within easy reach. Ironically, the same highway system that enhanced a sense of community across large parts of the United States served to interfere with that sense of community in many cities.

Because automobile exhaust is one of the major contributors to urban air pollution, moreover, the proliferation of freeways had dangerous consequences for the environment. The Los Angeles basin is particularly susceptible to air pollution because of its geography: When air cooled by the Pacific Ocean is blown into the basin, it may be trapped there beneath a layer of warmer air

hedged in by the surrounding mountains. Air pollutants produced in the basin are part of this layer. Given the staggering health costs that stem from the pollution caused by automobile traffic congestion, serious efforts to reduce both the pollution and the congestion gained high priority in the Los Angeles area by the end of the twentieth century.

—*Otto H. Muller*

FURTHER READING

Bottles, Scott L. *Los Angeles and the Automobile: The Making of the Modern City.* Berkeley: University of California Press, 1987. Well-researched, thorough history of the role of the automobile in the growth and development of Los Angeles. One of the most informative and comprehensive sources on the topic available.

Dasmann, Raymond F. *The Destruction of California.* New York: Collier Books, 1966. Argues that the freeway system in California is largely responsible for the demise of the state's cities. Characterizes Los Angeles as the city that "surrendered to the freeway system."

Davidson, Janet F., and Michael S. Sweeney. *On the Move: Transportation and the American Story.* Washington, D.C.: National Geographic Society, 2003. Companion volume to an exhibit at the National Museum of American History provides an overview of the evolution of transportation in the United States and how changes in transportation have affected other areas of American life. Includes illustrations.

Lents, James M., and William J. Kelly. "Clearing the Air in Los Angeles." *Scientific American* 269 (October, 1993): 32-39. Reports on improvements in air quality in Los Angeles and on plans for meeting federally mandated air-quality standards by 2010. Summarizes adverse health effects of smog and reviews the history of air-pollution abatement programs in Southern California.

Lewis, Tom. *Divided Highways: Building the Interstate Highways, Transforming American Life.* New York: Viking Penguin, 1997. Readable history of the building of the U.S. interstate highway system focuses in large part on the individuals involved in the enterprise and on the system's impacts on American society. Includes photographs.

Snow, W. Brewster, ed. *The Highway and the Landscape.* New Brunswick, N.J.: Rutgers University Press, 1959. Collection of essays written by landscape architects and others during the period when the inter-

1940

state system was in its active construction phase. Emphasizes the aesthetic qualities of well-designed expressways and points out the need for careful thought in the planning of highways, their plantings, and their interaction with the larger landscape. A refreshing and thought-provoking approach to the topic.

SEE ALSO: Mar. 4, 1902: American Automobile Association Is Established; Mar. 1, 1913: Ford Assembly Line Begins Operation; Nov. 5, 1913: Completion of the Los Angeles Aqueduct; 1922: First Major U.S. Shopping Center Opens; 1927: Number of U.S. Automakers Falls to Forty-Four.

Appendixes

BIBLIOGRAPHY

CONTENTS

INTRODUCTION

This bibliography is a starting point for general research in the various topics indicated by the headings below. It is by no means exhaustive, nor could it be for a century in which technology has made publication so relatively easy and in which virtually every country in the world has come to have a voice in the process. Emphasis here is placed on broad studies rather than on more narrowly targeted works. More recent works are also emphasized over older ones, although many of the best older works are also included. Most biographies, autobiographies, and general country studies are not included, as they are innumerable and easily found through standard catalog and database searches. No magazine or journal articles are included. Thorough research on any topic will require a literature search in databases that are updated regularly as well as a search of the World Wide Web, where an increasing number of excellent sites are daily being added to the surfeit of personal and propaganda portals. The works included in this bibliography will, however, help interested readers locate many of the most important

studies relative to twentieth century themes and will serve as aids in framing research.

Of the many general historical resources that might be helpful for those beginning to research early twentieth century themes, two are globally conceived and especially helpful. First, *The Encyclopedia of World History*, edited by Peter N. Stearns (Boston: Houghton Mifflin, 2001), is one of the most detailed and comprehensive compendiums of world events available. This work is arranged chronologically and extensively annotated to provide an invaluable reference narrative; it is supported by an exhaustive index and an excellent, searchable CD-ROM. Second, the two-volume third edition of *The American Historical Association's Guide to Historical Literature*, edited by Mary Beth Norton et al. (New York: Oxford University Press, 1995), is one of the most comprehensive annotated bibliographies of historical sources available, covering the most important works in all areas of research for all parts of the world—a tall task but one that specialist section editors achieve remarkably well. Although this work is increasingly dated, it is still an essential point of departure for research into unfamiliar areas.

Since the last decades of the twentieth century, three kinds of studies have produced an exceptionally long list of both monographs and reference works that are readily found through general catalog and database searches: (1) works on the major themes of twentieth century history, including the two world wars, the Holocaust, imperialism and decolonization, civil rights, the rise of environmentalism, women's issues, immigration, the Cold War, and international migration; (2) country and area studies, such as John King Fairbank and Merle Goldman's *China: A New History* (Cambridge, Mass.: Harvard University Press, 1998) and Ian Richard Netton's *Encyclopedia of Islamic Civilization and Religion* (New York: Routledge, 2006); and (3) works on contentious social issues, which vary from year to year but in the early twenty-first century have included topics such as energy supply, global terrorism, abortion, the death penalty, and immigration. Some of the best of these works are cited in their appropriate sections in this bibliography, although many others are not.

The sheer diversity of topics, cultures, and technologies in the twentieth century precludes the kinds of comprehensive treatments of the century on the World Wide Web that are more common for earlier centures. Amid a bewildering profusion of sites, an excellent guide to both research and historical Web sites is Richard Jensen's "Scholar's Guide to WWW" (http://tigger.uic.edu/~rjensen), which is especially useful for recommendations within categories. The Open Directory Project includes almost 3,000 websites devoted to the twentieth century, organized in a wide variety of topics and by decade (http://dmoz.org/Society/History/By_Time_Period/Twentieth_Century). The Historical Text Archive provides links to more than 6,500 Web sites, many of which cover twentieth century topics (http://historicaltextarchive.com). Yahoo has a growing collection of good history sites (http://dir.yahoo.com/Arts/Humanities/History/By_Time_Period/20th_Century). The Organization of American Historians keeps a list of "Links for the History Profession" (http://www.oah.org/announce/links.html), although it is less comprehensive than one might expect. The Avalon Project at Yale Law School collects hundreds of twentieth century documents, focusing on but not limited to international and foreign policy issues (http://www.yale.edu/lawweb/avalon/20th.htm). One general reference site deserving special mention is the "Historical Atlas of the Twentieth Century" (http://users.erols.com/mwhite28/20centry.htm), which illustrates much of the history of the entire world through maps. Finally, more than one hundred academic discussion networks, most of which cover twentieth century topics, can be accessed through the well-established academic portal H-Net (http://www.h-net.org/lists).

                  —*John Powell*

GENERAL REFERENCE

Barraclough, Geoffrey, ed. *HarperCollins Atlas of World History.* 2d rev. ed. Ann Arbor, Mich.: Borders Press, 1998.

Bothamley, Jennifer. *Dictionary of Theories.* London: Gale Research International, 1993.

Bullock, Alan, and Stephen Tromby, eds. *The Norton Dictionary of Modern Thought.* New York: W. W. Norton, 1999.

Christopher, A. J. *The Atlas of States: Global Change, 1900-2000.* Chichester, England: John Wiley & Sons, 1999.

Daniel, Clifton, ed. *Twentieth Century Day by Day.* American ed. London: Dorling Kindersley, 2000.

Dictionary of World Biography: The Twentieth Century. Pasadena, Calif.: Salem Press, 1999.

Encyclopedia of World History. Oxford, England: Oxford University Press, 1998.

Great Events: 1900-2001. Rev. ed. 8 vols. Pasadena, Calif.: Salem Press, 2002.

Great Stories of the Century: The Major Events of the Twentieth Century as Reported in the Pages of "The New York Times." New York: Galahad Books, 1999.

Horowitz, Maryanne Cline, ed. *New Dictionary of the History of Ideas.* 6 vols. Detroit: Thomson Gale, 2005.

McNeill, William H., ed. *Berkshire Encyclopedia of World History.* 5 vols. Great Barrington, Mass.: Berkshire Publishing Group, 2005.

Merriam-Webster's Biographical Dictionary. 3d rev. ed. Springfield, Mass.: Merriam Webster, 1995.

Merriam-Webster's Geographical Dictionary. 3d ed. Springfield, Mass.: Merriam Webster, 1997.

Minahan, James, ed. *Encyclopedia of the Stateless Nations.* 4 vols. Westport, Conn.: Greenwood Press, 2002.

Ramirez-Faria, Carlos, ed. *The Historical Dictionary of World Political Geography: An Encyclopedic Guide to the History of Nations.* New York: Palgrave, 2001.

Sherby, Louise S. *The Who's Who of Nobel Prize Winners, 1901-2000.* 4th ed. Westport, Conn.: Oryx, 2002.

Wintle, Justin, ed. *New Makers of Modern Culture*. New York: RoutledgeFalmer, 2006.

World Leaders of the Twentieth Century. 2 vols. Pasadena, Calif.: Salem Press, 2000.

GENERAL STUDIES

Appiah, Kwame Anthony, and Henry Louis Gates, Jr., eds. *Africana: The Encyclopedia of the African and African American Experience*. 2d ed. 5 vols. Oxford, England: Oxford University Press, 2005.

Brower, Daniel R. *The World in the Twentieth Century: From Empires to Nations*. 6th ed. Upper Saddle River, N.J.: Pearson Prentice Hall, 2006.

Davis, R. Hunt, Jr. ed. *Encyclopedia of African History and Culture*. Rev. ed. 5 vols. New York: Facts On File, 2005.

Duiker, William J. *Twentieth-Century World History*. 3d ed. Belmont, Calif.: Wadsworth, 2004.

Fernandez-Armesto, Felipe. *The World: A History*. Upper Saddle River, N.J.: Pearson Prentice Hall, 2007.

Fromkin, David. *A Peace to End All Peace: The Fall of the Ottoman Empire and the Creation of the Modern Middle East*. New York: Henry Holt, 1989.

Gilbert, Felix, and David Clay Large. *The End of the European Era: 1890 to the Present*. 5th ed. New York: W. W. Norton, 2002.

Goff, Richard. *The Twentieth Century: A Brief Global History*. 6th ed. New York: McGraw-Hill, 2001.

Jelavich, Barbara. *History of the Balkans*. 2 vols. New York: Cambridge University Press, 1983.

Johnson, Paul. *Modern Times: A History of the World from the Twenties to the Nineties*. Rev. ed. New York: HarperCollins, 1991.

Keylor, William R. *The Twentieth-Century World and Beyond: An International History Since 1900*. New York: Oxford University Press, 2006.

Mansfield, Peter, and Nicholas Pelham. *A History of the Middle East*. Rev. ed. New York: Penguin Books, 2004.

Mansoor, Menahem, ed. *1900-1941*. Vol. 1 in *Political and Diplomatic History of the Arab World, 1900-1967*. Washington, D.C.: NCR/Microcard Editions, 1972.

Overfield, James. *Sources of Twentieth Century Global History*. New York: Houghton Mifflin, 2001.

Paxton, Robert. *Europe in the Twentieth Century*. Belmont, Calif.: Wadsworth, 2004.

Roberts, J. M. *Twentieth Century: The History of the World*. New York: Penguin Books, 2000.

Schraeder, Peter J. *African Politics and Society: A Mosaic in Transformation*. 2d ed. Boston: Bedford/St. Martin's Press, 2000.

Stavrianos, Leften. *The Balkans Since 1453*. New York: New York University Press, 2000.

Tarling, Nicholas, ed. *From c. 1800 to the 1930's*. Vol. 3, part 1, in *The Cambridge History of Southeast Asia*. Cambridge, England: Cambridge University Press, 1999.

Wilkinson, James, and H. Stuart Hughes. *Contemporary Europe: A History*. 9th ed. Upper Saddle River, N.J.: Prentice Hall, 1997.

Zinn, Howard. *The Twentieth Century: A People's History*. New York: Harper Perennial, 2003.

AGRICULTURE AND THE LAND

Bonnifield, Mathew Paul. *The Dust Bowl: Men, Dirt, and Depression*. Albuquerque: University of New Mexico Press, 1979.

Cawley, R. McGreggor. *Federal Land, Western Anger: The Sagebrush Rebellion and Environmental Politics*. Lawrence: University Press of Kansas, 1993.

Cochrane, Willard W., and C. Ford Runge. *Reforming Farm Policy: Toward a National Agenda*. Ames: Iowa State University Press, 1992.

Cunfer, Geoff. *On the Great Plains: Agriculture and Environment*. College Station: Texas A&M University Press, 2005.

Curtis, Byrd C., Sanjaya Rajaram, and H. Gómez Macpherson, eds. *Bread Wheat: Improvement and Production*. Rome: Food and Agriculture Organization of the United Nations, 2002.

Donahue, Debra L. *The Western Range Revisited: Removing Livestock from Public Lands to Conserve Native Biodiversity*. Norman: University of Oklahoma Press, 1999.

Hamilton, David E. *From New Day to New Deal: American Farm Policy from Hoover to Roosevelt, 1928-1933*. Chapel Hill: University of North Carolina Press, 1991.

Hansen, John M. *Gaining Access: Congress and the Farm Lobby, 1919-1981*. Chicago: University of Chicago Press, 1991.

Howkins, Alun. *The Death of Rural England: A Social History of the Countryside Since 1900*. London: Routledge, 2003.

Saloutos, Theodore. *The American Farmer and the New Deal*. Ames: Iowa State University Press, 1982.

Steiner, Frederick R. *Soil Conservation in the United States: Policy and Planning*. Baltimore: The Johns Hopkins University Press, 1990.

Worcester, Donald. *Dust Bowl: The Southern Great Plains in the 1930's*. New York: Oxford University Press, 1979.

ARCHAEOLOGY AND ANTHROPOLOGY

Birx, H. James, ed. *Encyclopedia of Anthropology*. 2d ed. 5 vols. Thousand Oaks, Calif.: Sage, 2006.

Bohannan, Paul, and Mark Glazer, eds. *High Points in Anthropology*. 2d ed. New York: McGraw-Hill, 1988.

Freeman, Derek. *The Fateful Hoaxing of Margaret Mead: A Historical Analysis of Her Samoan Research*. Boulder, Colo.: Westview Press, 1998.

McGee, R. Jon, and Richard L. Warms. *Anthropological Theory: An Introductory History*. 3d ed. New York: McGraw-Hill, 2003.

Mead, Margaret. *Coming of Age in Samoa*. 1928. Reprint. New York: Harper Perennial, 2001.

Murray, Tim, ed. *Encyclopedia of Archaeology: History and Discoveries*. 3 vols. Santa Barbara, Calif.: ABC-Clio, 2001.

ARTS: PERFORMING

Adorno, Theodor W. *Philosophy of New Music*. Translated and edited by Robert Hullot-Kentor. Minneapolis: University of Minnesota Press, 2006.

Anderson, Jack. *Art Without Boundaries: The World of Modern Dance*. Iowa City: University of Iowa Press, 1997.

_____. *The One and Only: The Ballet Russe de Monte Carlo*. New York: Hudson Hills Press, 2003.

Bek, Mikuláš, Geoffrey Chew, and Petr Macek, eds. *Socialist Realism and Music*. Brno, Czech Republic: Institute of Musicology, Masaryk University, 2004.

Bordman, Gerald. *American Theatre: A Chronicle of Comedy and Drama, 1930-1969*. New York: Oxford University Press, 1996.

Charters, Samuel Barclay. *The Blues Makers*. New York: Da Capo Press, 1991.

Cook, Susan C. *Opera for a New Republic*. Ann Arbor, Mich.: UMI Research Press, 1988.

Fitz-Simon, Christopher. *The Abbey Theatre: Ireland's National Theatre—The First Hundred Years*. New York: Thames and Hudson, 2003.

Friedwald, Will. *Jazz Singing: America's Great Voices from Bessie Smith to Bebop and Beyond*. New York: Charles Scribner's Sons, 1990.

Garafola, Lynn. *Legacies of Twentieth-Century Dance*. Middletown, Conn.: Wesleyan University Press, 2005.

Hagan, Chet. *Grand Ole Opry*. New York: Henry Holt, 1989.

Hansen, Peter S. *An Introduction to Twentieth Century Music*. 4th ed. Boston: Allyn & Bacon, 1978.

Hinton, Stephen. *The Idea of Gebrauchsmusik*. New York: Garland, 1989.

Jasen, David A. *Tin Pan Alley: An Encyclopedia of the Golden Age of American Song*. Rev. ed. New York: Routledge, 2003.

Kerman, Joseph. *Opera as Drama*. 50th anniversary rev. ed. Berkeley: University of California Press, 2005.

Knapp, Raymond. *The American Musical and the Formation of National Identity*. Princeton, N.J.: Princeton University Press, 2004.

Krasner, David. *A Beautiful Pageant: African American Theatre, Drama, and Performance in the Harlem Renaissance, 1910-1927*. New York: Palgrave Macmillan, 2002.

Leach, Robert. *Makers of Modern Theatre: An Introduction*. New York: Routledge, 2004.

Lee, Carol. *Ballet in Western Culture: A History of Its Origins and Evolution*. New York: Routledge, 2002.

Malone, Bill C. *Don't Get Above Your Raisin': Country Music and the Southern Working Class*. Champaign: University of Illinois Press, 2002.

Malone, Bill C., and David Stricklin. *Southern Music/American Music*. Rev. ed. Lexington: University Press of Kentucky, 2003.

Miller, Terry E., and Andrew Shahriari. *World Music: A Global Journey*. New York: Routledge, 2005.

Nettl, Bruno. *Folk and Traditional Music of the Western Continents*. 3d ed. Englewood Cliffs, N.J.: Prentice-Hall, 1989.

Riddle, Peter H. *The American Musical: History and Development*. New York: Mosaic Press, 2004.

Rubin, Don, ed. *World Encyclopedia of Contemporary Theatre*. 6 vols. New York: Routledge, 2000.

Salzman, Eric. *Twentieth-Century Music: An Introduction*. 4th ed. Upper Saddle River, N.J.: Prentice Hall, 2001.

Schwartz, Bonnie Nelson. *Voices from the Federal Theatre*. Madison: University of Wisconsin Press, 2003.

Schwarz, Boris. *Music and Musical Life in Soviet Russia, 1917-1970*. London: Barrie & Jenkins, 1972.

Smith, Frederick Key. *Nordic Art Music: From the Middle Ages to the Third Millennium*. New York: Praeger, 2002.

Thomas, Helen. *Dance, Modernity, and Culture: Explorations in the Sociology of Dance*. New York: Routledge, 1995.

Titon, Jeff Todd, et al. *Worlds of Music: An Introduction*

to the Music of the World's People. Belmont, Calif.: Schirmer/Thomson Learning, 2005.

Wardlow, Gayle Dean. *Chasin' That Devil Music: Searching for the Blues*. San Francisco: Backbeat Books, 1998.

Welch, Robert. *The Abbey Theatre, 1899-1999: Form and Pressure*. New York: Oxford University Press, 1999.

Whiteman, Paul, and Mary Margaret McBride. *Jazz*. 1926. Reprint. New York: Arno Press, 1974.

Witham, Barry B. *The Federal Theatre Project: A Case Study*. New York: Cambridge University Press, 2003.

Wolfe, Charles K. *A Good-Natured Riot: The Birth of "The Grand Ole Opry."* Nashville: Vanderbilt University Press, 1999.

ARTS: VISUAL

Adlmann, Jan E. *Vienna Moderne, 1898-1918*. Houston, Tex.: Sarah Campbell Blaffer Gallery, 1978.

Apollinaire, Guillaume. *The Cubist Painters*. Translated by Peter Read. Berkeley: University of California Press, 2004.

Arnason, H. H. *History of Modern Art: Painting, Sculpture, Architecture, Photography*. 5th ed. Upper Saddle River, N.J.: Prentice Hall, 2003.

Art: A World History. New York: Dorling Kindersley, 2002.

Arwas, Victor. *Art Deco*. Rev. ed. New York: Harry N. Abrams, 1998.

Barron, Stephanie, ed. *Exiles and Emigres: The Flight of European Artists from Hitler*. Los Angeles: Los Angeles County Museum of Art, 1997.

Barron, Stephanie, and Maurice Tuchman, eds. *The Avant-Garde in Russia, 1910-1933: New Perspectives*. Los Angeles: Los Angeles County Museum of Art, 1980.

Bendavid-Val, Leah. *Propaganda and Dreams: Photographing the 1930's in the U.S.S.R. and the U.S.* New York: Edition Stemmle, 1999.

Bowlt, John E., ed. *Painting Revolution: Kandinsky, Malevich, and the Russian Avant-Garde*. Bethesda, Md.: Foundation for International Arts and Education, 2000.

Bown, Matthew Cullerne. *Socialist Realist Painting*. New Haven, Conn.: Yale University Press, 1998.

Cheetham, Mark A. *The Rhetoric of Purity: Essentialist Theory and the Advent of Abstract Painting*. New York: Cambridge University Press, 1991.

Doss, Erika. *Twentieth-Century American Art*. New York: Oxford University Press, 2002.

Doty, Robert. *Photo-Secession: Photography as a Fine Art*. Rochester, N.Y.: George Eastman House, 1960.

Finch, Christopher. *The Art of Walt Disney*. Rev. ed. New York: Harry N. Abrams, 2004.

Goldwater, Robert. *Primitivism in Modern Art*. Rev. ed. Cambridge, Mass.: Belknap Press, 2002.

Janson, Anthony. *Janson's History of Art*. 7th ed. Upper Saddle River, N.J.: Prentice Hall, 2006.

Lloyd, Jill. *German Expressionism: Primitivism and Modernity*. New Haven, Conn.: Yale University Press, 1991.

McShane, Megan. *Genesis of a Revolution from Dada to Surrealism*. New York: Parkstone Press, 2006.

Rochfort, Desmond. *Mexican Muralists: Orozco, Rivera, Siqueiros*. San Francisco: Chronicle Books, 1998.

Rosenblum, Naomi. *A World History of Photography*. 3d ed. New York: Abbeville Press, 1997.

Sandler, Martin W. *Photography: An Illustrated History*. New York: Oxford University Press, 2002.

Seaton, Elizabeth. *WPA Federal Art Project: Printmaking in California, 1935-1943*. San Francisco: Book Club of California, 2005.

Tuchman, Maurice, ed. *The Spiritual in Art: Abstract Painting, 1890-1985*. New York: Abbeville Press, 1999.

Valkenier, Elizabeth. *Russian Realist Art: The State and Society*. New York: Columbia University Press, 1989.

West, Shearer. *The Visual Arts in Germany, 1890-1937: Utopia and Despair*. New Brunswick, N.J.: Rutgers University Press, 2001.

Williams, Robert C. *Artists in Revolution: Portraits of the Russian Avant-Garde, 1905-1925*. Bloomington: Indiana University Press, 1977.

Wood, John. *The Art of the Autochrome: The Birth of Color Photography*. Iowa City: University of Iowa Press, 1993.

AVIATION AND TRANSPORTATION

American Automobile Manufacturers Association. *Automobiles of America*. 5th ed. Lakeland, Fla.: Cars & Parts, 1997.

Berger, Michael L. *The Automobile in American History and Culture: A Reference Guide*. Westport, Conn.: Greenwood Press, 2001.

Bilstein, Roger E. *Flight in America: From the Wrights to the Astronauts*. 3d ed. Baltimore: The Johns Hopkins University Press, 2001.

Botting, Douglas. *Dr. Eckener's Dream Machine: The Great Zeppelin and the Dawn of Air Travel*. New York: Henry Holt, 2001.

Bottles, Scott L. *Los Angeles and the Automobile: The Making of the Modern City.* Berkeley: University of California Press, 1987.

Brooks, Peter W. *Zeppelin: Rigid Airships, 1893-1940.* Washington, D.C.: Smithsonian Institution Press, 1992.

Christy, J., and L. R. Cook. *American Aviation: An Illustrated History.* 2d ed. Blue Ridge Summit, Pa.: TAB Books, 1994.

Corn, Joseph J. *The Winged Gospel: America's Romance with Aviation.* 1983. Reprint. Baltimore: The Johns Hopkins University Press, 2001.

DeVorkin, David H. *Race to the Stratosphere: Manned Scientific Ballooning in America.* New York: Springer-Verlag, 1989.

Durban, Enoch S., et al., eds. *The Encyclopedia of Ships.* San Diego, Calif.: Thunder Bay Press, 2001.

Flink, James. *The Car Culture.* Cambridge, Mass.: MIT Press, 1975.

Georgano, Nick, ed. *The Beaulieu Encyclopedia of the Automobile.* 3 vols. Oxford, England: Fitzroy Dearborn, 2000.

Gruntman, Mike. *Blazing the Trail: The Early History of Spacecraft and Rocketry.* Reston, Va.: American Institute of Aeronautics and Astronautics, 2004.

Holden, Henry M. *The Boeing 247: The First Modern Commercial Airplane.* Blue Ridge Summit, Pa.: TAB Books, 1991.

Kane, Robert M. *Air Transportation.* 14th ed. Dubuque, Iowa: Kendall/Hunt, 2002.

Kunz, Tom. *The Titanic Disaster Hearings.* New York: Pocket Books, 1998.

Lynch, Donald, and Ken Marschall. *Titanic: An Illustrated History.* Secaucus, N.J.: Chartwell Books, 2005.

Macmillan Encyclopedia of Transportation. New York: Macmillan Reference Books, 1999.

Moore, John. *The World's Railroads.* Secaucus, N.J.: Chartwell Books, 2000.

Pattillo, Donald M. *Pushing the Envelope: The American Aircraft Industry.* Ann Arbor: University of Michigan Press, 2001.

Syon, Guillaime de. *Zeppelins: Germany and the Airship, 1900-1939.* Baltimore: The Johns Hopkins University Press, 2002.

Taylor, Michael J. H. *Aviators: A Photographic History of Flight.* New York: HarperCollins, 2005.

Villard, Henry Serrano. *Contact! The Story of the Early Aviators.* 1968. Reprint. Mineola, N.Y.: Dover, 2002.

Wells, Alexander T., and John G. Wensveen. *Air Transportation: A Management Perspective.* 5th ed. Monterey, Calif.: Brooks/Cole, 2003.

Winter, Frank H. *The First Golden Age of Rocketry.* Washington, D.C.: Smithsonian Institution Press, 1990.

Zimmerman, Karl R. *Twentieth Century Limited.* St. Paul, Minn.: MBI Publishing, 2002.

BUSINESS, ECONOMICS, AND FINANCE (*see also* INDUSTRY AND LABOR)

Ake, Claude. *A Political Economy of Africa.* Harlow, England: Longman, 1981.

Berend, Ivan T. *An Economic History of Twentieth-Century Europe: Economic Regimes from Laissez Faire to Globalization.* Cambridge, England: Cambridge University Press, 2006.

Bliss, Michael. *Northern Enterprise: Five Centuries of Canadian Business.* Toronto: McClelland & Stewart, 1987.

Boyce, Robert. *British Capitalism at the Crossroads, 1919-1932.* New York: Cambridge University Press, 1988.

Brown, Anthony Cave. *Oil, God, and Gold.* New York: Houghton Mifflin, 1999.

Brownlee, W. Elliot. *Federal Taxation in America: A Short History.* 2d ed. Washington, D.C.: Woodrow Wilson Center Press, 2004.

Calomiris, Charles W. *U.S. Bank Deregulation in Historical Perspective.* New York: Cambridge University Press, 2000.

Castaneda, Christopher James. *Invisible Fuel: Manufactured and Natural Gas in America, 1800-2000.* Boston: Twayne, 1999.

Clarence-Smith, William Gervase, and Steven Topik, eds. *The Global Coffee Economy in Africa, Asia, and Latin America, 1500-1989.* Cambridge, England: Cambridge University Press, 2003.

Clarke, Peter. *The Keynesian Revolution in the Making, 1924-1936.* New York: Oxford University Press, 2006.

Cox, Howard. *The Global Cigarette: Origins and Evolution of British American Tobacco, 1880-1945.* New York: Oxford University Press, 2000.

Derks, Scott. *The Value of a Dollar: Prices and Income in the United States, 1860-2004.* Millerton, N.Y.: Grey House, 2004.

Dickerson, Kitty G. *Textiles and Apparel in the International Economy.* New York: Macmillan, 1991.

Eatwell, John, Murray Milgate, and Peter Newman, eds.

The New Palgrave: A Dictionary of Economics. 4 vols. London: Macmillan, 1987.

Eckes, Alfred E., Jr. *Opening America's Market: U.S. Foreign Trade Policy Since 1776.* Chapel Hill: University of North Carolina Press, 1995.

Eichengreen, Barry. *Golden Fetters: The Gold Standard and the Great Depression.* New York: Oxford University Press, 1992.

Feldman, Gerald D. *The Great Disorder: Politics,Economics, and Society in the German Inflation, 1914-1924.* New York: Oxford University Press, 1996.

Fenichell, Stephen. *Plastic: The Making of a Synthetic Century.* New York: Collins, 1996.

Fraser, Steve. *Every Man a Speculator: A History of Wall Street in American Life.* San Francisco: HarperCollins, 2005.

Geisst, Charles R. *One Hundred Years of Wall Street.* New York: McGraw-Hill, 1999.

Grant, James. *Money of the Mind: Borrowing and Lending in America from the Civil War to Michael Milken.* New York: Farrar, Straus and Giroux, 1992.

Gup, Benton E., ed. *Too Big to Fail: Policies and Practices in Government Bailouts.* Westport, Conn.: Praeger, 2004.

Hughes, Jonathan, and Louis P. Cain. *American Economic History.* 6th ed. Boston: Addison-Wesley, 2002.

International Directory of Company Histories. 79 vols. Detroit: Thomson Gale, 1988-2006.

Keller, Morton. *Regulating a New Economy: Public and Economic Change in America, 1900-1930.* Cambridge, Mass.: Harvard University Press, 1990.

Kindleberger, Charles P. *Manias, Panics, and Crashes: A History of Financial Crises.* 4th ed. New York: John Wiley & Sons, 2000.

_____. *The World in Depression, 1929-1939.* Rev. ed. Berkeley: University of California Press, 1986.

Koistinen, Paul A. C. *Mobilizing for Modern War: The Political Economy of American Warfare, 1865-1919.* Lawrence: University Press of Kansas, 1997.

Kuisel, Richard F. *Capitalism and the State in Modern France: Renovation and Economic Management in the Twentieth Century.* Cambridge, England: Cambridge University Press, 1981.

Lutz, Mark A. *Economics for the Common Good: Two Centuries of Social Economic Thought in the Humanistic Tradition.* New York: Routledge, 1999.

Naylor, R. T. *The History of Canadian Business, 1867-1914.* 1975. Reprint. Montreal: Black Rose Books, 1997.

Nove, Alec. *An Economic History of the U.S.S.R., 1917-1991.* New York: Penguin Books, 1992.

Odagiri, Hiroyuki, and Akira Goto. *Technology and Industrial Development in Japan: Building Capabilities by Learning, Innovation, and Public Policy.* New York: Oxford University Press, 1996.

Pomeranz, Kenneth. *The Great Divergence: China, Europe, and the Making of the Modern World Economy.* Princeton, N.J.: Princeton University Press, 2001.

Pomeranz, Kenneth, and Steven Topik. *The World That Trade Created: Society, Culture, and the World Economy, 1400 to the Present.* 2d ed. Armonk, N.Y.: M. E. Sharpe, 2005.

Rosenof, Theodore. *Economics in the Long Run: New Deal Theorists and Their Legacies, 1933-1993.* Chapel Hill: University of North Carolina Press, 1997.

Salazar-Carrillo, Jorge, and Bernadette West. *Oil and Development in Venezuela During the Twentieth Century.* Westport, Conn.: Praeger, 2004.

Sampson, Anthony. *The Seven Sisters: The Giant Oil Companies and the World They Shaped.* New York: Viking Press, 1975.

Sobel, Robert. *Panic on Wall Street: A History of America's Financial Disasters.* 1988. Reprint. New York: Beard Books, 1999.

Spellman, Paul N. *Spindletop Boom Days.* College Station: Texas A&M University Press, 2001.

Weber, Max. *The Protestant Ethic and the Spirit of Capitalism.* Translated by Talcott Parsons. 1904. Reprint. Oxford, England: Routledge, 2001.

Wilkins, Mira. *The Emergence of Multinational Enterprise: American Business Abroad from the Colonial Era to 1914.* Cambridge, Mass.: Harvard University Press, 1970.

_____. *The Maturing of Multinational Enterprise: American Business Abroad, 1914-1970.* Cambridge, Mass.: Harvard University Press, 1974.

Yergin, Daniel. *The Prize: The Epic Quest for Oil, Money, and Power.* New York: Simon & Schuster, 1991.

CIVIL RIGHTS, HUMANITARIANISM, AND SOCIAL ACTIVISM (*see also* GOVERNMENT AND POLITICS)

Bentley, Eric, ed. *Thirty Years of Treason: Excerpts from Hearings Before the House Committee on Un-American Activities, 1938-1968.* New York: Viking Press, 1971.

Ceadel, Martin. *Semi-detached Idealists: The British Peace Movement and International Relations, 1854-1945.* New York: Oxford University Press, 2000.

Cottrell, Robert C. *Roger Nash Baldwin and the American Civil Liberties Union.* New York: Columbia University Press, 2000.

Davis, Allen F. *Spearheads for Reform: The Social Settlements and the Progressive Movement, 1890-1914.* New York: Oxford University Press, 1967.

Donovan, Brian. *White Slave Crusades: Race, Gender, and Anti-vice Activism, 1887-1917.* Champaign: University of Illinois Press, 2005.

Du Bois, W. E. B. *The Souls of Black Folk: One Hundred Years Later.* Edited by Dolan Hubbard. Columbia: University of Missouri Press, 2003.

Gengarelly, W. Anthony. *Distinguished Dissenters and Opposition to the 1919-1920 Red Scare.* Lewiston, N.Y.: Edwin Mellen Press, 1996.

Goodman, Walter. *The Committee: The Extraordinary Career of the House Committee on Un-American Activities.* New York: Farrar, Straus and Giroux, 1968.

Hagan, William T. *The Indian Rights Association: The Herbert Welsh Years, 1882-1904.* Tucson: University of Arizona Press, 1985.

Haksar, Vinit. *Rights, Communities, and Disobedience: Liberalism and Gandhi.* 2d ed. New York: Oxford University Press, 2003.

Hill, Robert A., et al., eds. *The Marcus Garvey and Universal Negro Improvement Association Papers.* 10 vols. Berkeley: University of California Press, 1983-2006.

Johnson, Donald. *The Challenge to American Freedoms: World War I and the Rise of the American Civil Liberties Union.* Lexington: University Press of Kentucky, 1963.

Jonas, Gilbert. *Freedom's Sword: The NAACP and the Struggle Against Racism in America, 1909-1969.* New York: Routledge, 2004.

Kaplowitz, Craig A. *LULAC, Mexican Americans, and National Policy.* College Station: Texas A&M University Press, 2005.

Kraus, Harry P. *The Settlement House Movement in New York City, 1886-1914.* New York: Arno Press, 1980.

Laity, Paul. *The British Peace Movement, 1870-1914.* New York: Oxford University Press, 2001.

Lundarini, Christine A. *The American Peace Movement in the Twentieth Century.* Santa Barbara, Calif.: ABC-Clio, 1994.

Miers, Suzanne. *Slavery in the Twentieth Century: The Evolution of a Global Pattern.* Walnut Creek, Calif.: AltaMira Press, 2003.

Moore, Jacqueline M. *Booker T. Washington, W. E. B. Du Bois, and the Struggle for Racial Uplift.* Lanham, Md.: SR Books, 2003.

Murphy, Paul L. *World War I and the Origins of Civil Liberties in the United States.* New York: W. W. Norton, 1979.

Preston, William, Jr. *Aliens and Dissenters: Federal Suppression of Radicals, 1903-1933.* 2d ed. Champaign: University of Illinois Press, 1995.

United Nations. *International Agreement for the Suppression of the White Slave Traffic, Signed at Paris on 18 May 1904 Amended by the Protocol Signed at Lake Success New York, 4 May 1949.* Lake Success, N.Y.: United Nations Publications, 1950.

Walker, Samuel. *In Defense of American Liberties: A History of the ACLU.* 2d ed. Carbondale: Southern Illinois University Press, 1999.

Whipple, Leon. *The Story of Civil Liberty in the United States.* New York: Vanguard Press, 1927.

Zangrando, Robert. *The NAACP Crusade Against Lynching, 1909-1950.* Philadelphia: Temple University Press, 1980.

Zuckerman, Phil, ed. *The Social Theory of W. E. B. Du Bois.* Thousand Oaks, Calif.: Pine Forge Press, 2004.

COLONIALISM, EMPIRE, AND DECOLONIZATION

Abrahamian, Ervand. *Iran Between Two Revolutions.* Princeton, N.J.: Princeton University Press, 1982.

Aburish, Said K. *The Rise, Corruption, and Coming Fall of the House of Saud.* New York: St. Martin's Press, 1995.

Asante, S. K. B. *Pan-African Protest: West Africa and the Italo-Ethiopian Crisis, 1934-1941.* London: Longman, 1977.

Austen, Ralph A. *Northwest Tanzania Under German and British Rule: Colonial Policy and Tribal Politics, 1889-1939.* New Haven, Conn.: Yale University Press, 1968.

Banana, Canaan S., ed. *Turmoil and Tenacity: Zimbabwe, 1890-1990.* Harare, Zimbabwe: College Press, 1989.

Banani, Amin. *The Modernization of Iran, 1921-1941.* Stanford, Calif.: Stanford University Press, 1961.

Barber, James. *South Africa in the Twentieth Century.* Malden, Mass.: Blackwell, 1999.

Beachey, R. W. *The Warrior Mullah: The Horn of Africa Aflame, 1892-1920.* London: Bellew, 1990.

Berman, Karl. *Under the Big Stick: Nicaragua and the United States Since 1848.* Boston: South End Press, 1986.

Bley, Helmuth. *South West Africa Under German Rule, 1894-1914.* Translated by Huth Ridley. Evanston, Ill.: Northwestern University Press, 1971.

Boyce, D. G. *The Irish Question and British Politics, 1868-1986.* 2d ed. New York: St. Martin's Press, 1996.

Burnett, Christina Duffy, and Burke Marshall, eds. *Foreign in a Domestic Sense: Puerto Rico, American Expansion, and the Constitution.* Durham, N.C.: Duke University Press, 2001.

Cabán, Pedro A. *Constructing a Colonial People: Puerto Rico and the United States, 1898-1932.* Boulder, Colo.: Westview Press, 1999.

Cain, P. J. *Hobson and Imperialism: Radicalism, New Liberalism, and Finance 1887-1938.* New York: Oxford University Press, 2002.

Coupland, Reginald. *The Indian Problem: Report on the Constitutional Problem in India.* New York: Oxford University Press, 1944.

Delmendo, Sharon. *The Star-Entangled Banner: One Hundred Years of America in the Philippines.* New Brunswick, N.J.: Rutgers University Press, 2004.

Drechsler, Heinrich, and Bernd Zöllner. *Let Us Die Fighting: The Struggle of the Herero and the Nama Against German Imperialism.* London: Zed Press, 1980.

Dudden, Alexis. *Japan's Colonization of Korea.* Honolulu: University of Hawaii Press, 2005.

Edgerton, Robert B. *The Troubled Heart of Africa: A History of the Congo.* New York: St. Martin's Press, 2002.

Feuer, A. B. *America at War: The Philippines, 1898-1913.* New York: Praeger, 2002.

Fieldhouse, D. K. *The West and the Third World: Trade, Colonialism, Dependence, and Development.* Malden, Mass.: Blackwell, 1999.

_____. *Western Imperialism in the Middle East, 1914-1958.* New York: Oxford University Press, 2006.

Gann, Lewis H., and Peter Duignan. *The Rulers of Belgian Africa, 1884-1914.* Princeton, N.J.: Princeton University Press, 1979.

Gewald, Jan Bart. *Herero Heroes: A Socio-political History of the Herero of Namibia, 1890-1923.* Oxford, England: James Currey, 1999.

Goldstein, Melvyn C. *The Snow Lion and the Dragon: China, Tibet, and the Dalai Lama.* Berkeley: University of California, 1997.

Hill, George Francis. *The Ottoman Province, the British Colony, 1571-1948.* Vol. 4 in *A History of Cyprus.*

Cambridge, England: Cambridge University Press, 1972.

Hobson, John A. *Imperialism: A Study.* 1902. Reprint. London: Unwin Hyman, 1988.

Hochschild, Adam. *King Leopold's Ghost.* New York: Mariner Books, 1999.

Hopkirk, Peter. *The Great Game: The Struggle for Empire in Central Asia.* New York: Kodansha International, 1994.

Judd, Dennis, and Peter Shinn. *The Evolution of the Modern Commonwealth, 1902-1980.* London: Palgrave Macmillan, 1982.

Karnow, Stanley. *In Our Image: America's Empire in the Philippines.* New York: Random House, 1989.

Kennedy, Dane. *Islands of White: Settler Society and Culture in Kenya and Southern Rhodesia.* Durham, N.C.: Duke University Press, 1987.

Kitchen, Martin. *The British Empire and Commonwealth: A Short History.* London: Palgrave Macmillan, 1996.

Langley, Lester D. *The Banana Wars: An Inner History of American Empire, 1900-1934.* Lexington: University of Kentucky Press, 1983.

Lugard, Frederick J. D. *The Dual Mandate in British Tropical Africa.* London: Frank Cass, 1965.

McCullough, David. *The Path Between the Seas: The Creation of the Panama Canal, 1870-1914.* New York: Simon & Schuster, 1977.

Marks, Stephen G. *Road to Power: The Trans Siberian Railroad and the Colonization of Asian Russia, 1850-1917.* Ithaca, N.Y.: Cornell University Press, 1991.

Mommsen, Wolfgang J. *Theories of Imperialism.* Translated by P. S. Falla. Chicago: University of Chicago Press, 1982.

Morel, Edmond Dene. *E. D. Morel's History of the Congo Reform Movement.* Edited by W. Roger Louis and Jean Stengers. Oxford, England: Clarendon Press, 1968.

Munro, Dana G. *Intervention and Dollar Diplomacy in the Caribbean, 1900-1921.* Princeton, N.J.: Princeton University Press, 1964.

Mutambirwa, James A. Chamunorwa. *The Rise of Settler Power in Southern Rhodesia, 1898-1923.* Madison, N.J.: Fairleigh Dickinson University Press, 1981.

Page, Melvin E, ed. *Colonialism: An International Social, Cultural, and Political Encyclopedia.* 3 vols. Santa Barbara, Calif.: ABC-Clio, 2003.

Pérez, Louis A., Jr. *Cuba Under the Platt Amendment: 1902-1934.* Pittsburgh: University of Pittsburgh Press, 1986.

Porter, Bernard. *Critics of Empire: British Radical Attitudes to Colonialism in Africa, 1895-1914*. New York: Cambridge University Press, 1968.

Samatar, Said S. *In the Shadow of Conquest: Islam in Colonial Northeast Africa*. Trenton, N.J.: Red Sea Press, 1992.

Sbacchi, Alberto. *Legacy of Bitterness: Ethiopia and Fascist Italy, 1935-1941*. Trenton, N.J.: Red Sea Press, 1997.

Simon, Reeva S., and Eleanor H. Tejirian, eds. *The Creation of Iraq, 1914-1921*. New York: Columbia University Press, 2004.

Sluglett, Peter. *Britain in Iraq, 1914-1932*. London: Ithaca Press, 1978.

Thompson, L. M. *The Unification of South Africa, 1902-1910*. Oxford, England: Clarendon Press, 1960.

Tinker, Hugh. *The Foundations of Local Self-Government in India, Pakistan, and Burma*. New York: Praeger, 1968.

Wilder, Gary. *The French Imperial Nation-State: Negritude and Colonial Humanism Between the Two World Wars*. Chicago: University of Chicago Press, 2005.

Willoughby, William F. *Territories and Dependencies of the United States: Their Government and Administration*. New York: Century Press, 1905.

Wilson, Sandra. *The Manchurian Crisis and Japanese Society, 1931-1933*. New York: Routledge, 2002.

COMMUNISM AND FASCISM
(*see also* GOVERNMENT AND POLITICS)

Abel, Theodore. *Why Hitler Came into Power*. Cambridge, Mass.: Harvard University Press, 1986.

Applebaum, Anne. *Gulag: A History*. New York: Doubleday, 2003.

Baron, Salo W. *The Russian Jew Under Tsars and Soviets*. 2d ed. New York: Macmillan, 1987.

Bauer, Yehuda. *Jews for Sale? Nazi-Jewish Negotiations, 1933-1945*. New Haven, Conn.: Yale University Press, 1994.

Borkenau, Franz. *World Communism: A History of the Communist International*. Ann Arbor: University of Michigan Press, 1962.

Bosworth, R. J. B. *The Italian Dictatorship: Problems and Perspectives in the Interpretation of Mussolini and Fascism*. New York: Oxford University Press, 1998.

Bracher, Karl Dietrich. *The German Dictatorship: The Origins, Structure, and Effects of National Socialism*. New York: Praeger, 1970.

Brovkin, Vladimir, ed. *The Bolsheviks in Russian Society: The Revolution and the Civil Wars*. New Haven, Conn.: Yale University Press, 1997.

Brown, Anthony Cave, and Charles B. MacDonald. *On a Field of Red: The Communist International and the Coming of World War II*. New York: G. P. Putnam's Sons, 1981.

Browning, Christopher R. *The Origins of the Final Solution: The Evolution of Nazi Jewish Policy, September 1939-March 1942*. Lincoln: University of Nebraska Press, 2004.

Burleigh, Michael. *The Third Reich: A New History*. New York: Hill & Wang, 2000.

Cannistraro, Philip V., ed. *Historical Dictionary of Fascist Italy*. Westport, Conn.: Greenwood Press, 1982.

Carr, E. H. *The Bolshevik Revolution, 1917-1923*. 3 vols. Reprint. New York: Norton, 1985.

_____. *Socialism in One Country, 1924-1926*. 3 vols. New York: Macmillan, 1958-1964.

Carsten, Francis L. *The Rise of Fascism*. 2d ed. Berkeley: University of California Press, 1982.

Cohen, Stephen F. *Rethinking the Soviet Experience: Politics and History Since 1917*. New York: Oxford University Press, 1985.

Conquest, Robert. *The Great Terror: A Reassessment*. New York: Oxford University Press, 1990.

_____. *The Harvest of Sorrow: Soviet Collectivization and the Terror-Famine*. New York: Oxford University Press, 1986.

_____. *Stalin and the Kirov Murder*. New York: Oxford University Press, 1989.

Courtois, Stéphane, et al. *The Black Book of Communism: Crimes, Terror, Repression*. Translated by Jonathan Murphy and Mark Kramer. Cambridge, Mass.: Harvard University Press, 1999.

Dalin, David G. *The Myth of Hitler's Pope*. Washington, D.C.: Regnery, 2005.

Davies, R. W. *The Socialist Offensive: The Collectivization of Soviet Agriculture, 1929-30*. Cambridge, Mass.: Harvard University Press, 1980.

De Grand, Alexander J. *Italian Fascism: Its Origins and Development*. 3d ed. Lincoln: University of Nebraska Press, 2000.

Des Pres, Terrence. *The Survivor: An Anatomy of Life in the Death Camps*. New York: Oxford University Press, 1976.

Draper, Theodore. *The Roots of American Communism*. 1957. Reprint. New Brunswick, N.J.: Transaction, 2003.

Evans, Richard J. *The Coming of the Third Reich.* New York: Penguin Books, 2004.

_____. *The Third Reich in Power, 1933-1939.* New York: Penguin Books, 2005.

Fairbank, John King. *The Great Chinese Revolution, 1800-1985.* New York: Harper & Row, 1986.

Figes, Orlando. *A People's Tragedy: The Russian Revolution, 1891-1924.* New York: Penguin Books, 1998.

Fischer, Klaus P. *A History of Nazi Germany.* New York: Continuum, 1995.

Fitzpatrick, Sheila. *Cultural Revolution in Russia, 1928-1931.* Bloomington: Indiana University Press, 1984.

_____. *The Russian Revolution.* 2d ed. New York: Oxford University Press, 1994.

_____. *Stalin's Peasants: Resistance and Survival in the Russian Village After Collectivization.* New York: Oxford University Press, 1994.

Friedlander, Saul. *The Years of Persecution, 1933-1939.* Vol. 1 in *Nazi Germany and the Jews.* New York: HarperCollins, 1997.

Gasman, Daniel. *The Scientific Origins of National Socialism.* Somerset, N.J.: Transaction, 2004.

Getty, J. Arch, and Oleg V. Naumov. *The Road to Terror: Stalin and the Self-Destruction of the Bolsheviks, 1932-1939.* New Haven, Conn.: Yale University Press, 1999.

Godman, Peter. *Hitler and the Vatican: Inside the Secret Archives That Reveal the New Story of the Nazis and the Church.* New York: Free Press, 2004.

Harding, Neil. *Leninism.* 2 vols. Durham, N.C.: Duke University Press, 1996.

Horn, Gerd-Rainer. *European Socialists Respond to Fascism: Ideology, Activism, and Contingency in the 1930's.* New York: Oxford University Press, 1996.

Hoyt, Edwin P. *Mussolini's Empire: The Rise and Fall of the Fascist Vision.* New York: John Wiley & Sons, 1994.

Hutchings, Raymond. *Soviet Economic Development.* 2d ed. Oxford, England: Basil Blackwell, 1982.

Iroshnikov, M., D. Kovalenko, and V. Shishkin. *Genesis of the Soviet Federative State, 1917-1921.* Moscow: Progress, 1982.

Kallis, Aristotle A. *Fascist Ideology: Expansionism in Italy and Germany, 1922-1945.* New York: Routledge, 2000.

Khlevniuk, Oleg V. *The History of the Gulag: From Collectivization to the Great Terror.* Translated by Vadim A. Staklo. New Haven, Conn.: Yale University Press, 2004.

Kuromiya, Hiroaki. *Stalin's Industrial Revolution: Politics and Workers, 1928-1932.* New York: Cambridge University Press, 1988.

Levytsky, Boris. *The Stalinist Terror in the Thirties: Documentation from the Soviet Press.* Stanford, Calif.: Hoover Institution Press, 1974.

Lincoln, W. Bruce. *Red Victory: A History of the Russian Civil War, 1918-1921.* 1989. Reprint. New York: Da Capo Press, 1999.

Lyttelton, Adrian. *The Seizure of Power in Italy, 1919-1929.* 2d ed. London: Weidenfeld & Nicolson, 1987.

McDermott, Kevin, and Jeremy Agnew. *The Comintern: A History of International Communism from Lenin to Stalin.* New York: St. Martin's Press, 1997.

Mawdsley, Evan. *The Russian Civil War.* 2d ed. Edinburgh: Birlinn, 2005.

Medvedev, Roy. *Let History Judge: The Origins and Consequences of Stalinism.* Translated by George Shriver. New York: Columbia University Press, 1989.

Mortimer, Edward. *The Rise of the French Communist Party, 1920-1947.* London: Faber & Faber, 1984.

Nation, R. Craig. *War on War: Lenin, the Zimmerwald Left, and the Origins of Communist Internationalism.* Durham, N.C.: Duke University Press, 1989.

Pipes, Richard. *Communism: A History.* New York: Random House, 2003.

_____. *Formation of the Soviet Union: Communism and Nationalism, 1917-1923.* Rev. ed. Cambridge, Mass.: Harvard University Press, 1997.

_____. *Russia Under the Bolshevik Regime.* New York: Vintage Books, 1995.

Read, Anthony, and David Fisher. *The Deadly Embrace: Hitler, Stalin, and the Nazi-Soviet Pact, 1939-1941.* New York: W. W. Norton, 1989.

Salisbury, Harrison E. *The Long March: The Untold Story.* New York: Harper & Row, 1985.

Smelser, Ronald, and Rainer Zitelmann, eds. *The Nazi Elite.* Translated by Mary Fischer. New York: New York University Press, 1989.

Snow, Edgar. *Red Star Rising over China.* Rev. ed. New York: Grove Press, 1968.

Soucy, Robert. *French Fascism: The Second Wave, 1933-1939.* New Haven, Conn.: Yale University Press, 1995.

Spielvogel, Jackson J. *Hitler and Nazi Germany: A History.* Englewood Cliffs, N.J.: Prentice-Hall, 1988.

Swain, Geoffrey. *The Origins of the Russian Civil War.* London: Longman, 1996.

Thurston, Robert W. *Life and Terror in Stalin's Russia: 1934-1941.* New Haven, Conn.: Yale University Press, 1996.

Tiersky, Tonald. *French Communism, 1920-1972.* New York: Columbia University Press, 1974.

Ulam, Adam B. *The Bolsheviks: The Intellectual and Political History of the Triumph of Communism in Russia.* 1965. Reprint. Cambridge, Mass.: Harvard University Press, 1997.

_____. *Expansion and Coexistence: The History of Soviet Foreign Policy, 1917-67.* New York: Frederick A. Praeger, 1968.

Viola, Lynne. *The Best Sons of the Fatherland: Workers in the Vanguard of Soviet Collectivization.* New York: Oxford University Press, 1999.

Von Laue, Theodore H. *Why Lenin? Why Stalin? Why Gorbachev? The Rise and Fall of the Soviet System.* 3d ed. New York: Longman, 1997.

Waldman, Eric. *The Spartacist Uprising of 1919 and the Crisis of the German Socialist Movement.* Milwaukee: Marquette University Press, 1958.

Wohl, Robert. *French Communism in the Making, 1914-1924.* Stanford, Calif.: Stanford University Press, 1966.

CRIME, GENOCIDE, AND ATROCITIES

Abarinov, Vladimir. *The Murderers of Katyn.* New York: Hippocrene Books, 1993.

Barrow, Blanche, and John Neal Tebo Phillips. *My Life with Bonnie and Clyde.* Norman: University of Oklahoma Press, 2004.

Bauer, Yehuda. *Rethinking the Holocaust.* New Haven, Conn.: Yale University Press, 2001.

Bloxham, Donald. *The Great Game of Genocide: Imperialism, Nationalism, and the Destruction of the Ottoman Armenians.* New York: Oxford University Press, 2005.

Bornstein, Joseph. *The Politics of Murder.* Toronto: George J. McLeod, 1950.

Bruns, Roger. *The Bandit Kings: From Jesse James to Pretty Boy Floyd.* New York: Crown, 1995.

Burrough, Bryan. *Public Enemies: America's Greatest Crime Wave and the Birth of the FBI, 1933-34.* New York: Penguin Books, 2004.

Dadrian, Vahakn N. *The History of the Armenian Genocide: Ethnic Conflict from the Balkans to Anatolia to the Caucasus.* Providence, R.I.: Berghahn Books, 1995.

Encyclopedia of Genocide and Crimes Against Humanity. 3 vols. Detroit: Thomson Gale, 2004.

Feig, Konnilyn G. *Hitler's Death Camps: The Sanity of Madness.* New York: Holmes & Meier, 1979.

Fisher, David. *Hard Evidence: How Detectives Inside the FBI's Sci-Crime Lab Have Helped Solve America's Toughest Cases.* New York: Simon & Schuster, 1995.

Fogel, Joshua A., ed. *The Nanjing Massacre in History and Historiography.* Berkeley: University of California Press, 2000.

Friedlander, Henry. *The Origins of Nazi Genocide: From Euthanasia to the Final Solution.* Chapel Hill: University of North Carolina Press, 1995.

Gutman, Israel, ed. *Encyclopedia of the Holocaust.* 4 vols. New York: Macmillan, 1990.

Helmer, William J., and Arthur J. Bilek. *The St. Valentine's Day Massacre: The Untold Story of the Gangland Bloodbath That Brought down Al Capone.* Nashville: Cumberland House, 2004.

Hilberg, Raul. *The Destruction of the European Jews.* 3d ed. New Haven, Conn.: Yale University Press, 2003.

Hovannisian, Richard G. *The Armenian Genocide: History, Politics, Ethics.* New York: St. Martin's Press, 1992.

Knight, James, and Jonathan Davis. *Bonnie and Clyde: A Twenty-First Century Update.* Austin, Tex.: Eakin Press, 2003.

Laqueur, Walter, and Judith Tydor Baumel, eds. *The Holocaust Encyclopedia.* New Haven, Conn.: Yale University Press, 2001.

Lykken, David T. *A Tremor in the Blood: Uses and Abuses of the Lie Detector.* 2d ed. New York: Plenum, 1998.

Marrus, Michael R., ed. *The Nazi Holocaust: Historical Articles on the Destruction of European Jews.* 9 vols. Westport, Conn.: Meckler, 1989.

Melson, Robert. *Revolution and Genocide: On the Origins of the Armenian Genocide and the Holocaust.* Chicago: University of Chicago Press, 1992.

Nash, Jay Robert, ed. *Encyclopedia of World Crime: Criminal Justice, Criminology, and Law Enforcement.* Wilmette, Ill.: Crime Books, 1990.

Oney, Steve. *And the Dead Shall Rise: The Murder of Mary Phagan and the Lynching of Leo Frank.* New York: Pantheon Books, 2003.

Prassel, Frank Richard. *The Great American Outlaw: A Legacy of Fact and Fiction.* Norman: University of Oklahoma Press, 1993.

Read, James Morgan. *Atrocity Propaganda, 1914-1919.* New Haven, Conn.: Yale University Press, 1941.

Rubenstein, Richard L., and John K. Roth. *Approaches to Auschwitz: The Holocaust and Its Legacy.* Atlanta: John Knox Press, 1987.

Ruth, David E. *Inventing the Public Enemy: The Gang-*

ster in American Culture, 1918-1934. Chicago: University of Chicago Press, 1996.

Sanford, George. *Katyn and the Soviet Massacre of 1940: Truth, Justice, and Memory.* New York: Routledge, 2005.

Syriax, Oliver, Colin Wilson, and Damon Wilson, eds. *The Encyclopedia of Crime.* New York: Penguin Books, 2006.

Tanaka, Yuki. *Hidden Horrors: Japanese War Crimes in World War II.* Boulder, Colo.: Westview Press, 1998.

Tolczyk, Dariusz. *See No Evil: Literary Cover-Ups and Discoveries of the Soviet Camp Experience.* New Haven, Conn.: Yale University Press, 1999.

Wistrich, Robert S. *Hitler and the Holocaust.* New York: Random House, 2001.

Wyman, David S. *The Abandonment of the Jews: America and the Holocaust, 1941-1945.* New York: Pantheon Books, 1984.

Zuckoff, Mitchell. *Ponzi's Scheme: The True Story of a Financial Legend.* New York: Random House, 2005.

DIPLOMACY AND INTERNATIONAL RELATIONS
(*see also* GOVERNMENT AND POLITICS, WORLD WAR I, WORLD WAR II)

Ambrosius, Lloyd E. *Woodrow Wilson and the American Diplomatic Tradition: The Treaty Fight in Perspective.* New York: Cambridge University Press, 1987.

Andrew, Christopher. *Théophile Delcassé and the Making of the Entente Cordiale.* New York: St. Martin's Press, 1968.

Baer, George W. *Test Case: Italy, Ethiopia, and the League of Nations.* Stanford, Calif.: Hoover Institution Press, 1976.

Bailey, Thomas Andrew. *A Diplomatic History of the American People.* 10th ed. Englewood Cliffs, N.J.: Prentice-Hall, 1980.

Barnhart, Michael A. *Japan and the World Since 1868.* London: Edward Arnold, 1995.

Bartlett, C. J. *The Global Conflict: The International Rivalry of the Great Powers, 1880-1990.* 2d ed. New York: Longman, 1994.

Blasier, Cole. *The Hovering Giant: U.S. Responses to Revolutionary Change in Latin America, 1910-1985.* Rev. ed. Pittsburgh: University of Pittsburgh Press, 1985.

Bridge, F. R. *From Sadowa to Sarajevo: The Foreign Policy of Austria-Hungary, 1866-1914.* 1972. Reprint. New York: Routledge, 2001.

Carr, E. H. *German-Soviet Relations Between the Two Wars, 1919-1939.* Westport, Conn.: Greenwood Press, 1983.

Cooper, John Milton, Jr. *Breaking the Heart of the World: Woodrow Wilson and the Fight for the League of Nations.* New York: Cambridge University Press, 2001.

Dallek, Robert. *Franklin D. Roosevelt and American Foreign Policy, 1932-1945.* 1979. Reprint. New York: Oxford University Press, 1995.

Dockrill, Michael, and John Fisher, eds. *The Paris Peace Conference, 1919: Peace Without Victory?* New York: Palgrave Macmillan, 2001.

Ewell, Judith. *Venezuela and the United States: From Monroe's Hemisphere to Petroleum's Empire.* Athens: University of Georgia Press, 1996.

Ferrell, Robert H. *Peace in Their Time: The Origins of the Kellogg-Briand Pact.* New York: W. W. Norton, 1969.

Fischer, Conan. *Ruhr Crisis, 1923-1924.* New York: Oxford University Press, 2003.

Glantz, Mary E. *FDR and the Soviet Union: The President's Battles over Foreign Policy.* Lawrence: University Press of Kansas, 2005.

Griffiths, Martin, ed. *Encyclopedia of International Relations and Global Politics.* London: Taylor & Francis, 2005.

Hall, Christopher. *Britain, America, and Arms Control, 1921-1937.* New York: St. Martin's Press, 1987.

Hall, Linda B., and Don M. Coerver. *Revolution on the Border: The United States and Mexico, 1910-1920.* Albuquerque: University of New Mexico Press, 1988.

Hayne, M. B. *The French Foreign Office and the Origins of the First World War, 1898-1914.* Oxford, England: Oxford University Press, 1993.

Hiden, John. *The Baltic States and Weimar Ostpolitik.* 1987. Reprint. New York: Cambridge University Press, 2002.

Iriye, Akira. *Pacific Estrangement: Japanese and American Expansion, 1897-1911.* Cambridge, Mass.: Harvard University Press, 1972.

Jacobson, Jon. *Locarno Diplomacy: Germany and the West, 1925-1929.* Princeton, N.J.: Princeton University Press, 1972.

_____. *When the Soviet Union Entered World Politics.* Berkeley: University of California Press, 1994.

Jayne, Catherine E. *Oil, War, and Anglo-American Relations: American and British Reactions to Mexico's Expropriation of Foreign Oil Properties, 1937-1941.* Westport, Conn.: Greenwood Press, 2001.

Jelavich, Barbara. *Russia's Balkan Entanglements, 1806-1914.* 1991. Reprint. New York: Cambridge University Press, 2004.

Kennan, George F. *Russia and the West Under Lenin and Stalin.* Boston: Little, Brown, 1961.

Kennedy, Paul. *The Rise of Anglo-German Antagonism, 1860-1914.* London: Allen & Unwin, 1980.

Khouri, Fred J. *The Arab-Israeli Dilemma.* Syracuse, N.Y.: Syracuse University Press, 1985.

Kirk, John M., and Peter McKenna. *Canada-Cuba Relations: The Other Good Neighbor Policy.* Gainesville: University Press of Florida, 1997.

Knock, Thomas J. *To End All Wars: Woodrow Wilson and the Quest for a New World Order.* New York: Oxford University Press, 1992.

LaFeber, Walter. *The Clash: U.S.-Japanese Relations Throughout History.* New York: W. W. Norton, 1997.

_____. *Inevitable Revolutions: The United States in Central America.* New York: W. W. Norton, 1984.

McHenry, James A. *The Uneasy Partnership on Cyprus, 1919-1939: The Political and Diplomatic Interaction Between Great Britain, Turkey, and the Turkish Cypriot Community.* New York: Garland, 1987.

Marks, Sally. *The Illusion of Peace: International Relations in Europe, 1918-1933.* 2d ed. New York: Palgrave Macmillan, 2003.

Morley, James William, ed. *The China Quagmire: Japan's Expansion on the Asian Continent, 1933-1941.* New York: Columbia University Press, 1983.

_____. *Japan's Foreign Policy, 1868-1941.* New York: Columbia University Press, 1974.

Morris, Benni. *Righteous Victims: A History of the Zionist-Arab Conflict, 1881-1999.* New York: Alfred A. Knopf, 1999.

Nimmo, William F. *Stars and Stripes Across the Pacific: The United States, Japan, and the Asia/Pacific Region, 1895-1945.* New York: Praeger, 2001.

Nish, Ian. *The Anglo-Japanese Alliance: The Diplomacy of Two Island Empires, 1848-1907.* 2d ed. London: Athlone Press, 1985.

O'Brien, Conor Cruise. *The Siege: The Saga of Israel and Zionism.* New York: Simon & Schuster, 1986.

O'Brien, Phillips, ed. *The Anglo-Japanese Alliance, 1902-1922.* New York: RoutledgeCurzon, 2004.

Paasivirta, Juhani. *Finland and Europe: The Early Years of Independence, 1918-1939.* Helsinki, Finland: SHS, 1988.

Perras, Galen Roger. *Franklin Roosevelt and the Origins of the Canadian-American Security Alliance, 1933-1945: Necessary, but Not Necessary Enough.* Westport, Conn.: Praeger, 1998.

Pérez, Louis A., Jr. *Cuba and the United States: Ties of Singular Intimacy.* 2d ed. Athens: University of Georgia Press, 1997.

Rhodes, Benjamin D. *United States Foreign Policy in the Interwar Period, 1918-1941: The Golden Age of American Diplomatic and Military Complacency.* Westport, Conn.: Praeger, 2001.

Roorda, Eric Paul. *The Dictator Next Door: The Good Neighbor Policy and the Trujillo Regime in the Dominican Republic, 1930-1945.* Durham, N.C.: Duke University Press, 1998.

Rosenberg, Emily S. *Financial Missionaries to the World: The Politics and Culture of Dollar Diplomacy, 1900-1930.* Durham, N.C.: Duke University Press, 2004.

Ryan, Paul B. *The Panama Canal Controversy.* Stanford, Calif.: Hoover Institution Press, 1977.

Sanders, Ronald. *The High Walls of Jerusalem: A History of the Balfour Declaration and the Birth of the British Mandate for Palestine.* New York: Holt, Rinehart and Winston, 1983.

Schuker, Stephen A. *The End of French Predominance in Europe: The Financial Crisis of 1924 and the Adoption of the Dawes Plan.* 1976. Reprint. Chapel Hill: University of North Carolina Press, 1988.

Schuler, Frederich. *Mexico Between Hitler and Roosevelt: Mexican Foreign Relations in the Age of Lázaro Cárdenas, 1934-1940.* Albuquerque: University of New Mexico Press, 1998.

Schwabe, Klaus. *Woodrow Wilson, Revolutionary Germany, and Peacemaking, 1918-1919.* Translated by Robert Kimber and Rita Kimber. Chapel Hill: University of North Carolina Press, 1985.

Sherman, A. J. *Mandate Days: British Lives in Palestine, 1918-1948.* Baltimore: The Johns Hopkins University Press, 1997.

Shwadran, Benjamin. *The Middle East, Oil, and the Great Powers.* 3d rev. ed. New York: John Wiley & Sons, 1973.

Sibley, Katherine A. S. *Loans and Legitimacy: The Evolution of Soviet-American Relations, 1919-1933.* Lexington: University Press of Kentucky, 1996.

Sicker, Martin. *Reshaping Palestine: From Muhammad Ali to the British Mandate, 1831-1922.* Westport, Conn.: Praeger, 1999.

Smith, Sara. *The Manchurian Crisis, 1931-1932: A Tragedy in International Relations.* New York: Columbia University Press, 1948.

Sokolsky, Joel J., and Joseph T. Jockel, eds. *Fifty Years of Canada-United States Defense Cooperation: The Road from Ogdensburg.* Lewiston, N.Y.: Edwin Mellen Press, 1992.

Somakian, Manoug. *Empires in Conflict: Armenia and the Great Powers, 1912-1920.* London: Tauris Academic Studies, 1995.

Spengler, Oswald. *The Decline of the West.* Translated by Charles Francis Atkinson, edited by Arthur Helps. New York: Alfred A. Knopf, 1962.

Steiner, Zara. *The Lights That Failed: European International History 1919-1933.* New York: Oxford University Press, 2005.

Tarulis, Albert N. *American-Baltic Relations, 1918-1922: The Struggle over Recognition.* Washington, D.C.: Catholic University Press, 1965.

Tohmatsu, Haruo, and H. P. Willmott. *A Gathering Darkness: The Coming of War to the Far East and the Pacific, 1921-1942.* Lanham, Md.: SR Books, 2005.

Traina, Richard. *American Diplomacy and the Spanish Civil War.* 1968. Reprint. Westport, Conn.: Greenwood Press, 1980.

Ulfstein, Geir. *The Svalbard Treaty: From Terra Nullius to Norwegian Sovereignty.* Oslo, Norway: Scandinavian University Press, 1995.

Vardys, V. Stanley, and Romuald J. Misiunas, eds. *The Baltic States in Peace and War, 1917-1945.* University Park: Pennsylvania State University Press, 1978.

Venn, Fiona. *Oil Diplomacy in the Twentieth Century.* New York: St. Martin's Press, 1986.

Vinson, John C. *William E. Borah and the Outlawry of War.* Athens: University of Georgia Press, 1957.

Walker, William O. *Opium and Foreign Policy: The Anglo-American Search for Order in Asia, 1912-1954.* Chapel Hill: University of North Carolina Press, 1991.

Watt, Donald Cameron. *How War Came: The Immediate Origins of the Second World War, 1938-1939.* New York: Pantheon Books, 1989.

Weissman, Benjamin M. *Herbert Hoover and Famine Relief to Soviet Russia, 1921-23.* Stanford, Calif.: Hoover Institution Press, 1974.

White, John A. *The Diplomacy of the Russo-Japanese War.* Princeton, N.J.: Princeton University Press, 1964.

Williamson, Samuel R. *The Politics of Grand Strategy: Britain and France Prepare for War, 1904-1914.* Cambridge, Mass.: Harvard University Press, 1969.

Wilson, Joe F. *The United States, Chile, and Peru in the Tacna and Arica Plebiscite.* Washington, D.C.: University Press of America, 1979.

Woods, Randall Bennett. *The Roosevelt Foreign-Policy Establishment and the "Good Neighbor": The United States and Argentina, 1941-1945.* Lawrence: Regents Press of Kansas, 1979.

EDUCATION

Armytage, W. H. G. *Four Hundred Years of English Education.* 2d ed. Cambridge, England: Cambridge University Press, 1970.

Cochran, Judith. *Education in Egypt.* London: Croom-Helm, 1986.

Duiker, William J. *Ts'ai Yuan-p'ei: Educator of Modern China.* University Park: Pennsylvania State University Press, 1977.

Erlich, Haggai. *Students and University in Twentieth Century Egyptian Politics.* London: Frank Cass, 1989.

Faruqi, Ziya-ul-Hasan. *The Deoband School and the Demand for Pakistan.* New York: Asia Publishing, 1963.

Guthrie, James W. *Encyclopedia of Education.* Rev. 2d ed. Detroit: Thomson Gale, 2002.

Harrison, Brian, ed. *The Twentieth Century.* Vol. 8 in *The History of the University of Oxford.* Oxford, England: Oxford University Press, 1994.

Hoggart, Richard. *An English Temper: Essays on Education, Culture, and Communications.* New York: Oxford University Press, 1982.

Hurt, J. S. *Elementary Schooling and the Working Classes, 1860-1918.* London: Routledge & Kegan Paul, 1979.

Kenney, Anthony, ed. *The History of the Rhodes Trust, 1902-1999.* Oxford, England: Oxford University Press, 2001.

Lawson, John, and Harold Silver. *A Social History of Education in England.* London: Methuen, 1973.

Lowndes, G. A. N. *The Silent Social Revolution: An Account of the Expansion of Public Education in England and Wales, 1895-1965.* 2d ed. London: Oxford University Press, 1969.

Mazon, Patricia M. *Gender and the Modern Research University: The Admission of Women to German Higher Education, 1865-1914.* Stanford, Calif.: Stanford University Press, 2003.

Moon, Bob. *Routledge International Companion to Education.* New York: RoutledgeFalmer, 2000.

Reid, Donald M. *Cairo University and the Making of Modern Egypt.* Cambridge, England: Cambridge University Press, 2002.

Schaeper, Thomas J., and Kathleen Schaeper. *Cowboys into Gentlemen: Rhodes Scholars, Oxford, and the*

Creation of an American Elite. Providence, R.I.: Bergahn Books, 1998.

Shook, John. *Dewey's Empirical Theory of Knowledge and Reality.* Nashville: Vanderbilt University Press, 2000.

Simon, Brian. *Education and the Labour Movement, 1870-1920.* London: Lawrence & Wishart, 1965.

Szyliowicz, Joseph S. *Education and Modernization in the Middle East.* Ithaca, N.Y.: Cornell University Press, 1973.

Veysey, Lawrence R. *The Emergence of the American University.* Chicago: University of Chicago Press, 1965.

ENGINEERING, ARCHITECTURE, AND URBAN PLANNING
(*see also* ARTS: VISUAL, FASHION AND DESIGN)

Arieff, Allison, and Bryan Burkhart. *Prefab.* New York: Gibbs Smith, 2002.

Baborsky, Matteo Siro. *Twentieth Century Architecture.* Translated by Jay Hyams. Chichester, England: Wiley-Academy Press, 2003.

Bayer, Herbert, Walter Gropius, and Ise Gropius, eds. *Bauhaus, 1919-1928.* 1938. Reprint. New York: Museum of Modern Art, 1975.

Benton, Tim, and Charlotte Benton, eds. *Architecture and Design, 1890-1939.* New York: Whitney Library of Design, 1975.

Blake, Peter. *The Master Builders: Le Corbusier, Mies van der Rohe, Frank Lloyd Wright.* Rev. ed. 1976. Reprint. New York: W. W. Norton, 1996.

Campbell, Joan. *The German Werkbund: The Politics of Reform in the Applied Arts.* Princeton, N.J.: Princeton University Press, 1978.

Curtis, William J. R. *Modern Architecture Since 1900.* 3d ed. Upper Saddle River, N.J.: Prentice Hall, 1996.

De Souza Briggs, Xavier, and William Julius Wilson, eds. *The Geography of Opportunity: Race and Housing Choice in Metropolitan America.* Washington, D.C.: Brookings Institution, 2005.

Donnelly, Marion C. *Architecture in the Scandinavian Countries.* Cambridge, Mass.: MIT Press, 1992.

Droste, Magdalena. *Bauhaus, 1919-1933.* Cologne, Germany: Benedikt Taschen Verlag, 1998.

Fishman, Robert, ed. *The American Planning Tradition: Culture and Policy.* Washington, D.C.: Woodrow Wilson Center Press, 2000.

Frampton, Kenneth. *Modern Architecture: A Critical History.* 3d ed. New York: Thames and Hudson, 1992.

Goldberger, Paul. *The Skyscraper.* New York: Alfred A. Knopf, 1981.

Gropius, Walter. *The New Architecture and the Bauhaus.* Boston: Charles T. Branford, 1955.

Gutfreund, Owen D. *Twentieth Century Sprawl: Highways and the Reshaping of the American Landscape.* New York: Oxford University Press, 2004.

Huxtable, Ada Louise. *The Tall Building Artistically Reconsidered: The Search for a Skyscraper Style.* 1984. Reprint. Berkeley: University of California Press, 1992.

Johnson, Stephen, and Roberto T. Leon. *Encyclopedia of Bridges and Tunnels.* New York: Facts On File, 2002.

Kentgens-Craig, Margret. *The Bauhaus and America: First Contacts, 1919-1936.* Cambridge, Mass.: MIT Press, 1999.

Kostof, Spiro. *A History of Architecture: Settings and Rituals.* 2d ed. New York: Oxford University Press, 1995.

Lane, Barbara Miller. *National Romanticism and Modern Architecture in Germany and the Scandinavian Countries.* Edited by Richard A. Etlin. New York: Cambridge University Press, 2000.

Le Corbusier. *Precisions: On the Present State of Architecture of City Planning.* Translated by Edith Schreiber Aujame. Cambridge, Mass.: MIT Press, 1991.

Lindner, Rolf. *The Reportage of Urban Culture: Robert Park and the Chicago School.* New York: Cambridge University Press, 1996.

Messler, Norbert. *The Art Deco Skyscraper in New York.* Rev. ed. New York: Peter Lang, 1986.

Pevsner, Nikolaus. *Pioneers of Modern Design: From William Morris to Walter Gropius.* Rev. ed. New Haven, Conn.: Yale University Press, 2005.

Roth, Leland M. *American Architecture: A History.* 2d ed. Boulder, Colo.: Westview Press, 2003.

Schleier, Merrill. *The Skyscraper in American Art, 1890-1931.* Ann Arbor, Mich.: UMI Research Press, 1986.

Schock, James W. *The Bridge: A Celebration.* Sherman Oaks, Calif.: Shock Ink, 1997.

Scott, Mel. *American City Planning Since 1890.* 1971. Reprint. Chicago: American Planning Association, 1995.

Snapp, Jeremy Sherman. *Destiny by Design: The Construction of the Panama Canal.* With photographs by Gerald Fitzgerald Sherman and Jeremy Sherman Snapp. Lopez Island, Wash.: Pacific Heritage Press, 2000.

Snow, W. Brewster, ed. *The Highway and the Landscape*. New Brunswick, N.J.: Rutgers University Press, 1959.

Stevens, Joseph E. *Hoover Dam: An American Adventure*. Norman: University of Oklahoma Press, 1988.

Tauranac, John. *The Empire State Building: The Making of a Landmark*. New York: Scribner, 1995.

Van Der Zee, John. *The Gate: The True Story of the Design and Construction of the Golden Gate Bridge*. New York: Simon & Schuster, 1987.

FASHION AND DESIGN (*see also* ENGINEERING, ARCHITECTURE, AND URBAN PLANNING)

Bigelow, Marybelle S. *Fashion in History: Apparel in the Western World*. Minneapolis: Burgess, 1970.

Boucher, François. *Twenty Thousand Years of Fashion: The History of Costume and Personal Adornment*. New York: Harry N. Abrams, 1967.

Byrde, Penelope. *A Visual History of Costume: The Twentieth Century*. New York: Drama Book, 1986.

Clark, Robert Judson, et al. *Design in America: The Cranbrook Vision, 1925-1950*. New York: Harry N. Abrams, 1983.

De Marly, Diana. *Fashion for Men: An Illustrated History*. New York: Holmes & Meier, 1985.

_____. *The History of Haute Couture, 1850-1950*. London: B. T. Batsford, 1980.

Ewing, Elizabeth. *History of Twentieth Century Fashion*. Rev. ed. Totowa, N.J.: Rowman & Littlefield, 1992.

Johnson, J. Stewart. *American Modern, 1925-1940: Design for a New Age*. New York: Harry N. Abrams, 2000.

Kallir, Jane. *Viennese Design and the Wiener Werkstätte*. New York: George Braziller, 1986.

Laver, James. *Costume and Fashion: A Concise History*. 4th ed. New York: Thames and Hudson, 2002.

Ley, Sandra. *Fashion for Everyone: The Story of Ready-to-Wear, 1870's-1970's*. New York: Charles Scribner's Sons, 1975.

Loewy, Raymond. *Never Leave Well Enough Alone*. 1951. Reprint. Baltimore: The Johns Hopkins University Press, 2002.

Martin, Richard. *Fashion and Surrealism*. New York: Rizzoli, 1987.

Mulvagh, Jane. *"Vogue" History of Twentieth Century Fashion*. London: Viking Press, 1988.

Noyes, Eliot F. *Organic Design in Home Furnishings*. New York: Museum of Modern Art, 1941.

Nunn, Joan. *Fashion in Costume, 1200-2000*. 2d ed. New York: New Amsterdam Books, 2000.

Pendergast, Tom, and Sara Pendergast, eds. *St. James Encyclopedia of Popular Culture*. 5 vols. Farmington Hills, Mich.: St. James Press, 2000.

Sparke, Penny. *An Introduction to Design and Culture: 1900 to the Present*. 2d ed. New York: Routledge, 2004.

Steele, Valerie, ed. *Encyclopedia of Clothing and Fashion*. 2 vols. New York: Gale Thomson, 2005.

_____. *Women of Fashion: Twentieth Century Designers*. New York: Rizzoli, 1991.

Tortora, Phyllis, and Keith Eubank. *A Survey of Historic Costume*. 4th ed. New York: Fairchild Books, 2005.

Waugh, Norah. *Corsets and Crinolines*. 1954. Reprint. New York: Theatre Arts Books, 2000.

GENDER AND WOMEN'S ISSUES (*see also* SOCIAL AND CULTURAL HISTORY)

Adam, Ruth. *A Woman's Place, 1910-1975*. 1975. Reprint. London: Persephone Books, 2000.

Alberti, Johanna. *Beyond Suffrage: Feminists in War and Peace, 1914-1928*. New York: St. Martin's Press, 1989.

Anderson, Bonnie S., and Judith P. Zinsser. *A History of Their Own: Women in Europe from Prehistory to the Present*. Rev. ed. Vol. 2. New York: Oxford University Press, 2000.

Antrobus, Peggy. *The Global Women's Movement: Origins, Issues, and Strategies*. London: Zed Press, 2004.

Baker, Jean H. *Sisters: The Lives of America's Suffragists*. New York: Hill & Wang, 2005.

Boxer, Marilyn, and Jean H. Quataert, eds. *Socialist Women: European Socialist Feminism in the Nineteenth and Early Twentieth Centuries*. New York: Elsevier North-Holland, 1978.

Cleverdon, Catherine L. *The Woman Suffrage Movement in Canada: The Start of Liberation*. 2d ed. Toronto: University of Toronto Press, 1974.

Clift, Eleanor. *Founding Sisters and the Nineteenth Amendment*. New York: John Wiley & Sons, 2003.

Crawford, Patricia, and Philippa Maddern, eds. *Women as Australian Citizens: Underlying Histories*. Carlton, Vic.: Melbourne University Press, 2001.

Davidson, Caroline. *A Woman's Work Is Never Done: A History of Housework in the British Isles, 1650-1950*. London: Chatto & Windus, 1983.

Doumato, Eleanor Abdella, and Marsha Pripstein Poususney, eds. *Women and Globalization in the*

Arab Middle East: Gender, Economy, and Society. Boulder, Colo.: Lynne Rienner, 2003.

Flexner, Eleanor, and Ellen Fitzpatrick. *Century of Struggle: The Woman's Rights Movement in the United States.* Enlarged ed. Cambridge, Mass.: Belknap Press, 1996.

Forbes, Geraldine. *Women in Modern India.* New York: Cambridge University Press, 1996.

Frevert, Ute. *Women in German History: From Bourgeois Emancipation to Sexual Liberation.* New York: Berg, 1989.

Gordon, Linda. *Woman's Body, Woman's Right: A Social History of Birth Control in America.* Rev. ed. New York: Penguin Books, 1990.

Harvey, Anna L., and Randall Calvert. *Votes Without Leverage: Women in American Electoral Politics, 1920-1970.* New York: Cambridge University Press, 1998.

Holton, Sandra Stanley. *Feminism and Democracy: Women's Suffrage and Reform Politics in Britain, 1900-1918.* 1986. Reprint. New York: Cambridge University Press, 2002.

Kealey, Linda, ed. *A Not Unreasonable Claim: Women and Reform in Canada, 1880's-1920's.* Toronto: Women's Press, 1979.

Kent, Susan Kingsley. *Sex and Suffrage in Britain, 1860-1914.* Princeton, N.J.: Princeton University Press, 1987.

Kramarae, Cheris, and Dale Spender, eds. *Routledge International Encyclopedia of Women: Global Women's Issues and Knowledge.* 4 vols. New York: Routledge, 2000.

Lunardini, Christine A. *From Equal Suffrage to Equal Rights: Alice Paul and the National Woman's Party, 1910-1928.* 1986. Reprint. Lincoln, Nebr.: iUniverse, 2000.

Maguire, Daniel C., ed. *Sacred Rights: The Case for Contraception and Abortion in World Religions.* New York: Oxford University Press, 2003.

Mayhall, Laura E. Nym. *The Militant Suffrage Movement: Citizenship and Resistance in Britain, 1860-1930.* New York: Oxford University Press, 2003.

Momsen, Janet. *Women and Development in the Third World.* New York: Routledge, 1991.

Offen, Karen. *European Feminisms, 1700-1950: A Political History.* Stanford, Calif.: Stanford University Press, 2000.

Oldfield, Audrey. *Woman Suffrage in Australia.* New York: Cambridge University Press, 1992.

Orleck, Annelise. *Common Sense and a Little Fire: Women and Working-Class Politics in the United States, 1900-1965.* Chapel Hill: University of North Carolina Press, 1995.

Sanger, Margaret. *International Birth Control Conference.* 4 vols. New York: American Birth Control League, 1925-1926.

Sawer, Marian, and Marian Simms. *A Woman's Place: Women and Politics in Australia.* Sydney: George Allen & Unwin, 1984.

Schneider, Carl J., and Dorothy Schneider. *Into the Breach: American Women Overseas in World War I.* New York: Viking Press, 1991.

Seager, Joni. *The Penguin Atlas of Women in the World.* Rev. ed. New York: Penguin Books, 2003.

Sharer, Wendy B. *Vote and Voice: Women's Organizations and Political Literacy, 1915-1930.* Carbondale: Southern Illinois University Press, 2004.

Smith, Harold L., ed. *British Feminism in the Twentieth Century.* Amherst: University of Massachusetts Press, 1990.

Stephenson, Marylee. *Women in Canada.* Rev. ed. Don Mills, Ont.: General Publishing, 1977.

Storrs, Ladon R. Y. *Civilizing Capitalism: The National Consumers' League, Women's Activism, and Labor Standards in the New Deal Era.* Chapel Hill: University of North Carolina Press, 2000.

Strong-Boag, Veronica, Mona Gleason, and Adele Perry, eds. *Rethinking Canada: The Promise of Women's History.* 4th ed. New York: Oxford University Press, 2003.

Thönnessen, Werner. *The Emancipation of Women: The Rise and Decline of the Woman's Movement in German Social Democracy, 1863-1933.* Glasgow: Pluto Press, 1976.

Tilly, Louise A., and Joan W. Scott. *Women, Work, and Family.* 1978. Reprint. New York: Routledge, 1987.

Vickery, Amanda, ed. *Women, Privilege, and Power: British Politics, 1750 to the Present.* Stanford, Calif.: Stanford University Press, 2001.

Woloch, Nancy. *Women and the American Experience: A Concise History.* 3d ed. New York: McGraw-Hill, 1999.

Woollacott, Angela. *To Try Her Fortune in London: Australian Women, Colonialism, and Modernity.* New York: Oxford University Press, 2001.

Woolum, Janet. *Outstanding Women Athletes: Who They Are and How They Influenced Sports in America.* 2d ed. Phoenix, Ariz.: Oryx Press, 1998.

Young, Helen Praeger. *Choosing Revolution: Chinese Women Soldiers on the Long March.* Urbana: University of Illinois Press, 2001.

Young, Louise M. *In the Public Interest: The League of Women Voters, 1920-1970.* New York: Greenwood Press, 1989.

GEOGRAPHY, TRAVEL, AND EXPLORATION

Baines, John D., ed. *The Encyclopedia of World Geography: A Country by Country Guide.* San Diego, Calif.: Thunder Bay Press, 2002.

Bedesky, Baron. *Matthew Henson and Robert Peary: The Race to the North Pole.* New York: Crabtree, 2006.

Berton, Pierre. *The Arctic Grail: The Quest for the Northwest Passage and the North Pole, 1818-1909.* 1988. Reprint. New York: Lyons Press, 2000.

Bickel, Lennard. *Mawson's Will.* New York: Dorset Press, 1988.

Bingham, Hiram. *Machu Picchu: A Citadel of the Incas.* New Haven, Conn.: Yale University Press, 1930.

Confrey, Mick, and Tim Jordan. *Icemen: A History of the Arctic and Its Explorers.* New York: TV Books, 1998.

Cook, Frederick Albert. *My Attainment of the Pole.* 1913. Reprint. New York: Cooper Square Press, 2001.

De Porti, Andrea. *Explorers: The Most Exciting Voyages of Discovery—From the African Expeditions to the Lunar Landing.* Richmond Hill, Ont.: Firefly Books, 2005.

Fernandez-Armesto, Felipe, ed. *The Times Atlas of World Exploration.* New York: HarperCollins, 1991.

Fleming, Fergus. *Ninety Degrees North: The Quest for the North Pole.* New York: Grove Press, 2001.

Goetzmann, William H. *New Lands, New Men: America and the Second Great Age of Discovery.* 1986. Reprint. Austin: Texas State Historical Association, 1995.

Guberlet, Muriel L. *Explorers of the Sea: Famous Oceanographic Expeditions.* New York: Ronald Press, 1964.

Henderson, Bruce. *True North: Peary, Cook, and the Race to the Pole.* New York: W. W. Norton, 2005.

Huntford, Roland. *Scott and Amundsen: The Race to the South Pole.* New York: Atheneum, 1984.

McGregor, Alasdair. *Mawson's Huts: An Antarctic Expedition Journal.* Sydney: Hale & Iremonger, 1998.

Matsen, Brad. *Descent: The Heroic Discovery of the Abyss.* New York: Pantheon Books, 2005.

Roerich, Nicholas. *Heart of Asia: Memoirs from the Himalayas.* Rochester, Vt.: Inner Traditions, 1990.

Soule, Gardner. *The Greatest Depths: Probing the Seas to Twenty-Thousand Feet and Below.* Philadelphia: Macrae Smith, 1970.

Stein, Aurel M. *Innermost Asia: A Detailed Report of the Explorations in Central Asia, Afghanistan, Iran, Tibet, and China.* 2d ed. Delhi: Cosmo, 1991.

_____. *Serindia: Detailed Report of Explorations in Central Asia and Westernmost China.* 5 vols. London: Clarendon Press, 1921.

Thomson, David. *Scott, Shackleton, and Amundsen: Ambition and Tragedy in the Antarctic.* New York: Thunder's Mouth Press, 2002.

Unwin, Peter. *The Narrow Sea: Barrier, Bridge, and Gateway to the World—The History of the Channel.* London: Review, 2003.

Waldman, Carl, and Alan Wexler. *Encyclopedia of Exploration.* New York: Facts On File, 2004.

GOVERNMENT AND POLITICS
(*see also* DIPLOMACY AND INTERNATIONAL RELATIONS)

Agulhon, Maurice. *The French Republic, 1879-1992.* Oxford: Blackwell, 1993.

Alter, Jonathan. *The Defining Moment: FDR's Hundred Days and the Triumph of Hope.* New York: Simon & Schuster, 2006.

Altman, Nancy J. *The Battle for Social Security: From FDR's Vision to Bush's Gamble.* Hoboken, N.J.: John Wiley & Sons, 2005.

Anderson, Kristi. *The Creation of a Democratic Majority, 1928-1936.* Chicago: University of Chicago Press, 1979.

Ascher, Abraham. *The Revolution of 1905: A Short History.* Stanford, Calif.: Stanford University Press, 2004.

Balderston, Theo. *Economics and Politics in the Weimar Republic.* Cambridge, England: Cambridge University Press, 2002.

Ball, Stuart. *Baldwin and the Conservative Party: The Crisis of 1929-1931.* New Haven, Conn.: Yale University Press, 1988.

Barton, H. Arnold. *Sweden and Visions of Norway: Politics and Culture, 1814-1905.* Carbondale: Southern Illinois University Press, 2003.

Bassel, Richard. *Germany After the First World War.* New York: Oxford University Press, 1995.

Bates, J. Leonard. *The Origins of Teapot Dome: Progressives, Parties, and Petroleum, 1909-1921.* Urbana: University of Illinois Press, 1963.

Berkowitz, Edward D. *America's Welfare State: From Roosevelt to Reagan.* Baltimore: The Johns Hopkins University Press, 1991.

Bernstein, Irving. *A Caring Society: The New Deal, the Worker, and the Great Depression.* Boston: Houghton Mifflin, 1985.

Bischof, Gunter, Anton Pelinka, and Alexander Lassner,

eds. *The Dollfuss-Schuschnigg Era in Austria: A Reassessment.* New Brunswick, N.J.: Transaction, 2003.

Bliss, Michael. *Right Honourable Men: The Descent of Canadian Politics from MacDonald to Mulroney.* Toronto: HarperCollins, 1994.

Boller, Paul F., Jr. *Presidential Campaigns: From George Washington to George W. Bush.* New York: Oxford University Press, 2004.

Brenner, Anita. *The Wind That Swept Mexico: The History of the Mexican Revolution of 1910-1942.* 1971. Reprint. Austin: University of Texas Press, 1984.

Brinkley, Alan. *The End of Reform: New Deal Liberalism in Recession and War.* New York: Alfred A. Knopf, 1995.

Brown, Judith M. *Gandhi's Rise to Power: Indian Politics, 1915-1922.* Cambridge, England: Cambridge University Press, 1972.

Burner, David. *The Politics of Provincialism: The Democratic Party in Transition, 1918-1932.* 1968. Reprint. Cambridge, Mass.: Harvard University Press, 1986.

Burton, David H. *The Learned Presidency: Theodore Roosevelt, William Howard Taft, Woodrow Wilson.* Rutherford, N.J.: Fairleigh Dickinson University Press, 1988.

Cahm, Eric. *The Dreyfus Affair in French Society and Politics.* London: Longman, 1996.

Chodakiewicz, Marek Jan. *Between Nazis and Soviets: Occupation Politics in Poland, 1939-1947.* Lanham, Md.: Lexington Books, 2004.

Chow Tse-tsung. *The May Fourth Movement: Intellectual Revolution in Modern China.* Cambridge, Mass.: Harvard University Press, 1964.

Coddington, George A., Jr., and William B. Safran. *Ideology and Politics: The Socialist Party of France.* Boulder, Colo.: Westview Press, 1979.

Cole, Wayne S. *Roosevelt and the Isolationists, 1932-1945.* Lincoln: University of Nebraska Press, 1983.

Crankshaw, Edward. *The Shadow of the Winter Palace: Russia's Drift to Revolution, 1825-1917.* 1976. Reprint. New York: Da Capo Press, 2000.

Creese, Walter L. *TVA's Public Planning: The Vision, the Reality.* Knoxville: University of Tennessee Press, 1990.

Cronin, Thomas E. *Direct Democracy: The Politics of Initiative, Referendum, and Recall.* Cambridge, Mass.: Harvard University Press, 1989.

Crunden, Robert M. *Ministers of Reform: The Progressives' Achievement in American Civilization, 1889-1920.* New York: Basic Books, 1982.

Cullingworth, J. Barry, and Roger W. Caves. *Planning in the USA: Policies, Issues, and Processes.* 2d ed. New York: Routledge, 2003.

Cumberland, Charles C. *Mexican Revolution: The Constitutionalist Years.* Austin: University of Texas Press, 1972.

Duus, Peter. *Party Rivalry and Political Change in Taisho Japan.* Cambridge, Mass.: Harvard University Press, 1968.

Eidelberg, Philip Gabriel. *The Great Romanian Peasant Revolt of 1907: Origins of a Modern Jacquerie.* Leiden, the Netherlands: Brill, 1974.

Emmons, Terence. *The Formation of Political Parties and the First National Elections in Russia.* Cambridge, Mass.: Harvard University Press, 1983.

Feeny, Brian. *Sinn Féin: A Hundred Turbulent Years.* Madison: University of Wisconsin Press, 2003.

Franke, Wolfgang. *A Century of Chinese Revolution, 1851-1949.* Columbia: University of South Carolina Press, 1970.

Garcia, Mario T. *Mexican-Americans: Leadership, Ideology, and Identity, 1930-1960.* New Haven, Conn.: Yale University Press, 1989.

Ghani, Cyrus. *Iran and the Rise of Reza Shah: From Qajar Collapse to Pahlevi Power.* New York: I. B. Tauris, 1998.

Glassford, Larry. *Reaction and Reform: The Politics of the Conservative Party Under R. B. Bennett, 1927-1938.* Toronto: University of Toronto Press, 1992.

Gould, Lewis L., ed. *The Progressive Era.* Syracuse, N.Y.: Syracuse University Press, 1974.

_____. *Reform and Regulation: American Politics from Roosevelt to Wilson.* 2d ed. Prospect Heights, Ill.: Waveland Press, 1986.

Granatstein, J. L. *Canada's War: The Politics of the Mackenzie King Government, 1939-1945.* Toronto: University of Toronto Press, 1974.

Granatstein, J. L., and Norman Hillmer. *Prime Ministers: Ranking Canada's Leaders.* Toronto: HarperCollins, 1999.

Grieder, Jerome B. *Hu Shih and the Chinese Renaissance: Liberalism in the Chinese Revolution, 1917-1937.* Cambridge, Mass.: Harvard University Press, 1970.

Hadenius, Stig. *Swedish Politics During the Twentieth Century.* Translated by Victor Kayfetz. 3d rev. ed. Stockholm: Swedish Institute, 1990.

Hamilton, Richard F. *Who Voted for Hitler?* Princeton, N.J.: Princeton University Press, 1982.

Hanioğlu, M. Şükrü. *Preparation for a Revolution: The Young Turks, 1902-1908*. New York: Oxford University Press, 2000.

Harrison, Robert. *Congress, Progressive Reform, and the New American State*. New York: Cambridge University Press, 2004.

Hart, John Mason. *Revolutionary Mexico. The Coming and Process of the Mexican Revolution*. 10th anniversary ed. Berkeley: University of California Press, 1997.

Heidar, Knut. *Norway: Elites on Trial*. Boulder, Colo.: Westview Press, 2001.

Himmelberg, Robert F. *The Great Depression and the New Deal*. Westport, Conn.: Greenwood Press, 2000.

Holt, James L. *Congressional Insurgents and the Party System, 1909-1916*. Cambridge, Mass.: Harvard University Press, 1968.

Howell, Peter. *South Australia and Federation*. Kent Town, S.Aust.: Airlift, 2002.

Hughes, Michael. *Ireland Divided: The Roots of the Modern Irish Problem*. New York: St. Martin's Press, 1994.

Ilincioiu, Ion, ed. *The Great Romanian Peasant Revolt of 1907*. Bucharest, Hungary: Editura Academiei Romane, 1991.

Jachymek, Jan, and Waldemar Paruch. *More than Independence: Polish Political Thought, 1918-1939*. Lublin, Poland: Marie Curie-Sklodowska University Press, 2003.

Jenkins, Roy. *Mr. Balfour's Poodle: People v. Peers*. 1954. Reprint. New York: Chilmark Press, 1968.

Keddie, Nikki. *Iran: Religion, Politics, and Society*. Totowa, N.J.: Frank Cass, 1980.

Kelly, Lawrence C. *The Assault on Assimilation: John Collier and the Origins of Indian Policy Reform*. Albuquerque: University of New Mexico Press, 1983.

Kessler, Ronald. *The Bureau: The Secret History of the FBI*. New York: St. Martin's Press, 2002.

Kloppenberg, James T. *Uncertain Victory: Social Democracy and Progressivism in European and American Thought, 1870-1920*. New York: Oxford University Press, 1988.

Knight, Alan. *The Mexican Revolution*. 2 vols. Cambridge, England: Cambridge University Press, 1986.

Kohler, Peter A., and Hans F. Zacher, eds. *The Evolution of Social Insurance, 1881-1981: Studies of Germany, France, Great Britain, Austria, and Switzerland*. London: Frances Pinter, 1982.

Kollmann, Geoffry, and Carmen Solomon-Fears. *Social Security: Major Decisions in the House and Senate, 1935-2000*. New York: Novinka Books, 2002.

Lamour, Peter J. *The French Radical Party in the 1930's*. Stanford, Calif.: Stanford University Press, 1964.

Lauren, Paul Gordon. *Power and Prejudice: The Politics and Diplomacy of Racial Discrimination*. 2d ed. Boulder, Colo.: Westview Press, 1996.

Lee, J. J. *Ireland, 1912-1985: Politics and Society*. New York: Cambridge University Press, 1989.

Left, Carol Skalnik. *National Conflict in Czechoslovakia: The Making and Remaking of a State, 1918-1987*. Princeton, N.J.: Princeton University Press, 1988.

McGerr, Michael E. *A Fierce Discontent: The Rise and Fall of the Progressive Movement in America, 1870-1920*. New York: Oxford University Press, 2005.

McLynn, Frank. *Villa and Zapata: A History of the Mexican Revolution*. New York: Carroll & Graf, 2001.

May, Arthur J. *The Hapsburg Monarchy, 1867-1914*. Cambridge, Mass.: Harvard University Press, 1960.

Meaker, Gerald. *The Revolutionary Left in Spain, 1914-1923*. Stanford, Calif.: Stanford University Press, 1974.

Meli, Francis. *A History of the ANC: South Africa Belongs to Us*. Harare: Zimbabwe Publishing House, 1988.

Miller, Karen A. J. *Populist Nationalism: Republican Insurgency and American Foreign Policy Making, 1918-1925*. Westport, Conn.: Greenwood Press, 1999.

Mommsen, Hans. *The Rise and Fall of Weimar Democracy*. Translated by Elborg Forster and Larry Eugene Jones. Chapel Hill: University of North Carolina Press, 1998.

Montgomery, Tommie Sue. *Revolution in El Salvador: From Civil Strife to Civil Peace*. 2d ed. Boulder, Colo.: Westview Press, 1995.

Paludan, Ann. *Chronicles of the Chinese Emperors*. New York: Thames and Hudson, 1998.

Parkman, Patricia. *Nonviolent Insurrection in El Salvador: The Fall of Maximiliano Hernández Martínez*. Tucson: University of Arizona Press, 1988.

Payne, Stanley G. *The Collapse of the Spanish Republic, 1933-1936: Origins of the Civil War*. New Haven, Conn.: Yale University Press, 2006.

Pérez, Louis A., Jr. *Cuba: Between Reform and Revolution*. 2d ed. New York: Oxford University Press, 1995.

Perry, Duncan. *The Politics of Terror: The Macedonian Revolutionary Movements, 1893-1903*. Durham, N.C.: Duke University Press, 1988.

Pfannestiel, Todd J. *Rethinking the Red Scare: The Lusk Committee and New York's Crusade Against Radicalism, 1919-1923*. New York: Routledge, 2003.

Pugh, Martin. *The Making of Modern British Politics, 1867-1945*. 3d ed. Oxford, England: Blackwell, 2002.

Rawson, Don C. *Russian Rightists and the Revolution of 1905*. New York: Cambridge University Press, 1995.

Reichley, A. James. *The Life of the Parties: A History of American Political Parties*. Lanham, Md.: Rowman & Littlefield, 2000.

Richmond, Douglas W. *Venustiano Carranza's Nationalist Struggle, 1893-1920*. Lincoln: University of Nebraska Press, 1983.

Rogger, Hans. *Jewish Policies and Right-Wing Politics in Imperial Russia*. Berkeley: University of California Press, 1986.

Rothschild, Joseph. *Piłsudski's Coup d'État*. New York: Columbia University Press, 1966.

Ryder, A. J. *The German Revolution of 1918*. New York: Cambridge University Press, 1967.

Sarasohn, David. *The Party of Reform: Democrats in the Progressive Era*. Jackson: University Press of Mississippi, 1989.

Schantz, Harvey L., ed. *American Presidential Elections: Process, Policy, and Political Change*. Albany: State University of New York Press, 1996.

Schiffrin, Harold Z. *Sun Yat-sen and the Origins of the Chinese Revolution*. Berkeley: University of California Press, 1970.

Schirazi, Asghar. *The Constitution of Iran: Politics and the State in the Islamic Republic*. Translated by John O'Kane. New York: I. B. Tauris, 1997.

Schlesinger, Arthur M., Jr. *The Crisis of the Old Order*. 1957. Reprint. Boston: Houghton Mifflin, 2003.

Schmidt, David D. *Citizen Lawmakers: The Ballot Initiative Revolution*. Philadelphia: Temple University Press, 1989.

Schorske, Carl E. *Fin de Siècle Vienna: Politics and Culture*. New York: Vintage Books, 1981.

Schrems, Suzanne H. *Who's Rocking the Cradle? Women Pioneers of Oklahoma Politics from Socialism to the KKK, 1900-1930*. Norman, Okla.: Horse Creek, 2004.

Sexton, Patricia Cayo. *The War on Labor and the Left: Understanding America's Unique Conservatism*. Boulder, Colo.: Westview Press, 1991.

Sked, Alan. *The Decline and Fall of the Habsburg Empire, 1815-1918*. New York: Dorset Press, 1991.

Smith, Bradley. *Unfree Speech: The Folly of Campaign Finance Reform*. Princeton, N.J.: Princeton University Press, 2001.

Stone, Ralph A. *The Irreconcilables: The Fight Against the League of Nations*. Lexington: University Press of Kentucky, 1970.

Taylor, Graham D. *The New Deal and American Indian Tribalism: The Administration of the Indian Reorganization Act, 1934-1945*. Lincoln: University of Nebraska Press, 1980.

Tyler, S. Lyman. *A History of Indian Policy*. Washington, D.C.: U.S. Department of the Interior, Bureau of Indian Affairs, 1973.

Verner, Andrew M. *The Crisis of Russian Autocracy: Nicholas II and the 1905 Revolution*. Princeton, N.J.: Princeton University Press, 1990.

Waldron, Peter. *Between Two Revolutions: Stolypin and the Politics of Renewal in Russia*. De Kalb: Northern Illinois University Press, 1998.

Waters, Walter W. *B.E.F.: The Whole Story of the Bonus Army*. New York: John Day, 1933.

Weber, Eugen. *Action Française: Royalism and Reaction in Twentieth Century France*. Stanford, Calif.: Stanford University Press, 1962.

_____. *The Hollow Years: France in the 1930's*. New York: W. W. Norton, 1994.

Weisman, Steven R. *The Great Tax Wars: Lincoln to Wilson—The Fierce Battles over Money and Power That Transformed the Nation*. New York: Simon & Schuster, 2002.

Wheeler, Douglas L. *Republican Portugal: A Political History, 1910-1926*. 1978. Reprint. Madison: University of Wisconsin Press, 1999.

Whitehorn, Alan. *Canadian Socialism: Essays on the CCF-NDP*. Toronto: Oxford University Press, 1992.

Witte, John F. *The Politics and Development of the Federal Income Tax*. Madison: University of Wisconsin Press, 1985.

Young, Walter D. *The Anatomy of a Party: The National CCF, 1932-61*. Toronto: University of Toronto Press, 1969.

HEALTH AND MEDICINE

Allen, Peter Lewis. *The Wages of Sin: Sex and Disease, Past and Present*. Chicago: University of Chicago Press, 2002.

Bailey, Herbert. *The Vitamin Pioneers*. Emmaus, Pa.: Rodale Books, 1968.

Barry, John M. *The Great Influenza: The Epic Story of the Deadliest Plague in History*. New York: Penguin Books, 2005.

Batstone, Kay. *Outback Heroes: Seventy-Five Years of the Royal Flying Doctor Service of Australia*. Melbourne, Vic.: Lothian Books, 2003.

Black, Kathryn. *In the Shadow of Polio: A Personal and Social History*. New York: Perseus Books, 1996.

Bliss, Michael. *The Discovery of Insulin.* Toronto: McClelland & Stewart, 1982.

Burnham, Bruce S., Iris H. Hall, and Alex Gringauz. *Introduction to Medicinal Chemistry: How Drugs Act and Why.* 2d ed. New York: Wiley-Interscience, 2006.

Burrow, James G. *Organized Medicine in the Progressive Era.* Baltimore: The Johns Hopkins University Press, 1977.

Cameron, J. S. *History of the Treatment of Renal Failure by Dialysis.* Oxford, England: Oxford University Press, 2002.

Carpenter, Kenneth J. *Beriberi, White Rice, and Vitamin B: A Disease, a Cause, a Cure.* Berkeley: University of California Press, 2000.

_____. *The History of Scurvy and Vitamin C.* Cambridge, England: Cambridge University Press, 1986.

Critchlow, Donald T., ed. *The Politics of Abortion and Birth Control in Historical Perspective.* University Park: Pennsylvania State University Press, 1996.

Crosby, Alfred W., Jr. *America's Forgotten Pandemic: The Influenza of 1918.* 2d ed. New York: Cambridge University Press, 2003.

Duffy, John. *A History of Public Health in New York City, 1625-1866.* New York: Russell Sage Foundation, 1968.

Erling, Jonathon, and Joseph Spillane, eds. *Federal Drug Control: The Evolution of Policy and Practice.* Binghamton, N.Y.: Pharmaceutical Products Press, 2004.

Farley, John. *To Cast out Disease: A History of the International Health Division of the Rockefeller Foundation, 1913-1951.* New York: Oxford University Press, 2004.

Feldman, David, J. Wesley Pike, and Francis H. Glorieux, eds. *Vitamin D.* 2d ed. 2 vols. New York: Academic Press, 2004.

Fink, Max. *Electroshock: Restoring the Mind.* New York: Oxford University Press, 1999.

Friedrich, Wilhelm. *Vitamins.* New York: Walter de Gruyter, 1988.

Gallo, Robert. *Virus Hunting.* New York: Basic Books, 1991.

Gregg, Charles T. *Plague: An Ancient Disease in the Twentieth Century.* Rev. ed. Albuquerque: University of New Mexico Press, 1985.

Hawthorne, Fran. *Inside the FDA: The Business and Politics Behind the Drugs We Take and the Food We Eat.* New York: John Wiley & Sons, 2005.

Hilts, Philip J. *Protecting America's Health: The FDA, Business, and One Hundred Years of Regulation.* New York: Alfred A. Knopf, 2003.

Hobby, Gladys L. *Penicillin: Meeting the Challenge.* New Haven, Conn.: Yale University Press, 1985.

Kennedy, David M. *Birth Control in America: The Career of Margaret Sanger.* New Haven, Conn.: Yale University Press, 1970.

Kolata, Gina. *Flu: The Story of the Great Influenza Pandemic of 1918 and the Search for the Virus That Caused It.* Morongo Valley, Calif.: Sagebrush, 2001.

Krieg, Joann. *Epidemics in the Modern World.* New York: Twayne, 1992.

Lax, Eric. *The Mold in Dr. Florey's Coat: The Story of the Penicillin Miracle.* New York: Henry Holt, 2004.

Lerner, Barron H. *Breast Cancer Wars: Hope, Fear, and the Pursuit of a Cure in Twentieth-Century America.* New York: Oxford University Press, 2001.

McIntosh, Elaine N. *American Food Habits in Historical Perspective.* New York: Praeger, 1995.

Mullan, Fitzhugh. *Plagues and Politics: The Story of the United States Public Health Service.* New York: Basic Books, 1993.

Nuland, Sherwin B. *Doctors: The Biography of Medicine.* New York: Alfred A. Knopf, 1988.

Oldstone, Michael B. A. *Viruses, Plagues, and History.* New York: Oxford University Press, 1998.

Orent, Wendy. *Plague: The Mysterious Past and Terrifying Future of the World's Most Dangerous Disease.* New York: Free Press, 2004.

Pan American Health Organization. *Pro Salute Novi Mundi: A History of the Pan American Health Organization.* Washington, D.C.: Author, 1992.

_____. *Public Health in the Americas: Conceptual Renewal, Performance, Assessment, and Tools for Action.* 2 vols. Washington, D.C.: Author, 2006.

Patrick, Bill. *The Food and Drug Administration.* New York: Chelsea House, 1988.

Pettigrew, Eileen. *The Silent Enemy: Canada and the Deadly Flu of 1918.* Saskatoon, Sask.: Western Producer Prairie Books, 1983.

Pierce, John R., and Jim Writer. *Yellow Jack: How Yellow Fever Ravaged America and Walter Reed Discovered Its Deadly Secrets.* New York: John Wiley & Sons, 2005.

Rosner, David, and Gerald Markowitz, eds. *Dying for Work: Workers' Safety and Health in Twentieth-Century America.* Bloomington: Indiana University Press, 1987.

Ryan, Frank. *The Forgotten Plague: How the Battle Against Tuberculosis Was Won—and Lost.* Boston: Little, Brown, 1993.

Schneider, William E., ed. *Rockefeller Philanthropy and Modern Biomedicine: International Initiatives from World War I to the Cold War*. Bloomington: Indiana University Press, 2002.

Sellers, Christopher C. *Hazards of the Job: From Industrial Disease to Environmental Health Science*. Chapel Hill: University of North Carolina Press, 1997.

Silverstein, Arthur M. *A History of Immunology*. New York: Academic Press, 1989.

_____. *Paul Ehrlich's Receptor Immunology: The Magnificent Obsession*. New York: Academic Press, 2001.

Sneader, Walter. *Drug Prototypes and Their Exploitation*. New York: John Wiley & Sons, 1996.

Starr, Douglas P. *Blood: An Epic History of Medicine and Commerce*. New York: Alfred A. Knopf, 1998.

Starr, Paul. *The Social Transformation of American Medicine*. New York: Basic Books, 1982.

Tauber, Alfred I., and Leon Chernyak. *Metchnikoff and the Origins of Immunology: From Metaphor to Theory*. New York: Oxford University Press, 1991.

Temin, Peter. *Taking Your Medicine: Drug Regulation in the United States*. Cambridge, Mass.: Harvard University Press, 1980.

Tilney, Nicholas L. *Transplant: From Myth to Reality*. New Haven, Conn.: Yale University Press, 2003.

Tobin, Kathleen A. *The American Debate over Birth Control, 1907-1937*. Jefferson, N.C.: McFarland, 2001.

Valenstein, Elliot S. *Great and Desperate Cures: The Rise and Decline of Psychosurgery and Other Radical Treatments for Mental Illness*. New York: Basic Books, 1986.

Vertosick, Frank T. *Why We Hurt: The Natural History of Pain*. New York: Harcourt, 2000.

Watson, Rita Esposito, and Robert Wallach. *New Choices, New Chances*. New York: St. Martin's Press, 1981.

Wintrobe, Maxwell M. *Hematology, the Blossoming of a Science: A Story of Inspiration and Effort*. Philadelphia: Lea & Febiger, 1985.

Young, James Harvey. *Pure Food: Securing the Federal Pure Food and Drug Act of 1906*. Princeton, N.J.: Princeton University Press, 1989.

IMMIGRATION, MIGRATION, AND REFUGEES

Bankston, Carl L., III, and Danielle Hidalgo. *Immigration in U.S. History*. Pasadena, Calif.: Salem Press, 2006.

Barkan, Elliott, ed. *A Nation of Peoples*. Westport, Conn.: Greenwood Press, 1999.

Ciment, James, ed. *Encyclopedia of American Immigration*. 4 vols. Armonk, N.Y.: Sharpe Reference, 2001.

Daniels, Roger. *Coming to America: A History of Immigration and Ethnicity in American Life*. 2d ed. New York: HarperCollins, 2002.

_____. *Guarding the Golden Door: American Immigration Policy and Immigrants Since 1882*. New York: Hill & Wang, 2004.

Foner, Nancy, Rubén G. Rumbaut, and Steven J. Gold, eds. *Immigration Research for a New Century: Multidisciplinary Perspectives*. New York: Russell Sage Foundation, 2000.

Gibney, Matthew J., and Randall Hansen, eds. *Immigration and Asylum from 1900 to the Present*. 3 vols. Santa Barbara, Calif.: ABC-Clio, 2005.

Higham, John. *Strangers in the Land: Patterns of American Nativism, 1860-1925*. 2d ed. New Brunswick, N.J.: Rutgers University Press, 1988.

Hutchinson, E. P. *Legislative History of American Immigration Policy, 1798-1965*. Philadelphia: University of Pennsylvania Press, 1981.

Kasinitz, Philip, and Josh DeWind, eds. *The Handbook of International Migration: The American Experience*. New York: Russell Sage Foundation, 1999.

Kessner, Thomas. *The Golden Door: Italian and Jewish Immigrant Mobility in New York City, 1880-1915*. New York: Oxford University Press, 1977.

LeMay, Michael, and Elliott Robert Barkan. *U.S. Immigration and Naturalization Laws and Issues: A Documentary History*. Westport, Conn.: Greenwood Press, 1999.

Marrus, Michael R. *The Unwanted: European Refugees in the Twentieth Century*. 2d ed. Philadelphia: Temple University Press, 2001.

Meier, Matt S., and Feliciano Ribera. *Mexican Americans and American Mexicans: From Conquistadors to Chicanos*. Rev. ed. New York: Farrar, Straus and Giroux, 1993.

Mobasher, Mohsen M., and Mahmoud Sadri. *Migration, Globalization, and Ethnic Relations: An Interdisciplinary Approach*. Upper Saddle River, N.J.: Pearson Prentice Hall, 2004.

Moody, Suzanna, and Joel Wurl, eds. *The Immigration History Research Center: A Guide to Collections*. Westport, Conn.: Greenwood Press, 1991.

Nugent, Walter. *Crossings: The Great Transatlantic Migrations, 1870-1914*. Bloomington: Indiana University Press, 1992.

Powell, John. *Encyclopedia of North American Immigration*. New York: Facts On File, 2005.

_____. *Immigration*. New York: Facts On File, 2006.

Pozetta, George E. *American Immigration and Ethnicity*. 20 vols. New York: Garland, 1990-1991.

Takaki, Ronald. *Strangers from a Different Shore: A History of Asian Americans*. Rev. ed. Boston: Back Bay Books, 1998.

Thernstrom, Stephen, ed. *Harvard Encyclopedia of American Ethnic Groups*. Cambridge, Mass.: The Belknap Press, Harvard University Press, 1980.

Tichenor, Daniel J. *Dividing Lines: The Politics of Immigration Control in America*. Princeton, N.J.: Princeton University Press, 2002.

INDUSTRY AND LABOR
(*see also* BUSINESS, ECONOMICS, AND FINANCE)

Abernathy, William, Kim Clark, and Alan Kantrow. *Industrial Renaissance*. New York: Basic Books, 1983.

Alexander, Robert J. *A History of Organized Labor in Uruguay and Paraguay*. Westport, Conn.: Praeger, 2005.

Ashby, Joe C. *Organized Labor and the Mexican Revolution Under Lázaro Cárdenas*. Chapel Hill: University of North Carolina Press, 1967.

Babson, Steve. *The Unfinished Struggle: Turning Points in American Labor, 1877-Present*. Lanham, Md.: Rowman & Littlefield, 1999.

Barnard, John. *Walter Reuther and the Rise of the Auto Workers*. Boston: Little, Brown, 1983.

Bartolomei de la Cruz, Héctor, Geraldo von Potobsky, and Lee Swepston. *The International Labor Organization: The International Standards System and Basic Human Rights*. Boulder, Colo.: Westview Press, 1996.

Bercuson, David Jay. *Confrontation at Winnipeg: Labour, Industrial Relations, and the General Strike*. Montreal: McGill-Queen's University Press, 1974.

Bernstein, Irving. *The Lean Years: A History of the American Worker, 1920-1933*. 1960. Reprint. New York: Da Capo Press, 1983.

_____. *Turbulent Years: A History of the American Worker, 1933-1941*. Boston: Houghton Mifflin, 1970.

Brody, David. *Steelworkers in America: The Nonunion Era*. Cambridge, Mass.: Harvard University Press, 1960.

Brown, Cliff. *Racial Conflicts and Violence in the Labor Market: Roots in the 1919 Steel Strike*. New York: Garland, 1998.

Buhle, Paul, and Nicole Schulman, eds. *Wobblies! A Graphic History of the Industrial Workers of the World*. London: Verso, 2005.

Compa, Lance A., and Stephen F. Diamond, eds. *Human Rights, Labor Rights, and International Trade*. Philadelphia: University of Pennsylvania Press, 1996.

Dubofsky, Melvyn. *We Shall Be All: A History of the Industrial Workers of the World*. Chicago: Quadrangle Books, 1969.

Dubofsky, Melvyn, and Foster Rhea Dulles. *Labor in America: A History*. 7th ed. Arlington Heights, Ill.: Harlan Davidson, 2004.

Fine, Sidney. *Sit-Down: The General Motors Strike of 1936-1937*. Ann Arbor: University of Michigan Press, 1963.

Florey, R. A. *The General Strike of 1926: The Economic, Political, and Social Causes of That Class War*. New York: Riverrun Press, 1987.

Galenson, Walter. *The CIO Challenge to the AFL: A History of the American Labor Movement, 1935-1941*. 1960. Reprint. Cambridge, Mass.: Harvard University Press, 1981.

_____. *The International Labor Organization: An American View*. Madison: University of Wisconsin Press, 1981.

Green, James R. *The World of the Worker: Labor in Twentieth-Century America*. 1980. Reprint. Champaign: University of Illinois Press, 1998.

Greene, Julie. *Pure and Simple Politics: The American Federation of Labor and Political Activism, 1881-1917*. New York: Cambridge University Press, 1998.

Hinton, James. *Labour and Socialism*. Amherst: University of Massachusetts Press, 1983.

Howell, David. *British Workers and the Independent Labour Party: 1888-1906*. Manchester, England: Manchester University Press, 1983.

Jacoby, Daniel. *Laboring for Freedom: A New Look at the History of Labor in America*. Armonk, N.Y.: M. E. Sharpe, 1998.

Katzman, David M. *Seven Days a Week: Women and Domestic Service in Industrializing America*. New York: Oxford University Press, 1978.

McCartin, Joseph A. *Labor's Great War: The Struggle for Industrial Democracy and the Origins of Modern American Labor Relations, 1912-1921*. Chapel Hill: University of North Carolina Press, 1998.

McKibbin, Ross. *The Evolution of the Labour Party, 1910-1924*. 1974. Reprint. Oxford, England: Clarendon Press, 1984.

Martin, Ross. *TUC: The Growth of a Pressure Group, 1868-1976*. Oxford, England: Clarendon Press, 1980.

Masters, D. C. *The Winnipeg General Strike*. Toronto: University of Toronto Press, 1950.

Montgomery, David. *The Fall of the House of Labor: The Workplace, the State, and American Labor Activism, 1865-1925*. New York: Cambridge University Press, 1987.

Reid, Alastair J., and Henry Pelling. *A Short History of the Labour Party*. 12th ed. London: Palgrave Macmillan, 2005.

Renshaw, Patrick. *The Wobblies: The Story of the IWW and Syndicalism in the United States*. Rev. ed. Chicago: Ivan R. Dee, 1999.

Ruiz, Ramón Eduardo. *Labor and the Ambivalent Revolutionaries: Mexico, 1911-1923*. Baltimore: The Johns Hopkins University Press, 1976.

Schlager, Neil. *Encyclopedia of Labor History Worldwide*. 3 vols. Detroit: Thomson Gale, 2003.

Stein, Leon. *The Triangle Fire*. 1962. Reprint. Ithaca, N.Y.: ILR Press, 2001.

Warne, Colston E., ed. *The Steel Strike of 1919*. Boston: D. C. Heath, 1963.

Winters, Donald E., Jr. *The Soul of the Wobblies: The I.W.W., Religion, and American Culture in the Progressive Era, 1905-1917*. Westport, Conn.: Greenwood Press, 1985.

Wogu, Ananaba. *The Trade Union Movement in Nigeria*. New York: Africana, 1970.

Zane, J. Robert. *1902! The Great Coal Strike in Shenandoah, PA*. Frackville, Pa.: Broad Mountain, 2004.

Zieger, Robert H. *The CIO, 1935-1955*. Chapel Hill: University of North Carolina Press, 1995.

LAW AND LEGAL ISSUES

Abraham, Henry J. *Justices and Presidents: A Political History of Appointments to the Supreme Court*. 3d ed. New York: Oxford University Press, 1991.

Amar, Akhil Reed. *America's Constitution: A Biography*. New York: Random House, 2005.

Auerbach, Jerold S. *Rabbis and Lawyers: The Journey from Torah to Constitution*. Bloomington: Indiana University Press, 1990.

_____. *Unequal Justice: Lawyers and Social Change in Modern America*. New York: Oxford University Press, 1976.

Baker, Leonard. *Back to Back: The Duel Between FDR and the Supreme Court*. New York: Macmillan, 1967.

Blackburn, John D., Elliott I. Klayman, and Martin H. Malin. *The Legal Environment of Business*. 6th ed. Boston: Pearson Custom Publishing, 2003.

Bortman, Eli C. *Sacco and Vanzetti*. Beverly, Mass.: Commonwealth Editions, 2005.

Boyle, Alan, and David Freestone, eds. *International Law and Sustainable Development: Past Achievements and Future Challenges*. New York: Oxford University Press, 1999.

Breyer, Stephen. *Active Liberty: Interpreting Our Democratic Constitution*. New York: Alfred A. Knopf, 2005.

Burt, Robert A. *Two Jewish Justices: Outcasts in the Promised Land*. Berkeley: University of California Press, 1988.

Carrington, Paul D. *Stewards of Democracy: Law as a Public Profession*. Boulder, Colo.: Westview Press, 1999.

Cox, Archibald. *The Court and the Constitution*. Boston: Houghton Mifflin, 1987.

Curry, Charles F. *Alien Land Laws and Alien Rights*. Washington, D.C.: Government Printing Office, 1921.

Cushman, Barry. *Rethinking the New Deal Court: The Structure of a Constitutional Revolution*. New York: Oxford University Press, 1998.

Detter, Ingrid. *The Law of War*. 2d ed. New York: Cambridge University Press, 2000.

Grittner, Frederick K. *White Slavery: Myth, Ideology, and American Law*. New York: Garland, 1990.

Hall, Kermit L. *The Magic Mirror: Law in American History*. New York: Oxford University Press, 1989.

_____. *The Oxford Companion to the Supreme Court of the United States*. New York: Oxford University Press, 1992.

_____, ed. *The Oxford Guide to United States Supreme Court Decisions*. New York: Oxford University Press, 1999.

Hall, Timothy L., ed. *Laws, Acts, and Treaties*. 3 vols. Pasadena, Calif.: Salem Press, 2003.

Hardin, Patrick, and John E. Higgins, Jr., eds. *The Developing Labor Law*. 4th ed. 2 vols. Chicago: Bureau of National Affairs, 2002.

Henkin, Louis. *Foreign Affairs and the U.S. Constitution*. 2d ed. New York: Oxford University Press, 1996.

Hovenkamp, Herbert. *Federal Antitrust Policy: The Law of Competition and Its Practice*. 2d ed. Eagan, Minn.: West, 1999.

Hudson, Manley O. *World Court Reports: A Collection of the Judgments, Orders, and Opinions of the Perma-

nent Court of International Justice. Reprint. Buffalo, N.Y.: William S. Hein, 2000.

Irons, Peter. *A People's History of the Supreme Court.* New York: Penguin Books, 2000.

Johansen, Bruce E., ed. *Enduring Legacies: Native American Treaties and Contemporary Controversies.* New York: Praeger, 2004.

Karst, Kenneth L. *Belonging to America: Equal Citizenship and the Constitution.* New Haven, Conn.: Yale University Press, 1989.

Kens, Paul. *Judicial Power and Reform Politics: The Anatomy of "Lochner v. New York."* Lawrence: University Press of Kansas, 1990.

Larson, Edward J. *Summer for the Gods: The Scopes Trial and America's Continuing Debate over Science and Religion.* New York: Basic Books, 1997.

Leuchtenburg, William E. *The Supreme Court Reborn: The Constitutional Revolution in the Age of Roosevelt.* New York: Oxford University Press, 1995.

Levy, Leonard, et al., eds. *Encyclopedia of the American Constitution.* 4 vols. New York: Macmillan, 1986.

Lewis, Thomas Tandy, ed. *U.S. Supreme Court.* 3 vols. Pasadena, Calif.: Salem Press, 2006.

Mason, Alpheus T., and Donald Grier Stephenson, Jr. *American Constitutional Law: Introductory Essays and Selected Cases.* 12th ed. Englewood Cliffs, N.J.: Prentice Hall, 1998.

Newton, Nell Jessup, ed. *Cohen's Handbook of Federal Indian Law.* Rev. ed. New York: Matthew Bender, 2005.

Olasky, Marvin, and John Perry. *Monkey Business: The True Story of the Scopes Trial.* Nashville: Broadman & Holman, 2005.

Prucha, Francis Paul. *American Indian Treaties: The History of a Political Anomaly.* Berkeley: University of California Press, 1994.

Scott, James Brown. *The Hague Peace Conferences of 1899 and 1907.* Baltimore: The Johns Hopkins University Press, 1909.

Tan, Alan Khee-Jin. *Vessel-Source Marine Pollution: The Law and Politics of International Regulation.* New York: Cambridge University Press, 2005.

Tanenhaus, David S. *Juvenile Justice in the Making.* New York: Oxford University Press, 2004.

Theoharis, Athan G. *The FBI and American Democracy: A Brief Critical History.* Lawrence: University Press of Kansas, 2004.

Von Glahn, Gerhard. *Law Among Nations: An Introduction to Public International Law.* 7th ed. New York: Longman, 1995.

Walzer, Michael. *Just and Unjust Wars: A Moral Argument with Historical illustrations.* 3d ed. New York: Basic Books, 2000.

Washburn, Wilcomb E. *Red Man's Land/White Man's Law.* 2d ed. Norman: University of Oklahoma Press, 1995.

Wilkins, David E., and K. Tsianina Lomawaima. *Uneven Ground: American Indian Sovereignty and Federal Law.* Norman: University of Oklahoma Press, 2002.

LITERATURE AND LITERARY STUDIES

Adell, Sandra. *Double-Consciousness/Double Bind: Theoretical Issues in Twentieth-Century Black Literature.* Urbana: University of Illinois Press, 1994.

Beach, Christopher. *The Cambridge Introduction to Twentieth-Century American Poetry.* New York: Cambridge University Press, 2003.

Bernstein, Michael André. *Five Portraits: Modernity and Imagination in Twentieth-Century German Writing.* Evanston, Ill.: Northwestern University Press, 2000.

Brennan, Joseph G. *Three Philosophical Novelists: James Joyce, André Gide, Thomas Mann.* New York: Macmillan, 1964.

Brown, Nicholas. *Utopian Generations: The Political Horizon of Twentieth-Century Literature.* Princeton, N.J.: Princeton University Press, 2005.

Casanova, Pascal. *The World Republic of Letters.* Cambridge, Mass.: Harvard University Press, 2005.

Clark, Katerina. *The Soviet Novel: History as Ritual.* 3d ed. Bloomington: Indiana University Press, 2000.

Clerk, Jayana, and Ruth Siegel. *Modern Literatures of the Non-Western World: Where Waters Are Born.* London: Longman, 1995.

Damrosch, David. *What Is World Literature?* Princeton, N.J.: Princeton University Press, 2003.

Disch, Thomas M. *The Dreams Our Stuff Is Made Of: How Science Fiction Conquered the World.* New York: Free Press, 1998.

Frye, Northrop. *Anatomy of Criticism: Four Essays.* Updated ed. Princeton, N.J.: Princeton University Press, 2000.

Jack, Belinda E. *Negritude and Literary Criticism.* New York: Greenwood Press, 1996.

Kestelhoot, Lilyan. *Black Writers in French: A Literary History of Negritude.* Washington, D.C.: Howard University Press, 1991.

Marcus, Laura, and Peter Nicholls, eds. *The Cambridge History of Twentieth-Century English Literature.* New York: Cambridge University Press, 2004.

Owomoyela, Oyekan, ed. *A History of Twentieth-Century African Literatures*. Lincoln: University of Nebraska Press, 1993.

Pendergast, Christopher, ed. *Debating World Literature*. London: Verso, 2004.

Schmidgall, Gary. *Literature as Opera*. New York: Oxford University Press, 1977.

Simmons, Ernest J. *Russian Fiction and Soviet Ideology: Introduction to Fedin, Leonov, and Sholokhov*. New York: Columbia University Press, 1958.

Stringer, Jenny, ed. *The Oxford Companion to Twentieth-Century Literature in English*. New York: Oxford University Press, 1996.

Struve, Gleb. *Russian Literature Under Lenin and Stalin, 1917-1953*. Norman: University of Oklahoma Press, 1971.

Stuckey, W. J. *The Pulitzer Prize Novels*. Norman: University of Oklahoma Press, 1966.

Taylor, Helen. *Circling Dixie: Contemporary Southern Culture Through a Transatlantic Lens*. New Brunswick, N.J.: Rutgers University Press, 2001.

Toklas, Alice B. *What Is Remembered*. New York: Holt, Rinehart and Winston, 1963.

Tolstoy, Leo. *What Is Art?* Translated by Almyer Maude. New York: Bobbs-Merrill, 1960.

Watson, Steven. *The Harlem Renaissance: Hub of African-American Culture, 1920-1930*. New York: Pantheon Books, 1995.

Wintz, Cary D. *Black Culture and the Harlem Renaissance*. 1988. Reprint. College Station: Texas A&M Press, 1997.

MATHEMATICS

Fischbein, Efraim. *Intuition in Science and Mathematics*. Dordrecht, the Netherlands: D. Reidel, 1987.

Gigerenzer, Gerd, et al. *The Empire of Chance: How Probability Theory Changed Science and Everyday Life*. New York: Cambridge University Press, 1989.

Goldstein, Rebecca. *Incompleteness: The Proof and Paradox of Kurt Gödel*. New York: W. W. Norton, 2005.

Kline, Morris. *Mathematical Thought from Ancient to Modern Times*. Vol. 3. 1972. Reprint. New York: Oxford University Press, 1990.

Potter, Michael. *Set Theory and Its Philosophy: A Critical Introduction*. New York: Oxford University Press, 2004.

Temple, George. *One Hundred Years of Mathematics: A Personal Viewpoint*. New York: Springer-Verlag, 1981.

Tiles, Mary. *The Philosophy of Set Theory: An Historical Introduction to Cantor's Paradise*. Mineola, N.Y.: Dover, 2004.

Van Heijenoort, Jean, comp. *From Frege to Gödel: A Source Book on Mathematical Logic, 1879-1931*. 1967. Reprint. Cambridge, Mass.: Harvard University Press, 2002.

Whitehead, Alfred North, and Bertrand Russell. *Principia Mathematica*. 3 vols. Cambridge, England: Cambridge University Press, 1910-1913.

MILITARY HISTORY
(*see also* WORLD WAR I, WORLD WAR II)

Alpert, Michael. *A New International History of the Spanish Civil War*. 2d ed. New York: Palgrave Macmillan, 2004.

Baer, George W. *One Hundred Years of Sea Power: The U.S. Navy, 1890-1990*. Stanford, Calif.: Stanford University Press, 1994.

Best, Geoffrey. *Humanity in Warfare*. New York: Columbia University Press, 1980.

Bradford, James, ed. *International Encyclopedia of Military History*. New York Routledge, 2006.

Brown, Frederick J. *Chemical Warfare: A Study in Restraints*. 1968. Reprint. New Brunswick, N.J.: Transaction, 2005.

Coffey, Thomas M. *Lion by the Tail: The Story of the Italian-Ethiopian War*. New York: Viking Press, 1974.

Coleman, Kim. *A History of Chemical Warfare*. New York: Palgrave Macmillan, 2005.

De Arcangelis, Mario. *Electronic Warfare: From the Battle of Tsushima to the Falklands and Lebanon Conflicts*. Poole, England: Blandford Press, 1985.

Dingman, Roger. *Power in the Pacific: The Origins of Naval Arms Limitation, 1914-1922*. Chicago: University of Chicago Press, 1976.

Doughty, Robert A. *The Seeds of Disaster: The Development of French Army Doctrine, 1919-1939*. Hamden, Conn.: Archon Books, 1985.

Elshtain, Jean Bethke, and Sheila Tobias, eds. *Women, Militarism, and War*. Savage, Md.: Rowman & Littlefield, 1990.

Farwell, Byron. *The Great Boer War*. London: Penguin Books, 1976.

Forrest, Andrew. *The Spanish Civil War*. New York: Routledge, 2000.

French, David. *Raising Churchill's Army: The British Army and the War Against Germany, 1919-1945*. New York: Oxford University Press, 2000.

Graff, David A., and Robin Higham. *A Military History of China*. Boulder, Colo.: Westview Press, 2002.

Gray, Colin S. *The Leverage of Sea Power: The Strategic Advantage of Navies in War*. New York: Free Press, 1992.

Gray, Edwyn. *Hitler's Battleships*. London: Leo Cooper, 1992.

Habib, John S. *Ibn Saʿud's Warriors of Islam: The Ikhwan of Najd and Their Role in the Creation of the Saʿudi Kingdom, 1910-1930*. Leiden, the Netherlands: Brill, 1978.

Hodges, Peter. *The Big Gun: Battleship Main Armament, 1860-1945*. Annapolis, Md.: Naval Institute Press, 1981.

Holden, Robert H. *Armies Without Nations: Public Violence and State Formation in Central America, 1821-1960*. New York: Oxford University Press, 2004.

Hughes, Judith M. *To the Maginot Line: The Politics of French Military Preparation in the 1920's*. Cambridge, Mass.: Harvard University Press, 1971.

Hull, Isabel V. *Absolute Destruction: Military Culture and the Practices of War in Imperial Germany*. Ithaca, N.Y.: Cornell University Press, 2005.

Høiback, Harald. *Command and Control in Military Crisis: Devious Decisions*. Portland, Oreg.: F. Cass, 2003.

Keegan, John. *The Price of Admiralty: The Evolution of Naval Warfare*. New York: Viking, 1988.

Kemp, Anthony. *The Maginot Line: Myth and Reality*. New York: Stein & Day, 1982.

Kolinski, Charles J. *Independence or Death: The Story of the Paraguayan War*. Gainesville: University of Florida Press, 1965.

McKercher, B. J. C., ed. *Arms Limitation and Disarmament: Restraints on War, 1899-1939*. Westport, Conn.: Praeger, 1992.

Manchester, William. *The Arms of Krupp, 1587-1968*. 1968. Reprint. Boston: Back Bay Books, 2003.

Mason, Herbert Molloy. *The Great Pursuit: Pershing's Expedition to Destroy Pancho Villa*. 1970. Reprint. New York: Smithmark, 1995.

Massie, Robert K. *Dreadnought: Britain, Germany, and the Coming of the Great War*. 1991. Reprint. New York: Vintage Books, 2003.

Mockler, Anthony. *Haile Selassie's War: The Italian-Ethiopian Campaign, 1935-1941*. Northampton, Mass.: Olive Branch Press, 2002.

Nasson, Bill. *The South African War, 1899-1902*. London: Arnold, 1999.

O'Connell, Robert. *Sacred Vessels: The Cult of the Battleship and the Rise of the U.S. Navy*. Boulder, Colo.: Westview Press, 1991.

Padfield, Peter. *Battleship*. Rev. ed. Edinburgh: Birlinn, 2001.

Pakenham, Thomas. *The Boer War*. London: Weidenfeld & Nicolson, 1979.

Powell, John, ed. *Magill's Guide to Military History*. 5 vols. Pasadena, Calif.: Salem Press, 2001.

Preston, Paul. *The Spanish Civil War, 1936-1939*. Chicago: Dorsey Press, 1986.

Rouguié, Alain. *The Military and the State in Latin America*. Berkeley: University of California Press, 1987.

Sandler, Stanley. *Battleships: An Illustrated History of Their Impact*. Denver, Colo.: ABC-Clio, 2004.

Shaw, Stanford J. *From Empire to Republic: The Turkish War of National Liberation: A Documentary Study, 1918-1923*. Ankara, Turkey: Turk Tarih Kurumu Basimevi, 2000.

Smyth, Henry De Wolf. *Atomic Energy for Military Purposes*. 1945. Reprint. Stanford, Calif.: Stanford University Press, 1990.

Steinberg, John W., et al., eds. *The Russo-Japanese War in Global Perspective: World War Zero*. Leiden: Brill Academic, 2006.

Tarbush, Mohammad A. *The Role of the Military in Politics: A Case Study of Iraq to 1941*. London: Kegan Paul, 1982.

Terraine, John. *The U-Boat Wars, 1916-1945*. New York: G. P. Putnam's Sons, 1989.

Thomas, Hugh. *The Spanish Civil War*. Rev. ed. 1977. Reprint. New York: Modern Library, 2001.

Townshend, Charles, ed. *Oxford Illustrated History of Modern War*. New York: Oxford University Press, 1997.

NATURE AND THE ENVIRONMENT

Albright, Horace M. *The Birth of the National Park Service: The Founding Years, 1913-33*. Salt Lake City: Howe Brothers, 1985.

Allen, Thomas B. *Guardian of the Wild: The Story of the National Wildlife Federation*. Bloomington: Indiana University Press, 1987.

Barry, John, and E. Gene Frankland, eds. *International Encyclopedia of Environmental Politics*. New York: Routledge, 2002.

Belanger, Dian Olson. *Managing American Wildlife: A History of the International Association of Fish and Wildlife Agencies*. Amherst: University of Massachusetts Press, 1988.

Benedick, Richard E. *Ozone Diplomacy: New Directions in Safeguarding the Planet*. Cambridge, Mass.: Harvard University Press, 1991.

Berenbaum, May R. *Bugs in the System: Insects and Their Impact on Human Affairs*. Boston: Addison-Wesley, 1995.

Bortman, Marci, et al., eds. *Environmental Encyclopedia*. 3d ed. 2 vols. Detroit: Gale Thomson, 2003.

Bradford, Marlene, ed. *Natural Disasters*. 3 vols. Pasadena, Calif.: Salem Press, 2000.

Cech, Thomas V. *Principles of Water Resources: History, Development, Management, and Policy*. 2d ed. Hoboken, N.J.: John Wiley & Sons, 2005.

Chetham, Deirde. *Before the Deluge: The Vanishing World of the Yangtze's Three Gorges*. Brookline, Mass.: Palgrave Macmillan, 2002.

Cohen, Michael P. *The History of the Sierra Club, 1892-1970*. San Francisco: Sierra Club Books, 1988.

Cohen, Stan. *The Tree Army: A Pictorial History of the Civilian Conservation Corps, 1933-1945*. Missoula, Mont.: Pictorian Histories, 1980.

Davis, Charles, ed. *Western Public Lands and Environmental Politics*. 2d ed. Boulder, Colo.: Westview Press, 2001.

Dorgan, Charity Anne, ed. *Statistical Record of the Environment*. 3d ed. New York: Gale Research, 1995.

Elvin, Mark, and Liu Ts'ui-jung, eds. *Sediments of Time: Environment and Society in Chinese History*. New York: Cambridge University Press, 1998.

Flader, Susan L. *Thinking Like a Mountain: Aldo Leopold and the Evolution of an Ecological Attitude Toward Deer, Wolves, and Forests*. 1974. Reprint. Madison: University of Wisconsin Press, 1994.

Gillespie, Alexander. *Climate Change, Ozone Depletion, and Air Pollution: Legal Commentaries Within the Context of Science and Policy*. Boston: M. Nijhoff, 2006.

Goldman, Marshal I. *The Spoils of Progress: Environmental Pollution in the Soviet Union*. Cambridge, Mass.: MIT Press, 1972.

Golley, Frank Benjamin. *A History of the Ecosystem Concept in Ecology: More than the Sum of the Parts*. New Haven, Conn.: Yale University Press, 1993.

Gore, Al. *Earth in the Balance: Ecology and the Human Spirit*. New York: Houghton Mifflin, 1992.

Gottlieb, Robert. *A Life of Its Own: The Politics and Power of Water*. San Diego: Harcourt Brace Jovanovich, 1988.

Graham, Frank. *The Audubon Ark: A History of the National Audubon Society*. New York: Alfred A. Knopf, 1990.

Grzimek, Bernhard, and Michael Grzimek. *Serengeti Shall Not Die*. New York: E. P. Dutton, 1961.

Hagen, Joel B. *An Entangled Bank: The Origins of Ecosystem Ecology*. New Brunswick, N.J.: Rutgers University Press, 1992.

Huth, Hans. *Nature and the American: Three Centuries of Changing Attitudes*. Rev. ed. Lincoln: University of Nebraska Press, 1990.

Knight, Richard L., and Susanne Riedel, eds. *Aldo Leopold and the Ecological Conscience*. New York: Oxford University Press, 2002.

Krech, Shepard, III, J. R. McNeill, and Carolyn Merchant, eds. *Encyclopedia of World Environmental History*. 3 vols. New York: Routledge, 2004.

Lothian, William Fergus. *History of Canada's National Parks*. Vol. 2. Ottawa, Ont.: Parks Canada, 1977.

Lowry, William R. *The Capacity for Wonder: Preserving National Parks*. Washington, D.C.: Brookings Institution, 1994.

McKibben, Bill. *The End of Nature*. 10th anniversary ed. New York: Random House, 1999.

MacLennan, Hugh. *The Rivers of Canada*. Toronto: Macmillan of Canada, 1977.

Magill, Frank N. *Great Events from History II: Ecology and the Environment Series*. 5 vols. Pasadena, Calif.: Salem Press, 1995.

Merchant, Carolyn. *The Columbia Guide to American Environmental History*. New York: Columbia University Press, 2002.

Merrill, Perry H. *Roosevelt's Forest Army: A History of the Civilian Conservation Corps, 1933-1942*. Montpelier, Vt.: Perry H. Merrill, 1981.

Mitchell, Ronald B. *Intentional Oil Pollution at Sea: Environmental Policy and Treaty Compliance*. Cambridge, Mass.: MIT Press, 1994.

Mnatsakanian, Ruben A. *Environmental Legacy of the Former Soviet Republics*. Edinburgh: Center for Human Ecology, 1992.

Nash, Roderick Frazier. *The American Environment: Readings in the History of Conservation*. Reading, Mass.: Addison-Wesley, 1968.

_____. *The Rights of Nature: A History of Environmental Ethics*. Madison: University of Wisconsin Press, 1989.

_____. *Wilderness and the American Mind*. 4th ed. New Haven, Conn.: Yale University Press, 2001.

Parson, Edward A. *Protecting the Ozone Layer: Science*

and Strategy. New York: Oxford University Press, 2003.

Pavl'nek, Petr, and John Pickles. _Environmental Transitions: Transformation and Ecological Defence in Central and Eastern Europe_. London: Routledge, 2000.

Pelloso, Andrew J. _Saving the Blue Heart of Siberia: The Environmental Movement in Russia and Lake Baikal_. Bloomington: Indiana University School of Public and Environmental Affairs, 1993.

Pepper, David. _Modern Environmentalism: An Introduction_. New York: Routledge, 1996.

Reisner, Marc. _Cadillac Desert: The American West and Its Disappearing Water_. Rev. ed. New York: Viking Penguin, 1993.

Revkin, Andrew. _Global Warming: Understanding the Forecast_. New York: Abbeville Press, 1992.

Schmandt, Jurgen, Judith Clarkson, and Hilliard Roderick, eds. _Acid Rain and Friendly Neighbors: The Policy Dispute Between Canada and the United States_. Durham, N.C.: Duke University Press, 1988.

Schneider, Stephen H. _Global Warming: Are We Entering the Greenhouse Century?_ San Francisco: Sierra Club Books, 1989.

Searle, Rick. _Phantom Parks: The Struggle to Save Canada's National Parks_. Toronto: Key Porter Books, 2000.

Sellars, Richard West. _Preserving Nature in the National Parks: A History_. New Haven, Conn.: Yale University Press, 1997.

Sinclair, Kevin. _The Yellow River: A Five Thousand-Year Journey Through China_. London: Weidenfeld & Nicolson, 1987.

Social Learning Group. _Learning to Manage Global Environmental Risks_. 2 vols. Cambridge, Mass.: MIT Press, 2001.

Steinberg, Ted. _Down to Earth: Nature's Role in American History_. New York: Oxford University Press, 2002.

Taber, Richard D., and Neil F. Payne. _Wildlife, Conservation, and Human Welfare: A United States and Canadian Perspective_. Malabar, Fla.: Krieger, 2003.

Taylor, Bob Pepperman. _Our Limits Transgressed: Environmental Political Thought in America_. Lawrence: University Press of Kansas, 1992.

Turner, Myles. _My Serengeti Years: The Memoirs of an African Game Warden_. New York: W. W. Norton, 1987.

Weiner, Douglas R. _Models of Nature: Ecology, Conservation, and Cultural Revolution in Soviet Russia_.

1988. Reprint. Pittsburgh, Pa.: University of Pittsburgh Press, 2000.

Weiner, Ruth F., and Robin Matthews. _Environmental Engineering_. 4th ed. Burlington, Mass.: Elsevier Science, 2003.

Winchester, Simon. _The River at the Centre of the World_. London: Picador, 2004.

Worcester, Donald. _Nature's Economy: A History of Ecological Ideas_. Cambridge, England: Cambridge University Press, 1985.

PHILOSOPHY, HISTORIOGRAPHY, AND INTELLECTUAL HISTORY

Arrington, Robert L., ed. _A Companion to the Philosophers_. Oxford: Blackwell, 1999.

Bergson, Henri. _The Creative Mind_. Translated by Mabell L. Andison. New York: Philosophical Library, 1946.

Borchert, Donald M., ed. _Encylopedia of Philosophy_. 4 vols. Detroit: Thomson Gale, 2006.

Boyd, Kelly, ed. _Encyclopedia of Historians and Historical Writings_. Chicago: Fitzroy Dearborn, 1999.

Buber, Martin. _I and Thou_. Translated by Walter Kaufmann. New York: Scribner's, 1970.

Craig, Edward, ed. _Routledge Encyclopedia of Philosophy_. New York: Routledge, 1998.

Durant, Will. Preface to _The Story of Philosophy_. 2d ed. New York: Simon & Schuster, 1961.

Everdell, William R. _The First Moderns: Profiles in the Origins of Twentieth-Century Thought_. Chicago: University of Chicago Press, 1997.

Farrenkopf, John. _Prophet of Decline: Spengler on World History and Politics_. Baton Rouge: Louisiana State University Press, 2001.

Friedman, Michael. _Reconsidering Logical Positivism_. Cambridge, England: Cambridge University Press, 1999.

Gorman, Anthony. _Historians, State, and Politics in Twentieth-Century Egypt: Contesting the Nation_. London: Routledge Curzon, 2003.

Iggers, Georg G. _Historiography in the Twentieth Century: From Scientific Objectivity to the Postmodern Challenge_. Hanover, N.H.: Wesleyan University Press, 1997.

Kelley, Donald R. _Faces of History: Historical Inquiry from Herodotus to Herder_. New Haven, Conn.: Yale University Press, 1998.

Menand, Louis. _The Metaphysical Club: A Story of Ideas in America_. New York: Farrar, Straus and Giroux, 2001.

Mosse, George Lachmann. *Toward the Final Solution: A History of European Racism.* Madison: University of Wisconsin Press, 1985.

Roth, John K., ed. *World Philosophers and Their Works.* 3 vols. Pasadena, Calif.: Salem Press, 2000.

Russell, Bertrand. *My Philosophical Development.* 1959. Rev. ed. New York: Routledge, 1995.

Savickey, Beth. *Wittgenstein's Art of Investigation.* New York: Routledge, 1999.

Schwarcz, Vera. *The Chinese Enlightenment: Intellectuals and the Legacy of the May Fourth Movement of 1919.* 1986. Reprint. Berkeley: University of California Press, 1990.

Sluga, Hans. *Heidegger's Crisis: Philosophy and Politics in Nazi Germany.* Cambridge, Mass.: Harvard University Press, 1933.

Stadler, Friedrich. *The Vienna Circle: Studies in the Origins, Development, and the Influence of Logical Empiricism.* New York: Springer, 2000.

Windschuttle, Keith. *The Killing of History.* New York: Free Press, 1997.

Wittgenstein, Ludwig. *Philosophical Investigations.* Translated by G. E. M. Anscombe. 3d ed. Upper Saddle River, N.J.: Prentice Hall, 1999.

PUBLISHING AND JOURNALISM

Abrahamson, David. *Magazine-Made America: The Cultural Transformation of the Postwar Periodical.* Cresskill, N.J.: Hampton Press, 1996.

Carruthers, Susan L. *The Media at War: Communication and Conflict in the Twentieth Century.* New York: Palgrave Macmillan, 2000.

Doss, Erika Lee, ed. *Looking at "Life" Magazine.* Washington, D.C.: Smithsonian Institution Press, 2001.

Douglas, George H. *The Smart Magazines.* Hamden, Conn.: Archon Books, 1991.

Epstein, Jason. *Book Business: Publishing Past, Present, and Future.* New York: W. W. Norton, 2001.

Forsyth, David P. *The Business Press in America.* Philadelphia, Pa.: Chilton Books, 1964.

Gill, Brendan. *Here at "The New Yorker."* 1975. Reprint. New York: Da Capo Press, 1997.

Gramling, Oliver. *AP: The Story of News.* New York: Farrar & Rinehart, 1940.

Hall, Carolyn. *The Thirties in "Vogue."* New York: Harmony Books, 1985.

Hamilton, Ian. *The Little Magazines: A Study of Six Editors.* London: Weidenfeld & Nicolson, 1976.

Herzstein, Robert E. *Henry R. Luce, "Time," and the American Crusade in Asia.* New York: Cambridge University Press, 2005.

Lee, Charles. *The Hidden Public: The Story of the Book-of-the-Month Club.* Garden City, N.Y.: Doubleday, 1958.

Lubar, Robert, et al. *Writing for "Fortune": Nineteen Authors Remember Life on the Staff of a Remarkable Magazine.* New York: Time Inc., 1980.

Lupoff, Richard A. *The Great American Paperback: An Illustrated Tribute to the Legends of the Book.* Portland, Oreg.: Collectors Press, 2001.

Mahon, Gigi. *The Last Days of "The New Yorker."* New York: McGraw-Hill, 1988.

Mott, Frank Luther. *A History of American Magazines.* 5 vols. Cambridge, Mass.: Harvard University Press, 1938-1968.

Okren, Daniel, ed. *"Fortune": The Art of Covering Business.* New York: Gibbs Smith, 1999.

Peterson, Theodore. *Magazines in the Twentieth Century.* 2d ed. Urbana: University of Illinois Press, 1964.

Sharp, Joanne P. *Condensing the Cold War: "Reader's Digest" and American Identity.* Minneapolis: University of Minnesota Press, 2000.

Smith, Jeffery A. *War and Press Freedom: The Problem of Prerogative Power.* New York: Oxford University Press, 1999.

Tebbel, John. *A History of Book Publishing in the United States.* 4 vols. New York: R. R. Bowker, 1972-1981.

Tebbel, John, and Mary Ellen Zuckerman. *The Magazine in America, 1741-1990.* New York: Oxford University Press, 1991.

Williams, William E. *The Penguin Story.* Harmondsworth, Middlesex, England: Penguin Books, 1956.

RADIO, TELEVISION, AND MOTION PICTURES

Abel, Richard. *The French Cinema: The First Wave, 1915-1929.* Princeton, N.J.: Princeton University Press, 1984.

Abramson, Albert. *The History of Television, 1880-1941.* Jefferson, N.C.: McFarland, 1987.

Aitken, Hugh G. J. *The Continuous Wave: Technology and American Radio, 1900-1932.* Princeton, N.J.: Princeton University Press, 1985.

Balio, Tino, ed. *Grand Design: Hollywood as a Modern Business Enterprise, 1930-1939.* Berkeley: University of California Press, 1995.

Balk, Alfred. *The Rise of Radio: From Marconi Through the Golden Age.* Jefferson, N.C.: McFarland, 2006.

Barlow, John D. *German Expressionist Film.* Boston: Twayne, 1982.

Barnouw, Eric. *Tube of Plenty: The Evolution of American Television.* 2d rev. ed. New York: Oxford University Press, 1990.

Birkos, Alexander S. *Soviet Cinema: Directors and Films.* Hamden, Conn.: Archon Books, 1976.

Bogle, Donald. *Toms, Coons, Mulattoes, Mammies, and Bucks: An Interpretive History of Blacks in American Films.* 4th ed. New York: Continuum, 2001.

Bordwell, David, Janet Staiger, and Kristin Thompson. *The Classical Hollywood Cinema: Film Style and Mode of Production to 1960.* New York: Columbia University Press, 1985.

Bowser, Eileen. *The Transformation of Cinema, 1907-1915.* Reprint ed. Berkeley: University of California Press, 1994.

Briggs, Asa. *The BBC: The First Fifty Years.* Oxford, England: Oxford University Press, 1985.

Cain, John. *The BBC: Seventy Years of Broadcasting.* London: British Broadcasting Corporation, 1996.

Chanan, Michael. *Repeated Takes: A Short History of Recording and Its Effects on Music.* London: Verso, 1995.

Clurman, Richard M. *To the End of Time: The Seduction and Conquest of a Media Empire.* New York: Simon & Schuster, 1992.

Cook, David A. *A History of Narrative Film.* 4th ed. New York: W. W. Norton, 2004.

Cooke, Paul. *German Expressionist Film.* Harpenden, Hertfordshire, England: Pocket Essentials, 2002.

Crisell, Andrew. *An Introductory History of British Broadcasting.* 2d ed. New York: Routledge, 2002.

Dick, Bernard. *The Star-Spangled Screen: The American World War II Film.* 1985. Reprint. Lexington: University Press of Kentucky, 1996.

Douglas, George H. *The Early Days of Radio Broadcasting.* 1987. Reprint. Jefferson, N.C.: McFarland, 2001.

Douglas, Susan J. *Inventing American Broadcasting, 1899-1922.* Baltimore: The Johns Hopkins University Press, 1987.

Eyman, Scott. *The Speed of Sound: Hollywood and the Talkie Revolution, 1926-1930.* New York: Simon & Schuster, 1997.

Fabe, Marilyn. *Closely Watched Films: An Introduction to the Art of Narrative Film Technique.* Berkeley: University of California Press, 2004.

Inglis, Andrew F. *Behind the Tube: A History of Broadcasting Technology and Business.* Boston: Focal Press, 1990.

Kenez, Peter. *Cinema and Soviet Society: From the Revolution to the Death of Stalin.* New York: I. B. Tauris, 2001.

Koppes, Clayton R., and Gregory D. Black. *Hollywood Goes to War: How Politics, Profits, and Propaganda Shaped World War II Movies.* New York: Free Press, 1987.

Lanzoni, Rémi Fournier. *French Cinema: From Its Beginnings to the Present.* New York: Continuum International, 2002.

Levy, Emmanuel. *All About Oscar: The History and Politics of the Academy Awards.* New York: Continuum, 2003.

Newman, Kathy M. *Radio Active: Advertising and Consumer Activism, 1935-1947.* Berkeley: University of California Press, 2004.

Nowell-Smith, Geoffrey, ed. *Oxford History of World Cinema.* New ed. New York: Oxford University Press, 1999.

Pendergrast, Tom, and Sara Pendergrast, eds. *International Dictionary of Films and Filmmakers.* 4th ed. 4 vols. Detroit: St. James Press, 2000.

Ritchie, Michael. *Please Stand By: A Prehistory of Television.* Woodstock, N.Y.: Overlook Press, 1994.

Roman, James. *Love, Light, and a Dream: Television's Past, Present, and Future.* New York: Praeger, 1996.

Rotha, Paul. *The Film Till Now: A Survey of World Cinema.* Rev. ed. London: Spring Books, 1967.

Schatz, Thomas. *The Genius of the System: Hollywood Filmmaking in the Studio Era.* New York: Pantheon Books, 1988.

Scheuneman, Dietrich. *Expressionist Film: New Perspectives.* Rochester, N.Y.: Camden House, 2003.

Schoenbrun, David. *On and Off the Air: An Informal History of CBS News.* New York: E. P. Dutton, 1989.

Shindler, Colin. *Hollywood in Crisis: Cinema and American Society, 1929-1939.* New York: Routledge, 1996.

Smith, Anthony, ed. *Television: An International History.* 2d ed. New York: Oxford University Press, 1998.

Smulyan, Susan. *Selling Radio: The Commercialization of American Broadcasting, 1920-1934.* Washington, D.C.: Smithsonian Institution Press, 1994.

Standish, Isolde. *A New History of Japanese Cinema: A Century of Narrative Film.* New York: Continuum, 2005.

Sterling, Christopher H., and John M. Kittross. *Stay Tuned: A History of American Broadcasting.* 3d ed. Mahwah, N.J.: Lawrence Erlbaum, 2001.

Taylor, Richard. *Film Propaganda: Soviet Russia and Nazi Germany.* Rev. ed. New York: I. B. Tauris, 1998.

Udelson, Joseph H. *The Great Television Race: A History of the American Television Industry, 1925-1941.* Tuscaloosa: University of Alabama Press, 1989.

Vorontsov, Iu, and Igor Rachuk. *The Phenomenon of the Soviet Cinema.* Translated by Doris Bradbury. Moscow: Progress, 1980.

Webb, Richard C. *Tele-visionaries: The People Behind the Invention of Television.* Hoboken, N.J.: John Wiley & Sons, 2005.

RELIGION AND ETHICS

Algar, Hamid. *Wahhabism: A Critical Essay.* Oneonta, N.Y.: Islamic Publications International, 2002.

Almond, Gabriel A., R. Scott, and Emmanuel Sivan. *Strong Religion: The Rise of Fundamentalisms Around the World.* Chicago: University of Chicago Press, 2003.

Anderson, Allan. *An Introduction to Pentecostalism: Global Charismatic Christianity.* New York: Cambridge University Press, 2004.

Arjomand, Saïd Amir, ed. *Authority and Political Culture in Shīʿism.* Albany: State University of New York Press, 1988.

Armstrong, Karen. *The Battle for God.* New York: Ballantine, 2001.

Bartov, Omer, and Phyllis Mack. *In God's Name: Genocide and Religion in the Twentieth Century.* Oxford: Berghahn Books, 2001.

Carpenter, Joel A. *Revive Us Again: The Reawakening of American Fundamentalism.* New York: Oxford University Press, 1999.

Cox, Harvey. *Fire from Heaven: The Rise of Pentecostal Spirituality and the Reshaping of Religion in the Twenty-First Century.* Reading, Mass.: Perseus Books, 1995.

Davis, Nathaniel. *A Long Walk to Church: A Contemporary History of Russian Orthodoxy.* 2d ed. Boulder, Colo.: Westview Press, 2003.

DeLong-Bas, Natana J. *Wahhabi Islam: From Revival and Reform to Global Jihad.* New York: Oxford University Press, 2004.

Duffy, Eamon. *Saints and Sinners: A History of the Popes.* 2d ed. New Haven, Conn.: Yale University Press, 2002.

Greeley, Andrew. *The Catholic Imagination.* Berkeley: University of California Press, 2000.

Hawkins, Bradley. *Asian Religions: An Illustrated Introduction.* London: Longman, 2003.

Hay, Malcolm. *Thy Brother's Blood: The Roots of Christian Anti-Semitism.* New York: Hart, 1975.

Holden, Andrew. *Jehovah's Witnesses: Portrait of a Contemporary Religious Movement.* London: Routledge, 2002.

Jones, Lindsay, ed. *Encyclopedia of Religion.* 2d ed. 17 vols. Detroit: Thomson Gale, 2005.

Lawson, E. Thomas. *Religions of Africa: Traditions in Transformation.* Reprint. Prospect Heights, Ill.: Waveland Press, 1991.

Lewy, Guenther. *The Catholic Church and Nazi Germany.* New York: Da Capo Press, 2000.

Lincoln, C. Eric. *The Black Muslims in America.* 3d ed. Grand Rapids, Mich.: Wm. B. Eerdmans, 1994.

Lippman, Thomas W. *Understanding Islam: An Introduction to the Muslim World.* 2d rev. ed. New York: Penguin Books, 1995.

McBrien, Richard. *Lives of the Popes: The Pontiffs from St. Peter to John Paul II.* San Francisco: HarperSanFrancisco, 2000.

Marsden, George M. *Fundamentalism and American Culture: The Shaping of Twentieth Century Evangelicalism, 1870-1925.* New York: Oxford University Press, 1980.

Meyer, Donald. *The Positive Thinkers: Popular Religious Psychology from Mary Baker Eddy to Norman Vincent Peale and Ronald Reagan.* Rev. ed. Middletown, Conn.: Wesleyan University Press, 1988.

Porterfield, Amanda. *The Transformation of American Religion: The Story of a Late Twentieth-Century Awakening.* New York: Oxford University Press, 2001.

Pospielovsky, Dimitry. *The Orthodox Church in the History of Russia.* Crestwood, N.Y.: St. Vladimir's Seminary Press, 1998.

Reher, Margaret Mary. *Catholic Intellectual Life in America: A Historical Study of Persons and Movements.* New York: Macmillan, 1989.

Sánchez, José M. *Pius XII and the Holocaust: Understanding the Controversy.* Washington, D.C.: Catholic University of America, 2002.

_____. *The Spanish Civil War as a Religious Tragedy.* Notre Dame, Ind.: University of Notre Dame Press, 1985.

Sernett, Milton C. *Bound for the Promised Land: African American Religion and the Great Migration.* Durham, N.C.: Duke University Press, 1997.

Smith, Huston. *The World's Religions.* Rev. ed. San Francisco: HarperSanFrancisco, 1991.

Synan, Vinson. *The Holiness-Pentecostal Tradition:*

Charismatic Movements in the Twentieth Century. Rev. ed. Grand Rapids, Mich.: Wm. B. Eerdmans, 1997.

Timasheff, Nicholas S. *Religion in Soviet Russia, 1917-1942.* 1942. Reprint. Westport, Conn.: Greenwood Press, 1980.

Walker, Dennis. *Islam and the Search for African American Nationhood: Elijah Muhammad, Louis Farrakhan, and the Nation of Islam.* Atlanta, Ga.: Clarity Press, 2005.

Young, Glennys. *Power and the Sacred in Revolutionary Russia: Religious Activists in the Village.* University Park: Pennsylvania State University Press, 1997.

SCIENCE

Asimov, Isaac. *Asimov's Biographical Encyclopedia of Science and Technology.* 2d rev. ed. Garden City, N.Y.: Doubleday, 1982.

Ball, Philip. *The Ingredients: A Guided Tour of the Elements.* New York: Oxford University Press, 2003.

Barrow, John D., and Joseph Silk. *The Left Hand of Creation: The Origin and Evolution of the Expanding Universe.* 1983. Reprint. New York: Oxford University Press, 1994.

Bowler, Peter J. *Evolution: The History of an Idea.* 3d ed. Berkeley: University of California Press, 2003.

Carlson, Elof Axel. *Mendel's Legacy: The Origin of Classical Genetics.* Cold Spring Harbor, N.Y.: Cold Spring Harbor Laboratory Press, 2004.

Cathcart, Brian. *The Fly in the Cathedral: How a Group of Cambridge Scientists Won the International Race to Split the Atom.* New York: Farrar, Straus and Giroux, 2005.

Chown, Marcus. *The Magic Furnace: The Search for the Origins of Atoms.* New York: Oxford University Press, 2001.

Christie, Maureen. *The Ozone Layer: A Philosophy of Science Perspective.* New York: Cambridge University Press, 2001.

Clancey, Gregory. *Earthquake Nation: The Cultural Politics of Japanese Seismicity, 1868-1930.* Berkeley: University of California Press, 2006.

Clark, David H., and Matthew D. H. Clark. *Measuring the Cosmos: How Scientists Discovered the Dimensions of the Universe.* New Brunswick, N.J.: Rutgers University Press, 2004.

Crease, Robert P., and Charles C. Mann. *The Second Creation: Makers of the Revolution in Twentieth-Century Physics.* Rev. ed. New Brunswick, N.J.: Rutgers University Press, 1996.

Cropper, William H. *Great Physicists: The Life and Times of Leading Physicists from Galileo to Hawking.* New York: Oxford University Press, 2001.

Einstein, Albert. *Relativity: The Special and General Theory.* Translated by Robert W. Lawson. Reprint. New York: Routledge, 2001.

Ferris, Timothy. *The Red Limit: The Search for the Edge of the Universe.* Rev. ed. New York: HarperPerennial, 2002.

Feynman, Richard P. *The Feynman Lectures on Physics.* Rev. ed. 3 vols. Reading, Mass.: Addison-Wesley, 2005.

Foot, Robert. *Shadowlands: Quest for Mirror Matter in the Universe.* Parkland, Fla.: Universal, 2002.

Ford, Kenneth W. *The Quantum World: Quantum Physics for Everyone.* Cambridge, Mass.: Harvard University Press, 2004.

Gribbin, John. *In Search of the Big Bang: The Life and Death of the Universe.* Rev. ed. New York: Penguin Books, 1998.

Harrison, Edward R. *Masks of the Universe: Changing Ideas on the Nature of the Cosmos.* 2d ed. New York: Cambridge University Press, 2003.

Hawking, Stephen A. *A Brief History of Time.* 10th anniversary ed. New York: Bantam Books, 1996.

Heilbron, J. L., and Robert W. Seidel. *Lawrence and His Laboratory: A History of Lawrence Berkeley Laboratory.* Berkeley: University of California Press, 1989.

Heisenberg, Werner. *Physics and Philosophy: The Revolution in Modern Science.* 1958. Reprint. Amherst, N.Y.: Prometheus Books, 1999.

Kevles, Daniel J. *The Physicists: The History of a Scientific Community in Modern America.* 1977. Reprint. Cambridge, Mass.: Harvard University Press, 2005.

Kohler, Robert E. *Partners in Science: Foundations and Natural Scientists, 1900-1945.* Chicago: University of Chicago Press, 1991.

Krebs, Robert E. *The History and Use of Our Earth's Chemical Elements.* 2d ed. Westport, Conn.: Greenwood Press, 2006.

Laidler, Keith J. *To Light Such a Candle: Chapters in the History of Science and Technology.* New York: Oxford University Press, 2005.

Piel, Gerard. *The Age of Science: What Scientists Learned in the Twentieth Century.* New York: Basic Books, 2001.

Polkinghorne, John. *Quantum Theory: A Very Short Introduction.* New York: Oxford University Press, 2002.

Rowan-Robinson, Michael. *Cosmology.* 4th ed. New York: Oxford University Press, 2004.

Sapp, Jan. *Genesis: The Evolution of Biology.* New York: Oxford University Press, 2003.

Schneider, Stephen H., and Penelope J. J. Boston, eds. *Scientists Debate Gaia: The Next Century.* Cambridge, Mass.: MIT Press, 2004.

Silk, Joseph. *The Big Bang.* 3d ed. New York: W. H. Freeman, 2000.

_____. *On the Shores of the Unknown: A Short History of the Universe.* New York: Cambridge University Press, 2005.

Stuewer, Roger H. *The Compton Effect: Turning Point in Physics.* New York: Science History Publications, 1975.

Susskind, Leonard, and James Lindesay. *An Introduction to Black Holes, Information, and the String Theory Revolution: The Holographic Universe.* Hackensack, N.J.: World Scientific, 2004.

Todes, Daniel P. *Pavlov's Physiology Factory: Experiment, Interpretation, Laboratory Enterprise.* Baltimore: The Johns Hopkins University Press, 2001.

Trigg, George L. *Landmark Experiments in Twentieth Century Physics.* 1975. Reprint. Mineola, N.Y.: Dover, 1995.

Verschuur, Gerrit L. *Interstellar Matters: Essays on Curiosity and Astronomical Discovery.* New York: Springer-Verlag, 1989.

Vucinich, Alexander S. *Science in Russian Culture, 1861-1917.* Stanford, Calif.: Stanford University Press, 1970.

Watson, Fred. *Stargazer: The Life and Times of the Telescope.* New York: Da Capo Press, 2005.

Wilson, Edward O. *The Diversity of Life.* Rev. ed. Cambridge, Mass.: Belknap Press, 1999.

Zirker, J. B. *An Acre of Glass: A History and Forecast of the Telescope.* Baltimore: The Johns Hopkins University Press, 2005.

SOCIAL AND CULTURAL HISTORY

Allen, Frederick Lewis. *Only Yesterday: An Informal History of the 1920's.* 1931. Reprint. New York: HarperCollins, 2000.

_____. *Since Yesterday: The Nineteen-Thirties in America, September 3, 1929-September 3, 1939.* 1940. Reprint. New York: HarperPerennial, 1986.

Axinn, June, and Mark J. Stern. *Social Welfare: A History of the American Response to Need.* 6th ed. Newton, Mass.: Allyn & Bacon, 2004.

Billington, James H. *The Icon and the Axe: An Interpretive History of Russian Culture.* New York: Alfred A. Knopf, 1966.

Bowlby, Rachel. *Carried Away: The Invention of Modern Shopping.* New York: Columbia University Press, 2001.

Bullough, Vern L., and Bonnie L. Bullough. *Women and Prostitution: A Social History.* Buffalo, N.Y.: Prometheus Books, 1987.

Burns, Rob, ed. *German Cultural Studies: An Introduction.* New York: Oxford University Press, 1995.

Carmichael, Joel. *A Cultural History of Russia.* New York: Weybright and Talley, 1968.

Cole, G. D. H., and Raymond Postgate. *The British People, 1746-1946.* New York: Barnes & Noble, 1961.

Dangerfield, George. *The Strange Death of Liberal England, 1910-1914.* 1935. Reprint. Stanford, Calif.: Stanford University Press, 1997.

Davidson, Janet F., and Michael S. Sweeney. *On the Move: Transportation and the American Story.* Washington, D.C.: National Geographic Society, 2003.

Degler, Carl N. *Out of Our Past: The Forces That Shaped Modern America.* 3d ed. New York: Harper & Row, 1984.

D'Emilio, John, and Estelle B. Freedman. *Intimate Matters: A History of Sexuality in America.* 2d ed. Chicago: University of Chicago Press, 1998.

Egan, Timothy. *The Worst Hard Time: The Untold Story of Those Who Survived the Great American Dust Bowl.* Boston: Houghton Mifflin, 2006.

Fitzpatrick, John, ed. *Encyclopedia of American Social History.* 3 vols. New York: Charles Scribner's Sons, 1993.

Gavron, Daniel. *The Kibbutz.* Boston: Brown & Littlefield, 2000.

Gordon, Linda. *Pitied but Not Entitled: Single Mothers and the History of Welfare, 1890-1935.* New York: Free Press, 1994.

Goulart, Ron. *The Assault on Childhood.* London: Gollancz, 1970.

Graves, Robert, and Alan Hodge. *The Long Week-End: A Social History of Great Britain, 1918-1939.* 1940. Reprint. New York: W. W. Norton, 2001.

Gregory, James N. *American Exodus: The Dust Bowl Migration and Okie Culture in California.* New York: Oxford University Press, 1989.

Hau, Michael. *The Cult of Health and Beauty in Germany: A Social History, 1890-1930.* Chicago: University of Chicago Press, 2003.

Horsfield, Margaret. *Biting the Dust: The Joys of Housework.* New York: St. Martin's Press, 1998.

Hurt, R. Douglas. *The Dust Bowl: An Agricultural and Social History.* Chicago: Nelson Hall, 1981.

Katz, Michael B. *In the Shadow of the Poorhouse: A Social History of Welfare in America*. Rev. ed. New York: Basic Books, 1996.

Kyvig, David E. *Daily Life in the United States, 1920-1940: How Americans Lived During the Roaring Twenties and the Great Depression*. Chicago: Ivan R. Dee, 2004.

Lange, Dorothea, and Paul Taylor. *An American Exodus: A Record of Human Erosion*. New York: Reynal & Hitchcock, 1939.

Leach, William R. *Land of Desire: Merchants, Power, and the Rise of a New American Culture*. New York: Vintage, 1994.

Lemann, Nicholas. *The Promised Land: The Great Black Migration and How It Changed America*. New York: Alfred A. Knopf, 1991.

Lewis, David Levering. *When Harlem Was in Vogue*. 1981. Reprint. New York: Penguin Books, 1997.

Lincoln, W. Bruce. *In War's Dark Shadow: The Russians Before the Great War*. 1984. Reprint. De Kalb: Northern Illinois University Press, 2003.

McKibbin, Ross. *Classes and Culture: England, 1918-1951*. New York: Oxford University Press, 1998.

Miller, Nathan. *New World Coming: The 1920's and the Making of Modern America*. New York: Scribner, 2003.

Parrish, Michael. *Anxious Decades: America in Prosperity and Depression, 1920-1941*. New York: W. W. Norton, 1992.

Pugh, Martin. *State and Society: A Social and Political History of Britain, 1870-1997*. 2d ed. London: Arnold, 2000.

Robertson, Una A. *The Illustrated History of the Housewife, 1650-1950*. New York: Palgrave Macmillan, 1999.

Root, Waverly, and Richard de Rochemont. *Eating in America: A History*. New York: Ecco Press, 1995.

Rubin, Joan Shelley. *The Making of Middlebrow Culture*. Chapel Hill: University of North Carolina Press, 1992.

Sivulka, Juliann. *Soap, Sex, and Cigarettes: A Cultural History of American Advertising*. Belmont, Calif.: Wadsworth, 1997.

Sklar, Robert. *Movie-Made America: A Cultural History of American Movies*. Rev. ed. New York: Vintage Books, 1994.

Stearns, Peter W., ed. *Encyclopedia of European Social History, from 1350 to 2000*. 6 vols. New York: Charles Scribner's Sons, 2001.

Stevens, Jay. *Storming Heaven: LSD and the American Dream*. New York: Perennial Library, 1987.

Ward, Colin. *Cotters and Squatters: The Hidden History of Housing*. Nottingham, England: Five Leaves, 2002.

SOCIOLOGY, PSYCHOLOGY, AND THE SOCIAL SCIENCES (*see also* EDUCATION)

Albrow, Martin. *Max Weber's Construction of Social Theory*. New York: St. Martin's Press, 1990.

Carnegie, Dale. *How to Win Friends and Influence People*. Rev. ed. New York: Simon & Schuster, 1981.

Craighead, W. Edward, and Charles B. Nemeroff, eds. *The Corsini Encyclopedia of Psychological and Behavioral Science*. 3d ed. 4 vols. New York: John Wiley and Sons, 2001.

Ellenberger, Henri F. *The Discovery of the Unconscious: The History and Evolution of Dynamic Psychology*. New York: Basic Books, 1970.

Giddens, Anthony. *Capitalism and Modern Social Theory: An Analysis of the Writings of Marx, Durkheim, and Max Weber*. Cambridge, England: Cambridge University Press, 1973.

James, William. *Essays in Psychology*. Cambridge, Mass.: Harvard University Press, 1983.

Jones, Ernest. *The Life and Work of Sigmund Freud*. 3 vols. New York: Basic Books, 1953-1957.

Jung, Carl Gustav. *Memories, Dreams, Reflections*. 1961. Reprint. New York: Vintage Books, 1989.

_____. *Modern Man in Search of a Soul*. 1933. Reprint. Translated by W. S. Dell and Cary F. Baynes. London: Routledge, 2001.

_____. *Psychology of the Unconscious*. 1916. Reprint. Princeton, N.J.: Princeton University Press, 1991.

Pareto, Vilfredo. *The Rise and Fall of the Elites: An Application of Theoretical Sociology*. New Brunswick, N.J.: Transaction, 1991.

Ritzer, George, and Douglas J. Goodman. *Sociological Theory*. 6th ed. New York: McGraw-Hill, 2003.

Shamdasani, Sonu. *Jung and the Making of Modern Psychology: The Dream of a Science*. New York: Cambridge University Press, 2003.

Wallace, Ruth A., and Alison Wolf. *Contemporary Sociological Theory: Continuing the Classical Tradition*. 6th ed. Upper Saddle River, N.J.: Prentice Hall, 2005.

SPORT AND LEISURE

Alexander, Charles. *Our Game: An American Baseball History*. New York: Henry Holt, 1991.

Bachrach, Susan D. *The Nazi Olympics: Berlin, 1936*. Boston: Little, Brown, 2000.

Baker, William J. *Sports in the Western World*. Urbana: University of Illinois Press, 1988.

Barrett, John. *Wimbledon: The Official History of the Championships*. New York: HarperCollins Willow, 2001.

The Baseball Chronicle: Year-by-Year History of Major League Baseball. Lincolnwood, Ill.: Publications International, 2003.

Carroll, Bob, Michael Gershman, David Neft, and John Thorn, eds. *Total Football II: The Official Encyclopedia of the National Football League*. New York: HarperCollins, 1999.

Colwin, Cecil M. *Breakthrough Swimming*. Champaign, Ill.: Human Kinetics, 2002.

Dauncey, Hugh, and Geoff Hare, eds. *The Tour de France, 1903-2003: A Century of Sporting Structures, Meanings, and Values*. London: Frank Cass, 2003.

Falla, Jack. *NCAA: The Voice of College Sports*. Mission, Kans.: National Collegiate Athletic Association, 1981.

Fife, Graeme. *Tour de France: The History, the Legend, the Riders*. Edinburgh, Scotland: Mainstream, 2005.

Frost, Mark. *The Grand Slam: Bobby Jones, America, and the Story of Golf*. New York: Hyperion, 2004.

Garrett, Richard. *The Motor Racing Story*. London: Stanley Paul, 1969.

Gillette, Gary, and Pete Palmer. *The 2006 ESPN Baseball Encyclopedia*. New York: Sterling, 2006.

Gillmeister, Heiner. *Tennis: A Cultural History*. Washington Square, N.Y. : New York University Press, 1998.

Greenspan, Bud. *Frozen in Time: The Greatest Moments at the Winter Olympics*. Toronto: Stoddart, 1997.

Hart-Davis, Duff. *Hitler's Games: The 1936 Olympics*. New York: Harper & Row, 1986.

Hietala, Thomas R. *The Fight of the Century: Jack Johnson, Joe Louis, and the Struggle for Racial Equality*. New York: M. E. Sharpe, 2002.

Hilton, Christopher. *Grand Prix Century: The First One Hundred Years of the World's Most Glamorous and Dangerous Sport*. Yesvie, England: Haynes, 2006.

Hodges, David. *Classic Racing Cars: Grand Prix and Indy*. London: Regency House, 1995.

Hutchinson, Roger. *Empire Games: The British Invention of Twentieth-Century Sport*. London: Mainstream Publising, 1997.

James, Bill. *The Bill James Historical Baseball Abstract*. New York: Villard Books, 1988.

Krüger, Arnd, and William Murray, eds. *The Nazi Olympics: Sport, Politics, and Appeasement in the 1930's*. Urbana: University of Illinois Press, 2003.

Lazenby, Roland. *The Pictorial History of Football*. San Diego, Calif.: Thunder Bay Press, 2000.

Levinson, David, and Karen Christensen, eds. *Encyclopedia of World Sport, from Ancient Times to the Present*. Great Barrington, Mass.: Berkshire Publishing Group, 2005.

Luby, Mort. *The History of Bowling*. Chicago: Luby, 1983.

MacCambridge, Michael. *America's Game: The Epic Story of How Pro Football Captured a Nation*. New York: Random House, 2004.

_____, ed. *ESPN College Football Encyclopedia: The Complete History of the Game*. New York: ESPN Books, 2005.

Martin, James A., and Thomas F. Saal. *American Auto Racing: The Milestones and Personalities of a Century of Speed*. New York: McFarland, 2004.

Olympic Games: Athens 1896-Athens 2004. New York: Dorling Kindersley, 2004.

Ours, Robert M. *Bowl Games: College Football's Greatest Tradition*. Yardley, Pa.: Westholme, 2004.

Rader, Benjamin G. *American Sports: From the Age of Folk Games to the Age of Televised Sports*. 2d ed. Englewood Cliffs, N.J.: Prentice Hall, 1990.

Smith, Lissa, ed. *Nike Is a Goddess: The History of Women in Sports*. New York: Atlantic Monthly Press, 1998.

Tygiel, Jules. *Past Time: Baseball as History*. New York: Oxford University Press, 2001.

Wallechinsky, David. *The Complete Book of the Summer Olympics*. Toronto: SportClassic Books, 2006.

Woodland, Les. *The Unknown Tour de France: The Many Faces of the World's Biggest Bicycle Race*. San Francisco: Van der Plas, 2000.

Woolum, Janet. *Outstanding Women Athletes: Who They Are and How They Influenced Sports in America*. 2d ed. Phoenix, Ariz.: Oryx Press, 1998.

Wukovits, John. *The Encyclopedia of the Winter Olympics*. Princeton, N.J.: Franklin Watts, 2002.

TECHNOLOGY AND COMMUNICATIONS
(*see also* AVIATION AND TRANSPORTATION, SCIENCE)

Ashurst, F. Gareth. *Pioneers of Computing*. London: Frederick Muller, 1983.

Asimov, Isaac. *Eyes on the Universe: A History of the Telescope*. Boston: Houghton Mifflin, 1975.

Bowers, Brian. *Lengthening the Day: A History of Lighting Technology*. New York: Oxford University Press, 1998.

Brinkley, Douglas G. *Wheels for the World: Henry Ford, His Company, and a Century of Progress.* New York: Penguin Books, 2004.

Brooks, John. *Telephone: The First Hundred Years.* New York: Harper & Row, 1976.

Brown, L. *A Radar History of World War II: Technical and Military Imperatives.* Boca Raton, Fla.: Taylor & Francis, 1999.

Buderi, Robert. *The Invention That Changed the World: How a Small Group of Radar Pioneers Won the Second World War and Launched a Technical Revolution.* Carmichael, Calif.: Touchstone Books, 1998.

Burns, Russell W., ed. *Radar Development to 1945.* London: Peregrinus, 1988.

Campbell-Kelly, Martin, and William Aspray. *Computer: A History of the Information Machine.* 2d ed. Boulder, Colo.: Westview Press, 2004.

Ceruzzi, Paul E. *A History of Modern Computing.* 2d ed. Cambridge, Mass.: MIT Press, 2003.

DeFleur, Melvin L., and Everette E. Dennis. *Understanding Mass Communication.* 7th ed. Boston: Houghton Mifflin, 2001.

Dunlap, Orrin E., Jr. *Communications in Space: From Marconi to Man on the Moon.* New York: Harper & Row, 1970.

Du Vall, Nell. *Domestic Technology: A Chronology of Developments.* Boston: G. K. Hall, 1988.

Fagen, M. D., ed. *A History of Engineering and Science in the Bell System: The Early Years, 1875-1925.* Murray Hill, N.J.: Bell Telephone Laboratories, 1975.

Fang, Irving. *A History of Mass Communication: Six Information Revolutions.* Burlington, Mass.: Focal Press, 1997.

Freiman, Fran Locher, and Neil Schlager. *Failed Technology: True Stories of Technological Disasters.* New York: Gale Research International, 1995.

Gelatt, Roland. *The Fabulous Phonograph, 1877-1977.* 2d rev. ed. New York: Macmillan, 1977.

Head, Sydney W., et al. *Broadcasting in America: A Survey of Electronic Media.* 9th ed. Boston: Houghton Mifflin, 2000.

Hong, Sungook. *Wireless: From Marconi's Black-Box to the Audion.* Cambridge, Mass.: MIT Press, 2001.

Katz, Mark. *Capturing Sound: How Technology Has Changed Music.* Berkeley: University of California Press, 2004.

McMaster, Susan E. *The Telecommunications Industry.* Westport, Conn.: Greenwood Press, 2002.

Marcus, Alan I., and Howard P. Segal. *Technology in America: A Brief History.* 2d ed. Belmont, Calif.: Wadsworth, 1998.

Millard, Andre. *America on Record: A History of Recorded Sound.* New York: Cambridge University Press, 1995.

Newhouse, Elizabeth L., ed. *Inventors and Discoverers: Changing Our World.* Washington, D.C.: National Geographic Society, 2000.

Reich, Leonard S. *The Making of American Industrial Research: Science and Business at GE and Bell, 1876-1926.* 1985. Reprint. New York: Cambridge University Press, 2002.

Williams, Trevor I. *A Short History of Twentieth-Century Technology.* New York: Oxford University Press, 1982.

Winston, Brian. *Media Technology and Society: A History—From the Telegraph to the Internet.* New York: Routledge, 1998.

WORLD WAR I

Albertini, Luigi. *The Origins of the War of 1914.* Updated ed. Vol. 1. Translated by Isabella M. Massey. New York: Enigma Books, 2005.

Barker, A. J. *The Neglected War: Mesopotamia, 1914-1918.* London: Faber, 1967.

Braim, Paul F. *The Test of Battle: The American Expeditionary Forces in the Meuse-Argonne Campaign.* 2d ed. Shippensburg, Pa.: White Mane, 1998.

Butler, Daniel Allen. *The Lusitania: The Life, Loss, and Legacy of an Ocean Legend.* Mechanicsburg, Pa.: Stackpole Books, 2000.

Carver, Michael. *The National Army Museum Book of the Turkish Front, 1914-1918: The Campaigns of Gallipoli, Mesopotamia, and Palestine.* London: Sidgwick & Jackson, 2003.

Cooke, James J. *The Rainbow Division in the Great War, 1917-1919.* Westport, Conn.: Praeger, 1994.

De Groot, Gerard J. *The First World War.* New York: Palgrave, 2001.

Erickson, Edward J. *Ordered to Die: A History of the Ottoman Army in the First World War.* Westport, Conn.: Greenwood, 2001.

Feldman, Gerald D. *Army, Industry, and Labor in Germany, 1914-1918.* Rev. ed. Princeton, N.J.: Princeton University Press, 1992.

Fischer, Fritz. *Germany's Aims in the First World War.* London: W. W. Norton, 1967.

Fussell, Paul. *The Great War and Modern Memory.* 25th anniversary ed. New York: Oxford University Press, 2000.

Gibson, R. H., and Maurice Prendergast. *The German Submarine War, 1914-1918*. 1931. Reprint. Annapolis, Md.: Naval Institute Press, 2003.

Gilbert, Martin. *First World War*. New York: HarperCollins, 1995.

Groom, Winston. *A Storm in Flanders: The Ypres Salient, 1914-1918—Tragedy and Triumph on the Western Front*. New York: Grove Press, 2002.

Haber, L. F. *The Poisonous Cloud: Chemical Warfare in the First World War*. Oxford, England: Clarendon Press, 1986.

Halpern, Paul. *A Naval History of World War I*. Annapolis, Md.: Naval Institute Press, 1994.

Kennedy, David M. *Over Here: The First World War and American Society*. 25th anniversary ed. New York: Oxford University Press, 2004.

Kocka, Jürgen. *Facing Total War: German Society, 1914-1918*. Translated by Barbara Weinberger. Cambridge, Mass.: Harvard University Press, 1984.

Lawson, Eric, and Jane Lawson. *The First Air Campaign, August 1914-November 1918*. 1996. Reprint. New York: Da Capo Press, 2002.

Lincoln, W. Bruce. *Passage Through Armageddon: The Russians in War and Revolution*. New York: Simon & Schuster, 1986.

Mosier, John. *The Myth of the Great War: A New Military History of World War I*. New York: HarperCollins, 2001.

Richter, Donald C. *Chemical Soldiers: British Gas Warfare in World War I*. Lawrence: University Press of Kansas, 1992.

Schmitt, Bernadotte E. *Triple Alliance and Triple Entente*. New York: Howard Fertig, 1971.

Steiner, Zara S., and Keith Neilson. *Britain and the Origins of the First World War*. 2d ed. New York: Palgrave Macmillan, 2003.

Stevenson, David. *The First World War and International Politics*. Oxford, England: Oxford University Press, 1988.

Strachan, Hew, ed. *World War I: A History*. New York: Oxford University Press, 1999.

Tuchman, Barbara W. *The Guns of August*. 1962. Reprint. New York: Presidio Press, 1994.

Tucker, Spencer C., ed. *Encyclopedia of World War I: A Political, Social, and Military History*. 5 vols. Santa Barbara, Calif.: ABC-Clio, 2005.

Vincent, C. Paul. *The Politics of Hunger: The Allied Blockade of Germany, 1915-1919*. Athens: Ohio University Press, 1985.

Winter, J. M. *The Experience of World War I*. New York: Oxford University Press, 1989.

Winter, Jay, and Blaine Badgett. *The Great War and the Shaping of the Twentieth Century*. New York: Penguin Books, 1996.

WORLD WAR II

Blet, Pierre. *Pius XII and World War II: According to the Archives of the Vatican*. Translated by Lawrence J. Johnson. New York: Paulist Press, 1999.

Chapman, Guy. *Why France Fell: The Defeat of the French Army in 1940*. New York: Henry Holt, 1968.

Diamond, Hanna, and Simon Kitson, eds. *Vichy, Resistance, Liberation: New Perspectives on Wartime France*. New York: Berg, 2005.

Fischer, Bernd. *Albania at War, 1939-1945*. West Lafayette, Ind.: Purdue University Press, 1999.

Footitt, Hilary. *War and Liberation in France: Living with the Liberators*. New York: Palgrave Macmillan, 2004.

Garliński, Jozef. *Poland in the Second World War*. New York: Hippocrene Books, 1985.

Gilbert, Adrian. *Germany's Lightning War: The Campaigns of World War II*. Newton Abbot, England: David and Charles, 2000.

Goda, Norman J. W. *Tomorrow the World: Hitler, Northwest Africa, and the Path Toward America*. College Station: Texas A&M University Press, 1998.

Gross, Jan. *Polish Society Under German Occupation: The General Government, 1939-1944*. Princeton, N.J.: Princeton University Press, 1979.

Harries, Meirion, and Susie Harries. *Soldiers of the Sun: The Rise and Fall of the Imperial Japanese Army*. New York: Random House, 1991.

Horne, Alistair. *To Lose a Battle: France, 1940*. Rev. ed. Boston: Little, Brown, 1990.

Hoyt, Edwin P. *Japan's War: The Great Pacific Conflict*. New York: Da Capo Press, 1986.

Ienaga, Saburo. *The Pacific War, 1931-1945: A Critical Perspective of Japan's Role in World War II*. New York: Pantheon Books, 1978.

Jakobson, Max. *Finland Survived: An Account of the Finnish-Soviet Winter War, 1939-1940*. Helsinki, Finland: Otava, 1961.

Kaufmann, J. E., and H. W. Kaufmann. *Fortress France: The Maginot Line and French Defenses in World War II*. Westport, Conn.: Praeger Security International, 2006.

Koistinen, Paul A. C. *Arsenal of World War II: The Polit-*

ical Economy of American Warfare, 1940-1945. Lawrence: University Press of Kansas, 2004.

Krakowski, Shmuel. *The War of the Damned: Jewish Armed Resistance in Poland, 1942-1944*. New York: Holmes & Meier, 1984.

Kynoch, Joseph. *Norway, 1940: The Forgotten Fiasco*. Shrewsbury, Shropshire, England: Airlife, 2002.

Latimer, Jon. *Operation Compass, 1940: Wavell's Whirlwind Offensive*. Westport, Conn.: Praeger, 2004.

Lebra, Joyce C. *Japan's Greater East Asia Co-prosperity Sphere in World War II*. New York: Oxford University Press, 1975.

Moorehead, Alan. *Desert War*. 1941. Reprint. London: Penguin Books, 2001.

Moulton, J. L. *The Norwegian Campaign of 1940: A Study of Warfare in Three Dimensions*. London: Eyre and Spottiswode, 1966.

Robinson, Derek. *Invasion, 1940: The Truth About the Battle of Britain and What Stopped Hitler*. New York: Carroll & Graf, 2005.

Stacey, C. P. *Arms, Men, and Governments: The War Policies of Canada, 1939-1945*. Ottawa: Queen's Printers, 1970.

Taylor, A. J. P. *The Origins of the Second World War*. 1961. Reprint. New York: Touchstone, 1996.

Toland, John. *The Rising Sun: The Decline and Fall of the Japanese Empire, 1936-1945*. New York: Random House, 1970.

Trotter, William R. *A Frozen Hell: The Russo-Finnish Winter War of 1939-1940*. Chapel Hill, N.C.: Algonquin Books, 2000.

Tucker, Spencer C., ed. *Encyclopedia of World War II: A Political, Social, and Military History*. 5 vols. Santa Barbara, Calif.: ABC-Clio, 2005.

Upton, Anthony F. *Finland, 1939-1940*. Newark: University of Delaware Press, 1974.

U.S. Civilian Production Administration. *Industrial Mobilization for War: History of the War Production Board and Predecessory Agencies, 1940-1945*. Washington, D.C.: Government Printing Office, 1947.

Van Dyke, Carl. *The Soviet Invasion of Finland, 1939-1940*. Portland, Oreg.: F. Cass, 2001.

Walker, Ian J. *Iron Hulls, Iron Hearts: Mussolini's Elite Armored Divisions in North Africa*. Marlborough, Wiltshire, England: Crowood Press, 2003.

Weinberg, Gerald L. *A World at Arms: A Global History of World War II*. New York: Cambridge University Press, 1994.

Wilson, Dick. *When Tigers Fight: The Story of the Sino-Japanese War, 1937-1945*. New York: Viking Press, 1982.

Young, Louise. *Japan's Total Empire: Manchuria and the Culture of Wartime Imperialism*. Berkeley: University of California Press, 1998.

Electronic Resources

Web Sites

The sites listed below were visited by the editors of Salem Press in 2006. Because URLs frequently change or are moved, the accuracy of these addresses cannot be guaranteed; however, long-standing sites, such as those of university departments, national organizations, and government agencies, generally maintain links when sites move or upgrade their offerings.

General

The Long Nineteenth Century, VII: The End of European Hegemony

http://www.fordham.edu/halsall/mod/
    modsbook4.html#hegend

The highly regarded Internet Modern History Sourcebook includes an extensive collection of primary source materials and Web links about the early twentieth century. This part of the site includes a section titled "World War I: Tragic War and Futile Peace," containing information about the causes, battles, key people, and aftermath of World War I. Information is also available about the Russian Revolution, including links to Internet archives of the works of Vladimir Ilich Lenin, Leon Trotsky, and Joseph Stalin, as well as information about the revolutions of 1905 and 1917 and Bolshevik rule before and during Stalin's leadership. In addition, the site includes documents about life in the United States, Europe, and Latin America between the world wars, including information about the Great Depression.

WebChron: Web Chronology Project Then Again

http://www.thenagain.info/WebChron/index.html

The Web Chronology Project was created by the History Department at North Park University in Chicago. It is now administered by David Koeller, the project's originator, as part of his Then Again Web site. The site contains a series of hyperlinked time lines tracing developments in the United States, Africa south of the Sahara, the Middle East and west Asia, India and southern Asia, China and East Asia, Russia and Eastern Europe, and Western and Central Europe. Other chronologies provide information about Islam, Christianity, and Judaism and about art, music, literature, and speculative thought in the Western tradition.

World History @fsmitha.com: 1901 to World War II

http://www.fsmitha.com/h2/index.html

Historian Frank Smitha has created this collection of essays, maps, and time lines providing a broad range of historical information. This page features essays about significant events that occurred between 1901 and the end of World War II, including conditions in the Middle East, the Mexican Revolution, politics and economic conditions in Latin America, world order in the 1920's, and the United States in the 1920's.

Africa

The Story of Africa: Between World Wars (1914-1945)

http://www.bbc.co.uk/worldservice/africa/features/
    storyofafrica/index_section13.shtml

This is a section from The Story of Africa, a Web site that accompanied a series of radio programs of the same name produced by the British Broadcasting Corporation (BBC). The section contains information about Africa's role in World War I; the aftermath of the war; early nationalist movements in Sudan, Nigeria, South Africa, and other African countries; and the rise of the pan-African movement. Site users can also listen to the radio programs in the series as well as other relevant information. A bibliography and a list of Web links are included for further research.

Art and Architecture

Art History Resources on the Web, Part 13: Twentieth Century Art

http://witcombe.sbc.edu/ARTH20thcentury.html

Chris Witcombe, a professor of art history at Sweet Briar College in Virginia, compiled this unusually extensive list of Web sites about art history. This page of the site deals specifically with twentieth century painting, sculpture, and architecture, featuring hundreds of links to information about Art Deco, Art Nouveau, Dadaism, Fauvism, and other art movements, as well as information about individual artists, sculptors, and architects of the early twentieth century, including Paul Klee, Edward Hooper, Gustav Klimt, Henri Matisse, Pablo Picasso, Georgia O'Keeffe, Diego Rivera, Frida Kahlo, and many others.

Art of the First World War
http://www.art-ww1.com/gb/visite.html

This site features a collection of one hundred paintings organized in 1998 to commemorate the eightieth anniversary of the end of World War I. Included are essays about the war and the artists who represented it as well as paintings by Marc Chagall, Otto Dix, George Grosz, Oskar Kokoschka, Fernand Léger, Pablo Picasso, John Singer Sargent, and others. The paintings can be viewed in both thumbnail and enlarged formats.

A Digital Archive of Architecture: Twentieth Century Architecture
http://www.bc.edu/bc_org/avp/cas/fnart/arch/
20arch_europe.html

A Digital Archive of American Architecture: Twentieth Century Architecture
http://www.bc.edu/bc_org/avp/cas/fnart/fa267/
fa267_20.html

These two Web sites, which provide an overview of architecture in the twentieth century, were designed by Jeffery Howe, a professor at Boston College. The first site features photographs of buildings designed by Frank Lloyd Wright and Le Corbusier; the second contains photographs of public and commercial buildings, homes, churches, universities, and skyscrapers constructed in the United States in two periods: 1900-1925 and 1925-1945. The photographs can be viewed in both thumbnail and enlarged formats.

Frank Lloyd Wright: Designs for an American Landscape
http://www.loc.gov/exhibits/flw

This is a digitized version of a Library of Congress exhibition of the work of architect Frank Lloyd Wright. The site features designs that Wright developed from 1922 to 1932 for five projects that used advanced building techniques and innovative geometric patterns. The projects include a summer colony of homes at Lake Tahoe, a resort in the Arizona desert, and the Doheny Ranch in Beverly Hills, California.

Metropolitan Museum of Art: Timeline of Art History
http://www.metmuseum.org/toah/splash.htm

The museum's Web site describes itself as a "chronological, geographical, and thematic exploration of the history of art from around the world, as illustrated especially by the Metropolitan Museum of Art's collection." The time line for the period from 1900 to the present contains works of art, maps, and chronologies organized by regions of the world, including North America, South America, Europe, Central America and Mexico, Africa, Oceania, and several areas of Asia. In addition to the time lines, the site offers a broad range of information accessible through alphabetical lists of artists and subjects as well as through a list of special themes in specific nations and geographic areas of the world.

On-Line Picasso Project
http://csdll.cs.tamu.edu:8080/picasso

This enormous catalog of 9,681 works by Pablo Picasso has been compiled by Enrique Mallen, professor of Hispanic studies at A&M University, and other university faculty and staff. The site features a year-by-year listing of the events in Picasso's life and a similar chronology of his works. The paintings and other works can be viewed in thumbnail and enlarged formats. The site also provides a list of museums, galleries, and other places in which Picasso's work is exhibited and an archive of more than 3,300 articles about Picasso written in English, Spanish, German, and other languages.

ASIA

China in the Twentieth Century
http://departments.kings.edu/history/20c/china.html

This page from the Twentieth Century Resource Site, created by members of the History Department at Kings College, focuses on Chinese history. It includes information about the Boxer Rebellion, Sun Yat-sen (Sun Yixian), and Chiang Kai-shek as well as a bibliography of books and links to other Web sites for additional information.

Internet East Asian History Sourcebook

http://www.fordham.edu/halsall/eastasia/
    eastasiasbook.html

This site provides primary source materials tracing historical and cultural developments in China, Japan, Korea, and other East Asian nations. It includes separate sections that focus on Japan as a world power and Chinese history from 1840 through 1949.

CANADA

Canadian Economy Online: Key Economic Events

http://canadianeconomy.gc.ca/english/economy/
    key.html

This chronology of key economic events in Canadian history is part of a Web site created by the government of Canada. The time line contains several pages describing the condition of the nation's economy in the period 1910-1939, including information about the economic impacts of World War I, the imposition of a national income tax, the Winnipeg General Strike of 1919, the stock market crash of 1929, and the Great Depression. The site provides information in both English and French.

The Canadian Encyclopedia

http://thecanadianencyclopedia.com/
    index.cfm?PgNm=Homepage&Params=A1

This Web site provides authoritative information on "all things Canadian." The "Feature Articles" section is organized by various subject areas and includes articles about the stock market crash of 1929, the Winnipeg General Strike in 1919, and the discovery of insulin by Canadians John J. R. Macleod and Frederick G. Banting. The site also features several pages pertaining to the early twentieth century from an extensive time line of Canadian history, covering "Expansion, 1885-1913," World War I (1914-1919), the 1920's, and the 1930's.

ECONOMICS

The History of Economic Thought

http://cepa.newschool.edu/het

Created by the Department of Economics at the New School for Social Research, this site features biographical information and excerpts of texts from more than five hundred economists who can be accessed through an alphabetical index. It also describes various schools of economic thought, including a section devoted to the ideas of John Maynard Keynes and some of his followers, such as Joan Robinson and the Cambridge Keynesians.

Looking Back at the Crash of '29

http://www.nytimes.com/library/financial/index-1929-
    crash.html

This page from the Web site of *The New York Times* features reproductions of the newspaper's front pages from Monday, October, 28, 1929, through November 1, 1929, the week the stock market crash dominated the headlines. The page links to other articles published in *The New York Times* that week about various changes and events surrounding the stock market crash, including the rise in the number of telephone calls made in the period and the decisions of many women stockbrokers to resign from their profession.

McMaster University Archive for the History of Economic Thought

http://socserv2.socsci.mcmaster.ca/~econ/ugcm/3ll3

This site provides an extensive collection of texts about economics, organized by author. The site features an excerpt from John Maynard Keynes's book *The Economic Consequences of the Peace* (1919) as well as works by other twentieth century economists.

1929 Stock Market Crash

http://mutualfunds.about.com/od/1929marketcrash

This portion of About.com's Web site about mutual funds contains links to several pages about the great stock market crash, including articles about the condition of the stock market on Black Monday, Black Tuesday, and Black Thursday as well as charts depicting stock market fluctuations and a collection of historical photographs depicting American life during the Great Depression.

FRANCE

France 1900-1945

http://www.spartacus.schoolnet.co.uk/France.htm

This is one of the many excellent sites created by Spartacus Educational, a British organization that seeks to provide Internet-based lessons for students. The site contains separate pages of information about French politicians and military leaders in the periods

1900-1920 and 1920-1945, including excerpts from speeches and other primary source documents as well as referrals to books on related topics. It also provides a highly detailed chronology of World War I and information about France and the nation's armed forces from 1914 through 1918. All of the site's pages contain numerous links to other Web pages with related information.

GERMANY

Germany 1900-1945

http://www.spartacus.schoolnet.co.uk/Germany.htm

This site created by Spartacus Educational focuses on life in Germany before and during the Nazi regime. The site includes separate pages of information about political and military figures in the periods 1914-1918 and 1918-1945, the Weimar Republic, political parties, German art, and World War I. In addition, a separate page devoted to Nazi Germany contains information about foreign policy from 1932 through 1945, biographies of Adolf Hitler and other Nazi figures, and information on German laws, anti-Semitism, education, major historical events, and other aspects of life under the Nazi regime.

Weimar Germany, 1919-1933

http://www.historyhome.co.uk/europe/weimar.htm

Hitler: The Rise to Power

http://www.historyhome.co.uk/europe/hitrise.htm

Hitler's Foreign Policy

http://www.historyhome.co.uk/europe/hitfor.htm

These three pages are presented on A Web of English History, which, despite its name, also provides information about other European countries. These pages contain articles written by Stephen Tonge, head of history at Catholic University School in Dublin, Ireland, describing, respectively, the Weimar government, Adolf Hitler's rise to power, and Hitler's foreign policy from 1933 to 1939.

GREAT BRITAIN

British Timeline: Early Twentieth Century, 1901-1944

http://www.bbc.co.uk/history/timelines/britain/cen_science.shtml

This part of the British Broadcasting Corporation (BBC) Web site contains a series of time lines tracing British history from the Mesolithic era to the early twenty-first century. This section of the time line features information about key events in the early twentieth century, including the campaign for woman suffrage, liberal reforms adopted from 1906 to 1914, World War I, the Easter Rising and Irish independence, the economy and the Great Depression, and the Munich Agreement and appeasement. The site also contains similar time lines outlining early twentieth century events specifically in England, Scotland, Wales, and Northern Ireland.

The Monarchy, 1042-1952

http://www.spartacus.schoolnet.co.uk/monarchy.htm

This site contains individual pages about each of the British monarchs who reigned from 1042 through 1952, with portraits, biographical details, significant historical facts about their reigns, and links to sites with additional information.

Prime Ministers, 1760-1960

http://www.spartacus.schoolnet.co.uk/pm.htm

This site designed by Spartacus Educational provides portraits, biographies, and information about significant events that occurred during the terms of Britain's prime ministers from 1760 through the mid-twentieth century, with links to sites with additional information. H. H. Asquith, David Lloyd George, and Neville Chamberlain are among the prime ministers represented. The individual pages about each prime minister are accessed through a list of the prime ministers presented in chronological order of their terms in office.

IRELAND

Irish History on the Web

http://larkspirit.com/history

This site includes a page with links to information about the Easter Rising of 1916 and the creation of the Irish Republic. It also provides access to historical documents, including the Proclamation of the Republic in 1916, as well as a separate page of links to information about Northern Ireland.

A Web of English History: The Home Rule Crisis, 1910-1914

http://www.historyhome.co.uk/peel/ireland/
　　homerule.htm

This page outlines the Irish battle for home rule. It profiles some of the Unionist leaders and members of Parliament involved in the struggle and details the significant events that occurred in the period 1910-1914.

ITALY

Benito Mussolini

http://en.wikipedia.org/wiki/Benito_Mussolini

This biography of the Italian premier is found in Wikipedia, a free Web-based encyclopedia. The biography provides an overview of Mussolini's life and describes the rise of Italian Fascism.

LATIN AMERICA

Casahistoria: Latin American Home Page

http://www.casahistoria.net/latam.html

Casahistoria was created by a teacher in Buenos Aires, Argentina, who wanted to provide a list of Web resources for his undergraduate history students. The site contains information in English and Spanish, including a page of links about Latin American history and culture, with a section devoted to the twentieth century. The site also features individual pages with links to information about Argentina, Bolivia, Brazil, Chile, Cuba, Mexico, Paraguay, Peru, and Uruguay.

LITERATURE

American Literature on the Web: American Literature, 1865-1914

http://www.nagasaki-gaigo.ac.jp/ishikawa/amlit/19re/
　　overview_19re.htm

American Literature on the Web: American Literature, 1914-1945

http://www.nagasaki-gaigo.ac.jp/ishikawa/amlit/20/
　　overview_20.htm

This comprehensive compendium of Web links, maintained by Akihito Ishikawa of the Nagasaki College of Foreign Languages, includes a separate section about late nineteenth and early twentieth century American literature and another section about early and mid-twentieth century American literature. Each section has a page that provides access to information about individual authors, including Theodore Dreiser, William Dean Howells, William Faulkner, F. Scott Fitzgerald, Ernest Hemingway, Langston Hughes, Sinclair Lewis, Dorothy Parker, Ezra Pound, T. S. Eliot, and John Steinbeck. The "Related Resources" page provides links to Web sites about modernism, the Harlem Renaissance, and other literary topics of the period. Additional pages contain time lines, links to Web sites about music and the visual arts during each period, and links to sites placing the period's literature within a broader social context.

English Literature by Period: Modern (British and American)

http://vos.ucsb.edu/browse.asp?id=2747

This page is part of Voice of the Shuttle, a highly regarded Web site created by professors at the University of California, Santa Barbara. The page contains links to numerous Web sites, journals, Listservs, and other resources about twentieth century British and American literature. It also provides links to sites about individual authors.

Introduction to First World War Poetry

http://www.oucs.ox.ac.uk/ltg/projects/jtap/tutorials/
　　intro

Created by a professor at Oxford University, this Web-based tutorial contains poetry of the World War I era written by Wilfred Owen, Rupert Brooke, Siegfried Sassoon, and other British poets. It also features the work of women poets during this period, "trench poems" written by a soldier, and some popular trench songs.

Literary Resources: Twentieth Century British, Irish, and Commonwealth

http://andromeda.rutgers.edu/~jlynch/Lit/20th.html

One of the pages created by Rutgers University professor Jack Lynch in his Literary Resources, a compendium of Web links about literature. This page features links to several sites containing World War I poetry as well as links to information about individual authors, including Joseph Conrad, T. S. Eliot, Aldous Huxley, James Joyce, D. H. Lawrence, Virginia Woolf, and William Butler Yeats.

MATHEMATICS

The MacTutor History of Mathematics Archive

http://www-groups.dcs.st-and.ac.uk/~history/
index.html

This comprehensive Web site is maintained by the School of Mathematics and Statistics at the University of St. Andrews, Scotland. It features biographies of prominent mathematicians that can be accessed through alphabetical or chronological indexes. It also contains information about math history, with separate pages explaining important mathematical discoveries and concepts. Emmy Noether, Bertrand Russell, and Alfred North Whitehead are among the mathematicians included.

MEXICO

Mexico: Revolution and Twentieth Century

http://www.casahistoria.net/
mexicorevolution.htm#2.%20The%20Mexican%
20Revolution%201910-1920

This page of the Casahistoria Web site provides links to information in English and Spanish about twentieth century Mexico, with separate sections about the Mexican Revolution of 1910-1920, documents from the revolution, and the nation's history following that period.

MUSIC

Carolina Classical Connection: Twentieth Century Music Links

http://www.carolinaclassical.com/twentieth.html

This site provides a collection of links to a wide variety of music-related Web sites, with biographical information on composers, descriptions of musical genres and types of compositions, and encoded music files. The page with links to the twentieth century includes information on Gustav Mahler, Erik Satie, Claude Debussy, Arnold Schoenberg, George Gershwin, and many other composers.

The Classical MIDI Connection: The Twentieth Century

http://www.classicalmidiconnection.com/cmc/
twenty.html

This site offers a collection of music MIDI files.

MIDI, or musical instrument digital interface, is a digital technology that allows electronic musical instruments and computers to communicate with one another and enables people to listen to music on their computers. The site has an alphabetized list of composers with links to MIDI files of their music. The twentieth century period page contains links and MIDI files for Alban Berg, Edward Elgar, Manuel de Falla, George Gershwin, Sergei Prokofiev, and many other composers.

Public Domain Music

http://www.pdmusic.org

This collection of MIDI and text files of lyrics for American music in the public domain contains a separate page featuring popular American songs from 1900 through 1922. The page about the blues features a number of selections from the early twentieth century, and the page about ragtime includes compositions written from 1897 through 1915 by Scott Joplin and other composers.

The Red Hot Jazz Archive: A History of Jazz Before 1930

http://www.redhotjazz.com/index.htm

This site's name is something of a misnomer, as this multimedia collection of essays, film clips, and sound files contains not only voluminous information about early American jazz but also pages about blues music in the early twentieth century. Users can access information about bands led by Louis Armstrong, Duke Ellington, Paul Whiteman, Jelly Roll Morton, and Tommy Dorsey as well as about hundreds of other musicians. The site also provides pages of information about individuals such as Bessie Smith, Ma Rainey, and other classic women blues singers of the 1920's.

The Roaring 1920's Concert Extravaganza

http://bestwebs.com/roaring1920/index.shtml

This site creates an imaginary radio broadcast featuring performances by many popular entertainers of the 1920's, including Al Jolson, Maurice Chevalier, Bert Williams, Fanny Brice, Eddie Cantor, Ruth Etting, and Helen Kane, better known as the "boop boop a doop girl." The sound files are in Real Audio 2 Sound Format, with each selection lasting about sixty seconds.

PHILOSOPHY

Stanford Encyclopedia of Philosophy

http://plato.stanford.edu/contents.html

This site presents a collection of articles about philosophers and philosophical ideas that can be accessed through an alphabetical table of contents. Among the materials included are articles about John Dewey, Edmund Husserl, Bertrand Russell, George Santayana, and Ludwig Wittgenstein, as well as an article detailing Albert Einstein's contributions to the philosophy of science.

RUSSIA

Russia, 1860-1945

http://www.spartacus.schoolnet.co.uk/
RussiaIssues.htm

This examination of Russian history from 1860 until the end of World War II contains several pages of information about issues and events in Russian history in the period 1901-1914, including the 1905 revolution. It also features an extensive collection of links to other Web sites about the Russian Revolution of 1917 and related topics, as well as several pages of lessons about the 1917 revolution.

SCIENCE AND MEDICINE

Albert Einstein Online

http://www.westegg.com/einstein/index.htm

This lengthy list of links to information about Einstein includes links to Web sites that provide overviews of his life and scientific achievements, photos, quotations from his works and interviews, excerpts from his writings, and information on his Nobel Prize in Physics.

Eric Weisstein's World of Science

http://scienceworld.wolfram.com

This online reference, compiled by a research scientist and former professor of astronomy, contains several encyclopedias of information about astronomy, chemistry, mathematics, and physics. It also provides brief biographies and portraits of noteworthy twentieth century scientists, including Albert Einstein, Edwin Powell Hubble, and Enrico Fermi.

History of Western Biomedicine

http://www.mic.ki.se/West.html#West3

Compiled by the Karolinska Institutet in Sweden, this site contains links to Web sites that address various aspects of medical and scientific history from ancient times through the twenty-first century. The "Modern Period" section includes a list of sites related to twentieth century scientific and medical developments, including significant events in microbiology, the histories of blood transfusion and uranium, the discoveries of insulin and antibiotics, and the development of the electrocardiogram.

A Science Odyssey: People and Discoveries

http://www.pbs.org/wgbh/aso/databank

This site, which provides 120 entries about twentieth century scientists and their stories, is part of the Public Broadcasting System's (PBS) Web site. The entries can be accessed through a time line of significant scientific discoveries between 1900 and 1996 or through an alphabetical list of scientists. In addition, separate pages provide access to entries about medicine and health, physics and astronomy, human behavior, technology, and earth and life sciences.

SPAIN

Spanish Civil War

http://www.spartacus.schoolnet.co.uk/Spanish-Civil-
War.htm

Spartacus Educational has prepared this series of Web pages describing the main events and issues of the war and the political and military organizations involved in the conflict. The site also features biographies about Spaniards as well as people from other countries who played significant roles in the conflict and information about the participation of world leaders and countries other than Spain.

A Web of English History: European History, the Spanish Civil War

http://www.historyhome.co.uk/europe/spaincw.htm

This page provides an examination of the causes of the Spanish Civil War, a description of the outbreak and main events of the war, details about foreign involvement in the conflict, and an explanation why Francisco Franco was the war's victor. The site also recommends books and links to other Web sites for further information.

TECHNOLOGY

The History of the Automobile
http://inventors.about.com/library/weekly/
aacarssteama.htm

About.com's Inventors Web site includes a four-part history of the automobile, tracing the various phases in automotive invention from the eighteenth century through the twentieth century. The last of the four parts focuses on developments in automotive technology during the early years of the twentieth century, describing the introduction of the assembly line and mass-produced vehicles as well as the contributions of Ransom Eli Olds and Henry Ford to the automobile's development.

Inventing Entertainment: The Motion Pictures and Sound Recordings of the Edison Company
http://memory.loc.gov/ammem/edhtml/edhome.html

This site, created by the Library of Congress, contains digitized versions of 341 motion pictures and 81 disc recordings that were released by Thomas Alva Edison's entertainment company. The site provides detailed explanations of how users can view the videos and listen to the sound recordings. It also features a time line outlining significant events in Edison's life and links to pages describing Edison's role in creating the phonograph and his contributions to the motion-picture industry.

The Invention of Radio
http://inventors.about.com/library/inventors/
blradio.htm

About.com's Inventors Web site includes this page summarizing the history of the invention and development of radio, including information about Guglielmo Marconi, Nikola Tesla, and other inventors. The page also provides links to Web sites about radio broadcasting history.

Twentieth Century Inventions: 1900-1925
http://inventors.about.com/library/weekly/
aa121599a.htm

Twentieth Century Inventions: 1926-1950
http://inventors.about.com/library/weekly/
aa122299a.htm

These two pages from About.com's time line of inventions are devoted to the first half of the twentieth century. The time line links to additional pages describing inventors and inventions of the period, including information about the invention of the safety razor, vacuum cleaner, airplane, bubble gum, and Pez candy.

UNITED STATES

American Leaders Speak: Recordings from World War I and the 1920 Election
http://memory.loc.gov/ammem/nfhtml/nfhome.html

Created by the Library of Congress, this site allows users to hear fifty-nine sound recordings of speeches delivered by American leaders in the period 1918-1920. The topics of these speeches include World War I, the presidential election of 1920, home rule for Ireland, the labor movement, the League of Nations, and internationalism. Among the speakers are Presidents Warren G. Harding and Calvin Coolidge, labor leader Samuel Gompers, General John J. Pershing, and businessman John D. Rockefeller.

AmericanPresident.org
http://www.americanpresident.org

This accessible and inclusive site was created by the Miller Center of Public Affairs at the University of Virginia, a research institution devoted to the study of the American presidency. The section titled "Presidency in History" contains several pages of information about each of the presidents. Brief biographies are illustrated with period drawings, photographs, and other images and are followed by more extensive pages of information about the presidents' lives before and after their terms in office, their campaigns and elections, and significant domestic and foreign affairs during their administrations. The site also provides biographies of all the First Ladies, brief biographies of key cabinet members, lists of presidential staff members and advisers, and links to additional resources.

Fireside Chats of Franklin D. Roosevelt
http://www.mhric.org/fdr/fdr.html

During Franklin D. Roosevelt's administration, the president described the state of the nation and his political programs in his radio-broadcast "fireside chats." This site contains complete transcripts of thirty chats broadcast from March 12, 1933, through June 12, 1944. The topics of Roosevelt's talks include the national bank crisis of 1933, the New Deal and other programs aimed at helping the American economy recover from the Great Depression, the president's proposed judicial reorganization, the unemployment crisis, and the European war that began in 1939.

The Marcus Garvey and Universal Negro Improvement Association Papers Project

http://www.international.ucla.edu/africa/mgpp

Created by the James S. Coleman African Studies Center at the University of California, Los Angeles, this site provides a wide range of information about Marcus Garvey and his role in the pan-Africanism movement. The site contains excerpts from the papers of the Universal Negro Improvement Association as well as portions of Garvey's biography and editorials. It also features photographs and sound files of some of Garvey's speeches.

New Deal Network

http://newdeal.feri.org/index.htm

This Web-based research and teaching resource devoted to the public works and art projects of the New Deal era is the result of a collaboration among the Franklin and Eleanor Roosevelt Institute, the Franklin D. Roosevelt Presidential Library, and others. The site features more than five thousand Great Depression-era photographs and a library of some nine hundred articles, speeches, letters, historical documents, and other texts. It also contains a photographic essay about the impact of the Great Depression and the New Deal on a small town in Alabama as well as lesson plans for teachers and information on a variety of other resources about the period.

Prosperity and Thrift: The Coolidge Era and the Consumer Economy, 1921-1929

http://memory.loc.gov/ammem/coolhtml/coolhome.html

This Library of Congress compilation of materials concerns the prosperity of the United States during the administration of President Calvin Coolidge, the transition to a mass consumer economy, and the role of the American government in the transition. The site includes legislative documents, books, pamphlets, personal papers, photographs, five short films, and audio selections from Coolidge's speeches.

Theodore Roosevelt Association

http://www.theodoreroosevelt.org

The association, which, in its own words, seeks to "perpetuate the memory and ideals" of the twenty-sixth American president, features a great deal of information about Theodore Roosevelt on its site. Included are a time line, a lengthy biography, numerous photos, lists of books and other research resources, and links to other sites about Roosevelt. The site also provides a link to a Web site created by the Library of Congress containing film clips of Roosevelt, who is described as "the first U.S. president to have his career and life chronicled on a large scale by motion picture companies." Site visitors can view 140 films recording the events of Roosevelt's life from his participation in the Spanish-American War in 1898 until his death in 1919.

WOMEN

By Popular Demand: "Votes for Women," Suffrage Pictures, 1850-1920

http://memory.loc.gov/ammem/vfwhtml/vfwhome.html

Votes for Women: Selections from the National American Woman Suffrage Association Collection, 1848-1921

http://memory.loc.gov/ammem/naw/nawshome.html

These companion sites, created by the Library of Congress, provide information about the campaign for woman suffrage in the United States, which culminated in 1920, when women achieved the right to vote. The first site contains thirty-eight photographs, including portraits of feminist leaders, suffragist parades and picketing, and political cartoons. The photos can be viewed in either thumbnail or enlarged formats. The second site holds 167 books, pamphlets, and other artifacts documenting the suffrage movement, many of which were donated to the Library of Congress by Carrie Chapman Catt, longtime president of the National American Woman Suffrage Association.

WORLD WAR I

Teacher Oz's Kingdom of History: World War I

http://www.teacheroz.com/wwi.htm

Tracey Oz, a high school history teacher in Dallas, Texas, compiled the encyclopedic history site that includes this page on World War I. The page provides a broad range of materials, including time lines, primary source documents such as letters and diaries, first-person accounts of battles, statistics, discussions of international diplomacy during and after the war, and descriptions of battles, weapons, and types of warfare. Numerous images are also available, including maps, as well as examples of wartime propaganda, audio clips, descriptions of women's role in the war and the home front in wartime, and examples of the poetry, music, and art produced during the war years.

The World War I Document Archive

http://www.lib.byu.edu/%7Erdh/wwi

This collection of primary documents and other materials about the war was compiled by Brigham Young University. One of the site's best features is its collection of digitized books, in English and French, about various aspects of the war. It also includes the texts of conventions, treaties, and official papers related to the war, including the Treaty of Versailles, as well as dia-

ries, memorials, and personal reminiscences. One section of the site describes the various maritime battles fought during the war; another details the military and civilian medical aspects of the conflict.

World War I: Trenches on the Web

http://www.worldwar1.com

Regarded as one of the best sources of information about World War I available on the Internet, this site is maintained by the Great War Society, an organization that encourages discussion, learning, and scholarship about the events surrounding the war. The comprehensive offerings include a detailed time line listing the events that led to war and the battles fought during the conflict. It also contains biographies of the major figures involved in the war, articles provided by historians, maps and information about the European nations that fought in the war, and links to numerous other Web sites.

SUBSCRIPTION WEB SITES

The following sites are posted on the World Wide Web but are available only to paying subscribers. Many public, college, and university libraries subscribe to these sources; readers can ask reference librarians if they are available at their local libraries.

GENERAL

Oxford Reference Online

http://www.oxfordreference.com

The Core Collection of Oxford Reference Online is a virtual reference library of more than one hundred dictionaries, language reference, and subject reference books published by the Oxford University Press. The electronic versions of the books are fully indexed and cross-searchable and provide information on a wide range of subjects, including art, architecture, biological sciences, economics and business, history, law, literature, mathematics, medicine, military history, performing arts, political science, social science, religion, and philosophy. The Premium Collection contains all of the features of the Core Collection plus electronic versions of the Oxford Companions Series.

Oxford Scholarship Online

http:www.oxfordscholarship.com

Oxford Scholarship Online contains the electronic versions of more than one thousand books about eco-

nomics, finance, philosophy, political science, and religion that are published by the Oxford University Press. The site contains the full texts of these books couple with advanced searching capabilities.

ART

Grove Art Online

http://www.groveart.com

Grove Art Online provides authoritative and comprehensive information about the visual arts from prehistory to the present. In addition to its more than 130,000 art images, the site contains articles on a range of subjects, including fine arts, architecture, and the art of China, South America, Africa, and other world cultures, as well as biographies and links to hundreds of museum and gallery Web sites.

BIOGRAPHY

Oxford Dictionary of National Biography Online

http://www.oxforddnb.com

The online version of the recently revised *Oxford Dictionary of National Biography* is a highly authoritative reference source of biographical information. According to the site's description, the dictionary contains more than "50,000 biographies of people who shaped the history of the British Isles and beyond, from the earliest times to the year 2002."

HISTORY

Daily Life Through History Online

http://dailylife.greenwood.com/login.asp

Daily Life Through History Online, created by Greenwood Electronic Media, contains articles describing the religious, domestic, economic, material, political, recreational, and intellectual lives of people throughout history. It contains information from *The Greenwood Encyclopedia of Daily Life* as well as other books, reference works, and primary source documents. Users can also access chronologies, time lines, and hundreds of Web links.

MUSIC

Grove Music Online

http://www.grovemusic.com

This online version of the highly regarded *New Grove Dictionary of Music and Musicians* features more than 4,500 articles on musicians, instruments, musical techniques, genres, and styles. In addition to articles and biographies, the site provides more than five hundred audio clips of music and links to images as well as to related Web sites.

SCIENCE

Access Science: McGraw-Hill Encyclopedia of Science and Technology Online

http://www.accessscience.com

The online version of the *McGraw-Hill Encyclopedia of Science and Technology* and *McGraw-Hill Dictionary of Scientific and Technical Terms* contains the information found in the latest editions of these books. Users can access biographies, more than eight thousand articles, and science news.

ELECTRONIC DATABASES

Electronic databases usually do not have their own URLs. Instead, public, college, and university libraries subscribe to these databases and install them on their Web sites, where they are available only to library card holders or specified patrons. Readers can check their library Web sites to see if these databases are installed or ask reference librarians if the databases are available at their local libraries.

BIOGRAPHY

Biography Resource Center

Produced by Thomson Gale, this database includes biographies of more than 335,000 prominent people throughout history that were previously published in Thompson Gale reference sources. It also features biographical articles from almost three hundred magazines.

Biography Resource Center: African Americans

This electronic collection features almost 30,000 biographies of African Americans who have attained prominence in a number of areas, including the arts, business, government, history, literature, politics, and science. Produced by Thomson Gale, the database's biographies have been culled from the company's Biography Resource Center database. In addition to the biographies, the database provides links to related Web sites, about 2,000 portraits, and more than 42,000 articles from almost three hundred magazines.

Wilson Biographies Plus Illustrated

Produced by H. W. Wilson Co., this database contains more than 140,000 narrative profiles, more than 36,000 images, bibliographies, and links to related material. The database's content derives from some of Wilson's reference books, including *Current Biography* and the World Authors Series, as well as from information licensed from other reference publishers.

HISTORY

American History Online

This database, produced by Facts On File, contains information about more than five hundred years of political, military, social, and cultural history. Its content derives from the company's publications, including the *Encyclopedia of American History*, as well as the Landmark Documents in American History database. Users can access information about historical events and topics, biographies of significant people, more than 1,300 primary source documents, time lines, essays providing overviews of significant time periods, maps, charts, and more than 1,300 images.

American Women's History Online

This database is devoted to five hundred years of American women's history. Produced by Facts On File, it contains more than 2,300 biographies as well as entries about issues pertaining to women, such as court cases and legislation, events, and social issues. It also features primary source documents, time lines containing hyperlinked entries (including a time line of woman suffrage), and more than six hundred images, maps, and charts.

History Reference Center

A product of EBSCO Information Services, the History Reference Center is a comprehensive world history database. It includes the contents of more than one thousand encyclopedias, reference works, and nonfiction books as well as the full texts of articles published in about sixty history periodicals. It also features thousands of historical documents, biographies, photographs, maps, and historical film and video.

History Resource Center: U.S.

This database, produced by Thomson Gale, contains primary source documents from digital archives, articles from current periodicals, and multimedia reference articles about U.S. history. Users also can access audio and video clips of historic speeches and events and link to digitized special collections.

History Resource Center: World

This electronic collection compiled by Thomson Gale features information from the company's publications as well as primary source documents and complete articles from academic journals and periodicals.

MagillOnHistory

Available on the EBSCO Host platform, Salem Press's MagillOnHistory database offers the full contents of the company's Great Lives from History and Great Events from History series as well as entries from its many history and social science encyclopedias, such as the award-winning *Ready Reference: American Indians* and its decades volumes, *The Fifties*, *The Sixties*, and *The Seventies*. Several thousand full-length essays cross-link to coverage of historical events and to biographies about prominent persons from ancient times to the twenty-first century.

World History Online

Created by Facts On File, this database covers a wide range of historical events, from ancient times to the present. It includes more than 10,000 biographies and subject entries describing more than 14,000 events, places, and cultural events. Also available are hundreds of primary source documents, time lines, and more than 650 maps and charts.

LITERATURE

Literary Reference Online

Facts On File has compiled this electronic examination of the lives and works of writers throughout history. Among the database's features are author biographies searchable by type of writing or time period and information about the plots, themes, social contexts, and importance of literary works. Also available is a guide to more than 35,000 literary characters, a glossary of literary terms, and articles on literary movements, literary groups, magazines, and newspapers.

Literature Resource Center

This database produced by Thomson Gale includes biographies, bibliographies, and critical analyses of authors from a wide range of literary disciplines, countries, and eras. It also features plot summaries, complete articles from literary journals, and critical essays.

MagillOnLiteraturePlus

Available on the EBSCO Host platform, MagillOn LiteraturePlus is a comprehensive, integrated literature database produced by Salem Press. The database incorporates the full contents of Salem's many literature-related reference works, including information from *Masterplots* (series I and II), *Cyclopedia of World Authors*, *Cyclopedia of Literary Characters*, *Cyclopedia of Literary Places*, *Critical Surveys of Literature*, *Magill's Literary Annual*, *World Philosophers and Their Works*, and *Magill Book Reviews*. Among the materials available are articles on more than 35,000 works and more than 10,000 writers, poets, dramatists, essayists, and philosophers. Essays feature critical analysis as well as plot summaries, biographical information, character profiles, and authoritative listings of authors' works with the dates of publication. The majority of the essays also include annotated bibliographies to help users conduct additional research.

—*Rebecca Kuzins*

CHRONOLOGICAL LIST OF ENTRIES

1901

Early 20th cent.: Elster and Geitel Study Radioactivity

Early 20th cent.: Mahler Directs the Vienna Court Opera

1901: Creation of the First Synthetic Vat Dye

1901: Discovery of Human Blood Groups

1901: Grijns Suggests the Cause of Beriberi

1901: Hewitt Invents the Mercury-Vapor Lamp

1901: Hopkins Announces the Discovery of Tryptophan

1901: Ivanov Develops Artificial Insemination

1901-1904: Kipping Discovers Silicones

1901-1911: China Allows Some Western Reforms

1901-1925: Teletype Is Developed

Jan., 1901: American Bowling Club Hosts Its First Tournament

Jan. 1, 1901: Commonwealth of Australia Is Formed

Jan. 10, 1901: Discovery of Oil at Spindletop

Feb. 4, 1901: Reed Reports That Mosquitoes Transmit Yellow Fever

Feb. 26, 1901: Morgan Assembles the World's Largest Corporation

May 27, 1901: Insular Cases

July 1, 1901: Canada Claims the Arctic Islands

Aug. 30, 1901: Booth Receives Patent for the Vacuum Cleaner

Sept. 14, 1901: Theodore Roosevelt Becomes U.S. President

Dec. 10, 1901: First Nobel Prizes Are Awarded

Dec. 10, 1901: Röntgen Wins the Nobel Prize for the Discovery of X Rays

Dec. 12, 1901: First Transatlantic Telegraphic Radio Transmission

Dec. 19, 1901: Completion of the Mombasa-Lake Victoria Railway

1902

1902: Bateson Publishes *Mendel's Principles of Heredity*

1902: Carrel Rejoins Severed Blood Vessels

1902: Cement Manufacturers Agree to Cooperate on Pricing

1902: *Heart of Darkness* Critiques Imperialism

1902: Hobson Critiques Imperialism

1902: James Proposes a Rational Basis for Religious Experience

1902: Johnson Duplicates Disc Recordings

1902: Levi Recognizes the Axiom of Choice in Set Theory

1902: McClung Contributes to the Discovery of the Sex Chromosome

1902: Philippines Ends Its Uprising Against the United States

1902: Zsigmondy Invents the Ultramicroscope

1902-1903: Pavlov Develops the Concept of Reinforcement

1902-1913: Tiffany Leads the Art Nouveau Movement in the United States

Jan., 1902: French Expedition at Susa Discovers Hammurabi's Code

Jan. 1, 1902: First Rose Bowl Game

Jan. 30, 1902: Anglo-Japanese Treaty Brings Japan into World Markets

Feb. 17, 1902: Stieglitz Organizes the Photo-Secession

Mar. and June, 1902: Kennelly and Heaviside Theorize Existence of the Ionosphere

Mar. 4, 1902: American Automobile Association Is Established

Apr., 1902: Rhodes Scholarships Are Instituted

Apr.-June, 1902: Bayliss and Starling Establish the Role of Hormones

Apr. 11, 1902: Caruso Records for the Gramophone and Typewriter Company

May 8, 1902: Mount Pelée Erupts

May 12-Oct. 23, 1902: Anthracite Coal Strike

1903

1904

1905

1906

1907

1908

1909

1910

1910's: Garbage Industry Introduces Reforms

1910's: Handy Ushers in the Commercial Blues Era

1910: Angell Advances Pacifism

1910: Electric Washing Machine Is Introduced

1910: *Euthenics* Calls for Pollution Control

1910: Gaudí Completes the Casa Milá Apartment House

1910: Rous Discovers That Some Cancers Are Caused by Viruses

1910: Steinmetz Warns of Pollution in "The Future of Electricity"

1910: Thomson Confirms the Possibility of Isotopes

1910-1913: *Principia Mathematica* Defines the Logistic Movement

1910-1930: Great Northern Migration

Spring, 1910: Poiret's Hobble Skirt Becomes the Rage

Apr., 1910: Ehrlich Introduces Salvarsan as a Cure for Syphilis

Apr. 5, 1910: First Morris Plan Bank Opens

May 31, 1910: Formation of the Union of South Africa

June 25, 1910: *The Firebird* Premieres in Paris

July 1, 1910: U.S. Bureau of Mines Is Established

Aug. 22, 1910: Japanese Annexation of Korea

Oct. 5, 1910: Republic of Portugal Is Proclaimed

Mid-Oct., 1910-Dec. 1, 1920: Mexican Revolution

Nov. 25, 1910: Carnegie Establishes the Endowment for International Peace

1911

1911: Boas Publishes *The Mind of Primitive Man*

1911: Hashimoto Founds the Nissan Motor Company

1911-1912: Italy Annexes Libya

1911-1920: Borden Leads Canada Through World War I

1911-1923: Rilke's *Duino Elegies* Redefines Poetics

Mar. 15, 1911: Scriabin's *Prometheus* Premieres in Moscow

Mar. 25, 1911: Triangle Shirtwaist Factory Fire

Mar. 28, 1911: Baro-Kano Railroad Begins Operation in Nigeria

Apr. 3, 1911: Sibelius Conducts the Premiere of His Fourth Symphony

Apr. 14, 1911: Lever Acquires Land Concession in the Belgian Congo

May 15, 1911: U.S. Supreme Court Establishes the "Rule of Reason"

May 29, 1911: U.S. Supreme Court Breaks Up the American Tobacco Company

July 1, 1911: Agadir Crisis

July 24, 1911: Bingham Discovers Machu Picchu

Sept., 1911: Der Blaue Reiter Abandons Representation in Art

Sept. 4-15, 1911: Students Challenge Corporal Punishment in British Schools

Sept. 14, 1911: Assassination of Pyotr Arkadyevich Stolypin

Fall, 1911: Sturtevant Produces the First Chromosome Map

Oct. 10, 1911: Sun Yixian Overthrows the Qing Dynasty

Nov. 20, 1911: Mahler's Masterpiece *Das Lied von der Erde* Premieres

Dec. 2, 1911: Australasian Antarctic Expedition Commences

Dec. 14, 1911: Amundsen Reaches the South Pole

Dec. 31, 1911: Parliament Nationalizes the British Telephone System

1912

1912: Grey's *Riders of the Purple Sage* Launches the Western Genre

1912: Jung Publishes *The Psychology of the Unconscious*

1912: Kandinsky Publishes His Theory of Abstract Art

1913

1914

1914: Rutherford Discovers the Proton
1914: U.S. Government Begins Using Cost-Plus Contracts
Jan. 5, 1914: Ford Announces a Five-Dollar, Eight-Hour Workday
Feb. 13, 1914: ASCAP Forms to Protect Writers and Publishers of Music
Mar., 1914: Gilbreth Publishes *The Psychology of Management*
June 28-Aug. 4, 1914: Outbreak of World War I
June 28, 1914-Nov. 11, 1918: World War I
Aug. 15, 1914: Panama Canal Opens
Sept. 1, 1914: Last Passenger Pigeon Dies
Sept. 5-9, 1914: First Battle of the Marne

Sept. 15, 1914: Irish Home Rule Bill
Sept. 22, 1914: Germany Begins Extensive Submarine Warfare
Sept. 26, 1914: Federal Trade Commission Is Organized
Oct. 15, 1914: Clayton Antitrust Act
Oct. 15, 1914: Labor Unions Win Exemption from Antitrust Laws
Oct. 30, 1914: Spain Declares Neutrality in World War I
Nov. 5, 1914: British Mount a Second Front Against the Ottomans
Nov. 7, 1914: Lippmann Helps to Establish *The New Republic*

1915

1915: Merrill Lynch & Company Is Founded
1915: *The Metamorphosis* Anticipates Modern Feelings of Alienation
1915-1919: National Birth Control League Forms
Jan. 19, 1915: Germany Launches the First Zeppelin Bombing Raids
Jan. 25, 1915: First Transcontinental Telephone Call Is Made
Feb. 19, 1915-Jan. 9, 1916: Gallipoli Campaign Falters
Mar., 1915: Defense of India Act Impedes the Freedom Struggle
Mar. 3, 1915: Griffith Releases *The Birth of a Nation*
Apr. 22-27, 1915: Germany Uses Poison Gas Against Allied Troops
Apr. 24, 1915: Armenian Genocide Begins
Apr. 28-May 1, 1915: International Congress of Women
May, 1915: Fokker Aircraft Are Equipped with Machine Guns

May 7, 1915: German Torpedoes Sink the *Lusitania*
May 20, 1915: Corning Glass Works Trademarks Pyrex
Summer, 1915: Denishawn School of Dance Opens
Sept., 1915-Feb., 1916: McLean Discovers the Natural Anticoagulant Heparin
Sept. 5-8, 1915, and Apr. 24-30, 1916: Zimmerwald and Kienthal Conferences
Sept. 11, 1915: Women's Institutes Are Founded in Great Britain
Oct., 1915-Mar., 1917: Langevin Develops Active Sonar
Oct. 21, 1915: First Demonstration of Transatlantic Radiotelephony
Nov. 25, 1915: Einstein Completes His Theory of General Relativity
Dec. 8, 1915: Poppies Become a Symbol for Fallen Soldiers
Dec. 17, 1915: Malevich Introduces Suprematism

1916

1916: Completion of the Trans-Siberian Railroad
1916: Dada Movement Emerges at the Cabaret Voltaire

1916: Dewey Applies Pragmatism to Education
1916: Ives Completes His Fourth Symphony

1916: Schwarzschild Solves the Equations of General Relativity

Jan.-June, 1916: Lenin Critiques Modern Capitalism

Feb. 21-Dec. 18, 1916: Battle of Verdun

Mar. 15, 1916-Feb. 5, 1917: Pershing Expedition

Apr. 24-29, 1916: Easter Rebellion

May 31-June 1, 1916: Battle of Jutland

June 5, 1916: Brandeis Becomes the First Jewish Supreme Court Justice

July, 1916: Fayol Publishes *General and Industrial Management*

July, 1916: New York City Institutes a Comprehensive Zoning Law

Aug., 1916: Hindenburg Program Militarizes the German Economy

Aug. 25, 1916: National Park Service Is Created

Sept. 8, 1916: United States Establishes a Permanent Tariff Commission

Sept. 11, 1916: First Self-Service Grocery Store Opens

Sept. 19, 1916: American Institute of Accountants Is Founded

Oct. 16, 1916: First American Birth Control Clinic Opens

Nov. 7, 1916: First Woman Is Elected to the U.S. Congress

1917

1917: American Farmers Increase Insecticide Use

1917: Birdseye Invents Quick-Frozen Foods

1917: National Woman's Party Is Founded

1917: *De Stijl* Advocates Mondrian's Neoplasticism

1917: Yeats Publishes *The Wild Swans at Coole*

1917-1918: Bolsheviks Suppress the Russian Orthodox Church

1917-1920: Ukrainian Nationalists Struggle for Independence

1917-1924: Russian Communists Inaugurate the Red Terror

1917-1970: Pound's *Cantos* Is Published

Jan. 31, 1917: Mexican Constitution Establishes an Advanced Labor Code

Feb. 5, 1917: Immigration Act of 1917

Feb. 26, 1917: Mount McKinley National Park Is Created

Mar.-Nov., 1917: Lenin Leads the Russian Revolution

Mar. 2, 1917: Jones Act of 1917

Apr. 6, 1917: United States Enters World War I

Apr. 13, 1917: U.S. Curtails Civil Liberties During World War I

Apr. 30, 1917: Formation of the American Friends Service Committee

May, 1917: Universal Negro Improvement Association Establishes a U.S. Chapter

May 13-Oct. 17, 1917: Marian Apparitions in Fátima, Portugal

June, 1917: First Pulitzer Prizes Are Awarded

June 15, 1917, and May 16, 1918: Espionage and Sedition Acts

July 8, 1917: United States Establishes the War Industries Board

Sept. 15, 1917: *Forbes* Magazine Is Founded

Sept. 20, 1917: Canadian Women Gain the Vote

Oct. 3, 1917: U.S. Congress Imposes a Wartime Excess-Profits Tax

Oct. 15, 1917: France Executes Mata Hari

Nov., 1917: Hooker Telescope Is Installed on Mount Wilson

Nov. 2, 1917: Balfour Declaration Supports a Jewish Homeland in Palestine

Nov. 6-7, 1917: Bolsheviks Mount the October Revolution

Dec. 6, 1917: Halifax Explosion

Dec. 6, 1917-Oct. 14, 1920: Finland Gains Independence

1918

1918: Cather's *My Ántonia* Promotes Regional Literature

1918: Noether Shows the Equivalence of Symmetry and Conservation

1918-1919: Germans Revolt and Form a Socialist Government

1918-1919: Rietveld Designs the Red-Blue Chair

1918-1921: Russian Civil War

Jan. 8, 1918: Shapley Proves the Sun Is Distant from the Center of Our Galaxy

Feb. 6, 1918: British Women Gain the Vote

Feb. 24, 1918-Aug. 11, 1920: Baltic States Gain Independence

Mar., 1918-1919: Influenza Epidemic Strikes

Mar. 3, 1918: Treaty of Brest-Litovsk

Summer, 1918: Rise of Cultural Relativism Revises Historiography

July 3, 1918: Migratory Bird Treaty Act

Sept. 26-Nov. 11, 1918: Meuse-Argonne Offensive

Nov., 1918-June, 1920: Demobilization of U.S. Forces After World War I

Nov. 5, 1918-Nov. 2, 1920: Republican Resurgence Ends America's Progressive Era

Dec. 1, 1918: Kingdom of the Serbs, Croats, and Slovenes Declares Independence

Dec. 21, 1918: Birth of Czechoslovakia

1919

1919: Aston Builds the First Mass Spectrograph and Discovers Isotopes

1919: Founding of the World Christian Fundamentals Association

1919: German Artists Found the Bauhaus

1919: Mises Develops the Frequency Theory of Probability

1919: Principles of Shortwave Radio Communication Are Discovered

1919-1920: Ponzi Cheats Thousands in an Investment Scheme

1919-1921: Bjerknes Discovers Fronts in Atmospheric Circulation

1919-1933: Racist Theories Aid Nazi Rise to Political Power

Jan. 15, 1919: Assassination of Rosa Luxemburg

Jan. 19-21, 1919: Paris Peace Conference Addresses Protection for Minorities

Feb. 1, 1919: Lenin Approves the First Soviet Nature Preserve

Mar. 2-6, 1919: Lenin Establishes the Comintern

Mar. 15-May 9, 1919: Formation of the American Legion

Spring, 1919: Frisch Discovers That Bees Communicate Through Body Movements

Apr. 13, 1919: British Soldiers Massacre Indians at Amritsar

Apr. 28, 1919: League of Nations Is Established

May 4, 1919: May Fourth Movement

May 15-June 26, 1919: Winnipeg General Strike

May 19, 1919-Sept. 11, 1922: Greco-Turkish War

May 20, 1919: National Parks and Conservation Association Is Founded

June 28, 1919: International Labor Organization Is Established

June 28, 1919: Treaty of Versailles

July 31, 1919: Weimar Constitution

Aug., 1919-May, 1920: Red Scare

Sept. 10, 1919: Saint-Germain-en-Laye Convention Attempts to Curtail Slavery

Sept. 22, 1919-Jan. 8, 1920: Steelworkers Strike for Improved Working Conditions

Oct. 1-9, 1919: Black Sox Scandal

Nov. 6, 1919: Einstein's Theory of Gravitation Is Confirmed over Newton's Theory

Nov. 16, 1919: Horthy Consolidates Power in Hungary

1920

1921

Mar. 20, 1921: Plebiscite Splits Upper Silesia Between Poland and Germany

May 10, 1921: Pirandello's *Six Characters in Search of an Author* Premieres

May 19, 1921: Emergency Quota Act

Aug., 1921: Moplah Rebellion

Sept. 8, 1921: First Miss America Is Crowned

Nov. 11, 1921: Harding Eulogizes the Unknown Soldier

Nov. 11-13, 1921, and Mar. 25-31, 1925: Sanger Organizes Conferences on Birth Control

Nov. 12, 1921-Feb. 6, 1922: Washington Disarmament Conference

Nov. 23, 1921-June 30, 1929: Sheppard-Towner Act

1922

1922: Eliot Publishes *The Waste Land*

1922: First Major U.S. Shopping Center Opens

1922: First Meeting of the Vienna Circle

1922: McCollum Names Vitamin D and Pioneers Its Use Against Rickets

Jan., 1922: Izaak Walton League Is Formed

Feb., 1922: *Reader's Digest* Is Founded

Feb. 2, 1922: Joyce's *Ulysses* Redefines Modern Fiction

Apr. 16, 1922: Treaty of Rapallo

June, 1922: New Wimbledon Tennis Stadium Is Dedicated

July 24, 1922: League of Nations Establishes Mandate for Palestine

Sept. 22, 1922: Cable Act

Oct. 24-30, 1922: Mussolini's "March on Rome"

Nov. 4, 1922: Carter Discovers the Tomb of Tutankhamen

Nov. 13, 1922: *Ozawa v. United States*

Dec. 10, 1922: Nansen Wins the Nobel Peace Prize

Dec. 14, 1922: Oil Is Discovered in Venezuela

1923

1923: A. C. Nielsen Company Pioneers in Marketing and Media Research

1923: Andrews Expedition Discovers the First Fossilized Dinosaur Eggs

1923: Buber Breaks New Ground in Religious Philosophy

1923: De Broglie Explains the Wave-Particle Duality of Light

1923: Discovery of the Compton Effect

1923: Federal Power Commission Disallows Kings River Dams

1923: Germans Barter for Goods in Response to Hyperinflation

1923: Kahn Develops a Modified Syphilis Test

1923: *The Ten Commandments* Advances American Film Spectacle

1923-1939: *Cambridge Ancient History* Appears

Jan. 11, 1923-Aug. 16, 1924: France Occupies the Ruhr

Feb. 15, 1923: Bessie Smith Records "Downhearted Blues"

Mar. 3, 1923: Luce Founds *Time* Magazine

Mar. 5, 1923: Nevada and Montana Introduce Old-Age Pensions

Mar. 14, 1923: American Management Association Is Established

Apr. 9, 1923: U.S. Supreme Court Rules Against Minimum Wage Laws

Summer, 1923: Zdansky Discovers Peking Man

June 26, 1923: Oklahoma Imposes Martial Law in Response to KKK Violence

Aug. 27-Sept. 29, 1923: Corfu Crisis

Sept. 1, 1923: Earthquake Rocks Japan

Oct., 1923: Teapot Dome Scandal

Oct. 1, 1923: Great Britain Grants Self-Government to Southern Rhodesia

Oct. 18, 1923: Stravinsky Completes His Wind Octet

Nov. 8, 1923: Beer Hall Putsch

Dec. 10, 1923: Proposal of the Equal Rights Amendment

Dec. 29, 1923: Zworykin Applies for Patent on an Early Type of Television

1924

1924: Hubble Determines the Distance to the Andromeda Nebula

1924: Mann's *The Magic Mountain* Reflects European Crisis

1924: Soviets Establish a Society for the Protection of Nature

1924: Steenbock Discovers Sunlight Increases Vitamin D in Food

1924: Svedberg Develops the Ultracentrifuge

1924: U.S. Government Loses Its Suit Against Alcoa

1924-1932: Hawthorne Studies Examine Human Productivity

1924-1976: Howard Hughes Builds a Business Empire

Jan. 25-Feb. 5, 1924: First Winter Olympic Games

Feb., 1924: IBM Changes Its Name and Product Line

Feb. 12, 1924: Gershwin's *Rhapsody in Blue* Premieres in New York

Mar., 1924: Eddington Formulates the Mass-Luminosity Law for Stars

Mar. 31, 1924: Formation of the Blue Four Advances Abstract Painting

May 21, 1924: Farmers Dynamite the Los Angeles Aqueduct

May 26, 1924: Immigration Act of 1924

May 28, 1924: U.S. Congress Establishes the Border Patrol

June 2, 1924: Indian Citizenship Act

June 3, 1924: Gila Wilderness Area Is Designated

June 7, 1924: Oil Pollution Act Sets Penalties for Polluters

Summer, 1924: Dart Discovers the First Australopithecine Fossil

Sept. 1, 1924: Dawes Plan

Oct., 1924: Surrealism Is Born

Oct. 21, 1924: Halibut Treaty

Nov. 4, 1924: Coolidge Is Elected U.S. President

Dec., 1924: Hubble Shows That Other Galaxies Are Independent Systems

Dec. 4, 1924: Von Stroheim's Silent Masterpiece *Greed* Premieres

Dec. 10, 1924: Hoover Becomes the Director of the U.S. Bureau of Investigation

1925

1925: *The City* Initiates the Study of Urban Ecology

1925: Cranbrook Academy Promotes the Arts and Crafts Movement

1925: Eisenstein's *Potemkin* Introduces New Film Editing Techniques

1925: Gide's *The Counterfeiters* Questions Moral Absolutes

1925: Hamilton Publishes *Industrial Poisons in the United States*

1925: McKinsey Founds a Management Consulting Firm

1925: New Objectivity Movement Is Introduced

1925: Sears, Roebuck Opens Its First Retail Outlet

1925: Whipple Discovers Importance of Iron for Red Blood Cells

1925: Woolf's *Mrs. Dalloway* Explores Women's Consciousness

1925-1926: Mussolini Seizes Dictatorial Powers in Italy

1925-1927: Gance's *Napoléon* Revolutionizes Filmmaking Techniques

1925-1935: Women's Rights in India Undergo a Decade of Change

1925-1979: Pahlavi Shahs Attempt to Modernize Iran

Jan. 1, 1925: Bell Labs Is Formed

Jan. 5, 1925: First Female Governor in the United States

Feb. 2, 1925: U.S. Congress Authorizes Private Carriers for Airmail

Feb. 21, 1925: Ross Founds *The New Yorker*

1926

1927

1928

1929

1930

1931

Apr. 14, 1931: Second Spanish Republic Is Proclaimed

May 1, 1931: Empire State Building Opens

May 8, 1931: Credit-Anstalt Bank of Austria Fails

May 27, 1931: Piccard Travels to the Stratosphere by Balloon

July, 1931: Yellow River Flood

July 26, 1931: International Bible Students Association Becomes Jehovah's Witnesses

Nov. 17, 1931: Whitney Museum of American Art Opens in New York

Dec. 11, 1931: Formation of the British Commonwealth of Nations

1932

1932: Berle and Means Discuss Corporate Control

1932: Céline's *Journey to the End of the Night* Expresses Interwar Cynicism

1932: Gilson's *Spirit of Medieval Philosophy* Reassesses Christian Thought

1932-1935: Domagk Discovers That Sulfonamides Can Save Lives

1932-1940: Development of Negritude

Jan.-Feb., 1932: El Salvador's Military Massacres Civilians

Jan. 7, 1932: Stimson Doctrine

Jan. 22, 1932: Reconstruction Finance Corporation Is Created

Feb., 1932: Chadwick Discovers the Neutron

Mar. 9, 1932: De Valera Is Elected President of the Irish Dáil

Mar. 19, 1932: Dedication of the Sydney Harbour Bridge

Mar. 23, 1932: Norris-La Guardia Act Strengthens Labor Organizations

Apr., 1932: Cockcroft and Walton Split the Atom

Apr. 23, 1932: Stalin Restricts Soviet Composers

Apr. 23, 1932-Aug., 1934: Socialist Realism Is Mandated in Soviet Literature

May 20-21, 1932: First Transatlantic Solo Flight by a Woman

July 3, 1932: Jooss's Antiwar Dance *The Green Table* Premieres

July 18, 1932: St. Lawrence Seaway Treaty

July 21-Aug. 21, 1932: Ottawa Agreements

July 28, 1932: Bonus March

Aug. 1, 1932: Canada's First Major Socialist Movement

Sept., 1932: Anderson Discovers the Positron

Sept. 25, 1932: Poona Pact Grants Representation to India's Untouchables

Oct., 1932: Wright Founds the Taliesin Fellowship

Nov., 1932: Antitrust Prosecution Forces RCA to Restructure

Nov. 8, 1932: Franklin D. Roosevelt Is Elected U.S. President

Dec., 1932-Spring, 1934: Great Famine Strikes the Soviet Union

Winter, 1932: Huxley's *Brave New World* Forecasts Technological Totalitarianism

1933

1933: Billie Holiday Begins Her Recording Career

1933: *Forty-Second Street* Defines 1930's Film Musicals

1933: Kallet and Schlink Publish *100,000,000 Guinea Pigs*

1933-1934: First Artificial Radioactive Element Is Developed

Jan. 2, 1933: Coward's *Design for Living* Epitomizes the 1930's

Jan. 23, 1933: Italy Creates the Industrial Reconstruction Institute

Jan. 30, 1933: Hitler Comes to Power in Germany

Feb. 24, 1933: Japan Withdraws from the League of Nations

Feb. 27, 1933: Reichstag Fire

Feb. 28, 1933: Perkins Becomes First Woman Secretary of Labor

Mar., 1933: Nazi Concentration Camps Begin Operating

Mar. 4, 1933-1945: Good Neighbor Policy

Mar. 9-June 16, 1933: The Hundred Days

Mar. 23, 1933: Enabling Act of 1933

Apr. 5, 1933: U.S. Civilian Conservation Corps Is Established

May 18, 1933: Tennessee Valley Authority Is Created

June 16, 1933: Banking Act of 1933 Reorganizes the American Banking System

June 16, 1933: Roosevelt Signs the National Industrial Recovery Act

July 6, 1933: First Major League Baseball All-Star Game

Aug. 2, 1933: Soviets Open the White Sea-Baltic Canal

Aug. 11-13, 1933: Iraqi Army Slaughters Assyrian Christians

Sept., 1933: Marshall Writes *The People's Forests*

Sept. 8, 1933: Work Begins on the Grand Coulee Dam

Fall, 1933-Oct. 20, 1949: Lewis Convenes the Inklings

Oct. 18, 1933: Roosevelt Creates the Commodity Credit Corporation

Nov.-Dec., 1933: Fermi Proposes the Neutrino Theory of Beta Decay

Nov. 16, 1933: United States Recognizes Russia's Bolshevik Regime

Dec. 8, 1933: Canonization of Bernadette Soubirous

Dec. 17, 1933: End of the Thirteenth Dalai Lama's Rule

1934

1934: Benedict Publishes *Patterns of Culture*

1934: Discovery of the Cherenkov Effect

1934: Lubitsch's *The Merry Widow* Opens New Vistas for Film Musicals

1934: Soviet Union Bans Abstract Art

1934: Squier Founds Muzak

1934: Toynbee's Metahistorical Approach Sparks Debate

1934: Zwicky and Baade Propose a Theory of Neutron Stars

1934-1935: Hitchcock Becomes Synonymous with Suspense

1934-1938: Production Code Gives Birth to Screwball Comedy

1934-1939: Dust Bowl Devastates the Great Plains

1934-1945: Radar Is Developed

Feb., 1934: Rivera's Rockefeller Center Mural Is Destroyed

Feb. 6, 1934: Stavisky Riots

Mar. 16, 1934: Migratory Bird Hunting and Conservation Stamp Act

Mar. 24, 1934: Philippine Independence Act

May 23, 1934: Police Apprehend Bonnie and Clyde

June 6, 1934: Securities and Exchange Commission Is Established

June 10, 1934: Federal Communications Commission Is Established by Congress

June 18, 1934: Indian Reorganization Act

June 26, 1934: Federal Credit Union Act

June 28, 1934: Taylor Grazing Act

June 30-July 2, 1934: Great Blood Purge

Sept. 1, 1934: Miller's *Tropic of Cancer* Stirs Controversy

Fall, 1934-May 6, 1953: Gibbon Develops the Heart-Lung Machine

Oct. 16, 1934-Oct. 18, 1935: Mao's Long March

Oct. 19, 1934: Marshall and Leopold Form the Wilderness Society

Nov., 1934: Yukawa Proposes the Existence of Mesons

Dec., 1934: Stalin Begins the Purge Trials

Dec. 1, 1934: Goodman Begins His *Let's Dance* Broadcasts

Dec. 6, 1934: Balanchine's *Serenade* Inaugurates American Ballet

Dec. 29, 1934: Japan Renounces Disarmament Treaties

1935

1935: Chapman Determines the Lunar Atmospheric Tide at Moderate Latitudes

1935: Penguin Develops a Line of Paperback Books

1935-1936: Turing Invents the Universal Turing Machine

Jan., 1935: Richter Develops a Scale for Measuring Earthquake Strength

Jan., 1935: Schiaparelli's Boutique Mingles Art and Fashion

Feb., 1935-Oct. 27, 1938: Carothers Invents Nylon

Feb. 12, 1935: Exhibition of American Abstract Painting Opens in New York

Feb. 19, 1935: Odets's *Awake and Sing!* Becomes a Model for Protest Drama

Feb. 27, 1935: Temple Receives a Special Academy Award

Apr. 8, 1935: Works Progress Administration Is Established

Apr. 15, 1935: Arbitration Affirms National Responsibility for Pollution

Apr. 27, 1935: Soil Conservation Service Is Established

May 27, 1935: Black Monday

June 10, 1935: Formation of Alcoholics Anonymous

July, 1935: Tansley Proposes the Term "Ecosystem"

July 5, 1935: Wagner Act

Aug. 14, 1935: Roosevelt Signs the Social Security Act

Aug. 23, 1935: Banking Act of 1935 Centralizes U.S. Monetary Control

Aug. 29, 1935-June 30, 1939: Federal Theatre Project Promotes Live Theater

Aug. 31, 1935-Nov. 4, 1939: Neutrality Acts

Sept. 6, 1935: *Top Hat* Establishes the Astaire-Rogers Dance Team

Oct. 10, 1935: Gershwin's *Porgy and Bess* Opens in New York

Oct. 11, 1935-July 15, 1936: League of Nations Applies Economic Sanctions Against Italy

Oct. 23, 1935-Nov. 15, 1948: King Returns to Power in Canada

Nov.-Dec., 1935: Egas Moniz Develops the Prefrontal Lobotomy

Nov. 5, 1935: Armstrong Demonstrates FM Radio Broadcasting

Nov. 10, 1935: Congress of Industrial Organizations Is Founded

Nov. 27, 1935: New Zealand's First Labour Party Administration

1936

1936: Lehmann Discovers the Earth's Inner Core

1936: Müller Invents the Field Emission Microscope

1936-1946: France Nationalizes Its Banking and Industrial Sectors

Jan.-Mar., 1936: Consumers Union of the United States Emerges

Jan. 1, 1936: Ford Foundation Is Established

Jan. 26, 1936: Tudor's *Jardin aux lilas* Premieres in London

Jan. 28, 1936: Soviets Condemn Shostakovich's *Lady Macbeth of the Mtsensk District*

Feb. 4, 1936: Darling Founds the National Wildlife Federation

Feb. 4, 1936: Keynes Proposes Government Management of the Economy

Feb. 17, 1936: Corporatism Comes to Paraguay

Mar. 7, 1936: German Troops March into the Rhineland

Mar. 11, 1936: Boulder Dam Is Completed

Apr. 15, 1936-1939: Great Uprising of Arabs in Palestine

June 19, 1936: Robinson-Patman Act Restricts Price Discrimination

June 25, 1936: The DC-3 Opens a New Era of Air Travel

July 17, 1936: Spanish Civil War Begins

Aug. 1-16, 1936: Germany Hosts the Summer Olympics

Aug. 2-18, 1936: Claretian Martyrs Are Executed in Spain

Nov., 1936: Carnegie Redefines Self-Help Literature

1937

1938

Apr. 5, 1938: Ballet Russe de Monte Carlo Debuts
May 26, 1938: HUAC Is Established
June 7, 1938: Chinese Forces Break Yellow River Levees
June 21, 1938: Natural Gas Act
June 25, 1938: Fair Labor Standards Act
June 25, 1938: Federal Food, Drug, and Cosmetic Act
July 6-15, 1938: Evian Conference
Sept. 17, 1938: First Grand Slam of Tennis

Sept. 29-30, 1938: Munich Conference
Oct. 5, 1938: Death of Maria Faustina Kowalska
Oct. 22, 1938: Carlson and Kornei Make the First Xerographic Photocopy
Oct. 30, 1938: Welles Broadcasts *The War of the Worlds*
Dec., 1938: Hahn Splits the Uranium Atom
Dec. 10, 1938: Buck Receives the Nobel Prize in Literature

1939

1939: Bourbaki Group Publishes *Éléments de mathématique*
1939: Ford Defines the Western in *Stagecoach*
1939: Müller Discovers the Insecticidal Properties of DDT
1939-1945: Nazi Extermination of the Jews
1939-1949: Bill Monroe and the Blue Grass Boys Define Bluegrass Music
Jan. 2, 1939: Marian Anderson Is Barred from Constitution Hall
Feb. 15, 1939: Oppenheimer Calculates the Nature of Black Holes
Mar. 2, 1939: Pius XII Becomes Pope
Mar. 31, 1939: Sherlock Holmes Film Series Begins
Apr., 1939: *The Grapes of Wrath* Portrays Depression-Era America
Apr. 7, 1939: Italy Invades and Annexes Albania

Apr. 30, 1939: American Television Debuts at the World's Fair
May 16, 1939: First U.S. Food Stamp Program Begins
June 12, 1939: Dedication of the Baseball Hall of Fame
Summer, 1939: Stalin Suppresses the Russian Orthodox Church
Aug., 1939: United States Begins Mobilization for World War II
Aug. 17, 1939: *The Wizard of Oz* Premieres
Aug. 23-24, 1939: Nazi-Soviet Pact
Sept. 1, 1939: Germany Invades Poland
Sept. 10, 1939: Canada Enters World War II
Nov. 1, 1939: Rockefeller Center Is Completed
Nov. 30, 1939-Mar. 12, 1940: Russo-Finnish War
Dec. 15, 1939: *Gone with the Wind* Premieres

1940

1940: García Lorca's *Poet in New York* Is Published
1940: Wright's *Native Son* Depicts Racism in America
1940-1941: Moore's Subway Sketches Record War Images
Apr.-May, 1940: Soviets Massacre Polish Prisoners of War
Apr. 9, 1940: Germany Invades Norway
May, 1940: Florey and Chain Develop Penicillin as an Antibiotic
May, 1940: Roosevelt Uses Business Leaders for World War II Planning
May 10-June 22, 1940: Collapse of France

May 16, 1940-1944: Gypsies Are Exterminated in Nazi Death Camps
May 26-June 4, 1940: Evacuation of Dunkirk
June 14, 1940: United States Begins Building a Two-Ocean Navy
June 30, 1940: Congress Centralizes Regulation of U.S. Commercial Air Traffic
July 1, 1940: U.S. Fish and Wildlife Service Is Formed
July 10-Oct. 31, 1940: Battle of Britain
Aug., 1940: Japan Announces the Greater East Asia Coprosperity Sphere
Aug. 3, 1940-Mar., 1941: Italy Invades British Somaliland

Geographical Index

List of Geographical Regions

GHANA

GREAT BRITAIN. *See* ENGLAND, IRELAND, SCOTLAND, WALES

GREECE

CATEGORY INDEX

LIST OF CATEGORIES

ASTRONOMY

Business and Labor

CHEMISTRY

ETHICS. *See* **RELIGION, THEOLOGY, AND ETHICS**

EXPANSION AND LAND ACQUISITION

HEALTH AND MEDICINE

HISTORIOGRAPHY

JOURNALISM. *See* PUBLISHING AND JOURNALISM

LABOR. *See* BUSINESS AND LABOR

LAND ACQUISITION. *See* EXPANSION AND LAND ACQUISITION

LAWS, ACTS, AND LEGAL HISTORY

LEGAL HISTORY. *See* **LAWS, ACTS, AND LEGAL HISTORY**

LITERATURE

MUSIC

NATURAL RESOURCES

ORGANIZATIONS AND INSTITUTIONS

PHILANTHROPY. *See* **HUMANITARIANISM AND PHILANTHROPY**

PHILOSOPHY

PHOTOGRAPHY

RADIO AND TELEVISION

REBELLIONS. *See* WARS, UPRISINGS, AND CIVIL UNREST

RECREATION. *See* TRAVEL AND RECREATION

REFORM. *See* SOCIAL ISSUES AND REFORM

RELIGION, THEOLOGY, AND ETHICS

RELOCATION. *See* **IMMIGRATION, EMIGRATION, AND RELOCATION**

REVOLUTIONS. *See* **WARS, UPRISINGS, AND CIVIL UNREST**

RIOTS. *See* **WARS, UPRISINGS, AND CIVIL UNREST**

SCANDAL. *See* **CRIME AND SCANDAL**

SCIENCE AND TECHNOLOGY

SOCIAL ISSUES AND REFORM

TRANSPORTATION

TRAVEL AND RECREATION

UPRISINGS. *See* WARS, UPRISINGS, AND CIVIL UNREST

URBAN PLANNING

WAR CRIMES. *See* ATROCITIES AND WAR CRIMES; WORLD WAR I; WORLD WAR II

WARS, UPRISINGS, AND CIVIL UNREST. *See also* WORLD WAR I; WORLD WAR II

WOMEN'S ISSUES

WORLD WAR I

Great Events from History

Indexes

Personages Index

Subject Index